QUALITY OF LIFE THERAPY

QUALITY OF LIFE THERAPY

Applying a Life Satisfaction Approach to
Positive Psychology and Cognitive Therapy

MICHAEL B. FRISCH

WILEY

JOHN WILEY & SONS, INC.

*To Martin E. P. Seligman, PhD
founder of the Positive Psychology Movement*

Foreword

Michael B. Frisch's book presents state-of-the-art findings in positive psychology, brought to life with practical exercises that make the research findings accessible to readers. This book presents a new, comprehensive approach to positive psychology that is equally applicable to clients with or without a psychiatric or psychological disturbance. With respect to the latter, this is a guidebook for mental health professionals who wish to integrate positive psychology theory and interventions into their practice. For the past century, clinical practitioners have focused on helping people overcome misery. Although this is a laudable goal, it is not enough to just remove the misery; clients may need help to further build upon their strengths and to create new strengths and personal resources. Clinical psychologists are in an excellent position to assist people to move from negative numbers through zero and well into the positive range on the quality of life scale. It is this latter goal that is a major focus of Dr. Frisch's book. Dr. Frisch sets a broad and ambitious goal for mental health and behavioral medicine practitioners—improving all aspects of quality of life. He has greatly expanded the role of practitioners in what is likely to be a revolution for the helping professions.

Frisch's book brings new emphasis to improving clients' total quality of life as the major goal of interventions. This is important for several reasons. First, people want rewarding lives and do not merely want to overcome severe problems. Second, sometimes solutions to problems need not be solely based on a direct attack on the problem; part of the solution might come from developing strengths and resources. Third, more and more people are seeking a fulfilled life and turn to professionals to help them in their quest. Although many counseling psychologists and humanistic psychologists have long advocated focusing on client strengths and positive change, the recent upsurge of interest in positive psychology has expanded the number of supported intervention techniques in this area.

This book is both science based and theory based. Frisch builds on the work of cognitive behavioral clinicians such as Aaron T. Beck, activity theories such as that of Mihalyi Csikszentmihalyi, and positive psychologists such as Martin E. P. Seligman. The author also incorporates work on metaphor in therapy, research on relaxation and meditation, and emotion theory. Readers can be reassured that Frisch's book is research based; at the same time the author recognizes the human touch and the need for a skilled practitioner. Frisch is a Fellow in the Academy of Cognitive Therapy and is very involved in positive psychology activities—thus he weaves together expertise in these two areas to create interventions for enhancing quality of life.

The book encourages readers to go beyond the disease model of psychological disturbance. Although severe problems must be dealt with, and in the case of serious mental disorders these problems sometimes must be the focus, fostering better quality of life is a final aim of *all* therapy. Fostering better quality of life can also help clients in adapting to chronic or short-term physical illness and disability. In all of these cases, the author suggests three goals for positive practice: (1) increasing and improving "inner abundance" and experience, (2) increasing the amount of "quality time" the client experiences, and (3) increasing the client's meaning and purpose in life. To accomplish these goals, the therapist is given exercises that focus on what the client does well.

In addition, four principles are described that can be applied to all clients:

1. Make happiness a habit.
2. Learn forgiveness.
3. Be optimistic.
4. Learn to find and cultivate "Expert Friends" whatever your life situation.

In contrast with therapies that focus only on problems, Frisch emphasizes learning, helping, and creativity. The interventions teach clients that happiness is a choice. Although happiness matters in the author's approach, learning loving kindness also counts. That is, the interventions do not just focus on the self, but focus on helping the client to grow by learning compassion and kindness.

Clients are taught to put their time where their values are. Many people spend much time on tasks they do not value, often for extrinsic reasons. Frisch's approach emphasizes the need for clients to clarify their important values, and then provides exercises to help them to focus their activities on these values.

The exercises offered by Frisch are concrete and detailed and are built around his CASIO model. The CASIO model incorporates five concepts: life circumstances, attitudes, standards, the importance of values, and overall satisfaction. Within this model, 30 principles for a happy life are described. The CASIO model and the 30 principles give practitioners very concrete ways to move their clients in positive directions.

Accompanying the book is a Toolbox CD that provides copies and details of all of the exercises, handouts, and worksheets needed to fully implement the material discussed in the book. This is a valuable resource on its own and will save the practitioner time in preparing session material and will generate additional ideas as the practitioner works with this material.

Frisch's book can be used by therapists working with individual clients, as well as in workshops and educational settings. Many of the exercises are appropriate both in one-on-one therapy and in group settings. There are homework exercises for some of the interventions, but many of them can be completed within a group setting such as in a workshop or lecture venue.

The exercises and interventions can be easily understood by practitioners, and most can be easily mastered with some practice. Practitioners can add their own positive interventions to those presented in the book. In reading this book with a clinical psychologist, that is, my wife, Carol Diener, we found ourselves thinking of additional new interventions that skillful therapists might try. Therefore, it seems likely that other clinicians will find themselves generating new positive interventions when they read Frisch's work, and therefore they will become broader and more positive in their practice.

Frisch's book is filled with specific principles and exercises that can be readily adopted by practitioners. The therapists and life coaches using this book can be assured that Frisch has carefully reviewed the psychological literature for support for his approach, and they can adapt the many ideas to fit their own practice.

This book can jump-start the work of any practitioner in terms of integrating positive approaches into his or her practice. Not only can the exercises be integrated with the therapist's other successful tools, but many practitioners will find themselves reorienting their practice in a strength-based direction. The book is simultaneously both practical in giving many specific principles for educating clients and exercises to use with them, but also conceptual in giving practitioners a positive theoretical framework around which to build quality-of-life interventions.

I heartily recommend Dr. Frisch's book to positive psychology and clinical practitioners of all persuasions—counselors, psychologists, social workers, life coaches, organizational psychologists, health psychologists, and other practitioners who work with clients with the goal of improving their quality of life and personal happiness. This book is a highly readable work for professionals in all the human intervention disciplines. Not only is it clear and interesting, but the book is filled with scores of specific interventions that are based on scholarship in positive psychology, cognitive therapy, and quality of life research. This book will greatly assist readers in expanding their treatment tools in the direction of strength-based positive psychology counseling.

Ed Diener
University of Illinois Distinguished
    Professor of Psychology
Senior Research Scientist at the Gallup
    International Positive Psychology Center
Distinguished Researcher and Past
    President of the International Society
    of Quality of Life Studies

Foreword

There is a well-worn adage that I am sure every cognitive therapist has used more than once while working with a clinically depressed client. When engaging a depressed client in a process of Socratic questioning, a cognitive therapist might end the intervention with an astute observational analogy that refers to biased personal evaluations in terms of "the glass being half full or half empty." This metaphor is meant to highlight the depressed person's automatic tendency to form the most negative construction of one's self, personal world, or future. For the person suffering from clinical depression, life does appear empty. Personal loss, deprivation, and failure are all too obvious and the positives, the half-full aspect of the adage, are completely lost from the depressed person's perspective.

In some respects, clinical psychology and psychiatry generally and cognitive therapy more specifically have exhibited a depressive thinking style in their theories, research, and treatment of psychological disorders. We have tended to focus exclusively on the negative, the "half-empty" portion of the proverbial glass. Our preoccupation has been the relief of suffering, the alleviation of negative emotions, the restructuring of negative cognitions and dysfunctional schemas, and the modification of problematic behavioral responses. This maladaptive side of human functioning is viewed as critical to the etiology and persistence of emotional and behavioral disorders. And yet, as critical as this focus is to the effectiveness of our therapies, it is clearly not the whole story. As psychotherapists, we have ignored the "half-full" side of the equation. That is, we rarely address issues of happiness, contentment, and quality of life. At last psychologists like Ed Diener, Martin Seligman, and now Michael B. Frisch have begun to readdress this imbalance in our perspective on human emotion with their positive psychology and quality of life research.

In this book, Michael B. Frisch proposes a bridge or integration of the positive psychology and cognitive therapy perspectives. To my knowledge, this is the first

such venture and it has the potential to enrich both cognitive therapy and positive psychology. Frisch's Quality of Life Therapy (QOLT) adheres strongly to the positive psychology movement's concern with human happiness, strengths, and a better quality of life for all. Happiness is understood as the fulfillment of cherished goals, needs, and wishes in valued areas of life. It should not be confused with positive affect, joy, or elation. In fact, happiness and depressed mood are not opposite poles on a single continuum but instead independent affective states. The implication of this finding for the treatment of emotional disorders should not be lost to the clinician. Treating negative mood will not automatically lead to happiness and life satisfaction in our patients. Instead the single most important message from this volume is that a new and expanded therapeutic perspective is needed that directly addresses issues of positive affect, life satisfaction, and contentment. Frisch's book provides some interesting insights into how this more holistic cognitive therapy of emotion and life satisfaction might evolve.

According to Frisch, QOLT is conceptualized in terms of the constructive mode that Aaron T. Beck and I described in *Scientific Foundations of Cognitive Theory and Therapy of Depression* (Clark & Beck, 1999). We noted that depression is characterized not only by hypervalent activation of negative self-referent schemas but also a failure to access more positive, constructive self-schemas involved in the promotion of productive activities that increase the vital resources of the individual. The constructive mode provides the cognitive basis for healthy living; to achieve; to relate intimately; to be creative and independent; and to exhibit resilience, optimism, and a sense of mastery. Standard cognitive therapy developed interventions aimed at deactivating negative dysfunctional schematic processing in anxiety and depression. However, the therapy has been relatively silent on how to address the inaccessibility of the constructive mode. QOLT has broken new ground by providing some of the first insights for cognitive therapists who recognize the need to enhance their patients' access to constructive schematic thinking.

The conceptual basis of QOLT adheres closely to a stress-cognition perspective, with core cognitive processes playing a critical role in the creation of life satisfaction and happiness. Frisch's CASIO model provides the theoretical foundation for understanding individual differences in life satisfaction. We see in this model a recognition that external circumstances interact with three cognitive processes in the production of life satisfaction, an evaluation of one's circumstances or area of life, personal standards for judging goal attainment in particular areas, and a personal value or importance that is attached to various life goals. This cognitive conceptualization of goal attainment and life satisfaction is entirely compatible with Aaron T. Beck's cognitive theory by elaborating specific cognitive processes that might be relevant for activation of the constructive mode.

The QOLT model outlined in Chapter 3 is then applied to 16 areas of life that range from spiritual development and self-esteem to home, neighborhood, and community. The CASIO model is then applied to each of these life domains and the reader is provided information on how life satisfaction or happiness could be achieved in each domain. The clinician will find this part of the book most helpful because Frisch provides practical intervention strategies that can be used both within-session and as between-session homework assignments. The Toolbox CD is rich with a variety of forms, rating scales, educational hand-outs, and other resource materials that the clinician may find particularly helpful when offering interventions. They are aimed at quality of life issues.

This book is broad in its scope and application. For example, Frisch shows how his approach can be applied to an entirely new area of practice, that is, "positive psychology clients" such as professionals devoid of psychological disorders who nevertheless wish to be happier and more content with their lives. Frisch speaks first, however, as clinician and so the clearest application of the book will be found in the clinical setting. QOLT can be viewed as an adjunct to standard cognitive therapy for anxiety or depression. In the forthcoming years, QOLT may come to be recognized as an important component of relapse prevention and treatment maintenance programs. We look forward to further developments and clinical applications in this emerging field of positive psychology and quality of life research.

David A. Clark, PhD
Department of Psychology at the University of
    New Brunswick, Canada
Founding Fellow of Academy of Cognitive Therapy

REFERENCE

Clark, D. A., & Beck, A. T. (with Alford, B.). (1999). *Scientific foundations of cognitive theory and therapy of depression.* New York: Wiley.

Contents

NOTE TO READER: Please note the CD has been converted to URL. Go to the following website www.wiley.com/go/frisch.

Toolbox CD of Personal Growth Exercises for Clients

ACT Model

Areas of Life

Basket-of-Eggs Worksheet

BAT Exercise

Beck Theory Diagram

Budget Skills

Cognitive Errors

Couple's Serenity Prayer

Creativity Skills

Daily Activity Plan

Feeling Dictionary

Five Paths or CASIO Model

Five Paths to Happiness

Five Paths Summary

Frisch Essential Symptom Scale

Frisch Essential Symptom Scale: Test Manual

Good Not Great Exercise

Guide for Worry Warts

Habit Control Diary

Happiness Pie Exercise

Lie Detector and Stress Diary

Lie Detector Questions

Mental Health Day or Hour Technique

Mindful Breathing and Mediation

My Most Feared Obituary

Neighborhood or Community Checklist

New Life Script

Occupational Survey

Personal Stress Profile

Play List

Pro versus Con Technique

Relapse Emergency Checklist

Relapse Prevention Worksheet

Relationship Skills

Relaxation Rituals

Schemas That Drive Us Crazy

Self Sympathy and Loving Kindness

Street Signs to Success

Strength Exercise

Success Log

Tenets of Contentment

Tenets of Contentment in Separate Documents (Folder)

Vision Quest Exercise

What's Wrong

Work That Satisfies

PART ONE
INTRODUCTION AND THEORY

CHAPTER 1

Quality of Life Therapy (QOLT):
An Introduction

WHY QUALITY OF LIFE THERAPY[1] (QOLT)? THE BENEFITS OF HAPPINESS AND LIFE SATISFACTION

Why do we put happiness and satisfaction ahead of money as life goals (Diener & Oishi, in press)? Certainly, feeling good, that is, being happy and satisfied with life, is its own reward. Other more tangible rewards accrue to the generally or consistently happy. For example, the generally happy in Western societies appear to have more rewarding and longer-lasting marriages, more friends, higher incomes, superior work performance, more community involvement, better mental and physical health, and even greater longevity relative to their less-happy peers (see review by Lyubomirsky, King, & Diener, in press).

Greater happiness and contentment lead to greater success in life, better health, and more rewarding relationships; clients need not be unhappy to benefit and grow from a positive psychology program like Quality of Life Therapy (QOLT) since *any* growth in happiness can affect these outcomes and make individuals more

satisfied with life. This is the rationale for QOLT with nonclinical or *pure positive psychology clients* such as the professional groups of lawyers, teachers, businesspeople, physicians, clergy of all stripes and persuasions, university student life professionals, quality of life researchers and their students from around the world, and police or probation personnel who make up half of my positive psychology practice.

QOLT for Boosting Acute Treatment Response and Relapse Prevention in Cognitive Therapy

QOLT may also be seen as a way to boost the acute treatment response of clients undergoing evidence-based cognitive therapies for *DSM* disorders, in part, because of QOLT's hypothesized activation of the constructive mode, a necessary part of successful cognitive therapy. According to the latest formulation of cognitive theory expanded now to include most psychopathology and not just clinical depression (Clark & Beck, 1999—also see details in Chapter 3). QOLT also has a role to play in relapse prevention. Just as schema work used to be considered relapse prevention work in cognitive therapy and just as mindfulness training is often now seen in this way (interestingly, mindfulness training is also a part of QOLT—see Chapters 7 and 10). QOLT is viewed as a new, comprehensive, and *positive psychology-oriented approach to relapse prevention* in cognitive therapy that goes well beyond the very simple and limited interventions of Fava and his colleagues (Fava & Ruini, 2003) who pioneered the approach of enhancing relapse prevention in cognitive therapy with positive psychology or so-called well-being

---

[1] A simpler exposition of QOLT for the layperson can be found in the companion book and CD to this book authored specifically for clients and the general public titled, *Finding Happiness with Quality of Life Therapy: A Positive Psychology Approach,* © 2006 by Michael B. Frisch, Woodway, TX: Quality of Life Press. Foreword by Ed Diener; E-mail contact: michael_frisch@baylor.edu.

Interventions described in this book are positive psychology interventions that can be used with both clinical and nonclinical/general public/professional samples in the same way that Seligman (2002) has begun to apply his *Authentic Happiness* interventions to both groups. Interventions aimed at nonclinical groups are sometimes referred to as "coaching"; the term and acronym *Quality of Life Therapy* and *QOLT* encapsulates both types of interventions, that is, *Quality of Life Therapy and Coaching.*

interventions. QOLT tries to represent the current state-of-the-art and *totality* of what positive psychology has to say about improving human functioning. Much of this knowledge was simply unavailable at the time of Fava's pioneering work. In contrast to Seligman's (2002) approach to positive psychology training that was written for a lay audience, QOLT is geared more to practitioners, is more life satisfaction-oriented, and more directly interconnected to Beckian cognitive theory and therapy than *Authentic Happiness*. The specific mechanisms of action for relapse prevention in QOLT are presented in Chapter 22 on *Relapse Prevention and Maintenance*.

The Birth of QOLT: A Journey from Cognitive Therapy to Positive Psychology and Back Again

This book—and a simpler companion book for clients and the general public entitled, *Finding Happiness with Quality of Life Therapy: A Positive Psychology Approach* (Frisch, 2006)—represents a new approach to positive psychology and, to a lesser extent, a new approach or addition to cognitive therapy. My primary mentor in cognitive therapy was John Rush who graciously supervised my work and taught me not to trust authors who wrote about therapy without having a passion for doing it themselves. Other influences include Aaron Beck, Art Freeman, and Robin Jarrett.

After exploring the issues of quality of life assessment and intervention in the 1980s, I presented a little noticed paper in 1989 at the World Congress on Cognitive Therapy at Oxford University. In this paper, I described my work in developing an early version of the Quality of Life Inventory or QOLI (Frisch, 1994; Frisch et al., 2005; Frisch, Cornell, Villanueva, & Retzleff, 1992). I was attempting the classic exercise of many cognitive behavior therapies taught to me by Tom Stampfl of the University of Wisconsin-Milwaukee by applying findings from the experimental laboratory to the clinical enterprise. In this case, I wanted to synthesize and apply the vast literature on subjective well-being or happiness in nonclinical populations to the understanding, assessment, and treatment of clients with depression and related disorders. I was also interested in assessing and promoting life satisfaction and a better quality of life in nonclinical groups such as older persons and the unemployed, using community psychology interventions and social programs. I found encouragement and inspiration in these efforts from the vast subjective well-being literature, in general, and the

work of Ed Diener, Alex Michalos, John Flanagan, Angus Campbell, Hans Strupp, and others, in particular.

I hoped that the QOLI could help in carrying out the under-elaborated problem-solving component of cognitive therapy by assessing problems in living as well as strengths or assets. Robin Jarrett allowed me to work with her research group at the University of Texas Southwestern Medical School in Dallas; for a time, Dr. Jarrett used the QOLI (Frisch, 1994) to train cognitive therapists in assessing problem areas of life. Dr. Beck (Aaron T. Beck) encouraged me to continue elaborating traditional cognitive therapy tools, and develop new ones based on the happiness literature. He also encouraged me to share my ideas with Art Freeman, who published my work in his *Comprehensive Casebook of Cognitive Therapy* (Frisch, 1992). The need for measures of problems in living or quality of life concerns was raised in this chapter along with the need to consider these concerns in cognitive therapy case formulations. More recently, Jackie Persons and her colleagues have raised these issues again, bemoaning the scarcity of measures like the QOLI that allow for problem assessment and, therefore, adequate case formulation in cognitive therapy (Persons & Bertagnolli, 1999; Persons, Davidson, & Thompkins, 2001). According to Dr. Persons and her colleagues, cognitive therapists in training often miss crucial problems in living or quality of life concerns without use of a formal assessment instrument aimed at assessing these concerns and problems in living.

With the encouragement of Alan Kazdin and Ed Diener, I continued my work in quality of life assessment and intervention, culminating in several papers and a revision of the QOLI (Frisch, 1994, 1998b; Frisch et al., 1992, 2005). While pursuing a program of research on the psychometrics of the QOLI, including the development of a nationwide normative sample, I continued to develop my own approach to positive psychology intervention for clinical and positive psychology applications (Frisch, 1998b). Additional testing and refinement with clinical and nonclinical or *positive psychology* clients has led to the intervention approach described in this book. Along the way, QOLT has also been refined and updated based on the most current positive psychology literature—research findings and theories. As a *Founding Fellow* in Dr. Beck's Academy of Cognitive Therapy, I have tried to represent current cognitive theory and therapy accurately, using my clinical practice to develop some elaborations of venerable cognitive therapy techniques like the thought record and activity schedule—see Chapter 10—as well as some new approaches such as the *Five Paths* rubric and exercise for problem solving and enhancing quality of life in *any* area of life (see the accompanying Toolbox CD and Chapter 10). To gain some firsthand experience in mindfulness training and to learn about the current state of affairs in various spiritual traditions, I attempted to gain an understanding of mindfulness and mediation approaches as part of a study of contemplative practices of diverse religions, including Christianity, Judaism, Buddhism, and Islam. The Reverend Barbara Kohn along with Drs. Peg Syverson and T. Flint Sparks, psychologist and founder of the Austin Zen Center, were invaluable in this regard as were ministers, priests, and rabbis in the Waco and Woodway area, especially the Reverend Dr. Jimmie Johnson, Reverend Mike Toby, Rev. Dr. W. Winfred Moore Sr., and Rabbi Seth Stander.

DEFINITION OF POSITIVE PSYCHOLOGY AND QOLT

Diener (2003) defines the good life and the *positive* in positive psychology as the relative predominance of happiness (i.e., "subjective well-being" or "well-being," a pleasant or "positive" affect) over unpleasant/negative affective experiences (e.g., anxiety, depression, anger) in our conscious experience. He emphasizes happiness and life satisfaction over other positive affects (see Lazarus, 1991, for a discussion of these) perhaps because these are associated with fulfillment and accomplishment of personal goals in the areas of life that we value. To avoid moral relativism and the celebration of happy psychopaths, he further emphasizes happiness achieved in an ethical manner without harming others. Finally, he defines positive psychology as a loose confederation of those interested in studying happiness and other positive human strengths and virtues and in helping people achieve a better quality of life. *Quality of Life Therapy* (QOLT) defines positive psychology similarly as *the study and promotion of human happiness, strengths, and a better quality of life for all.* As one of many positive psychology approaches to enhancing human happiness and quality of life, QOLT advocates a life satisfaction approach in which clients are taught a theory, tenets, and skills aimed at helping them to identify, pursue, and fulfill their most cherished needs, goals, and wishes in valued areas of life. In order to preserve relationships

and social harmony, this pursuit should be an ethical one in which the legitimate rule of law is not violated and in which harm to others is minimized and avoided. QOLT attempts to incorporate the most current theory and research with respect to happiness, positive psychology, and the management of negative affect along with insights from my clinical and positive psychology practice.

QUALITY OF LIFE THERAPY AS A "PURE" POSITIVE PSYCHOLOGY APPROACH WITH NONCLINICAL POPULATIONS

QOLT consists of an approach to increasing happiness or to *positive psychology intervention* (see Seligman (2002) or Snyder (Cheavens, Feldman, Gum, Michael, & Snyder, in press) for a different approach). QOLT can be applied to clinical and nonclinical clients. Nonclinical clients are defined here as groups without a psychological or psychiatric disturbance as defined by the presence of one or more *DSM-IV-TR* disorders (American Psychiatric Association, 2000a). For example, QOLT has been shared with nonclinical professionals—physicians, lawyers, clergy, university professors or academics, quality of life researchers and their students, university student life professionals, police personnel, psychologists, and other mental health professionals as well as undergraduate and graduate university students. In the context of professional training and instruction, QOLT has been joined with the American Psychological Association's Ethics Code principle of *competency* and the related constructs of impaired performance, burnout, professional/personal growth, and self-care (American Psychological Association, 2002); in this context, QOLT aims to increase professional self-care or "inner abundance" (Chapter 3) and to prevent burnout. It has been estimated that 50 percent of ethical lapses on the part of psychologists stem, in part, from personal problems and unhappiness at the time of the infraction (Koocher & Keith-Spiegel, 1998). Similar rates of unhappiness are likely involved in sub-standard care and service in other professions. If so, some ethical lapses could be prevented or minimized with QOLT which is aimed at boosting happiness by addressing problems of fulfillment in all valued areas of life (while at the same time, invoking evidence-based treatments for any psychological disturbance that may also be present).

It is likely that personal problems and unhappiness lead to reduced competence, impaired performance, and sub-standard care by preoccupying, isolating, and clouding the judgment of professionals who otherwise are not prone to the self-serving "cognitive distortions" so often seen in professional misconduct and unethical behavior (Koocher & Keith-Spiegel, 1998). In QOLT, self-caring is equated with Inner Abundance and is defined as feeling deeply calm, rested, centered, loving, alert, and ready to meet the challenges of your day and your life after caring for yourself in a thoughtful, loving, compassionate, and comprehensive way. It is assumed that such self-caring attitudes and behaviors will, by themselves, and in concert with other QOLT interventions, improve professionals' quality of life while at the same time protecting them from the kind of burnout, ethical lapses, and professional errors born of harried lifestyles and personal problems.

QOLT interventions described in this book are positive psychology interventions that can be used with both clinical and nonclinical/general public/professional samples in the same way that Seligman (2002) has begun to apply his *Authentic Happiness* interventions to both groups. Interventions aimed at nonclinical groups are sometimes referred to as "coaching"; the term and acronym *Quality of Life Therapy and QOLT* encapsulates both types of interventions, that is, *Quality of Life Therapy and Coaching*.

TWO-TRACK THERAPY: QOLT WITH CLINICAL POPULATIONS

QOLT is about teaching clinicians how to incorporate the latest in positive psychology into their "negative" or traditional mental health treatments. The QOLT approach to positive psychology or increasing happiness is combined with evidence-based Beckian cognitive therapy for various *DSM-IV-TR* disorders when clients present with a *DSM-IV-TR* diagnosis (American Psychiatric Association, 2000). The goal here is a seamless integration of cognitive therapy and positive psychology that is consonant with the latest formulation of Beck's cognitive therapy and cognitive theory of depression and psychopathology, as expressed in the book he coauthored with David A. Clark of the University of New Brunswick, entitled *The Scientific Foundations of Cognitive Theory and Therapy for Depression* (Clark & Beck, 1999).

Characteristics of QOLT

Some of the unique characteristics or emphases of QOLT include:

1. A Whole Life or Life Goal perspective in which each phase of intervention is related to clients' overall life goals in valued areas of life so that clients see a direct connection between an intervention or homework assignment and the fulfillment of their most important needs, goals, and wishes (although developed independently, Lyubomirsky, Sheldon, & Schkade, in press, review evidence—e.g., Sheldon & Elliot, 1999—supporting the usefulness of this strategy in boosting the effects of happiness-enhancing interventions). Similarly, assessment and conceptualization of clients' problems and strengths assume a Whole Life perspective in which functioning in 16 areas of everyday life are considered along with any psychological or physical problems, disorders, or disabilities.
2. A therapy of meaning in so far as QOLT is concerned with helping clients find out what is most meaningful to their happiness and well-being both now and over the course of their lifetime.
3. A therapy of awareness- and skill-building aimed at giving clients the understanding and skills that they need to gain satisfaction in areas of life that they most value and cherish.
4. A life satisfaction approach to the positive psychology goal of increasing happiness and contentment.
5. The Five Path or CASIO rubric or model of life satisfaction as a blueprint for quality of life and positive psychology interventions.

The CASIO model suggests that satisfaction (the perceived gap between what one wants and has) with a particular area of life is made up of four components: the objective Circumstances or Characteristics of an area; the person's Attitude about, perception, and interpretation of an area in terms of his or her well-being; a person's evaluation of fulfillment in an area based on the application of Standards of fulfillment or achievement; and the value or Importance a person places on an area for overall happiness or well-being. These four components, combined with a fifth concerned with Overall satisfaction in other areas of life that are not of immediate concern, make up the CASIO model for increasing satisfaction and happiness.

6. A blueprint for bringing positive psychology theory and interventions to traditional clinical or "negative psychology" practice. Specifically, QOLT offers an integration of current positive psychology findings and the QOLT theory of life satisfaction with Beck's cognitive theory of psychopathology and depression. For example, QOLT can be used in the clinical context of cognitive therapy to activate the constructive mode in Beck's latest model of depression and psychopathology, in general. Activation of this constructive mode is now seen as an important part of cognitive therapy for the entire range of psychopathology. QOLT can be used clinically to augment clients' *acute treatment* response to cognitive therapy, to provide *continuation therapy* when needed, and to prevent relapse—*relapse prevention* as predicted by Clark and Beck (1999) and Diener and Seligman (2004).

7. Suggests how activation of Beck's constructive mode with QOLT can benefit *nonclinical* or "pure" *positive psychology* populations, that is, the general public or professional groups interested in personal growth and often at risk for burnout and other disorders that may impair their work performance. With respect to the latter, QOLT is conceptualized as an avenue for personal growth and for primary and secondary prevention of mental disorders such as depression and anxiety, in keeping with Clark and Beck (1999).

8. Acknowledges the real limitations of happiness interventions in terms of clients' family backgrounds, genetic heritage, and temperament.

9. Acknowledges the need for *negative* emotional control as part of a comprehensive approach to happiness.

10. Views happiness as a complex "stew" of varied ingredients that vary from person to person.

The First Clinical Trial of QOLT and Research on the Quality of Life Inventory

Given the impossibility at the time of finding enough "purely" depressed volunteers, adequate control groups were not possible in the first and, so far, only clinical trial of QOLT (Grant, Salcedo, Hynan, & Frisch, 1995). Although all depressed clients in the study were no longer depressed and showed clinically significant gains in quality of life and life satisfaction at posttreatment

and follow-up assessments, the results of this trial must be viewed as preliminary when applying the highest standards of clinical trial outcome research (Kazdin, 2003). That is, the use of QOLT for acute, continuation, maintenance/relapse prevention phase treatment of depression and other *DSM-IV-TR* psychological disturbances—as well as the use of QOLT for nonclinical, "pure" positive psychology populations—requires further efficacy and effectiveness studies to "prove its salt" as an evidence-based approach. Of course, almost all positive psychology approaches have been published and presented with little or no supportive outcome research whatsoever (see Frisch, 2000, for review).

The cornerstone of QOLT is the QOLI® or Quality of Life Inventory, a positive psychology test used throughout QOLT in planning and evaluating individual interventions. This instrument was also used in the first clinical trial of QOLT and in many other clinical trials to evaluate the effectiveness of various other treatments in the context of randomized controlled clinical trials. Psychometric research on the QOLI is extensive, including my own research (e.g., see Frisch, 1994; Frisch et al., 1992, 2005) as well as *independent* studies and evaluations by other researchers at other laboratories (e.g., Ben-Porath, 1997; Crits-Christoph & Connolly, 1997; Crowley & Kazdin, 1998; Eng, Coles, Heimberg, & Safren, 2001a; Heimberg, 2002; Horowitz, Strupp, Lambert, & Elkin, 1997; Kazdin, 1993a, 1993b, 1994, 2003; Mendlowicz & Stein, 2000; Moras, 1997; Ogles, Lambert, & Masters, 1996; Persons & Bertagnolli, 1999; Rabkin, Griffin, & Wagner, 2000; Safren, Heimberg, Brown, & Holle, 1997; Forrest Scogin, personal communication, August 22, 2005). Figure 1.1 depicts the pre-intervention/treatment QOLI profile of Tom, a disguised case study used to illustrate QOLT throughout this book; both Tom's overall score and profile of specific areas of satisfaction and dissatisfaction are used in planning and evaluating interventions after the example of Kazdin (1993a, 2003) and others.[2] Notice the non-pathology, positive psychology items, overall score, and QOLI profile. These

---

[2] In keeping with the ethics code of the American Psychological Association (2002), the cases discussed in this book have been disguised and altered to protect the confidentiality of clients. Personally identifying information has been removed and, at times, fictionalized as in the person's name, gender, city, or occupation to further protect the privacy of clients.

INTRODUCTION

The Quality of Life Inventory (QOLI) provides a score that indicates a person's overall satisfaction with life. People's life satisfaction is based on how well their needs, goals, and wishes are being met in important areas of life. The information in this report should be used in conjunction with professional judgment, taking into account any other pertinent information concerning the individual.

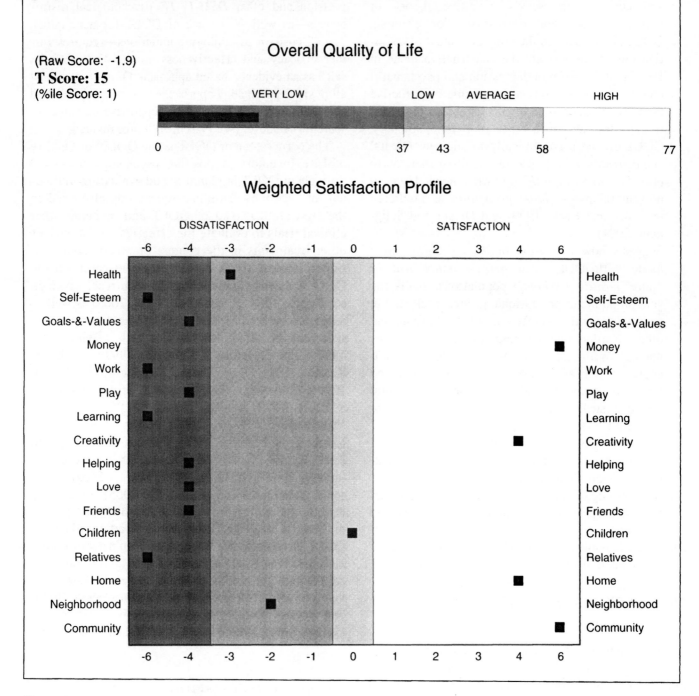

Figure 1.1 Tom's pretreatment QOLI Profile. *Source:* ©2006, 1994, Pearson Assessments and Michael B. Frisch. All rights reserved. Reprinted with permission.

OVERALL QUALITY OF LIFE CLASSIFICATION

The client's satisfaction with life is Very Low. This person is extremely unhappy and unfulfilled in life. People scoring in this range cannot get their basic needs met and cannot achieve their goals in important areas of life. This person is at risk for developing physical and mental health disorders, especially clinical depression. This risk remains until the client's score reaches or exceeds the Average range. The client should be assessed and treated for any psychological disturbances.

WEIGHTED SATISFACTION PROFILE

The Weighted Satisfaction Profile helps to explain a person's Overall Quality of Life by identifying the specific areas of satisfaction and dissatisfaction that contribute to the QOLI raw score. Clinical experience suggests that any negative weighted satisfaction rating denotes an area of life in which the individual may benefit from treatment; ratings of -6 and -4 are of greatest concern and urgency. Specific reasons for dissatisfaction should be investigated more fully with the client in a clinical interview. The *Manual and Treatment Guide for the Quality of Life Inventory* suggests treatment techniques for improving patient satisfaction in each area of life assessed by the QOLI.

The following weighted satisfaction ratings indicate areas of dissatisfaction for the client:

Area	Weighted Satisfaction Rating
Self-Esteem	-6
Work	-6
Learning	-6
Relatives	-6
Goals-and-Values	-4
Play	-4
Helping	-4
Love	-4
Friends	-4
Health	-3
Neighborhood	-2

OMITTED ITEMS

None omitted.

End of Report

Figure 1.1 *Continued*

features illustrate the general orientation of QOLT that tries to address all 16 areas of life depicted in the QOLI profile of Figure 1.1.

PLAN FOR THE BOOK

Part I continues with a discussion in Chapters 2 and 3 of the empirically based theory underlying the positive psychology approach of QOLT. A general understanding of this theory and some of the key terms like positive psychology and quality of life can be invaluable in carrying out QOLT. The theory is also meant to help therapists better understand their clients and to better plan interventions for these clients. Beginning with Chapter 3 and continuing throughout the book, Tom's case is used to show how QOLT, its theory and techniques, can be applied to a particular case; numerous other clinical and positive psychology cases are peppered throughout the book by way of illustration in how to conduct QOLT. Chapter 4 concludes Part I by offering the basic preparatory steps or "nuts and bolts" for conducting QOLT. The structure and format for clinical cases versus pure positive psychology sessions is discussed along with stylistic suggestions such as the use of groups or judicious self-disclosure by therapists or coaches.

To begin QOLT, therapists may simply apply the specific chapters of Part II *in order* to a particular case or group. That is, all of the core elements of QOLT are covered in the proper order of administration in Part II. All chapters in Part II and throughout this book allude to exercises, homework assignments, and mini-lectures/readings that clients can read and explore as part of QOLT; all of these resources such as blank copies of exercises are available for clinical and positive psychology use in the *Toolbox CD* that accompanies this book. The Toolbox CD contains printable Word documents that can be personalized for the therapist's use.

The first core technique presented in Chapter 5 is quality of life (QOL) assessment and how this is integrated with traditional assessments of psychological disorders and general medical conditions. A model of case conceptualization and treatment planning is presented and illustrated in Chapter 6 that allows therapists to easily apply the theoretical concepts from Chapter 3 to an actual clinical or positive psychology case. As set forth

in Chapter 6, the resulting case conceptualization and treatment/intervention plan is shared with clients in an effort to form a common understanding and close collaborative relationship between therapist and client. The "three pillars" or essential core QOLT interventions of Inner Abundance, Quality Time, and Find a Meaning are presented in Chapter 7.

QOLT offers both *general* CASIO interventions based directly on QOL theory for *any* and all areas of life along with area-specific interventions for specific areas like work or love. Chapter 8 presents these general CASIO interventions, including *Five Paths* (*Five Paths to Happiness*) a highly versatile tool for problem solving and gaining happiness throughout QOLT. The *Tenets of Contentment* in Chapter 9 constitutes an excellent summary of this book in the form of maxims, skills, and proverbs designed to resonate instantly with clients' experience; *Tenets* are easily selected, grouped, and tailored to a particular client's or group's needs using the Toolbox CD.

Unfortunately, positive psychologists often lose sight of the fact that scientific definitions of happiness refer to a predominance in frequency of positive to *negative* affect, neglecting interventions for the latter even though both clinical and nonclinical groups need help in managing negative affect (Diener, 2003) and in managing their lives. In QOL theory, effective goal striving—part of the area called *Goals-and-Values,* requires some basic (negative) emotional control and life management skills in order to achieve fulfillment in valued areas of life. These skills provide a powerful bridge to traditional cognitive therapy and are presented in Chapter 10 because of their importance in QOLT. Cognitive therapists should recognize some skills taught as part of Life Management and Emotional Control Skills in Goal Striving. Indeed this chapter concludes with a quick reference *Primer In Cognitive Therapy* for those who wish to brush up on their Beckian skills as they learn how to combine them with positive psychology interventions.

While general CASIO skills are useful, area-specific techniques add greatly to the power of QOLT. These additional area-specific interventions are presented in Part III with chapters on *Goals-and-Values, Spiritual Life, Self-Esteem, Health, Relationships, Work, Play, Helping, Learning, Creativity, Money,* and Surroundings—*Home, Neighborhood,*

Community.[3] Part III closes with a chapter on relapse prevention and maintenance of intervention gains.

Part IV consists of the *Toolbox CD,* some 50 or so growth exercises, maxims, tenets, or potential homework assignments presented as Word documents that therapists and coaches can "legally" download, edit, adapt, personalize, and distribute via e-mail or printing to clients in order to address their unique needs. Toolbox CD exercises summarize or *translate* QOLT concepts into action and into language that clients with little or no education can understand (Therapists may have to present growth exercises orally for those clients with little or no reading skills). Personal growth exercises from the Toolbox CD are designed to be fun and interesting for clients at the same time that they educate and instigate change in positive directions. When done outside of sessions as part of clients' "homework," the growth exercises and tenets of the Toolbox CD are designed to add to the effectiveness of in-session interventions by having clients think about and implement in-session ideas and techniques *between* sessions and even after therapy is over as clients learn how to be their own therapists or personal coaches—the ultimate skill in relapse preven-

tion. Therapists and coaches typically "prescribe," adapt, and tailor Toolbox CD exercises to meet the needs of particular clients.

A NOTE ON REFERENCES

To reduce the reference density and improve readability, when references are lacking for some assertions, the reader is referred to the following scholarly works on subjective well-being, quality of life, and positive psychology: Csikszentmihalyi (1997); Diener (1984); Diener and Seligman (2004); Diener and Suh (2000); Diener, Suh, Lucas, and Smith (1999); Frisch (1998b); Frisch (2006); Frisch et al. (2005); Kahneman, Diener, and Schwarz (1999); Peterson and Seligman (2004); Seligman (2002); Snyder and Lopez (in press); Suldo and Huebner (2005); and Vaillant (2002). With respect to Beck's cognitive theory and therapy, the reader is referred to Clark and Beck (1999), Judith S. Beck (1995), and McMillan and Fisher (2004).

---

[3] Areas of life like *Money* are capitalized and italicized throughout the book when referring to the specific theoretical terms and definitions for these areas of life as spelled out in QOL theory and the Quality of Life Inventory or QOLI®—see Chapter 3 and Table 3.1 for the precise definitions of these terms.

CHAPTER 2

Happiness through the Ages and Sages

PHILOSOPHICAL THEORIES AND THEORISTS

At least since the time of ancient Greece, philosophers and pundits have speculated on the necessary conditions for happiness (Veenhoven, 1984). Many of these musings on the nature of and recipes for happiness are tongue-in-cheek (although not without a large grain of truth). The Enlightenment philosopher Jean-Jacques Rousseau (1712–1778) thought happiness consisted of "a good bank account, a good cook, and a good digestion." One wonders why he didn't add "good sex" to his list given the scores of illegitimate children he fathered. In *Tristram Shandy* (1776), Dr. Samuel Johnson asserts that "there is nothing which has yet been contrived by man, by which so much happiness is produced as by a good tavern or inn." According to author John Gunther, "all happiness depends on a leisurely breakfast." Albert Schweitzer, the selfless humanitarian, says happiness is "nothing more than health and a poor memory." (A client of mine calls the latter a good "forgettory" and it indeed comes in handy at times.) In a similar vein, Mark Twain's recipe for happiness was "good friends, good books, and a sleepy conscience."

In a more serious vein, the ancient Greek philosophers had many differing views of happiness. Some felt happiness could best be achieved by suppressing desires and wants, whereas others saw the active fulfillment of desire as the key. Stoic philosophers like Epictetus (A.D. 50–130) exemplify the "suppressor-of-desire" school claiming that happiness comes from accepting fate and winnowing all desires down to one that we can control, that is, the desire to do your duty or fulfill your basic responsibilities in life as best you can. By wanting or desiring only that which is under your control and which isn't subject to outside forces, like being the best parent or person you can be given the constraints of your circumstances, Stoics reasoned you can never be disappointed, frustrated or . . . unhappy! The late-great philosopher Joel Feinberg (1992) used the metaphor of a card game to explain Stoicism; no matter what cards fate deals you in life, you can play each hand as well as possible whether you win or lose. Thus, the Stoic motto might be "Fortune (what happens to me) is up to Fate; excellence (in how I respond to Fate and carry my responsibilities in life) is up to me." So we can feel good about ourselves if we handle crises with "class," honoring our values and commitments as best we can whatever obstacles we face. Hemingway called this "grace under pressure" and used it to define masculinity. Not surprisingly, Stoics and other philosophers like Democritus saw happiness as a function more of our attitudes and frame of mind than of the objective circumstances of our existence. They saw happiness as a function of thought, not lot (in life). To them, it's not our situation that makes us happy or unhappy but our *attitude* about our situation. To paraphrase the old saw of Epictetus: We are disturbed not by things or circumstances, but by the view we take of them.

In contrast to Stoics, Epicureans saw the satisfaction of desire rather than its suppression as the key to happiness. Still, Epicureanism does not recommend unbridled hedonism or an "If-it-itches-go-ahead-and-scratch-it" mentality. The founder of this school of thought, Epicurus (342–270 B.C.) was no wild and crazy guy. For example, he lived on bread and water, adding only moderate portions of cheese on special occasions (Feinberg, 1992). What he and his followers promoted was a kind of selective hedonism in which we pick and choose which desires or goals to pursue or forsake based on what will make us happiest *in the long run.* This usually means fashioning a moderate lifestyle of simple pleasures like enjoying good books, friends, and nature instead of things like drugs, orgies, and gluttony merely because these things feel good at a given time.

The selective, restrained approach of pursuing pleasure in the service of happiness was abandoned by Romantic philosophers of the nineteenth century who, unlike the Epicureans, *did* counsel unbridled hedonism. Although they were a very diverse group, Romantic philosophers like Lord Byron seemed to agree that happiness could be achieved through total exploration of, immersion in, and full awareness of one's immediate experience including grand passions, adventures, and a celebration of one's uniqueness. This approach reemerged in the 1960s with a clear sentiment of "If it itches, *by all means,* go ahead and scratch it."

Plato (427–347 B.C.) saw happiness as the by-product of being just and moral. In Plato's *The Republic* (Plato, 2001), unscrupulous tyrants are depicted as basically miserable even though they are often admired and all-powerful. (We can only hope that this was Saddam Hussein's lot while he was in power.) Aristotle (384–322 B.C.) believed that all human endeavor is aimed at securing happiness in the sense of the good life or the life that goes well. His *Nicomachean Ethics* can be viewed as the first happiness self-help book in the sense that it was intended as a guide to building a fulfilling or happy life (Hughes, 2001).

Aristotle acknowledged the need for the basic necessities of life such as food, shelter, and good health, which could only be secured with some modicum of wealth (Aristotle, trans. 2000). Life goes well and we achieve happiness most however, if we realize, fulfill, and most importantly, act on, our potential or "higher (human) faculties" or virtues. These faculties or virtues include our capacity to reason and to contemplate, just as philosophers like Aristotle do, and numerous moral virtues such as fairness, honesty, sincerity, trustworthiness, courage, generosity toward others, self-control, and moderation in indulging our appetites for things like food and sex (see Nicomachean Ethics X 6–8). Aristotle's idea of achieving happiness by expressing our virtues or, in today's preferred term, *strengths,* is exactly mirrored in one approach to the new interdisciplinary field of positive psychology (Seligman, 2002); acting on general strengths, however, is only a small part of the QOLT approach to positive psychology that focuses more on the results of achieving our goals and desires in valued areas of life, addressing both weaknesses and strengths to fulfill those goals and wishes.

Once again, Aristotle felt it was not enough to *be* good or virtuous in a passive sense; we must act on or *express* our virtues behaviorally in everyday life in order to be content (Aristotle, trans. 2000). This implied theory of happiness through self-realization or actualization anticipates the work of humanistic psychologists and philosophers—self-fulfillment and existential—who followed him some 2,300 years later.

Bertrand Russell (1958), the eminent twentieth-century philosopher, devised a recipe for happiness in his book, *The Conquest of Happiness,* that includes (after basic needs for food and shelter are met) self-acceptance, compelling and wide-ranging interests and goals beyond the self, a "mental discipline" or "hygiene of the nerves" in which we control and counteract worrisome thoughts that flood our consciousness (see Negative Emotional Control in QOLT), and a balance between work, family, and recreational pursuits as we resist the cultural temptations toward workaholism and the pursuit of wealth for its own sake.

Another happiness philosopher, Robert Nozick (1989), in his book, *The Examined Life,* anticipates psychology in general and QOLT in particular by suggesting that we boost our happiness by "fiddling" with our standards of evaluation so that our current life situation looks good relative to some baseline or benchmark such as conditions in the past. Since we can control the benchmark or yardstick we use to evaluate whether our needs, goals, and wishes are being fulfilled, we can control our own level of happiness (at least to a point). Psychologist William James used this approach to happiness enhancement to treat his own depression by lowering his expectations and perfectionistic demands on himself. For example, he chose to study philosophy, instead of biology, believing that philosophy was the easier field of study (Reisman, 1966).

Another diverse group, the modern existentialist philosophers, may agree that what little happiness is possible in a random, indifferent universe can be achieved by facing the hard truths of existence, creating our own values and meaning in life, and, then, boldly acting out these values knowing full well that our actions may serve no useful purpose in an "absurd" or pointless universe. Albert Camus, for example, saw the ancient Greek myth of Sisyphus as a perfect metaphor for the absurdity of human life and striving: Sisyphus is condemned by the gods to an eternal life spent pushing a large rock to the top of a hill. Every time he reaches the top, the rock falls down the other side of the hill. Sisyphus must then push the rock to the top again and so on *ad infinitum.*

Joel Feinberg (1992) echoed Aristotle's view of happiness through self-actualization and cleverly overcomes the pessimism of other existentialists. He argues that while life may be pointless and absurd, it is still "good," worthwhile, and happy to the extent that we fulfill our human potentialities. According to Feinberg, we are all born with latent potentials and unique dispositions that can be perfected as we grow into useful skills and talents. When used to the fullest, these skills bring satisfaction and happiness because we have fulfilled our nature or "done what comes naturally." According to Feinberg, a self-fulfilled and therefore happy life is "one that comes into being, prone and equipped to do its thing," and then uses itself up doing things without waste, blockage, or friction. His ideas like those of other philosophers discussed previously are reflected throughout modern psychology, in general, and in QOLT, in particular. With respect to the latter, these ideas can be found both in the QOL theory of life satisfaction and depression (Chapter 3) and in Chapter 11 on Goals-and-Values, as one key component to a person's quality of life. Some of this "ivory tower" philosophy can be very useful when used to build a practical philosophy of life to guide and sustain us.

In contrast to the nontheistic perspective of existentialists, world religions or wisdom traditions have suggested a very different perspective on achieving happiness. For example, the Judeo-Christian tradition seems to identify happiness with the experience of God. This sense of transcendence and mystical union usually requires an inward journey that de-emphasizes the physical world and material possessions, reduces preoccupation with selfish concerns, and focuses on increasing our spiritual knowledge and capacity for love as seen in the Jewish Kabbalah tradition, versions of which are currently popular with rock stars like Madonna and Britney Spears and in the writings of Buddhist and Christian monastics or contemplatives (Kornfield, 2000; Merton, 1996a, 1996b).

In summing up philosophical and theoretical perspectives on happiness, the work of Richard Coan (1977) is useful. After reviewing the bulk of what philosophers, theologians, and theoretical psychologists had to say about happiness, fulfillment, "self-actualization," and mental health in his book, *Hero, Artist, Sage, or Saint?* Coan suggests that happiness can be achieved in five basic ways or "modes": (1) *Efficiency,* or competence in basic life skills so that one can focus on work, projects, or causes outside of the self. These include basic intellectual and relationship skills; (2) *Creativity,* in which we are imaginative, open to experience, and able to make original contributions to how we live and work whether we are bona fide "artists" or not; (3) *Inner harmony,* including a deep self-understanding and acceptance; (4) *Relatedness,* including a deep empathy, sensitivity, and compassion for both the individuals we care about in our lives and for humanity as a whole. This gives us nurturing and fulfilling relationships as well as a focus beyond ourselves, that is, a concern for humankind, in general; and (5) *Transcendence,* in which we no longer experience ourselves as separate or alienated from the world, nature, or the universe and in which we experience a mystical sense of unity with a larger whole whether it be referred to as God, the whole of nature, ultimate beauty, or love.

PSYCHOLOGICAL THEORIES AND THEORISTS

Like philosophers, psychologists have speculated on how to properly understand and achieve happiness. Like many philosophers, William James, the "father of American psychology," believed that "happiness is for most men at all times the secret motivation of all they do and all they willingly endure." Sigmund Freud also believed happiness is the ultimate human motivation; our purpose in life is to adhere to the "pleasure principle" as we strive to maximize pleasure and minimize pain. Ever the pessimist, he thought we could never be happy given the constraints of civilized society that outlaw unbridled hedonism or the "If-it-itches-scratch-it" mentality. For this reason, even psychoanalysis couldn't cure human misery; at best, it could "turn neurotic misery into everyday unhappiness." In *Civilization and Its Discontents* Freud (1929/1989) laid out ways to become at least a little happy, including the use of drugs or meditation to kill instinctual urges, isolation from others (to insulate one from the hurt of rejection), and immersing oneself in a fantasy world of goodness through involvement in art, religion, or even psychosis (Freud, 1929/1989). Nevertheless, our best bet for some modicum of happiness is, according to Freud, sublimation or channeling our sexual and aggressive urges and instincts into meaningful work, especially art or science. Like Plato with his "philosopher-king" idea, Freud is really championing his own personal solution to the happiness conundrum since he himself was a workaholic who saw patients all day and wrote scientific papers in the evening.

B. F. Skinner, probably the most influential psychologist of the previous century, saw happiness as a feeling derived from rewarding circumstances or a life situation in which one was richly rewarded and appreciated and not subject to "aversive control," that is, the use of punishments to mold and maintain one's behavior. The neo-Freudian and social philosopher Erich Fromm (1956) bemoaned the fact that happiness for most is now pursued through mindless consumerism in which we act like overstuffed babies in search of commodities and experiences designed to make ourselves feel good instead of finding happiness through the externally focused art of loving others.

More recent psychological thought based on both research and theory has emphasized the thinking component of happiness; people are happy to the extent that they see a favorable comparison between the way their life is and how they want or expect it to be. Inherent in these cognitive theories is a judgment or evaluation as to whether reality meets our expectations, standards, or aspirations. According to this approach, we may decide how satisfied or happy we are by comparing our current situation to numerous standards or benchmarks like other people (as we strive to "keep up with the Joneses"), the past (or conditions in the past), or personal goals and aspirations. When we see that our needs, goals, or wishes have been fulfilled in our daily lives, we feel satisfied and, then, happy in the emotional sense (Diener, 1984; Diener et al., 1999; Lyubomirsky, Sheldon, et al., in press; Michalos, 1991; Veenhoven, 1996). In a similar vein, Abraham Maslow's theory of a universal hierarchy of needs that emerge in the same order for all of us, reflects the popular view that we are happy when our

needs or goals are met. Theorists like Maslow have been called "telic" or "endpoint" theorists since they see the final achievement of goals or fulfillment of needs as essential to happiness (Diener, 1984).

Activity theorists (Diener, 1984), like Mihaly Csikszentmihalyi (1990) in his groundbreaking book, *The Psychology of Optimal Experience,* see happiness as the by-product of activity rather than the result of reaching some endpoint or goal. This view echoes earlier philosophers like Henry David Thoreau who felt that keeping busy was the key to happiness. According to Csikszentmihalyi, we are content, blissful, and "in flow" when we are involved in tasks that are worthwhile and challenging, that is, when it is not too easy to be boring or too difficult to be frustrating. Other activity theorists like Peter Lewinsohn of the University of Oregon see happiness as the simple sum of pleasures or pleasant events we experience. This explains how many people get depressed when their life becomes burdened by "should" or burdensome activities and drudgery instead of "want" activities involving pleasure, joy, and mastery (Witkiewitz & Marlatt, 2004). Presumably, one's happiness should increase as positive experiences accumulate, according to this view.

Finally, there are what Ed Diener of the University of Illinois refers to as "top-down" (as opposed to "bottom-up") or activity theorists who see happiness as a function of our overall attitudes and personality rather than our circumstances (including the accumulation of pleasant events or "flow" experiences). As the poet John Milton said, "the mind is its own place and can make a hell of heaven and a heaven of hell." The theory and research of psychologist, David Lykken (1999) and others (see, e.g., DeNeve & Cooper, 1998; McCrae et al., 2000) have supported the view that many of us are blessed with happiness-promoting temperaments and personality traits like high sociability or extraversion and low neuroticism or emotional stability or "even-keelness," being naturally warm and trusting of others and so forth. This book teaches coping skills and attitudes to *partially* counteract unhappy traits and foster happy traits as recommended by Seligman (2002) especially with the happiness trait of optimism, which he maintains is educable.

Scholars such as Ed Diener have asserted that there is some truth in all of these contemporary theories and that seemingly incompatible theories may hold true at the same time. For example, research suggests that happiness can be enhanced (and negative affects like depression reduced) both by changing general attitudes or beliefs ("top-down" theories) and by increasing the number of pleasant activities in our life ("bottom-up" theories). Aaron T. Beck's cognitive therapy for depression is an example of this "two-pronged" attack (Clark & Beck 1999). The integrative theory proposed here tries to marry these various happiness theories with Beck's latest formulation of cognitive theory and therapy.

HAPPINESS RESEARCH

Although the idea of promoting happiness may have originated with the ancient Greeks, scientific research on the topic did not begin until the twentieth century (see reviews by Diener, 1984; Veenhoven, 1984). The bulk of this research began in the 1960s with the birth of the Social Indicators Movement in which government leaders and researchers in sociology and economics searched for social indicators of citizens' subjective or psychological well-being and personal happiness to supplement purely objective, economic indicators of wealth and material prosperity such as the gross national product, consumer price index, and average annual income. As the late Angus Campbell (1981) observed in *The Sense of Well-Being in America,* the increased affluence and college education that followed World War II seemed to create a paradigm or attitude shift in people and government in which happiness was no longer identified with material wealth alone. In keeping with psychologist Abraham Maslow's hierarchical theory of needs (which was popular in the 1950s), it was as if the country as a whole became motivated by higher needs for social support, belongingess, love, self-esteem, and the respect of others now that the country's affluence took care of more basic needs for food and shelter for many Americans.

The idea of the *good life* involving more than material affluence was expressed in political discourse as the responsibility of government and it seemed to expand to include securing the happiness (and not just material wealth) of its all citizens. Thus, President Lyndon Johnson in a 1964 speech promoting his Great Society program said: "The task of the Great Society is to ensure our people the environment, the capacities, and the social structures which will give them a meaningful chance to pursue their individual happiness.

Thus, the Great Society is concerned not with how much, but with how good—not with the quantity of goods, but with the quality of our lives." This sentiment led affluent Western nations to implement a series of large-scale survey studies to assess the well-being of their citizens and to gauge the demand for more government programs aimed at improving the national quality of life. The first national survey of happiness in the United States was conducted in 1957 and found Americans to be happy in general, especially those who worried less and were younger, married, wealthier, and better educated (see Gurin, Veroff, & Feld's, 1960, book, *Americans View Their Mental Health*). Other large-scale studies in the United States were conducted by Angus Campbell, Phillip Converse, Willard Rogers, Frank Andrews, Stephen Withey, Norman Bradburn, and Hadley Cantril (see Diener, 1984; for a review).

Personality and social psychologists developed their own approaches to researching happiness aimed at understanding happiness on the individual-level of human personality (e.g., the groundbreaking study of college students by Wessman & Ricks, 1966; updated and extended by Diener & Seligman, 2002; also see Diener, 1984; for review). Some gerontologists also became interested in the subject as they studied the adjustment to retirement and old age (George & Bearon, 1980; Vaillant, 2002). Oddly enough, clinical psychologists and psychiatrists neglected the scientific study of happiness until very recently (see Frisch, 1998b; for review). In the words of the famous psychologist, Henry Murray, "one of the strangest . . . symptoms of our time is the neglect by psychologists of the problem of human happiness, the inner state which Plato, Aristotle, and almost all succeeding thinkers of first rank assumed to be the highest of all good achievable action."

Recent research on happiness has spawned innumerable, creative approaches to measuring and studying happiness, a concept that until recently was seen as too complex, private, and difficult to measure. With the aid of computers and pagers, Experience Sampling Methods allow us to record our mood and happiness randomly throughout the day to see how they fluctuate depending on our thoughts and experiences or circumstances (Csikszentmihalyi & Hunter, 2003; Diener, 2003). Paper-and-pencil tests of happiness and life satisfaction like the QOLI (Frisch, 1994) used in QOLT have been found to predict outcomes years in advance from job satisfaction (Diener & Seligman, 2004; Judge, Thoreson, Bono, & Patton, 2001) and performance to academic retention in college (Frisch et al., 2005) and social-psychiatric adjustment (see review in Chapter 3).

Clearly many of the ideas of ancient Greek philosophers are mirrored in contemporary psychological theories of happiness. For example, Freud was a hedonist and both cognitive judgment and "top-down" attitude theories are clearly reminiscent of the ancient Stoics like Epictetus. Given this discovery that there is "nothing new under the sun," one can wonder what progress we've made in understanding happiness over the past 2,300 years. As then-governor, Ronald Reagan asked about public support of university-based research, "Why subsidize intellectual curiosity?" especially if it results in nothing new. Indeed, QOLT maintains that the psychology of happiness and contentment is the greatest scientific challenge of our generation since increased wealth, technological advances, and advances in medicine and the "hard sciences" of physics and chemistry have not appreciably impacted human happiness (Diener & Seligman, 2004; Easterbrook, 2004; Myers, 2000; Putnam, 2001). Additionally, the current study of happiness is much more sophisticated than the Greeks on at least two counts: (1) current theories are infinitely more complex and precise and (2) the application of sophisticated research methodology has moved the study of happiness from the armchair (as in "armchair" philosophizing and pure speculation) to the scientific laboratory (for examples, see Diener & Seligman, 2004; Kahneman et al., 1999).

Perhaps the greatest contribution of contemporary thought to happiness is the development and implementation of sophisticated research techniques. These techniques now let us test and refine theories based on fact instead of speculation and have led to the precise scientific measurement of happiness on a global scale so that it is now possible to compare the contentment level of different countries. For example, an ambitious study of 39 countries using sophisticated measurement and statistical techniques by Alex Michalos (1991; also see Inglehart, 1990) found strong cross-cultural evidence for a key assumption of QOLT; happiness is closely tied to how we *think* about our lives, especially life satisfaction or the gap we perceive between what we have and what we want out of life. Michalos also found overall happiness to be best predicted by satisfaction in the specific areas of love relationship, self-esteem, standard of living, and friendships, areas of life highlighted in QOLT. Many other large-scale studies within and across countries can be found in the journals, *Social Indicators Research* and the *Journal of Happiness Studies* (e.g., see Cummins, 2003; Diener & Suh, 2000; and Veenhoven, 1999 for more international studies).

The findings of happiness research studies have sacrificed some "sacred cows" by disproving long-held beliefs. For example, we now know that positive feelings like happiness and joy are somewhat independent of negative feelings like depression and anxiety. So just because you don't feel *bad,* does not mean you feel *good.* In fact, research in this area has convinced many that we need to broaden our criteria for mental health and adjustment to include personal happiness, contentment, and a capacity for joy rather than focusing only on the negative side of mental illness and pathological symptoms (Diener & Seligman, 2004; Frisch et al., 1992; Kazdin, 1993a, 1993b, 2003; Ogles et al., 1996; Strupp, 1996). It is as if mental health professionals have excluded an entire realm of positive psychological functioning or positive mental health, which we need to include in any wholistic understanding of a person. Hans Strupp, a distinguished professor of psychology at Vanderbilt University, has argued this point for years, saying that a clients' happiness or contentment should be the ultimate criterion to see if psychotherapy or medication is effective in treating a psychological disturbance (Strupp, 1996; Strupp & Hadley, 1977). Tests of psychiatric symptoms and negative feelings simply do not give a full and complete picture of clients' "mental status," psychological well-being, or progress in treatment, according to Dr. Strupp. These findings and others from the research literature on happiness, positive psychology, and quality of life form the basis of Quality of Life Therapy.

CHAPTER 3

QOL Theory

QOL, HAPPINESS, AND LIFE SATISFACTION AS QUALITY OF CONSCIOUSNESS

Perhaps control of our consciousness, our thoughts, feelings, and physical sensations, is the greatest challenge to clinical psychologists, according to Albert Bandura (1986), as well as to the QOL theory[1] that underlies QOLT.[2] With QOL theory's emphasis on life satisfaction and subjective well-being—SWB, the researcher's term for happiness, quality of life or QOL refers, in part, to the quality of consciousness or the extent to which human inner experience (e.g., thoughts and feelings) is positive. It deals with the question, "Are you basically happy, content, or satisfied with your life?" Defining QOL in terms of inner, subjective, and personal experience is a hallmark of SWB research in general, and QOL theory, in particular. This inner subjective—SWB—approach yields different results from those obtained with a purely "objective" approach to QOL, well-being, and its measurement as when well-being is defined in terms of material wealth alone (Diener & Seligman, 2004). At the same time, the inner experience or subjective approach never denies the relevance of our objective living conditions. As we shall see, however, such conditions are only a part of the happiness equation.

In QOL theory, emotions—and related satisfaction judgments—are seen as adaptive in that they provide continuous feedback on progress toward personal goals. Whereas pleasant or positive affects stem from the perception that important needs, goals, and wishes have been, or are about to be, met, achieved, or fulfilled, unpleasant or negative affect signals setbacks or stagnation in the quest for fulfillment in valued areas of life (Diener, Diener, Tamir, Kim-Prieto, & Scollon, 2003; Diener & Larsen, 1993; Frisch, 1998a; Lyubomirsky, King, et al., in press). The affects usually associated with SWB include contentment, satisfaction, happiness, enjoyment, pleasure, and enthusiasm. Positive affect here also includes security, tranquility, hope, optimism, pride in accomplishments, love, affection, relief (from the reduction or elimination of a perceived threat, harm, loss, or yearning), positive "aesthetic emotions" (in response to art, nature, or religious activity) as defined by Lazarus (1991), as well as occasional moments of joy, rapture, or elation (see Diener, Scollon, & Lucas, 2004). According to Lyubomirsky, King, et al. (2004; also see Frisch et al., 2005), consistent happiness and life satisfaction signal to us that we are doing well in gaining fulfillment in valued areas of life, leading to a plethora of benefits.

THE BENEFITS OF HAPPINESS AND LIFE SATISFACTION

As mentioned in Chapter 1, feeling good is its own reward. A positive and pleasant conscious experience is rewarding in and of itself. QOL theory assumes that many additional benefits accrue to clients who maximize their happiness, especially to the point of stable,

---

[1] A simpler exposition of QOL theory and QOLT for the layperson can be found in the companion book and CD to this book authored specifically for clients and the general public entitled, *Finding Happiness with Quality of Life Therapy: A Positive Psychology Approach,* © 2006 by Michael B. Frisch, Woodway, TX: Quality of Life Press. Foreword by Ed Diener. E-mail contact: michael_frisch@baylor.edu.

[2] This theory is a revision and extension of that presented in Frisch (1998a) to the recent work of Aaron T. Beck, David A. Clark, and Ed Diener.

chronic, or high average happiness and satisfaction (those who experience high levels of happiness and life satisfaction most of the time). High average happiness and high average life satisfaction signal to us that we are doing well in gaining fulfillment in valued areas of life (Frisch et al., 2005; Lyubomirsky, King, et al., 2004). Success breeds success as this inner experience of stable happiness and satisfaction itself boosts our confidence, optimism, and self-efficacy; positive construals of others and likeability; sociability, activity, and energy; prosocial behavior; immunity and physical well-being; effective coping with challenge and stress; and originality, flexibility, and goal-oriented behavior. These characteristics of the very happy, in turn, lead stably happy people (those who experience positive emotions most of the time) to be *more* successful at achieving additional goals in valued areas of life, in keeping with the definition of life satisfaction here and elsewhere (Diener, 1984). In support of this hypothesis, happy people—relative to their less happy peers—in Western societies appear to have more rewarding and longer-lasting marriages, more friends, higher incomes, superior work performance, more community involvement, better mental and physical health, and even greater longevity (see review by Lyubomirsky, King, et al., 2004).

QUALITY OF LIFE THEORY: TOWARD A UNIFIED CONCEPTION OF QOL

Inconsistency in Measurement and in Conceptualization

The pervasive lack of articulated theory and the methodological inconsistency within and across healthcare disciplines (e.g., social work, nursing, psychology, medicine, gerontology) have resulted in QOL being equated with diverse constructs. Depending on the study, QOL refers to sex, pain, level of fatigue, life satisfaction, SWB, objective living conditions and circumstances (e.g., housing, standard of living), behaviors such as attending sporting events that a researcher (rather than a respondent) deems as "healthy" or "good," impairments in "functional ability" presumably caused by a particular disease or disorder, behavioral competencies needed to gain satisfaction in valued areas of life, self-esteem, personal control, mortality of disease, symptoms of psychological disturbance (e.g.,

depression and anxiety) and physical illness (Bowling, 1991; Salek, 1998; Spilker, 1996; Stewart & King, 1994). In addition, polyglot QOL scales that add to the theoretical confusion by confounding these diverse constructs in single measures are proliferating (Salek, 1998).

The inconsistency in measuring and conceptualizing quality of life threatens to trivialize the field in the eyes of clients or consumers and their families, third-party payers, and regulators who, at present, are willing to consider QOL in determining the cost-effectiveness of treatments and health plans (Diener & Seligman, 2004; Dimsdale & Baum, 1995; Gladis, Gosch, Dishuk, & Crits-Cristoph, 1999). In particular, an explicit, comprehensive, and testable theory seems to be an essential prerequisite for further advances in the understanding, assessment, and intervention of QOL problems in healthcare as well as in nonclinical, positive psychology settings.

QUALITY OF LIFE THEORY: BRIDGING QOL, POSITIVE PSYCHOLOGY, AND BECK'S COGNITIVE THEORY OF PSYCHOPATHOLOGY

QOL theory attempts to address the inconsistency and confusion in the literature of both positive psychology and health-related quality of life. Key terms are explicitly defined. The theory consists of an empirically—*based* and empirically—*validated* model of quality of life and life satisfaction applicable to clinical and positive psychology purposes. For clinical purposes—both psychological and medical—the theory is integrated with Beck's latest cognitive theory of psychopathology and depression.

KEY FEATURES OF QOL THEORY

More specifically, QOL theory:

1. Offers the Five Paths or CASIO rubric or model of life satisfaction as a blueprint for quality of life and positive psychology interventions called Quality of Life Therapy (QOLT) and Coaching.
2. Spells out how positive psychology interventions can be incorporated into clinical practice. Specifically, QOL theory spells out how QOLT can be used

in the clinical context of cognitive therapy to activate the "constructive mode" in Beck's latest model of depression and psychopathology, in general. Activation of this constructive mode is now seen as an important part of cognitive therapy for the entire range of psychopathology.

3. Delineates how QOLT can be used clinically to augment clients' *acute treatment* response to cognitive therapy, to provide *continuation therapy* when needed, and to *prevent relapse* as predicted by D. A. Clark and Beck (1999) and Diener and Seligman (2004).

4. Suggests how activation of Beck's constructive mode with QOLT can benefit *nonclinical or "pure" positive psychology* populations, that is, the general public or professional groups interested in personal growth.

DEFINING QUALITY OF LIFE

Quality of life refers to the degree of excellence in life (or living) relative to some expressed or implied standard of comparison, such as most people in a particular society (*Oxford English Dictionary*, 1989; "quality" entry; also see Veenhoven, 1984; for similar definition). The degree, grade, or level to which "the best possible way to live" or "the good life" is attained can range from high to low or good to poor (Veenhoven, 1984). Usually, QOL is explicitly or implicitly contrasted with the *quantity* of life (e.g., years), which may or may not be excellent, satisfying, or enjoyable. The Stoic philosopher Seneca (c. 4 B.C.–A.D. 65) clearly valued quality over quantity: ". . . it matters with life as with play; what matters is not how long it is, but how good it is" (Hadas, 1958, p. 63). In this vein, popular definitions center on excellence or goodness in aspects of life that go beyond mere subsistence, survival, and longevity; these definitions focus on "domains" or areas of life that make life particularly enjoyable, happy, and worthwhile, such as meaningful work, self-realization (as in the full development of talents and capabilities), and a good standard of living. These popular definitions and the origins of the phrase, QOL, may stem from the increased affluence and college education in Western societies following World War II and the accompanying fundamental attitude shift away from an emphasis on material wealth toward a concern with QOL issues (Campbell, 1981;

Patterson, 1996). Cross-cultural studies support the view that this shift in values continues to characterize postmodern, Western affluent societies (Diener & Suh, 2000; Inglehart, 1990).

Popular definitions of QOL found their way into political discourse, resulting in efforts by affluent Western governments to study and improve the QOL of their citizenry through a series of national QOL surveys begun in the United States in 1959 (Cantril, 1965; Gurin et al., 1960). Sociologists and economists created the "Social Indicators Movement," in part, to supplement "objective" indices of QOL (e.g., material well-being) with "subjective" measures of "well-being," "perceived QOL," life satisfaction, and personal happiness. Little correlation between objective and subjective indices of QOL were found (Michalos, 1991; Myers & Diener, 1995; see Davis & Fine-Davis, 1991, for an international review).

As with the fields of sociology and economics, the discussion of QOL issues in general medicine is a post-World War II phenomenon, dating from 1948 (Dimsdale & Baum, 1995) but beginning in earnest during the 1960s (Kaplan, 1988). Until recently, QOL was equated with symptoms of disease (or morbidity) and length of survival from an illness (or mortality; Taylor, 2002). While current conceptualizations include the constructs of happiness, well-being, SWB, and life satisfaction, most emphasis is placed on behavioral competencies or "functional ability" (Dimsdale & Baum, 1995; Spilker, 1996; Ware, 2004), which is often unrelated to happiness (e.g., Diener et al., 1999; Frisch, 1998b; Safren et al., 1997). Functional ability can be defined as perceived behavioral competencies, that is, clients' or medical patients' perceived ability to function effectively and successfully in valued areas of daily life. Functional ability includes social role performance (e.g., as a parent, spouse, employee) and the daily living skills needed for dressing, eating, transportation, handling money, maintaining a home or apartment, and the like.

QOL theory and measurement in gerontology began in the 1960s as part of an effort to define and to foster "successful aging" (Baltes & Baltes, 1990; L. George & Bearon, 1980). QOL in gerontology has been defined primarily as life satisfaction that is the primary outcome of successful aging from a variety of theoretical perspectives (Abeles, Gift, & Ory, 1994; L. George & Bearon, 1980). Gerontologists also define QOL in terms of functional ability and, to a lesser extent, happiness, pain, energy level, personal control, and self-esteem (Stewart & King, 1994).

Clinical and health psychologists have only recently begun to recognize the potential contribution of quality of life theory and research both to the clinical enterprise (Frisch et al., 1992; Kazdin, 1993a, 1993b, 1994; Ogles et al., 1996; Safren et al., 1997) and to nonclinical interventions (Frisch et al., 1992; see Frisch, 1998a; for a review of intervention studies).

DEFINING POSITIVE PSYCHOLOGY IN TERMS OF QUALITY OF LIFE

The field of positive psychology has ignored or given short shrift to the voluminous literature on QOL. For example, Seligman (2002) barely mentions the term much less its researchers, despite the fact that the construct fits positive psychology's rubric of a *positive* human characteristic and despite the fact that QOL has often been defined exclusively in terms of happiness and life satisfaction, core concerns of positive psychologists.

Recent work defines quality of life as what philosophers such as Plato have long referred to as "the good life" (Diener, 2003; Veenhoven, 2003a). As with Frisch (1998b), Diener (2003) defines the good life, quality of life, and the *positive* in positive psychology as happiness a.k.a. "subjective well-being" or "well-being." Happiness involves the relative predominance of pleasant or "positive" affect, over negative or unpleasant affective experiences—anxiety, depression, anger—in our conscious experience. Diener (2003) emphasizes happiness and life satisfaction over other positive affects (see Lazarus, 1991, for a discussion of these), perhaps because these are associated with fulfillment and accomplishment of personal goals in the areas of life that we value. To avoid moral relativism and the celebration of happy psychopaths, he further emphasizes happiness achieved in an ethical manner without harming others. Finally, he defines positive psychology as a loose confederation of those interested in studying happiness and other positive human strengths and virtues and in helping people achieve a better quality of life.

QOLT defines positive psychology similarly as the study and promotion of human happiness, strengths, and a better quality of life for all. As one of many positive psychology approaches to enhancing human happiness and quality of life, QOLT advocates a life satisfaction approach in which clients are taught a theory, tenets, and skills aimed at helping them to identify, pursue, and fulfill their most cherished needs, goals, and wishes in valued areas of life. In order to preserve relationships and social harmony, this pursuit should be an ethical one in which the legitimate rule of law is not violated and in which harm to others is minimized and avoided. The approach attempts to incorporate the most current theory and research with respect to happiness and the management of negative affect along with insights from positive psychology practice and various wisdom traditions such as philosophy and contemplative/mindfulness spiritual traditions.

DEFINING HAPPINESS, WELL-BEING, AND QOL

The terms *quality of life, perceived quality of life, subjective well-being* (SWB), *well-being, happiness,* and *life satisfaction* have been used interchangeably, and inconsistently, in the SWB literature. However, each term has unique theoretical nuances (Campbell, Converse, & Rogers, 1976; Diener, 1984; Diener & Seligman, 2004). The global constructs of SWB and happiness are equivalent and have, for the most part, been defined in terms of affect, cognition, or a combination thereof (Andrews & Robinson, 1991; Diener, 1984; Diener et al., 1999, 2003; Lyubomirsky, Sheldon, et al., in press). *Affective theorists* define SWB as either positive affect alone or as a preponderance of positive affect (such as joy, contentment, or pleasure) over negative affect (such as sadness, depression, anxiety, or anger) in an individual's experience (Andrews & Robinson, 1991; Bradburn, 1969).

LIFE SATISFACTION APPROACH

Cognitive theorists use the "life satisfaction approach," to SWB, defining happiness in terms of cognitive judgments as to whether a person's needs, goals, and wishes have been fulfilled (Campbell et al., 1976; Cantril, 1965). Thus, life satisfaction is defined as a "cognitive judgmental process dependent upon a comparison of one's circumstances with what is thought to be an appropriate standard" (Diener, Emmons, Larsen, & Griffen, 1985, p. 71). The smaller the perceived discrepancy between one's aspirations and achievements,

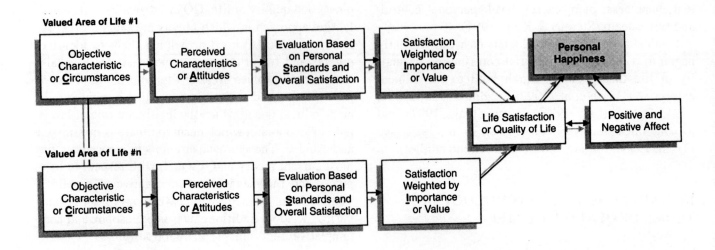

Figure 3.1 Five Path or CASIO model of life satisfaction, happiness, and positive psychology intervention. *Note:* The <u>O</u> element of CASIO refers to the assumption that overall satisfaction may be increased by boosting satisfaction in *any* valued area of life, even areas <u>O</u>ther than those of immediate concern. Interventions in any CASIO element may boost happiness in an area of life like love or work. In Beck's cognitive theory, moderate to high happiness or life satisfaction may be seen as part the positive schema cluster called the *constructive mode.*

the greater the level of satisfaction, according to this approach (Diener et al., 2003; Frey & Stutzer, 2001).

QOL AS THE LIFE SATISFACTION PART OF HAPPINESS

A consensus has emerged among some researchers who have found evidence for the cognitive theory of emotion, in general, and SWB, in particular, supporting a *combined cognitive-affective theory* or definition of SWB based on numerous studies, including factor-analytic and large-scale national and cross-cultural studies (Andrews & Withey, 1976; Diener, 1984; Diener & Larsen, 1993; Headey & Wearing, 1992; Lazarus, 1991; Michalos, 1991; Veenhoven, 1984; also see the cognitive theories of emotion posited by Beck and his colleagues; D. A. Clark & Beck, 1999; and by Lazarus, 1991). According to this view and QOL theory: SWB and well-being are synonymous with personal happiness. Personal happiness, in turn, is defined in terms of three parts: life satisfaction, positive affect, and negative affect. In high SWB or happiness, there is high life satisfaction and a preponderance (in duration) of positive versus negative affective experience in consciousness. That is, our conscious experience consists of much

more positive than negative emotional experiences (Diener, 1984; Diener et al., 1999). In other words, our degree of happiness is a positive function of the degree of life satisfaction and of the extent of positive affect preponderance in a person's daily experience.

QOL theory further assumes that the affective components of happiness stem largely from our cognitively based life satisfaction judgments or appraisals as when we feel happy, secure, and relieved once our standards for satisfying work have been met. In keeping with the cognitive theorists who take the "life satisfaction approach" just discussed, *in QOL theory, life satisfaction refers to our subjective evaluation of the degree to which our most important needs, goals, and wishes have been fulfilled.* Thus, the perceived gap between what we have and what we want to have in valued areas of life determines our level of life satisfaction or dissatisfaction.

Finally, in QOL theory, QOL is equated with life satisfaction (see Figure 3.1 and Table 3.1). In support of this view, QOL in psychology and psychiatry, and, to a lesser extent, in general medicine and cancer treatment is often equated with life satisfaction (Ferrans, 2000; Frisch, 1998b, 2000; Rabkin et al., 2000; A. G. Snyder, Stanley, Novey, Averill, & Beck, 2000). When not defined *solely* in terms of life satisfaction, life sat-

Table 3.1   The 16 Areas of Life That May Constitute a Person's Overall Quality of Life

1. *Health* is being physically fit, not sick, and without pain or disability.

2. *Self-Esteem* means liking and respecting yourself in light of your strengths and weaknesses, successes and failures, and ability to handle problems.

3. *Goals-and-Values/Spiritual Life* (A person's Goals-and-Values or Philosophy of Life may or may not include Spiritual Life.) Goals-and-Values are your beliefs about what matters most in life and how you should live, both now and in the future. This includes your goals in life, what you think is right or wrong, and the purpose or meaning of life as you see it. *Spiritual Life* may or may not be an important part of a person's *Goals-and-Values*. *Spiritual Life* refers to spiritual or religious beliefs or practices, that you pursue on your own or as part of a like-minded spiritual community.

4. *Money* (or *Standard of Living*) is made of the money you earn, the things you own (like a car or furniture), and believing that you will have the money and things that you need in the future.

5. *Work* means your career or how you spend most of your time. You may work at a job, at home taking care of your family, or at school as a student. Work includes your duties on the job, the money you earn (if any), and the people you work with.

6. *Play* (or *Recreation*) means what you do in your free time to relax, have fun, or improve yourself. This could include watching movies, visiting friends, or pursuing a hobby like sports or gardening.

7. *Learning* means gaining new skills or information about things that interest you. Learning can come from reading books or taking classes on subjects like history, car repair, or using a computer.

8. *Creativity* is using your imagination to come up with new and clever ways to solve every day problems or to pursue a hobby like painting, photography, or needlework. This can include decorating your home, playing the guitar, or finding a new way to solve a problem at work.

9. *Helping* (Social Service and Civic Action) means helping others (not just friends or relatives) in need or helping to make your community a better place to live. Helping can be done on your own or in a group like a church, a neighborhood association, or a political party. Helping can include doing volunteer work at a school or giving money to a good cause.

10. *Love* (or *Love Relationship*) is a very close romantic relationship with another person. Love usually includes sexual feelings and feeling loved, cared for, and understood.

11. *Friends* (or *Friendships*) are people (not relatives) you know well and care about who have interests and opinions like yours. Friends have fun together, talk about personal problems, and help each other out.

12. *Children* includes a measure of how you get along with your child (or children). Think of how you get along as you care for, visit, or play with your child (or children).

13. *Relatives* means how you get along with your parents, grandparents, brothers, sisters, aunts, uncles, and in-laws. Think about how you get along when you are doing things together like visiting, talking on the telephone, or helping each other.

14. *Home* is where you live. It is your house or apartment and the yard around it. Think about how nice it looks, how big it is, and your rent or house payment.

15. *Neighborhood* is the area around your home. Think about how nice it looks, the amount of crime in the area, and how well you like your neighbors.

16. *Community* is the whole city, town, or rural area where you live (not just your neighborhood). Community includes how nice the area looks, the amount of crime, and how well you like the people. It also includes places to go for fun like parks, concerts, sporting events, and restaurants. You may also consider the cost of things you need to buy, the availability of jobs, the government, schools, taxes, and pollution.

isfaction is almost always a component of QOL theories and assessments (Gladdis et al., 1999; Spilker, 1996). Interestingly, QOL in gerontology is often equated with life satisfaction; indeed, life satisfaction is the primary outcome of "successful aging" from a variety of theoretical perspectives (L. George & Bearon, 1980; Stewart & King, 1994).

FURTHER SUPPORT FOR THE LIFE SATISFACTION APPROACH TO HAPPINESS AND QOL

Life satisfaction is also emphasized over positive and negative affect in QOL theory for pragmatic reasons. Practically speaking, life satisfaction is less susceptible to momentary online mood fluctuations and irrelevant contextual effects than is positive or negative affect (Diener, 2003). Additionally, life satisfaction is much easier to measure than the preponderance of positive over negative affect experiences over time (Campbell et al., 1976; Diener et al., 2003; Diener & Larsen, 1993; Michalos, 1991); this may explain the predominance of life satisfaction QOL measures in the American Psychiatric Association's listing in their *Handbook of Psychiatric Measures* and the relative exclusion of behavioral functional ability measures, which are relegated to chapters on functioning rather than QOL (American Psychiatric Association, 2000b).

Life satisfaction may best reflect the concepts of happiness and quality of life because life satisfaction best reflects the philosophical notion of the good life according to Veenhoven (1993), because it reflects *enduring* and *longstanding* well-being—Seligman (2002) would say "authentic happiness"—and because it is highly individualistic and flexible: "a strength of the life satisfaction measure is its flexibility because people can consider or ignore information that they personally consider to be relevant or irrelevant. Therefore, the measure is idiographic in that the individual respondent, not the experimenter, can weigh information in whatever way the individual prefers" (Diener et al., 2003, p. 24).

LIFE SATISFACTION AS A PREDICTOR OF HEALTH PROBLEMS AND HEALTH-RELATED EXPENDITURES AS WELL AS FUTURE JOB PERFORMANCE AND SATISFACTION

Besides the reasons just cited, the relative emphasis on life satisfaction over affect in QOL theory reflects the plethora of predictive validity studies, whose findings support the view that low life satisfaction may predict a number of problems and maladaptive behaviors (with adaptive behaviors and outcomes associated with moderate to high satisfaction):

- Job performance and satisfaction as much as 5 years in advance (Judge & Hulin, 1993; Judge & Watanabe, 1993)
- Job accidents, unit profitability, and productivity (Harter, Schmidt, & Hayes, 2002)
- School performance (e.g., academic retention in college; see Predictive Validity of the QOLI above,

functioning in high school; Valois, Zullig, Huebmer, & Drane, 2001; Zullig, Valois, Huebner, Oeltmann, & Drane, 2001)
- Healthcare expenditures (e.g., treatment costs; Moreland, Fowler, & Honaker, 1994; Stewart, Ware, Sherbourne, & Wells, 1992; Ware, 1986)
- Suicide (Koivumaa-Honkanen, Honkanen, Viinamaki, Heikkila, Kaprio, et al., 2001)
- Deaths due to fatal injuries (Koivumaa-Honkanen, Honkanen, Koskenvuo, Viinamaki, & Kaprio, 2002)
- Response of depressed clients to pharmacotherapy and the need of both medication and psychotherapy treatments for some depressed clients (Miller et al., 1998)
- Chronic pain syndrome (Dworkin et al., 1992)
- Cardiovascular diseases such as myocardial infarction (Vitaliano, Dougherty, & Siegler, 1994; for a review)
- Other physical illnesses such as respiratory tract infections and colds in both healthy individuals and those afflicted with cancer (Anderson, Kiecolt-Glaser, & Glaser, 1994)
- Willingness to participate in prevention programs aimed at eliminating unhealthy behaviors like smoking (Wagner et al., 1990)
- Adolescent substance abuse (Gilman & Huebner, 2000)
- Adolescent and adult violent and aggressive behaviors (Valois et al., 2001)
- Peer relationship problems in adolescents (Ford, Fisher, & Larsen, 1997; Gilman & Huebner, 2000)
- Impulsive, reckless behavior such as unsafe sex practices (Kalichman, Kelly, Morgan, & Rompa, 1997)
- Somatoform disorders (Baruffol, Gisle, & Corten, 1995; Lundh & Sinonsson-Sarnecki, 2001)
- Anxiety disorders (Baruffol et al., 1995)
- Major depression—initial onset and relapse

In one of the few prospective studies of its kind, Lewinsohn and his colleagues (Lewinsohn, Redner, & Seeley, 1991) found that low life satisfaction preceded or predicted episodes of clinical depression in an undepressed subsample of community volunteers. Participants evidenced low life satisfaction just prior to the onset of clinical depression. Life satisfaction ratings tended to worsen during the depressive episode, only to move up into the average or normal range once the depression abated. Low life satisfaction was the only variable found to be "prodromal, or an early manifestation, of depression's onset" (p. 163) both in this study and in a prospective study of depressive relapse that followed clients who had been successfully treated for depression (Gonzales, Lewinsohn, & Clarke, 1985). The results of these studies were corroborated and extended in a prospective study of 184 randomly selected community volunteers in which levels of life satisfaction assessed 2 years earlier significantly predicted the onset of *DSM* depressive, anxiety, and somatoform disorders (Baruffol et al., 1995). The authors concluded that low life satisfaction is a major risk factor for psychological disturbance.

Besides identifying risks for health problems and related expenditures, life satisfaction seems to predict a person's ability to function in major life tasks or social roles such as work. Life satisfaction relates to and, at times, predicts a person's satisfaction at work—in the context of school, work includes the ability to stay in school and complete a degree, that is, academic retention—making QOL measures a potential screening device for employers and schools since those satisfied with their life generally are more likely to be successful in and satisfied with their work (see Diener et al., 1999; for review and Frisch et al., 2005; for an original research study on the topic). Life satisfaction seems to be discriminable from the constructs of psychiatric symptoms, negative and positive affect, depression, and anxiety in both clinical and nonclinical samples,making it less likely that the relationships reviewed here merely reflect the influence of a third variable like depression (Crowley & Kazdin, 1998; Diener, 2000; Frisch et al., 1992; Gonzales et al., 1985; Headey, Kelley, & Wearing, 1993; Lewinsohn et al., 1991; Lucas, Diener, & Suh, 1996; McNamara & Booker, 2000; Schimmack, Diener, & Oishi, 2002; A. G. Snyder et al., 2000).

AIMING FOR CONTENTMENT OVER GIDDINESS IN QOLT

The relative emphasis on life satisfaction over affect in QOL theory also reflects the QOLT intervention goal of reasonable contentment rather than perpetual positive affect whether it be rapturous joy—which is rare and may result in painful rebound effects—or to constant happiness—which is chimerical even in the very happy (e.g., see Diener & Seligman, 2002).

FIVE PATH OR "CASIO" MODEL OF LIFE SATISFACTION AND QOL INTERVENTIONS

The *CASIO* model of life satisfaction is, in many ways, the centerpiece of QOL theory.

Figure 3.1 presents the CASIO model of life satisfaction that is then joined with "Positive and Negative Affect" to explain the concept of SWB or personal happiness. The CASIO model of life satisfaction is used as the basis for many of the QOL interventions that make up Quality of Life Therapy since intervention in any CASIO element may lead to greater happiness in an area of life.

The "CASIO" model in Figure 3.1 is a linear, additive model of life satisfaction based on the work of Campbell et al. (1976), which assumes that an individual's overall life satisfaction consists largely of the sum of satisfactions with particular "domains" or areas of life deemed important by the individual. (Those areas most closely related to *personal goals* are usually considered most important; Diener et al., 2003.) This additive assumption has been empirically validated in numerous studies and reviews (e.g., Andrews & Withey, 1976; Campbell et al., 1976; Davis & Fine-Davis, 1991; Diener & Diener, 1995; Diener & Larsen, 1984; Diener & Oishi, 2003; Diener et al., 1999, 2003; Evans, 1994; Groenland, 1990; Headey, Holmstrom, & Wearing, 1985; Headey & Wearing, 1992; Kozma & Stones, 1978; Linn & McGranahan, 1980; McGee, O'Boyle, Hickey, O'-Malley, & Joyce, 1990; Michalos, 1983, 1991; Rice, Frone, & McFarlin, 1992; Szalai & Andrews, 1980). For example, when asked about the source of their global life satisfaction judgments, research participants spontaneously—without any prompts—and consistently report basing these judgments on their satisfaction with particular domains or areas of their life that they deem important such as romantic relationships, family, health, and finances (Schimmack et al., 2002).

A corollary to the additive assumption is that *satisfying* areas of life may compensate for areas of *dissatisfaction* or *low satisfaction* (Campbell et al., 1976; Diener et al., 2003; Frisch, 1998a). For example, some working mothers may be more content than homemakers because satisfactions in one domain (e.g., work, family life) may mitigate the effects of dissatisfaction in other areas of life.

CASIO ELEMENTS OF QOL THEORY

As illustrated in Figure 3.1, a person's satisfaction with a particular area of life is made up of four parts: (1) the objective characteristics or circumstances of an area, (2) how a person perceives and interprets an area's circumstances, (3) the person's evaluation of fulfillment in an area based on the application of standards of fulfillment or achievement, and (4) the value or importance a person places on an area regarding his or her overall happiness or well-being.

The C in the CASIO Model: Objective Characteristics and Living Conditions

Objective life circumstances or living conditions refer to the objective physical and social characteristics of an area of life whose effects on life satisfaction and SWB are cognitively mediated. According to Michalos (1991), about half of the SWB equation reflects a persons' perception and evaluation of their circumstances, while their actual or objective circumstances constitute the other half. The objective characteristics of an area of life contribute to satisfaction judgments, such as when a person's satisfaction with work is based on the work itself, pay, relationships with coworkers and bosses, the work environment, and job security (Diener & Larsen, 1984; Diener et al., 2003; Frisch, 1998a).

The role of perceptions and satisfaction judgments may help to explain the lack of significant correlations between objective and subjective indices of QOL such as wealth and housing after years of research carried out as part of the Social Indicators Movement (Michalos, 1991; Myers & Diener, 1995; see Davis & Fine-Davis, 1991, for a review of the Social Indicators Movement). By way of illustration, two people in identical circumstances will often respond differently to the circumstances as in the case of two janitors, one who appreciates his work conditions and enjoys his work, and another who sees the work as beneath her.

In QOL theory, objective living conditions vary in their rewardingness or potential for yielding human fulfillment or satisfaction. Reasonable rewardingness in a living environment is a prerequisite for QOL enhancement. When individuals accurately perceive the objective characteristics of an area of life as extremely impoverished or destructive to their well being, efforts

to alter or remove themselves from the environment should take precedence over purely cognitive coping efforts, a point lost in some purely cognitive formulations of depression and SWB. This does not, however, preclude biased interpretations of accurately perceived situations to enhance self-esteem and optimism, which is reflected in the A in the CASIO model (Taylor & Brown, 1988).

A in CASIO Model: Attitude

In addition to objective characteristics, individuals' subjective *perception* of an area's characteristics will also influence their satisfaction with the area as when they distort the objective reality of a situation in either a positive or negative way. In addition to this "reality testing" aspect, the *Attitude* component of CASIO satisfaction judgments includes how a person *interprets* reality or a set of circumstances once it is perceived. This interpretation includes deciding the implications that a given set of circumstances has for a person's self-esteem (e.g., causal attributions) and present or future well-being (Lazarus, 1991).

The S in the CASIO Model: Standards of Fulfillment

The *evaluated* characteristics of an area of life in Figure 3.1 refer to the application of personal standards to the *perceived* characteristics of an area. Specifically, the perceived characteristics of an area of life are evaluated through the application of standards of fulfillment that reflect a person's goals and aspirations for that particular area of life (Diener et al., 2003). That is, a person will decide whether his or her needs and aspirations have been met in a valued area of life. The level of achievement of standards for key characteristics in an area of life are combined subjectively via a "hedonic calculus" (Andrews & Withey, 1976) to form an overall judgment of satisfaction for a particular area of life (i.e., "Overall Satisfaction" *with the area* in Figure 3.1).

People will feel more satisfied when they perceive that their standards of fulfillment have been met and less satisfied when they have not been met (Diener et al., 2003; Schimmack et al., 2002). The standards, aspirations, and goals an individual holds for an area of life can dwarf the influence of objective living conditions in determining his or her satisfaction with an area as when goals and standards are set unrealistically high (i.e., not commensurate with functional abilities or the potential rewardingness of a given environment to provide rewards), a common scenario in depression (see, e.g., Ahrens, 1987; Bandura, 1986; Rehm, 1988).

The I in the CASIO Model: Weighing Area Satisfaction by Importance

QOL Theory proposes that a person's satisfaction with a particular area of life is weighed according to its importance or value to the person before the area's satisfaction enters into the subjective "equation" of *overall* life satisfaction (see Figure 3.1). Thus, satisfaction in highly valued areas of life is assumed to have a greater influence on evaluations of overall life satisfaction than areas of equal satisfaction judged of lesser importance. For example, a person equally satisfied with work and recreational pursuits who values work more highly will have his or her overall judgments of life satisfaction influenced more by work than recreational satisfaction. In QOL theory, the value or importance attributed to specific domains or areas of life reflects a person's most cherished goals and values; it also can dramatically affect overall judgments and ratings of satisfaction. In a clinical or coaching intervention context, life satisfaction may increase when an extremely important area of dissatisfaction is de-emphasized as less important in the process of reexamining life priorities as when persons who are exposed to unsolvable problems at work relegate work to a marginal place in their life and commit themselves instead to being a better spouse or parent or vice versa (Frisch, 2005).

The O in the CASIO Model: Overall Satisfaction

Since individuals' overall satisfaction in life reflects, in part, the sum of satisfactions in all valued areas of life, they may boost their overall satisfaction by increasing satisfaction in any or all areas they value, even areas that are not of immediate concern or that have not been considered recently. The gist of the O positive psychology strategy is to focus on these areas of lesser concern or focus in order to increase overall positive affect.

LIFE SATISFACTION APPROACH TO HAPPINESS

There are implications of the CASIO model of life satisfaction. As noted previously, QOLT theory maintains that happiness comes largely from having needs, wants, and goals fulfilled in the areas of life that we care about; this includes satisfaction and happiness as we meet subgoals along the way. While real time or online *flow* experiences may not generate happiness or its elements—life satisfaction, positive over negative affect, *at the time* (Seligman, 2002), a deep sense of satisfaction or contentment follow such experiences. As, for example, when therapists "at the top of their game" see clients all day, only to feel content and, at times, joyful at the end of the day, reflecting on their use of skill with challenging clients in the service of therapeutic goals. Similarly, parents playing with their children, teens doing challenging homework all evening, and a guitarist practicing all afternoon on a complex piece of music, experience satisfaction and/or other elements of happiness at the conclusion of their labors and for as long as the related memories persist and are recalled even savored, perhaps as a way to bask or self-soothe oneself with pleasant memories of engaging and challenging activities.

Our level of satisfaction with an area of life that we care about along with our emotions about the area tell us if we are making progress toward long-term goals and short-term subgoals. Thus, our feelings and satisfaction with an area tell us our *progress and prospects:* they tell us our progress in gaining fulfillment so far, and they tell us our prospects for future fulfillment in the area.

HAPPINESS *INGREDIENTS*

Overall happiness may be likened to a salad or a stew with different ingredients for different people and tastes. QOL theory assumes that a finite number of areas of human aspiration and fulfillment may be identified that will be applicable to both clinical and nonclinical populations; numerous researchers have found support for this assumption (e.g., Andrews & Withey, 1976; Campbell et al., 1976; Diener, 1984; Headey & Wearing, 1992; Veenhoven, 1984, 1993). That is, people tend to want the same things, although the areas valued by a particular individual will vary as will the subjective importance of those areas to that individual's overall life satisfaction or happiness. Thus, an area of life such as work may be highly valued by one individual but judged irrelevant to overall happiness by another who is retired.

Based on an exhaustive review of the literature in general, "cognitive mapping" studies of human concerns (Andrews & Inglehart, 1979; Andrews & Withey, 1976) and studies identifying particular areas of life associated with overall life satisfaction and happiness (Andrews & Withey, 1976; Campbell et al., 1976; Cantril, 1965; Diener, 1984; Flanagan, 1978; Inglehart, 1990; Michalos, 1991; Veenhoven, 1984), a comprehensive list of human concerns, "domains," or areas of life was developed; evidence for the importance of these chosen domains has accumulated since 1994 and the publication of the QOLI by Pearson Assessments. An effort was made to be comprehensive but to limit the areas of life to those empirically associated with overall satisfaction and happiness. The 16 *potential* Valued Areas of Life related to overall life satisfaction are listed in Table 3.1 (and make up the QOLI; Frisch, 1994). These areas of life such as *Money* are capitalized and italicized throughout the book when referring to the specific theoretical terms and definitions for these areas of life as spelled out in QOL theory and the Quality of Life Inventory or QOLI®.

HAPPINESS FROM GOAL STRIVING AND ACHIEVEMENT NOT MATERIALISM PER SE

QOL theory maintains that happiness comes largely from having our needs, wants, and goals fulfilled in the areas of life that we care about; this includes happiness as we meet subgoals in the journey toward fulfillment in valued areas of life, such as when college students make the grades they need to apply to graduate school later on. This assumption is supported by much research (see Diener, 1984; Diener & Seligman, 2004; Diener et al., 1999, for reviews). At times, happiness is associated with the achievement of developmental tasks or milestones at certain ages including the ability to make friends as a child, succeed in school, and find a partner in adulthood (and not in early adulthood as many have assumed, according to Dr. Rebecca Shiner of Colgate University;

Shiner, 2003). Of course, these milestones are often related to our conscious goals of making friends and so forth.

Achievement in QOL theory is *not* equated with materialistic wealth, although this is important to many. Indeed, an undue emphasis on materialism may interfere with lasting happiness and contentment (see, e.g., Myers, 2000). We also can achieve intimacy in love relationships and friendships as well as proficiency in pastimes that amuse, entertain, and distract us, for a time, from stressors, hassles, and problems we face.

THE IMPORTANCE OF WEIGHTING SATISFACTION BY IMPORTANCE: THEORY

The weighting of an area's satisfaction by its importance to an individual is considered essential according to many theorists in the fields of both quality of life/SWB and clinical psychology/psychiatry. Indeed, satisfaction in areas of life deemed unimportant or "goal irrelevant" should have no influence on overall life satisfaction or SWB according to these theorists (Campbell et al., 1976; Diener, Emmons, et al., 1985; Diener et al., 2003, 2004; Ferrans & Powers, 1985; Flanagan, 1978, 1982; Frisch, 1998a; Lazarus, 1991; Pavot & Diener, 1993; also see Abramson, Metalsky, & Alloy, 1989; Bandura, 1986; D. A. Clark & Beck, 1999), who make the same point with respect to the impact of life events on measures of negative well-being and clinical depression. Also see Pelham (1995) who makes the same point with respect to self-esteem judgments—weighted esteem of self-aspects is more strongly related to global self-esteem that unweighted esteem of self-aspects judgment.

By omitting importance ratings in theories and scale scoring schemes, researchers, clinicians, and coaches will allow unimportant—or relatively unimportant—areas to be weighed the same as a client's most cherished areas of life since all domains are considered to be of equal value; this may lead to distortions and inaccuracies in estimates of overall life satisfaction, SWB, or quality of life, along with a misunderstanding of a person's fundamental values and goals in life. For example, scale items about satisfaction with marriage, children, or work are assumed important in unweighted scoring schemes or theories even when a respondent is widowed, childless, and retired, respectively, and no longer interested in these areas.

THE IMPORTANCE OF WEIGHTING SATISFACTION BY IMPORTANCE: RESEARCH

Weighing satisfaction by importance is an implicit part of the process of making global satisfaction judgments according to empirical findings. Studies of source reports support the view that individuals estimating their SWB vary systematically in their valuing—or importance ratings—of different life domains such as work, health, leisure, school, or love life (e.g., Schimmack et al., 2002; Schwarz & Strack, 1999). Furthermore, only valued domains, that is, domains cited in source reports of overall life satisfaction judgments, impact overall life satisfaction judgments; unimportant domains seem to have no impact on such overall ratings. Finally, Schimmack et al. (2002) also found that weighing domain satisfaction judgments by importance improves the relationship between domain satisfaction and global life-satisfaction, presumably by reflecting the domains that really matter to a person's overall quality of life (also see Campbell et al., 1976).

RISK AND PROTECTIVE FACTORS FOR LIFE SATISFACTION AND HIGH QOL: "TOP-DOWN" AND "BOTTOM-UP" INFLUENCES ON LIFE SATISFACTION

In keeping with findings that support both approaches, the QOL theory of life satisfaction is both a top-down and bottom-up theory (Diener & Larsen, 1993). Rewarding or pleasurable objective life circumstances and events foster life satisfaction as do superordinate cognitive styles and traits. Individual difference or environmental variables that increase the probability for high life satisfaction are called protective factors, while factors that decrease the probability for high life satisfaction are called vulnerability or risk factors. The vulnerability factors proposed by QOL theory are supported by research findings (for reviews see Argyle, 2001; D. A. Clark & Beck, 1999; Diener, 1984; Diener & Seligman, 2004; Headey & Wearing, 1992) and include: (1) inadequate coping skills or functional abilities, especially social skills related to valued

areas of life; (2) any of the following generalized cognitive styles or personality traits: neuroticism/negative affectivity, self-focused attention, trait low self-esteem, self-blame and criticism for negative outcomes, the depressive or pessimistic attributional style for interpreting the causes of negative events (i.e., internal, stable, and global attributions for negative events), negative cognitive schemas, low self-efficacy, pessimism, introversion—especially low sociability and low interpersonal warmth, low hope, and perfectionism or the tendency to set unrealistically high standards for personal accomplishment or satisfaction in valued areas of life; (3) biological (heritable) vulnerabilities to anxiety, depression, and low trait SWB/unhappiness; exaggerated neuroendrocrine reactions to stress, including the stress of repeated frustration in gaining life satisfaction (Lazarus, 1991); (4) social isolation or lack of social support, especially *close* friends, mates, or confidants; (5) early experiences with loss, uncontrollable events, and unpredictable events (e.g., Barlow, 2002); (6) negative parenting experiences with unengaged, neglectful or overprotective, and emotionally reactive caretakers who may model ineffective coping skills or who fail to foster autonomy and self-efficacy (e.g., Barlow, 2002; Hammen & Brennan, 2002); and (7) a low frequency of pleasant events, which is often indicative of unrewarding life circumstances, inadequate functional/coping abilities or both. Protective factors or "immunities" to low life satisfaction simply consist of the opposites of vulnerabilities or risk factors (e.g., adequate coping and interpersonal competencies, optimism, high self-esteem).

QOL IS MORE THAN FUNCTIONAL ABILITY

Functional ability can be defined as perceived behavioral competencies, that is, clients' or medical patients' perceived ability to function effectively and successfully in valued areas of daily life (see Defining Quality of Life section earlier in the chapter). From the *psychological* perspective of QOL theory, particular functional impairments may or may not discourage, demoralize, or ruin individuals' basic contentment or quality of life, suggesting the need to assess life satisfaction, or SWB first and foremost (Diener et al., 1999; Diener, 2000; Frisch, 1998b) in order to assess quality of life and to gain the needed context for understanding assessments of objective circumstances and functional abilities. For example, even clients who value the ability to drive (or walk more than one mile) equally can be expected to differ to the extent that driving (or walking) restrictions affect their satisfaction with life; one person may be devastated while another, who pursues interests close to home or lives in a self-contained retirement community, may suffer little, if any, impairment in life satisfaction or SWB. Very often the impact of problems in abilities/functioning or in objective living circumstances will be drastically tempered by the cognitive aspects of the last four CASIO elements along with other psychological risk and protective factors proposed by QOL theory and described later in the chapter. As Taylor (2002) asserts, QOL in medicine should consist of patients' reports of their *subjective* experience (e.g., life satisfaction) rather than behavioral or functional ability measures alone.

QOL IS NOT DEFINED IN TERMS OF SYMPTOMS OR MORBIDITY

The entire rationale for QOL assessment rests upon the discriminability of the construct from morbidity, otherwise this "extra" assessment would be a waste of time, yielding no additional information than that gleaned from symptom measures. When QOL and symptoms are confounded, valuable information may be lost according to Gladis et al. (1999) who present compelling evidence for the discriminability of life satisfaction from depressive symptoms (also see Lewinsohn et al., 1991, and Gonzales et al., 1985). Unfortunately, some health-related QOL measures still confound psychiatric symptoms with the QOL components of SWB and functional ability as in the case of the Global Assessment of Functioning (GAF) Scale or Axis V of the *DSM-IV-TR* (American Psychiatric Association, 2000; see Bowling, 1991, and Spilker, 1996, for other examples).

QOL THEORY OF CHANGE

The QOL theory of change hypothesizes that we always do our best to find happiness and to cope with difficulties given our limited skills and awareness

(and, less amenable to change, our genetic inheritance). QOLT aims to enhance skills and awareness so that clients may exercise their will over those aspects of contentment that are amenable to change so as to make themselves happier and more successful. According to one theory, we can potentially influence and control 50 percent of our happiness because we can control or learn to control our goals, activities, coping skills, and even to an extent, our life circumstances—the C in CASIO model outlined here; the remaining 50 percent of our happiness is determined by a genetically determined happiness set point or set range (Lyubormirsky, Sheldon, et al., in press).

LIFE IN THE CONSTRUCTIVE MODE: QOL THEORY AND A BRIDGE BETWEEN COGNITIVE THEORY AND POSITIVE PSYCHOLOGY

As seen in Figure 3.2 and as illustrated with Tom's case at the end of this chapter, psychopathology comes about when a significant stressor or unpleasant life event activates negative core beliefs or schemas, hurling clients into an all-encompassing primal mode of thinking, feeling, and behaving.

QOL theory bridges Beck's cognitive theory of psychopathology and positive psychology by delineating, for the first time in the literature, a suggested general mechanism for "constructive mode" functioning regardless of the specific type or area of personal striving. According to Beck and colleagues, constructive modes are acquired primarily through learning and are schema clusters aimed at increasing the resources of individuals (A. T. Beck, 1996; D. A. Clark & Beck, 1999). In terms of *etiology*, inactivity or weakness in constructive mode functioning contributes to the maintenance and chronicity of depression and related disorders, according to cognitive theory (A. T. Beck, 1996; D. A. Clark & Beck, 1999). In terms of *treatment*, the strengthening of constructive mode functioning and schemas, in addition to the deactivation of depressogenic schemas—paramount in cognitive therapy—is also important, according to Beck and his colleagues:

Intensely negative affective states such as depression may continue in part because of the inactivity or rela-

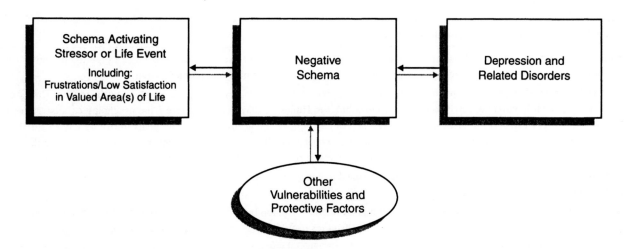

Figure 3.2 Integration of *QOL Theory* with Beck's Cognitive Theory of Depression and Related Disorders. *Note:* Based on Barlow (2002), Beck (1995), D. A. Clark and Beck (1999), and Persons et al. (2001). *Related disorders* include anxiety, anger, substance abuse, and personality disorders. Weakness in the schemas of the *constructive* or *satisfaction mode* may be a maintaining factor in depression just as their strengthening may be an essential part of cognitive therapy treatment according to Beck and colleagues (Beck, 1996; Clark & Beck, 1999). Frustrations/low satisfactions may include repeated failures to find satisfaction as in long-term *under*employment, loneliness, or a "loveless marriage."

tive weakness of the constructive modes. Thus a shift from a negative to a euthymic mood state may not be possible until the constructive modes have been activated. (Clark & Beck, 1999, p. 91)

A TWO-TRACK APPROACH TO COGNITIVE THERAPY

This latest formulation of Beck's model suggests a two-track approach to cognitive therapy, which is the essence of QOLT for clinical cases: application of traditional cognitive therapy techniques to deactivate depressogenic schemas and the application of the interventions to activate constructive schemas and modes. QOLT consists of a host of positive psychology interventions to activate constructive schemas and modes along with an underlying theoretical framework to guide these interventions. While important, QOLT interventions are limited at the start of cognitive therapy as therapists go about the most important order of business, that is, the deactivation of pathognomic or psychopathological schemas, as for example in major depression, depressogenic schemas (associated with the primal

loss mode). Of course, in nonclinical, personal growth, or positive psychology cases without *DSM* disorders, the use of QOLT interventions to activate constructive schemas and modes makes up the entirety of treatment.

In QOL theory, all constructive mode functioning is driven and activated by the processes outlined in the CASIO model life satisfaction, happiness, and positive psychology intervention delineated in Figure 3.1. Once activated, the constructive mode is hypervalent—dominating information processing and coloring experience in terms of the mode so that success in meeting needs is expected, that is, optimism ensues. Features of the mode color or dominate experience in that features of the mode itself will largely determine interpretations of situations and experience, rather than the characteristics of the situations themselves. Once activated, the mode becomes relatively autonomous and even somewhat impervious to experience as in the pathological mode functioning characteristic of clinical anxiety, anger, and depression wherein the threat, victim, and deprivation/loss modes predominate, respectively. Once activated, the constructive mode is relatively automatic and effortless, characterized by the *flow* state of consciousness (Csiksentmihalyi, 1997; Csikszentmihalyi & Hunter, 2003) as a person

Table 3.2   Delineation of the Constructive Mode(s), in General. Cluster of Schemas Characteristic of Constructive Mode Activation Regardless of Particular Area of Life or Strivings

1. Cognitive-Conceptual Schemas—Basically content and satisfied with life; appraisals of fulfillment and a high likelihood of fulfillment in most valued and cherished areas of life or optimism; personal planning and problem solving.

2. Affective Schemas—basically content and happy—moderate to high subjective well-being (SWB) along with frequent flow states of consciousness while pursuing fulfillment (Csikszentmihalyi & Hunter, 2003); relatively free from psychological distress and negative affect precisely because many or most of the individual's cherished needs, wishes, and goals in life have been fulfilled or will be (optimistic expectation for success); occasional activating dysphoria when fulfillment in a valued area of life dips (see Diener & Seligman, 2002 for this phenomenon in even extremely happy individuals); other positive affects (Lazarus, 1991).

3. Motivational Schemas—Very active with high energy aimed at engagement with environment to gain satisfactions and to savor pleasures and successes; optimistic zest for life.

4. Behavioral Schema—Energetic engagement in planning and in goal-directed behavior along with the ability to stop and savor experience as goals are met; perseverance in the face of obstacles to fulfillment; resourceful and assertive.

5. Physiological Schema—High energy and enthusiasm, moderate physiological arousal, alert though calm, centered and able to focus attention on immediate task or goal at hand.

---

pursues cherished goals and values with the expectation of success.

The schemata and categories of schemata in the constructive mode are reciprocally influenced among themselves and with the external environment. In keeping with the demarcations of Clark and Beck (1999), the constructive mode consists of five categories of schemas with particular schemas making up each category—see Table 3.2.

ACTIVATION OF THE CONSTRUCTIVE MODE AND POSITIVE AFFECT THROUGH QUALITY OF LIFE, POSITIVE PSYCHOLOGY, AND WELL-BEING INTERVENTIONS

David A. Clark and Aaron T. Beck (1999, pp. 91) explicitly predict that success in building satisfaction in valued areas of life may activate constructive mode functioning:

The relation between the *constructive modes [emphasis added]* and emotion is evident in two ways. First, the fulfillment of personal goals and expectations (this is a common definition for life satisfaction in the QOL and happiness literatures, the enhancement of which is the explicit goal of Quality of Life Therapy) . . . will be associated with positive emotions such as happiness. . . . Second . . . depression may continue in part because of the inactivity or relative weakness of the construc-

tive modes. Thus a shift from a negative to a euthymic mood state may not be possible until the constructive modes have been activated. The key to effective treatment of depression, then, involves strengthening of constructive modes of thinking to maintain a shift in mood state from a negative to positive valence. (p. 91)

The revolutionary import of this therapeutic advice is that depression (and other psychopathologies) subsides with success experiences in achieving personal goals and with the processing of these personal success experiences (constructive mode activation) and not merely with the processing of negative mode functioning (deactivation of primal loss mode) and schemas in therapy (also see Persons et al., 2001, who make the same point as does Frisch, 1992, 2005). Empirical support for this postulate of Beck and his colleagues is found in many of the previously listed predictive life satisfaction studies; for example, in the case of school functioning, constructive mode functioning as reflected in higher QOLI scores is predictive of future success in college as measured by academic retention 1 to 3 years in advance (Frisch et al., in press).

The mechanism of action in QOLT, like other well-being and positive psychology interventions (Fava & Ruini, 2003; Seligman, 2002), may be the activation of constructive mode functioning. QOLT attempts to achieve this activation by teaching clients practical skills for and steps to fulfillment in valued areas of life.

QOL THEORY: VULNERABILITIES AND PROTECTIVE FACTORS TO DISSATISFACTION, UNHAPPINESS, DEPRESSION, AND RELATED DISORDERS

QOL theory includes consideration of predisposing characteristics or moderator variables (Denney & Frisch, 1981; Frisch & McCord, 1987) that may either increase or decrease the likelihood of experiencing unhappiness, and low life satisfaction (or dissatisfaction), as well as depression and related disorders, especially anxiety disorders (see Barlow, 2002; D. A. Clark & Beck, 1999; and Persons et al., 2001; for the close relationship between, and similar diathesis-stress models of, anxiety and depression). Individual difference or environmental variables that increase the probability for the occurrence of depression/anxiety refer to risk factors or "vulnerabilities," while factors that decrease the probability for the occurrence of dissatisfaction or depression/anxiety refer to "Protective Factors" or "Immunities." The vulnerability factors proposed by QOL theory are supported by research findings (e.g., Abramson et al., 1989; Barlow, 2002; D. A. Clark & Beck, 1999; Diener et al., 2003; Headey & Wearing, 1992; Seligman, 2002; C. R. Snyder & Lopez, 2002) and include: (1) inadequate coping skills, problem-solving skills, and/or social skills related to valued areas of life—these are also called *functional abilities* in QOL Theory as a bridge to the literature on health-related QOL; (2) any of the following generalized cognitive styles or personality traits: neuroticism/negative affectivity or temperament, anxious and depressive schemas and modes such as negative self-referential schemas and the loss/deprivation primal mode, self-focused attention, low self-esteem, self-blame, and criticism for negative outcomes, the depressive or pessimistic attributional style for interpreting the causes of negative events (i.e., internal, stable, and global attributions for negative events), sociotropic or autonomous personality styles (D. A. Clark & Beck, 1999), low self-efficacy, pessimism, external locus of control, introversion and especially low sociability and interpersonal warmth, low hope (Snyder & Lopez, 2002), and a tendency to set unrealistically high standards for personal accomplishment and satisfaction in valued areas of life; (3) biological (heritable) vulnerabilities to anxiety, depression, low SWB/unhappiness or exaggerated neuroendocrine reactions to stress, including the stress of repeated frustration in gaining life satisfaction; (4) lack of social support, especially a close friend or confidant; (5) early experiences with loss, uncontrollable events, and unpredictable events; (6) negative parenting experiences with unengaged, neglectful or overprotective, and emotionally reactive caretakers who model ineffective coping skills and who fail to foster autonomy and self-efficacy; and (7) a low frequency of pleasant events. Protective factors or "immunities" to dissatisfaction and depression simply consist of the opposites of vulnerabilities or risk factors (e.g., adequate coping and interpersonal competencies, optimism, high self-esteem).

EMOTIONAL CONTROL AND LIFE MANAGEMENT SKILLS: PROTECTIVE FACTORS OR "IMMUNITIES" NEEDED FOR GOAL STRIVING

(Negative) Emotional Control and Life Management Skills are seen as protective coping skills or functional abilities in QOL theory. Specifically, a modicum of proficiency in Life Management and (Negative) Emotional Control Skills is seen as essential to goal striving, and to basic happiness or *positive mental health* in both clinical and nonclinical populations.

Happiness, according to researchers, includes life satisfaction as measured by the QOLI and the preponderance of positive to negative emotional experiences. We want the frequency of positive feelings to be much greater than the frequency of negative feelings. Despite this widely held definition, positive psychologists too often ignore the need for what QOLT calls *Negative Emotional Control.* All of our positive psychology efforts to be happy can be vitiated by frequent negative feelings.

Control or management of Negative Affectivity or what Barlow, Allen, and Choate (2004) call Negative Affect Syndrome is essential for goal striving and functioning in the modern, or postmodern, world and therefore a required prerequisite to the successful pursuit of happiness. Somewhat independent, strong negative affect will trump any positive affect, making us miserable and unhappy, however, we also need emotional control skills because high negative affectivity interferes with the complex social problem solving and thinking needed for goal striving, the essence in some ways of happiness. Finally, negative affect causes addictive relapse and may be the primary motivation for drug and alcohol abuse and dependency (Witkiewitz &

Marlatt, 2004). QOLT refers to the "'Big Three'" negative affects of anger, anxiety, and depression that so often co-occur in clients as its client-oriented name for negative affectivity. Negative affectivity, also called neuroticism is a huge stumbling block to happiness according to the latest research findings (Diener & Seligman, 2002, 2004). This makes sense given definitions of happiness as life satisfaction and the preponderance of positive over negative affective experience. If our feelings are predominantly unpleasant and negative, it will suppress or drown out any positive feelings of happiness (see *Emotional Control* "Tenet of Contentment" in the Toolbox CD).

LIFE MANAGEMENT SKILLS

Clients can gain control of their lives and make steady progress in solving problems and in achieving life goals and subgoals, including happiness, if they are reasonably organized in how they manage their day-to-day affairs and especially their time. If our time is planned and managed in the Graded Task Assignment sense of cognitive therapy (A. T. Beck, Rush, Shaw, & Emery, 1979) so that *small steps* of progress toward long-term goals are made every day, then we will feel happier and more content instead of dysphoric and frustrated, the feelings associated with unsuccessful goal-strivings and coping. Indeed, successful goal striving is negatively reinforced to the extent that dysphoria and frustration are reduced with goal attainment. In QOLT, skills in managing our day-to-day affairs and time in the service of goal striving define Life Management Skills, along with basic Relationship Skills—see Toolbox CD—or social skills required for any level of goal attainment. A modicum of ability in these skills is seen as essential to happiness in QOL theory, since happiness goal strivings will lead to nothing without them.

THE REALITY OF NONCOGNITIVE EXTERNAL INFLUENCES IN QOL AND COGNITIVE THEORIES

In contrast to popular perceptions, cognitive theory shows a thoroughgoing appreciation for external stressors and negative life events in the etiology of depression, although the impact of these and other factors on

depression is always cognitively mediated—the same point is true with respect to QOL theory. Objective circumstances are part of the definition of QOL and are an integral part of the CASIO model, although their effect is always cognitively mediated.

USE OF THE CASIO MODEL OF LIFE SATISFACTION IN FORMULATING POSITIVE PSYCHOLOGY AND CLINICAL INTERVENTIONS FOR CLINICALLY DISTURBED AND NONCLINICAL CLIENT POPULATIONS

Given that many researchers are agnostic about the ultimate cause of depression and related disorders, it is important to note that regardless of the ultimate etiology, QOL theory assumes that the construct of life satisfaction is a useful heuristic for understanding and treating QOL concerns by themselves, reflecting a positive psychology perspective, as well as treating QOL concerns related to psychiatric disorders like major depression from a clinical psychology or psychiatric perspective.

One of the major contributions that QOLT makes to cognitive therapy and to positive psychology intervention programs is the CASIO rubric for problem solving and QOL enhancement. QOL theory says that happiness comes largely from achieving one's goals and living one's values in the areas of life that one cares about. QOLT offers five general strategies that can boost satisfaction with any area of life. These general strategies flow from the underlying CASIO theory of life satisfaction. The CASIO model is illustrated in the *Five Paths to Happiness and Problem Solving* worksheet and the *Five Paths* (or CASIO) *Summary Reading Assignment and Exercise* in the Toolbox CD that accompanies this book. It is also illustrated in the completed *Five Paths* worksheet from a client introduced in Part III.

APPLICATION OF QOL AND COGNITIVE THEORY TO A CLINICAL CASE

The disguised case history of Tom is used throughout this text to illustrate the application of QOLT theory and procedures. After some background information on Tom, we will see the application of QOL theory, including its integration with the latest formulation of Beck's cognitive theory/therapy (Clark & Beck, 1999).

Background

Tom is the pseudonym used for a 22-year-old college student undergoing QOLT. Tom was drawn to the work of tortured artists such as Kurt Cobain and Sylvia Plath whose book *The Bell Jar* presaged her own suicide. He also immersed himself in the writings of existentialists whose emphasis on inner angst and the inherent meaninglessness and absurdity of life mirrored his own inner experience. All of his energy seemed to go into maintaining a high average in premedical undergraduate courses. His Type-A lifestyle seemed to reflect a core belief—depressogenic schema—that he was only worthwhile when he was achieving near-perfect levels of performance in school.

Tom occasionally overeats and abuses alcohol to self-medicate his depression. When feeling deeply down and depleted, alcohol helps Tom to forget his problems and to feel more confident in approaching women. He feels guilty about several furtive one-night stands, which, at the time, seemed to relieve his depression momentarily by providing him with some level of intimacy.

He felt guilty later, however, for violating his personal moral code and values by using women in this way and by pretending he was close to the person and interested in a committed relationship when he was not.

For a while, Tom was able to function as a "workaholic." A depressive crisis developed insidiously, however, because he increasingly had no time for anything but school work. For example, he started using any free time for more schoolwork. He often went to the library to read all of the latest research articles that he could to impress his teachers. There was no sense of moderation or balance in his life. In QOLT terms, he put all of his "emotional eggs" in one basket which was work, making him vulnerable to deep unhappiness should anything ever go wrong in this area of life.

Application of CASIO Theory of Happiness to Tom

In terms of the CASIO model of life satisfaction and happiness, Tom's overall satisfaction plummeted as

he put more and more time into his work/schoolwork, completely neglecting other valued areas such as *Friends, Spiritual Life,* and love life—all areas of deep unhappiness. This unbalanced lifestyle failed to render even his schoolwork satisfying. In CASIO terms, Tom's S or Standards for fulfillment in work were perfectionistic and impossible to meet on a consistent basis. He was dissatisfied with anything but an "A" on an assignment and constant signs of approval from all of his professors. Since he evaluated his performance as substandard most of the time, he did not really enjoy or feel satisfied with his work, even though he had an A average at pretreatment!

The CASIO model in Figure 3.1 shows overall life satisfaction as the additive sum of satisfactions in all valued areas of life. Since Tom neglected all valued areas except for his school-*Work*, his pretreatment satisfaction in non-Work areas was quite low, contributing to a very low overall level of QOL as seen in his pretreatment QOLI profile shown in Chapter 1, Figure 1.1.

Application of Beck's Cognitive Theory of Depression to Tom

As seen in Figure 3.2, psychopathology, in this case, major depression, comes about when significant stressors or unpleasant life events activate negative core beliefs or schema, hurling clients into an all-encompassing primal mode of thinking, feeling, and behaving. For Tom, the stress—or stressors—of trying to maintain a perfect "A" average in all of his academic work on the one hand, and an increasingly impoverished lifestyle of academic drudgery with little or no pleasure or fun, on the other hand, activated "ghosts from the past" or negative core schemas that led directly to Tom's depression (see "Schemas That Drive You Crazy" in the Toolbox CD for a listing of many core schemas). In other words, his frustration in meeting his goals for perfect work and his dissatisfaction with other areas of life that he cared about but ignored seemed to serve as stressors in Tom's case; more than discrete and obvious stressors like the end of a relationship or losing a job (Clark & Beck, 1999).

This barren and bleak lifestyle seemed to potentiate all of Tom's negative core beliefs or depressogenic schemas. He could not always get "As" on assignments and tests. He could not always make professors like him. In his private world of twisted logic, this was "proof" that he was somehow a defective person, unworthy of love and care. Here we see the interplay of schemas of perfectionism, approval, and what Dr. Judy Beck (1995) calls unloveability.

Other diverse schemas and complex cognitive processing characteristic of Beck's loss/deprivation primal mode took hold of Tom. Tom was certainly *deprived* of self-respect and a rewarding daily life. This deprivation *mode,* a full body and mind experience of misery that goes beyond simple cognitive schemas alone (see Clark & Beck's, 1999, exposition of *mode theory* for details), colored Tom's consciousness every waking minute, leading ultimately, to the diagnosis of Major Depressive Disorder (American Psychiatric Association, 2000). The pervasiveness of the deprivation mode is captured in Tom's metaphors. He said it was like being possessed by a "Mr. Hyde personality." He also referred to the experience as "my personal Auschwitz."

In terms of key schemas, Tom believed that he was basically an unlovable, flawed, and defective person. His academic achievements were a smoke screen that, as he saw it, hid his rotten inner core, keeping those he cared about from abandoning him completely. Indeed, he was sure that friends would reject him if they ever got to know him. Tom was ruthlessly critical of himself in order to keep his performance perfect and to jump on any mistake or interpersonal problem that might arise. If a problem came up, he wanted to "nip it in the bud" and effect "damage control," before rejection, abandonment, or criticism took place. If he was not eternally vigilant and successful in staving off failure or big mistakes, others might see what a loser he was and abandon or reject him. In this vein, his online conscious experience was like that of the spider-like machines in the *Matrix* movie whose only purpose was to sniff out problems (as in human beings) and destroy them before they could do any serious damage (see Wells & Papageorgiou, 2004). This depressive rumination and generalized anxiety-type worry maintained and intensified Tom's depression as he endlessly focused on and analyzed his negative feelings, looking for mistakes he made and convincing himself that any dysphoria or bad feeling whatsoever was a sign of deep psychopathology or "craziness" (McMillan & Fisher, 2004).

A detailed case conceptualization of Tom can be found in the Toolbox CD (ACT model worksheet).

Poor Little Rich Boy: The Childhood Etiology of Tom's Schemas

How did Tom's negative core schemas develop? To begin with, Tom was an unwanted child born into a materially wealthy family. His father took sadistic pleasure in reminding him that he was an "accident" and that his mother wanted to take him to an orphanage when he was born. For his first 9 years, his parents basically ignored Tom. His mother was working on becoming a prominent socialite in the community and his father was building a medical practice; they simply had no time for the boy. After coming home from day care all day, he would be left alone as his mother pursued her community volunteer work and his father worked in the evenings. The pain and confusion from being ignored and rejected by his own parents was intensified by their constant fighting. Tom blamed himself for their fights, believing that he was flawed, defective, and the extra burden that caused his parents to fight. Tom also blamed himself for his parents divorce when he was 9. His mother really didn't want him to live with her, fearing that living with a single mother would make him gay. Instead, Tom lived with his father from ages 9 to 17. For the most part, Tom was lucky if he saw his father for 15 minutes a day over dinner. From the age of 6 to 13, Tom was sent away to summer camp for 11 weeks where he was always the last child to be picked up by his parents, an experience that haunts him to this day. His father did not handle the divorce well; he withdrew further from Tom except to scold or beat him for such egregious offenses as leaving an apple core on the kitchen table. In anger he would tell Tom what a "rotten little shit" he was and how his mother never wanted him. The few times in which Tom's father was not scolding, berating, or ignoring him involved sexual molestation. Tom was "rescued" by his mother at the age of 17 when she heard of Tom's abuse. Older and wiser, his mother now resolved to try to make up for the years of neglect and abuse that Tom had experienced.

CHAPTER 4

How to Do QOLT

QUALITY OF LIFE THERAPY (QOLT) AND COACHING: POSITIVE PSYCHOLOGY VERSUS CLINICAL APPLICATIONS

QOLT defines positive psychology as the study and promotion of human happiness, strengths, and a better quality of life for all. As one of many positive psychology approaches to enhancing human happiness and quality of life, QOLT advocates a life satisfaction approach in which clients are taught a theory, tenets, and skills aimed at helping them to identify, pursue, and fulfill their most cherished needs, goals, and wishes in valued areas of life. This book describes positive psychology interventions that can be used with both clinical and nonclinical/general public/professional samples in the same way that Seligman (2002) applies his *Authentic Happiness* interventions to both groups. Interventions aimed at nonclinical groups are sometimes referred to as "coaching"; the term and acronym *Quality of Life Therapy* and *QOLT* encapsulates both types of interventions, that is, *Quality of Life Therapy and Coaching*.

This chapter explains how to conduct QOLT for both pure *positive psychology clients* devoid of psychiatric disorders and *clinical clients* with psychiatric disorders who can benefit from a *combination* of positive psychology and mental health interventions. Beginning with Chapter 3 and continuing throughout the book, the disguised case history of "Tom" is used to show how QOLT, its theory and techniques, can be applied to a particular *clinical* case; numerous other clinical and positive psychology cases are peppered throughout the book to illustrate QOLT.

CLINICAL APPLICATION OF QOLT

With clinical clients, QOLT always involves a two-track approach in which core techniques are combined with an evidence-based cognitive therapy for any comorbid *DSM* disorder. In this way, both quality of life and disorder-specific problems are comprehensively addressed. Since activation of the construction mode is now recommended in cognitive therapy for many *DSM* disorders (Clark & Beck, 1999), and since it may boost clients' acute treatment response and facilitate lasting therapeutic change and the prevention of relapse (see Chapters 1 and 22 for details as well as D. A. Clark and Beck, 1999; Diener & Seligman, 2004; Fava & Ruini, 2003; Frisch et al., 1992), QOLT core techniques from Part II (Chapters 5 through 10) are presented in order from the start of therapy to its conclusion along with standard cognitive therapy techniques. Chapter 22 gives additional details on conducting QOLT for relapse prevention purposes for clinical, chronic clinical, and *pure* positive psychology clients.

PURE POSITIVE PSYCHOLOGY APPLICATIONS OF QOLT: USE OF QOLT WITH NONCLINICAL POPULATIONS

For clients or groups without *DSM* disorders, such as those seeking growth-oriented coaching or burnout prevention, or people with physical illnesses or disabilities who might profit from quality of life enhancement, QOLT core techniques are presented in order followed by all of the area specific interventions, with an emphasis on areas of special concern and interest to the individual or group. For example, *Play* or recreation may be of greater interest to a group of retirees with no interest in paid employment or *Work;* for this reason *Play* interventions would be emphasized, and *Work* interventions would de-emphasized for this QOLT group.

Although QOLT therapists may emphasize specific areas of interest or concern depending on clients' interests and needs, it is recommended that all area-specific chapters be covered since topics and techniques of relevance are inevitably found in areas that clients initially thought would be irrelevant to their situation. For example, the *Work* area of intervention contains guidance on managing work-related problems that are relevant to volunteer positions as well as paid employment. Additionally, some clients' self-esteem and gratitude may be boosted in useful ways by that chapter's interventions even though these clients expressed little interest in the area to start with. Use of readings from the companion book for clients, *Finding Happiness* (Frisch, 2006) can be an efficient way to expose clients to all areas of QOLT so that potent interventions are not missed.

The O strategy in the CASIO model of QOLT provides the final rationale for covering all topics and area-specific interventions in QOLT. This strategy aims to boost <u>O</u>verall life satisfaction and quality of life by boosting satisfaction in areas of life not considered heretofore. Such a strategy urges clients to consider *all* areas of life that they value for intervention. This strategy may pay huge dividends in cases where progress is slow in certain areas of dissatisfaction as in a chronically unhappy marriage, chronic illness, or complex work situation.

NUMBER OF SESSIONS AND BRIEF THERAPY GUIDELINES

QOLT and related approaches have been effective in improving clients' quality of life in 10 to 15 sessions (Frisch, 2004a, 2000; Grant et al., 1995; Kazdin, 1993a, 2003). Clinical experience suggests that more or less time (or a smaller or larger "dose" of QOLT) may be needed depending on a particular client's personality and comorbid difficulties (Frisch, 1992). Most QOLT treatment techniques can be beneficial if practiced for 1 to 2 weeks, assuming that the client understands and has faithfully applied the exercise (e.g., Five Paths to Happiness worksheet, Lie Detector, and Stress

Diary a.k.a. Thought Record). After successfully applying a technique for 1 to 2 weeks, clients may then use the technique on an ongoing basis during intervention and after therapy ends to prevent relapse. Clients may also use some techniques on an as-needed basis, especially when they are under stress. Major life stressors often seem to contribute to relapses.

BEGINNING QOLT WITH THE CORE CASIO INTERVENTIONS IN PART II

The rest of this book provides a road map to doing QOLT. To begin QOLT, therapists should go through the chapters of Part II in order. These chapters represent the foundation of QOLT. As indicated earlier in this chapter, the QOLT approach has been used successfully in both group and individual therapy for *pure* positive psychology clients with no *DSM* disorders and with *clinical* cases or clients diagnosed with *DSM* disorders or emotional problems—especially, depression, anxiety, addictions/compulsive behaviors, and couples distress—in addition to quality of life difficulties.

Part I begins with a detailed chapter on QOL assessment and describes how this is integrated with traditional assessments of psychological disorders and general medical conditions. A model of case conceptualization and treatment planning is illustrated, which allows therapists to easily apply theory concepts from Chapter 3 in an effort to organize their thoughts about a client's problems and appropriate interventions. This case conceptualization is shared with clients in an effort to form a common understanding and close collaborative relationship between therapist and client. The essential core strategies and tenets of Inner Abundance, Quality Time, and Find a Meaning are included in Chapter 9.

QOLT offers both general CASIO Interventions based directly on QOL theory for all areas of life along with area-specific interventions like Work or relationships. Part II emphasizes general CASIO strategies, whereas the area-specific interventions are covered in Part III.

Unfortunately, positive psychologists often lose sight of the fact that scientific definitions of happiness refer to the predominance in frequency of positive to negative affect, neglecting interventions for the latter when negative affect is often a huge factor in the experience of happiness for both clinical and nonclinical groups (Diener, 2003). In QOL theory, effective goal striving—part of the area called *Goals-and-Values*—requires some basic (negative) emotional control and life management skills in order to achieve fulfillment in valued areas of life. Everyone needs skills to effectively manage these emotions to prevent immobilization in coping and to prevent them from becoming a chronic problem. Similarly, clients need some basic organization skills in order to pursue life goals and subgoals effectively. These skills provide a powerful bridge to traditional cognitive therapy and are presented in Chapter 10 because of their importance in QOLT.

WHEN TO APPLY AREA-SPECIFIC INTERVENTIONS IN QOLT

QOLT group and individual therapists urge clients to skim the relevant area chapters in the client-oriented companion guide to this book, *Finding Happiness* (Frisch, 2006), in order to transfer some responsibility for choosing interventions to clients. Area-specific interventions are applied in QOLT whenever clients express an interest or express dissatisfaction with the area and when it is clear that the area is important to a client. Additionally, both clients and therapists must see the area as important to work on in the context of therapy. In this vein, therapists may suggest work in an area that they see as relevant to the client's happiness even though clients did not spell out the area in the assessment phase of QOLT. Therapists provide an invaluable service when they gently make clients aware of area dissatisfactions of which they may be unaware or to which they will not admit. Graciella,[1] for example, appreciated being exposed to Goals-and-Values interventions, when the therapist suggested it; her initial Vision Quest exercise lacked goals for her marriage even though she felt stranded at home alone while her husband put in long hours at the office.

ASSESSING UNHAPPINESS IN ONE AREA OF LIFE IN THE CONTEXT OF WHOLE LIFE ASSESSMENT

Before charging ahead with interventions for one area of concern in life-like work, therapists and clients

[1] In keeping with Standard 4.07 of the Ethics Code of the American Psychological Association (American Psychological Association, 2002), the use of pseudonyms and other steps have been taken to disguise the personal identity of all case histories discussed.

should together examine clients' *overall* Goals-and-Values for the present and long-term with the QOLI and Vision Quest (described in Chapter 5) techniques. Other problems in living such as an impending divorce or a *DSM* disorder should be considered in formulating a conceptualization that incorporates all of the sources or causes of dissatisfaction with a particular area like Work. CASIO related problems can be examined with the *What's Wrong?* assessment in Chapter 5. In sum, first consider *all* of the possible sources or causes of clients' dissatisfaction and then choose the appropriate interventions. This *whole life* assessment perspective should be used with each of the specific areas addressed in Part III.

PRESENTING AREA-SPECIFIC INTERVENTIONS TO CLIENTS

As the core techniques of QOLT are being presented to clients or after they have been introduced, therapists may apply interventions from Part III. Chapter 5 presents a model of case conceptualization and intervention planning that can aid in this regard.

Thus, if Part III chapters are presented in order, clients first identify Goals-and-Values and related Tenets of Contentment conducive to happiness and weave these into an individually tailored Life Script of positive schemas. Next, clients learn techniques for building and maintaining basic self-acceptance or *Self-Esteem*—a significant ingredient of happiness and a big issue in both clinical and pure positive psychology populations. Next, it often helps to deal with *Health,* including dealing with chronic illnesses and disabilities along with positive and negative health habits or addictions.

Chapter 13 on health also considers positive *mental* health and a plethora of related happiness precepts, tenets, and strategies.

Relationship enhancement, a vital part of QOLT, constitutes the next part of this book. *Work.* considered in Chapter 15, is applicable even for retirees or for those on disability, given the broad definition of work in QOLT. Next, therapy continues by considering challenging and active *Play,* recreation, and socializing. Subsequent chapters look at ways to boost happiness in the areas *of Helping, Learning, Creativity, Money,* and *Surroundings.* Part III ends with a chapter on maintaining gains and relapse prevention.

LIFE SATISFACTION AND THE *WHOLE LIFE* PERSPECTIVE

Overall life goals are always considered in QOLT as therapists explain to clients how each therapy task, exercise, or homework assignment will move them closer to a cherished life goal. Therapists help clients develop life goals when they are lacking. For each life goal, QOLT therapists offer awareness and skills training as well as positive schemas or *Tenets of Contentment* (see Chapter 9) associated with fulfillment in that particular area of life. Expanding our life skills and awareness is viewed as a major avenue toward personal growth, happiness, and contentment in QOLT. In addition to teaching attitudes or tenets didactically, QOLT asks clients to test their efficacy *in vivo*, that is, in everyday life. Skill building is pursued via practice and small success experiences via small and doable homework assignments; for example, talking to a grocery clerk is related to the life goal of finding a mate for shy, depressed clients as they gradually improve their skills and confidence.

STRUCTURE OF SESSIONS

Each session of QOLT begins with an open-ended question such as, "How are you doing this week?" In this way, therapists communicate a willingness and openness to "tune in" to where the client is and to hear his or her agenda for the session rather than imposing their own agenda on clients without considering clients' immediate feelings and problems, which could include a suicidal crisis!

SETTING THE AGENDA

After checking in with clients as to how they are feeling, therapists should collaborate with them in setting an agenda for the session. Clients should be asked if there is anything in particular they would like to discuss. They may include crises or problems revealed in the initial "checking in" portion of the session.

A task-oriented way of checking in or setting an agenda with the client is to ask the question, "What would you like to work on today?" This is a great question for setting the tone of QOLT, that is, the idea that QOLT depends on clients taking responsibility to learn

and implement new ways to fulfillment in valued areas of life. This active orientation is integral to cognitive therapy (Beck, 1995).

After hearing the client's agenda, therapists can add their own agenda items and prioritize a master list. Often the list includes some immediate crises or problems brought in by the client to the session as well as ongoing interventions aimed at boosting satisfaction in valued areas of life. Near the top of the agenda or priority list should be homework from the last session. Unless homework assignments are discussed early in the session, the client may see them as unnecessary "busy work" that is not intimately tied to progress toward his or her personal life goals.

If there were problems in the last session, therapists may wish to inquire about any resistance or difficulties noted in the last session by asking the client a question such as, "How did you feel about our last session? Do you feel that we're on the right track in our counseling? Can you see how our work might help you to realize some of the Vision Quest goals you set for yourself? Was there anything I did or said during the last session that was unclear or rubbed you the wrong way?"

HOMEWORK PROCEDURES

Therapists should complete all of the QOLT exercises and instruments introduced in this book before trying them with clients in session. In turn, therapists should do part or all of the exercise or assessment during the session collaboratively with the client, before exercises, tenets, and skills are assigned as homework for clients to apply in real-world or in vivo circumstances. This procedure allows for the gradual shaping of skills and understanding that are essential for the design of small and consecutive success experiences engineered by therapists to minimize failures and to maximize excitement, enthusiasm, and optimism for the approach.

CLIENT NOTE TAKING DURING SESSIONS

Clients who can write are usually provided with a pen and a notepad when they arrive for therapy so that they can take notes or write down key points during the session for review later and so that they may record any homework assignments during the therapy session.

QOLT therapists encourage note-taking by telling clients that they will have a stronger chance of positive change and will "get more bang for their buck" if they think about their sessions during the week using their written notes. Therapists further encourage clients by saying that the more that they think about, practice, and work over concepts from sessions by taking notes and by putting them in their own words, the greater chance they will have of storing information in their long-term memories for future recall.

QOL THEORY OF CHANGE: USING METAPHORS IN THERAPY

The QOL Theory of Change is the rationale for QOLT. This theory represents a hopeful and optimistic view of human change that reflects the capacity for growth and resilience in each of us.

QOLT and its underlying theory assumes that clients are doing their best to cope with the problems in their life and really want to change, but lack the necessary skills and awareness to do so on their own. This assumption should be communicated clearly to clients since it can relieve them of self-defeating and undue guilt that often blocks efforts at positive change. This assumption also motivates clients with a message of hope since a lack of awareness and skills is remediable and is not the client's "fault" in the sense that he or she intentionally or willfully adopts self-defeating thoughts, feelings, and behaviors. This assumption and rationale should be communicated in the first session of treatment through the use of metaphor. For example:

> People who are not at their peak in happiness or who are downright *unhappy* are like mountain climbers trying to climb a mountain without the necessary skills, awareness, or even equipment needed to do it. For example, one of the major trails at the north end of the Grand Canyon, Bright Angel Trail, is full of hikers wearing sandals and shorts without any water going down into the canyon in the hottest time of the summer. While these people walk into the canyon with a definite spring to their step, they're usually huffing, puffing, thirsty, and sunburned by the time they try to climb back up. They simply haven't prepared for the trip. Many of them are unaware of what awaits them on the sizzling canyon floor beneath. Many have never learned the basics of

hiking or how to prepare for an adequate and safe journey. Many lack the basic skills in climbing and stumble over the difficult parts of the trail and are unable to navigate the loose rocks. For all of these reasons, some people aren't able to make the climb.

If you think of a mountain as a metaphor for self-realization, fulfillment, and success, you could say that we spend our life climbing the mountain of personal fulfillment. The journey of life or the journey up the mountain of self-realization is difficult and long but with each step up we can feel greater wholeness and confidence as we realize our potential and become all that we can be. Those "stuck in the rut" of unhappiness lack the necessary skills and awareness needed to make the climb to the top. Many never had a proper mentor or guide. They may have had neglectful or abusive parents. In addition to their ignorance, they may bear some psychic wounds or disabilities that make it hard for them to climb and succeed. They are unable to fulfill the key needs, wishes, and goals that are essential to their self-fulfillment.

Just like baby eagles thrust out of the nest before they are ready to fly on their own, these people lack the skills and awareness necessary to navigate life. They aren't inherently bad or incompetent. They aren't particularly responsible for the fix they're in. They've done the best they could with the limited skills and awareness they have. What they need is a guide or mentor to teach them the skills to fly or climb the "mountain of personal fulfillment." This, in large part, is the goal of QOLT that is used in counseling.

While you may not be responsible for the fix that you're in or your problems, you *are* responsible for getting help and for using or applying the help and skills you learn on a routine or day-to-day basis to make yourself happier and more fulfilled. Then, once you are aware of your problems and learn new ways to cope in counseling, it is up to you to apply these solutions and to do what is necessary to succeed. So while you can say "good-bye to guilt" for the fix that you're in, you have to bear the responsibility of moving forward.

JUDICIOUS SELF-DISCLOSURE

QOLT recommends regular and judicious self-disclosure by therapists to normalize problems and model positive self-change. This is especially helpful with same-sex/gender clients. For example, I share struggles with relationship issues such as equality in decision making, checking in on schedules, controlling anger, and really listening to my partner as though she were an equal business partner as a way of showing male clients that they are not alone, that it is "manly" to invest in their marriage, and that there is hope for real change.

Judicious refers to an effort to limit the extent of self-disclosure so as to not sully the "positive transference" clients have toward therapists who seem to be functioning well across life domains. It is said in the Dzogchen religious tradition of Tibet that one's guru should be from a village far away from your own so that you do not become too familiar with his human frailties; the same may apply to therapists who preserve the special *one-way* relationship of psychotherapy by not burdening clients and by not tarnishing their sterling images by being overly disclosing.

NONCOMPLIANCE AND "RESISTANCE" IN QOLT

Like traditional cognitive therapy, noncompliance or resistance is dealt with as a therapy issue in QOLT. That is, a time out from the general agenda is called as therapists ask clients for their reasons and even automatic thoughts—revealed by an in-session Lie Detector and Stress Diary exercise—related to "homework" that was not completed and so on.

Resistance can sometimes be seen when the QOLT case conceptualization is first shared with clients. Unless clients agree with the basic assumptions of QOLT, their specific case formulation and treatment plan, and the specific sequence of techniques developed by their counselor, resistance, a lack of cooperation, and noncompliance with treatment may sabotage the efforts of even the most skillful professional. Thus, before QOLT can begin, the therapist must reconcile the differing agendas of the client, the therapist, and at times, the referral source (such as a physician), or even significant others, such as partners, children, or coworkers. Finally, the QOLT case conceptualization and treatment plan should be shared with and approved by the client to assure a positive working relationship or therapeutic alliance.

Whenever resistance to change is encountered in QOLT, therapists should reexamine their case formulation or treatment contract with clients to be sure that there is no confusion or substantial disagreement about the goals and strategies of QOLT. Clients' case formulations should be presented to them in such a

way that they see a direct connection between the activities of QOLT and the achievement of personal life goals. In this vein, therapists should continuously relate specific techniques to clients' goals for QOLT.

NONCOMPLIANCE PREVENTION FOR HOMEWORK ASSIGNMENTS

Possible or anticipated noncompliance with homework is dealt with or prevented in two ways in QOLT. First, it is always best to first successfully complete an exercise like a thought record during a session with a client *before* assigning it as homework. Whether it is a thought record (or "structured journaling" as I call it) or a meditation exercise for Quality Time, do it in session with the client saying, "I understand how this works and it does make me feel better," *before* you assign it as homework. The principle of shaping should be applied to homework assignments, growth exercises, or skill training such that failure experiences are minimized or eliminated.

Second, by asking clients just before they leave a session to share all of the reasons and excuses for not doing homework that they are likely to come up with at the next session and then challenging and disputing each of these reasons, such as when clients say "I have no time," with a positive reframe like "I'll get more bang for my buck. I'll get more for my money if I make efforts in between sessions to think about and practice what I've discussed in session."

ADAPTING QOLT FOR GROUP WORK

QOLT is especially well suited to the context of group therapy. In addition to the considerable cost savings of providing QOLT in a group format, client groups provide invaluable social support as clients struggle together to build a more meaningful and satisfying life (e.g., Grant et al., 1995). Group members typically support the change efforts of each member. Finally, the group can function as an "interpersonal laboratory" in which clients may role-play and test out new interpersonal strategies for dealing with QOL problems. The relative safety of the group allows clients to get feedback on how they are coming across and to hone their new QOLT skills before taking risks in their everyday life (for an early example of this, see

Frisch, Elliot, Atsaides, Salva, & Denney, 1982). Such practice and feedback in groups especially increase a client's chances of success when implementing QOLT *relationship* strategies in real-life situations.

Just as with Individual QOLT, therapists should present the core techniques of QOLT in order with therapy groups. Although it is possible for a group to decide among themselves which areas of Part III to cover first, second, and so on, experience suggests that the order presented in this book is usually very well received.

QOLT WITH NONCLINICAL WORK GROUPS

With respect to *organization training,* this book and accompanying homework exercises can be utilized by a leader trained in this approach. Work groups particularly appreciate their managers' willingness to budget time for personal growth or QOL training. Satisfied workers are much more happy and productive on the job, so it clearly benefits employers as well as workers to provide this type of training.

ADAPTING QOLT WITH DISADVANTAGED, ILLITERATE, AND YOUNGER CLIENTS

QOLT can be easily adapted for use with disadvantaged, intellectually impaired, and illiterate clients. In these cases, exercises and concepts may be translated into simpler language that is easier to understand. Rather than carrying out homework assignments in written form, clients may be asked to verbally report on assignments. In addition, thoughts and behaviors may be recorded on a digital recorder or IPod, rather than in written form. Also, clients with reading difficulties or intellectual impairments can benefit from doing homework assignments during therapy sessions with the expert guidance of their therapists. Finally, therapists can and should involve significant others (e.g., family members) in the treatment so that they can encourage clients with disabilities and help them gain the most from QOLT.

Although QOLT has been successfully used with a few child and adolescent clients, further research is needed to validate this approach with this population. As a general rule of thumb, QOLT should be tailored to the developmental level of the client being treated. QOLT has been used successfully with college students in workshop, classroom, and counseling center settings (Frisch, 2004b; Frisch et al., 2005).

BURIED IN TECHNIQUES: THE ART AND SCIENCE OF PSYCHOTHERAPY

Therapy is both an art and a science. Even the most evidenced-based treatment manual such as that for cognitive therapy of depression (A. T. Beck et al., 1979) has much room for creativity as in how negative schemas are challenged by a therapist. In fact, many have not noticed that the case example in the manual involved *couples* cognitive therapy because the authors judged traditional individual cognitive therapy insufficient for the case. Likewise, this book requires creativity in case formulation and in the application of techniques. Lest readers be overwhelmed by the plethora of techniques herein, keep in mind that these tools may be used selectively according to what best fits a client and according to how much the therapist and client can handle at one time. While some clients can handle and integrate multiple readings and handouts, illiterate, apathetic, and intellectually challenged clients cannot. In the latter instance, a therapist may improvise by doing Stress Diaries or thought records in sessions with the therapist doing all of the writing and with the clients using *Second Opinions* from others more than their own rational disputations. Once again, therapy is an art as well as a science. Just as a skilled jazz musician improvises and riffs on a favorite theme, so, too, may experienced cognitive therapists adapt techniques and presentations to fit their personality as well as to the needs and personalities of their clientele.

The techniques presented in this book are meant to be ideas for moving therapy forward and for keeping it fresh and on-target. Rather than slavishly applying every technique, the therapist is encouraged to take a "kid in a candy store" attitude, experimenting in new, fun, and creative ways to apply QOLT to the unique problems, challenges, and assets of their clients.

QOLT AS A SUPPORT AND NOT ANOTHER BURDEN IN CLIENTS' LIVES

Be careful not to "guilt trip" clients into completing QOLT exercises outside of sessions. You can communicate a tolerant attitude toward QOLT by saying the following to clients:

> Since QOLT is a support for you to use when you feel like it, never criticize yourself for not doing an exercise like Quality Time on a regular basis. QOLT is something you do for you and should not be an extra burden in your life. We will want to notice what type of routines and exercises seem to foster greater contentment, but there will be times when you will not have time for these.

THE TONE OF THIS BOOK

This book and the accompanying Toolbox CD exercises for clients are written in a client-friendly tone that has been successful in communicating ideas and skills in a readily understandable and interesting way. The use of idioms and everyday language is aimed at making the material accessible to clients. Technical jargon is avoided in places where it has been a hindrance to clients' understanding, interest, and enthusiasm for the approach.

PART TWO
CORE TECHNIQUES IN QOLT

CHAPTER 5

QOLT Assessment: Integrating QOL with Traditional Health Assessments

As early as 1992, psychologists decried the exclusive emphasis on psychiatric symptoms of "ill-being" to the neglect of *positive* mental health and functioning (Frisch et al., 1992). Now, leaders from opposing theoretical camps in clinical psychology, psychiatry, health psychology, and general medicine encourage the development of nonpathology-oriented measures of QOL, SWB, life satisfaction, positive psychology, and "positive mental health" to augment those that focus on *negative* affect and symptoms (see Diener & Seligman, 2004; Frisch, 1998a; Keyes, 2005). For example, some cognitive-behavioral, psychodynamic, and humanistic theorists agree that a client's happiness or satisfaction with life is an essential criterion for mental health and for a positive outcome in psychotherapy, and that happiness or satisfaction with life should be routinely assessed by researchers and clinicians alike (Berzon, 1998; Fava & Ruini, 2003; Frisch, 1992; Kazdin, 1993a, 1993b, 1994, 2003; Seligman, 2002; Strupp, 1996; Strupp & Hadley, 1977). For example, according to Alan Kazdin, "there are few constructs as clinically important as quality of life," and that "measures of quality of life add an important domain to treatment (outcome) evaluation since clinicians are usually interested in improving patients' quality of life as a result of either psychological or medical treatment" (1993b, p. 296). Similarly, Strupp and his colleagues (Strupp, 1996; Strupp & Hadley, 1977) maintain that contentment, satisfaction, or SWB is the most important criteria of "mental health" and positive outcome in psychotherapy from a client's perspective (see also Ogles, Lambert, & Masters, 1996): "the individual wishes first and foremost to be happy, to feel content. He or she thus defines

mental health in terms of highly subjective feelings of well-being, feelings that have an incontrovertible validity of their own" (Strupp, 1996, p. 1019).

The World Health Organization defines health as "a state of complete physical, mental, and social well-being and not merely the absence of disease or infirmity" (World Health Organization, 1948). In keeping with this definition, the goal of healthcare today is to improve clients' QOL in addition to affecting a biological cure for physical illness or disability (Hyland, 1992; Muller, Montaya, Shandry, & Hartl, 1994). QOL is increasingly viewed as an essential health care outcome or "medical endpoint" which is at least as important as symptomatic status and survival in evaluating the effectiveness of any health care intervention. For this reason, general medicine and health psychology researchers are saying that biological measures of health should be supplemented with QOL and happiness measures to adequately represent the health of an individual or a group (American College of Physicians, 1988; Berzon, 1998; Diener & Seligman, 2004; Faden & Leplege, 1992; Fallowfield, 1990; Frisch et al., 1992; Ogles et al., 1996).

QOLT defines *positive mental health* as happiness with its core constituents of life satisfaction and preponderance in the duration of positive affective experiences over negative affective experience. Either happiness overall or one of its core constituents qualify as an indicator of positive mental health in QOL theory (see Chapter 3).

In keeping with QOL theory, in general, and the *CASIO* model of life satisfaction, in particular (see Chapter 3 or, for clients, see the Five Paths model diagram in the Toolbox CD), and in keeping with

Table 5.1   Essential Constructs for Integrated Positive Psychology and Clinical Assessment

Pure positive psychology or nonclinical assessments are identical to clinical assessments of those with a *DSM* disorder except for the omission of the first-order construct of Symptoms of Disorder or Disease. Despite this omission, QOLT requires a medical evaluation or report from a client's personal physician to the effect that no serious physical or psychiatric problems are evident that would militate against doing QOLT.

First-Order Construct

It is recommended that these constructs be assessed at the outset for all clients or patients:

- Symptoms of Disorder or Disease
- Overall Positive Psychology Indicator of Well-Being, Quality of Life, or Life Satisfaction (Area-based or domain-based measures whose overall scores are explained in terms of specific areas of life like work, relationships, and recreation are preferred because they suggest areas of intervention).

Second-Order CASIO Constructs

Assess these constructs only when particular areas of dissatisfaction or low satisfaction (e.g., love, work, recreation) are the focus of treatment or intervention as when overall quality of life is found to be low:

- Objective Circumstances or Living Conditions
  Related to Areas of Dissatisfaction (or Low Satisfaction)
- Cognitive Constructs Related to Areas of Dissatisfaction
  Including Perception of and Interpretation of Objective Circumstances; Goals or Standards of Fulfillment for Areas; and Personal Importance or Value of Areas
- Personal Competencies or "Functional Abilities" Related to Areas of Dissatisfaction (e.g., social skills for relationships, budgeting for Money or Standard of Living, and daily living skills for Health and personal safety)

current findings in the fields of QOL and SWB reviewed here, Table 5.1 lists the essential constructs for assessment in psychology and medicine. These constructs are based on a definition of health as the absence of physical disease or disability along with the presence of positive mental health and QOL to a level commensurate with well-functioning and nonclinical peers. As part of an initial and general macroanalysis (Emmelkamp, 1982) or overview, it is recommended that the clinician construct a comprehensive list of psychological disturbances and physical diseases or disabilities from which a client suffers. The client's level of QOL or life satisfaction should also be assessed to determine whether it falls within or above the average or normal range of the client's well-functioning nonclinical peers. Only if a client's QOL is significantly lower than his or her peers (i.e., one or two standard deviations below the mean for functional peers; Ogles et al., 1996) will the assessment of second-order constructs (see Table 5.1) and subsequent QOL interventions be necessary. The clinician, with the client's consent, may choose to treat or intervene in any specific area of life dissatisfaction deemed relevant to the client's symptoms. In general, people whose life satisfaction scores are average or above enjoy a good QOL and are mentally

healthy (e.g., positive mental health) to the point where further QOL assessment and intervention may be unnecessary (Frisch, 1994).

Implicit in this recommended assessment procedure is the assumption that clinical significance refers to both (1) clinically meaningful and relevant constructs (such as QOL) that reflect how clients feel and function in everyday life, and (2) the extent to which treatment-related change in these clinically significant, relevant, and important constructs indicates moving into the average range or level for nonclinical well-functioning peers (Kazdin, 1992; Ogles et al., 1996; Ogles, Lunnen, & Bonesteel, 2001; also see Kazdin for review of other methods).

SCREENING FOR PSYCHOLOGICAL DISTURBANCES AND SYMPTOMS

Clinical, health, and positive (with clinical training) psychologists may quickly and efficiently screen for psychological disturbances and symptoms by utilizing a symptom checklist such as the SCL-90-R (Derogatis & Lynn 1999), or the Frisch Essential Symptom Scale (FESS) and its test manual available at no charge in the Toolbox CD (also see Frisch, 2002). A clinical interview with the client, and, when possible, significant others (e.g., spouse) is also recommended; this interview should yield a comprehensive listing of symptoms as revealed by the client's behavior during the interview, presenting complaints, current medications, response to stressful life events, and history (e.g., psychiatric, medical, family, and social). The goal of this phase of assessment of first-order constucts (Table 5.1) is to generate a comprehensive list of possible psychiatric symptoms and associated *DSM-IV-TR* disorders.

Next, potential *DSM-IV-TR* diagnoses can be conclusively ruled in or out by directly questioning patients with respect to the criteria for each suspected disorder as spelled out in the *DSM*. Time can be saved by asking patients about "essential" symptoms first, as in the case of major depressive disorder where either anhedonia or depressed mood must be present, making it unnecessary to inquire about other depressive symptoms when these two are absent (Frisch, 2000; Othmer & Othmer, 1994). When it comes to diagnosing psychological disturbances, informal but direct questioning about specific *DSM-IV-TR* criteria may be adequately reliable and is certainly less time consuming and costly than standardized, structured diagnostic interviews, according to Lambert and his colleagues (Ogles et al., 1996).

SCREENING FOR NONPSYCHIATRIC OR GENERAL MEDICAL CONDITIONS

Nonpsychiatric or general medical conditions can be assessed via clients' personal physicians, an important step in QOLT assessment. Symptoms of physical disease or disability revealed by clients should be corroborated through consultation with their physician.

"Pure" positive psychology or nonclinical assessments are identical to clinical assessments of those with a *DSM* disorder except for the omission of screening for or assessing *DSM* disorders, part of the first-order construct of Symptoms of Disorder or Disease.

QOL is the second first-order construct listed in Table 5.1. Clients' level of life satisfaction or QOL can be assessed through use of a brief screening measure. In cases where clients' overall QOL is not commensurate with well-functioning peers, further assessment is called for to (1) identify the sources of

dissatisfaction and (2) assess the second-order constructs (Table 5.1) associated with each area of dissatisfaction. The former can be accomplished by using a domain- or area-based QOL screening measure (examples appear later in this chapter). The latter constitutes a microanalysis (Emmelkamp, 1982) or functional analysis, which specifies the reasons for and parameters (e.g., controlling variables, causes) of low satisfaction in a particular area of life. Initial, domain-based QOL assessment can also be viewed as screening for "problems in living," which can be as important as symptom screenings (Frisch, 1992). An urgent need exists for brief measures of problems in living (Othmer & Othmer, 1994). An example of an initial QOL assessment for a client, "Sandy," is presented in Figure 5.1; the same assessment can be shared with clients by way of illustration.

ASSESSING SECOND-ORDER CONSTRUCTS

Multimodal assessments can be used for assessing and changing the second-order constructs (Table 5.1). For example, role-play assessments have been invaluable in assessing both patient's social capabilities and actual behavior in real-life situations (Frisch & Higgins, 1986). Both the objective circumstances and clients' personal competencies in conducting relationships can be assessed by observing the interaction of those who are dissatisfied with their relationships with their "antagonists" (e.g., family members, coworkers) in sessions. Clients' problem-solving ability, standards of fulfillment, perceptions, and goals for particular areas of life can be assessed via interview and various instruments such as the Vision Quest and "What's Wrong?" exercises in the Toolbox CD. Home visits can be helpful in assessing the objective living conditions of clients reporting dissatisfaction with their surroundings, especially for older patients (Frisch, 1996). Clinicians may simply discuss the Areas of Life to Consider for Greater Happiness handout in the Toolbox CD with clients to gain information on particular areas of life.

Based on a sample of 281 outpatients, Frisch (1992, 1994) has identified the specific and recurrent, or typical, reasons (i.e., second order factors) clients give for dissatisfaction with each of the sixteen areas of life in

INTRODUCTION

The Quality of Life Inventory (QOLI) provides a score that indicates a person's overall satisfaction with life. People's life satisfaction is based on how well their needs, goals, and wishes are being met in important areas of life. The information in this report should be used in conjunction with professional judgment, taking into account any other pertinent information concerning the individual.

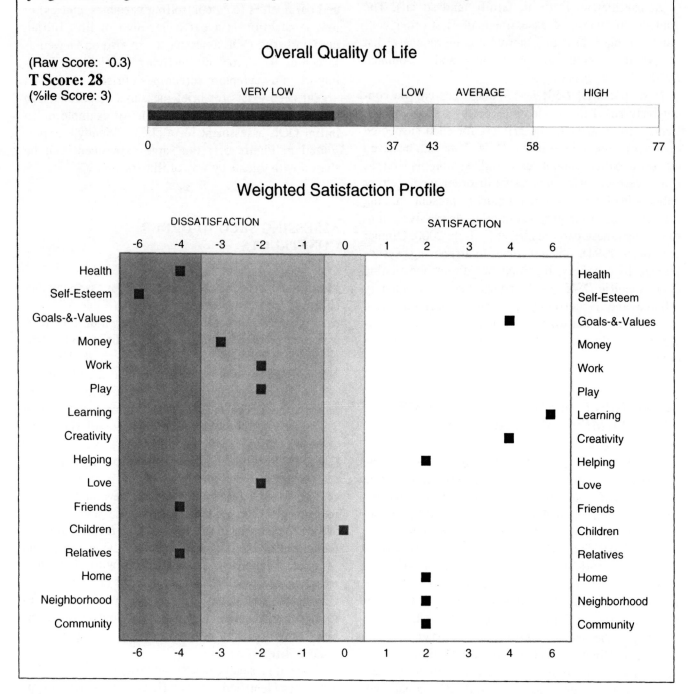

Figure 5.1 Pre-intervention QOLI profile of client "Sandy." ©2006, 1994, Pearson Assessments and Michael B. Frisch. All rights reserved. Reprinted with permission.

OVERALL QUALITY OF LIFE CLASSIFICATION

The client's satisfaction with life is Very Low. This person is extremely unhappy and unfulfilled in life. People scoring in this range cannot get their basic needs met and cannot achieve their goals in important areas of life. This person is at risk for developing physical and mental health disorders, especially clinical depression. This risk remains until the client's score reaches or exceeds the Average range. The client should be assessed and treated for any psychological disturbances.

WEIGHTED SATISFACTION PROFILE

The Weighted Satisfaction Profile helps to explain a person's Overall Quality of Life by identifying the specific areas of satisfaction and dissatisfaction that contribute to the QOLI raw score. Clinical experience suggests that any negative weighted satisfaction rating denotes an area of life in which the individual may benefit from treatment; ratings of -6 and -4 are of greatest concern and urgency. Specific reasons for dissatisfaction should be investigated more fully with the client in a clinical interview. The *Manual and Treatment Guide for the Quality of Life Inventory* suggests treatment techniques for improving patient satisfaction in each area of life assessed by the QOLI.

The following weighted satisfaction ratings indicate areas of dissatisfaction for the client:

Area	Weighted Satisfaction Rating
Self-Esteem	**-6**
Health	**-4**
Friends	**-4**
Relatives	**-4**
Money	**-3**
Work	**-2**
Play	**-2**
Love	**-2**

OMITTED ITEMS

None omitted.

End of Report

NOTE: This and previous pages of this report contain trade secrets and are not to be released in response to requests under HIPAA (or any other data disclosure law that exempts trade secret information from release). Further, release in response to litigation discovery demands should be made only in accordance with your profession's ethical guidelines and under an appropriate protective order.

Figure 5.1 *Continued*

QOL theory and the QOLI. For example, patients dissatisfied with their level of self-esteem usually feel inadequate because of their failure to meet their standards of performance and success in highly valued areas of life, such as work, school, parenthood, love relationship, or weight control. These possible explanations for unhappiness in specific areas of life can be presented to clients by therapists as a start in identifying the second order constructs that explain dissatisfaction in a particular area for a particular client. Using the CASIO model diagram from the Toolbox CD, the CASIO model presented in Figure 3.1 is often discussed with clients as part of a collaborative effort to identify their reasons for their dissatisfaction with particular areas of life.

Once a client's QOL and symptomatic status is comprehensively assessed, the process of clinical case conceptualization and treatment planning can be advanced through the final two steps of case conceptualization and establishing intervention priorities and strategies. One parsimonious approach to case conceptualization involves applying both the Beck model for any *DSM* disorder (Clark & Beck, 1999) and, at the same time, invoking QOL theory in the form of the CASIO model to explain dissatisfaction in valued areas of life that may or may not have *contributed* to clients' *DSM* disorders. This QOLT approach to case conceptualization is detailed and illustrated in the next chapter on Sharing Case Conceptualizations.

THE STEPS IN QOLT ASSESSMENT

Step 1: Assess Clients' Overall QOL

QOLT begins with an evaluation of a clients' *overall life goals and overall QOL* compared to nationwide norms to determine whether his or her QOL is substandard. Client feedback can be very motivating as in those cases in which clients acclimated to misery in a high-stress job deny their misery only to find themselves in the low or very low range on a test like the QOLI that puts them at risk for a host of physical and psychological maladies. The QOLI or a similar instrument is administered before treatment, at 3-week intervals during treatment, and at the end of treatment, as well as at follow-ups or booster sessions. The QOLI yields an overall score, a profile of specific areas of happiness and unhappiness that make up the overall

score, and a list of problems that hurt or hinder satisfaction in specific areas of life.

Step 2: Life (or Lifetime) Goal Assessment

The second step involves the assessment of life goals. Implementing life goal assessment involves administering:

1. QOLI
2. The Vision Quest exercise
3. Happiness Pie exercise (Optional)
4. My Most Feared Obituary (Optional)

The Vision Quest exercise, Happiness Pie, and My Most Feared Obituary are all found in the Toolbox CD.

Life goal assessment is at the heart of QOLT. The Vision Quest exercise can be assigned along with the QOLI either 15 minutes before the first session or assigned as homework after the first session. The QOLI takes about 10 minutes to complete, and the Vision Quest exercise takes about 5 minutes. The Happiness Pie and My Most Feared Obituary are optional life goal assessments that may or may not be given along with the QOLI and Vision Quest exercise at the start of QOLT.

Step 3: Assess Specific Areas of Life or "Domains" Contributing to Clients' Overall QOL

Step 3 involves finding which specific areas of life contribute to overall unhappiness or dissatisfaction. As a follow-up to assessing clients' overall QOL with nationwide norms, it is important to know which specific areas of life are assets or strengths to clients (strengths are areas of happiness or satisfaction) and which areas are contributing to *unhappiness* (weaknesses are areas of dissatisfaction or unhappiness) and thus, are good targets for intervention (e.g., see Figure 5.1).

The QOLI[1] (Frisch, 1994) is especially suited in this regard since it generates both an overall score and a profile of strengths and weaknesses in the same spe-

---

[1] To order the *Hand-Scoring Starter Kit* (least expensive) or the computer version of the QOLI, telephone Pearson Assessments at (800) 627-7271 (8 A.M. to 6 P.M. U.S. Central Standard Time). For special arrangements like obtaining a discount or using an electronic version of the QOLI, you may contact Ms. Kristie Heisick, Pearson Assessments (formerly NCS Assessments), 5601 Green Valley Drive, 5th Floor, Bloomington, MN 55437, U.S.A.; Telephone: (800) 627–7271 ext. 3340 (8 A.M. to 6 P.M. U.S. Central Standard Time); e-mail: Kristie.Heisick@pearson.com. For additional QOLI information, go to http://www.pearsonassessments.com/tests/qoli.htm.

cific areas of life found in QOLT. An initial assessment or preintervention profile of "Sandy" without the accompanying text of a full report is illustrated in Figure 5.1. As can be seen, clients' overall QOL is pictured at the top of the computer-generated QOLI report; the *Weighted Satisfaction Profile* clearly divides clients' areas of satisfaction and dissatisfaction with the latter, providing targets for intervention and the former, providing a listing of clients' assets and strengths in valued areas of life. These are not character strengths in the traditional positive psychology sense but are pockets of joy and fulfillment in clients' lives that may mitigate the impact of areas of dissatisfaction as predicted by the CASIO model of QOL theory depicted in Figure 3.1. The Toolbox CD handout, Areas of Life to Consider for Greater Happiness, can also be useful in ferreting out areas of unhappiness that underlie overall dissatisfaction with life.

The background, psychometrics, and use of the QOLI to assess overall QOL and QOL in specific areas of life are explained and illustrated at the end of this chapter.

Step 4: Finding the Causes of Dissatisfaction in Particular or Specific Areas of Life

Once identified, each specific area of dissatisfaction can be analyzed or assessed in terms of the CASIO model to see which CASIO factors are causing the dissatisfaction and how. This can be accomplished by asking clients why they feel dissatisfied with an area. Another optional way that each area of dissatisfaction in life can be analyzed is by using the What's Wrong? Exercise found in the Toolbox CD. It can also help to know clients' Vision Quest goals. For example, dissatisfaction with health on the QOLI can be better understood in the context of a goal for health cited in Vision Quest of "quitting smoking and losing weight."

Step 5: Medical Consultation or Report from a Physician

In QOLT, a medical consultation or report from the client's personal physician is sought to be sure that the client is free from major physical or psychological disturbances that would require treatment by mental health and general medicine professionals in addition to any positive psychology intervention program.

In cases of serious physical illness or disability, QOLT is often conducted as a behavioral medicine treatment aimed at improving or sustaining clients' overall QOL even though the QOLT interventions do not directly impact the disease or disability. In these situations, close and frequent consultation is a must between therapists and physicians along with taking great care to tailor interventions to clients' unique physical constraints and limitations.

Step 6: Screening for DSM Disorders

In clinical situations, clients are evaluated for *DSM* symptoms and disorders as well as their QOL. Therapists with training in assessment and psychopathology can administer this screening themselves. Where possible, time is saved by using brief symptom or essential symptoms measures such as the FESS (Frisch, 2002), which is available in the Toolbox CD.

Step 7: Sharing an Integrated Case Conceptualization and Treatment/Intervention Plan with Clients

Although not technically part of the assessment phase of QOLT, in the next step in the process of QOLT, which is described in the following chapter, the results of the initial assessment are integrated via the ACT model of case formulation illustrated in the next chapter. The resulting Case Conceptualization and Treatment/Intervention Plan is then shared with clients to build their understanding and motivation for treatment and to bring a common understanding to clients and therapists as to what the clients' assets and problems are and what intervention plan would best serve the clients' goals.

ILLUSTRATION OF LIFE GOAL ASSESSMENT PROCEDURES: TOM'S VISION QUEST EXERCISE

Chapter 3 introduced "Tom," the case we are following throughout this book. This chapter describes the QOL assessment process with Tom, especially the application of the QOLI, Vision Quest, Happiness Pie, and My Most Feared Obituary. Tom's pretreatment/intervention QOLI profile and results can be found in Figure 1.1; these results were shared with him along with the rest of the overall case conceptualization in Chapter 6.

Chapter 6 explains how to share case conceptualizations with clients in a therapeutically beneficial way using Tom's results as an example.

In spite of his intelligence, Tom really didn't know what he wanted from life. The QOLI, Vision Quest exercise, Happiness Pie technique, and My Most Feared Obituary represented Tom's first step toward establishing some meaningful goals and priorities and provided a "Whole Life" framework for positive psychology or clinical interventions.

It took Tom less than 5 minutes to complete the Vision Quest exercise after finishing the QOLI. Here are some excerpts detailing Tom's lifetime goals:

. . . . My Long-Term Goals for Love

More than anything I want someone to share my life with but I'm scared. I haven't dated in 3 years of college!

My Long-Term Goals for My Work

I want to find some work that is fun and challenging, but doesn't make me crazy. I don't need a lot of money to be happy. (I don't know where do I begin?) . . . Teaching at a small school like Beloit would be a helluva lot easier and happier than some tier 1 research factory like UT— University of Texas—where all the profs seem nuts.

Money . . . My Long-Term Goals

I don't need a lot of money to be happy.

Health . . . My Long-Term Goals

I need a way to handle my moods and my life day to day, some kind of routine that works . . . a way to blow off steam without getting "blown away" with beer and doing things I regret later.

Children . . . My Long-Term Goals

Not a priority for me.

Relatives . . . My Long-Term Goals

Stay close to Mom. Dad is more of a burden than a friend.

Learning . . . My Long-Term Goals

I want to study and learn without the pressure or the misery.

Helping . . . My Long-Term Goals

I miss doing stuff through my church.

Self-Esteem . . . My Long-Term Goals

I feel flawed and defective, a broken person with a lot of pain and shame. I plan to do the program—stay in ther-

apy, do my Quality Time each day I feel crappy, and read even a few sentences of Finding Happiness, *my bible for happiness—as long as it takes to feel better about myself. Accomplishing my other goals will help in this department.*

Spiritual Life . . . My Long-Term Goals

My faith really matters to me. I want to keep studying philosophy and religion on the side and find a sympatico church to find a stable spiritual vision to keep me in touch with the Infinite.

Clients find the process of spelling out life goals illuminating as was the case for Ashley, a positive psychology client and trial lawyer who felt on-call 24 hours a day:

The Vision Quest exercise forced me to look at each area of my life, evaluate my weaknesses in it, and devise a plan to strengthen those areas. I have never physically written down goals for different aspects of my life. I found that the written word holds me more accountable than do my thoughts. Although I did not stay true to some of my goals, the quality of my life in the other areas where I did pursue my goals increased.

In terms of Tom's case, whenever possible, his therapy goals and work were tied into his lifetime goals revealed by Vision Quest so that Tom could see a direct connection and regard therapy as a way to keep his "eye on the prize" of cherished lifetime goals. Tom was also encouraged to pursue these lifetime goals on his own *outside* of therapy both during QOLT and after therapy had ended. The latter instance may constitute a kind of self-continuation, maintenance, or relapse prevention therapy for clients as discussed in Chapter 4.

SETTING GOALS AND PRIORITIES: THE HAPPINESS PIE TECHNIQUE

The Happiness Pie technique is an optional exercise aimed at establishing meaningful goals and priorities for clients. In preparation for using this assessment and intervention technique, with Tom, I first showed Tom the CASIO model diagram from the Toolbox CD (which is Figure 3.1 in this book) and told him about the CASIO theory that our overall happiness is made up of the satisfactions we feel in particular valued areas of life. We then went over the specific areas of life that, according to QOL theory, seem to account for most of human happiness—these *Areas of Life* are available in

Figure 5.2   Tom's Happiness Pie at the start of therapy.

THE QUALITY OF LIFE INVENTORY: DESCRIPTION AND TREATMENT UTILITY

Description

The QOLI (Frisch, 1994; Frisch et al., 1992) was developed for both nonclinical and clinical uses. With respect to the *nonclinical* positive psychology application, the QOLI was intended to be a measure of *quality of life* and life satisfaction based on an articulated theory that could guide interventions and serve as a reliable and valid outcome indicator. With respect to the *clinical* application, the QOLI was intended to be a measure of *positive mental health* or life satisfaction based on an articulated theory that could augment existing measures of negative affect and symptoms of disease or psychological disturbance and that would be useful in:

1. *Clinical/mental health screening;*
2. *Progress and outcomes assessment* of mental health and general medicine/behavioral medicine programs and treatments; and
3. *Treatment planning* in mental health and general medicine/behavioral medicine contexts.

the Toolbox CD as Areas of Life to Consider for Greater Happiness and are also part of QOLI profiles.

Next, I said, "Tom, draw me a picture of what your life is like right now." He was told to "Look at his overall happiness like a 'big pie' composed of particular parts of life or 'slices' that together make up his overall happiness. Some 'slices' or areas will be bigger than others depending on how important they are to you and how much they add to your overall happiness. Not everyone makes time for or values all of the 16 areas of life that can contribute to people's happiness. That's normal. So what I'd like you to do now is to draw me a picture of what areas seem to dominate your life most. In other words, where is the most of your time and mental energy going?"

Here is a picture of Tom's pretreatment Happiness Pie (see Figure 5.2).

Next, I asked Tom to do some soul-searching and come up with a *new* pie that would reflect the priorities that he felt he really needed and wanted in his life, independent of any "guilt trips" that other people were laying on him as to who he should be and how he should behave. The more balanced pie became the centerpiece or guide for much of our work in therapy. Here Figure 5.3 is Tom's revised or ideal Happiness Pie.

Furthermore, according to Persons and Bertagnolli (1999), the QOLI may be one of the only available tools for assessing problems in living, an essential part of cognitive therapy and cognitive case conceptualization.

The QOLI is a domain-based life satisfaction measure that attempts to overcome some of the situational biases (see Diener et al., 2004) encountered with purely global measures of life satisfaction by reminding respondents of all areas of life that may or may not be important to them, while at the same time, yielding an overall or "global" score or measure of life satisfaction based on these very same areas of importance.

The QOLI consists of 16 items selected to include all domains of life that have been empirically associated with overall life satisfaction (see Weighted Satisfaction Profile portion of Figure 5.1, Table 3.1, and Areas of Life to Consider for Greater Happiness in the Toolbox CD). Respondents rate how important each of the 16 domains is to their overall happiness and satisfaction (0 = Not at all important, 1 = Important, 2 = Very important) they then rate how satisfied they are in the area (−3 = Very dissatisfied to 3 = Very satisfied). The importance and satisfaction ratings for each item

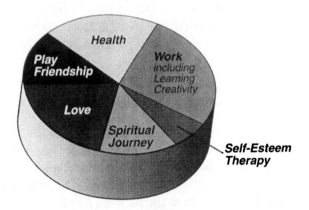

Figure 5.3   Tom's Ideal Happiness Pie.

are multiplied to form weighted satisfaction ratings ranging from −6 to 6. A *Weighted Satisfaction Profile* of problems in living and life strengths in 16 areas of life is generated that is akin to an MMPI profile of symptoms and disorders (see Figure 5.1 for illustration).

A brief examination of a client's Weighted Satisfaction Profile can suggest both targets for treatment or intervention (i.e., any area with a negative rating) and treatment or intervention priorities (i.e., areas rated −6 to −4 are given top priority). Weighted Satisfaction Profiles also suggest areas of strength and fulfillment (i.e., any area rated positively) that can be used to enhance intervention effects. For example, in a positive psychology context, satisfaction and abilities related to friends, may be used to build more positive relationships at work, thereby enhancing satisfaction at work and making cooperation, team building, and leadership signature strengths at work (Seligman, 2002). In a clinical situation, an agoraphobic or depressed client's spouse may be enlisted as an ally/participant in treatment when the client reports satisfaction with this love relationship on the Weighted Satisfaction Profile. The use of weighted satisfaction ratings in psychotherapy/treatment planning is further illustrated elsewhere (Frisch, 1992, 1993, 1998b, 2006; Kazdin, 1993a, 2003; Persons & Bertagnolli, 1999).

Once the Weighted Satisfaction Profile is completed, overall life satisfaction is then computed by averaging all weighted satisfaction ratings with nonzero importance ratings—unimportant areas of life not valued by test takers are thereby eliminated; the total score thus reflects one's satisfaction in only those areas of life one considers important. Respondents can also "write in" or indicate what problems interfere with their satisfaction in each area on a brief written or narrative section of the QOLI test booklet labeled Part II.

Treatment Utility

The treatment utility of a measure refers to its contribution to a positive treatment outcome, usually by facilitating the ease, efficiency, or accuracy of assessment, treatment planning, and/or treatment (Hayes, Nelson, & Jarrett, 1987). The QOLI's treatment utility has been demonstrated with 281 clients from five outpatient and inpatient clinics (Frisch, 1992) and in numerous case studies reported by Kazdin (1993a, 2003) and Frisch (1992, 2004a). The QOLI's overall life satisfaction score (and related nationwide norms) and its Weighted Satisfaction Profile (see Figure 5.1) of ratings for each area of life have been valuable to clinicians conducting a macroanalysis or overview in which clients' problems-in-living are comprehensively assessed, conceptualized, and prioritized for treatment (Frisch, 1992, 2004a; Kazdin, 1993a, 2003; Persons & Bertagnolli, 1999).

QOLI PSYCHOMETRICS

Initial QOLI Studies

When the QOLI was first developed, it assessed the satisfaction and importance of 17 areas of life (Frisch et al., 1992). In an effort to refine the instrument, the language used was simplified to a 6th-grade reading level and the closely related areas of, Social Service and Civic Action, were combined into one area named Helping. The original QOLI is highly correlated with the revised QOLI. A summary of the validity and reliability coefficients for the original QOLI can be found in Frisch et al. (1992).

Nationwide Normative Study

The current version of the QOLI was distributed to individuals drawn from the nonclinical population throughout the continental United States. These individuals were sampled from 12 states from the four major U.S. geographical regions: the Northeast, the South, the Midwest, and the West. The final standardization sample consisted of 798 individuals who closely approximate the ethnic composition of the 1990 U.S. Census. This nonclinical functional norm group is useful in interpreting scores of clients from both clinical and positive psychology intervention programs and settings (Frisch, 2003a, 2004a, 2006; Frisch et al., 2005).

Clinical Norms Based on Dysfunctional Samples

Clinical significance is defined both in terms of (1) a *construct*, such as quality of life or life satisfaction, that is clinically and practically important, a basic or central aspect of a client's experience or functioning that is easily noticeable to the patient (Kazdin, 1993a) and (2) the amount of change on a measure deemed to be of clinical or practical importance (Kazdin, 2003; Ogles et al., 1996). In terms of the latter, change to within one standard deviation of a functional, nonclinical norm group or change that is two standard deviations or more away from a clinical, dysfunctional norm group can be considered to be a clinically significant amount of change, using the most stringent standards (Kazdin, 2003; Ogles et al., 1996).

Although comparisons of clients to nonclinical functional peers is the preferred "gold standard" for establishing clinical significance in the amount of change on a measure (Kazdin, 2003; Ogles et al., 1996), clinical, dysfunctional norm groups can be necessary as in cases of highly impaired or chronic samples in which change approaching a nonclinical sample is unrealistic even when treatment has been successful, as in the case of clients with schizophrenic disorders or very few resources (Frisch & MacKenzie, 1991). Dysfunctional norms can also be helpful in cases of overlapping nonclinical and clinical distributions (Jacobson & Truax, 1991).

Clinical or dysfunctional norms for the QOLI have been developed by collecting data from naturalistic samples of community mental health center (CMHC) clients and university counseling center clients. These norms along with guidelines for their use are available in Frisch et al. (2005).

Test-Retest Reliability

Temporal stability of QOLI T scores were examined with test-retest reliability coefficients from a subsample of 55 participants in the normative study. The retest coefficient of .73 was significant at $p < .001$ over an interval of about 2 weeks.

Internal Consistency Reliability

Internal consistency reliability (coefficient alpha) computed in the normative study for the sum of the QOLI Weighted Satisfaction ratings was .79.

Predictive Validity

Frisch et al. (2005) aimed to extend quality-of-life predictive validity studies to an entirely new domain by assessing the ability of life satisfaction to predict academic retention in university counseling center clients.

By using the QOLI in this analysis, its predictive validity could be assessed for the first time in the literature. Over a 4-year period, 2,179 clients referred for individual psychotherapy at a large public midwestern university were administered the QOLI and a demographic questionnaire prior to their first session. As part of this process, clients who had a planned termination from therapy were asked by their counselor to complete a second, posttreatment QOLI. In an effort to predict academic retention and assess outcome, retention status was checked in 1998 for students who had either completed counseling or dropped out of counseling in 1995 to 1997 and in 2000 for students who had either completed counseling or dropped out of counseling in 1997 to 1999. Students who were still enrolled or had graduated at the time that their enrollment status was checked were considered *retained*, whereas students who were no longer enrolled and had not graduated were considered *not retained*. The time between QOLI testing and the check on students' retention status ranged from 12 to 36 months with a mean of 24.8 months. In the discriminant analysis, the most recent QOLI score the client had obtained prior to terminating services was utilized. For those students who failed to follow through on counseling, the pretest was their most recent QOLI. For those students who completed a planned termination from counseling, the posttest was used.

Using the cross-validation approach of Butcher and his colleagues at the University of Minnesota (Rouse, Butcher, & Miller, 1999), a discriminant analysis was conducted to determine the predictive utility of clients' QOLI scores and cumulative GPA in assessing academic retention 1 to 3 years in advance. Three discriminant function equations were generated from the validation sample with GPA and QOLI scores considered separately as predictors of retention, followed by a step-wise discriminant analysis in which *both* variables were included. Of the three discriminant equations, all reached statistical significance. The correct classification rate for the cross-validation sample was nearly identical to that of the validation sample. Furthermore, the efficiency statistics generated for the cross-validation sample actually increased in accuracy from those of the validation sample, suggesting no shrinkage when the predication equation from the first sample was applied to the second sample. In sum, the QOLI was able to predict academic retention both by itself and in conjunction with cumulative GPA 1 to 3 years in advance. This finding lends further credence to the view that life satisfaction may be a transtheoretical and interdisciplinary construct of great heuristic and practical value.

Convergent and Discriminant Validity

Data from two other measures of life satisfaction were collected in order to assess the convergent validity of the QOLI. The QOLI was significantly and positively correlated with both measures: $r = .56$, $p < .001$ with the Satisfaction with Life Scale (Pavot & Diener, 1993), and $r = .75$, $p < .001$ with the Quality of Life Index (Ferrans & Powers, 1992). The correlation found between QOLIT-scores and scores on the Marlowe-Crowned Social Desirability Scale was .25. Although statistically significant at $p < .001$, the small size of this suggests that the impact of the social desirability response set on QOLI scores is minimal since it accounts for only about 6 percent of the variance in QOLI scores.

Treatment Validity or Sensitivity to Treatment-Related Change

In the interest of parsimony and clarity, the cumbersome phrase, sensitivity to treatment-related change, may also be referred to as *treatment validity*. Although it is a requirement for psychometric adequacy (Frisch et al., 2005; Guyatt et al., 1987; Ogles et al., 1996), treatment validity is often not documented for health-related quality of life measures (Hays et al., 1998; Spilker, 1996). In a study carried out at the Center for Stress and Anxiety Disorders on the treatment of social phobia, QOLI scores were low at pretreatment (9th percentile of nonclinical standardization sample) and improved significantly after therapy (Safren et al., 1997); these findings have been replicated with other social phobic and Generalized Anxiety Disorder samples at the Adult Anxiety Clinic of Temple University (Eng, Coles, et al., 2001; Eng, Coles, Heimberg, & Safren, 2001a; Eng, Heimberg, Hart, Schneier, & Liebowitz, 2001b; Turk, Mennin, Fresco, & Heimberg, 2000). In a related finding from this clinic, supporting the construct validity of the QOLI, a cluster analysis of social phobics revealed lower life satisfaction in clients with disordered adult attachment styles versus those with mature attachment styles (Eng, Heimberg, Hart,

Schneider, & Liebowitz, 2001). After administration of Heimberg's treatment in a different laboratory, social phobics' QOLI scores moved to within one standard deviation of a nationwide nonclinical normative sample, suggesting clinically significant change in response to treatment (Woody & Adessky, 2002). Evidence for the QOLI's sensitivity to treatment-related change has also been found in studies of cognitive behavior therapy and exposure therapies for refugees with PTSD (Paunovic & Ost, 2001), an Internet-delivered treatment for Panic Disorder (Carlbring, Setling, Ljungstrand, Ekselius, & Andersson, 2001), contingency management treatment for cocaine abuse (Petry et al., 2001), major depression (Frisch, 1992; Grant et al., 1995; Kazdin, 2003), schizophrenia and the chronically mentally ill (Stanard, 1999), and inpatient PTSD treatment (Ford, Fisher, & Larson, 1997). The QOLI also seems to be sensitive to treatment-related change in the National Institute on Aging's Project to Enhance Aged Rural Living (PEARL) study in so far as the quality of life of older rural home healthcare clients and their caregivers improved following a psychosocial intervention aimed at improving their emotional well-being and quality of life, while the quality of life of delayed treatment clients and caregivers did not, according to initial findings (Forrest Scogin, personal communication, August 22, 2005).

Frisch et al. (2005) attempted to extend these QOLI treatment validity findings to larger samples in more naturalistic settings, that is, a managed care, HMO program for substance abuse and the ongoing treatment program of a university counseling center. The QOLI was found to be sensitive to treatment-related change in each of these samples. Specifically, in both the managed care/substance abuse and counseling center samples QOLI scores increased significantly with treatment and moved to within one standard deviation of the functional, nonclinical normative sample mean after treatment, that is, from a mean T score of 38 to a score of 47 for both samples at posttest with scores of 48 and 50 at the 3- and 6-month follow-ups for the managed care/substance abuse sample. This change signifies a clinically, and not just a statistically, significant amount of change as previously discussed. Additional clinical trials using the QOLI are underway. For example, in the largest clinical trial ever attempted in the treatment of PTSD, the QOLI is being used along with measures of PTSD symptoms and severity to gauge the effects of treatment carried out in 10 Veterans Affairs medical centers (VA Cooperative Study 420; Schnurr, Friedman, Lavori, & Hsieh, 2001).

Factor Analytic Studies

In response to Rabkin et al.'s (2000) call for factor analytic studies of the QOLI, QOLI scores from a large clinical sample were factor analyzed (Frisch & Sanford, 2005). Preliminary results favor a unidimensional factor solution in keeping with the scoring scheme of the QOLI that rests upon a single score.

Conclusion

According to several independent evaluations and reviews (see, e.g., Ben-Porath, 1997; Crits-Christoph & Connolly, 1997; Crowley & Kazdin, 1998; Eng, Coles, et al., 2001; Horowitz et al., 1997; Kazdin, 1993a, 1993b, 1994, 2003; Mendlowicz & Stein, 2000; Moras, 1997; Ogles et al., 1996; Persons & Bertagnolli, 1999; Rabkin et al., 2000), the QOLI appears to meet the eleven criteria for useful assessment instruments identified by a panel of experts assembled by NIMH (Newman, Ciarlo, & Carpenter, 1999) including psychometric strength, clinical usefulness, understanding by nonprofessional audiences, compatibility with diverse theories and clinical practices, low measure costs relative to its uses, usefulness in assessing treatment progress as well as outcome, and relevance to a broad target group since it is the aim of *all* health interventions to enhance patients' QOL in addition to ameliorating symptoms of disorder or disease. Positive predictive validity results and nationwide norms are especially unique among psychological tests, in general, and QOL measures, in particular.

GENERAL APPLICATIONS OF THE QOLI

Interpretation of *Overall* Quality of Life

Detailed interpretive statements associated with high, average, and low QOLI scores can be found in the QOLI Test Manual available from Pearson Assessments—see footnote 1 (Frisch, 1994). Guidelines for determining clinically significant or, in the case of nonclinical intervention assessment, practically

significant change as a result of intervention can also be found in the test manual. In keeping with QOL theory, high scorers are generally seen as happy and fulfilled and successful in getting what they want out of life, in contrast to low scorers who: (1) are at risk for future health problems; (2) merit close monitoring for QOL changes and for the development of related health problems like depression and substance abuse; (3) could benefit from QOL interventions to move their level of satisfaction to a level commensurate with more functional, nonclinical peers. Clients who begin treatment or intervention at a low level and stay there may be considered "treatment failures" who require a different type or "dose" of intervention (Frisch, 1994).

Identifying Reasons for Dissatisfaction

The QOLI requests that clients list problems that get in the way of their satisfaction in each of the 16 areas of life assessed by the QOLI. Written responses here often tell why a client is unhappy with a particular area of life. This information can be used in treatment planning or positive psychology intervention planning (see Frisch, 1992; for clinical illustrations). QOLI results can quickly suggest areas to work on even to novice therapists and students (Frisch, 1992, 2004b). As illustrated in Figure 5.1, the QOLI instructions, items, scoring, and profiles are generally clear and understandable to clients, clinicians, and family members. Clients see how areas of *dis*-satisfaction can contribute to their problems of unhappiness just by hearing the theory, seeing the Five Path/CASIO model depicted in Figure 3.1 or the Five Paths model diagram from the Toolbox CD, or observing the scoring scheme of the QOLI in which the average of satisfactions in valued areas determines the overall score. Clients can readily see that their areas of dissatisfaction are logical targets for treatment since their overall QOLI will go up if their happiness with specific, valued parts of life increases (see example in Figure 5.1). A simple examination of a QOLI profile suggests areas for a client to work on; for example, areas in the darkest part of the dissatisfaction range in Figure 5.1, Health, Self-Esteem, Friends, and Relatives, are obvious targets of intervention because they are the areas of deepest unhappiness to the client. (Recall that unimportant areas are excluded from profiles and scoring.)

The Use of the QOLI in Treatment Planning and Problems in Living Assessment

The QOLI can be used to screen for problems in living and strengths to use in treatment planning in the same way that symptom checklists efficiently identify symptoms that need to be the focus of treatment (Othmer & Othmer, 1994). For example, because therapists often miss important life problems that bear on etiology and treatment, Persons and Bertagnolli (1999) maintain that cognitive therapists should use a formal assessment device to identify problems in living that can then be used in cognitive therapy case formulations and treatment plans; Frisch (1992) identified a similar need given the focus of cognitive therapy on both symptoms and problems in living. Persons and Bertagnolli (1999) go so far as to say that the QOLI may be the only available screening assessment for problems in living at this time. The QOLI has been used in this way in the training of cognitive therapists at the University of Texas Southwestern Medical School and elsewhere (Frisch, 1992, 2004a; Robin Jarrett, personal communication, January 5, 2004). The ability of the QOLI to efficiently identify problems in living in addition to providing an overall score interpretable with nationwide nonclinical norms adds to its treatment planning utility.

The Use of the QOLI as a Universal Outcomes Measure

Because the QOLI is not a disorder- or disease-specific measure (Spilker, 1996) and because all healthcare interventions aim to improve a client's QOL, the QOLI may be used to evaluate the effectiveness of both psychological and medical treatments for most mental or physical disorders based on numerous different theoretical perspectives, including QOLT. Findings from all studies to date support the view that the QOLI is sufficiently sensitive to treatment-related change to merit its use as an outcome measure. Since the goal of all health interventions (i.e., medical and psychological, see Kazdin, 1993a) is to enhance clients' quality of life, it may be useful to conduct quality of life assessments using the QOLI or similar measures on a routine basis in medicine, psychology, and other mental health professions (Berzon, 1998; Strupp, 1996). With respect to outcome evaluation in mental health—whether in psychiatry, psychology, social work, or counseling—the QOLI may meet the need for a measure of individual contentment cited by Strupp (Ogles et al., 1996; Strupp, 1996; Strupp & Hadley, 1977) as the *primary* criterion of positive outcome and mental health from the perspective of a patient.

Use of the QOLI in QOLT whether in mental health, positive psychology, or behavioral medicine outcome evaluation (and treatment planning) typically involves administering the QOLI prior to, during, and at the conclusion of QOLT in order to chart a client's progress and to detect specific areas of life that may warrant intervention (Frisch, 1992, 2004b; Kazdin, 1993a, 2003). QOLT therapists administer the QOLI on a monthly or biweekly basis much like the Beck Depression Inventory (BDI) in order to closely monitor clients' progress. With nonclinical populations the QOLI has been successfully applied in business and professional settings for organizational development programs and workshops on positive psychology.

The following is an example of an outcome-oriented *termination summary* or posttreatment evaluation using the QOLI and BDI with a depressed client with an eating disorder who denied some problems at the start of therapy both to herself and to her therapist, a not uncommon problem with clients with these difficulties; nevertheless, this client's QOLI score climbed to the average range, indicating clinically significant change:

> After further inspection of her QOLI profile, it became evident that the areas in which Katie was experiencing discontent had changed. Prior to treatment, Katie had been unhappy with her self-esteem, health, and relationships. However, her posttreatment QOLI reflected Katie's satisfaction with her self-esteem and health, while indicating her continued displeasure with relationships. The area of "Love" actually became a greater source of dissatisfaction through treatment as Katie realized that her "needs were not being met and [she] wasn't being emotionally honest with herself or her boyfriend." Katie openly acknowledged her unhappiness with her relationships, but was not overly disturbed by this as she stated, "I see this as a good thing. I *know* what I want and need now; before I had no idea. I didn't even know what I felt! Now I know why I am dissatisfied and I know what to do about it. Plus, I believe I have the ability to change my relationships, so I think that score will continue to improve." Overall, Katie denied feeling unhappy and she was functioning in a manner comparable to well-adjusted, healthy college students.

The QOLI as a *Progress/Outcome Assessment Measure and a Measure for Fine-Tuning Treatments.* The QOLI can potentially provide therapists with outcome accountability in three to ten minutes given its brevity and readability. The QOLI has been used to document clients' progress and outcome in both traditional mental health/behavioral medicine and managed care settings (Chambliss, 2000; Frisch, 1992, 1994, 1998a, Frisch et al., 2005; Kazdin, 1993a, 2003). According to Kazdin (2003), treatment monitoring or progress/outcome assessment involves regular (e.g., weekly, biweekly, monthly) assessments during the course of treatment. The aim of treatment monitoring is to document progress toward therapeutic goals so that treatment for a particular problem or goal can either be terminated (once goal attainment has been documented) or fine-tuned if it fails to ameliorate a disorder/disease or quality of life difficulty.

Kazdin (1993a, 2003) and Frisch (1992, 1994, 1998a, 2004b) illustrate the usefulness of the QOLI in treatment/intervention monitoring. For example, Kazdin (1993a) used the overall QOLI scores of a depressed homemaker to document clinically significant, treatment-related change. Additionally, Kazdin used the weighted satisfaction ratings associated with areas of dissatisfaction to chart the progress toward area-specific treatment goals. For example, although the client's satisfaction with several areas of life increased after 14 weeks of treatment, her low satisfaction with her love relationship remained essentially unchanged. This prompted the therapist to institute couples therapy in place of the previous interventions that were unsuccessful. The QOLI would serve the same purpose in QOLT.

Use of the QOLI in Managed Care Settings

Use of the QOLI in managed care settings is specifically recommended in the book, *Psychotherapy and Managed Care* (Chambliss, 2000). Indeed, the QOLI has been used for high risk/relapse risk assessment (e.g., screening), outcome assessment (e.g., "behavioral healthcare report card development"), problems-in-living assessment, treatment planning, and treatment at several managed care companies such as MCC Behavioral Healthcare, United Behavioral Health, Health Empowerment, and Allina Health System. For example, the Allina Health System chose the QOLI as its primary behavioral healthcare measure for evaluating the effectiveness of its inpatient and outpatient chemi-

cal dependency treatment programs (Frisch et al., 2005). The QOLI has also been used successfully in EAPs (Frisch, 1998a). Problems-in-living assessment with the QOLI is particularly useful in managed care settings where about 75 percent of clients present with problems in living and related adjustment concerns (Chambliss, 2000; Ludden & Mandell, 1993).

Positive Psychology, Organizational, and Other Nonclinical Applications of the QOLI

With regard to nonclinical/positive psychology uses, the QOLI was designed, in part, to assess the outcome of programs, such as job training and quality of life enrichment programs for the elderly, aimed at improving the quality of life of general, nonclinical populations (Frisch et al., 1992). In this vein, the QOLI has been useful in individual, group, and classroom settings where programs such as Authentic Happiness (Seligman, 2002) or QOLT for the general public and for particular nonclinical groups—for example, various professionals, employees, clergy, and students—were presented (Frisch, 2004b). These programs were aimed at personal growth, the prevention of burnout, and quality of life enhancement.

Given the ability of life satisfaction to predict job performance/satisfaction and health-related problems and expenditures, the QOLI and its related interventions may also be useful in personnel selection and employee evaluation (Frisch, 1998a, 2003a, 2004a). In a similar vein, the QOLI may also be useful in career counseling in so far as low satisfaction suggests the need to prevent possible future work problems and in so far as the QOLI Weighted Satisfaction Profile is a beginning step in identifying broad interests and life goals that should be considered when planning a career or looking for employment (Frisch, 2004b). Despite encouraging initial results, these nonclinical applications await more formal outcome and efficacy evaluations as recommended by Seligman (2002).

Use in Organizations to Justify Additional Resources

In an era of shrinking budgets and increased demands for service, measures like the QOLI may provide the "proof" and accountability that funding agencies are demanding if healthcare services are to be maintained or expanded. In this vein, QOLI results have already been used successfully to secure additional resources, that is, more space and additional staff in a university counseling center (M. P. Clark & Mason, 2001).

Use of the QOLI in University Counseling Centers

In the context of college counseling centers, the QOLI may be used as a harbinger of academic failure that can alert both therapists and students to the need for intervention. Specifically, a counseling center clinician or admissions officer can predict whether a student will drop out of the university 1 to 3 years in advance if the student's QOLI score and GPA are known (see Frisch et al., 2005, for specific instructions). A comprehensive program of outcomes assessment for a university counseling center based on the QOLI is described by M. P. Clark and Mason (2001).

Use of the QOLI in Risk Assessment

QOL scales may significantly predict such practical, "bottom-line" variables as subsequent physical illness, psychological disorders, and related healthcare expenditures, academic retention in college, and future job performance and satisfaction (e.g., see Frisch et al., 2005). These variables and associated studies are listed in the *Life Satisfaction as a Predictor* and *Psychometrics/Predictive Validity* sections herein; the QOLI has the potential to identify those at risk for each of the problems listed. In this regard, the QOLI may be a useful screening device for organizations (e.g., universities, businesses) and health delivery service systems (e.g., group private practices, managed care, employee assistance programs [EAPs]), high-risk clients, employees, or *potential* employees relative to a nationwide normative sample.

CHAPTER 6

Sharing Case Conceptualizations with Clients

Once a QOLT assessment is complete, the results of positive psychology/QOL, *DSM,* and medical assessments are integrated via the ACT model of case formulation. Positive psychology *areas for growth* that are not a problem to clients may be listed alone or in addition to positive psychology *problems areas* as in dissatisfaction with Play or Recreation. The resulting case conceptualization and treatment/intervention plan are then shared with clients to build their understanding and motivation for treatment and to bring a common understanding to clients and therapists as to what the clients' assets and problems are and what intervention plan would best serve the clients' goals. Many wonder why this step is necessary since it delays treatment and intervention.

THE NEED FOR SOUND CASE CONCEPTUALIZATION AND FORMULATION

Too often therapists are taught to blindly apply treatment techniques to particular problems and disorders, skipping the important first step of case formulation and conceptualization. Authors from all major schools of psychotherapy have criticized this approach to treatment planning as simplistic and superficial (e.g., see Kazdin, 1993a, 2003; Persons et al., 2001; Strupp & Binder, 1984). Therapist-scholars are not the only ones insisting on thoughtful case conceptualizations as a prerequisite to adequate treatment planning and implementation. Increasingly, licensing boards for all mental health professions (including psychology, psychiatry, and social work) are requiring candidates for licensure to show the ability to conceptualize cases as

a necessary first step in treatment planning (Othmer & Othmer, 1994). Assessing this ability has become *de rigueur* in oral exams for licensure in which test cases are presented to candidates in order to assess their "in-the-trenches" conceptualization skills.

The essential problem with assigning treatments or interventions to specific disorders or positive psychology areas of life without prior case conceptualization or formulation is that the unique causal factors or *dynamics* of a case are ignored. Without considering the unique factors responsible for a particular client's problems, the therapist runs the risk of choosing interventions that fail because they do not address the root causes of the client's problems. At best, this may result in ineffective treatment; at worst, the intervention may be iatrogenic, making the client worse, that is, more unhappy and with a more severe *DSM* disorder than prior to treatment.

A simple listing of positive psychology targets for intervention, QOL problems, or *DSM* disorders, does not address the issue of etiology, that is, how the problems develop, how the problems are maintained, and how they interrelate. In fact, many diagnostic systems such as the *DSM-IV-TR* are designed to be atheoretical and agnostic with respect to the issue of etiology. Psychopathology research has repeatedly supported the view that most diagnoses and clinical problems represent the "final common pathway" for multiple causes that vary from client to client. The same can be said for QOL problems or areas for growth. Thus, for example, in unhappiness or dissatisfaction with *Love,* the CASIO dynamics or causes may be completely different for different clients as when one couple struggles with impossibly high standards adopted from the media, for example, *Sex In the City* norms for sexual athleticism and infidelity—an S problem in CASIO terms—and another couple suffers because neither partner makes the relationship a priority for time and effort, a decidedly I problem in CASIO terms. Without considering the CASIO and other factors unique to each client, or in this case, couple, the "wrong" interventions aimed at the wrong factors could easily be applied as when I-oriented CASIO interventions are applied for S-oriented CASIO problems.

BRIEF CASE CONCEPTUALIZATION

Sharing a case conceptualization with clients may be as simple as going over a QOL profile to show clients how their particular areas of dissatisfaction contribute to an overall unhappiness in CASIO terms, followed by an examination of how *Five Path* strategies could improve clients' satisfaction in these valued areas of life. Alternatively, Positive psychology areas for growth that are not a problem to clients may be directly plugged into the *Five Path* exercise. For example, Work may be the focus of a *Five Path* or CASIO intervention effort to boost satisfaction and productivity even though this is not a problem per se but only an area for growth. This approach can be applied for pure positive psychology clients who do not have a specified *DSM* disorder.

ACT MODEL CASE CONCEPTUALIZATION

The three-step ACT model of case formulation in QOLT includes a complete problem Assessment, including a consideration of diagnosis/symptoms, client assets, problems in living, and theory-based problems, Conceptualization of problems and establishment of treatment priorities in a detailed Treatment plan.

The ACT model case conceptualization allows for a more in-depth case conceptualization that is preferred over the Brief Case Conceptualization discussed here if time allows. The model will be illustrated in detail shortly using our familiar case of Tom introduced in earlier chapters. The ACT model of case formulation and treatment planning addresses the common deficits in case formulation training found across mental health disciplines. The model also attempts to provide guidance in brief, but comprehensive assessment and in prioritizing and planning specific treatment strategies for particular problems, symptoms, and disorders. The

model goes beyond traditional diagnosis by including QOLT's *Whole Life Assessment* view in which overall life goals, situations, and QOL assets and problems are assessed along with symptoms of disturbance. Furthermore, all of these *Whole Life* factors are used in conceptualizing the causal factors that lead to a particular QOL profile and diagnosis in a particular case.

Although the ACT model can be used with most theoretical approaches, including theoretically integrative or technically eclectic approaches, its use here will be illustrated in the context of QOL and cognitive theories where it is especially useful. A reusable ACT model form for case conceptualization and intervention/treatment planning can be found in the Toolbox CD; a completed clinical example follows the blank form.

Once a client's QOL and symptomatic status is (1) *comprehensively assessed*, the process of clinical case formulation and treatment planning can be advanced through the final two steps of (2) *case conceptualization* and (3) *establishing treatment priorities and strategies*. One parsimonious approach to case conceptualization involves applying both the *Beck model* diagrammed in the Toolbox CD—for clients to see—and in Chapter 3 for any *DSM* disorder (Clark & Beck, 1999) and, at the same time, invoking QOL theory in the form of the *CASIO model* also diagrammed in the Toolbox CD to explain dissatisfaction in valued areas of life that may or may not have contributed to clients' *DSM* disorders. This ACT model approach to case conceptualization is based on the QOL definition of health (see Chapters 3 and 13 for elaboration) that invites therapists with clinical cases to have as their goal both to reduce (or eliminate) symptoms of disorder or disability, and to increase or maintain the QOL and personal happiness or contentment of every client that they see. Of course, case conceptualization is simplified in nonclinical or pure positive psychology cases in so far as the CASIO model is employed without invoking the Beck model to explicate *DSM* disorders.

STEP 1: COMPLETE PROBLEM ASSESSMENT AND/OR LISTING OF POSITIVE PSYCHOLOGY AREAS OF GROWTH

The first step in the ACT model is to conduct a complete problem assessment, which was discussed and illustrated in Chapter 5. This assessment component addresses the basic question of what is wrong with a particular client and/or what are the areas to be considered for growth in satisfaction. Positive psychology areas for growth that are not a problem to clients should also be listed here. For example, Work may be the focus of a *Five Path* or CASIO intervention *effort to boost satisfaction and productivity even though this is not a problem per se but only an area for growth.*

It is useful to conduct this assessment at the beginning of therapy and on a periodic basis during the course of therapy to monitor progress toward specific outcome goals (Kazdin, 1993a). Once the assessment of treatment progress reveals that positive outcome goals have been achieved, the assessment ends; this, in effect, makes the last progress assessment an assessment of final outcome, which verifies that the treatment has been effective.

There are four components to the problem assessment (DAPT): **D**iagnosis/Symptoms, **A**ssets, Strengths, and/or Areas for Growth, **P**roblems in Living, and **T**heory-Based Problems. These four components are based on the assumption that a thorough and complete assessment must be done, including questions about problems and complaints that clients do not bring up on their own, in order to develop a conceptualization and treatment plan that treats the underlying problems and causes rather than just the "symptoms" or presenting problems. It is believed that in the long run this will reduce the number of client visits, reduce the amount of healthcare expenditures, and prevent current problems from getting worse, thereby accomplishing *secondary prevention* in public health terms.

The basic task in this part of client assessment is to *translate* the client's problems or symptoms into the language of any theory or theories that a clinician wishes to apply. Assessing and conceptualizing clients' problems and symptoms in terms of particular theories of psychopathology and positive psychology is an important prerequisite to case formulation, treatment planning, and outcome assessment. With respect to the latter, although it is essential to consider a client's perspective on therapeutic outcome, it is also important to consider the therapist's view, which is usually expressed in terms of theory-based concepts when it comes to assessing the outcome of any healthcare intervention (Strupp, 1996; Strupp & Hadley, 1977).

Theory-based problems and concepts, such as CASIO deficits, negative schemas, coping skill deficits, and happiness protective and risk factors can provide the basis for the conceptualization of causes of clients' particular difficulties. These concepts also reflect important intervening variables that reflect the process of psychotherapy according to various the-oretical perspectives. These processes can often be assessed in their own right, as in the case of a dysfunctional attitude scale assessing negative schemas. Although a few theoretical constructs can and should be listed here, most of them belong in the next step. For the purposes of QOLT, QOL and Beck's theories are used here to identify theory-based problems.

STEP 2: *CONCEPTUALIZATION OF PROBLEMS*

Irrespective of theoretical orientation, case conceptualization and intervention/treatment planning appears to consist of therapist-generated answers to a series of questions. These key questions are embedded in a model and a related worksheet for case conceptualization and intervention or treatment/intervention planning called the *ACT model.* For the purposes of QOLT, the ACT worksheet has some QOLT and cognitive therapy examples.

Once an assessment of a client is completed, it is the therapist's task to "make order out of the chaos," that is, to construct a case conceptualization by answering the following four questions:

1. *What are the most important problems or areas for growth?* Here therapists must sort out the most important problems, diagnoses, or symptoms (or a combination of these) that are amenable to therapy and that are related to the presenting complaints or referral questions, and that can adequately be addressed in the amount of time available for treatment.

2. *What factors caused the problem initially? What factors contribute to areas for growth that are going well but may always be improved?* Here the therapist is challenged to invoke a particular theoretical orientation(s) to explain what initially caused the particular problem or problems in the client. For QOLT, CASIO factors and Beckian stressors and schemas may be invoked. This question of causation or etiology is essential to the development of a treatment plan that will effectively address the underlying problems of the client as well as presenting complaints so as to reduce the need for future treatment and expenditures.

DSM disorder case conceptualizations can be improved by including empirically supported factors or causes from the literature or an empirically based book that identifies the likely causes for specific problems or disorders that a client has and that have been verified in the clinical interview and assessment (Davison, Neal, & Kring, 2004). For example, current research suggests that Antisocial Personality Disorder may be the result of growing up in a home environment with inconsistent discipline and antisocial role models as well as a genetic defect resulting in chronic under-arousal, such that some psychopaths commit antisocial acts as thrill-seeking behaviors (Davison et al., 2004). If such a characterization fits a particular client with Antisocial Personality Disorder, this information could be used to formulate the following conceptualization of cause:

> Jonathan's Antisocial Personality Disorder appears to stem from a chaotic home environment in which as a child he was exposed to an antisocial model—his father—by whom he was disciplined both inconsistently and harshly. In addition, Jonathan may suffer from the same type of genetic underarousal found in other sociopaths that leads him to commit antisocial acts as a form of thrill seeking.

It may not be essential for case conceptualizations to be completely accurate or verifiable. The state of knowledge with regard to psychopathology in mental health has large gaps in terms of etiology (Davison et al., 2004). Even though a case conceptualization may not be true or verifiable, it can service a very useful purpose in initially guiding treatment. One way to assess whether the case conceptualization is inadequate or "untrue," is to see whether a particular treatment plan based on the conceptualization is effective or not. In cases where the treatment approach is effective, one may assume that the conceptualization is "true" or at least useful. In this sense we may speak of the *treatment utility of case conceptualization* in the same manner that the treatment utility of assessment has been discussed by Hayes et al. (1987). Hayes et al. defined the treatment utility of assessment as the degree to which assessment is shown to contribute to beneficial treatment outcome regardless of the psychometric validity or reliability of the assessment approach used. Likewise, a thoughtful, but somewhat incomplete or inaccurate case conceptualization may effectively guide the therapist to an effective treatment, thereby proving its treatment utility by contributing to a beneficial treatment outcome (Yalom, 1980).

One way to test the treatment utility of case formulations, in general, and case conceptualizations, in particular, would be to perform outcome studies in which the formulization or conceptualization step is omitted from some cases, but not others, comparing the treatment outcome of cases whose treatment plan was based on a conceptualization versus those whose treatment plan was not based on a thoughtful case conceptualization. It is this author's view, and that of others (Persons, 1989; Persons & Bertagnolli, 1999; Strupp & Binder, 1984) that the treatment utility of a thoughtful case conceptualization would definitely contribute to beneficial treatment outcome in such a study.

3. *What factors maintain the problem(s) or keep it going in the present? What factors maintain an identified area for growth or keep it going in the present?* This question refers to the maintaining factors or causes of a problem or diagnosis, as opposed to those factors that originally caused the problem. In those cases where the original causes or initial causes do not differ from the maintaining causes, this step in case conceptualization may be omitted. It should be noted, however, that initial and maintaining factors often differ. For example, clients addicted to smoking often begin the habit in order to secure peer approval as teenagers, only to continue the life-threatening habit as adults because of physical and psychological dependence. When maintaining causal factors have been identified, the treatment plan should address these rather than the initial causes in order to get at the key etiological factors of a client's disorder.

Before charging ahead with interventions for one area of concern in life like Work, therapists should consider clients' overarching Goals-and-Values for the present and long-term with the QOLI and Vision Quest techniques. Other problems in living such as an impending divorce or a *DSM* disorder should also be considered in formulating a conceptualization that considers all of the sources or causes of dissatisfaction with a particular area like Work. CASIO related problems can be made very clear with results from the *What's Wrong?* assessment in the Toolbox CD. In sum, *all* possible sources or causes of clients' dissatisfaction with a particular life area must be considered and *plugged into* a brief conceptualization well *before* therapists choose the appropriate interventions. This *Whole Life Assessment* perspective should be used with each area of life. The ACT may even be applied to a single *area* of life for clients seeking a very detailed conceptualization of dissatisfaction in one area of life.

4. *How do the different problems or areas for growth interrelate to each other?* It is important for therapists to speculate on the causal relationships

among different problems and diagnoses in order to come up with an efficient and effective treatment or intervention plan. Answering this question can dramatically simplify the number of problems addressed as in the case where a client's depression appears to be caused by the loss of a job and related negative schemas. An evidence based approach such as cognitive therapy for depression in the context of QOLT designed to boost the acute treatment response of cognitive therapy and to prevent relapse would be expected to alleviate this depression and, quite possibly, a host of symptoms and QOL problems that are conceptualized as the result of the depression such as marital discord, occasional alcohol abuse, insomnia, and problems at home, in a mosque/church/synagogue/zendo or a volunteer group due to an inability to concentrate.

In conceptualizing how problems and symptoms interrelate, the therapist can begin by looking at two major factors, or potential causal agents, at a time and speculating on the direction of causation. For any two factors, such as marital discord (or x) and depression (or y), the direction of causality can differ in three ways:

1. x causes y
2. y causes x
3. z causes x and y

In this example, the related problems of marital discord and depression can be conceptualized in three different ways. The marital discord may be largely causing the depression experienced by the client. In contrast, the depressive symptoms of the client may be irritating the other spouse to the extent that they produce the marital discord or distress. Finally, a third variable, such as a chemical imbalance among catecholamines, may be causing both the depressive symptoms and marital difficulties in a particular clinical case.

To begin to conceptualize the interrelationships of a particular client's problems or disorders, the clinician may isolate two key hypothesized causal factors at a time and look at each of the three possibilities. Whichever causal connection best fits the assessment data at hand may be chosen by the clinician to conceptualize the interrelationship of problems in this case. Of course, case conceptualizations are regularly revised based on a client's response to treatment or based on new information and insights of the therapist.

The Diathesis-Stress model (see Beck's model in Chapter 3 and the Toolbox CD for an example) can be invaluable in conceptualizing the interrelationships of a particular client's problems; the model can be applied to most cases with empirical justification for the factors included according to Davison et al. (2004) and others (who discuss additional, more complicated expressions of the model than those used here). Here the problem or disorder can be expressed mathematically wherein the disorder is a function of an interacting Diathesis and Stress:

DSM disorder $= f$ (*Diathesis or predisposition,* which can be biological, psychological, or social × *Stress, stressor, or trigger* in the form of a stressful life event such as losing a job).

DSM disorder $= f$ (Predisposition × Negative life event or trigger)

Likewise, here is an equation for Positive Psychology:

Satisfaction in QOL/Positive Psychology Area for Growth $= f$ (Happiness protective or risk factors from Chapter 3 × CASIO features of the area that may or may not be stressful to the client)

If present, *DSM* disorders could be added to the equation of Satisfaction in QOL/Positive Psychology Area for Growth:

Satisfaction in QOL/Positive Psychology Area for Growth $= f$ (*DSM* disorder × CASIO features of the area that may or may not be stressful to the client)

Even when the CASIO conditions are not experienced as stressful, they can be manipulated via intervention to increase happiness and productivity in the area (see Box 6.1).

QOL area for growth: Work

Work performance and happiness $= f$ (Happiness Protective or Risk Factors × CASIO features of work that may or may not be stressful).

NARRATIVE EXAMPLES SHARED WITH CLIENTS OF ACT STEP 2: CONCEPTUALIZATION OF PROBLEMS

The following conceptualization, which was shared with a client and the client's referral source, illustrates the application of the Diathesis-Stress model to Beck's

---

BOX 6.1

Example of Case *Conceptualization* or Step 2 in ACT Based on QOL Theory

Work performance and happiness =

f (Negative affectivity and chronically low self-esteem × CASIO features of work including crowded noisy conditions)

Or with protective factors:

Work performance and happiness =

f (Optimism and Calm Temperament × CASIO features of work including crowded noisy conditions and a supportive boss)

Note: See Chapter 3 for detailed exposition of QOL Theory.

---

cognitive therapy. It also relates problem drinking to the problem of depression:

Therapist to client: Jane, I believe your depression is a product of your unhappy childhood and the recent stresses of your job loss and divorce. It appears that your primary caretaker, your mother, was emotionally abusive and neglectful and that she constantly criticized you as a child and seemed basically to reject you and not want you around. This, I believe created a predisposition to depression or diathesis in the form of your chronic low self-esteem. Once you got zapped by losing your job and having your husband file for divorce, I think this interacted with your low self-esteem and beliefs that you are only worthwhile if you were in a love relationship and successful in your work to produce the depression you are suffering from now. In addition, I think you've tried to treat your own depression by drowning your sorrows in alcohol. This helps you to forget about your problems, at least for a little while, and is the only way you have learned to cope with problems.

QOLT CASE CONCEPTUALIZATION EXAMPLE

The following is a case example of a case conceptualization based specifically on QOLT:

Therapist to client: John, I think your subclinical depression and conflicts with your friends and coworkers is related to your poor quality of life. You just haven't been able to get your needs met in the areas of life you consider most important, such as love, friends, work, and money. It seems like you've coped with your inability to succeed in these areas in life by blaming yourself and getting more down on yourself, which only makes matters worse. You've been in this negative spiral of hopelessness and self-hate that I think led you to come here today. I think if we can try to apply some techniques from this new approach called Quality of Life Therapy to your life, we can get you out of this pit of depression by engineering small, gradual success experiences in each of these areas of life that you care about until your realistic needs and goals have been met.

STEP 3: ESTABLISH TREATMENT PRIORITIES AND TREATMENT PLAN

The final step in the ACT model involves *five substeps.*

1. *Rank order the problems or areas for growth you need to treat to achieve a positive outcome.* Based on their conceptualization done as part of Step 2, the therapist must decide on the problems (or growth areas) and rank order them in terms of their priority for treatment.

   You may prioritize particular problems, areas, or diagnoses for intervention based on the following factors:

   a. *The conceptualization.* Priortize problems for treatment that seem to be causing or maintaining the client's difficulties in the present. For example, if you decide that a client's depression is due primarily to marital discord, you probably would put the marital discord and couples therapy as the primary treatment priority to get at the key cause for the depression.

   b. *The urgency of a problem.* Any suicidal problem is urgent and must be treated to reduce suicidal risk before any other problem can be addressed in treatment. Similarly, a client facing an imminent divorce that could destroy a basically positive social support may be exposed to couples therapy before any other treatment. Resistance to treatment or noncompliance to treatment itself should be included in a treatment plan and should move to the top of the list of treatment priorities when it is obstructing therapeutic progress.

c. *The potential to provide some immediate relief for easily treated problem(s).* Another factor to consider in establishing treatment priorities is the therapist's desire to provide immediate relief for immediate problems. Therapists can often establish their authority, helpfulness, and create considerable "positive transference" as they alleviate symptoms and distress by, at first, treating problems that are easily managed or resolved. For example, some basic tips on sleep hygiene, such as not taking naps during the day and going to bed and waking up at the same time each day, may "cure" a depressed client's insomnia, but the client with energy, hopefulness, and confidence in the therapist needed to make further progress.

d. *The client's or referral agent's (or both) priorities or agenda for change.* In pure positive psychology cases, this amounts to which areas for growth are most important to the client.

2. *Specifically name and define each problem or area for growth.* Any area of life dissatisfaction on the QOLI can be listed as a problem to be treated. A client's depression may be listed or defined further in terms of the specific *DSM-IV-TR* symptoms the client exhibits, such as feelings of worthlessness, insomnia, or anhedonia, with each symptom representing a problem.

3. *State a long-term or termination goal for each problem or area that is measurable* and observable to others, and will show definite and clear progress. For each problem that will be addressed in the treatment plan, clinicians should clearly define how they would like to see the client's thoughts, feelings, behaviors, and life circumstances change at the end of successful treatment. This goal(s) should be specific and measurable and realistic to the time frame available for treatment. Having a termination goal enables a therapist to clearly know when treatment has been successful and can be terminated, as opposed to when treatment has *not* been successful, at which point the therapist should go back to Step 1 of the ACT model. For example, a therapist may aim for a termination goal of a BDI score of less than 20 (or less than 5 for complete remission of depression) in cases of clinical or Major Depression. In terms of

the *DSM*, therapists should aim for a *DSM* interview in which the client no longer meets the criteria for Major Depression or other diagnosis.

4. *Choose specific treatments, techniques, and interventions that will allow clients to achieve their termination goal(s).* Interventions should be tied to specific goals so that it is clear to the reader of the treatment plan what interventions will achieve which particular intermediate goals. For example, the goal of eliminating a particular client's panic attacks by the fifteenth session of therapy may be specifically achieved through the intervention of Clarks' cognitive therapy for panic disorder, which has been empirically validated for this specific purpose.

TOM AND THE ACT MODEL OF CASE CONCEPTUALIZATION

Tom's (the case introduced in Chapter 3) background was presented along with a detailed QOLT case conceptualization drawing on both Beck's theory and the CASIO model. This background information and conceptualization of Tom is included to illustrate the use of the ACT Model Worksheet (see Toolbox CD) that can organize a therapist's understanding of a case and that can be shared with clients to build a common understanding of their problems, strengths, and plans for growth.

DISCUSSION OF TOM'S ACT MODEL CASE CONCEPTUALIZATION

Tom's case conceptualization is simplified and demystified by breaking it into the three components of ACT. *DSM* symptoms are listed until particular diagnoses are ruled in and out. Assets and strengths are taken directly from his pretreatment/intervention QOLI depicted in Figure 1.1. *Likewise, problems in living and areas for growth are quickly and efficiently taken from the QOLI by simply listing areas of dissatisfaction pictured on the QOLI profile* (see Figures 1.1 and 5.1 for sample profiles). Obstacles to satisfaction cited by clients in Part II of the QOLI test booklet called "Problems That Get in the Way of Your Satisfaction" may also be listed as problems in living. The theory-based problems section of ACT allows therapists to include their favorite and applicable theoretical concepts to a case going well

Date: _January 1, 2525_

Client Name: _____ _Thomas_ _____ _"Tom"_ _____ _T._

Last   First   MI

Age: _22_   Gender: _Male_   ID#: _1234654_

Ethnicity: _White_   Marital Status: _Single_   Religious Preference: _Methodist_

Setting: _____

Clinician's Name: _____

Reason for referral and presenting problems or areas for growth: _Sad, blue, life has no meaning, burned out, lonely, shut down_ _and can't work anymore._

STEP 1: COMPLETE PROBLEM ASSESSMENT

Key Questions: What's wrong?
                     What does **D.A.P.T.** (STEP 1 A-D) assessment reveal?

A. Diagnosis/Symptoms

List all psychological and physical symptoms and diagnoses verified by clinical interview, chart, symptom checklist, significant others, testing, and history. Skim *DSM* list of disorders (American Psychiatric Association, 2000) for disorders to include, exclude, or explore further.

Major Depressive Disorder, Recurrent

Perfectionism and Workaholism parts of subclinical Obsessive Compulsive Personality Disorder

Depressive rumination and worry that could relate to subclinical Generalized Anxiety Disorder

Subclinical and occasional binge eating and alcohol abuse

Subclinical social anxiety symptoms

B. Assets and Areas for Growth

List the client's strengths, skills, assets, and resources. List areas of satisfaction on the quality of life tests like the Quality of Life Inventory (QOLI) as well as any positive personal characteristics, skills, strengths, or resources. For pure positive psychology cases with no current area of dissatisfaction in life, list areas identified for growth or greater satisfaction by clients such as work in which the client is doing well but would like to do better.

Tom is very bright and is motivated to feel and function better.

Tom's QOLI profile shows that he feels satisfied, that is, his needs are being met in the areas of "Money," "Creativity," "Home," and "Community." He chooses not to try and improve satisfaction further in these areas so he has no "areas for growth" in a pure positive psychology sense.

More specifically, Tom's profile and written comments in the QOLI narrative section suggest that Tom is comforted by the following assets and strengths: clear religious beliefs, financial security, ability to get good grades, creative ideas, close

Figure 6.1   Case example of QOLT conceptualization and treatment (intervention) plan.

friends that he has not seen lately, and involvement in a local church and service club. He also feels safe, comfortable, and stimulated by the university community and likes his "home" or apartment complex.

C. Problems in Living or Quality of Life Problems

List any real-life practical problems faced by the client. For example, list and describe areas of dissatisfaction on the QOLI.

His QOLI Profile reveals that Tom is deeply dissatisfied (Weighted Satisfaction Score is −4 or −6) with Self-Esteem ("I feel flawed and defective . . ."), Work ("I'm driven to perform well and worry too much about school work."), Play ("I have no time to 'goof' around, exercise, and hang out with my friends 'cause of school."), Goals-and-Values ("I don't live my values about a balanced, kind, spiritual life and feel guilty about some one night stands I've had—I don't like leading women on . . . Some of it has been weird. For example, a friend watched me have sex with his girlfriend when I had been drinking and I felt really weird afterward."). Relatives said I was abused as a kid. I'm still trying to prove I'm not a bad person by doing good in school." and Love ("I have chosen to isolate and not date. I couldn't attract the kind of girl I'd like.") He is also dissatisfied with his Health ("I'm out of shape, drink too much, and eat too much. At times I want to 'make the world go away.' I can't get motivated to exercise. I don't play b-ball anymore with 'the guys.'").

D. Theory-Based Problems and Concepts

"Translate" the client's problems or symptoms into the language of any theory or theories that you wish to apply. Keep this brief, putting details in the upcoming Step 2: Conceptualization of Problems.

Cognitive Therapy Examples: Stressors, Negative Core Beliefs/Schemas, Coping Skill Deficits, Childhood Abuse/Neglect, Genetic Predisposition, Deactivation of Constructive Mode Functioning, and Activation of Primal Modes—loss/deprivation in depression, threat in anxiety, victim in anger.

QOLT Examples: Areas for Growth, Low Quality of Life or Life Satisfaction, Inability to get needs met in valued areas of life (specify areas), CASIO factors—Unrewarding Life Circumstances, Negative Attitudes about an Area of Life, Unrealistic Standards of Fulfillment in Valued Areas of Life, Poor Priorities in What Is Deemed Important—Undue Emphasis on Dissatisfying or Uncontrollable Parts of Life, Unbalanced Lifestyle—O in CASIO, Lack of Goals or Purpose, Self-Hate (or Negative Self-Evaluation), Hopelessness, Low Self-Esteem, Low Self-Efficacy, Excessive Self-Blame, or Criticism, Excessive Self-Focused Attention and/or Performance Fears, Self-Medication (through drug abuse), Lack of Social Support, Poor Social Skills Needed for Developing Mutually Beneficial Relationships, Poor Coping Skills for Dealing with Stress and Frustration including Poor Emotional Control, Problem-Solving, or Time Management Skills. Life Management Problems as in Difficulty in Setting and Following Priorities, Difficulty in Setting Challenging but Realistic and Attainable Goals.

Tom is a "Type A workaholic" who puts all his energy into work which he doesn't currently enjoy and which keeps him from getting satisfaction from other parts of life like Play and Love which he values but neglects in favor of work. His standards of fulfillment (CASIO model of life satisfaction) are so high for Work that he never fulfills them, feels frustrated, and has no time for anything else. Also shows signs of Depressionogenic Schemas of self-hate, perfectionism; Childhood Abuse/Neglect, Deactivation of Constructive Mode Functioning and Activation of loss/deprivation Primal Mode; Very Low Quality of Life or Life Satisfaction, Inability Unrewarding Life Circumstances, Negative Attitudes about Play and Friends which are completely ignored and neglected for Work that has perfectionist and Unrealistic Standards of Fulfillment; Unbalanced Lifestyle—O in CASIO, Poor Coping Skills for Dealing with Stress and Frustration including overeating and alcohol use. Poor Emotional Control and Life Management Skills.

Figure 6.1 *Continued*

71

STEP 2: <u>C</u>ONCEPTUALIZATION OF PROBLEMS OR AREAS OF GROWTH

Key Questions: What are the most important problems?
                   What factors <u>caused</u> the problems?
                   What factors <u>maintain</u> the problem (or area for growth) or keep it going now?
                   (Answer <u>only</u> if these factors differ from those that caused the problem in the first place)
                   How do the different problems <u>interrelate</u> to each other?
                   What <u>T</u>heory-Based Problems and Concepts (1D) apply here? List them for a conceptualization.
                   Apply your preferred theory or theories if you wish to be eclectic, integrationist, or diathesis-stress-oriented, and so on.

<u>Cognitive Therapy Examples</u>:   Low self-esteem (predisposition) from an abusive/neglectful childhood interacted with the stress of rejection in love or failure at work (stress) to activate depressogenic schemas to produce depression that is self-medicated with alcohol abuse (illustrates Beck's latest cognitive theory, a diathesis-stress model).

<u>QOLT Examples</u>:   Client is dissatisfied in love because of her unrealistic standards for husband and her marriage (S in CASIO) and her exclusive devotion to the marriage over other valued areas of life like friends, work, and play that are being woefully neglected. Depression and overeating over her unhappiness with love and generally poor quality of life or low life satisfaction may get worse until progress toward her life goals as shown on Vision Quest is realized. (List specific areas of dissatisfaction such as learning and see also QOLT Examples in Step (1D).

In cognitive therapy terms, the stress—or "stressors"—of trying to maintain a perfect A average in all of his academic work on the one hand, and an increasingly impoverished lifestyle of academic drudgery with little or no pleasure or fun, on the other hand, activated negative core depressogenic schemas—unlovable/defective self, perfectionism, approval—that led directly to Tom's depression. He has felt as if in a fog, as this "full body" deprivation mode seems to take over his body and mind. In QOL theory terms, Tom's Standards of Fulfillment (CASIO model of life satisfaction) for Work are so high that he never fulfills them, feels frustrated, and has no time for anything else, resulting in impoverished and unfulfilling Circumstances in the areas of Friends, Play, and Love. Tom lacks confidence in dating. Tom self-medicates his depression with occasional and alcohol abuse, overeating, and furtive one night stands which he feels guilty about later.

STEP 3: ESTABLISH TREATMENT AND INTERVENTION PRIORITIES AND PLAN

Key Questions:

A. Based on your conceptualization, the urgency of a problem (e.g., suicide risk, resistance to treatment, imminent divorce), the client's and referral agent's priorities or agenda for change, and/or desire to provide immediate relief for easily treated problems, <u>rank order the problems and areas for growth you need to treat to have a positive treatment outcome</u>. Rank the top priority goal #1, the second priority goal #2, and so on.

B. Specifically name and define each problem or area for growth.

C. State a long-term or termination goal(s) for each problem or area for growth, saying how you'd like the client's thoughts, feelings, behaviors, and circumstances to be different <u>if treatment is successful</u>. Be specific and offer a time line to check and see later if the goal is accomplished. Make sure *Goals* are <u>measurable and observable to others</u>. For example, in 15 sessions aim for a subclinical BDI-II score of less than 15 or aim for a *DSM* interview in which the client no longer meets the *DSM* criteria for Major Depressive Disorder. For positive goals aim for an overall QOLI T score within one standard deviation of the nationwide nonclinical mean, therefore, a score of 41 or greater. Include goals for specific areas for growth such as "find and form a second close friendship (to supplement my relationship with my husband) with a woman at work with whom I can be totally open and can visit with daily or weekly."

D. Choose specific treatments, interventions, and techniques that will allow you to achieve each Termination Goal. Try and reference interventions with specific books, treatment manuals, studies, and/or theorists.

Figure 6.1   *Continued*

Problem (or Area for Growth) #1:

Major Depression

Measurable Termination Goal:

Tom will no longer meet the DSM criteria for Major Depressive Disorder and will have a BDI-II within the functional or nonclinical range (that is, within one standard deviation; Kazdin, 2003; Ogles, Lambert, & Masters, 1996) according to college norms.

Interventions:

1. *Quality of life therapy (Frisch, 2006), including Beck's cognitive therapy of depression and positive psychology interventions for valued areas of life with which Tom is unhappy right now.*
   Note: This entry by itself can be a sufficient treatment plan. If the reader wishes to consider each problem in more detail, this problem 1 entry can be expanded to the following problems and interventions.

Problem #2:
Low Self-Esteem and Self-Hate

Measurable Termination Goal:

Movement to within one standard deviation of functional sample on Rosenberg Self-Concept scale.

Interventions:

1. *QOLT Self-Esteem interventions from both professional and client handbooks.*

2. *Traditional cognitive therapy schema work.*

3. *Self-schema work via QOLT Goals-and-Values' Life Script Technique and Tenets of contentment.*

Problem #3:

Work/School Dissatisfaction

Measurable Termination Goal:

Movement to within one standard deviation of nonclinical functional sample on College Adjustment scale.

Interventions:

1. *QOLT Work interventions esp, Good Not Great Technique for perfectionism.*

2. *QOLT Learning interventions that relate specifically to the school problems that Tom is having.*

3. *Readings in books **Mind Over Mood** and **Feeling Good** on perfectionism and achievement schemas.*

Figure 6.1 *Continued*

Problem #4:

Play and Health Dissatisfaction

Measurable Termination Goal:

Meeting target—30 minutes per day of aerobic physical activity on behavioral exercise log.

Interventions:

1. *QOLT Play interventions such as Playlist.*

2. *Habit Change Program to increase physical activity and exercise for their antidepressant and anxiolytic properties.*

3. *Time management via Happiness Pie and activity scheduling—QOLT's Daily Activity Plan—to plan for daily recreation activities and exercise which is Health as well as recreational concern for Tom.*

Problem #5:

Relatives Dissatisfaction

Measurable Termination Goal:

1. *Movement to within one standard deviation of functional sample on Dyadic Adjustment scales.*

2. *Interacts weekly with mom and both report in session that the relationship is mutually supportive and satisfying.*

3. *No longer reports guilt about limited relationship with father that is totally one sided as dad discusses his suicidal ruminations with Tom!*

Interventions:

1. *QOLT Relationships/In General and Relative interventions such as Surrogate Family Technique, Take-a-Letter #1 and 2.*

2. *Emotional Honesty and QOLT Relationship Tenets and Skills for setting boundaries with dad and sharing specific hurts and needs with mom.*

Problem #6:

Addictions or subclinical and occasional overeating, alcohol abuse, and one-night stands

Measurable Termination Goal:

1. *Each behavior moves to within target goal range on behavioral log/Habit Control Diary in QOLT.*

2. *Movement to within one standard deviation of non-clinical, functional sample on Addiction Severity Index with norms available in Ogles, Masters, & Lambert, 1996.*

Figure 6.1 *Continued*

Interventions:

1. *These "self-medication" practices should cease once Tom's depression starts to remit.*

2. *If intervention #1 is not successful in 10 weeks, the Health chapter's Habit Change Program will be invoked.*

Problem #7:

Depressive rumination and GAD-type worry which seem to be equivalent (Papageorgiou & Wells, 2004)

Measurable Termination Goal:

1. *Movement to within one standard deviation of nonclinical functional sample on Response Styles Questionnaire (Luminet, 2004)*

Interventions:

1. *QOLT "Guide for Worry Warts" protocol from Toolbox CD*

2. *QOLT Emotional control techniques (Chapter 10) that overlap with cognitive therapy techniques with the same purpose*

3. *New cognitive therapy techniques of McMillan & Fisher (2004)*

Figure 6.1   *Continued*

beyond the theory-neutral *DSM*. Some basic CASIO model musings on Tom are listed here in preparation for the fuller conceptualization of Tom's case that is in the next section of the ACT worksheet. The conceptualization of Tom's case also draws on Beck's latest cognitive theory summarized in Chapter 3 and diagrammed in the Toolbox CD as the *Beck Theory Diagram*. Finally, a straightforward treatment/intervention plan is offered to Tom based on QOLT. The plan could stop with the listing of only problem 1 and prescribed intervention/treatment: Depression, and the prescription of QOLT, understanding that QOLT in this case would also include Beck's cognitive therapy for depression. Nevertheless, six more problems and associated interventions are presented to give readers a flavor of a more detailed and comprehensive treatment/intervention plan using the QOLT approach. The detail of an intervention plan is only limited by the time available to "flesh out" such a plan in the ACT format.

Sharing the Case Conceptualization with Tom

At the second and third meetings, the therapist and Tom went over a copy of Tom's ACT Model Work-

sheet and discussed the results of the various assessments used to diagnose Tom's problem. The process made Tom feel understood and enhanced his confidence in the therapist who not only accurately described Tom's problems in terms of QOLT and cognitive therapy, but who also had a specific and clear plan of attack (i.e., treatment/intervention plan) for addressing these problems. The therapist discussed Tom's particular *DSM* symptoms before introducing the ACT worksheet.

In explaining Tom's QOLI profile to him, the therapist first shared the CASIO diagram from the Toolbox CD and mentioned the CASIO theory, which states that a person's overall happiness is made up of the satisfaction he feels with particular areas of life that he or she personally values.

Tom's QOLI profile (Figure 1.1 in Chapter 1) was explored collaboratively with his therapist, the author. Tom could see that the CASIO theory was illustrated in the way the QOLI was scored and in how the QOLI profile was laid out in terms of overall score followed by the underlying profile of satisfactions and dissatisfactions in valued areas of life. He understood that his QOLI score was very poor relative to the standardization sample (his score placed him in the 15th percentile), putting him at risk for future health problems in addition to his current depression and other problems.

Tom was reminded of his assets and strengths on the QOLI by going over areas of *satisfaction* such as Money and Surroundings in his QOLI profile (see Chapter 5 for detailed instructions for interpreting QOLI results). Likewise, his problems in living were discussed in terms of areas of *dissatisfaction* on the QOLI (as well as Problems That Get in the Way in the narrative or "write in" section of Part II of the QOLI, which is not shown in Figure 6.1).

After sharing the ACT model of case conceptualization, the therapist presented Tom with a straightforward QOLT treatment/intervention plan that would address seven identified problems. Once again, Tom felt cared for, understood, and hopeful about a clearcut intervention plan specifically tailored to his particular assets and problem areas.

Tom, We Hardly Knew Ye: Implementation of ACT and Outcome

Tom was willing to "play with," to experiment with all manner of QOLT ideas and techniques in order to gradually sculpt a life that fit his truest, most personal goals and values—and less so the one's foisted on him by his parents and teachers. He quickly separated the "wheat from the chaff" in terms of techniques that were clearly helpful to him and his circumstances and those that were not. The specific cognitive therapy treatment techniques found useful by Tom included the classic activity schedule, thought record—in this case the *Lie Detector,* and schema change techniques as presented here along with techniques unique to QOLT such as the *Five Paths* approach to problem solving— see Chapter 8 for excerpts from Tom's many *Five Paths* exercises completed during his daily Quality Time. Weekly QOLI profiles and scores helped to determine the current focus of treatment whether it be on dealing with work/school/achievement issues, planning for recreation, or dealing with dating or familial relationship problems.

After 15 sessions of therapy, Tom would talk at length about how he had taken up rollerblading and was zipping through the campus at frenetic speed at all hours of the day and night—he also moved to a safer neighborhood where he could walk and rollerblade without fears of getting mugged. Further-

more, he was extolling the gospel of rollerblading to many of his uptight friends who seemed to think that graduate school was all that mattered in life. Besides rollerblading, Tom would play, re-create, and recharge himself by volunteering through his church at a local food bank. The food bank work was very renewing as predicted by Lyubomirsky et al. (in press) and allowed him to lose himself in the *flow* of interacting with and helping others (Csikszentmihalyi, 1997). The food bank and church also did wonders for his subclinical social anxiety problems and added to the web of relationships in his life, a prominent aspect of the lives of the "very happy" (Diener & Seligman, 2002; also see *Tangled Web Tenet*). On weekends, Tom took up sailing, a love from his youth that he had almost forgotten.

In building his self-esteem, Tom resonated to the QOLT approach that builds self-esteem through small success experiences in *other* areas of life. The major Tenet of Contentment that he used in developing a new philosophy of life and in countering negative schemas was the *Happiness Matters Principle.* Specifically, Tom accepted that, in some ways, depression was a choice for him. Every day he made hundreds of choices that could lead him down the path to either fulfillment or depression. For example, by making time to connect with others and to exercise, rather than indulging in his self-hate ruminations or work worries, he knew that he was choosing a path that was more life-affirming and offered growth. Chapter 12 details Tom's other self-esteem work, including revised self-related schemata and a revised or *New Life Script* as suggested in the Goals-and-Values chapter.

In the area of Relationships, with time and therapy, Tom used skills in Emotional Honesty and *Relationship Enhancement* to become clearly aware or mindful of what he wanted from the people in his life and how he was coming across to them in day-to-day interactions. At my request, Tom's mother attended several therapy sessions with him. He gained from this as well as from the use of the Take-a-Letter Technique in which he first clarified his hurts, feelings, and wants about his mother to himself, and then *carefully* planned how to share these hurts, feelings, and wants in an emotionally honest but considerate way in order to improve the relationship. Tom began to make peace with his mother and to see her as a new-found friend. His father continued to be distant and cruel. In their occasional contacts, his father would speak *ad nau-*

seam about his own personal problems (including suicidal tendencies) instead of playing the part of a nurturing father who keeps his own worst burdens to himself. When told of his son's plan to abandon medicine and biology for the field of history, his father ridiculed him in public, only to "come begging" in order to share in his son's academic honors, including his admission to a prestigious West Coast university. Also in the area of relationships, Tom used the Surrogate Family Tenet to build a support network of friends in place of that part of his family that he had "lost" or more correctly, never had, as a bastion of emotional support.

In terms of his schoolwork or *Learning*, Tom was able to keep his high grades and have a lot more fun and time for friends by lowering his standards and goals *slightly* via the *Good Not Great* exercise—see Chapter 8 for details of Tom's efforts in this regard.

In terms of his work, after taking career interest tests and after exploring career issues and options via QOLT techniques, Tom settled on a plan for a relatively low-stress, but stimulating and challenging job at a small, liberal arts college when he graduated. In terms of his surroundings, Tom was careful to pick a two-bedroom apartment or *Home* in a safe *Neighborhood* that allowed for him to exercise and rollerblade outside. He found his new university *Community* to be as stimulating, open, and tolerant as Austin had been, which was a relief for him given his fundamentalist upbringing in rural Texas.

When stressed, Tom would take time out from his schedule for *Quality Time* and *Inner Abundance* in the evening to calm down—through meditation, prayer, or moving music that he found touching. He would process problems with a thought record/Lie Detector or *Five Paths* exercise, review his Goals-and-Values, and plan a modest but interesting and challenging schedule or flow for next day. Given enough external stress, Tom could still get depressed and lapse or relapse, but he learned to curtail these episodes by recognizing their *Early Warning Signals*—in his case, problems with sleeping, and diarrhea—and following his *Relapse Emergency Checklist* from Chapter 22 and in the Toolbox CD. Rather than get down on himself for these blue periods, he would "drag himself back on top of the horse" of QOLT and get back to feeling good once he had reestablished his *Happiness Habits*—see Tenets.

Outcome

By the end of treatment, Tom no longer met *DSM-IV* criteria for major depression or alcohol abuse. His occasional binge eating episodes had ceased. Reductions in anxiety were reflected in scores on the Trait Anxiety Scale of the State Trait Anxiety Inventory that moved to within one standard deviation of a nonclinical sample; the same result was evident on the BDI (see Ogles et al., 1996, for graphs of reliable change used for both measures). Tom's pretreatment QOLI score soared from a T score of 29 to a T score of 60, a clinically significant move to within one standard deviation of the nationwide nonclinical sample (Ogles et al., 1996). Tom's treatment gains were maintained for 2 years that included several booster sessions or maintenance therapy sessions during times of stress including the breakup of a romantic relationship.

CHAPTER 7

The Three Pillars of QOLT: Inner Abundance, Quality Time, and Find a Meaning

QOLT can begin in earnest with the three pillars or foundational *Tenets of Contentment*. Each Tenet is included in the Toolbox CD; they are also listed for therapists to examine both here and in Chapter 9. These three core principles are to be shared with all clients at the start of QOLT because they are basic to the approach. For this reason, therapists must be well acquainted with these principles along with some specific techniques for their implementation; these tenets will often be "the answer" or an answer to clients' unhappiness, stuckness or resistance to intervention, or life problem/challenge. It can help to present them to clients as a regular practice that should be considered or reviewed *daily* for QOLT to have its intended effect. In general, *happiness practices* that are routine, habitual, and daily seem to have the greatest effect and are most likely to be continued after QOLT has ceased.

After introducing the "three pillars" in session, therapists should assign the three core Tenets of Contentment as reading homework for clients (and themselves!) early in therapy along with other *Tenets* that seem to fit clients unique needs—see Tenets in the Toolbox CD. After Tenets are assigned, it is then essential to discuss them near the start of the next session (to show that they are important tools for realizing clients' personal goals), designing specific implementation plans for carrying out the Tenets in daily life on a regular or routine basis, and following up on these plans throughout QOLT to see if implementation has worked in terms of increased contentment and effectiveness in pursuing cherished life goals.

INNER ABUNDANCE PRINCIPLE

Inner Abundance means feeling deeply calm, rested, centered, loving, alert, and ready to meet the challenges of the day and life after caring for oneself in a thoughtful, loving, compassionate, and comprehensive way. It suggests that when people do the very best for themselves, they have a lot more of themselves available for other people and activities (see Giving Tree or Self-Other Tenet). People must feel centered, calm, and good on the inside, hence the "inner" of Inner Abundance, to serve others or to pursue happiness in any of the areas of life in QOLT.

Inner Abundance demands that people do a good job of self-care, which means putting in a lot of time, effort, and thinking into what renews them each day and then making time to do it.

Inner Abundance means getting necessary rest and caring for one's body. It often means engaging in regular exercise. It can mean regular mediation, prayer, and review of goals and planning (all things that make up Quality Time in QOLT). Above all, Inner Abundance relies on routines, that is, over learned actions that require no thinking.

Inner Abundance is also about creating space for oneself in life as in time alone to reflect and recharge one's batteries. Creating space for Inner Abundance also means not overwhelming oneself with responsibilities and projects at work and elsewhere.

Inner Abundance is highly personal; what works for others may not work for a particular person. Encourage clients to experiment and discover routines for

Inner Abundance that they can practice every day or nearly every day.

Committing to Inner Abundance means making happiness, peace, and contentment priorities (see Happiness Matters Principle or Tenet). It may sound trite but it is no less true that if you do not care for yourself, who else will? Clients should stop putting off the things they know that they need to experience Inner Abundance. Stop waiting for vacation and make time for mini-vacations every day, interludes of self-renewing routines that make your current life circumstances livable and decent right now . . . without any drastic changes. QOLT speaks of Daily Inner Abundance (IA Goals). To concretize this principle along with a question, clients are urged to ask themselves when upset and throughout the day, "What would Inner Abundance be for me in this moment?" (Inner Abundance in the Moment).

Emergency Abundance means doing a few small things to care for yourself even when things get hairy, crazy, or too busy and difficult to make any changes in your routine. It can mean a full-body massage in lieu of a 5-day church/temple/meditation retreat. If you are using a bad habit to get you through these times and provide some self-nurturing, Emergency Abundance advocates a harm-reduction strategy in which you indulge but limit the damage as in smoking 10 cigarettes a day instead of 30 or eating a 600-calorie binge of delicious self-soothing junk food rather than a 3,000-calorie hit. Of course, Emergency Abundance assumes that you won't let the bad times last forever and that once things calm down in several months or even a year in a difficult marriage or job, and so on, you will pursue a program of real Inner Abundance with no corners cut and with unhealthy habits challenged, managed, controlled, or eradicated (see Box 7.1).

QUALITY TIME PRINCIPLE

People should allow themselves time alone in a quiet place with no distractions to relax; get centered; get in touch with feelings, goals, and values; plan their day; and make a plan to solve or manage personal problems. Quality Time is time alone (5 to 30 minutes) used to renew, to relax, to get in touch with the key overarching goals in your life, and to process any worries or problems.

Although it is best to do this regularly, even daily, Quality Time is a must when people are particularly busy and upset. Since QOLT is a support for people to

---

BOX 7.1
Quality Time Principle

Allow yourself time alone in a quiet place with no distractions to relax; get centered; get in touch with your feelings, goals, and values; plan your day; and make a plan to solve or manage personal problems.

---

use when they feel like it, people should never criticize themselves for not practicing Quality Time on a regular basis. QOLT should not be an extra burden in your life. Encourage clients to consider Quality Time as a necessary and enjoyable part of their day. Rather than being selfish, this basic kind of self-caring can give people more energy and love to give to others.

Quality Time is not time spent with other people. It is time devoted to your relationship with yourself.

To prevent a major upset, self-destructive behavior, or addiction, it is important for clients to learn and identify the first signs of stress. These early warning signals of stress vary from person to person so clients must learn to recognize their own unique *Personal Stress Profile* (PSP). At the first inkling of stress, worry, or anger, clients can carve out some Emergency Quality Time to calm down and deal with the situation.

It helps for Quality Time to start off with a Relaxation Ritual to calm and make the person deeply aware of personal thoughts and feelings. Quality Time could begin with lighting a candle, taking a hot bath, playing soft music, prayer, meditation, or taking a few deep breaths. The Toolbox CD includes two sample Relaxation Rituals that can be shared with clients. Whatever method clients choose, the idea is for them to quiet down enough to become aware of anything that is bothering them (see Thou Shalt Be Aware or Psychephobia Principle in Chapter 9). Clients may wish to keep a journal or fill in the first column of the Lie Detector and Stress Diary labeled Upsetting Thoughts. The Feelings Dictionary can help clients when they have difficulty putting what they are feeling or thinking into words.

Once clients have relaxed and are aware of a problem or area of life that they would like to work on, they may choose to complete some QOLT exercises, such as *Five Paths* to help them find solutions. The Lie Detector and Stress Diary can also guide clients in coming up with a realistic and positive answer to painful, distorted, and unhealthy thoughts. As noted earlier, all of these exercises are available in the Toolbox CD that accompanies this book. These exercises can be printed out and given to clients at the start of therapy.

The following script introduces clients to the idea of carving out Structured Quality Time as a regular practice—like their daily workout:

> Make time every day to get away by yourself to calm down, process your worries, and come up with a plan for dealing with the problem. The first part of this Quality Time should be devoted to a Relaxation Ritual that will calm you down so that you can think clearly, feel centered, and be in touch with your most cherished Goals-and-Values. It's especially easy to forget what's most important, lose perspective, and do something stupid that is not in our best long-term interest when we feel confused, scared, or depressed; a good Relaxation Ritual will lessen these upset feelings.
>
> Once you feel composed *physically* through a Relaxation Ritual, compose your thoughts by doing a Lie Detector and Stress Diary about what is troubling you. Once your thinking about the situation is straightened out, it is time to use the Five Paths worksheet (*Five Paths*) to work out a plan of attack that won't be too costly but that will solve or manage the problem. Later, after you've finished your Quality Time exercises for the day, use the Second Opinion technique to talk to a trusted friend about your problem to be sure that you are seeing the problem and its possible solutions clearly. A friend who knows you well and loves and accepts you as you are, including your frailties and imperfections, can also boost your confidence as you plan to implement the solutions you have settled on. You may remember these steps with the acronym, QRSPS:

QRS . . . PS Routine for Quality Time

Step 1	*Q*	*Take a Time-Out for Quality Time, and do the following . . .*
Step 2	*R*	*Relaxation Ritual*
Step 3	*S*	*Stress Diary or Lie Detector*
Step 4	*P*	*Problem Solving with Five Paths worksheet*
Step 5	*S*	*Second Opinion technique*

QUALITY TIME AND COGNITIVE THERAPY TOOLS

Many of the tools used during Quality Time include essentials of cognitive therapy for depression and other negative affects like anger and anxiety (Beck, 1995); these cognitive therapy elements are discussed in more detail in Chapter 10. For example, the Lie Detector and Stress Diary is designed to be a client-friendly thought record that also teaches clients to name their feelings and to take action toward solving problems after cognitively restructuring a situation. Relaxation Rituals help clients to calm down enough to complete an effective thought record. As Frisch (1992) suggested, problem solving is an under-elaborated part of cognitive therapy. Problem solving is spelled out in QOLT in the form of the Five Paths worksheet that directly flows from the CASIO model of life satisfaction detailed in Chapter 3 (see Figure 3.1). The Daily Activity Plan is an expanded activity schedule, the venerable cognitive therapy technique that should be used before the thought record or Stress Diary in cases of severe depression or psychopathology (Beck, 1995).

EMERGENCY QUALITY TIME

Although it is best to make time for Quality Time regularly, even daily, Quality Time is a must when people are particularly busy or upset. Quality Time can be grabbed for a few minutes in a bathroom stall if need be. To prevent a major upset or some self-destructive behavior or relapse, it is important for clients to learn and identify the first signs of stress. These early warning signals vary from person to person so clients must learn to recognize their unique Personal Stress Profile. For example, one abusive father knew that when he clinched his teeth, it was a warning sign of anger. At the first inkling of stress or worry or anger, clients can carve out some Emergency Quality Time in order to calm down and deal with the situation in a way that will be best for clients and others in the long run. Emergency Quality Time can also break through or eradicate major stress or upset that has built up over time. Suggest to clients options such as spending a few minutes in Mindful Breathing (Toolbox CD) in a bathroom stall, walking around the block, or taking a drive if they can drive safely.

STRESS AND THE RATIONALE FOR RELAXATION RITUALS IN QUALITY TIME

QOLT defines stress as the feeling or perception of being overwhelmed by an unpleasant situation. We feel as though we lack the ability or help needed to cope effectively. We know that we are feeling stress by one of the Big Three negative emotions. Indeed, stresses/stressors and daily hassles reduce well-being and quality of life by reducing the ratio of positive to negative affect experiences that define the equation of happiness (see QOL theory in Chapter 3 and Diener & Seligman, 2004). Stress can be experienced in thoughts, feelings, behavior, and physical sensations. With respect to the latter, people often experience physical tension with stress and daily hassles (whereas "uplifts" often reduce tension and stress overall—see Diener & Seligman, 2004). Without even being aware of it, tension can gradually build in the neck, in the forehead, and throughout the body. Sometimes the tension can produce headaches, so-called tension or muscle contraction headaches.

Whether clients get headaches or not, the physical tension that accompanies stress and feeling upset feeds the negative thoughts and feelings they already have, making matters worse. For example, if we're afraid of something like meeting with our boss to get some performance feedback, the fears we have about getting negative feedback can produce physical tension, which then causes more fearful thoughts. People in a situation like this may take physical cues of tension and unease as a sign that they really are in danger, whether or not that is the case. A spiral of anxiety, worry, and fear can easily develop, as upsetting thoughts and physical tension feed on each other to make people more and more emotionally upset. Of course, being anxious or afraid doesn't help clear thinking either. It is hard to think clearly when we are upset. It is easy to lose perspective on a problem or our overall quality of life when we are upset.

Fortunately, our bodies and minds have a capacity to create and cultivate a center of calm and peace amid a storm of worries. Just as people are biologically programmed with the fight-flight-freeze-or-faint-tend-and-befriend reaction to handle extreme danger, we also have an internal calming mechanism or response (Barlow, 2002), what Herbert Benson called "the relaxation response." With proper training, we can teach clients to access this response, get centered, gain perspective on their lives, and solve the problems that they are facing with skill and deep understanding.

People need to access their relaxation response reliably since we do not problem solve well when we are upset and in the throes of the fight-or-flight reaction to

stress. People also do not process negative thoughts and upsetting feelings well when they are upset. This is why Relaxation Rituals are important to QOLT. A Relaxation Ritual is a discipline or routine that people use to help them calm down when upset or under stress. Although the techniques are very effective in and of themselves, the ritual is also designed as a first step toward attitude change and problem solving. Rather than asking clients to fill in a Stress Diary, for example, or a Problem-Solving worksheet when they are upset, it's best if they first do a Relaxation Ritual to take the edge off the tension and get to a place where they can thoughtfully consider the problems and upsetting thoughts that they face.

Relaxation training has been called the "aspirin" of psychology because it is so useful, calming, and even pain relieving. QOLT suggests several approaches to relaxation. Clients may also be encouraged to develop their own techniques.

RELAXATION RITUAL: PROGRESSIVE MUSCLE RELAXATION (PMR) RITUAL

One of the best, most reliable relaxation exercises is the PMR technique, which takes about 30 minutes and is transcribed in detail in the Toolbox CD. Clients may make a recording of the procedure to listen to. The PMR approach involves progressive muscle relaxation during which clients do a series of tensing and releasing exercises for various muscle groups in their body. This approach also includes some deepening exercises from hypnosis and breathing exercises common to meditation approaches. The sequence of exercises is based on that of Dr. David Barlow and his colleagues at Boston University (Barlow, 2002). Some clients prefer to make a recording of PMR instructions so they can concentrate solely on the physical sensations and not worry about what muscle group to tense and when (although with regular practice, this sequence is easily memorized). The end of the transcript for the PMR ritual (see Toolbox CD) alludes to cue-controlled relaxation in which a person recalls or re-creates the pleasant and warm feelings of relaxation by simply saying a keyword like "relax" that brings about or cues the relaxation by virtue of its association with the full procedure. Since the word "calm" is used during the procedure we outline, tell clients that by simply saying this word to themselves softly as they exhale, they can actually become relaxed, recalling many of the sensations felt during a full session of PMR.

Differential relaxation refers to the tensing and relaxing of a specific muscle group, one at a time, without drawing attention to ourselves as we face an anxious situation in real life. For example, therapists may suggest that clients shrug their shoulders and then relax them while driving in order to reduce the anxiety brought about by being late to an appointment. Clients often can tense and relax leg muscles without others noticing it. After clients practice the entire PMR Ritual in a quiet place, encourage them to experiment by applying selected parts of the PMR Ritual to everyday situations in which they would like to feel more relaxed as in relaxing a few parts of the body or breathing slowly and steadily during a tense business meeting or presentation.

RELAXATION RITUAL: REVIEWING THE TENETS OF CONTENTMENT TECHNIQUE

Reading and reviewing the Tenets of Contentment in a comfortable chair in a quiet place for 10 minutes to an hour with no distractions, can constitute a Relaxation Ritual for clients to calm down and access their body's inner Relaxation Response and personal wisdom (look under Relaxation Rituals in the Toolbox CD for a copy of this procedure; a copy of the master list of Tenets is also needed for enacting this procedure and can be found in the companion book, *Finding Happiness*).

Rationale

Reviewing the *Tenets* can remind clients of the wisdom and skills available to them for handling their problems no matter how great they seem at the moment. Too often people forget about these resources when upset. Additionally, reading in a quiet place with no distractions is a reliable relaxation.

Dealing with Distractions

If clients are distracted with upsetting thoughts as they read the Tenets, tell them to acknowledge or "greet" their worries and then gently refocus their attention on the Tenets. Tell them to do this "a thousand times" if they have to during relaxation time. They will gradu-

ally improve as they learn to carve out time and psychic space for themselves to relax without obsessing about the problems of the day. If they still feel distracted with upsetting thoughts, have them review the Tenets while practicing Mindful Breathing (see Toolbox CD).

Once relaxed, clients may circle Tenets that resonate with themselves or with a problem that they are working on.

MINDFUL BREATHING AND THE GUIDE FOR WORRY WARTS

QOLT includes a variation on mindfulness training aimed at becoming fully aware of episodes of dysphoria and their meanings to clients, while controlling distractions during everyday tasks. The QOLT approach to mindfulness is called *Mindful Breathing* and can be found in the Toolbox CD; the rationale for learning to accept and become aware of dysphoric episodes is expressed in the Thou Shalt Be Aware Tenet of Contentment. Essentially, clients are taught, to paraphrase Freud's famous saying, that *feelings are the royal road to meaning*. For this reason, clients need to accept negative feelings in order to become acquainted with the meanings and negative schemas that often accompany them. Only through deep openness and awareness can these meanings be brought to light and eventually challenged or restructured into more positive schemas. Often the processing of these meanings and attendant cognitive restructuring is put off until Quality Time; in the meantime, clients are taught to use Mindful Breathing as a way to accept and reduce distracting worries during everyday tasks. With respect to the latter goal, clients are encouraged to ask themselves "The Question" from the Tenet of the same name over and over, whenever they get distracted from the task at hand:

- What am I doing?
- What are my goals for this situation?

By asking themselves "What am I doing?" clients can then refocus their attention on the task at hand and try to do the best that they can at that task since, in mindfulness terms, the present moment is all that we have. From this perspective, the past is just a memory and the future, a fantasy or expectation.

By asking "What are my goals for this situation?" the essence of QOLT is tapped since clients are enjoined to consider an activity in terms of personal goals. For example, a badgering father, Nate, who loved to tell his teenage daughter how to raise her child, changed his behavior after realizing that his main goal was to provide his daughter with a safe and comfortable haven from an abusive boyfriend and *not* to teach her child-rearing skills for her toddler who was driving him crazy. This change of heart saved a relationship that, if it had turned sour, would have encouraged a return to the abusive boyfriend. Rod, a business person undergoing positive psychology training, bathed his children each night in a mindful way, thereby reconnecting with his wife and family and managing his rampant worry about a serious business downturn that he had made a plan to deal with.

Mining the Moment is a related mindfulness Tenet challenging clients to "milk" or "mine" each situation they face for any and all possible satisfactions, so that these satisfactions can be savored even if it is the feeling of satisfaction gained from cleaning the toilet after letting it go too long!

In the Toolbox CD's Guide for Worry Warts, anxious clients who worry or ruminate too much and who have problems with negative affect and distress tolerance are given process interventions aimed at limiting task-interfering worry experienced outside of Quality Time or QOLT Meditation, which is described in the Toolbox CD's Mindful Breathing handout. Chapter 10 discusses the application of these mindfulness interventions in the context of building distress tolerance and reducing the negative affect that can swamp the positive feelings and satisfactions necessary for the experience of happiness.

Play It Again Technique

Another way for some clients to relax is to listen to soothing, relaxing, and moving music of their choice. One client made an MP3 recording with Pachebel's *Canon in G* playing over and over for 90 minutes. She would listen to this file to relax herself when feeling upset about something. Besides relaxing her, it helped her get in touch with her thoughts and feelings. In this way, Play It Again can prepare clients for attacking a problem with a *Five Path* or Lie Detector worksheet.

To do the Play It Again Relaxation Ritual, tell clients to find music that really moves them. Tell them not to worry whether others might think that the music is too "sappy," maudlin, or sentimental or to worry if they get teary eyed while playing the music. Next, have them make a recording of the music that lasts for 30 to 90 minutes. They can then play the recording at times when they want to relax or get in touch with their feelings and concerns as a prelude for getting some distance from and perspective on their problems.

Crying Time Technique

Years ago, the late Ray Charles had a hit blues song titled "It's Crying Time Again." Sometimes we need a good cry to get in touch with our feelings and hurtful thoughts, calm down, and get ourselves ready to tackle a problem head-on. This is the rationale for Crying Time.

More is not better in the crying or worry department. It is better to limit our worry time, make a plan for solving or managing a problem, and then get on with and enjoy our life moment to moment. Clients can't enjoy the moment if they are worrying about something else. Mark, a real-estate salesperson in financial trouble found this out. He was oblivious to his loving wife and wonderful kids because he worried about his work all the time, even when he was with his family. The Crying Time technique addresses Mark's problem. It is based on the ideas of many mental health professionals over the years, including Thomas Borkovec, Milton Erikson, and Victor Frankl. Use the following as an introduction for your clients:

> The Crying Time technique is simple, when you are really upset about a problem or lack of fulfillment in your life, you give yourself 30 minutes to get really upset about the problem. (It can make you more upset to give yourself less time.) If you feel like crying, you cry your eyes out. If you feel like yelling, you yell (be sure no one else is around or can hear you as in the case of one of my patients who rolls up the windows in her car to vent her frustration).

Crying Time is based on a distinction that I like to make between problem solving and worry. I define worry as a destructive rumination or spinning of wheels in which we worry about problems, think about them over and over, but never come up with good solutions. Often, worry involves thinking about things that are unlikely to change or are never likely to happen, like our child being kidnapped or being fired from a job even though the odds of those things happening are slim. Mark Twain once said, "My life has been plagued with misfortunes, most of which never happened!" Problem solving, on the other hand, is defined as a constructive process whereupon we come up with realistic solutions to highly probable or unpleasant events that we're going to face. Use the problem-solving tips in QOLT to help clients tackle the challenges that face them, but help them to not indulge in destructive worry that can color or discolor much of their waking consciousness if it is not controlled (see the Toolbox CD's Guide for Worry Warts and Chapter 10 for additional suggestions for clients with clinical and subclinical but bothersome worry. EBT or evidence-based treatment manuals are also available to treat the associated conditions of Generalized Anxiety and Social Anxiety/Social Phobia disorders).

Client-Generated Relaxation Rituals

You may wish to encourage your clients to develop their own Relaxation Rituals based on what has relaxed them in the past. It might be sitting quietly or reading a magazine or novel. It might involve puttering around in their garden, or visiting an old friend. Whatever it takes to relax them so that they can gain some perspective on problems and tackle them more effectively can be considered a Relaxation Ritual.

Other Quality Time Techniques

Street Signs to Success or 5 Minutes to Joy Technique. To keep up the needed ratio of positive self-talk to negative self-talk to 2 or 3 to 1, have your clients try the Street Signs technique during Quality Time. Have them place a Word document in the start-up menu of their computer or buy some 3″ × 5″ index cards or both. As they decide on life goals, take notes during therapy sessions, complete Stress Diaries or journal about their worries, ask them to identify key phrases or thoughts that help them get focused, relaxed, and centered as they go about their day. They may then write each helpful thought or phrase on an index card or type it into the Word document.

When very upset and barraged with negative thoughts, patients can counter these negative thoughts by going through their Street Signs of positive thoughts. For example, Joan, a perfectionistic patient,

was never satisfied with her work. She felt that she should be so "saintly" that she shouldn't have to take time off for relationships or recreation. Joan carried around an index card to battle her perfectionism. The card simply read, "Saint Joan doesn't live here anymore." More examples can be found in Box 7.2.

Mental Health Day or Hour Technique   Sometimes clients feel so upset or bad that all they want to do is crawl into bed and hide under the covers. At times, they become so agitated, depressed, or upset that it may be helpful to simply take a few hours or the day off. During this "time off" or "vacation" time, clients may get a babysitter, take time off from work, and fill their day with relaxing and pleasurable activities as they try to get re-centered and relaxed.

Mental Health Day or Hour does not mean wallowing in our sorrows. It means taking some time off to recharge our batteries, get deeply relaxed, and stay productively busy around the house or wherever we happen to be. Taking a Mental Health Day can reduce clients' arousal levels and improve their attitude so that we are ready to tackle problems with renewed vigor. For the technique to be effective, remind clients to stay busy doing things that they love on the day they take off—see Frivolous Flow Tenet. For example, they should include some Quality Time and pure "fun" activities (the Toolbox CD contains a Play List of ideas). It can also help tremendously to simply get out of the house or office and stay in a hotel for a day or two with no daily responsibilities—in clients' own or a nearby city.

Clients may visit a close friend out of town, take a day trip, go to a spa, or attend a spiritual retreat of some kind. As a continuation treatment/intervention strategy this can be done every 3 to 6 months to prevent relapse into unhealthy old habits or an episode of unhappiness.

Mental Health Days and Hours must be used judiciously and sparingly; overdoing this could compromise clients' precious vacation time or even their jobs. Also, Mental Health Days should not be used to avoid facing problems directly, an action going against the very foundation of QOLT that counsels accepting and facing problems directly and honestly. Rather, an occasional Mental Health Day or hour can help clients regroup so that they can tackle their problems with renewed vigor and sagacity.

BOX 7.2

Street Signs to Success: Clinical and
Positive Psychology Examples

Instructions: Street Signs are phrases or sayings on computer postings or index cards that maintain a positive attitude that is constructive and therefore happiness-producing. Here are some examples from clients—try writing some of your own:

Stay optimistic—I'm going to get through this and eventually survive and thrive.

Be a ray of sunshine toward others today.

Stop gossiping and breeding dissension!

I'm a decent person even when I make a mistake or others are unhappy with me.

What's the best use of my time right now?

Keep goals modest. One thing at a time.

My job: have a good time pursuing commitments.

It's up to me to cope and feel better. Take care of myself!

I'm going to stop thinking about that right now and do something for someone else.

I'm as good as anyone else. I have a right to be here.

I can control my thoughts, feelings, and behaviors, but not the world or other people.

Stop judging and complaining . . . let it be.

Stop fretting! What do I want? How can I get it?

What have I done right today? What's been accomplished?

What do I have to be thankful for?

People mean more to me than fortune or fame.

It will work out fine eventually!

What needs doing, right now?

Favor Bank your buds, helpmates, even enemies!!! to move on with your life.

Happiness is a choice (see Tenet).

I'm going to work on me right now. Screw the rest.

What's the best use of my time right now?

I'm going to save my worries till *Crying Time* at 2 P.M.—I'm relaxed then and usually don't need to process problems anymore!!!! (See *Guide for Worry Warts.*)

You feel helpless and down when you demand the impossible from yourself and others.

Try to *enjoy* instead of *changing* the world!

(Continued)

Keep goals modest.

Of my million things to do, just pick one—what looks most important—and forget the rest.

My job: Have a good time pursuing commitments.

It's up to me to cope and feel better.

What do I have to be grateful for? Count my blessings.

I'm sorry you feel rotten. Be kind and gentle with yourself today.

FIND A MEANING/FIND A GOAL

The third pillar or Tenet of QOLT can be assigned as part of the work to be done during Quality Time. Clients are happier when they find a meaning or life goals to pursue that fits their unique values, skills, strengths, and interests. This challenge is summarized for clients in the Find a Meaning Tenet in the Toolbox CD.

Find a Meaning/Goal Principle

We all need a guiding vision of what matters most in life and how we should live, both now and in the future. Whether secular, spiritual, or both, this guiding vision answers the question, "What is the meaning or purpose of life?" These Goals-and-Values are basic and essential to a sense of security and happiness. QOLT defines Goals-and-Values as "your beliefs about what matters most in life and how you should live—both now and in the future. This includes your goals in life, what you think is right or wrong, and the purpose or meaning of life as you see it."

Goals-and-Values include your personal and career goals for the future. Identifying some lifetime goals for yourself is an essential part of QOLT. The QOLI and Vision Quest exercise are designed to help you identify life goals. Once identified, the idea is to think about and recall your lifetime goals daily as you plan your days and your life. Also try to embrace beliefs, habits, and routines that help you in this endeavor and shun those influences, habits, beliefs, and routines that block your progress. Even the media, books, and TV that you watch or "consume" may help you or hinder you in your "diet" of influences needed for change and reaching personal goals.

More secular purposes. Secular purposes in life beyond the self are often seen as sacred or spiritual callings by believers in these paths to fulfillment. Secular purposes can include raising a family, pursuing excellence in our work or hobbies, fighting for a cause we believe in, and even avidly following a nontheistic faith or philosophy as in being a fervent Bright, Humanist, Buddhist, Universist, or Unitarian. For some, the idea of fulfilling their own potential—self-actualization—is a useful goal along with just enjoying life to the fullest. Still and all, some meanings beyond the self seem necessary to happiness even if there is a selfish component, as in raising children, a wonderful type of life work. Of course, multiple meanings and goals are typical, leaving room for both altruistic and more selfish pursuits.

Purely secular meanings can be reflected in QOLT areas of life such as love, children, creativity—defined broadly as originality in any area of human endeavor and service to others. The need for secular meaning can spring from the existentialist assumption that since life has no inherent or absolute meaning, we must, therefore, invent one and dedicate ourselves to a meaning in order for our lives to cohere, make sense, or be coherent. Psychologist Alfred Adler held this position as did the existential philosophers, Jean Paul Sartre and Albert Camus (Yalom, 1980).

More Spiritual and Religious Meanings and Goals. While not important to everyone, religious and spiritual activities can greatly enhance a person's satisfaction with life, and deserve consideration by all of us interested in boosting our happiness or contentment. In the most un-evangelical way imaginable, the Dalai Lama, spiritual leader of the Dzogchen lineage of Buddhism, exiled from his home country of Tibet by Communist China, suggests in his book, *The Art of Happiness,* that we should have as many religions as people in the world because all of us have different personalities and spiritual needs! He goes on to say that Buddhism is not for everyone and that we can be quite principled and moral without any religion at all as long as we adhere to general ethical principles. In this vein, QOLT defines spiritual life *broadly* as spiritual or religious beliefs or practices, that you pursue on your own or as part of a like-minded community. For those who value and want a spiritual life, QOLT "proselytizes" for a spiritual life or journey in which those interested freely explore spiritual meaning systems, practices, and communities until they find one—or more—that is truly inspiring, uplifting, and personally meaningful. A religious or spiritual life should provide some useful personal "answers" for those of us spiritual pilgrims looking for causes and meanings beyond our own selfish desires as well as "selfish" tips on how to understand, live and cope with an often insane world of conflicting beliefs, tremendous beauty, and horrific hatred and violence.

For those interested, QOLT advocates a search for a Spiritual Life that is renewing, invigorating, and inspiring. It should function in the same way that a love relationship should, as a shelter or safe haven in the storm of life. It should also function as a refueling station, inspiring us, making us feel good about ourselves, and girding our loins, that is, giving us confidence and optimism to cope with the challenges of our life. Speaking of optimism, the quintessential positive psychology trait, what forum could be better suited for its cultivation than a spiritual community, practice, and belief system? *Whatever spiritual approach or approaches are embraced should be followed and practiced on a daily basis for 5 to 20 minutes in order to get the maximum happiness-producing effect.* Spiritual beliefs can be reviewed and need to be followed, rituals and practices can and need to be practiced, and spiritual guidance needs to be put into action for Spiritual Life to have a real benefit in terms of increased happiness or contentment. Being part of a like-minded spiritual community can also be extremely important, even essential.

Our Spiritual Life may be most powerful and fulfilling if it includes a community of spiritual friends and teachers who can support us and whom we can support—helper therapy principle—as we try to walk the walk of a spiritual approach 24/7, even with our most difficult family members and work colleagues. This more complete spiritual approach, including a community of like-minded people whom we socialize with on a regular basis, a particular teacher/leader or spiritual friend who sees the goodness and potential in you, and the belief system of the approach can completely change our lives, making us much more happy and fulfilled. Consider the success of Alcoholics Anonymous (AA) as well as the other myriad communities and approaches from Judaism to Christianity to Islam, Hinduism, and Buddhism—American or Eastern. A spiritual life and discipline with regular, preferably daily practice for even 5 to 10 minutes daily, can make you more patient and kind, but likely will not change your basic temperament, personality, and potential happiness range or set point.

Happiness-Enhancing Goals-and-Values.   You may wish to consider adopting some of the Tenets of Contentment themselves as part of your Goals-and-Values. All of the Tenets are meant to foster a life of greater happiness and contentment. The Tenets, *Happiness Matters* and *Happiness is a Choice*, may be especially important for you to adopt if being happy is important to you.

Put Your Time Where Your Values Are.   What may be unique to the QOLT approach is that QOLT tries to make a connection in how clients order their daily routines and their overarching life goals. To paraphrase the saying "Put your money where your mouth is," clients are told, "Put your time and effort where your values are." This sub-tenet or corollary of *Find a Meaning* suggests that we as therapists try telling clients to "Enshrine your personal goals with related activities in your schedule for each day *so that your acts follow your Goals-and-Values.*" Such a schedule constitutes your "Marching Orders" for the day and can really help in the process of "sculpting" days that fit your innermost values and personal goals (see Meanings Are Like Buses; Marching Orders Principle and Feed the Soul Principle).

Happiness-Enhancing Goals-and-Values

Clients may wish to consider adopting some of the Tenets of Contentment from the Toolbox CD as part of their Goals-and-Values. All of the Tenets are meant to foster a life of greater happiness and contentment.

The Tenets, Happiness Matters and Happiness Is a Choice, are especially important for clients in QOLT to be exposed to early on. Ask clients to consider adopting these Tenets as personal Goals-and-Values. Perhaps more than any other Tenet, these should be adopted by clients who value happiness as an important life goal.

Happiness Matters Principle or Tenet of Contentment. If people want to be happy, they have to make happiness a top priority in their lives and engage in activities that they know will foster contentment and fulfillment. They should try to do and think nothing that will harm their basic contentment and happiness and always try to make efforts to do and think what they know will help. For example, if socializing makes a client less depressed, he or she should plan to visit with a friend each day. People will also be happier if they are actively doing things and accomplishing things they care about. People tend to feel unhappy or bored when they are passively "doing nothing" or pursuing pleasure all the time.

Happiness Is a Choice or It's Up to You Principle or Tenet of Contentment. To some degree, people choose their happiness or unhappiness by deciding how to think, act, and structure their time during every moment of every day. The lifestyle and attitudes we choose can have as much to do with our happiness or depression as our childhood, genetics, or circumstances. For example, we often know what to do to be happier but refuse to do it. This principle begs us to ask ourselves how we contribute to the problems in our life, likely the greatest challenge in personal growth and self-improvement. This principle challenges us to think, act, and live in ways that we know foster contentment instead of unhappiness. While we probably aren't responsible for developing self-defeating thoughts, feelings, and behaviors in the first place, we are responsible for asking for help (e.g., get counseling) or for managing the problem once you've gained the tools to do so (e.g., positive coping skills). Thus, therapists can remind clients of the adage "You're not responsible for being down, but you are responsible for getting up." Suggest to clients: "You are the master of your fate in that you can at least choose how you cope with problems in your health, habits, and inner life of thoughts and feelings (Inner Life Responsibility)." No matter how bad our

circumstances or how badly we've been mistreated, it is our problem to find a way out of negative feelings and unhealthy behaviors and to cultivate positive satisfactions and emotions. No one else will do it for us. If we don't take responsibility and do something about it, it won't get done. Don't count on anyone else to fix it; that may never happen! It's up to *us* to find answers to how to live and then, this is so hard, to implement the "answers" that work for us in our daily life. Suggest to clients: "You are the master of your fate in that you can at least choose how you cope with any particular life situation (Responsibility for Circumstances and Behavior)." Even when fate deals a cruel blow or throws a roadblock or temptation in our way, we can decide how to deal with the problem. We can always exercise some Stimulus Control, that is, we can refuse to let some outside stimulus, stress, conflict, tragedy, obstacle, frustration, or person in our life control our actions and behaviors. We can use the Expert Friend Principle to find people in similar circumstances to ours who are coping well and can share their secrets of success. According to one recent theory, 40 percent of our happiness is under voluntary control (Lyubomirsky, Sheldon, et al., in press). That is, 40 percent of happiness is controlled by our choices or intentional activities that we pursue. The figure rises to 50 percent if we view our life circumstances as changeable or livable through our own best efforts (Lyubomirsky, Sheldon, et al., in press).

Meanings Like Buses Rule. Some parents console their kids who have been jilted by saying, "Don't worry, men/women are like buses, there is always another one coming around the corner." This is especially true for meanings and flows. One engaging activity or flow can be found to substitute for another in a world of almost infinite hobbies, pastimes, and jobs. The same may be said for meanings or life goals. When disappointed with one avenue of flow or meaning as in a difficult job or marriage, we can find other flows and meanings to look forward to and to soften the blow, if we but believe that other avenues exist for us—optimism—and make the effort to explore the avenues as in trying out these Tenets of Contentment in QOLT. The happiness literature is replete with accounts of many who have survived tragedy or even the loss of loved ones or limbs in terrible accidents, regaining their pretragedy level of happiness in most cases (widowhood and hugely disabling injuries may be tragedies from which we never fully recover).

Introducing your clients to the Three Pillars of QOLT gives them some important attitudes and skills that are basic to lasting happiness. They learn the importance of deep self-caring and self-awareness (Inner Abundance) along with the necessity for meaningful life goals and values, including some that go beyond the self. With Quality Time, they learn a mechanism of renewal and review in which they remind themselves of what is important and problem solve obstacles along the way. The Dalai Lama says that prayer often consists of reminding ourselves of what is important and what our most cherished Goals-and-Values are; this is, in many ways, what Quality Time is all about. Relaxation Rituals and mindfulness training can help clients to calm down enough to use Quality Time to good effect.

CHAPTER 8

Five Paths to Happiness and Other CASIO Techniques

One of the major contributions that QOLT attempts to make to cognitive therapy and to positive psychology intervention programs is the CASIO rubric for problem solving, positive psychology intervention, and QOL enhancement. Chapter 3 details the empirically tested theory that underlies the CASIO model. Suffice it to say here that the model assumes that happiness comes largely from achieving goals and gaining fulfillment in the areas of life that we value. QOLT offers five general strategies that can boost satisfaction with any area of life. These general strategies flow from the underlying CASIO theory of life satisfaction, which suggests that satisfaction (the perceived gap between what one wants and has) with a particular area of life is made up of four components: (1) the objective circumstances or characteristics of an area; (2) the person's attitude about, perception, and interpretation of an area in terms of personal well-being; (3) a person's evaluation of fulfillment in an area based on the application of standards of fulfillment or achievement; and (4) the value or importance a person places on an area for overall happiness or well-being. These four components, combined with a fifth concerned with overall satisfaction in other areas of life that are not of immediate concern, make up the CASIO model for increasing satisfaction and happiness: the objective Circumstances of an area, the Attitude or perception of an area, the Standards of fulfillment for an area, the Importance placed on an area for one's overall happiness, or the satisfaction one experiences in Other areas not of immediate concern.

EXPLAINING FIVE PATHS OR CASIO TO CLIENTS

Along with some visual aids in the form of the Toolbox CD's CASIO diagram and it's Five Paths worksheet,

the five CASIO strategies for boosting happiness can be explained to clients as follows:

What Is Happiness? Happiness, or quality of life, can be defined as the extent to which your most important needs, goals, and wishes have been fulfilled. For any area of life that you are unsatisfied with and that is important to you, there are five strategies you can use to boost your satisfaction and thereby increase you overall happiness.

Change Your Circumstances. The first strategy involves changing your circumstances to improve a particular area of your life. You could change your circumstances by changing things like your relationships, where you live, where you work, or where and how you play. For example, if you are married and unhappy with your marriage, you may seek couples counseling in order to change the nature of your relationship with your partner. Or, if you are a college student and unhappy with your grades, you may seek the advice of a counselor in order to improve your study skills.

Change Your Attitude. The second way to improve your happiness in a particular area of life is to change your attitude about the situation, to correct any distortions or negativity in your thinking. Changing your attitude involves reevaluating or taking a new look at any part of your life by asking two key questions: (1) "What is really happening here?" and (2) "What does it mean to me?" Many times our view of a situation or what we think the situation means for our well-being and our future is not based on facts; our view may be distorted or in error. For example, you may believe that your boss is unhappy with your work because he or she seems to be ignoring you, when in fact your boss is preoccupied with a personal problem. Because of our tendency to jump to conclusions without having all the facts, it is important to gather information about the situation before deciding what is really going on in an area of life that we care about. We do not want to prematurely decide that things are hopeless, for example, when they really are not.

After you clear up any distortion of the facts about a problem or an area of life that you care about, you can then reevaluate or take a new look at your *interpretation* of the facts. Interpretation often amounts to a question we answer to ourselves like, "How will this situation affect me and my future prospects for happiness?" or "What does this situation say about my abilities or my worth as a person?" Often our interpretation of a situation is biased in a self-defeating and upsetting way, for example, when we conclude that we are unlovable because one relationship did not work out. Often the situation isn't as bad or as gloomy as we think. It is important to develop the capacity to picture yourself eventually surviving and thriving even if your worst fears came true. For example, even if you had to leave your present job, it is important that you be able to picture yourself finding some other meaningful work in the future. Of course, the type of work will depend on a realistic appraisal of your skills and what is available.

In summary, the essence of the Changing **A**ttitude Strategy from the CASIO model is to find out what is really happening in an important area of your life and to carefully evaluate what it means for you and your future in an objective and realistic way that preserves your self-esteem and gives you some reason to hope for fulfillment and happiness in the future.

Change Your Goals and Standards. The third strategy for boosting your satisfaction in an area of life such as work or love is to change your goals and standards for that area. The key idea here is to set realistic goals and to experiment with raising and lowering your standards of fulfillment for particular areas or life that you are unhappy with. To do this you have to answer questions like "What do I really want in this part of life? How much is enough? What realistic goals and standards can I set for success in this particular part of my life?" Often it helps to lower your standards slightly so that you can gain some fulfillment in that part of your life.

Change Your Priorities. The fourth strategy for improving life satisfaction or happiness is to change your priorities or consider changing what your think is important in your life. This strategy involves reevaluating your priorities and emphasizing those areas that are most important to you and that are most under your control, that is, areas that you can do something about. For example, if you have an untreatable health problem, you may de-emphasize the importance of health in your life and instead focus on relationships or your work. These may be two areas you can change to make yourself happier. To pursue this strategy, you have to ask "What are my priorities?" Remember, you can boost your overall quality of life by de-emphasizing specific areas you cannot change and putting more importance on areas you can change or control.

Boost Your Satisfaction in Other Areas Not Previously Considered. The fifth and final strategy for improving your quality of life is to boost your satisfaction in areas that you haven't previously considered. You can boost or increase your overall quality of life by increasing your satisfaction with other areas of life that are not of immediate concern. This is especially helpful when you are working on an area that is very difficult and slow to change, such as a love relationship. While a particular area of concern, like love, may be moving slowly toward improvement, you can boost your overall quality of life by focusing on other areas of life that you care about, such as recreation and friendships, even though these areas are not your number one concern at the moment. The essence of this strategy is to try to increase your quality of life by increasing satisfaction in any area you care about, even one that doesn't seem to be a problem right now.

Using the Five Paths to Become Happier. To apply any or all of these five CASIO strategies or paths to happiness to your situation, all you need to do is (1) identify the areas of life that you are unhappy with and want to change and (2) creatively brainstorm about ways to apply one or more of these five strategies with the goal of improving your quality of life satisfaction. As these strategies suggest, you can improve your satisfaction in any area of life by actually changing your *circumstances* or by changing your *attitudes, goals, standards,* and *priorities.* Finally, because your overall quality of life is made up of your happiness with all of the particular parts of life that your care about, you can increase your overall quality of life by doing what you can to boost your satisfaction in *any* area that you care about, even ones that are not of pressing concern right now.

This explanation of CASIO strategies for solving problems can be shared with clients in the form of homework by assigning the Five Paths Summary "Cheat Sheet" in the Toolbox CD. The CASIO strategies are neatly packaged for clients in the form of a structured exercise, the Five Paths worksheet that can be downloaded from the Toolbox CD.

FIVE PATHS TO HAPPINESS: USING THE CASIO MODEL AS A GUIDE FOR PROBLEM SOLVING OR FOR BOOSTING SATISFACTION IN *ANY* AREA OF LIFE

Frisch (1992) argues that problem solving is under-elaborated in cognitive therapy. Persons and Bertagnolli (1999) agree that too few instruments like the QOLI exist that can assess problems in living or "external problems" as Aaron T. Beck et al. (1979) refer to them. Assessing problems in life and earmarking them for intervention is a necessary part of cognitive therapy case formulation and treatment planning (Persons & Bertagnolli, 1999; Persons et al., 2001).

Whereas the QOLI may aid in *assessing* life problems and strengths, the Five (CASIO) Paths to Happiness exercise, referred to as *Five Paths* here and in the Toolbox CD, presents a scheme for *solving* or managing problems based directly on the CASIO theory of life satisfaction and happiness. It is inspired, in part, from the pioneering work of Thomas D'Zurilla, Marvin Goldfried, and Arthur Nezu along with the CASIO model of life satisfaction and happiness presented in Chapter 3.

Five Paths is repeatedly used throughout the course of QOLT—both as homework and as an in-session exercise—to brainstorm ideas for improving satisfaction in valued areas of life. It is also used as a general scheme for solving problems that may come up in QOLT. Five Paths is a central intervention that directly applies QOL theory to real-world problems and issues. Its versatility lies in its general applicability to any area of life that clients may bring up.

Clinical and Positive Psychology Case Examples Illustrating the Five Paths Technique

Returning to the clinical case of Tom, consider the following excerpts from Tom's Five Paths homework as-

signments and in-session exercises summarized in Table 8.1—also see the client version of Five Paths in the Toolbox CD, which has additional examples attached to a reusable Five Paths form. Tom claimed to use the exercise to good effect whenever he was in a quandary regarding how to boost his satisfaction with a valued area or simply had to deal with a hassle or problem that had come up in his life:

The excerpts in Table 8.1 illustrate Tom's successful efforts at applying CASIO strategies to myriad areas of life, including problems in the areas of Relatives and Self-Esteem ("My folks taught me garbage I don't have to listen to, like I'm no good. I think they were no good as parents. No kid is inherently bad."), Learning ("Try for a B or B+ in my classes for one week and see if the sky falls"), finding a Love relationship ("Try to just be kind and connect to folks with a simple hello, including girls as I make a String of Pearls or a string of positive interactions each day with folks I see."), Play/Friends ("Feed my soul with shooting hoops, talking to John or Ron every day. Without some 'Inner Abundance' I'm no good to anybody."), Play/Spiritual Life/Friends. ("Sailing club and church are ways to play and meet people.") This exemplifies the versatility of the CASIO model in generating interventions for many areas of life as opposed to those in Part III that apply to only one area of life. Tom's examples also demonstrate classic cognitive restructuring or reframes of his problems that reduce distress and foment contentment. Behavioral examples of happiness interventions are also clearly evident as in his plans to visit friends, say hello to others, and go to church.

Box 8.1 shares the story of an accountant who benefited from Five Paths in the context of positive psychology counseling or coaching.

USING FIVE PATHS WITH CLIENTS WITH READING DIFFICULTIES OR DEVELOPMENTAL DELAYS

As with all QOLT interventions, therapists should always complete an exercise in session with a client first before assigning it as homework. Clients get no benefit from the assignment if its steps and purposes are not made clear. After successfully completing one Five Paths exercise in session, therapists usually assign it along with the Five Paths Summary Cheat

Table 8.1 *Excerpts from Tom's Five Paths to Happiness Exercises during QOLT*

Brainstorm possible solutions under each CASIO strategy by listing attitudes or actions for managing or solving the problem.

C	A	S	I	O
Changing Circumstances	Changing Attitudes	Changing Goals and Standards	Changing Priorities or What's Important	Boost Satisfaction in Other Areas not Considered Before
		Basic Strategy		
Problem Solve to improve situation.	Find out what is really happening and what it means for you and your future.	Set realistic goals and experiment with raising and lowering standards. What new goals and standards can you come up with?	Reevaluate priorities in life and emphasize what is most important and controllable.	Increase satisfaction in any areas you care about for an overall boost to happiness.
I need to decide whether to make peace with Mom and accept her overtures or keep "blowing her off."	*My folks taught me garbage I don't have to listen to like I'm no good. I think they were no good as parents. No kid is inherently bad!*	*Try for a B or B+ in my classes for one week and see if the sky falls.*	*Feed my soul with shooting hoops, talking to John or Ron every day. Without some "Inner Abundance" I'm no good to anybody.*	*Sailing club and church are ways to Play and meet people.*
	Talk back to negative thoughts like "I'm a loser" or distract via Mindful Breathing.	*Try to just be kind and connect to folks with a simple "hello," including girls as I make a String of Pearls or a string of positive interactions each day with folks I see.*	*Quit beating your head against the wall. Dad can't be a dad or a friend. Stop trying and move on.*	

93

BOX 8.1

In Her Own Words: *Five Paths* in the Positive Psychology Case of Elise

The *Five Paths to Happiness* exercise was where I benefited the most in QOLT. At the beginning of my positive psychology program, I was struggling with overwork and a breakup. I applied the CASIO strategies to my life, and they drastically helped me turn my life around. I changed my Circumstances—the C in CASIO, developed a less distorted Attitude—the A CASIO—about my situation, and set more realistic goals and Standards for success in my accounting practice—the S in CASIO. Most importantly, I changed my priorities, what's Important or the I in CASIO. I put my focus more on my friendships and spiritual life. In terms of Other areas of life I hadn't thought much about, the O in CASIO, I acknowledged and embraced the other relationships and friendships in my life that I had previously taken for granted. I also sought enhancement in other areas of my life, such as Learning by taking classes to expand my work skills. My satisfaction in the areas of recreation and Community compensated for some of the unhappiness I felt in the Work and Love parts of my life. This upped my overall satisfaction. My spirits have lifted and my bouts with depression have subsided. I never got clinically depressed according to my psychologist, which is amazing in itself.

Sheet to clients with a 6th-grade reading level or above and an intellectual functioning level of Low Average or above.

For clients who do not meet these criteria, the QOLT therapist summarizes the main points for clients, usually suggesting specific CASIO interventions to carry out the next week saying:

I would like you to aim for just passing your GED tests this week, rather than insisting on impressing your teachers with getting every question right. If this doesn't work, we can go back to the high-pressure strategy without hurting your performance overall. We call this playing with standards or goals as a way to boost your happiness. Let us role-play the GED test now with these sample questions and you can tell me out loud what you are thinking as I suggest thoughts to you to practice.

OTHER CASIO INTERVENTIONS

QOLT offers *area-specific treatment strategies* for each area of life such as Love or Work. QOLT also offers general CASIO intervention strategies in addition to Five Paths that can boost a person's satisfaction in *any* area of life. A summary list of all CASIO interventions can be found in Table 8.2.

The techniques in Table 8.2 are described and illustrated in the remainder of this chapter and may be applied to *any* area of life. In contrast to Five Paths that considers *all* CASIO factors at once, these other

CASIO interventions are based on only one CASIO factor whether it be: changing the objective Circumstances of an area, the Attitude or perception of an area, the Standards of fulfillment for an area, the Importance placed on an area for their overall happiness, or the satisfaction one experiences in Other areas not of immediate concern. It is usually best to introduce clients to the general CASIO strategies and techniques first, and then the techniques for specific areas of life from Part III, although when time is limited therapists often choose an array of strategies from both CASIO and area-specific interventions that best suit clients' needs, assets, and strengths.

Strategy 1: Changing Circumstances

The objective Circumstances or characteristics of an area is that part of the CASIO model that suggests that dissatisfaction or unhappiness is not always "in a person's head" or based on cognitive distortions as some mental health professionals believe. Circumstances include the specific characteristic of an area. For example, the circumstances of Work may include characteristics such as the work itself, pay, surroundings, job security, relationships with coworkers, and availability of needed equipment and supervision. If clients really dislike what they do all day, are grossly underpaid, or don't get along with their bosses or coworkers, they will be dissatisfied with this area no matter what mental gymnastics, cognitive restructur-

Table 8.2 Five Path or CASIO Strategies and Techniques for Increasing Satisfaction in Any Area of Life

<u>C</u>	<u>A</u>	<u>S</u>	<u>I</u>	<u>O</u>
Changing Circumstances	Changing Attitudes	Changing Goals and Standards	Changing Priorities or What's Important	Boost Satisfaction in Other Areas not Considered Before
		Basic Strategy		
Problem solve to improve situation.	Find out what is really happening and what it means for you and your future. Ask "Is there a better way too look at this situation? Can I survive and thrive the worst?"	Set realistic but challenging goals and experiment with raising and lowering standards.	Reevaluate priorities in life and emphasize what is most important and controllable.	Increase satisfaction in any area you care about for an overall boost to happiness.
		Specific Techniques		
Five Paths to Happiness	Lie Detector and Stress Diary	Ask Your Death Tenet	Vision Quest Exercise	Basket-of-Eggs
Strength Exercise	Emotional Control Skills and	Good-Not-Great Exercise	Happiness Pie Exercise	
Inner Abundance Tenet	Tenet (Ch. 10)	Process Goal Tenet	My Most Feared Obituary	
Quality Time Tenet			Quality of Life Inventory or	
Find a Meaning Tenet			QOLI (Ch. 5)	
Zen Steps to Success (Ch. 10)				
Daily Activity Plan				
Life Management Skills (Ch. 10)				

ing, or positive thinking they try to apply to the situation. Recent cognitive theories of depression such as hopelessness theory and that of Clark and Beck (1999) have been revised to reflect the assumption that objectively unrewarding circumstances and life stresses contribute significantly to depression (along with distortions in thinking that make the situation worse, or, more correctly, feel or seem worse or more hopeless than it is). The bottom line is that, at times, clients must alter or leave situations that are destructive to their well-being such as a "psychonoxious" job or relationship.

The primary intervention strategy for Changing Circumstances is a part of the Five Paths exercise from the Toolbox CD. Once this exercise is complete, plans for changing circumstances must be gradually implemented, one step at a time. This can be accomplished with the Zen Steps to Success from Chapter 11 along with the Daily Activity Plan from Chapter 10. Also central to consideration of any change strategy are the foundation Tenets of Inner Abundance, Quality Time, and Find a Meaning Tenets discussed in Chapter 7.

Strength Exercise. The Strength Exercise in the Toolbox is a classic positive psychology intervention for changing circumstances via personal strengths. The exercise contains QOLT's list of strengths as does Table 12.1 and the BAT gratitude and self-esteem exercise in Chapter 12. The Strength It Tenet is a less structured approach than the Strength Exercise for applying strengths to valued areas of life.

Strategy 2: Changing A̲ttitudes

The Changing A̲ttitudes strategy of boosting happiness is based on the concept of "reality testing" or the extent to which someone's perceptions of an area fit the objective reality of the situation. Someone's reality testing is good when the person's perceptions of situations match the reality. If reality testing is poor—a common problem since no one is graced with "immaculate perception"—a client can be dissatisfied in situations that really aren't that bad. In these cases, the client's satisfaction judgments are based on subjective not objective reality. This happens especially when clients are upset with a Big Three emotion (anxiety, depression, anger) as in the case of an accountant who was frantic because she was sure that her husband no

longer loved her when, in fact, he was putting extra time in at the office, not to avoid her, but to pay off their medical bills from a severe car accident.

Attitudes about an area of life also include our interpretation of what a situation will do to our well-being. When clients interpret the end of a relationship or business failure accurately (good reality testing), but then misinterpret the loss or failure in catastrophic terms, they can create more grief and dissatisfaction than they started with. For example, after such a failure they may conclude that they are unlovable or doomed to failure in all romantic or business pursuits. So patients can err in two major ways as they size up their circumstances. First, their reality testing may be poor, and they may *misperceive* the situation or answer the question, "What happened?" or "What is happening?" in an area of life incorrectly. Second, they can *misinterpret* the implications of a situation for their well-being as they answer the question, "What does this mean (to me and my future happiness)?"

The basic treatment strategy for Changing Attitudes about an area of life is cognitive restructuring aimed at giving clients an accurate perception of their situation and a positive interpretation that preserves clients' self-esteem and gives them hope for future happiness either in the area of concern or in some other part of life. The major QOLT tool for cognitive restructuring is the Lie Detector and Stress Diary and related thought record tools described and illustrated in Chapter 10.

Strategy 3: Changing Goals and Standards

The Vision Quest exercise, a required part of QOL assessment from Chapter 5 that is also discussed in Chapter 11 as a way to identify Goals-and-Values is designed to help clients develop a set of clear-cut goals for their life. The exercise asks clients to list lifetime goals related to areas of life that are important to them. The therapist should reassure clients that their goals can be changed at any time in the future. In fact, it can help clients to repeat the exercise annually or whenever they feel as though their goals are changing. At the same time, it is important (and often freeing) for clients to assertively say Yes to some goals and No to others.

Another important aspect of Changing Goals and Standards is clarifying values. One way clients can clarify their values is by reviewing the Ask Your Death Tenet or by completing the My Most Feared Obituary exercise from Chapter 11. Interestingly, Buddhists often recommend regular meditations on our own deaths to clarify our values and to clarify what we wish to stand for or to stand on in the way of accomplishments in our lives (Kornfield, 2000). Similarly, Irving Yalom (1980) included clients with terminal illnesses in his therapy groups to foster a similar awareness of finitude in clients.

Another aspect of Changing Goals and Standards is battling perfectionism. QOL theory contends that a big part of clients' happiness equations consists of the standards of fulfillment that they set for aspects of life that are important to them. Standards of fulfillment are the benchmarks or yardsticks for deciding if clients have enough of their needs met in an area to be satisfied. If people are getting what they want, they're satisfied and happy. If there is a gap between what they have and what they want in some part of their life, they are dissatisfied. This part of the happiness equation involves answering the question, "Have my goals and standards for an area been met or realized?" For example, a promising medical student became depressed with any grade less than an A in medical school. His reality testing or perception of the situation was good. He knew his grades only too well. The problem came in applying his own goals and standards to the situation to see if fulfillment was attained. His standards were too high.

Standards can move *down* as well as *up* to help clients cope with any kind of situation. Those faced with tragedy, such as a visual impairment or a spinal cord injury resulting in the loss of their arms or legs, seem to maintain their satisfaction with life by lowering their expectations for fulfillment in key parts of life, in keeping with their physical limitations. In other words, they adapt their standards and expectations to fit their changing circumstances. Unfortunately, people prone to depression or unhappiness are often plagued with impossibly high standards, no matter what the circumstances are in their life.

Although clients cannot always control what they get from life, they can control what they want. For example, they can decide what is enough to feel satisfied about things like Work, Love, or Money. For example, if a client decides that he makes enough money in his job to buy the things that he needs and wants, he can become satisfied with his standard of living even though his salary has not increased at all.

One way to moderate or soften tough goals and standards is to set "process" goals or standards that are within patients' control rather than "outcome" goals or standards in particular areas of life. For example, a client set a process goal of studying for 2 hours a day, rather than an outcome goal of getting a B in a difficult organic chemistry class. At the end of the two hours, the client felt a real sense of accomplishment for achieving her goal. This was much more fulfilling and stabilizing than when she goaded herself with the outcome goal of a B.

The basic strategy for clients to boost their happiness by changing Goals and Standards is for them to set realistic but challenging goals for each area of life that they care about; this approach to goal/standard setting in QOLT is called the Good-Not-Great technique. To do this, therapists can encourage patients to experiment with raising and lowering standards of success and fulfillment in valued areas of life until challenging but comfortable and realistic goals and standards are found. A structured Good-Not-Great worksheet is in the Toolbox CD.

Consider the case of Tom who before starting QOLT was never satisfied with anything less than a 4.0 or straight-A grade average. During QOLT, Tom successfully experimented with new, slightly more modest standards using the Good-not-Great technique. To make it easier, he started in small steps. He set his sights on a B+ rather than A average for 1 week of the semester, deciding that this still might be sufficient to get him into the professional school of his choice. Further, he tried the lower goal for only 1 week, allowing him to ratchet up his standard and performance should he decide to revert to his old ways. Tom was shocked to find that he could lower his standards and still be very successful. In fact, he got a 4.0 or A-average the semester he aimed for a B+ or 3.5 average. What amazed him even more was how much more he enjoyed the semester. He had been so deadly serious about school and grades that he rarely felt happy and never made time for anything but school work. But the B+ semester was different. He made time for friends, for daily Quality Time, for recreation and play, as well as for schoolwork. Even though the circumstances of his life did not change radically, he seemed to reduce his depression in large measure by simply experimenting with new standards thereby taking tremendous pressure off himself. As he faced his fear of failure with lower standards, he found that the fear gradually subsided as he saw that he could be successful without being a perfectionist. In fact, it can be argued that perfectionists often succeed in spite of their impossibly high standards rather than because of them. Impossibly high standards can get in the way more than they help, since many clients will try hard without placing impossible standards on themselves. In Tom's case, the intervention was done without paperwork or homework forms, an important option in QOLT for clients and therapists who do not like excessive paperwork and written homework assignments.

Strategy 4: Changing Priorities or What's Important

Another key piece of the satisfaction "puzzle" is the value or importance assigned to a particular area. QOL theory posits that satisfaction with an area is weighted by its perceived importance or value before an area's satisfaction is entered into the overall equation of life satisfaction or happiness. This assumption is reflected in the scoring scheme for the QOLI, which weights satisfaction by importance for all 16 areas of life. In fact, the QOLI omits areas of life from the overall satisfaction equation if a person deems them unimportant. The bottom line is that satisfaction in areas that people care about the most ("highly valued" areas) have a much greater influence on overall life satisfaction than areas of equal satisfaction in those areas people see as less important to their overall happiness and well-being. A client, Jane, for example, was a successful account executive for a public relations firm. She tended, however, to value her love relationships far above anything else in her life, including her work. For this reason, her considerable work satisfaction seemed to have little impact on her overall happiness when relationship problems surfaced. As this example illustrates, happiness in one area is always tempered by its importance or value relative to other areas.

Because the importance clients assign to areas of their life affects their overall happiness, it is possible, at times, for them to boost their overall satisfaction by rearranging their priorities as when clients assign more importance or value to areas that they can control and are happy with, and de-emphasize or emotionally disengage from areas they cannot control or that are going badly or both. This is the essence of the Changing Priorities (or What's Important?) strategy for increasing satisfaction: Clients are taught to reevaluate their priorities in life in order to emphasize the areas that are most important and controllable.

Problems in priorities usually come in three varieties. There can be a problem in *misplaced priorities.* Here clients put too much time and energy in areas they do not really care about and too little time into the areas that are most important to them. Second, they can suffer from *conflicting priorities* in which they unrealistically try to "serve two masters." For example, some women (and men) struggle with the desire to be both a stay-at-home parent *and* a highly successful professional. These conflicts can often be unconscious, pointing up the need for counseling to ferret them out. A third problem, a *lack of priorities,* arises when clients lack clear-cut goals and priorities and have not really decided what is most important to them in life. Techniques for addressing problems in priorities are discussed in Chapter 10 and can be highlighted by completing the Happiness Pie exercise.

To illustrate this technique, consider the case of Sarah, who had a problem with misplaced priorities. She was dependent on the use of pot to make herself relax at the end of the day and was dating a married man with two children. At the same time, she was completely neglecting her long-term career plans and her relationship with her family, which was her main emotional support system. Her Happiness Pie identified the following priorities in order of importance: (1) job; (2) boyfriend; (3) pot; (4) relationship with mom, dad, and grandparents; and (5) school and career. Sarah's job was a radio disc jockey, a goal she had pursued since junior high school. Still, she only worked the "graveyard" shift part-time, and, rather than announcing, spent most of the time playing cassettes and tapes of other people's announcements.

After discussing her Happiness Pie, it became clear that Sarah was not putting her energy into the areas or parts of her life that were most important to her in the long run, that is, her family (who gave her the most reliable emotional and financial support she had) and her school and career (which would provide a long-term job and career that would be infinitely more stable than her current radio job).

In QOLT, Sarah reordered her priorities by creating an Ideal Happiness Pie and rechanneled her energies in such a way as to find a meaningful career and "mend the fences" or repair her relationship with her family. She decided to be as responsible and conscientious about "being there" for her family and helping them out as she was in getting to her job. She also made looking for a stable career a priority. She talked to professors at a nearby university about areas she was interested in and made plans for enrolling in college in order to reach her dream of becoming a broadcast journalist. With time, she realized that her boyfriend was merely using her and "just wasn't in to her." She also saw that her dependence on marijuana sapped her motivation and confidence and stifled her social skills. She felt and looked "developmentally retarded" (in her words) during role-play tests in so far as she lacked the Relationship Skills of her peers that are detailed in the Toolbox CD. It was as if she stood still because of her pot use while her friends were honing their social skills and gaining confidence.

In addition to helping develop meaningful standards (the **S** in CASIO), the Ask Your Death Tenet and the Most Feared Obituary technique just discussed can also help in developing priorities (the **I** in CASIO) and life goals.

Strategy 5: Boosting Satisfaction in Other Areas

A client named Carol, who was in couples QOLT with her husband, Tim, put most of her energy into caring for her children. She neglected other basic needs like recreation and contact with other adults, which had been extremely important to her in the past. Carol put all her emotional eggs in the one basket of family life. She tried to derive all her happiness from one particular area. This is a dangerous strategy since when things go wrong with the one or two areas of life clients are over-invested in, it is easy for them to become depressed or to turn to an addiction to escape. In addition, people are complicated; few people have needs in only one or two areas. For example, people who take the QOLI usually endorse 15 or 16 of the 16 areas listed as important. People need some fulfillment in *all* (or most) areas they care about to maximize their happiness. If clients put all of their "emotional eggs" in one basket and fail to meet their needs in other areas that are important, they rob themselves of potential joy and put themselves at risk for severe depression and unhappiness. Instead, clients need to invest energy or "eggs" in every area or "basket" that is important to them to build or sculpt a balanced life.

QOL theory can be simplified into a math equation to reveal the general **O** of the CASIO model and the rationale for the specific treatment technique called Basket-of-Eggs:

> Love satisfaction + Work satisfaction + Health satisfaction + Recreational satisfaction = Overall satisfaction or happiness

Since our overall happiness and satisfaction is the sum of our satisfactions in particular valued areas of life, we can boost our overall satisfaction by increasing our satisfaction in any or all areas we value, even ones that are not of immediate concern or that we did not consider before. This is the gist of the Boost Satisfaction in Other Areas Not Considered Before strategy for increased happiness.

To implement the Basket-of-Eggs technique, have clients begin to complete the form from the Toolbox CD while in session. Carol did this to good effect; with her therapist's help, she applied the CASIO and area-specific treatment techniques to each area that she identified as personally important. In keeping with the **O** or Basket-of-Eggs approach, she problem solved about ways to boost her satisfaction in every area she cared about, including those that were not bothering her at the moment; her efforts are illustrated in Table 8.3.

Another client used the Basket-of-Eggs technique to work on the area of Friendships even though his main area of unhappiness was his Love life. He chose to focus on Friendships since he knew he could make friends more quickly than he could find a soulmate. This made him happier while he was looking for a lover even though he did not view friendships as a serious problem.

The Five Path or CASIO rubric is based directly on QOL theory, a theory based on years of research in quality of life and life satisfaction. The rubric and associated techniques are as versatile as they are applicable to *any* area of life. Other core techniques from Part II have wide applicability. They include the three pillars QOLT—Inner Abundance, Quality Time, and Find a Meaning, life management and emotional control skills, and the Tenets of Contentment.

Table 8.3 Carol's Basket-of-Eggs Worksheet: A Clinical Example

Instructions: One way to boost your overall happiness is to try and increase your happiness with particular parts of life, including parts that are not of immediate concern. Doing what we can to feel happier with every part of life that we care about can get us through the "tough times" when some parts of life just can't be changed quickly, if at all. For each area of life listed below, write down things you could do NOW to feel happier and more fulfilled. Even if you're happy with an area, write down things you could do to feel even happier. Skip any area that is not really important to you and your overall happiness. Also, skip any area where change is unlikely or is very slow to happen. (Talk about these slow-to-change areas with your counselor or therapist.)

Health _____ *Aerobics class takes the edge off my anxiety and gives me people to socialize with while Tim and I try to work out* _____
_____ *our differences.* _____

Self-Esteem _____ *I'm learning ways to build this in the* Finding Happiness *book. I'm discussing what I read there with friends* _____
_____ *and my therapist.* _____

Goals-and-Values/Spiritual Life _____ *Going to church is an easy thing I could do to feel better.* _____
_____

Money _____ *Not that important to me.* _____
_____

Work _____ *Having lunch with coworkers can meet social needs that Tim can't right now. I'm looking for an Expert Friend* _____
_____ *(Tenet) who can navigate the minefields at work.* _____

Play _____ *"Tennis anyone?" cross-stitching?* _____
_____

Learning _____
_____

Creativity _____ *I'd love to redecorate the living room.* _____
_____

Helping _____ *Just going to the PTA could make me feel like I'm doing something for the world. The world doesn't stop just* _____
_____ *because Tim and I are at loggerheads.* _____

Friends _____ *Making close "buds" will take awhile. Health, Helping, and Goals-and-Values ideas above will help get the ball rolling.* _____
_____

Love _____ *A long-term counseling project. No quick fixes here.* _____
_____

Children _____ *As the oldest of three girls, Kathleen, feels neglected. I'd like us to do more things together, just the two of us.* _____
_____

Relatives _____ *Too hard to change.* _____
_____

Home _____ *See Creativity.* _____
_____

Neighborhood _____ *No ideas here . . .* _____
_____

Community _____ *Not that important to me.* _____
_____

CHAPTER 9

The Tenets of Contentment: A Summary of Key Concepts and Skills in QOLT

The *Tenets of Contentment* in QOLT consist of core QOLT concepts, attitudes, skills, strengths, and positive schemas or beliefs (healthy mirror opposites to negative schemas or "irrational beliefs") aimed at promoting lasting happiness, contentment, and satisfaction with life. A Tenet can be seen as a personal strength of a client in the positive psychology sense if they act on it consistently in everyday life. Many Tenets are based on decades of research, representing the state of the art in positive psychology; indeed this list could also be called "What We Know about Happiness." Along with other exercises in the Toolbox CD, these Tenets provide a summary of much of this book. Two versions of Tenets for clients can be found in the Toolbox CD: an aggregate listing and a listing of each Tenet as a separate document in the Toolbox CD folder called "Tenets in Separate Documents." Because the files are alphabetized, this folder is useful for quickly finding a Tenet or for perusing Tenets to find Tenets applicable to a particular client.

In addition to listings here, Tenets related to a particular areas of life can be found in area-specific chapters. For example, the essential Tenets with respect to fostering fulfilling relationships in Chapter 14, Emotional Honesty and Favor Bank, can be found in Chapter 14 as well as in this chapter (and, of course, the Toolbox CD for clients).

All of the Tenets are presented together in this chapter in alphabetical order. While it is recommended that all Tenets be consulted for a particular client, the Top 30 or most important Tenets of Contentment are listed in Table 9.1.

Table 9.1 The Top 30 Tenets of Contentment: An Alphabetical Listing

1. Ask Your Death Tenet
2. Balanced Lifestyle Principle
3. Be the Peace You Seek or Worry Warts Principle
4. Be with People or Relationship Immersion Principle
5. Blind Dumb Optimism Principle
6. Bosom Friends Principle
7. Cocoon It Rule
8. Curb or Ignore Desires Principle or You Can't Have It All Principle
9. Don't Forgive Principle or Set Aside, Shelve, Accept, or Forget Principle
10. Emotional Control or the Big Three Make Us Dumb Principle
11. Emotional Honesty Principle
12. Expert Friend Principle
13. Favor Bank Principle or Favor Bank of Good Will from Good Deeds or Mind-Set of Constant Gratitude and Acts of Kindness Principle
14. Find a Meaning or Find a Goal Principle
15. Flow It Principle
16. Happiness Habits Principle
17. Happiness Is a Choice or It's Up to You Principle
18. Happiness Set Point Principle or Personality Stays the Same Principle
19. Inner Abundance Principle
20. Modest Goal
21. Overthinking Principle
22. Physical Activity Principle or Take Your Medication Principle
23. Positive Addiction Principle

(continued)

Table 9.1 *Continued*

24. Quality Time Principle
25. Serve Others Principle
26. Strength It Principle
27. String of Pearls Practice and Principle
28. Taoist Dodge Ball Rule
29. Thou Shalt Be Aware or Psychephobia Principle
30. We Are Family Principle

Note: In cases of Tenets with two names, they are listed by the first name (with the second name following).

QOLT is tailored to clients' unique needs when therapists peruse the Tenets for those most likely to be of help to particular clients. Particularly applicable Tenets can then be prescribed for clients to read and to follow as part of a homework assignment in QOLT. Reading over all of the Tenets is an invaluable review technique for clients and therapists alike who wish to reap the full benefit of ideas and skills in QOLT. Therapists find it invaluable to study and review the Tenets as a group in order to keep them in mind and to use them in conducting QOLT. Perusing the Tenets in aggregate is helpful for clients and is even prescribed as a Relaxation Ritual in Chapter 7. Use of the Tenets as a tool in QOLT may be introduced to clients in the following way:

> Please read over this list (Tenets from the Toolbox CD) in a slow and leisurely way. As you read, circle Tenets that apply to your situation and that you would like to "try out" and follow for a week or two to see if they can really boost your sense of happiness, calm, or contentment. To remind yourself, you may wish to put your favorite Tenets in a document in the Start-Up Menu of your computer so it pops up each time you restart your computer. You may also cut and paste your favorite Tenets onto your refrigerator, dresser, or car seat as a daily reminder. Simply reading over these Tenets in a quiet comfortable place with few or no distractions can constitute a Relaxation Ritual to calm yourself when you are upset or struggling with a difficult problem. For example, an impatient lawyer, "Hallie in a Hurry," read and carried out the Inner Abundance, Find a Meaning, String of Pearls, and Favor Bank Tenets and greatly improved her happiness, relationships, and work performance in the process.

Some Tenets have two names and are cross listed. Different names resonate more or less with certain clients. It is exciting when a name "clicks" for clients who seem to use the name to both remember a person-

ally relevant Tenet and to recall the gist of the Tenet at the same time. For example, a socially obtuse physician who meant well but tended to be arrogant and insensitive in relationships identified with the Favor Bank Tenet that he used to good effect in paying more attention to his wife as well as to the staff at the hospital where he performed surgery. Tenets are sometimes referred to as rules or principles ("Exercises" and "Skills" are never Tenets and can be found in the Toolbox along with Tenets.)

▶ ABUSE OR NEGLECT PRINCIPLE (SEE ACOAN PRINCIPLE)

Accept and Enjoy Your Body Principle

The reality is that attractive people are no more happy than the rest of us. This Tenet highlights the fact that being pretty will not solve problems. Clients should concentrate instead on developing inner beauty, calmness, and contentment. If clients decide to change their body, they should do it, but never hate what they are now. If they insist on listing problems, they should also make a list of physical attributes or positive characteristics. It's okay for clients to enjoy the instinctual high that can come from seeing attractive youth, this seems to be nature's way of telling us who can make good, healthy babies, but clients should not confuse this reproductive potential with human decency, kindness, or the potential to be a committed partner and lifelong friend (Etcoff, 1999). They should recall that potential mates are not stupid; inner beauty matters to them and should to clients as well. Inner beauty includes warmth, personality, loyalty, kindness, and intelligence. Clients should be thankful for their bodies, which allow them to feel pleasure, take them where they want to go, and give them senses to appreciate the world. Life is too short to let youth-oriented pop culture say who can and cannot enjoy life and feel beautiful.

Accept What You Cannot Change Principle

Although clients should be encouraged to leave no stone unturned in trying to change problematic situations and relationships, it can ultimately be freeing and helpful for them to accept situations and relationships that cannot be changed. Accepting unchangeable circumstances reduces frustration and frees clients to pursue other avenues of fulfillment.

► Acceptance Principle (See Nothing Human Disgusts Me Principle)

ACOAN Principle or Abuse or Neglect Principle

The ACOAN Principle in QOLT affirms the reality of and legacy of abuse and neglect in adults quite apart from personality or temperament problems, although the latter can, to an extent, be shaped by childhood experiences of abuse. While acknowledging the legacy of pain from childhood abuse and neglect, QOLT remains steadfastly optimistic that some measure of happiness and contentment can be found here and now through a few of the many avenues presented here, elsewhere, and through clients' own Personal Wisdom (see Be Your Own Guru or Personal Wisdom Tenet) about what kinds of friends, activities, and situations bring them a sense of contentment and even occasional joy.

Using the Alcoholics Anonymous phrase, many of us are Adult Children of Abuse and Neglect (ACOAN) whether from emotional, physical, or sexual acts of betrayal, many of which were perpetrated by alcoholic caretakers. One does not have to be a fan of inner child work, to acknowledge that ACOANs carry scars from childhood abuse and neglect that complicate their Inner Abundance needs. In short, such people need more TLC and understanding from others because of their scars. Even without *DSM* diagnoses, these individuals also may need lifelong periodic therapy, medication, or both to manage their legacies of shame, confusion, hurt, betrayal, sense of unworthiness, stress, fear, and abandonment. Another legacy is nervous systems racked by abuse or neglect because ACOANs' central nervous systems are permanently damaged. With neural wiring akin to a frayed electrical cord that shoots sparks whenever touched, ACOANs are nevertheless responsible for not visiting their pain on others as much as they can help it. There often are limits to such people's potential in terms of love, work, and schooling, which go against the positive psychology grain that all things are possible and that all people are equal. Despite a few Horatio Alger exceptions, their limits can be seen at private and public and correctional residential treatment centers in which thousands of ACOANs are unable to take advantage of college scholarships and the chance of upward mobility even after years of intervention. This does not mean that such individuals are without hope or optimism, for QOLT teaches that there is always hope for a meaningful, happy, and fulfilling life even as people look their situations square in the eye (see Thou Shalt Be Aware Prinicple). Nevertheless, QOLT eschews the false hope of those who say that the past of ACOANs bears little or nothing on their potential. This is the prison of positive thinking that leads people to blame victims or survivors for not always pulling themselves up by their own bootstraps.

Affirm the Spark (in Others) Principle

This principle encourages clients to try to see and affirm the spark or potential for goodness and greatness in others no matter their position in society. This is a social skill but also a part of serving others and mentoring others as we support, teach, and mentor as often as we can wherever we are. This means being a cheerleader for everyone in the client's life in whom he or she can find some potential. When lives are turned around among the most poor, hopeless, sick, and mean people in our society, it is because someone whom they respected affirmed the spark of potential goodness and greatness in them.

Anger Is the Enemy or Shift of Hate Principle

Like Shakespeare's King Lear, people often feel justified in their anger and adopt a victim role, believing they are a man more sinned against than sinning. It is useful to get out of this victim role and to get on with the importance of pursuing life goals. One way to do this is to have clients view their anger as the enemy and not just as the antagonist. Anger robs people of any joy in the moment so the antagonist wins by continuing to hurt them long after the incident in question. Anger also hurts a person's body (see Tenet of Care for My One Body) by releasing the stress hormone, cortisol, suppressing the immune system, and creating actual tissue damage as in the case of the link between chronic anger, hostility, and heart disease (Beck, 1999; Williams, 1998). In the words of Martin Luther King Jr., "I have decided to stick with love; hate is too great a burden." In a play on the expression, a shift of fate, people can experience a shift of hate or choose their fate by abandoning the victim role once they see how personally destructive it is. The alternative according to QOLT is to put hate into the background via Mindful Breathing. Consider exercising compassion and restraint toward aggressors to not perpetuate the conflict. QOLT also suggests Lie Detector exercises in order to reframe or dispute the core beliefs of insecurity, low self-esteem, injustice, vulnerability, distrust, superiority, and helplessness that so often fuel the fire of anger and hate (Eidelson & Eidelson, 2003).

Ask Your Death Tenet

On the 9/11 flight that crashed in Pennsylvania, United flight 93, passenger Tom Burnett called his wife. He knew that two planes had crashed into the World Trade Center and surmised that the hijackers on his plane would likely do a similar thing. Tom said, "I know we're going to die," something we could all say about ourselves. Then he said, "Some of us are going to do something about it." Clients can use the spirit that Tom Burnett showed during this tragedy and resolve that, in light of their impending death, which could be minutes or years away, they are going to do something positive with their life, forging the legacy they want and building the kind of life they want in their one time to live on earth.

Irving Yalom tried to include a client with terminal cancer in his groups in order to foster the awareness of our finiteness in his group therapy sessions. We can try to do something similar. When uncertain what to do or how to behave or what goals to strive for, Ask clients to think of themselves as being dead and ask their dead self, how shall I handle this? What shall my legacy be? How do I want to be remembered?

▶ Assessing Progress and Prospects Principle (See Taking Your Emotional Temperature Principle)

Assume the Best in Others Principle

Nice guys/gals finish first, not last according to research on people who are warm and trusting of others. As my Viennese analyst supervisor at the Menninger Foundation used to tell me, "It's far better to be taken advantage of, than to be mistrustful of others from the get go or start."

▶ Attack the Moment Principle (See Mine the Moment Principle)

Avoid Stress Carriers or I Never Bother with People I Hate Rule

Stress Carriers are people who carry stress themselves and infect others with their stress just as Typhoid Mary infected people with typhoid, knowing that she was a carrier and refusing to renounce restaurant and kitchen work. Everyone knows a worry wart who is always anxious and stressing about something that isn't even a problem yet. Everyone knows an angry person who is always gossiping and criticizing everyone. Everyone knows somebody who is paranoid of everyone and often abuses people in a lower position. Encourage clients to avoid and ignore these folks as much as possible. Encourage them to be polite and take care of the business at hand but avoid gossiping or criticizing anyone except when absolutely necessary.

Stress carriers freak people out constantly all to no avail. Stress carriers are psychonoxious: Some want to understand and help but are incompetent or have no power, while others do not really care a thing about others and their welfare.

Life is short. If we follow the admonitions of spiritual leaders to live each day as if it were our last, we would do as the self-actualized do according to Abraham Maslow (1982) and largely keep to ourselves and our loved ones and close friends, avoiding stress carriers like the plague.

Balanced Lifestyle Principle

The positive psychology and nonpathology oriented view of the CASIO theory explains unhappiness from the assumption that all valued areas of life contribute to the overall life satisfaction equation and that they must be honored or recognized by being included in one's life priorities and schedule if people wish to feel happier. This can often mean painful choices as clients parcel limited time toward their most important priorities, shelving many things or areas they might like to pursue if days were longer than 24 hours. . . . The process of balancing can take time in situations in which major life changes are in order as in changing jobs. In these cases people must stay optimistic that things will change with time and practice Emergency Inner Abundance if nothing else. Supportive friends, coworkers, or spiritual communities can help in these difficult transitions from an unbalanced to a more balance lifestyle. Lifestyle imbalance is a recurring theme in the professional self-care literature suggesting it is important to consider and address if clients wish to boost their happiness or satisfac-tion. QOLT prescribes such a balanced lifestyle. The Happiness Pie exercise expresses this principle in a powerful and pictorial way. Unfortunately, many suggest that imbalance is a necessary feature of job success in our culture especially if people wish to advance in the organization and be promoted (e.g., Lowman, 1993).

Be the Peace You Seek or Worry Warts Principle

People who worry too much, ruminate about problems ad nauseum, and are prone to the Big Three negative feelings of anger, anxiety, and depression need to control the process of anxious worry and depressive or angry rumination and not just try to fight every upsetting thought we ever have. As hard as it is to believe, everyone has a Calming Response within them just as everyone has the capacity for the Fight or Flight (Freeze, Faint, Tend, and Befriend) Stress Response. Help clients to access this response by searching for Inner Abundance and following the Guide for Worry Warts.

Be True to Your School Principle: BETTY'S Way

This principle is based on the time-honored notion that often happiness is a by-product of fulfilling commitments and doing things that we think are right. For example, be true to your school of thought. That is, encourage clients to honor and act on their values on a daily, moment-by-moment basis in order to feel good about themselves and maintain a sense of contentment and satisfaction. This sense of satisfaction comes from knowing that they are meeting their own personal standards of behavior on a day-to-day basis. Another way to put this is, **"Be ever true to your school"** (BETTY'S Way). Happiness will follow if clients "do the right thing," act in accord with their own standards of behavior, and ask to get their needs met when needed.

Be with People or Relationship Immersion Principle

Perhaps more than anything else, happiness comes from getting along with people and having a few friends who know you and care about you (for one example, see Diener & Seligman's, 2002, groundbreaking study of very happy people). Passionate love and sex may be fickle and inconsistent, but friendship even from a committed partner can be enduring and is what all people must have to live and cope with the ups and downs of life. The happiest people invest heavily in relationships and spend a lot of time with others (Diener & Seligman, 2002). We are not yet sure whether this is merely an artifact of being an extrovert, but until we know, this salient part of daily life in happy people begs for emulation. (Also see the Bosom Friends Principle that recommends people have two or more close friends.)

Be Your Own Guru or Personal Wisdom Principle

In Hinduism, a spiritual teacher is known as a guru or "darkness remover." This principle challenges clients to be their own "darkness removers" as they take final responsibility for choosing a lifestyle and choosing Goals-and-Values that they truly believe in and that foster contentment. Although clients may listen to the advice of others, *they* make the final decisions about what to believe and how to live their life. People are the best experts on themselves. To borrow a phrase from President Harry Truman, the "buck stops here" in deciding what principles to follow in your life.

▶ THE BIG THREE MAKES US DUMB PRINCIPLE (SEE EMOTIONAL CONTROL PRINCIPLE)

Blind Dumb Optimism Principle

Happy folks believe that things will turn out for the best and that they are the kind of person who succeeds in life. Obstacles are temporary setbacks in specific situations that you can learn from and not due to some immutable character flaw. Encourage clients to adopt this attitude. They might have to "fake it till they make it" (i.e., act as though the world is not going to hell in a handbasket even though in their heart of hearts they think that it is). Clients should never blame their mistakes on the assumption that they are bad people. They must never give up on themselves as people who can survive and thrive in life.

This principle does not mean that clients should pretend that things now are better than they are; instead, it means fully accepting where they are now, while believing that eventually they will succeed in finding paths to happiness and success.

Bosom Friends Principle

L. M. Montgomery, author of *Anne of Green Gables,* is a writer with an eye for human behavior who inspired

Mark Twain. In Montgomery's lexicon, a bosom friend is someone who knows and accepts you warts and all; a bosom friend is someone with whom you can share your innermost hopes and dreams with complete trust that they will put your best interests first and will keep a confidence or secret. QOLT urges people to find at least two such friends. If they are lucky and wise, one of these may be a partner or spouse. A close friend or two may be one of the most powerful happiness-boosters that there is; of course, it takes work and regular contact or time together to keep these relationships alive and flourishing.

Business Partner Principle

People who take their love relationships for granted at times, should consider them like they do a relationship between business partners. It is necessary to listen attentively and consult with business partners regularly before any major decisions are made. The Business Partner Principle also suggests that couples invest the same time commitment in their love and domestic relationships as they devote to their jobs and show the same care, attention, and respect they bring to a business partnership.

Calculated Risk Principle

It is almost impossible to grow, change, and find fulfillment without taking calculated risks. If clients always do what they have always done, they will always get what they always got (including depression, addictions, loneliness, etc.). The calculated part of this principle refers to the need for good problem solving prior to taking action on a problem. For example, it is best to take risks or take actions that have the best chance of succeeding and whose consequences are most likely to be positive (both in the short run and in the long run). Clients can improve their odds or increase their probability of success by committing themselves to a "good bet"; it helps to risk or try out a solution that is likely to succeed without a lot of costs. One way to minimize the risk of failure is to gain the necessary skills and understanding needed before taking on the risk. Depressed clients tend to "Yes . . . but" any suggestion to make them feel better; help clients to take the attitude of "I'll try anything once" and try out any reasonable strategy for feeling happier and more fulfilled.

Can't Buy Me Love or Forget Fame and Fortune Rule

Those who value money over love are often the least happy people. If fame and fortune happen that's great, but if not, that's okay, too. In the meantime, clients should seek out fulfillment in play, relationships, service to others, and intrinsically satisfying work.

Care for My One Body Principle

"If I knew I was going to live this long, I'd have taken a lot better care of myself!" How many times do we hear older adults say this? It's important for clients to remember that they are only given one body to live in, thus, they should strive to honor it and take good care of it.

Clients cannot pursue their goals or "passions" fully unless they satisfy their bodies' need for proper nutrition, rest, and regular exercise. Some basic self-control and moderation in personal habits, such as how much clients eat or drink is also essential to caring for their bodies. Engaging in risky sexual behaviors, using illegal substances, and other dangerous activities should be avoided. People who follow this principle will simply not let their health and body suffer no matter how stressful or difficult their lives become.

Check-In with Friends Principle

Since close supportive relationships are one of, if not the biggest, predictor of happiness, it makes sense that we regularly tend and nurture these relationships as we would water a garden or perform our expected duties at Work. To avoid the huge danger of taking close friends and family for granted, QOLT prescribes a check-in routine in which we visit, phone, or text message our close friends and family every month. Face-to-face contact is best. Remember that most of human communication and connection is nonverbal, that is, undecipherable in e-mail. A face-to-face meeting or videoconference is necessary every 6 months to a year if at all possible; whether it be meeting for coffee, lunch, or dinner, it is best to meet one-on-one to keep the closeness and support alive. This principle can be a recurring appointment in a datebook. Josh touches base with one or two friends and family on his Friend List at the start of work each day. This makes it routine and alleviates his sense of isolation from working at home for a software company (also see Favor Bank and Thank Everybody for Everything).

▶ CLEAR CONSCIENCE RULE (SEE DO THE RIGHT THING RULE)

Cocoon It Rule

Milton in *Paradise Lost* said, "the mind is its own place. It can make a heaven of hell or a hell of heaven." The happiness literature bears this out. Researchers are consistently finding that the happiest people keep a sacred place—their minds—cocooned off from the rest of the world. The happiest people are happy about what they've received from life, and are optimistic about achieving more in the future, independent of what is going on around them. They do not let other people impact this sacrosanct space between their ears. They don't compare themselves with others to keep up with the Joneses. They do not second-guess their decisions. They cocoon their mind so that nothing intrudes that would make them question their basic security, self-esteem, or optimism about the future. Encourage clients to practice Mindful Breathing whenever they catch themselves comparing themselves with others or second-guessing, worrying, or ruminating about a decision they have made. Another idea is to ask clients to record each instance when they catch themselves doing these things by writing it down in a journal.

Color Purple Principle

In Alice Walker's Pulitzer prize-winning novel about physical and sexual abuse, she admonishes people to never walk by a field of purple flowers without stopping to drink in, luxuriate in, and appreciate the flowers' beauty. The Color Purple Principle tells people to stop what they are doing for a moment to appreciate, to drink in the beauty and good that they come across each day. No matter how much pain or darkness clients see in their world, there are flashes of beauty or purple flowers every day. This principle tells us to stop what we are doing for a moment to appreciate, to drink in the beauty and good that we come across each day. To ignore this part of the world is to paint a jaded, pessimistic, and distorted perception that will only breed cynicism and unhappiness in the end. The Color Purple

Principle can also be seen as a practice or happiness habit: Encourage clients to practice this principle moment to moment as a perpetual homework assignment to look for and appreciate the good and beautiful in the world. We are to be on the look out perpetually for something or someone to appreciate, 24/7, and then to stop everything even for a few seconds to savor and enjoy the experience.

▶ COMMUNE WITH NATURE RULE (SEE LI PO RULE)

Creativity Routine Principle

Advise clients to adopt the attitude of "I'll try anything once" and search for a Creativity Routine, habitual activity, or positive addiction that gives them a chance to express themselves. Such expression can be habit-forming and happiness enhancing in a world full of passive entertainments and very few creative outlets. Remember that QOLT defines creativity broadly, including crafts, home decoration, and creative play with a child or adult friend!

Curb or Ignore Desires Principle or You Can't Have It All Principle

Popular culture and self-help books are all about fulfilling every desire or impulse. This mentality needs a counterweight, that is a philosophy and technology of behavior that helps people curb or ignore any desire or impulse that is not in their long-term best interest. Many religious traditions tackle this issue as do addiction treatments. Compulsive behaviors or addictions first require motivation to be controlled. It can help to have clients create a pro and con list for this purpose.

People get into trouble when they try to "have it all." It is difficult to be a centered, calm, contented, and reasonably happy person with a committed love relationship and a few supportive friends when faced with too many responsibilities—called role strain by sociologists—too many friendships or romantic relationships, acting unethically in work or personal life as a way to cut corners to get ahead. Even if you win the rat race, you are still a rat, that is, a person who is anything but centered, kind, and deeply contented.

QOLT prescribes a balanced lifestyle in which people recognize that all valued areas of life contribute to an overall life satisfaction equation and that all valued or important areas must be honored or recognized by being included in life priorities and daily schedule if they wish to feel happier. The Happiness Pie exercise expresses this principle in a powerful and pictorial way. People may have to make difficult choices between overall happiness and success in a particular area, like their career. QOLT never presumes to make choices for anyone; QOLT only counsels clients to consider the short- and long-term pros and cons of various courses of action, choosing the alternative that best serves clients' long-term interests at a reasonable cost (see Five Paths exercise). An example of trade-off challenges between Inner Abundance and Work involves the need for a humane workload with reasonable time constraints, which will add to the Intrinsic Satisfaction of a job. It has been suggested that working more than 45 hours a week can have a negative spillover on marriage and family life, suggesting a difficult choice between family harmony and the demands of many professional jobs that require much more than 45 hours per week.

Daily Vacation Principle

This principle advocates planning a 15-, 30-, or 60-minute break every day to do something fun and diverting, just like a vacation. It could mean shopping over the lunch hour and to get the feel of being physically away from the office as if on vacation. It could also mean stealing a few minutes from a hectic schedule at home to read a magazine or watch a favorite TV program. The idea is for clients to take a few minutes for themselves to just play and forget their worries each day. Long out-of-town vacations are great, too, but we need more. We need a sense of vacation in our daily routines. A daily time-out can bring a sense of calm to clients' frenzied lives.

Depression Is Not Normal Principle

Everyone feels great grief, sadness, and disappointment when facing tragedy or disappointment in life. But clinical depression (i.e., acute or chronic depression) is never normal. It is something clients should never accept no matter how awful their circumstances may be. It is a "disorder" in that our ability to keep a positive but realistic perspective on our life is lost. Depression is a treatable disorder that can be changed with professional help.

Don't Bring It Home or Work Spillover Principle

Just as no one is an island unto himself (or herself), neither is a love relationship an island unto itself. Besides being important to our happiness during working hours, satisfaction in their occupation "spills over" into clients' personal and home lives (Kahneman et al., 1999). So, if clients are unhappy at work, they are often preoccupied and irritable at home as they "take their work home" with them. Satisfying work can make people great company, that is, pleasant, content, and enthusiastic to be around when at home or play. A Negative Spillover Effect has been documented: Some people bring their work concerns home with them to the point that they cannot enjoy their free time. Lack of control in a person's job predicts a lack of energy on weekends, suggesting that people can run but not hide from serious work problems and dissatisfaction (Diener & Seligman, 2004; Grebner, Semmer, & Elfering, 2003). Sadly, one of the biggest predictors of relapse in couples therapy for marital distress is the devastation wrought by pressures and stresses outside the marriage like work woes (Jacobson & Christensen, 1996).

A Positive Spillover Effect can also be seen insofar as overall life satisfaction predicts future work performance and productivity up to 5 years in advance (Diener et al., 1999). For this reason, it may be important to embark on a happiness program just as we may pursue fitness or exercise, in order to boost overall happiness, since this can actually spillover into the work sphere. The Happiness Habit keeps clients balanced and sane when work problems arise and allows them to Mine the Moment at work by finding joy and satisfaction there.

Finally, a positive spillover takes place insofar as satisfaction with a person's job seems to lead to greater productivity (Diener & Seligman, 2004). Clients can increase their work productivity by finding ways to enjoy their work more, make it more enriching, and even appreciate it more. After all, most jobs beat the psychological devastation of unemployment; furthermore, there may be positive characteristics of work that some clients never fully appreciate.

Don't Forgive Principle or Set Aside, Shelve, Accept, or Forget Principle

Although forgiveness is not always possible, particularly in cases of severe abuse or neglect, clients can apply the Set Aside, Shelve, Accept, or Forget Principle. Hatred or holding grudges is one of the greatest hell-holes clients can create for themselves, a dungeon without a window to let any real happiness through. Starting with the easiest option, advise clients to Set Aside or Shelve the Wrong that has been done to them, practice Mindful Breathing and let the hurt stay in the back of their mind. The next, more difficult step, is to Accept the Wrong and the Enemy. Here clients accept other people's behavior and try to understand it, realizing that those people did the best they could given their limited awareness, skills, and understanding of the situation. This principle can help clients to reconcile themselves with people they resent or with whom they are in conflict. It especially helps to see a conflict from the other person's perspective; empathy can be a powerful tool for anger management (see To Understand All Is to Forgive All). The third and most difficult step will free clients the most from the hurt: Clients need to forgive their antagonist and wish them well every time that they think of that person. Doing this will stop the retraumatization that happens each time clients replay the hurt to themselves or tell others about it. The latter can be very destructive in keeping hate alive.

Do the Right Thing or Clear Conscience Rule or When in Doubt, Don't Rule

One benefit of decent and ethical behavior is a clear conscience. Clients cannot bring home concerns and worries about cutting corners ethically or morally, if they do the right thing from the start. Guilt over misdeeds can tax an already taxed mind or consciousness even further. It can especially exacerbate depression, which involves guilt prone tendencies anyway. As the French proverb says, "There is no pillow as soft as a clear conscience."

Do What You Love or Tune In to What Turns You on Principle

Encourage clients to spend as much time as possible or practical doing things that make them happy.

Emotional Control or the Big Three Makes Us Dumb Principle

Happiness, according to researchers, is measured in part by the preponderance of positive to negative emotional experiences. The frequency of positive feelings should optimally be much greater than the frequency of negative feelings. Despite this widely held definition, positive psychologists too often ignore the need for what QOLT calls Negative Emotional Control. Positive psychology efforts to be happy can be vitiated by frequent negative feelings. So clients must pay attention to this part of the equation. As predicted by Frisch (1998b), everyone will experience negative feelings or dysphoria when encountering roadblocks to satisfaction in valued areas of life; this is true of even the very happy (Diener & Seligman, 2002). Feeling bad is good if it gives clients a wake-up call to find a new or different path to getting their needs met, as when unhappy lovers realize their irreconcilable differences and find someone more suitable, that is, with differences that they can tolerate better (Gottman & Silver, 1999). Feeling bad often and for long periods of time is not good, however. Hence the need for (Negative) Emotional Control skills, which is part of QOLT. Since we all will experience the Big Three of negative emotions even if we never suffer from a bone fide *DSM* disorder.

As noted earlier in the book, the Big Three negative emotions are anger, anxiety, and depression. Although life circumstances and stresses elicit these feelings, people often magnify these emotions by their attitudes, habits, and backgrounds of abuse/neglect, which make them more sensitive than others, and their basic temperaments, which may be over-emotional anyway. The Emotional Control Principle says that it is clients' responsibilities to control themselves and their expression of these emotions. This control can add immeasurably to clients' happiness as they will not always overreact to stressors, upsetting themselves for hours and days when it is not necessary or appropriate. For this reason, Emotional Control skills are part of this principle and the QOLT approach to happiness (Guide for Worry Warts, Lie Detector and Stress Diary, Five Paths, and Relaxation Rituals associated with Quality Time and Inner Abundance can build these skills).

Fear and anger make people dumb. Higher cognitive processes are interrupted when the Fight or Flight Stress Response is invoked. Fear and anger enable people for Fight or Flight but not much else. When the Fight or Flight mode holds sway over people's consciousness, Daniel Goleman calls the experience a "limbic system hijacking." In a limbic system hijacking, the older more primitive part of the brain—the limbic system and its amygdala—runs the show and higher cortical brain functioning that is essential for solving complex twenty-first century interpersonal problems is short circuited. People make mistakes like taking a swing at an obnoxious stranger, running away from a social gathering, or insulting a boss, actions that may work fine in a Stone Age culture but that now could ruin a career or relationship. Likewise, depression makes it hard to concentrate and think clearly and is not suited to complex social problem solving.

Emotional Honesty Principle

The Emotional Honesty Principle is defined as a deep awareness of and honesty with oneself about what is wrong in a relationship, careful decision making about whether to share concerns or not, and, when deciding to share concerns, using QOLT skills and Tenets to express concerns in an honest, but considerate, compassionate, and respectful way that preserves the relationship as much as possible. These components constitute a three-step process:

1. Developing a deep emotional awareness and understanding of one's hurts, feelings, and wants in a troubled relationship. This is the goal of the core technique of Take-a-Letter 1 and is also reflected in the QOLT Tenet of Thou Shalt Be Aware, that is, individuals must face relationship problems head on and in an unflinching manner whether they decide to change them or not. This awareness process itself can be very helpful and healing, hence the usefulness of Take-a-Letter 1 even with those who are deceased or unavailable.

Emotional honesty also includes an individual's role and responsibility in creating relationship problems and not just that person's innermost feelings about the relationship.

Building a deep awareness of our feelings and our role in a relationship dispute requires some Quality

Time away from the situation. Expressing anger in the moment when a person is very upset and lacks perspective is not recommended in QOLT, although it is recognized that this often happens. Individuals can be honest about problems in ongoing relationships and still be optimistic about their capacity for happiness in general; as this book demonstrates there are myriad paths to contentment and happiness.

2. Deciding what to do if anything based on a deep awareness of the relationship. Because no one is graced with "immaculate perception" and because people can be clueless about their role in creating relationship problems, the Second Opinion technique in which individuals seek counsel about what happened and how to deal with it is highly recommended in QOLT. Whenever possible, it is best to consult a relationship expert, someone adroit at handling these situations who also has your best interests at heart and can keep a secret. Friends, loved ones, and therapists can often serve in this role. No matter how much advice is given, however, QOLT says the buck stops with you, since the individual must live with the consequences of his or her actions. For example, although often helpful, Second Opinions can be ineffective or even harmful, in that they may irritate the antagonist and make matters much worse. Thus, when deciding what actions, if any, to take when confronting a relationship difficulty, individuals must consider their rights in a situation and others' capacity to change. Often saying and doing nothing may be the best option, such as in work relationships in which the antagonist has no willingness or motivation to change.

John Gottman, marriage researcher, estimates that about two-thirds of problems between couples are "perpetual" or unsolvable (Gottman & Silver, 1999). Still individuals may feel it is worth the try to share their hurts, feelings, and wants with the person causing them distress. This is fine as long as they carefully consider the possible negative as well as positive consequences.

Emotional honesty depends on believing in some basic human rights in communication and in how individuals should live their lives. It is helpful to see if personal rights have been violated in situations as a first step in giving a person the confidence and assurance that it is justified to raise an issue. Nevertheless, QOLT and its relationship approach of Emotional Honesty, recommend compassionate and considerate speech when sharing hurts, feelings, and wants with another person. Individuals have the human and relationship right: (1) to act in ways that promote dignity and self-respect as long as others' rights are not violated in the process; (2) to be treated with respect; (3) to say no and to not feel guilty; (4) to experience and express feelings; (5) to take time to slow down and think; (6) to change their minds; (7) to ask for what they want; (8) to do less than they are humanly capable of doing; (9) to ask for information; (10) to make mistakes; and (11) to feel good about themselves.

3. Sharing hurts/feelings/wants: Applying relationship skills to problem situations or relationships. If an individual decides to share his or her concerns about a relationship problem with the antagonist, QOLT recommends that the individual practices and implements QOLT Relationship Tenets (see Tenets of Contentment) and Relationship Skills (found in the Toolbox CD). QOLT recommends retreating from angry situations when possible to avoid "poisoning" the relationship with insults that can never be taken back and to think about what brought about the problem. Using state of the art communication skills may not guarantee success, but it will increase the odds of success; Interestingly, Gottman and Silver (1999) contradict themselves on the importance of communication skills, saying that they are irrelevant early in their book and then resurrecting them later as they give advice on how to deal with relationship problems. Take-a-Letter 2 is the core technique in QOLT for preparing to confront the antagonist in a dispute by marshalling the Tenets and Relationship Skills of QOLT, many of which have been empirically supported in research (e.g., see Frisch & Froberg, 1987).

▶ EMPATHY PRINCIPLE (SEE TO UNDERSTAND ALL IS TO FORGIVE ALL PRINCIPLE)

Equality Principle

There is a growing consensus in the field of couples therapy that egalitarian relationships are the most healthy and long lasting. This means that both partners in a love relationship have equal power when it comes to making major decisions.

Expect the Unexpected Principle

People are doomed to constant frustration when they expect and insist that life will go smoothly. The more people can expect, plan for, and accept obstacles, frustrations, losses, episodes of disrespect, rejection by others, and disappointment in their lives on a regular, unexpected basis, the happier they will be. As much as possible, people should face obstacles and frustrations with a calm and graceful attitude and ask, "How can I deal with this problem?" instead of getting stuck asking, "Why did this happen to me? This isn't fair (as if life is fair!)."

Expert Friend Principle

Always, choose one or more friends who are in your same life situation and who are doing really well at handling the challenges and minefields associated with your situation and time of life. This may be the most important key to "Aging Well," according to Harvard psychiatrist George Vaillant (2002). It can also be crucial to young stay-at-home moms or career women, lawyers as well as mid-career male accountants with young children at home. Whatever your situation, do not take the easy route of befriending folks who simply like you or are easy friends to make. Indeed, the most accepting groups can be those who have failed to find happiness as those people in school and university settings who drown their sorrows with alcohol and drugs. Instead, pick friends you look up to, who are role models of who you want to be, and who cope well with the stresses and strains of their and your stage of human development. You may need to woo these friends as you would a spouse, but you only need one or two of them and the payoff is enormous. Expert Friends who are role models are fonts of wisdom on how to cope with the tragedies of life like sickness and death as well as the mundane details of finding a good pediatrician if you have children or climbing the corporate ladder. As the Bible proverb says, "Walk with the wise and you will become wise." QOLT also says, "You are who hang out with." Our friends say a lot about who we are and who we will become.

Face the Music Principle

Too often most people would rather sweep their problems under the rug than face them directly, hoping that they will somehow disappear on their own. Individuals should commit themselves to staying in touch with the reality of their world: Acknowledge problems and tackle them directly.

Failure Quota Principle

Individuals should expect to have failures, lapses, and relapses in their efforts at self-improvement. Whether they are trying to overcome an addiction, find a mate, or get a good job, it takes time and practice to master the coping and social skills needed to succeed. A certain number of failures or lapses are to be expected before they get it right and succeed. Individuals should view every effort as a chance to practice and fine-tune their coping skills whether they succeed or not. They must reach their quota of practice trials and failures before they can expect to succeed. This attitude will motivate them to learn from failures and persevere since they must "get through" their quota of failures before they can expect to succeed.

FAT Time Principle

FAT time refers to time with Family, time Alone, and Together or couple time with a lover. This principle suggests that people with families should assertively schedule time with them, time alone, and time together with their partner or spouse in order to maximize their enjoyment of life. By honoring each of these key relationships, including the relationship they have with themselves, people increase the chance of gaining fulfillment in life.

Favor Bank or Favor Bank of Good Will from Good Deeds Principle

This is a foundational relationship mind-set and skill in QOLT. Tom Wolfe, in his novel, *Bonfire of the Vanities,* talks about the "favor bank" system, in which Irish cops, judges, and lawyers do favors for each other with the understanding that when they need a favor their "friends" will come through for them because everyone has a full bank account of favors from each other. A full bank account of favors means that others have done so many helpful and kind things for us, that we are more than willing to return the favor.

It is helpful to think of relationships in terms of the Favor Bank metaphor. Indeed, QOLT assumes that the Favor Bank system is really the way of the world in relationships. QOLT views all relationships through this Favor Bank lens of mutuality and reciprocity. That is, QOLT assumes that every relationship has a "bank account" of good feelings that builds up as individuals do favors for their friends, loved ones, and coworkers. Usually, when people are in conflict, this bank account of good feelings is depleted or empty. To resolve disputes, it helps to build the bank account back up by doing genuine favors and little things to please or help the people they care about or work with in their lives. Even when there is no conflict, it's good to regularly, even daily, make efforts to please and help others to keep the Favor Bank full. This helps ensure that people will be treated fairly, considerately, and generously when problems or disagreements inevitably come up and they need a favor in return or a spirit of compromise and fairness and kindness as they negotiate a dispute.

The Favor Bank in many respects boils down to the concept of "What have you done for me lately?" which can be distasteful to some positive psychologists and other idealists who conceive of at least some relationships of unconditional positive regard. Except in cases of disability, such as in Alzhiemer's disease, people expect relationships of reciprocity in which individuals take turns doing favors for each other, meeting each other's needs, and responding to others' request for help (see Mutual Aid Society Tenet). Once Favor Banks are full on both sides of a relationship, it is pleasurable to do things for each other so the question of what have you done for me lately never comes up. Helping is not a burden hanging over someone's head. However, if people stop giving basic satisfactions to others that they know they are fully capable of giving, the relationship atrophies.

Even if they do not need a favor, building up a Favor Bank account with others is a social lubricant that makes daily interactions pleasant and rewarding. Just saying hello to someone for whom an individual has done a favor in the past brightens the interaction. One way to do a favor is to always, Thank Everybody for Everything (see Tenet). That is, anytime anyone does something special or helpful, the recipient should say thanks in a sincere and kind way. This can include doing something for that person, even if the person was just doing his or her job.

Starting with the groundbreaking work of social worker Richard Stuart in *Helping Couples Change* and his Love Days intervention, this general concept has been applied to couples in a rather contrived way. Modifying this intervention, you might give an assignment to a client saying:

> This homework involves doing at least one small thing a day that we know will please, affirm, or ease the burden of our lover/partner. To implement the technique, make a list of 10 small things you could do for the person you wish to "favor." One list of favors to please a partner includes "do the dishes, call partner at work to say I love you, bring food home for dinner, initiate making love, leave a love note in the partner's car, snuggle while watching TV, and bring partner a cup of coffee in the morning." After making a Favor List play "detective" by doing the favors and seeing if they really are pleasing to the other person. You may even let the other person see your list and give you ideas as to what favors please the person the most. Commit yourself to doing a favor or "act of love" whenever you think of it or have a break in your schedule (a quick e-mail or phone call could qualify). It's important to be sincere in doing favors; if you do them grudgingly, it will ruin their positive effects. It's best for partners in a love relationship to do the Favor Bank technique at the same time.

Clients should never feel compelled to do a favor they are uncomfortable with it.

In QOLT, the Favor Bank goes way beyond structured assignments. The Favor Bank is a philosophy of relationships that clients are taught to always keep in mind and to act on in a routine and habitual way. QOLT therapists ask clients to always have the Favor Bank of Good Will concept in their mind as they constantly remind themselves to thank and to do thoughtful/kind things for the people in their life that they interact with day after day. It is too easy and terribly mistaken to take these everyday people, including lovers and partners, for granted and to live without this Mind-Set of Constant Gratitude and Kindness Doing. As they do favors, they should not selfishly look for a payoff now or necessarily even in the future. We dispense kindness and happiness because it is fun and makes us feel good. We certainly notice, however, how smoothly things go when we do need to ask for something. We appreciate it when others seem to do kindnesses in return for us. However, when people do something kind for others, it is more likely that others will do kind things for them. The String of Pearls Principle and Practice (see Tenets

and Helping) is a similar concept that is less selfish than the Favor Bank approach.

Feed the Soul Principle

Although not important to everyone, a religious or Spiritual Life complete with beliefs, activities, and a spiritual community of like-minded friends can greatly enhance one's satisfaction with life. A Spiritual Life deserves consideration by anyone interested in boosting happiness or contentment. QOLT defines spiritual life broadly as spiritual or religious beliefs or practices that individuals pursue on their own or as part of a like-minded community. QOLT prosleytizes for a spiritual journey in which those interested freely explore various secular and spiritual meaning systems, practices, and communities until one finds one that is truly inspiring, uplifting, meaningful to those of us spiritual pilgrims looking for causes and meanings beyond our own selfish desires as well as "selfish" tips on how to live and cope with an often insane world of conflicting beliefs, tremendous beauty, and horrific hatred and violence. Primatologists like Jane Goodhall have observed that our nearest evolutionary cousin, the chimpanzee who shares 99 percent of our DNA is capable of tremendous kindness and tremendous cruelty, arguing for biological predispositions in all of us that may benefit from spiritual beliefs, practices, and communities to keep us somewhat calm and sane and decent to each other.

QOLT advocates a search for a Spiritual Life that is renewing, invigorating, and inspiring. It should function in the way a love relationship should, as a harbor in the storm of life. It should also function as a refueling station, making people feel good about themselves and giving them confidence and optimism to cope with the challenges of their life. Speaking of optimism, the quintessential positive psychology trait, what forum could be better suited for its cultivation than a spiritual community, practice, and belief system.

To really see what can be gained from a particular spiritual approach, QOLT recommends that 10 to 20 minutes of each day be devoted to the practices and readings associated with the approach. Involvement with a skilled teacher in the approach and a spiritual community is also highly recommended in light of the inevitable questions and ups and downs associated with a spiritual practice. Thus an evangelical Christian may do some Bible study each day. Catholics may go to

Mass as often as possible or take a class on Catholic teachings at a nearby church. Jews may observe high holidays and study the Torah. Buddhists may meditate daily. Retreats are highly recommended ways of learning a tradition and of clarifying our Goals-and-Values as well as stuck points or problems that reoccur within us no matter how much we try to blame others.

The meditative and contemplative practices of diverse religions such as Judaism, Christianity, Islam, Buddhism, and Hinduism offer a centuries-old system for managing emotional life, another potential benefit to a spiritual life that includes some form of meditation or meditative prayer (Foster, 1988; Kornfield, 2001; Merton, 1996a). In QOLT, the mind and consciousnesses are likened to a river. This raging or flowing river is full of flotsam, jetsam, jewels, and trash. Some thoughts and beliefs are full of truth and wisdom that help move people toward a more contented life. Others defeat, plague, and distract people from enjoying and partaking in the banquet of life. If consciousness is a river, feelings and thoughts will eventually flow by and go away. Meditation or meditative prayer is a way to watch the river of thoughts and feelings in a more detached way, allowing trash or negative feelings, thoughts, and beliefs to pass by as they are either ignored or later brought to the attention of a spiritual teacher or therapist for further study or resolution. Meditation is recommended in QOLT as a way for clients to become aware of negative feelings and thoughts when they are too upset to name exactly what is disturbing them. A regular meditation practice with an established group is recommended in QOLT as a system of emotional control for clients with high and chronic negative affectivity even though it is a major commitment of time and energy.

Since the river of consciousness is constantly flowing, people need not identify with any one thing in the river. The passive, nonjudgmental, "Nothing human disgusts me" attitude taken toward consciousness in Mindful Breathing or Meditation fosters an acceptance and deeper awareness of upsetting thoughts and impulses since they are not seen as identified with the self. Hence, as passing debris in the river, these items are no more the self or who I am than a passing fancy to buy a new dress or car. Additionally, awareness of the thoughts and impulses make them available for critical examination and thus, make them, if anything, less dangerous (see Thou Shalt Be Aware Principle).

QOLT distinguishes among spiritual beliefs, practices, and communities. Beliefs alone can be powerful. For example, the Zen teacher Joko Beck teaches that the spiritual answer to hate is love rather than a redressing of grievances, a powerful message to anyone struggling with chronic anger.

Many folks get all the religious support they need over the Internet and perhaps with a meditation mat or little altar in their closet to pray at when things get bad. Still, the community aspect is important. Remember that the very happy (Diener & Seligman, 2002) are steeped in relationships, spending hours each day socializing with friends and so forth. David Speigel maintains that lack of friendships is a bigger risk factor for early death or mortality than smoking or cholesterol.

One's spiritual community can provide support during tough battles and in loss, betrayal, and disappointment. In fact this may be one of the few constants even in those with highly disciplined spiritual practices and lives, according to an informal study of the spiritual path by Jack Kornfield (2001) in *After the Ecstasy, the Laundry*. As this book reveals, even devout Christians, Jews, and Buddhist teachers and leaders who pray and meditate "religiously" or regularly are prone to times of pain and depression and anxiety. A spiritual life cannot insulate people completely from the "slings and arrows of outrageous fortune" (Hamlet) that characterize life. For this reason, a spiritual community may be key to getting people through the tough times.

For some, spiritual life entails more secular meanings and paths. Purely secular meanings are reflected in QOLI areas of life such as love relationships, children, creativity (defined broadly as originality in any area of human endeavor, and service to others). The need for secular meaning can spring from existential concerns: For example, if life has no inherent or absolute meaning, people must, therefore, invent one and dedicate themselves to a meaning in order for their lives to cohere. Psychologist Alfred Adler who broke with Freud only to be branded by him as "a little pygmy" believed this as did the existential philosopher Jean Paul Sartre.

Fight for Much, Reap Frustration Principle

This gem from Lao Tzu, alludes to the truism that individuals pay a great price for being overly ambitious in trying to change themselves, others, and circumstances. Success as defined by great wealth, for example, can be as hard to win as the lottery. Additionally, it almost always requires huge sacrifices in terms of Inner Abundance, health, supportive relationships, and peace of mind. People with a manic or hypomanic temperament may be suited to this single-minded pursuit. For most, however, it is chimerical and self-destructive. One will not, for example, find inner peace by risking all he or she owns on an iffy business enterprise in a field full of competitors, especially when such a pursuit robs the person of needed sleep, a good diet, and supportive relationships that can be lost just as surely as a garden that is unattended for several weeks. For clients who are prone to negative feelings or who lack self-discipline and organizational skills, QOLT generally recommends salaried jobs without extensive travel away from the person's home base of friends and supportive relationships. Commission or piecework or by the hour salary structures can make for grossly imbalanced lifestyles and a work-dominated existence in these clients and others, leading to direct conflict with the Love Many Things Tenet.

Fight the Power Principle

This means refusing to accept unhealthy values purveyed, at times, in popular culture or popular media. Such values include using violence as a way to solve problems; materialism or pursuit of money over anything else; a frenzied pace of living that robs life of any joy; "lookism" and the worshipping of an impossible body ideal that speaks volumes about reproductive potential but nothing about human decency, warmth, intelligence, or well-considered goals and values; exploitation and devaluation of workers in various occupations, casual sex over any real intimacy or commitment to those we love in a sexual way, devaluation/ridicule/ prejudice of the poor and powerless including children; the elderly poor; people of color; prisoners; sex offenders; the old, sick, and infirm; people with schizophrenia and other chronic mental illness, physical illness, or disability.

Fighting the Power means everything from refusing to buy into these unhealthy distortions; to sharing this resistance with your friends, colleagues, and family; to actively campaign against particular values or instances of excess.

Find an Area or Go to Your Room Principle

This principle says that when individuals are bored upset, or looking for a way to boost happiness, they should pick an area of life that they care about, and do something safe that used to be satisfying. For example, if a client prizes Play, he should download a computer game; if she prizes Friends, she should call or visit a friend just to hang out and perhaps share her concerns. (See *Areas of Life to Consider for Greater Happiness* in the Toolbox CD for a list of all areas of potential joy or satisfaction to consider.)

Find a Friend, Find a Mate Principle

Individuals should focus efforts on the small area of overlap between the circles in Figure 9.1, People I Like and People Who Like Me, accepting that many will be unavailable (i.e., not in the Meet/Meat Market of friendship or love right now) or indifferent to for other reasons just as they will pass by or reject many potential dates/friends. Individuals should move on quickly from folks not in the overlap area of the circles using Mindful Breathing and the Lie Detector to deal with self-downing thoughts about rejection. Encourage them to remember, potential friends or mates are like buses, there is always another one coming around the corner. That is, encourage them to put themselves into circulation in contrast to the painfully shy butler in the beautiful novel, The *Remains of the Day,* who lost the love of his life by refusing to take any initiative (Ishiguro, 1989).

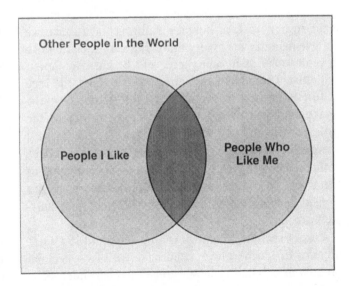

Figure 9.1   Find a Friend, Find a Mate principle.

▶ FIND A GOAL PRINCIPLE (SEE FIND A MEANING PRINCIPLE)

Find a Meaning/Find a Goal Principle

We all need a guiding vision of what matters most in life and how we should live, both now and in the future. Whether secular, spiritual, or both, this guiding vision answers the question, "What is the meaning or purpose of life?" These Goals-and-Values are basic and essential to a sense of security and happiness. QOLT defines Goals-and-Values as "your beliefs about what matters most in life and how you should live—both now and in the future. This includes your goals in life, what you think is right or wrong, and the purpose or meaning of life as you see it."

Goals-and-Values include your personal and career goals for the future. Identifying some lifetime goals for yourself is an essential part of QOLT. The QOLI and Vision Quest exercise are designed to help you identify life goals. Once identified, the idea is to think about and recall your lifetime goals daily as you plan your days and your life. Also try to embrace beliefs, habits, and routines that help you in this endeavor and shun those influences, habits, beliefs, and routines that block your progress. Even the media, books, and TV that you watch or "consume" may help you or hinder you in your "diet" of influences needed for change and reaching personal goals.

More Secular Purposes. Secular purposes in life beyond the self are often seen as sacred or spiritual callings by believers in these paths to fulfillment. Secular purposes can include raising a family, pursuing excellence in our work or hobbies, fighting for a cause we believe in, and even avidly following a nontheistic faith or philosophy as in being a fervent Bright, Humanist, Buddhist, Universist, or Unitarian. For some, the idea of fulfilling their own potential—self-actualization—is a useful goal along with just enjoying life to the fullest. Still and all, some meanings beyond the self seem necessary to happiness even if there is a selfish component as in raising children, a wonderful type of life work. Of course, multiple meanings and goals are typical, leaving room for both altruistic and more selfish pursuits.

Purely secular meanings can be reflected in QOLT areas of life such as love, children, creativity—defined broadly as originality in any area of human endeavor—and service to others. The need for secular meaning can spring from the existentialist assumption that since life has no inherent or absolute meaning, we must, therefore, invent one and dedicate ourselves to a meaning in order for our lives to cohere, make sense, or be coherent. Psychologist Alfred Adler held this position as did the existential philosophers, Jean Paul Sartre and Albert Camus (Yalom, 1980).

More Spiritual and Religious Meanings and Goals. While not important to everyone, religious and spiritual activities can greatly enhance a person's satisfaction with life and deserve consideration by all of us interested in boosting our happiness or contentment. In the most un-evangelical way imaginable, the Dalai Lama, spiritual leader of the Dzogchen lineage of Buddhism, an exile from his home country of Tibet by Communist China, speculates in the *Art of Happiness* that we should have as many religions as people in the world because all of us have different personalities and spiritual needs. He goes on to say that Buddhism is not for everyone and that we can be quite principled and moral without any religion at all as long as we adhere to general ethical principles. In this vein, QOLT defines spiritual life *broadly* as spiritual or religious beliefs or practices, that you pursue on your own or as part of a like-minded community. For those who value and want a spiritual life, QOLT "proselytizes" for a spiritual life or journey in which those interested freely explore spiritual meaning systems, practices, and communities until one finds one—or more—that is truly inspiring, uplifting, or personally meaningful. A religion or spiritual life should provide some useful personal "answers" for those of us spiritual pilgrims looking for causes and meanings beyond our own selfish desires as well as "selfish" tips on how to understand, live and cope with an often insane world of conflicting beliefs, tremendous beauty, and horrific hatred and violence.

For those interested, QOLT advocates a search for a Spiritual Life that is renewing, invigorating, and inspiring. It should function in the same way that a love relationship should, as a shelter or safe haven in the storm of life. It should also function as a refueling station, inspiring us, making us feel good about ourselves and girding our loins, that is, giving us confidence and optimism to cope with the challenges of our life. Speaking of optimism, the quintessential positive psychology trait, what forum could be better suited for its cultivation than a spiritual community, practice and belief system? *Whatever spiritual approach or approaches are embraced, they should be followed and practiced on a daily basis for 5 to 20 minutes in order to get the maximum happiness-producing effect.* Spiritual beliefs can be reviewed and need to be followed, rituals and practices can and need to be practiced, and spiritual guidance needs to be put into action for Spiritual Life to have a real benefit in terms of increased happiness or contentment. Being part of a like minded spiritual community can also be extremely important, even essential.

Our Spiritual Life may be most powerful and fulfilling if it includes a community of spiritual friends and teachers who can support us and whom we can support—helper therapy principle—as we try to walk the walk of a spiritual approach 24/7, even with our most difficult family members and work colleagues. This more complete spiritual approach, including a community of like-minded people that we socialize with on a regular basis, a particular teacher/leader or spiritual friend who sees the goodness and potential in you, and the belief system of the approach can completely change our lives, making us much more happy and fulfilled. Consider the success of Alcoholics Anonymous (AA) as well as the other myriad communities and approaches from Judaism to Christianity to Islam, Hinduism, and Buddhism—American or Eastern. A spiritual life and discipline—with preferably regular daily practice for even 5 to 10 minutes—can make you more patient and kind, but likely will not change your basic temperament, personality, and potential happiness range or set point.

Happiness-Enhancing Goals-and-Values. You may wish to consider adopting some of the Tenets of Contentment themselves as part of your Goals-and-Values. All of the Tenets are meant to foster a life of greater happiness and contentment. The Tenets, Happiness Matters and Happiness Is a Choice, may be especially important for you to adopt if being happy is important to you.

Put Your Time Where Your Values Are. What may be unique to the QOLT approach is that QOLT tries to make a connection in how clients order their daily routines and their overarching life goals. To paraphrase the saying "Put your money where your mouth is," clients are told, "Put your time and effort where your values are." This sub-tenet or corollary of Find a

Meaning suggests that we as therapists try telling clients to "Enshrine your personal goals with related activities in your schedule for each day so that your acts follow your Goals-and-Values." Such a schedule constitutes their "Marching Orders" for the day and can really help in the process of "sculpting" days that fit your innermost values and personal goals (see Meanings Are Like Buses, Marching Orders Principle, and Feed the Soul Principle).

Flow It Principle

Ask yourself this common survey question to find out if an activity is a flow for you—if it is, try to do it more often and try to do nonflows less often: Do you ever get involved in something so deeply that nothing else seems to matter, and you lose track of time? Many of our favorite activities are flows like making conversation with people, playing sports, or exercising—athletes refer to flow as in the zone, gardening, decorating, gaming, scrap booking, shopping, home improvement, surfing the net to answer a question, playing with children, arts and crafts, playing or listening to music; there is also a treasure trove of flows that each of us has never tried but need to in order to maximize our happiness like helping, creative problem solving at Work, and trying out entirely new and active hobbies (see Play List in the Toolbox CD). Since we are all different, we must try out various activities several times to see if an activity is a potential flow for us.

Flows are activities that we do for their own sake, that are intrinsically rewarding. The state of consciousness that results while we do flows is the sense of total engagement, loss of time, and loss of self-consciousness or worry. The state of consciousness that results when the activity is over and we reflect back on it is a deep sense of satisfaction and happiness. "Flow-ers," folks engaged in flow activities, are, in a sense, too busy or immersed to feel happiness at the time; that comes later.

Along with the importance of close relationships with others, flow activities in which people actively do something challenging that fits their level of skill may be as close to the Holy Grail or the key to happiness that science can offer right now (Csikszentmihalyi, 1997; Csikszentmihalyi & Hunter, 2003). As much as possible, we want to Flow It, that is, find and carry out flow activities in all spheres of life and at all possible times—at home, with family and friends, in hobbies, at work, and in retirement—in order to maximize our happiness and life satisfaction.

A flow is an activity that requires our total attention, during it we are not distracted with other worries or concerns. A flow is an activity with a definite challenge that requires us to use our maximum skill as in reading a book written at just our reading level or slightly above. In computer gaming, flow is playing a game you enjoy at a difficulty level that matches your skill level or exceeds it slightly. It cannot be too hard/challenging or too easy to be a flow; the activity must require all of your skill and attention to overcome an obstacle or challenge that is just slightly out of reach. You can use flows even if you have a grumpy temperament/personality and, as long as you keep raising the challenges to fit your skill level, it *never* stops working. You need only make the initial effort to start the activity and pick a goal or challenge that takes all of your skill and attention. This requires bigger challenges as your skill increases as when a gardener who cultivates solid color roses branches out to plant a rainbow colored rose of three different colors. If you get too good, you may need to switch hobbies or flows entirely, but there is always one out there for each of us, a major source of joy or fulfillment if we just make the effort and say no to the easy but cloying pleasures of passive activities like TV.

When feeling bored, unhappy, or discontented, we should be aware of the feeling and accept it fully but then make ourselves do something that has been challenging and engaging in the past. If not a past flow, we can try a potential new flow, practicing Mindful Breathing as we carry out the activity.

The FOOBS Principle or Switch Out of FOOBS Principle

Anh Minh, the Vietnamese cook protagonist in the heartbreaking and beautifully written, *The Book of Salt,* by Monique Truong (2003), cleans his drunken rageaholic father's filthy spittoon and grows up hearing how stupid, worthless, and incompetent he is. Minh carries this abuse across the ocean to Paris in 1929 as he serves in the home of Gertrude Stein and Alice B. Toklas; Minh hears his father's voice berating and criticizing him constantly. The ever-present voice of Minh's father in this book is a perfect metaphor for how people can carry unhealthy legacies from their past to their present circumstances.

As with Minh, many of the dysfunctional, unhealthy, and self-defeating thoughts, feelings, and behaviors people have come from their family of origin. These well-practiced routines will reliably rear their ugly heads whenever people are under stress or encounter a situation similar to ones in the past. Consider the case of Janie, who never got enough love or attention as a child and learned to demand it in an annoying way. Today she terrorizes her workgroup by keeping score of who is getting enough in terms of supplies, office space, and other perks. Her behavior comes from schemas or core beliefs that everything must be equal. Janie's family of origin or FOO created dysfunctional, unhealthy, and self-defeating Behaviors and Schemas that Janie learned as a coping response. QOLT sees FOOBS as behavior patterns so overlearned that they are in our bones. The situations from childhood that spawned these patterns have analogues in adult life that lead to the same thinking and behaving response learned from childhood which, while often adaptive then, is no longer adaptive in the adult world. According to Beck (1996; also Clark & Beck, 1999), these unhealthy schemas and behaviors can spawn unhealthy levels of anxiety, anger, and depression to the point that a full-blown psychiatric disorder blooms.

QOLT recommends that people closely watch out for FOOBS, that is situations and people that push their buttons or make them upset. When they experience a FOOBS reaction, QOLT asks them to switch out just like a basketball player who has been knocked on the floor by another player. "Switch out" means to figuratively get up off the floor and do something different. In this way, people can avoid stress carriers or those who push their FOOBS buttons. When practicing the switch out of FOOBS, clients should recall that the conscious mind is like a movie that they make. If they do not like the movie they are watching, change channels (see My Movie or Make Your Own Movie Principle). Let the Calm Self redirect clients' minds from reruns of the same old flicks of misery. Alternatively, people can approach in a new way the person who caused the FOOBS response. That is, they can carefully watch for and react differently to those people or situations that they know push their buttons. Thus, when Janie realizes that she is being overly concerned with equality in minor situations in which views or equality are subjective or unimportant, she tells herself to switch out by going to her default strategy of being silent or kind. Her silence means that she will refrain from criticizing or making any suggestions in the work meeting, being aware that her judgment is unreliable when in the throes of FOOBS and trusting others to be fair. The recommended behavioral default strategy to FOOBS at the time of upset is to be silent and leave the situation if possible or to stay in the situation and be silent and kindly, avoiding and postponing the concrete discussion of upsetting issues until another time when the person is calmer and centered. Since most decisions are not irrevocable, people can wait to get centered during Quality Time to decide what the FOOBS pattern was all about and to consider an Emotionally Honest response to the situation. The Lie Detector and Stress Diary (see the Toolbox CD) can be done to explore ways to dispute the core schemas and beliefs associated with a FOOBS episode. Another option is to stage a conversation between one's FOOBS state and one's more calm, centered, and stable self. This can be done with empty chairs as individuals take on one role in one chair and then move to another to assume another role. This can also be done in one's imagination by asking clients to close their eyes and have the Calm Self step away from the Crazy Self or FOOBS state that is overwhelming them. The Calm Self's job is to comfort and counsel the Crazy Self or FOOBS state like a loving parent as in "I know you have been terribly hurt but we can survive and thrive with time and perspective. What Inner Abundance can we do right now to care for you in a loving way?" By having various parts or modes interact with each other, the cognitive part of the modes, that is, core beliefs or schemas associated with the mode, can be examined and disputed. This approach to switching out of FOOBS and to schema change is called the Multiple Personality or Multiple Personality of Everyday Life technique. In this case, the full-body mode experiences that possess an individual are like alters or subpersonalities in a case of multiple personality disorder, which although debunked by many researchers, is a useful metaphor for people to understand their sometimes warring and disparate parts. While adhering strictly to D. A. Clark and Beck (1999) cognitive theory concept of a mode and not a reified construct of a true alter in a multiple personality sense, this approach to schema work or FOOBS control is inspired by Richard C. Schwartz (2001) and Fritz Perls (1971).

Although FOOBS usually concerns reactions to nonrelatives, it also occurs with relatives and family members. In fact, individuals may reenact a FOOBS dance every time that they return to their family of origin. After all, the FOOBS routines originated in the family of origin.

▶ FORGET FAME AND FORTUNE RULE (SEE CAN'T BUY ME LOVE RULE)

Get a Therapist Rule

Most of us can benefit from a great psychotherapist/ coach at times of crisis or pain. Those of us with chronic unhappiness and any psychological disorder probably need a therapist. Choosing the right therapist is a delicate task. Word of mouth is important. Years of experience—the more the better—is important. But it is also important for individuals to assess how you hit it off with a particular therapist and gauge the results honestly with yourself and your loved ones. Finally, it is important to shop around. Three to five sessions should tell you plenty about whether a particular therapist or therapy approach is going to help. Because of the impossible restrictions on mental health practice, many good therapists do not accept insurance or work "in network" for a particular health plan. Be willing to pay out of pocket like you do for a lawyers' service. You will gladly pay whatever it takes for great therapy. This kind of life-changing help is worth the cost.

Get Organized Principle

People can only achieve a modicum of happiness and contentment if their lives are reasonably organized and well managed. Unless people consciously plan each day in ways that promote happiness and further progress toward cherished needs, goals, and wishes, they will not experience a sustained sense of contentment.

Giving Tree or Self-Other Principle

Many people suffer from the Giving Tree Syndrome; they become depressed when overwhelmed by outside responsibilities. The Self-Other Principle suggests that people balance the time they devote to helping other people with time for themselves or Self-Caring. Self-Caring is not selfishness. It is a realistic understanding that people have some basic physical and psychological needs that have to be met before they can be there for anyone else or do anything else. Self-Caring can be thought of as self-maintenance. People need to find a balance between extremes of total self-sacrifice and extreme narcissism or selfishness.

Glow of Peace Tenet

In *After the Ecstasy,* Jack Kornfield talks of spiritual teachers, gurus, or darkness removers whose presence attracts, holds, and transforms their students into those who have touched God or experience a deep mystical peace. Everyone can bring this to relationships. In the Dzogchen tradition of Tibet, it is recommended that one's guru be at least three valleys away. Perhaps this ensures that the positive transference or idealism is not shattered by observing the human peccadilloes of our healers. Nevertheless, clients often size up their therapists to see whether they walk the walk of enlightened, centered, and joyful living. Practicing Inner Abundance usually enhances the Glow of Peace, a state and Tenet that makes people more attractive, effective, and inspiring to others with whom they live and work.

▶ GO TO YOUR ROOM PRINCIPLE (SEE FIND AN AREA PRINCIPLE)

The Grass Isn't Greener, It's Weeds Principle

Individuals should not second-guess their decisions and commitments, as a general rule, unless they want to be miserable, according to Lyubomirsky, Sheldon, et al. (in press) and QOLT, which came upon this idea from work with fretful and anxious (Big Three) folks. Until and when people decide to really act on their desire to explore a different committed relationship or a different job or career, they should assume that *The Grass Isn't Greener, it's Weeds.* Today's disposable, materialistic culture encourages people to treat relationships and jobs like disposable Kleenex, a dangerous and destructive attitude that feeds the normal human tendency to quickly adapt to and then take for granted anything that we have. As Joni Mitchell in *Big Yellow Taxi* bemoans, "you don't know what you've got 'til it's gone. . . ."

The Great Compromise Principle

In the spirit of Henry Clay's Great Compromise to avert the Civil War, committed love relationships are great compromises in the sense that we give up much for the sake of our partners and "The Relationship." In return, we get much as in having our needs met for stable, intimacy, companionship, and love. Ultimately, then, this is a "win-win" relationship or bargain. Nevertheless, the compromises are constant and can feel painful or unfair. QOLT teaches that big and little compromises on a regular even daily basis are essential to the health of long-term, committed relationships.

Habits Rule Rule or Routines Rule Rule

Although it is fine to accept themselves as they are (see Self-Acceptance Tenet), people who wish to change will only do so if the proposed change becomes a habit or routine for them. Whether it be daily physical activity or regular study of the Bible, Koran, or some other book, it isn't going to happen if it does not become part of our habitual routine.

Happiness Diet Principle

In the song, *White Rabbit,* Jefferson Airplane says "Feed your head" . . . with drugs. People "feed their heads" with influences from self-talk, the people with whom they associate, with the TV shows they watch, the movies they see, the magazines they read, even the bus billboard ads they observe. Everything that the head digests is either good, bad, or neutral in terms of its happiness-producing potential. The Happiness Diet Principle says people should ingest what makes them happy, sane, and content and restrict or remove other items.

Happiness Equation Tenet

Happiness Equation Tenet: One Happiness Equation in QOLT is the Five Path model diagram of life satisfaction available in the Toolbox CD and illustrated in the *Five Paths Exercise,* which says that our satisfaction and resulting happiness come from adding up our satisfactions with each area of life that we care about. More generally, the *Happiness Equation Tenet* refers to how much of our happiness is genetic versus under our control. In general, QOLT assumes that despite various constraints on our control of happiness such as the process of adaptation and our genetically determined set point of happiness. We can control about 50 percent of the Happiness Equation (Lyubormirsky, Sheldon, et al., in press).

Each area of satisfaction in the equation is made up of the CASIO elements that also constitute intervention strategies for happiness.

Happiness from Achievement Principle

QOL theory maintains that happiness comes largely from getting personal needs, wants, and goals fulfilled in the areas of life that one cares about; this includes happiness as people meet subgoals in the journey toward fulfillment in valued areas of life. Rebecca Shiner of Colgate University has longitudinal data in support of the view that happiness is associated with the achievement of developmental tasks or milestones at certain ages including the ability to make friends as a child, succeed in school, and find a partner in adulthood (and not in early adulthood as many have assumed). In the words of Ed Diener, "As people work for their goals, and achieve them, they experience subjective well-being. Thus happiness can be achieved by seeking those things that one values" (see Diener web site at http://www.psych.uiuc.edu/~ediener/faq.html).

Happiness Habits Principle

Happiness is based largely on how people choose to look at the world and the activities they choose to pursue. It is based on no brainer routines or Happiness Habits that they do not have to think about but that they do out of habit. These Happiness Habits or "no-brainer" routines honor Goals-and-Values in life and follow some of the suggestions supported by research and found in this book like the need to sacrifice for and to put regular time in to building and sustaining close relationships with friends and family (see Lyubomirsky, Sheldon, et al., in press, for empirical support and for a similar idea developed independently). People need to regard Happiness Habits like a job that they put time into every day, as in checking in with and helping friends, doing some physical activity or exercise, and looking over the Tenets of Contentment to challenge and to replace old thinking habits of pessimism, hopelessness, and fear (also see Lie Detector in the Toolbox CD). This view of happiness is shared by eminent researchers, including Mihaly Csikszentmihalyi (Csikszentmihalyi & Hunter, 2003) and

Sonja Lyubomirsky and her colleagues (Lyubomirsky, Sheldon, et al., in press).

Happiness Is a Choice or It's Up to You Principle

To some degree, people choose their happiness or unhappiness by deciding how to think, act, and structure their time during every moment of every day. The lifestyle and attitudes we choose can have as much to do with our happiness or depression as our childhood, genetics, or circumstances. For example, we often know what to do to be happier but refuse to do it. This principle begs us to ask ourselves how we contribute to the problems in our life, likely the greatest challenge in personal growth and self-improvement. This principle challenges us to think, act, and live in ways that we know foster contentment instead of unhappiness. While we probably aren't responsible for developing self-defeating thoughts, feelings, and behaviors in the first place, we are responsible for asking for help (e.g., get counseling) or for managing the problem once we have gained the tools to do so (e.g., positive coping skills). Thus, therapists can remind clients of the adage "You're not responsible for being down, but you are responsible for getting up." Suggest to clients: "You are the master of your fate in that you can at least choose how you cope with problems in your health, habits, and inner life of thoughts and feelings (Inner Life Responsibility)." No matter how bad our circumstances or how badly we've been mistreated, it is our problem to find a way out of negative feelings and unhealthy behaviors and to cultivate positive satisfactions and emotions. No one else will do it for us. If we don't take responsibility and do something about it, it won't get done. Don't count on anyone else to fix it; that may never happen! It's up to *us* to find answers to how to live and then, this is so hard, to implement the "answers" that work for us in our daily life. Suggest to clients: "You are the master of your fate in that you can at least choose how you cope with any particular life situation (Responsibility for Circumstances and Behavior)." Even when fate deals a cruel blow or throws a roadblock or temptation in our way, we can decide how to deal with the problem. We can always exercise some Stimulus Control, that is, we can refuse to let some outside stimulus, stress, conflict, tragedy, obstacle, frustration, or person in our life control our actions and behaviors. We can use the Expert Friend Principle to find people in similar circumstances to ours who are coping well and can share their secrets of success. According to one recent theory, 40 percent of our happiness is under voluntary control (Lyubomirsky, Sheldon, et al., in press). That is, 40 percent of happiness is controlled by our choices or intentional activities that we pursue. The figure rises to 50 percent if we view our life circumstances as changeable through our own best efforts (Lyubomirsky, Sheldon, et al., in press). One way we take responsibility for our own happiness is by deciding to make some basic contentment or life satisfaction a priority in our life that we are willing to work for; this is called the Happiness Matters Tenet.

Happiness Matters Principle

If people want to be happy, they have to make happiness a top priority in their lives and engage in activities that they know will foster contentment and fulfillment. They should try to do and think nothing that will harm their basic contentment and happiness and always try to make efforts to do and think what they know will help. For example, if socializing makes a client less depressed, he or she should plan to visit with a friend each day. People will also be happier if they are actively doing things and accomplishing things they care about. People tend to feel unhappy or bored when they are passively "doing nothing" or pursuing pleasure all the time.

Happiness Set Point Principle or Personality Stays the Same Principle

This principle alerts people to the need to accept their limitations in terms of how happy and positive they can become even with strenuous intervention; people will be happier accepting that they have some limits in just how happy they can be even with great effort or terrific circumstances.

Everyone has a happiness set point and potential range of happiness that they inherit from their parents much like intelligence. In the case of both IQ and happiness, people inherit a possible range so that with the right learning and experience they can get to the top of that range but no further. People also inherit a set point in the middle of their range, a level of happiness or satisfaction that they tend to gravitate toward after some-

thing unusually good or bad upsets them or makes them feel "on top of the world." While intelligence may be 70 percent genetic or inheritable in this way, happiness and positive affect and even basic personalities and temperaments are about 50 percent heritable (Diener & Seligman, 2004; Lyubomirsky, Sheldon, et al., in press; Myers, 2004).

People born with a shy or grumpy temperament or personality (a tendency to react to life with one of the Big Three negative emotions of anger, anxiety, or depression and possessing a very low happiness set point and potential happiness range) will continue to experience curmudgeon tendencies even with intervention. But QOLT will help such people to achieve the best degree of happiness and contentment within their range.

Temperament and personality are also heavily influenced by culture, upbringing, parental modeling, and experience of abuse (see FOOBS Tenet). Personality traits like high extroversion and low negative affectivity are closely related to happiness and life satisfaction and change little if at all after the age of 30 (McCrae et al., 2000). According to Lyubomirsky, Sheldon, et al. (in press) and others, there appear to be heritable set points and ranges for personality traits, temperaments, and specific emotions, all of which can limit our experience of pleasure, happiness, and satisfaction to a degree, perhaps 50 percent, allowing another 50 percent for environmental, psychological, cognitive, and behavioral factors that are, to an extent, under our control.

In addition to QOLT interventions, QOLT also asserts that a Spiritual Life and discipline with regular, preferably daily practice or participation can make you more patient and kind and content, but your basic quirks and personality—your Happiness Range, Personality, Temperament, and Neuroses—will stay. Nevertheless, individuals' attitudes and life circumstances have an enormous impact on happiness and can do much to move them to the high end of their happiness range (see Sensate Focus/Savor and Find a Meaning Principles for more on what people can change about their happiness potential).

Happiness Spillover Principle

Happiness or unhappiness in one area of life can spillover into other areas. This concept works both ways so, if people hate their jobs, they are often preoccupied and irritable at home as they "take their work home" (Negative Spillover Effect). Similarly, satisfying work can make people great company, that is, pleasant, content, and enthusiastic to be around when at home or while recreating (Positive Spillover Effect). This principle challenges people to find Positive Spillover Areas to compensate for areas of unhappiness (Campbell et al., 1976). A structured way to achieve this is the Basket-of-Eggs exercise in the Toolbox CD. Finally, this principle warns people to keep an eye out for Negative Spillover and to respond aggressively to areas of deep dissatisfaction with their lives with the knowledge that this dissatisfaction can spread like a cancer to other areas of life that were doing just fine—Five Paths can aid in finding ways to manage a Negative Spillover.

► HAPPINESS TAKES EFFORT PRINCIPLE (SEE
   KEEP BUSY WITH FLOWS PRINCIPLE)

How Kind Principle or Tender-Hearted Rule

All the spiritual practices, teachings, and readings that we have done should, if they have the desired effect, make us more kind. If not, something is wrong. Even outside the realms of spiritual traditions, this principle still is compelling. What better rule of thumb or benchmark exists than one's personal decency and kindness, day in and day out. . . . The benefit to others of this Tenet may be incalculable as stated in the conclusion of Middlemarch, written by George Eliot, in 1871. To paraphrase Eliot: The growing good of the world is dependent upon the myriad noble acts by we "insignificant" people. . . . That things are not so ill with you and me as they might have been is half owing to the daily acts of the nonfamous (the good and kind ordinary folk whose daily acts exert an incalculable effect on the world even as they are invisible to history).

Humble Servant or Servant Leader Principle

Whether out of a spiritual or religious commitment or out of a pragmatic, secular, humanistic framework, this principle gives guidance on how to conduct oneself in relationships. It is a marriage of the How Kind and Serve Other Principles, and says that seeking out ways to serve others is a wonderful orientation toward daily life that can make a person happy and successful in dealing with others. This principle suggests that people try to be positive and helpful to others in a kindly, quiet way that communicates a sense of "I

am no better than you or anyone else." A leader with this philosophy or mind-set will listen to employees, care about them, and know all aspects of the business since that person is not afraid to get his or her hands dirty doing the most mundane or dirty parts of the business, especially those that involve serving customers!

Humor Principle

People should foster a sense of humor in themselves, focus on the funny side of something, and pursue activities that make them laugh. When people are able to laugh at themselves and others in their circumstances, they take the sting out of misfortune, enjoy a pleasant diversion, and garner the strength they need to carry on.

I Can Do It Principle

In order to succeed, people must have some basic faith that they can do what it takes to achieve any reasonable goal they've set for themselves. QOLT suggests that all people need are the necessary skills and awareness to improve themselves in reasonable ways. This doesn't mean that they won't experience setbacks, but with time they can get it right. Even when they doubt themselves, it's best to act as if they believe that they can do what it takes to eventually succeed.

I'll Think about That Tomorrow Principle

After being jilted by Rhett Butler, Scarlett O' Hara in the film Gone with the Wind, says to herself something to the effect of, "I'll Think about That Tomorrow." This incident illustrates the Happiness Habit of postponing worry by distraction with some engaging flow type of activity to avoid the untoward effects of ruminative coping, which preoccupies us and promotes Big Three emotional blow ups to little avail. The habit of ruminative coping is usually self-defeating even though many people feel superstitiously that it will lead to some magic bullet solution to their problems or will forestall them from making any errors in the future. QOLT recommends that it be seen as a bad habit to be gently broken through Mindful Breathing (see Tenet or the Guide for Worry Warts), in which worry is always postponed to see if in fact it is necessary at all and, if it seems necessary, to problem solve as in Five

Paths at a time when they are relatively calm and graced with some measure of Inner Abundance.

I'm Going to See My Friends at Work Principle.

One way to boost happiness at work is to be friendly to all and to make friends with people one trusts and enjoys. People can also network in the sense of making friends who can help them navigate the system and get their jobs done. In either case, people can go to work with the pleasant idea, "I'm Going to See My Friends" today!

▶ **I Never Bother with People I Hate Rule (See Avoid Stress Carriers or Stress Carriers Rule)**

Inner Abundance Principle

This is a foundational principle in QOLT. Inner Abundance means feeling deeply calm, rested, centered, loving, alert, and ready to meet the challenges of the day and life after caring for oneself in a thoughtful, loving, compassionate, and comprehensive way. It suggests that when people do the very best for themselves, they have a lot more of themselves available for other people and activities (see Giving Tree or Self-Other Tenet). People must feel centered, calm, and good on the inside, hence the "inner" of Inner Abundance, to serve others or to pursue happiness in any of the areas of life in QOLT.

Inner Abundance demands that people do a good job of self-care, which means putting time, effort, and thinking into deciding what renews them each day and then making time to do it.

Inner Abundance means getting necessary rest and caring for one's body. It often means engaging in regular exercise. It can mean regular meditation, prayer, review of goals and planning (all things that make up Quality Time in Quality of Life Therapy). Above all, Inner Abundance relies on routines, that is overlearned actions that require no thinking.

Inner Abundance is also about creating space for oneself in life as in time alone to reflect and recharge one's batteries. Creating space for Inner Abundance also means not overwhelming oneself with responsibilities and projects at work and elsewhere.

Inner Abundance is highly personal; what works for others may not work for a particular person. Encourage clients to experiment and discover routines for Inner Abundance that they can practice every day or nearly every day.

Committing to Inner Abundance means making happiness, peace, and contentment a priority (see Happiness Matters Principle or Tenet). It may sound trite but it is no less true that if you do not care for yourself, who else will? Clients should stop putting off the things they know that they need to experience Inner Abundance. Stop waiting for vacation and make time for mini-vacations every day, interludes of self-renewing routines that make your current life circumstances livable and decent right now . . . without any drastic changes. QOLT speaks of Daily Inner Abundance (IA Goals). To concretize this principle, a question clients are urged to ask themselves when upset and throughout the day is, "What would Inner Abundance be for me in this moment?" (Inner Abundance in the Moment).

Emergency Abundance means doing a few small things to care for yourself even when things get hairy, crazy, or too busy and difficult to make any changes in your routine. It can mean a full-body massage in lieu of a 5-day church/temple/meditation retreat. If you are using a bad habit to get you through these times and provide some self-nurturing, Emergency Abundance advocates a harm-reduction strategy in which you indulge but limit the damage as in smoking 10 cigarettes a day instead of 30 or eating a 600-calorie binge of delicious self-soothing junk food rather than a 3,000-calorie hit. Of course, Emergency Abundance assumes that you won't let the bad times last forever and that once things calm down in several months or even a year in a difficult marriage or job, and so on, you will pursue a program of real Inner Abundance with no corners cut and with unhealthy habits challenged, managed, controlled, or eradicated.

Intellectual Masturbation Priniciple

This is a corollary to the Overthinking Rule. The Intellectual Masturbation Principle says that after people have carefully considered the "big questions" about the meaning of life and the existence of God, they should try to come to some resolution and get on with their lives. It is possible to get so caught up and mired in these questions that we get stuck in life. People can become guilty, confused, and down on themselves for not getting clear-cut answers to the Big Questions. In the meantime, they neglect their immediate needs and personal life goals and wants. When confused encourage clients to ask themselves the following questions: "What do I want? How am I going to get it?"

▶ It's Up to You (See Happiness Is a Choice Principle)

Judge Not, You Don't Know Principle

No one knows all of the pressures, problems, hurts, and health problems—both general medical and mental health—that make people do what they do. This principle says individuals should avoid judging other people since they are not privy to all of those people's reasons for various behaviors. People will be happier with themselves and more popular with others if they avoid being judgmental. People do not like being judged and criticized. For this reason, it is best to refrain from criticizing others in casual social relationships and to limit this to rare and special problem-solving discussion times with close friends and lovers.

Hypercriticalness born of perfectionism and ignorance of others' pain and difficult backgrounds makes people crazy and miserable. Demanding perfection in ourselves and others is a well-documented source of misery in both spiritual traditions and in the mental health professions and academic disciplines (Burns, 1999; Kornfield, 2001). Often when people judge others and even themselves, they do not know why an act of stupidity or cruelty was committed. As Mother Teresa said, it is better to forgive endlessly and move on.

Keep Busy with Flows or Happiness Takes Effort Principle

Katherine Hepburn said that staying busy was a key to her happiness in later years and research supports this as an avenue to contentment, especially when people are busy with activities that demand their close attention and from which they enjoy or feel a sense of accomplishment. Thus, keeping a clean home can be satisfying in a different way than having a meal with a friend. Engaging activities in which we participate—not passive activities like watching TV—and in which we lose track of time are called flows; flow activities should also be challenging—but not overwhelming—and require some skill to do effectively as in gardening or making conversation, according to Mihaly Csik-szentmihalyi, the seminal researcher in this area (see Csikszentmihalyi & Hunter, 2003; for his current theory and methodology as applied to the study of adolescents). This key to happiness says that people must make efforts to be happy; the pure pleasure routes of food and sex and passive entertainment like channel surfing on the TV will not lead to lasting happiness. Often people jump for the Easy Chair Passive Alternative when looking for something to do because it takes little effort. But it doesn't have to take a lot of energy to start a flow activity like taking out some paper and markers to draw or looking up a phone number to call a friend (Lyubomirsky, Sheldon, et al., in press; Seligman, 2002; Tatarkiewicz, 1976).

Keeping Up with the Joneses Principle

Very happy people do their own thing without comparing themselves to others or second guessing their decisions (see Cocoon It Rule).

Kill Them with Kindness or Love Bomb Principle

Margaret Sanger called it "love bombing," when cultists would shower a person with love, kindness, and attention in order to get them to visit and join a cult like the Moonies. QOLT redefines this as sincerely—and without hidden manipulation of any kind—showering others with everyday acts of kindness and consideration, not to mention a positive attitude and smile, in order to build a positive working or loving relationship (see Favor Bank Tenet). It can also be practiced in the course of asking a favor if people are up front about it, such as when a partner love bombs her spouse before asking the partner to watch the children for a week while she goes to a spiritual retreat, a mountain climbing trip, or a dog agility competition.

Kiss the Past Goodbye Principle

Encourage clients to wrestle any lessons from painful past experiences that can help them live happier today. Encourage them to try to understand where they came from and their personal history, but tell them to move on once they have learned what they can. People need to make the most of now and the future rather than focusing on the past. If they have been wronged, they should put it on the shelf, get over it or risk wasting their lives as a professional victim, full of hate but empty of fun, love, or real accomplishments. If they've made mistakes they should acknowledge them, learn from them and try to do better, and try to make amends to the people they've hurt, and then get on with their lives. They should stop reenacting troubled past relationships in current relationships. Too often people treat current friends and family as if they were the uncaring, unreasonable, or abusive people of their past. They should stop coping with stress and relating to others as they did in the past; what worked in the past often makes things worse in the new situation.

Leisurely Pace and Lifestyle Principle

Many great sages and philosophers became wise after leaving the stress and hub-bub of busy jobs in crowded places. According to legend, Lao Tse left a government bureaucratic job to live as a hermit in nature. Seneca composed his wisdom of Stoicism after becoming wealthy and financially secure. Their most happy and contented times with the greatest wisdom, corresponded to times with less outside responsibilities. To the extent that people's jobs and family responsibilities are less onerous, the more happy and content they may be. That is, living simply as the Buddhists recommend, in a not too crowded area with a workload that is manageable and that can be done at a leisurely or at least sane pace may be an important way to be happier.

Life Satisfaction Breeds Job/Work Satisfaction

Life satisfaction, as measured by the QOLI and as targeted for intervention in QOLT, predicts job satisfaction and productivity as much as 5 years in advance (see Diener et al., 1999, for review). This means that being happy overall in every area of life that a person cares about can spill over into personal happiness and effectiveness at work. Of course, work satisfaction or dissatisfaction can spill over, too, coloring happiness in other areas of life like family for good or ill.

Li Po or Commune with Nature Rule

You ask me,
Why I live here
In the mountains
Green as jade.

I laugh,
And give no answer.
But within my heart
Is peace.
Indeed
I have hidden in my breast
A paradise
Unknown to worldly men.

The petals of the peach
Fall from the bough
And float in silence
Down the stream.
—Li Po (A.D. 699–762)

As the Chinese poet, Li Po, suggests, living in an area with close access to nature and to natural beauty that is not too crowded may make a huge difference in quality of life and happiness. Many research findings also support the view that pleasant and safe and even beautiful, natural surroundings are related to life satisfaction and happiness. If an individual cannot live or work in such natural surroundings, encourage that person to try to recreate or vacation in such places to see if it makes a difference to quality of life. According to various researchers, noise and overcrowding are irritants that we may never get used to or adapt to; the only way to eliminate them is to move.

Live Your Dream or 24/7 Principle

Individuals should find something they really care about and do it. Putting all of one's energy and all of one's time—"24 hours a day, 7 days a week"—into activities that move one closer to his or her dreams and shunning the things that get in the way a person can achieve boundless happiness and contentment.

Love and Work Principle

It is important to be agreeable and conscientious in love and work to increase one's success, which then will register as increased happiness in these areas and increased happiness overall. Agreeableness includes being friendly, patient, and kind (see String of Pearls Principle). Nothing is more important than good and pleasant relationships at work since problems in this area are much more dangerous to losing one's job than are problems in technical competence.

▶ **LOVE BOMB PRINCIPLE (SEE KILL THEM WITH KINDNESS PRINCIPLE)**

Love Many Things Principle

Having a wide range of interests, particularly interests outside of work, makes for a well-rounded and happy person. Some outside interests and hobbies are essential to help people recharge their batteries and maintain their enthusiasm for life. The great philosopher, Bertrand Russell, in *The Conquest of Happiness* said, "Contented folks have a lot more shakin' than the dullards among us." Many things interest them so that when free time comes up, the question is not "what can I do?" but "which of my many hobbies, interests, or relationships can I pursue?"

Love What You Do Principle

According to Dave Myers, happiness is loving what you do. Individuals should find a job, pastimes, and avocations that they really love not necessarily what pays the best. They will be much happier than many people who hate their work, fret about it all the time, and are never satisfied. Of course, everyone needs enough money to pay the bills and live in a safe neighborhood, but individuals who can combine both are a real success in the happiness and contentment department.

▶ **LOVE WHERE YOU ARE PRINCIPLE (SEE TANGLED WEB PRINCIPLE)**

▶ **LOWER EXPECTATIONS PRINCIPLE (SEE NEVER GOOD ENOUGH PRINCIPLE)**

"Mad Col." Disease Rule

This principle is a riff on Mad Cow Disease, a great way to become permanently brain damaged and disabled. Col. stands for colleagues or managers at work who are often angry and bullying. Similar to the Stress Carrier Rule, this principle admonishes people to treat angry, sometimes bullying colleagues or managers with kid gloves, that is, very carefully and cautiously, avoiding them when possible. When they must interact with these folks, QOLT urges a "just the facts, Ma'am" approach in which individuals attend to the details or specifics of their colleagues' comments or criticisms while ignoring their angry tone or manner. Rather than venting at work, seek our friends and family to discuss frustration. Consider a change of employment if the situation becomes intolerable or health suffers.

Make Friends at Work Principle

Whether to network with others that help with one's job or whether to make a friend to share a hobby with, it helps to have friends at work. Then, work is not just about the paycheck. Instead, clients can say, "I'm going to work to see my friends."

▶ **MAKE IT ROUTINE PRINCIPLE (SEE ROUTINE IS EVERYTHING PRINCIPLE)**

Manage Your Time and Your Life Rule

A contented life requires organization to get the things done that need to be done each day. It also helps to have uncluttered living space. The Daily Activity Plan used in cognitive therapy is a godsend to anyone who lacks time management and life management skills.

Marching Orders Principle

What may be unique to the QOLT approach to time management is that QOLT tries to make a connection in how people order their daily routines and overarching life goals. To paraphrase the saying "Put your money where your mouth is," clients are told, "Put your time and effort where your values are. Enshrine your personal goals and related activities in your schedule for each day so that your acts follow your Goals-and-Values." Such a schedule constitutes their "marching orders" for the day. The Happiness Pie (see the Toolbox CD), forces clients to visualize their goals and can assist in the process of sculpting days that fit their innermost values and personal goals (also see Find a Meaning/Find a Goal Principle).

Meanings Like Buses Rule

Some parents console their kids who have been jilted by saying, "Don't worry, men/women are like buses, there is always another one coming around the corner." This is especially true for meanings and flows. One engaging activity or flow can be found to substitute for another in a world of almost infinite hobbies, pastimes, and jobs. The same may be said for meanings or life goals. When disappointed with one avenue of flow or meaning as in a difficult job or marriage, we can find other flows and meanings to look forward to and to soften the blow, if we but believe that other avenues exist for us—optimism—and make the effort to explore the avenues as in trying out these Tenets of Contentment in QOLT. The happiness literature is replete with accounts of many who have survived tragedy or even the loss of loved ones or limbs in terrible accidents, regaining their pre-tragedy level of happiness in most cases. (Widowhood and hugely disabling injuries may be tragedies from which we never fully recover.)

Men Are Just Desserts (and Women Are Just Desserts) Principle

As Erik Erikson, the father of developmental psychology said, people need a solid identity and interests and the ability to love and nurture themselves like a loving parent, along with the ability to manage their lives and moods, *before* they enter into a committed love relationship. This doesn't mean people have to be perfect. But it is better to be somebody in our own right than to marry somebody in order to take on their identity as our own. In this vein, people should enjoy relationships as something extra like a dessert after the main meal of personal success, identity, and self-esteem. They need to learn to love and care for themselves first, before seeking others to love.

Mental Health Day or Hour

When particularly hard pressed, overwhelmed or upset, it may be necessary for clients to take the day off from work or from other responsibilities in order to get their bearings, recharge their batteries, and luxuriate in some Inner Abundance and Quality Time (see Tenets). This is especially helpful with big decisions. The more relaxed and centered people are, the better they can think about long-term consequences. It can help tremendously to get out of the house as when clients stay in a hotel for a day or two with no daily responsibilities—at home or in a nearby city, visit a close friend out of town, take a day trip, go to a spa, or attend a retreat of some kind. As a continuation treatment/intervention strategy this can be done every 3 to 6 months to prevent relapse into unhealthy old habits or an episode of unhappiness.

▶ MINDSET OF CONSTANT GRATITUDE AND ACTS OF KINDNESS PRINCIPLE (SEE FAVOR BANK PRINCIPLE)

Mine the Moment or Attack the Moment Principle

All that exists is the present moment since the past is over and the future is not yet here. No matter what people are doing, they can experience joy, surprise, fulfillment, or least a feeling of accomplishment as they handle things with grace or class no matter what the situation is. It is a matter of "mining" the moment. Think of the metaphor of a gold mine. People may have to dig, and struggle, and search, but if they put themselves in a situation that likely has some "gold" or possible fulfillment around, they will eventually find it. This is the attitude to take every moment. Encourage clients to try to search or uncover potential meaning or fulfillment in whatever they are doing, and stop bemoaning the past or anticipating the future. Often this means finding enjoyment and fulfillment in everyday tasks. Suggest that clients "mine" or explore their current life situation for what it has to offer. They should look for any potential riches or fulfillment instead of assuming it's barren or "lusting" after potential riches and fulfillment somewhere else. Each moment quickly dies, and cannot be experienced again. This is it! The time to live fully is now. Attack the Moment is for people who worry about things such that their head is always in the past or future instead of the present. Here the encouragement is to focus hard on the sensations of the moment, such as the sights and sounds of the situation, feelings and body sensations, and even breathing (see Mindful Breathing and Guide for Worry Warts in the Toolbox CD for more tools in this regard).

Modest Goal Principle

For all activities, encourage clients to set a goal that is challenging but not overwhelming. This will allow them to achieve the contented state of consciousness called "flow" in which they are so focused on the activity that they are doing that they lose awareness of themselves, their problems, and time. Setting modest goals also ensures a sense of satisfaction at the end of each day since people usually achieve the modest goals they set for themselves. Depressed people tend to be especially poor at setting modest goals and pacing themselves throughout the day.

Multiple Personality or Multiple Personality of Everyday Life Principle (See also FOOBS Principle)

Many of the dysfunctional, unhealthy, and self-defeating thoughts, feelings and behaviors people have come from families of origin. These instinctive patterns often surface when people are under stress or encounter a situation similar to ones in the past.

The Multiple Personality Principle says that people can view their different strong emotional states as parts or even subpersonalities of themselves as though they have multiple personalities (see FOOBS Principle).

Mutual Aid Society Principle

Close friendships and love relationships are not volunteer work or one-way affairs in which one partner gives and the other does not. Unlike their families, people pick their friends; thus, they should be careful to pick ones who are emotionally healthy (not perfect, but healthy enough to want to and to be able to give love and support as well as receive it). These refueling relationships are crucial to basic well-being and happiness and should be reciprocal Mutual Aid Societies, in which people get what they give (or at least close to what they give). These core relationships should be relationships of strong equals, relationships of mutual support and caring. They are keys to Inner Abundance and self-care. Once these foundational needs have been met people can reach out and help those less fortunate through Helping activities (see Role Model Friends Principle).

Never Good Enough or Lower Expectations Principle

According to legions of cognitive therapists and spiritual teachers/disciplines, perfectionism, like anger, is one of the greatest enemies of happiness and contentment. We live in an imperfect world and universe. To the extent that people can extend loving kindness, compassion, and acceptance to themselves and to the other people in their lives, they will feel happy and contented. It all starts with self-compassion or forgiveness for foibles or peccadilloes. Ram Dass said, "Expect nothing. Appreciate everything. Be here now." as his prescription for living, capturing the essence of this principle.

No Conditions of Worth Rule

The great humanistic psychologist, and son of a minister, Carl Rogers, theorized that people disown and grow to fear and hate those parts of themselves that their parents reviled. That is, to win their parents' love and approval, they had to disown their shadow sides of fear, anger, sexual feelings, sadness, and the like. In order to reclaim their right to self-esteem, individuals can reject these Conditions of Worth and openly embrace, accept, and explore all parts of or facets of themselves, each of which has served them in some way either in their family of origin or even now. In the spirit of the "Nothing Human Disgusts Me" Tenet, people can accept all parts of themselves, never abandoning their right to full acceptance and forgiveness for whatever they have done given their limited awareness and understanding.

No Gossip/Criticism/Suggestions or Words as Daggers Rule

This principle recognizes the power of words, insults, and compliments to deeply hurt or help. To avoid hurting coworkers it is a good rule of thumb to refrain from gossiping or saying anything negative about people not present during a conversation, criticizing, insulting, judging, and even making task-oriented work-related suggestions during difficult times or all of the time when dealing with difficult people who are easily hurt and possibly vindictive. This avoids the inevitable cycle of retaliation and escalation. A corollary to this rule is to refrain from making close friends in your immediate work group. For many, this principle may be too difficult or extreme to put into practice except in emergency situations in which the atmosphere at work is very tense and interpersonal relationships are very strained.

No Mayo, Pickles, or Mustard Rule

People need to know the particular hopes, dreams, likes, and dislikes of their close friends, partners, and children if they expect to receive the huge happiness boost from harmonious relationships.

Nothing Human Disgusts Me or Acceptance Priniciple

As intolerance and judgmental attitudes without all of the facts are the mothers of misery, hate, and alienation, this principle suggests that people suspend judgment and accept reality for what it is (while remaining optimistic that things will turn out for the better in the end). It also suggests that people try to empathize with others and understand the reasons for their actions, instead of or before, making a judgment. A character in Tennessee Williams' play, *Night of the Iguana* says "Nothing human disgusts me." Although provocative and not literally true for most people, the sentiment points the way toward acceptance of others; of course, this acceptance does not mean that people should condone acts of cruelty or abuse, only that they not shrink from accepting the problems that exist.

▶ ORGAN RECITAL RULE (SEE SILENCE IS GOLDEN RULE)

OTAAT or One-Thing-at-a-Time Principle

Encourage clients to do one thing at a time with their utmost concentration, effectively tuning out other distractions such as worries about the future, and regrets about the past. By planning their day ahead of time based on cherished lifetime goals, clients can go about their business one small step at a time with full concentration and awareness. Any major task, like writing a book or making a friend, consists of thousands of tiny tasks that must be attended to one at a time, in order to get to the final end product. Break things down into tiny "pieces," worrying only about one piece of the "puzzle" at a time (see Baby Steps to Success technique).

Overthinking Principle

Professors love to tell their students that the unexamined life is not worth living. Consider the Zen ideal of in-the-moment living, being one with washing the dishes, making love, or performing heart surgery. Conscious Thinking is not a big part of the picture. In Zen, people strive to think less and happy people do this it turns out. In fact, it has been suggested that people think consciously only when a problem comes up. Being mindfully in the moment means not thinking as much as possible. Losing oneself in an activity means stopping the hateful barrage of self-talk people hurl at themselves. Happy people have more of a contented cow or coiled to strike lion mien since they are not obsessive ruminators. For the record, no one is always happy. Happy folks worry and stress about problems just like unhappy people. However, happy people spend less time worrying about problems. Mihaly Csikszentmihalyi (personal communication, Positive Psychology listserv, August 8, 2000) discusses the lack of deep reflection, worry, or rumination in happy people whom he speculates are in a flow state of consciousness oftentimes. People who struggle with intruding worries can benefit from the skills in Guide for Worry Warts and Mindful Breathing.

Parent-Teacher Support Principle

Having good, supportive parents and teachers are major predictors of happiness in children and youth (see, e.g., Suldo & Huebner, 2005). Uninvested and neglectful teachers, along with a few psychonoxious teachers, are the bane of children's existence according to the latest research. This can mean changing schools and even living arrangements after other efforts to improve the situation have failed, including efforts at remediating contributions that youths may make to the poor relationship.

The PCD Time for Couples Rule

PCD Time involves three important regular activities to maintain the relationship:

1. One hour of regularly scheduled joint **P**roblem-solving time each week, using *Five Paths* or just talking about disagreements or problems.
2. 20 minutes of uninterrupted **C**heck-in time each evening without being too upset about outside stressors. During check-in time, people should ask their partners if they want problem-solving advice about problems they bring up from their day or if they just want someone to listen. The latter is also called sympathy without problem solving or compassionate listening in QOLT.
3. One **D**ate per week or month, including Cheap Dates like a McDate to McDonalds for dinner or walk around the block or in a park.

▶ PERSONALITY STAYS THE SAME (SEE HAPPINESS SET POINT PRINCIPLE)

▶ PERSONAL WISDOM PRINCIPLE (SEE BE YOUR OWN GURU PRINCIPLE)

Physical Activity or Take Your Medication Principle

Nothing comes close to regular physical activity, not necessarily exercise as a fountain of youth and happiness (via emotional control of negative feelings). It can delay or minimize the physical and mental deterioration seen in aging until the age of 70 (Myers, 2004). Cardiac psychologist Jim Blumenthal and others have also found that its antidepressant effects may rival that of SSRIs like Prozac and Zoloft in late adulthood volunteers; thirty minutes of aerobic exercise three times a week seems to do the trick and exercising with others may help. Others have argued for its anxiolytic, that is anti-anxiety and anti-anger, effects. Physical activity is simply one, if not the most important, thing that individuals can do for their physical and mental health. For those clients who struggle with their weight and hate exercise and weight loss schemes, remember to tell them that this Tenet is not about losing weight or trying to look better: It is about feeling better and getting psychologically healthier. QOLT encourages a *daily* habit physical activity—especially activity that increases your heart rate—in the same way that people brush their teeth each day, so that the question becomes not will I exercise today? but *when* will I exercise today? Before beginning any program of physical activity, clients should consult with their physicians.

Pick a Role Model for a Friend Principle

Encourage clients to keep core relationships reciprocal and choose friends or lovers whom they look up to with qualities that they aspire to. As the Jewish and Christian Bible says, Walk with the wise and you will become wise (Proverbs 13:20).

Pick Your Battles/Pick No Battles Principle or Yes, Boss/Yes, Dear Rule

Work relationships like love relationships are about compromise. Interpersonal problems more often than technical competence are the issue when clients lose

their jobs or have problems at work. Couples therapists frequently have clients draw a circle within a circle on a piece of paper as shown in Figure 9.2.

The inner circle symbolizes issues that one partner cannot compromise on like adultery. The outer circle symbolizes the myriad issues that are not crucial deal breakers in a committed relationship like leaving the toilet seat up or down in the bathroom. QOLT urges people to apply this concept to the work setting and to be open to the influence of coworkers and managers to the point that their inner circle is minuscule, that is there is very little about which they feel rigid or uncompromising. It is best to learn to say, Yes, Boss or Yes, Friend to a coworker, or yes to all reasonable requests and preferences of coworkers and bosses since this honors their autonomy, makes them feel free and thankful, and increases the chances that they will say "Yes" to the client on deal-breaker work issues. It is an excellent idea to have this diagram handy or to draw a new one whenever problems are discussed in a work group as it reminds coworkers and administrators that many issues are simply not worth fighting over.

In a Taoist sense, it also makes sense that people pick their battles carefully and conserve their energy and peace of mind, choosing only those battles that are very important at a time when they have the strength and energy to pursue them fully. Taoism recommends that people stand aside and let others bloody themselves in fights with their enemies rather than taking

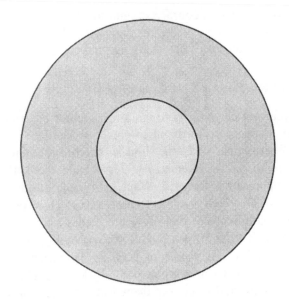

Figure 9.2 Pick Your Battles/Pick No Battles principle.

them on themselves. This principle asks people to consider the long-term costs of battle as fights can go on forever and can engender destructive retaliation that they may not consider. For example, in many work situations it is better to go along with the group instead of fighting for something that could engender long-term retaliation or hurt feelings. Because of the volatile political alliances at work, it is best whenever possible to avoid conflict completely, by cultivating your garden as Voltaire recommends instead of being distracted by and even hurt by lengthy office politics and their fallout. Political alliances can shift in a heartbeat leaving clients alone and vulnerable when they decide to take on an adversary at work. When it comes to one's livelihood, the pleasantness of the day-to-day work environment, and one's paycheck, survival may be much more important than being right.

Pick Your Friends Principle

Encourage clients to choose friends they respect and admire who have qualities they seek to develop. Encourage them to avoid people who have qualities that bring them down, bring out the worst in them, or prevent them from reaching their potential. Friends who share their Goals-and-Values will support them in acting in accord with these Goals-and-Values.

Play It Safe Principle

In work or play, encourage clients to play it safe by finding some simple, safe, innocuous, and legal pleasures, flows (activities that challenge and engage them).

Play Like a Kid or Frivolous Flow Principle

A 5-year-old plays for hours in a refrigerator box that is now a spaceship to the alien planet of Mordor. The poet Wordsworth said "the child is father to the man" in *Intimations on Immortality*. Jesus bade the little children to come forward. What can young children teach us? They can teach us to have a blast as we play unself-consciously at frivolous, fun games and flows (see Flow It) that are not productive work and that, in no way, add to our wealth or prestige. To paraphrase the Bible, unless you can play like a little child who is full of the joy and wonder of the world, who has a blast at pure fun activities with no merit, and who is blissfully unaware of how they are being judged, you will

not enter the kingdom of happiness here on earth. A key to Aging Well, is to pursue fun and games even as society sneers at us as over the hill (Vaillant, 2002). QOLT holds that this is important our whole lives as we search for and find recreation, play, and flow activities that give us joy by engaging us totally and using all of our skills even as it does nothing for our reputation or pocketbooks. Can you talk baby talk to your dog or cat as you play with them or train them for agility competitions? Can you color or paint shamelessly like you did as a child or sing at the top of your lungs or dance without lessons or putter around in your garden or read a trashy novel or play computer games just because they are fun, engaging flows that are intrinsically satisfying? Explore frivolous fun activities and flows throughout your life as you allow some time for yourself to simply play; limiting ourselves to productive hobbies or work, cuts us off from myriad sources of joy that this life offers. (See Chapter 10 and 12 for ways to cope with naysaying or killjoy thoughts about pure play.)

Pocket of Time to Relax Principle

People shouldn't wait for vacations. Rather, they should grab, steal, and enjoy brief pockets of time whether it be 5 to 30 minutes to take a walk, read a book, or call their partner to say hi. Intervals of pure play and relaxation are essential to happiness and contentment. No one can keep up a nonstop frenzied pace day in and day out.

Positive Addiction Principle

People will often turn to addictive behaviors like using drugs, overeating, or overspending on shopping sprees because of the immediate payoff or reward they get in feeling good. Instead, encourage clients to learn to "look down the road" at the negative consequences of addictions. QOLT teaches that there are at least 16 different areas of life or avenues of fulfillment that people can turn to instead of addictive behaviors. Encourage clients to find the gratification, fun, flow, thrills, and the love that they need in one of these areas. Also, encourage them to find a nonaddictive Relaxation Ritual to calm themselves down when stressed. They should also make a plan to avoid or cope with the specific triggers, situations, feelings, and decisions that lead to addictive behavior. A Frivolous Flow (see Tenet) can make a great positive addiction that perhaps most if not all of us need to be happy.

PRF Principle

This prescription for depression is based on research showing that everyone needs time with people, time to rest and relax, and time for fun each day to keep their spirits up. Socializing with others is a powerful antidote to depression. Depressed people are poor at pacing themselves and often do not provide times for relaxation and fun in their daily routine.

Process Goal Principle

This principle suggests that people attend to the process of their efforts to achieve goals and not the outcome in order to maximize happiness. This frees people to engage in here-and-now living and to enjoy here-and-now satisfactions, as opposed to some "pie in the sky" payoff when their work is complete. Since we often cannot control outcomes, the idea here is to focus on the process of goal-striving and to "pat themselves on the back" for taking the necessary steps needed to move toward the goal, whether the goal is ultimately reached or not. For example, people can congratulate themselves for studying an hour a day for a class instead of always worrying about their grade. One way to moderate or soften tough goals and standards is to set "process" goals or standards that are within clients' control rather than "outcome" goals or standards in particular areas of life. For example, a client set a "process goal" of studying for two hours a day, rather than an outcome goal of getting a B in a difficult organic chemistry class. At the end of the two hours, he felt a real sense of accomplishment for achieving his goal. This was much more fulfilling and stabilizing for him than when he pressured himself to get a B on a test.

Quality Time Principle

This is time alone (5 to 30 minutes) in a quiet place with no distractions to relax; get centered; get in touch with feelings, goals, and values; plan your day; and make a plan to solve or manage personal problems. Daily Quality Time helps you increase and plan your progress in QOLT. It is a great way to foster Inner Abundance.

It helps for Quality Time to start off with a Relaxation Ritual—there are two in the Toolbox CD—to calm you down and to make you deeply aware of personal thoughts, feelings, worries, or anything that is bothering you (see Thou Shalt Be Aware or Psychephobia Tenet). This is also a time to get in touch with the key overarching goals in your life and to do QOLT reading and exercises such as a Lie Detector and Stress Diary or Five Paths to get a handle on a problem. Since QOLT is a support for you to use when you feel like you can, don't get down on yourself for missing some Quality Time. That is, don't let Quality Time and QOLT become another burden for you to shoulder in your life. When you can, try to see Quality Time as a necessary and enjoyable part of your day. Make it fun or luxurious somehow as when you start it with a hot bath. Rather than being selfish, this basic kind of self-caring can give you more energy and love to give to others. Still and all, Quality Time is not time spent with other people because it is time devoted to your relationship with yourself. To prevent relapses or to prevent little problems from getting bigger, carve out some Emergency Quality Time when you see an Early Warning Sign of stress as on your Personal Stress Profile—or PSP from the Toolbox CD.

The Question Rule

Ruminations about the past or future can be short-circuited with the question, "What do I want and how am I going to get it, today, this week, this month, this lifetime?" This question can orient people to the present and what must be done today to take care of their responsibilities and to begin to move forward toward achieving their lifetime goals while being true to their basic Goals-and-Values.

▶ **REASONED PASSION PRINCIPLE (SEE SELECTIVE HEDONISM PRINCIPLE)**

▶ **RELATIONSHIP IMMERSION PRINCIPLE (SEE BE WITH PEOPLE PRINCIPLE)**

Relationship with Self or Self-Compassion Principle

People's ability to accept and care for themselves, that is to Self-Tend, is central to Inner Abundance, to the ability to help others, and to the ability to function successfully in valued roles and areas of life. People will only self-tend if they have a positive view of themselves. People must cultivate a positive, accepting, forgiving, and nonperfectionist relationship with themselves as a prerequisite for self-tending and caring for others. QOLT advocates for an attitude of deep compassion toward oneself; that is, people should forgive themselves for faults and mistakes, learn from them, and move on. Self-compassion is expressed in the attitude that a loving parent would have toward a beloved child. QOLT suggests that people take this loving parent role and attitude toward themselves and others (see How Kind Principle) even in cases and especially in cases, in which they did not have a loving parent figure like this as children (see Self-Acceptance Principle).

Ride It Out, Read It Out Principle

When they are upset, encourage clients to find a quiet place and time to review the Tenets of Contentment for 30 minutes to an hour. All things must pass, including upsetting mood states, for most people.

▶ Role Model Principle (See What Would My Role Model Do Principle)

Romantic Friendship or Take the Sex Out of Marriage Rule

QOLT assumes that long-term committed love relationships depend first and foremost on a deep friendship in which partners are essentially best friends who work hard at the relationship as if it were paid employment, and who compromise and forgive endlessly to borrow a phrase from Mother Teresa. People should strive to be the exception to the old lament, "I've Never Heard of Lovers Who Could Be Best Friends." QOLT maintains that sex in successful committed relationships is a symptom or expression of what the relationship is like outside of the bedroom, hence, couples therapists' interest in the last time a couple has made love. If it has been 6 to 12 months, the couple may already be "psychologically divorced."

Routine Is Everything or Make It a Routine Principle

When it comes to any self-change or self-improvement effort, routine is everything. If it becomes as automatic as brushing one's teeth before going to bed, chances are, the habit will stay whether it is physical activity, a

spiritual practice, calling a friend, or reading a book (see Happiness Habits Principle).

▶ Routines Rule Rule (See Habits Rule Rule)

Second Opinion Principle or Technique

In the normal give and take of friendship, it is appropriate to seek advice from trusted friends on vexing problems at home or work. At times, people may only want a sympathetic ear. At other times, specific advice can help. People prefer to ask friends questions within their area of expertise. Even with this caveat, of course, people may receive bad advice or advice that does not work and even makes things worse. Thus, clients must always weigh the consequences of actions, especially social actions, to see if they are willing to accept the potential negative consequences (see Take-a-Letter technique). Friends can also help with cognitive restructuring (CASIO strategies or thought records) as clients try to make sense of a loss in a positive way as in the friend who encouraged her gal pal to use a firing as a springboard to a new career more to her liking and aptitudes.

Because none of us is graced with immaculate perception and because we can be quite clueless about our role in creating relationship problems, the Second Opinion technique in which we get counsel about what is happening in a relationship dispute and how to deal with it is highly recommended in QOLT. Where possible, it is best to consult a relationship expert, someone adroit at handling these situations who also has your interests at heart and can keep a secret. Friends, loved ones, and therapists can often serve this role. Friends and loved ones who really know you and perhaps the history of the conflict are especially useful. Additionally, Second Opinions are usually essential in doing any cognitive work or cognitive restructuring as in the Lie Detector and Stress Diary exercises. It is easy for people to get stuck in coming up with powerful new attitudes to move them out of a rut in living or in thinking. Similarly, Second Opinion can be invaluable in considering specific CASIO changes.

See a Psychiatrist Principle

Go beyond the herbal remedies and nutritional supplements. If a client needs help with stress, anxiety or depression, encourage him to get pure pharmaceuticals from the best dealer around: psychiatrists. Psychiatric or psychotropic medication is hugely beneficial for many maladies that hurt QOL. Clients are not weak, soon-to-be drug addicts for exploring better living through chemistry. They are merely smart, educated consumers.

Selective Hedonism or Reasoned Passion Principle

This principle suggests that people pursue a few pleasures or goals that are reasonably within their grasp in life and forsake those that are clearly impossible or self-destructive. To do this, people must let their reason temper their passion and emotions so that they never get too "crazy" or self-destructive in pursuing the pleasures or meanings most important to them.

Self-Acceptance Principle

To be truly happy or content, we must see ourselves as basic miracles worthy of love. This requires active and constant consciousness and commitment as clients concretely show self-love, self-kindness, and self-forgiveness for all mistakes in the present moment and the past. People with low self-esteem, must do this moment to moment, day and night, for it to work, even as they hear in the background noise of their minds what a jerk or loser they are (see Mindful Breathing and FOOBS Principle). The Dalai Lama heartily laughs when he screws up or makes a mistake, "Ah, ha! I'm a fallible human as we all are." Clients can cultivate the same habit. Everyone needs to forgive themselves and each other endlessly to live together said Mother Teresa (1983).

People are basically good, decent, and deserving of happiness just because they are alive. The principle also assumes that people are not the product of their actions. Actions are what the "self," does to meet its goals given its limited abilities and awareness. When people do hurtful and destructive things to others, it is usually because they lack the necessary relationship skills to communicate more effectively or they are unaware of how hurtful their actions are. Although people do many good, bad, ugly, and neutral things, they should never, and cannot meaningfully, make an overall judgment of self-worth based on any of these acts. So while people may criticize themselves for a particular act they

should never confuse their "self" with the act. That is, hate the act without hating oneself. Bad or imperfect acts don't make a bad or inadequate person (overgeneralization), any more than the hundreds of good and neutral acts make a good or neutral person. If they always do their best, it is unfair and irrational for clients to blame and hate themselves for mistakes that they make.

In practical terms, following this Tenet means that clients accept themselves as good and decent no matter how they behave. They forgive themselves because of the knowledge that they, or their "self," do not equal their actions. They also forgive themselves because they accept that they always try to do their best, given their limited skills and awareness.

How people relate to themselves is just as important as how they relate to other people. Research clearly shows that people who are basically satisfied and accepting of themselves are much happier. The principle of self-acceptance suggests that people never give up on themselves and strive to become their own greatest fan, comforter, and friend. A big part of loving, accepting, or liking oneself is to accept the bad things that one does. "Warts and all," oneself is still the most important person in one's life and is worthy of basic respect as much as any other living thing. A person may choose to try to change a behavior and try to correct mistakes, but this doesn't mean the person has to earn approval or worth as a person. Self-acceptance does not mean self complacency, narcissism, or self-ishness. While not condemning oneself for wrong, bad, or hurtful acts, the person can still admit these and try to change the behavior. Healthy self-acceptance makes people more giving to others; selfish people usually feel deprived and "greedy" precisely because they lack self-acceptance and esteem, not because they have too much self-respect.

▶ SELF-COMPASSION PRINCIPLE (SEE RELATIONSHIP WITH SELF PRINCIPLE)

▶ SELF-OTHER PRINCIPLE (SEE GIVING TREE PRINCIPLE)

Sensate Focus/Savor or Vary Your Pleasures to Avoid Adaptation Tenet

Although not true for all tragedies and windfalls, people tend to quickly adapt or habituate to life conditions and circumstances so that the good ones do not feel so good and so that the bad ones do not feel so bad with time, perhaps as little as a year for major events such as winning the lottery or being seriously injured in a car crash (Brickman & Campbell, 1971; Brickman, Coates, & Janoff-Bulman, 1978; Lucas et al., 2003; Lyubormirsky, Sheldon, et al. in press). These authors review additional evidence of adaptation and cleverly describe adaptation as akin to trying to ride up on a down escalator, no matter how hard people try to go up, the escalator tries to bring them down to their happiness set point or range. That is, emotions dampen or lessen in response to good and bad life events and return to a positive rather than a neutral baseline at or near the middle of one's genetically determined happiness range or set point (Headey & Wearing, 1992; Lyubormirsky, Sheldon, et al., in press). For this reason, it is good to consciously savor or luxuriate in one's favorite pleasures even to the point of going very slow and giving a play by play of appreciation and joy (as in chewing desserts very slowly and talking to oneself about how great it looks/feels/tastes) since such pleasures lose their kick or high if repeatedly indulged in a short time. Similarly people can vary their favorite pleasures or space them out over time, so that they do not lose their power to excite and gratify. Such savoring is a treatment technique in highly regarded and empirically supported cognitive behavior therapies for obesity and bulimia (Brownell, 2000). Mindfully savoring involves single-minded concentration on the pleasure as well as full attention to how the pleasure affects our senses. Thus, people can luxuriate in the smell, texture, taste, and creamy brown color of chocolate just as they would try to be aware of all of their senses in a quiet place with no distractions while making love. In fact, savoring pleasures and enjoyable activities can be likened to Masters and Johnson's famous sensate focus exercises for enhancing the pleasure of making love. Additionally, flow activities in which people actively do something challenging that fits their level of skill may be an answer to adaptation or habituation in so far as people never get tired of these types of activities (see Flow It Tenet). Similarly, people never adapt to or get used to (or recover from fully) stimulus events like noise, sexual touching, the death of a loved one, or severe disabilities like quadriplegia from an accident. QOLT maintains that despite adaptation and the set point of happiness, people can control their goals, activities, life circumstances (the **C** in CASIO), focus of attention (see Mindful Breathing), **A**ttitudes in CASIO or thinking, and how they interpret stress, life events, and the good things in their lives.

▶ SERVANT LEADER PRINCIPLE (SEE HUMBLE SERVANT PRINCIPLE)

Serve Others Principle

Helping others day to day and making the world a better place to live can be a satisfying answer to the question of the meaning of life. According to several spiritual traditions, service *by itself* can lead to wisdom, and even enlightenment or nirvana. Serving Others or Helping in QOLT parlance can also be a major key to happiness for the giver. Consider that service has a greater happiness-boost than great food according to positive psychology researchers (Seligman, 2002). Service has also been found to prolong life. According to University of Michigan researchers, older adults who practically help or emotionally support friends, neighbors, or relatives reduce their risk of dying by nearly 60 percent even when the researchers controlled for the health, age, and gender of the helpers. Paid staff versus volunteer distinctions are likely meaningless so long as people see the work as really helping others. As it happens, it may truly be better to give than to receive!

Most spiritual traditions stress service to others, giving those who serve both a life meaning to pursue and an avenue to reduce painful self-consciousness and self-focused attention, which is endemic to a materialist culture in which few measure up to the ideal. Self-consciousness and self-focused attention are also endemic to depression and anxiety problems, making it a relief to focus on helping others, on one's spiritual community, and on one's religious practices instead of the self. The emphasis on service is illustrated from the beginning of the bestseller, *The Purpose Driven Life* (Warren, 2002) in which the author boldly proclaims that meaning in life from a Christian perspective goes way beyond any selfish concerns for self-actualization and the like. Similarly, the Zen master, Joko Beck says that spiritual maturity in Zen is characterized by an increasing focus on the welfare of others (and all sentient beings), and a decreasing concern for self.

▶ SET ASIDE, SHELVE, ACCEPT OR FORGET PRINCIPLE (SEE DON'T FORGIVE PRINCIPLE)

Share the Hurt behind the Anger Tenet

In close friendships and committed love relationships it is helpful to get in touch with, to really feel and to share the hurt behind strong negative emotions such as anger, hate, and contempt. Encourage clients to aim for a soft-disclosure of hurt or disappointment to accompany any strong emotional sharing (Jacobson & Christensen, 1996). Therapists can model this soft-disclosure by repeatedly speculating on the hurt behind the anger as in "Many of us feel hurt and not just angry when criticized by our mate since we really want to be seen as a good husband or wife."

▶ SHIFT OF HATE PRINCIPLE (SEE ANGER IS THE ENEMY PRINCIPLE)

Should-Want Principle

According to addiction specialist, Alan Marlatt, as people plan or sculpt their days, they should always provide a balance between "should" and "want" activities. "Should Activities" are things people feel they must do but don't enjoy. "Want Activities" are things they enjoy doing—they create such a feeling of pleasure or satisfaction that they *want* to do them. People are at high risk for addictive behavior when "Should Activities" dominate. Encourage clients to incorporate some "want" activities into each day's routine.

Silence Is Golden or Organ Recital Rule

Encourage clients to say nothing when they feel rotten or nasty or mean or when they experience a Big Three attack. Encourage them to say nothing while negative feelings and tendencies are holding sway. Feeling bad and even a *DSM* diagnosis is no excuse for bad manners. Of course a few loved ones need to hear when the client feels bad, but even then he or she need not do an Organ Recital of every complaint. Organ Recitals come from people who love to go over every little ache or pain in their body and mind with others.

Socializing Doubles Your Pleasure

Whatever the activity, whether the client is an introvert or an extrovert, being with others seems to boost the enjoyment or satisfaction of an activity.

Stop Second Guessing Principle

Very happy people make a decision and do not second guess it. They get on with their life (see Cocoon It Principle).

Street Signs to Success Principle

To keep up the needed ratio of positive self-talk to negative self-talk to 2 or 3 to 1, encourage clients to write down key phrases or ideas that move them and help them get focused, relaxed, and centered as they go about their day. Clients should display these ideas prominently or keep them close at hand for easy reference.

Strength It Principle

In addition to working on weaknesses or problem areas that could jeopardize or scuttle our happiness, we must remember to also apply our talents and strengths to areas of life that we care about. Ask your client, "What are some big and little things that I am good at and that people like about me right now without any changes in my personality?"

Have them consider any skill, talent, or positive personality trait that they possess. For positive *Traits,* personality characteristics, or "strengths," they may count any of the *Tenets of Contentment* that they follow consistently such as "good Inner Abundance."

Share the following list of strengths with your clients. A copy of the list and this Tenet written in language for clients is available in the Toolbox CD. Tell clients to consider any word or phrase that applies to them as a potential strength—as in I am consistently:

- Friendly and Affirming of Other People
- Kind, Loving, Loyal, Generous, or Sympathetic to Others
- Very Generous and Giving toward Others
- Accepting and Nonjudgmental of Others
- Self-Disciplined and Cautious about What I Say to Avoid Hurting People
- Thoughtful toward Others
- Thoughtful toward the Group or Society (Good Team Player)
- Gentle, Quiet and Respectful of Others
- Ethical, Honest, Fair, Straightforward
- Funny, Humorous, Playful, Fun to Be With
- In Love with Learning New Things

- Modest, Humble, Forgiving
- Able to Fix Things, Mechanically Gifted
- Self-Calming and Emotionally Intelligent in Controlling Feelings of Depression, Anxiety, or Anger (*Good Emotional Control*)
- Optimistic about Life and the Future
- Full of Energy and Enthusiasm
- A "Person on a Mission" in Life, That I Am a Person with Clear-Cut Life Goals-and-Values
- Self-Disciplined in Moving toward Long-Term Goals (Farsighted), Able to Control Self, Make Good Choices, and Steadily Move toward Long-Term Goals
- Self-Disciplined in Work Habits
- Self-Disciplined in Personal Habits Like Weight Control
- Self-Disciplined and Cautious about What I Say to Avoid Hurting People
- Good Self-Control *in General*
- Good Organizer, Well Organized, Very Organized, Conscientious about Getting Things Done
- Hard Working and Reliable, Persistent in Getting Things Done
- Neat and Clean
- Able to Take Good Care of Myself and Keep Myself Healthy—Good Fitness Habits or Inner Abundance
- Good Problem Solver
- Good Common Sense, Good Judgment, Problem Solving and Decision Making in Practical Everyday Matters
- Cautious and Careful
- Creative or Original
- Artistic
- Can Make and Keep Close Friends
- Spiritually Gifted; Spiritually at Peace, Kind, or Forgiving; Spiritually Gifted and In-Tune with What Really Matters in Life; Spiritually-Based Kindness, Patience, Optimism
- Good at Enjoying Life
- Mindful or Able to Focus All of My Attention on the Present Moment Rather Than Worry about the Past or Future—Mindfulness
- Not Obsessed with Fame or Fortune, Not Overly Concerned about Making Money or Achieving Fame
- Lover of Animals
- Lover of Nature
- Lover of Children
- Nurturing of Others, Loves to Teach and Help Others Grow in Skill

- Lover of Social Justice, Good Fighter for Justice, Crusader for Social Justice or the Environment, Dedicated Citizen of the Community and the World
- Courageous or Brave
- A Person with Many Outside Interests
- Very Knowledgeable, Wise
- Loyal, Caring, Fair
- Consistently Happy or Content
- Consistently Kind, Grateful, or Forgiving
- Humble or Modest
- Good Self-Esteem

Teach clients to pick out specific talents and (positive) traits that they have right now and Make a Plan to apply them in areas of life that they care about. Tell your clients: "Applying your skills, talents, and positive traits to areas you care about may make you more successful in getting your needs, goals, and wishes satisfied; greater satisfaction in one area leads to greater happiness overall. Use the Five Paths exercise to think of a specific way you could apply a strength on a regular or routine basis (if it becomes a no brainer Happiness Habit you will be much more successful). Once you have a specific idea of how to apply a strength, test it out and then see if it works. For example, you may decide to visit office mates each morning for a few minutes to check in on work tasks as a way to specifically implement your team player and hard working/conscientious strengths. Remember, without a plan to apply your skills, talents, and traits in specific ways, this principle won't work."

Stress Carriers or I Never Bother with People I Hate Rule

Life is short. If people follow the admonitions of spiritual leaders to live each day as if it were their last, they would be doing what the self-actualized do according to Abraham Maslow (1982) and largely keep to themselves and their loved ones and close friends, avoiding stress carriers like the plague. This rule, like others, is presented in a provocative way to get the clients' attention and need not be taken literally in contexts where they have to accept and live with people they do not particularly like. Still clients can minimize contact, staying as kind and cordial as they can when they have to deal with these folks if for no other reason than to get involved with them inevitably leads to unpleasant entanglements. Like stepping in fresh tar on the street, interactions with stress carriers tend to be sticky and hard to extricate from (also see Mad Col. Disease Rule).

String of Pearls Practice and Principle

> Fast as the rolling seasons bring
> The hour of fate to those we love,
> Each pearl that leaves the broken string
> Is set in Friendship's crown above.
> As narrower grows the earthly chain,
> The circle widens in the sky;
> These are our treasures that remain,
> But those are stars that beam on high.
> —*Songs of Many Seasons,* Our Classmate, F.W.C.

In "Our Classmate," Oliver Wendell Holmes Sr. talks about the death of a loved one as the removal of a pearl from a pearl necklace with each pearl denoting a treasured relationship. QOLT speaks of metaphorically building a pearl necklace each day from the positive, kind, and loving interactions that people have with others.

Encourage clients to think of every day as a series of interactions with others from loved ones to strangers on the street. Ask them to measure their day by these interactions. It can be fun to write them down to see all of the lives they touch or cross paths with each day. The String of Pearls Principle says that the goal each day is to be mindful of every social interaction; paying attention as one interaction starts, unfolds, stops, and another begins. With each interaction clients should try to do no harm in terms of being surly or rude or ignoring others. Besides doing no harm, clients should try to be kind and responsive in each daily interaction. If clients are kind, they can judge that interaction as a positive pearl for their necklace for the day. It matters not if others always respond to these pearls of kindness; the pearls are counted even if the other person is too grumpy to accept them.

String of Pearls is meant to become a habit of kindness toward others in every interaction. This principle will become a no brainer, something clients do without thinking that will build deep bonds with those they see on a regular basis (see Favor Bank) and will make them feel good about how they treat strangers. String of Pearls will also eliminate guilt from being rude or dismissive to others. As the How Kind and

Serve Others Tenets say, being kind and decent is the essential fruit of most spiritual practices and is something that will brighten one's day, increase one's enjoyment and satisfaction with life and oneself, and make the world a better place for others whose paths one crosses. Encourage clients to try to be aware and to stop time while in these interactions so they can fully attend to the other person (see Mine the Moment Principle).

Success Principle

Consistent happiness comes from achievement, success, or fulfillment in pursuit of worthwhile goals or challenges. It will not reliably come from pursuing pleasure alone.

Surrogate Family Principle

When clients have been unsuccessful in establishing healthy, mutually supportive relationships with family members, encourage them to satisfy their needs for social support, love, and encouragement by building a network of supportive friends or a "surrogate family." This may be done, even as they attempt to improve their family relationships. One loyal friend is worth a thousand relatives according to a Latin proverb.

Sweet Revenge Principle

The best way to respond to adversity, that is, some personal tragedy, a hurtful action by a perceived enemy, or hassles in life is to grab moments of joy and satisfaction wherever possible. Getting angry is often "playing into the hands" of antagonists who want to see people get upset. The greatest revenge is to *not* react to anger with anger. Instead people should pursue other sources of joy and satisfaction. (Also see Don't Forgive Principle.)

▶ Switch Out of FOOBS Principle (See FOOBS Principle)

Take a Stand Principle

Taking a stand and making a commitment is, ultimately, freeing and liberating rather than stifling and confining. Unless people "get off the fence" and commit themselves to particular goals and values, they lose the chance to gain fulfillment from *any* commitment in life. People gain nothing for interminably "keeping their options open."

▶ TAKE THE SEX OUT OF MARRIAGE
   PRINCIPLE (SEE ROMANTIC FRIENDSHIP
   PRINCIPLE)

▶ TAKE YOUR MEDICATION PRINCIPLE (SEE
   PHYSICAL ACTIVITY PRINCIPLE)

Taking Your Emotional Temperature or Assessing Progress and Prospects Principle

Clients' level of satisfaction with an area they care about along with their emotions about the area tell them if they are making progress to long-term goals and daily subgoals. Thus, their feelings and satisfaction with an area tell them their Progress and Prospects, they tell them their progress in gaining fulfillment so far, and they tell them their prospects for future fulfillment in the area. Clients can take their temperature formally with psychological tests like the QOLI, although tests that have not been subject to rigorous validity testing can yield false and misleading results. Additionally, clients can assess their progress informally by asking themselves how satisfied or good they feel about an area like love or work. They also get informal feedback on how they are doing—at times, unsolicited—from loved ones who may know better than they do how unhappy they are and seem to the world. These same loved ones can let clients know if they are cutting the mustard in terms of progress, especially when they are trying to enhance happiness in these very relationships.

Tangled Web or Web of Support or Love Where You Are Principle

QOLT regards close and friendly relationships as a major key to QOL and happiness. Wherever possible, this means having some friends at work and elsewhere in the community and neighborhood. It also means visiting a little bit with everyone you see and attempt to help them each day, whether it be help in getting coffee at a coffeeshop, ringing up a purchase, or getting their dry cleaning (see String of Pearls). Everyone is embedded in a web of supportive relationships that they too often take for granted even though this web is a major contributor to a sense of happiness and well-being each day.

Taoist Dodge Ball Rule

Lao Tse in the Tao De Ching suggests that people let others take the hit and get bloodied fighting their enemies instead of doing it themselves. Every battle exacts a cost to us in some way; counterattacks should be expected when a person attacks another. Clients can avoid the counterattack and energy expenditure of fighting if they dodge the battle to begin with. Academia is full of survivors who stay relentlessly pleasant without getting into the fray of vicious politics. Navigating highly politicized organizations requires adroit skills in dodging political problems and minefields. It is very much like playing dodgeball. Besides pure running ability, it requires cageyness and alertness to avoid getting hit, as when one stays behind and in back of the pack so that others get hit before you do. To avoid getting in the classic drama of persecutor-victim-rescuer, QOLT urges people to stay out of the fray by refusing to take sides or take one of these three roles, again, based on Taoist principles formed during warlike times in China.

▶ TENDER HEARTED RULE (SEE HOW
   KIND PRINCIPLE)

▶ TERRORIST PRINCIPLE (SEE YOU DO IT TO
   YOURSELF PRINCIPLE)

Thank Everyone for Everything Principle

This is a gratitude practice or ritual. Anytime someone does something special or helpful, people should say thanks in a sincere and kind way. It can help to send an e-card or just to jot a note or e-mail. The idea is not to just get something back. The act of saying thanks is service to others and is its own reward (also see Serve Others Principle). Nevertheless, such acts of kindness for those with whom we work and see every day, certainly builds up the Favor Bank Account of Good Will.

The Three Rs of Stress Management Principle

The natural order of dealing with overwhelming stress and other slings and arrows of outrageous fortune is for people to retreat, lick their wounds in a safe haven to renew, and finally to reengage themselves in the business of their lives, getting done what needs to be done and dealing with stressors along the way. Staying with a battle metaphor, this Tenet urges people to parry and thrust at challenges rather than staying in the fray of a situation ad nauseum, thereby depleting energy, enthusiasm, and hope. People need regular breaks in the action to not get stale, even when challenges are welcome. This principle underlies Quality Time and Mental Health Day as people retreat from the world and regroup before reentering the jungle out there that is life.

They Love to Help Me Tenet

We all need help from others in so many ways that it is important to know how to make it rewarding, fun, and mutually beneficial for others to help you in all of the ways you may need it from friendship, to encouragement in pursuing life goals, aid your professional advancement, to technical advice on how to operate a new computer program, replace a water heater, challenge a worry that is upsetting you, or suggest social skills to use in a touchy interpersonal situation. Be very thankful for such assistance (Thank Everyone for Everything Tenet). Find ways to help your helpers (Mutual Aid Tenet). Give your helpers face time as you visit with them, ask about their loved ones and encourage them in their pursuits. Find ways that you can share your skills and expertise with them so that the helping is a two way street. Pick wisely people whom you look up to, who share your Goals-and-Values, and who have great skills to share, good judgment, and can keep a secret. No man (or woman) is an island. Make it easy and fun for people to help you so that they will do it again and again. Of course, you must show some self-reliance by not asking for too much help or for help for things that you should have learned for yourself by now. In keeping with this Tenet, QOLT urges you to learn to become your own therapist and to, in a sense, get others to also be your coaches, helpers, and supporters to the extent that they are happy and willing to help you over and over again.

Thou Shalt Be Aware or Psychephobia Principle

Being aware of one's innermost thoughts, feelings, and hurts is essential in QOLT. Clients should not get excited or down on themselves for unpleasant thoughts, feelings, and images. They are but drops in a river of consciousness that is the wakeful mind. Rather than leading to unethical or even homicidal behavior, an awareness of impulses makes people stronger in resisting temptation as they are not "blind sided" by feelings that overtake them in the heat of passion.

Time of Departure Tenet

Some say, "Live today as though it were your last; one day, and it could be today, it really will be your last." Think of how long your parents and grandparents lived, your health risks, and then estimate your longevity in years and the time of your death, your *Time of Departure.* It can help to view your life years as a straight line as follows, marking an X where you think you are now:

Birth _____ Death

After guessing your *Time of Departure,* ask yourself, "What do I truly love? What is flow for me?" Try then to minimize time spent on other things. Stop unfulfilling activities that do not fit with your Goals-and-Values if you can and . . .

REMEMBER, time is running out FAST, like water down a large drain.
REMEMBER, you can't have any time back.
REMEMBER, you can't take it with you when you go.
REMEMBER, your next breath could be your last.

To Understand All Is to Forgive All or Empathy Principle

Encourage clients to forgive or at least accept other people's behavior as they try to understand them, realizing that they did the best they could given their limited awareness, skills, and understanding of the situation, a core part of QOL theory. This principle can help clients to reconcile themselves with people they resent or are in conflict with. It especially helps to see a conflict from the other person's perspective; empathy can defuse anger better than most interventions. The origin of this principle is a French proverb that is used here in a purposely provocative and idealistic way. While people often cannot either understand or forgive all, they can strive for understanding as a way to cope with their own destructive emotion of hate or anger.

Trust Principle

Until proven otherwise, people should trust others and assume that they have good intentions. Trusting people are happier and better liked by others than those who are mistrustful. Mistrustful people create a negative self-fulfilling prophecy, creating the very rejection in other people that they fear.

▶ Tune into What Turns You on Principle (See Do What You Love Principle)

Under the Influence or Yes, Dear Rule

The villain of Barbara Kingsolver's novel, *The Poisonwood Bible*, is Nathan, who takes the world on his shoulders without asking for help or being open to the interests of loved ones and friends. He tries to convert African pagans of the troubled Congo region while repeatedly misprouncing the word precious, saying that Jesus is poison in all of his sermonizing! He also subjects his family to bitter hardships while being obtuse and abusive toward his mate, who only leaves after losing a child (see Men Are Just Desserts). John Gottman stresses the importance of shutting up, listening, and often implementing the feedback of one's mate. I would argue that this openness to influence would extend to all loved ones and friends in all social systems, including work and home.

▶ Vary Your Pleasures to Avoid Adaptation Tenet (See Sensate Focus/Savor Tenet)

We Are Family Principle

Although it may have been hard living with family members growing up, most people got along with their family most of the time. You can pick your friends, but you *don't* pick your family. Likewise, you don't pick your colleagues, workmates, coworkers, or bosses. Despite differences in values and personalities try to get along with workmates as if they were family. (See Love and Work, No Gossip and Emotional Honesty Principles.)

▶ Web of Support Principle (See Tangled Web Principle)

We're Not Okay and That's Okay Rule

Recall the "I'm okay, You're okay" pop psychology of Transactional Analysis? Many people have tremendous family of origin pain or wounds (see FOOBS and ACOAN Principle). Some scars never fade. Clients may be neurotic and weird and quirky for life if they are now. At most, the therapy, meds, and spiritual practice may make them a little more patient or kind, but only a lobotomy will erase the pain and change their personality (see Personality Stays the Same Principle).

What Would My Role Model Do? or Role Model Principle

In solving difficult problems or in deciding how to act in day-to-day situations, it can help greatly to invoke a role model. Many of my clients usefully ask, What Would Jesus or Buddha or God or Allah or Rabbi Stander or Martin Luther King or Ghandi or Mother Theresa or Mom or Dad or My Best Friend with Good Judgment Do when faced with perplexing problems? One reason that the area of Spiritual Life can be so powerful is that a person can try to follow a role model as a way to foster inner peace, contentment, and decency in his day-to-day life. A variation of this called The Good Grief Principle instructs bereaved individuals to ask themselves how the deceased would have wanted them to live and carry on with the loss, a question they can repeat to themselves throughout the day. Many people pray to or visit their deceased loved ones to comfort themselves. In cases of complicated grief or mourning in which the bereaved seems stuck or mired in misery, it helps greatly to invoke this principle even in a guided imagery or empty chair format.

▶ **When in Doubt, Don't Rule (See "Do the Right Thing" Rule)**

Words as Daggers Rule (See No Gossip/Criticism/Suggestions Rule)

Work Spillover Principle (See Don't Bring It Home Principle)

Worry Warts Principle (See Be the Peace You Seek Principle)

Yes, Boss/Yes, Dear Rule (See Pick Your Battles/Pick No Battles Principle and Under the Influence Principle)

You Are What You Do Principle

QOLT says You are who your friends are; our friends say a lot about who we are and who we will become (see Expert Friend). In a similar way, we are what we do. Buddha said "all we have or own are our actions." What we do defines who we are to the world. The quality of life pioneer and researcher, Alex Michalos, says that the key to achieving Plato's good life is to do good things. Charles Barkley notwithstanding, we all are role models to ourselves, if not to our friends, neighbors, and kids. Find passions, causes, work, play, and day-to-day activities that reflect your values, that are good, and you will be a good and happy person, living the good life.

▶ **You Can't Have It All Principle (See Curb or Ignore Desires Principle)**

You Do It to Yourself or Terrorist Principle

Moment-to-moment self-talk is often hateful as people tell themselves, "you are lazy, a fat slob who will never amount to anything." Or people may scare themselves with, "If you don't watch out, you will lose your job or your lover." People are often unaware of this self-hating and terrorizing banter because it is such a habit. They may also be unaware of the core beliefs or schema that such thoughts spring from as in "I'm a flawed defective person that no one could love if they really knew me." QOLT maintains that the impact of these thoughts on mood and well-being is like dropping a hand grenade on the middle of a tea party or the inner sanctum of the bedroom as individuals ready themselves for sleep. It is so invasive and destructive that it is like a terrorist act.

The second part of this principle is that when clients find themselves in a deep hole psychologically, whether deeply sad, mad, scared, or depressed, You Do It to Yourself. As much as they may blame others or bad events for upsetting them, it would not happen if a part of them did not buy into the criticism of others deep down. It is not accurate to just blame others or their circumstances for their bad mood. This is especially true when people are in the throes of what Aaron T. Beck and David A. Clark call "modes" or full-body feelings or emotions that seem to take over completely, almost like the person is possessed except that this part of the person has taken possession of the person's body and mind *before*. At these times, clients should recognize that they are in some deep mode of misery, that it is not the "real" them, that it will pass, and that with time it will go away. Clients should also try to be aware of hurtful thoughts that may be fueling the misery and practice (see Mindful Breathing in the Toolbox CD). They should dispute their negative self-talk at these times with the Lie Detector exercise and refuse to let patterns picked up in their family of origin take over completely (see Switch Out of FOOBS and Silence is Golden Principle). The best response at these times is to try and kindly re-parent oneself with deep self-compassion, much like a parent would do for a distraught child; also be either silent or kind to others.

When clients are in a deep Big Three mode of feeling, be it deep anger, anxiety, or depression or a mixture of the three, they distort like crazy and see only bad things in their present and past. That is, they see others and the world and themselves in a way that fits their mode of misery as in seeing others as unloving or uncaring just because they hate themselves at times. Since the mind plays tricks on people at these times, it is best to try and stay silent or to act kindly rather than fly off the handle. Our loved ones can appear to be devils or angels depending on the mood we are in; this is called *mood congruent memory*.

CHAPTER 10

Emotional Control and Life Management Skills in Goal Striving

As part of Goals-and-Values, QOLT teaches clients basic life management and mood control skills aimed at controlling negative affect and organizing their lives in the service of striving for personal goals in valued areas of life. Although some techniques here are new, others are variations on venerable cognitive therapy techniques—adapted after years of testing to improve ease of use with both clinical and positive psychology clients:

- Activity scheduling and tying the use of your time to life Goals-and-Values and Inner Abundance
- Cognitive restructuring and schema work—including use of a thought record and consideration of positive schemas in the Tenets of Contentment and the New Life Script or Goals-and-Values
- Social Skills and Assertion Training—discussed in the relationship chapter (Chapter 14)
- Mindfulness Training and anxiety management—discussed here and earlier in Chapter 7 as part of Quality Time

For clients with *DSM* disorders, these techniques are almost always taught in both cognitive therapy and QOLT protocols. For positive psychology clients without *DSM* disorders, these techniques are only applied if clients have obvious deficits in the areas of time management for goal striving and control of any Big Three negative emotion—anxiety, depression, anger. With respect to the latter, nonclinical clients often have difficulty managing subclinical levels of anxiety, anger, and depression, especially during stressful life events such as a divorce, job change, or new develop-

mental task or challenge such as establishing a career, starting a family, retirement, or dealing with empty nest syndrome.

In Chapter 3 on QOL theory, we saw how a modicum of proficiency in Life Management and (Negative) Emotional Control Skills are essential to goal striving and to basic happiness or positive mental health in both clinical and nonclinical populations. Because of the connection with goal striving and Goals-and-Values, the definition of these skills is borrowed from Chapter 11 on Goals-and-Values in order to present the full core of QOLT here in Part II.

"MENTAL HYGIENE" FOR NEGATIVE AFFECT OR SENSITIVITY SYNDROME

QOLT refers to the Big Three negative affects of anger, anxiety, and depression, which so often co-occur in clients, as its client-oriented name for negative affectivity (see The Big Three Makes Us Dumb or Emotional Control Principle/Tenet). The less perjorative term, *Sensitivity Syndrome*, is also used in QOLT because it highlights the strength of extreme interpersonal and emotional sensitivity in some situations as well as the co-occurrence of sensitivity to positive and not just negative emotions in many clients.

Negative affectivity, also called neuroticism or over-emotionality, is a huge stumbling block to happiness (Diener & Seligman, 2002, 2004). This makes sense given definitions of happiness as life satisfaction plus the preponderance of positive over negative affective experience (Diener, 1984; Diener et al., 1999). *If clients' feelings are predominantly unpleasant and negative, it will suppress or drown out any positive feelings of happiness or cognitive evaluations of their lives as satisfying.* Control or management of Negative Affectivity or what Barlow, Allen, and Choate (2004) call *Negative Affect Syndrome* is essential for goal striving for several reasons. Unpleasant emotional experiences signal a lack of success in achieving needs, goals, and wishes in valued areas of life. Clients need to keep these managed and in check in order to respond effectively with new strategies for fulfillment. If unchecked, these affects can immobilize clients and interrupt needed problem-solving efforts (Frisch, 1998b). For example, high negative affectivity interferes with the complex social problem solving and thinking needed for goal striving. Episodes of negative affect also cause addictive relapse and may be a primary motivation for drug and alcohol abuse and dependency as clients "self-medicate" their unpleasant affects with drugs and alcohol (Witkiewitz & Marlatt, 2004). *Chronic* negative affect is another threat to effective goal striving that can be managed with some basic emotional control skills. These emotional control skills may be seen as part of what philosopher Bertrand Russell (1958) referred to as "mental discipline" or "hygiene of the nerves," which allow us to control and to counteract worrisome thoughts and feelings that flood people's consciousness from time to time as they pursue "the conquest of happiness." For example, both Authentic Happiness and QOLT approaches to positive psychology, tout cognitive restructuring as an avenue for emotional control in nonclinical populations—Seligman (2002) through an Ellis-type thought record and QOLT through the Lie Detector or Stress Diary discussed next.

Like Seligman (2002), QOLT believes that the tendency toward negative affectivity can be modified somewhat with positive psychology interventions. The *Whole Life* or *Life Goal Perspective* of QOLT can itself help with Big Three emotions, insofar as clients are taught to consider the big picture both horizontally in their life—that is, when one area of life is a problem, 15 others may be going better—and vertically insofar as any problem is smaller if seen in the perspective of one's lifetime or even in the space of the year. Cognitive restructuring tools can modify negative affectivity according to Seligman (2002).

RATIONALES FOR COGNITIVE RESTRUCTURING AND ATTITUDE CHANGE IN QOLT AND COGNITIVE THERAPY

A rationale for cognitive restructuring and attitude change in QOLT can be found in the Five Paths Summary Cheat Sheet in the Toolbox CD. Clients can reframe their thoughts and attitudes to promote happiness in a valued area of life. The same reframe skills can be used to manage unduly negative feelings:

One way to improve your happiness in a particular area of life is to change your attitude about the situation, to correct any distortions or negativity in your thinking. Changing your attitude involves reevaluating or taking a new look at any part of your life by asking two key questions: "What is really happening here?" and "What does it mean to me?" Many times our view of a situation or what we think the situation means for our well-being and our future is not based on the facts; that is, our view is distorted or in error. For example, you may believe that your boss is unhappy with your work because he or she seems to be ignoring you, when in fact your boss is preoccupied with a personal problem. Because of our tendency to jump to conclusions without having all the facts, it is important to gather information about the situation before deciding what is really going on in an area of life that we care about. We do not want to prematurely decide that things are hopeless, for example, when they really are not.

After you clear up any distortion of the facts about a problem or an area of life that you care about, you can then reevaluate or take a new look at your *interpretation* of the facts. Interpretation often amounts to a question we answer to ourselves like, "How will this situation affect me and my future prospects for happiness?" or "What does this situation say about my abilities or my worth as a person?" Often our interpretation of a situation is biased against us in a self-defeating and upsetting way, for example, when we conclude that we are unlovable because one relationship did not work out. Often the situation isn't as bad or as gloomy as we think. It is important to develop the capacity to picture yourself eventually surviving and thriving even if your worst fears came true. For example, even if you had to leave your present job, it is important that you be able to picture yourself finding some other meaningful work in the future. Of course, the type of work will depend on a realistic appraisal of your skills and what is available.

The essence of the Changing **A**ttitude Strategy from the C**A**SIO model is to find out what is really happening in an important area of the client's life and to carefully evaluate what it means for the client and his or her future in an objective and realistic way that preserves the client's self-esteem and gives the client some reason to hope for fulfillment and happiness in the future.

The following script can be used to introduce clients to cognitive restructuring and attitude change:

We live in a world of thoughts, images, and theories about what's going on in the world. Everything we see or understand around us is filtered through our eyes, ears, and brain. Difficult childhood backgrounds and just feeling bad or upset at the moment can distort our perception of the situation. We need to come up with a factual description of problems. Only after we have a clear picture of the situation can we make interpretations about what it means, or evaluations about how good or bad the situation is. These interpretations or evaluations themselves are subject to distortion or mistakes. They too must be carefully examined for their truthfulness and helpfulness in meeting the challenges of life. As the Roman philosopher Marcus Aurelius put it, "Very little is needed to make a happy life; it is all within yourself, in your way of thinking." While attitude isn't everything, it sure is a big part of human happiness. The great news is that this part of happiness is largely under our control.

In keeping with cognitive therapy, clients in QOLT are taught that they often respond to the world as they see it and not as it truly is, in keeping with the maxim, You feel—and often act—as you think. People's minds play tricks on them, in that people become convinced of ideas or perceptions of reality that are flat wrong. Often clients lack all of the relevant facts when they jump to such conclusions.

Additionally, even when clients are viewing and evaluating a situation accurately, they often make distorted, biased, inflammatory, unduly upsetting, and self-defeating interpretations or conclusions about what a particular situation means for their self-esteem, personal resources, or future well-being as when they conclude that they are failures and give up trying when they find that one job or career path does not suit their strengths.

Dysfunctional, Maladaptive, or "Unhealthy" Thinking and Evaluations

Thus, in keeping with cognitive therapy, clients are urged to challenge or evaluate both: (1) the accuracy of

their perceptions of a situation as in "Do I really have all the facts and know, for example, why someone did what he did"? and (2) the accuracy and usefulness of conclusions that he makes about what a situation means about his self-worth and his future. Evaluations or interpretations of events are not useful and are dysfunctional, maladaptive, or "unhealthy" when they lead to: (1) unwarranted and excessive emotionality; (2) the activation of negative schemas, modes, and emotions that derail appropriate problem solving and efforts to remedy problems that are likely to be effective; and (3) immobility, useless rumination that does not lead to productive action, and an unproductive wallowing in extremes of depression, anxiety, anger, or a combination of these feelings.

There are two kinds of attitude change techniques according to Dr. Robin Jarrett of the University of Texas Southwestern Medical School at Dallas (Jarrett et al., 2001). In "logical analysis" clients look at the logic or fairness of hurtful beliefs that they hold about themselves, the world, and the future. They attack the logic of their upsetting thoughts to come up with "Positive Answers" to use the parlance of the QOLT thought record, the Lie Detector. They reason their way out of a dysfunctional belief. The other approach is called "reality testing." It involves testing beliefs in reality as in the case of the person who went to a party to test out his belief that he was unattractive or unable to make conversation with people. This is also called "hypothesis testing" since thoughts, attitudes, and beliefs are really just hypotheses, hunches, or opinions people have about themselves in the world that have to be verified or tested (see Set Up a Test technique). Whichever approach clients use, they should get used to challenging the thoughts and beliefs that upset them. As clients set up tests to test the truth of their beliefs, they must take risks to show the lie of their negative thoughts. As Eleanor Roosevelt said, "You must do the thing you think you cannot do." By testing and challenging and acting against their beliefs, clients can effectively change their attitudes.

A NOTE ON QOLT TERMINOLOGY AND SELF-GENERATED OPTIMISTIC REFRAMES

Based on clinical experience with hundreds of clients over the past 20 years, QOLT uses terms that resonate with clients like Positive Answer, Unhealthy Beliefs, River of Consciousness, and Lie Detector and Stress

Diary for its thought record and cognitive work, without encouraging clients to do anything more than evaluate their thoughts in order to come up with a realistic reframe, alternative, or "positive answer" to those thoughts that are clearly maladaptive and self-defeating. Thoughts that immobilize clients when problem solving is in order or thoughts that fuel extreme negative emotions that are out of proportion to the situation are deemed maladaptive, unhealthy, dysfunctional, and self-defeating in QOLT. Clients are asked to reevaluate these maladaptive thoughts and to formulate alternative answers that correct for any self-demeaning or unduly scary "lie," "trash in the river," or error even though clients realize full well that they are not being asked to sugar coat situations with mindless platitudes, unrealistic reframes, or conclusions that they do not believe in nearly 100 percent. They also understand that they are to work with their therapist to find realistic answers or reframes to upsetting thoughts.

In terms of using the QOLT thought record or Lie Detector and Stress Diary, QOLT clients understand that there is always something patently self-defeating in thinking that leads to emotional extremes that are out of proportion to the situation or in thinking that pushes them into a passive, incapacitated loss/deprivation mode in which they wallow in their pain to no good effect. QOLT clients understand that even when there is not a literal "lie" or factual error in their negative thinking, their perceptions and conclusions may contain trash in the river of consciousness in the sense of jumping to conclusions without all the facts or in making unwarranted inflammatory conclusions about their self-worth or future well-being in light of their situation. These lies then lead to undue extremes of negative feeling and the engagement of passive modes that defeat or incapacitate them when a problem-solving approach containing an action plan, could move them forward in terms of reducing negative affect and in terms of engaging the constructive mode of positive feelings and goal striving (see Chapter 3). The Stress Diary makes it clear to clients that they must think about their worries in a structured way in order to feel and function better; that is, unstructured thinking that does not lead to realistic and productive reframes when clients are incapacitated with high levels of negative affect, will accomplish nothing or make the problem worse.

"Unhealthy" means self-defeating or maladaptive in QOLT parlance and can be applied even when clients'

thoughts are true; Richard Heimberg and his colleagues refer to these thoughts that upset people most and that interfere with goal-striving and performance as the thinking or cognitive error of "maladaptive thoughts" (Hope, Heimberg, Juster, & Turk, 2000). In an effort to be more client friendly and clear, QOLT uses the term Unhealthy Thinking.

TOOLS AND TECHNIQUES FOR CHANGING ATTITUDES AND CONTROLLING NEGATIVE AFFECTIVITY

The Lie Detector or Stress Diary

Gaining distance and realistic perspective on negative beliefs is a skill. Challenging automatic thoughts is a skill. It is like a muscle that must be exercised regularly to stay in shape. In this vein, clients are told not to be discouraged with relapses, it just means that they "got out of shape" and need to tone up by reacquainting themselves with the positive schemas such as those in the Tenets of Contentment and with cognitive techniques such as QOLT's version of a thought record.

One major QOLT tool for cognitive restructuring is the thought record or Lie Detector and Stress Diary (see Box 10.1). If clients really want to gain control of their consciousness, that is, the often-negative running banter or thoughts in their head or what Eugene O'Neill, the playwright, called "mosquitoes of the soul," they need to write them down and study them in a structured, careful way. The Lie Detector/Stress Diary in the Toolbox CD does exactly this. It is the single most important tool for attitude change of QOLT.

After years of supervising students working with probationers, some with sex and drug offenses and subject to polygraph testing, the metaphor of lie detecting seems useful in cognitive restructuring; clients are asked to reevaluate their thinking to find the "lie" or maladaptive thought process or content that is defeating them even when it is not a "lie" in the literal sense as when a mother who occasionally slapped her 3-year-old, branded herself a hopeless child abuser; in fact, she was "in recovery" from having a mother with schizophrenia herself.

With extreme emotions, clients are requested to ask themselves, "Where is the lie in my thinking or view that is upsetting me so much?" There may not be a literal lie, but there usually is an unhealthy or unhelpful conclusion, cognitive distortion, or negative schema

BOX 10.1
Clinical Example of Lie Detector and Stress Diary

Instructions: Fill out this form each time you feel upset. Try to complete the form as soon as possible after you realize that you are upset.

Name: _Bill_   Date and Time: _2:00 A.M. January 2, 2025_

Situation (Who-What-When-Where-Why): _At home after worrying about my bills._

Feelings (Circle): (Sad) (Mad) Down Depressed Hurt Lonely Hopeless Disappointed Lazy Tired Bored (Self-Hate) Unloved Guilty Ashamed Angry Frustrated Irritated Disgusted Defensive Worried (Afraid) Restless (Overwhelmed) (Confused) Jealous Envious

Upsetting Thoughts	Positive Answer
What's bothering me? What's happening? What does this mean for me and my future?	Do I have all the facts? Where is the lie in my thinking or view that is upsetting me so much? Is there a better way to look at this? What would a compassionate friend say?
I'm in trouble. I'm too broke to pay these bills. Arrested and disgraced. They'll turn off my utilities! What a jerk I am for getting into this mess!	_Wait a minute and stop calling yourself names. I'm a decent, good person even if I did screw up here. I don't really know how much I have and owe. I might be able to get or borrow money if I need it. Anyway, I'm not trying to rip someone off._

Action Plan: Do I need to test out my thoughts? How can I change this or learn to live with it?

Take some Quality Time, then figure out what you really owe. I can then call the utilities to see if I can work out a payment plan. The Consumer Credit Counseling Service gives free counseling on money management—I'll go there to avoid this in the future.

Note: If you don't feel better after completing this form, go over your responses to be sure that you: (1) Didn't miss an upsetting thought, (2) Really believe your positive answer, and (3) Have a *realistic* action plan. When all else fails, get involved in a fun, service-orientated, or worthwhile activity. For example, a small act of kindness for a sick friend can be service to others. Also make room in your life for some Quality Time.

that is defeating clients by adding to their upsetting circumstances like rubbing salt into a wound. For example, Jessica felt much better when she stopped thinking that her socially awkward husband was malevolent and out to hurt her. She reframed his inability to hug and console her exactly as she wished as, "He is just socially retarded or ignorant, not mean. He is a brain in business but a social schlep. I know down deep he cares even though he often doesn't react as I'd like him to."

To use the Stress Diary or Lie Detector most effectively, clients need multiple copies of it so that they can carry the copies with them wherever they go. At times that they feel upset, they should reach for a Stress Diary and find a quiet, private place to get a handle on their thoughts and feelings. It is important that they fill out a Stress Diary as soon as they can after they get upset. If they still feel upset about something at the end of the day, that's also a good time to do a Stress Diary.

To begin a Lie Detector, clients first write down the date and time. Next, they describe the upsetting situation briefly. What seems to be bugging them? Whatever the situation is, they should briefly describe it in their Stress Diary. This becomes very important later on when clients and therapists look for themes in the kinds of situations that upset them, giving them a window to their deepest fears, worries, and beliefs, that is, negative schemas. For example, Charley and his therapist looked at 12 Stress Diaries and could see a clear pattern. He always got upset or "lost it" in situations where his work was criticized. This gave him a clue that he was a "raving perfectionist" who could never accept any mistake or failing. For him, he was either "God or scum," with no middle ground of evaluation. When no one complained and everything seemed perfect, he was great; if he made one mistake, however, it "ruined" his performance and made him a "loser" and "failure" in his eyes (see Box 10.1).

Next, under "Feelings" clients should circle the feelings that apply to them while they're upset. Clients need to learn to name their feelings. Freud said, "Dreams are the royal road to the unconscious." I say, "Feelings are the royal road to cognitions or thoughts." For example, when clients are worried or afraid, that is almost always a sign that they're having thoughts like, "I'm in some kind of danger. Something bad is going to happen." Thoughts of danger like this are things that can be worked with, processed, and overcome. As they'll see, if clients can identify their feelings, they can then identify their thoughts, which is the first step to overcoming

negative emotions and feelings of unhappiness in some part of life.

The column "Upsetting Thoughts" is where clients write down their self-talk or "stream of consciousness." It's also where they write down what I call the "verbal diarrhea" that is often making them more upset than they have to be (no matter how awful a situation may seem). They can learn to be their own psychologist as they learn to catch and identify the thoughts that are running through their heads. A major goal of QOLT is to teach clients how to tune into their thoughts whenever they get upset. This gives them something clear and changeable to work with. Anytime they get upset then, it should be a signal for them to tune into their thoughts and ask, "What am I thinking to make myself so upset?" For days a client named Bill worried about paying his bills. His upsetting thoughts went something like this, "I'm going to be late paying some of these bills. I may have to call some of my utility companies and tell them I can't pay them on time. I'll be disgraced and laughed at. I should pay my bills on time like everyone else. I'm a loser and a jerk for not paying all my bills like everyone else, on time."

Be sure to have clients answer two questions when they write down their upsetting thoughts. First, they should write down their view of the situation. That is, say what they think is happening in the situation or what's bothering them. Often people jump to conclusions or get the facts wrong when they get upset. This happened to the client, Bill, when he assumed he was "broke" before balancing his checkbook, causing needless worry and anxiety. Next, they should think about what the upsetting situation means for them and their future. Often they assume that they can't handle or overcome a bad situation. This also happened to Bill when he assumed he'd be arrested for being late with a payment to the telephone company. Part of being your own psychologist, a major goal of QOLT, is to teach clients how to tune into their thoughts whenever they get upset. This gives them something clear and changeable to work on.

The next column is called "Positive Answer." Once clients put their upsetting thoughts on paper, it's time for them to look at them in the clear light of day. They need to try to come up with a realistic positive answer to their negative and immobilizing thoughts. This should not be some sugary, rosy picture that doesn't accurately describe the situation. The *positive answer* or reframe must be realistic, but also supportive and encouraging. It should be something that helps clients cope with the upsetting feelings and dissatisfaction that they feel in a positive way. It should help them solve a problem (or accept an unsolvable problem) and keep their optimism and self-esteem intact. The Stress Diary itself asks a couple of key questions to get the ball rolling. One question is, "Do I have all the facts?" Bill realized here that he didn't really know how much money was in his checking account. So for a positive answer, he wrote, "I may have enough money to pay these bills. Stop beating up on yourself and balance your checkbook to see where you stand."

Another key question for clients (and counselors) to ask when they are trying to come up with a positive answer is, "Is there a better way to look at this?" Bill came up with a good one here, "Nobody's perfect. Just because I can't pay my bills, doesn't mean I'm a bad person. I'm not trying to rip off my creditors. I'll only withhold the money if I don't have it. I know of some ways I can get more money if I need it." This positive answer counteracted the patient's upsetting thoughts that if he can't pay some bills, it means that he is a "no good jerk."

A third key question to ask is, "What would a compassionate friend say in this situation?" Depressed people often get into a habit of putting themselves down and being overly critical of themselves and other people. To overcome this they need to summon what I call "the compassionate friend" to come up with a positive answer to their worries and fears. They might conjure up a person in their life who's very loving or supportive and yet competent or skillful in handling tough situations. It could be a parent, a teacher, or some other role model in their life. If all else fails, they should pretend that someone is coming to them with these upsetting thoughts, for example, their best friend whom they love and cherish more than anyone else. What would they tell that person as a compassionate friend? Bill summoned a compassionate friend to come up with this positive answer:

You're a good, decent, person. No matter what happens, you're going to survive and thrive. Other good people get into financial binds. You don't know how others will react. Maybe they'll understand, especially since you want to do right by those you're indebted to. Stop putting yourself down. Treat yourself with care and respect. That's the way to get out of this situation, with some composure.

For a positive answer to work, clients have to really believe it, say 80 percent to 100 percent on a scale of be-

lief; therefore, encourage clients to only write things down that they truly believe.

Next, it's time for clients to do something about what's upsetting them. This is the Action Plan part of the Stress Diary. Clients may decide at first to get some more information. Getting information, especially facts, will help them test out their thoughts to see if they are true, for thoughts are opinions about the world, not facts. They must be verified to be believed. For example, Bill wrote here, "Find out how much money I have by balancing my checkbook." He did not have all the facts to see whether in fact he really was going to be late in paying bills.

Once clients get the facts about a problem, they need to think about ways to change a difficult situation or an unfulfilling area of life. In cases where they can't change it, they must think of ways they can learn to live with it. To do this, they should answer the second question under the Action Plan part of the Stress Diary, which asks "How can I change this or learn to live with it?" They can brainstorm solutions to the situation upsetting them. For example, a client who was unhappy in her marriage did several Stress Diaries about fights with her husband and decided to ask her husband to pursue couples counseling as part of her Action Plan.

The point with the Action Plan is that clients decide to try something to solve a problem now that they've got some composure and a little perspective after developing a positive answer to their upsetting thoughts. It isn't usually enough to have insight into a problem. Clients have to do something about it to make it better. This "Face-the-Music" principle of QOLT sets it apart from many other approaches. In one client's Action Plan for a difficult marriage that did not respond to counseling, she decided to put more of her efforts into cultivating friendships and hobbies outside of her marriage. She didn't want a divorce and so decided not to put all of her "emotional eggs" in the basket of her troubled marriage. This strategy helped her to cope with an unsolvable problem that couldn't be changed.

Some Action Plans are simple, but powerful. For example, a client, Judy, took her temperature to see whether she had the flu or was descending into some kind of terrible depressive tailspin. She found out, in fact, that she woke up sick and was not getting depressed as she had feared. Counselors can provide clients who have trouble arriving at Action Plans and

Solutions copies of Five Paths to Happiness from the Toolbox CD to facilitate problem solving.

Once they complete a Stress Diary or Lie Detector, clients should see if they feel better. If they don't feel substantially better, there's a problem. They may not have identified the key upsetting thoughts and need to think harder about what's upsetting them. Doing an "instant replay" in their mind of the upsetting situation will help to ferret out more upsetting thoughts. They might also look at the positive answers they came up with. Maybe they don't really believe in the answers. Maybe they don't address the upsetting thoughts sufficiently. Finally, they need to take a look at their Action Plan. Are they addressing the problem in a realistic, doable fashion? Doing a Stress Diary is a skill that takes weeks to develop properly, so tell clients not to give up on the idea. Just becoming aware of some of their upsetting thoughts and feelings is an important first step.

Lie Detector Questions or Questions-in-Court Technique

The Questions-in-Court handout should be given to clients along with the Stress Diary in order to help them generate positive answers to upsetting thoughts listed in a Stress Diary. These questions include virtually all of the avenues for cognitive restructuring used today. Counselors should keep these questions in mind when doing in-session cognitive restructuring. The following script may be used to introduce clients to this technique:

When using these questioning techniques, it's helpful to think of yourself in a courtroom. Pretend that your upsetting thoughts are on trial. You want to question such upsetting thoughts as, "I'm a bad person" or "I'm a bad father" by looking objectively at the evidence, just as one might in a court of law. Usually people never challenge or examine their upsetting thoughts. They just swirl around in their mind, making them crazy and upset. By looking at them objectively, through questioning techniques, people can see the extent to which they "hold water," are valid, or are really true. Another useful metaphor for this process is that of a lie detector. Be your own "lie detector." To do this, check out whether your perceptions of yourself, your world, and other people are truthful and accurate or in error, that is, a "lie." The Questions in Court summarizes the work of many great cognitive thera-

pists including Aaron T. Beck and his colleagues, Albert Ellis, and David Barlow; this tool is full of good questions to use in challenging upsetting and self-defeating thoughts.

Set up a Test Technique

Setting up a fair test of a painful attitude or belief in the real world is often more powerful than clients talking or reasoning their way out of the belief. Sometimes a carefully crafted positive answer won't cut it. Often clients must test out the belief in the real world to be convinced that it is false or unfair. A red-headed teenager tested her belief that redheads were "yucky" and unappealing to guys by clipping all the ads she could find in teen magazines that featured red-headed models. After finding numerous ads, she reasoned that red-headed models wouldn't be used to sell stuff to guys if redheads were "yucky." The test of her belief was so convincing that immediately she began to date. She also became sexually active, which created another slew of problems to deal with in QOLT! Nevertheless, she no longer felt ugly. Another client tested the assumption that he couldn't make small talk or enjoy himself by actually going to a party. He was determined to show an active interest in other people at the party and to try not to think about himself as much as possible. The test worked. He had a great time and really made a connection with people.

Clients can also use the Set Up a Test technique to conquer compulsions or strong urges to act in self-destructive ways as when they indulge in addictions, workaholism, perfectionism, or undue dependency on others (codependency). Counselors may use the following script to introduce clients to this technique:

In the case of compulsions, you can best test the irrational belief that you MUST act on the compulsion to feel good or avoid harm by doing what psychologists call Response Prevention. Response prevention consists of avoiding indulging in a compulsive response in order to gain control of the compulsion. For example, you may postpone having a cigarette right after a meal for 30 minutes in order to gain control of the compulsion to smoke right after every meal. With time and practice, you can avoid or prevent the response even longer—say an hour after each meal. By this time, you may no longer associate mealtimes with smoking. You may have gradually eliminated the compulsion. Response prevention can also be used to combat perfectionism and workaholism as when you refuse to bring work home with you each night in order to build a more balanced life with time for recreation and family as well as work. This will be tough the first 10 times. You'll go through "withdrawal" and have irrational fears about losing your job, being criticized by your boss, or losing your self-respect. These fears will pass with time (and a few Stress Diaries!). Just stick to your guns and prevent the response. With time and practice, you'll lose the chicken-little mentality that says that your world will fall apart if you don't indulge in the self-destructive compulsion.

Responsibility Pie Technique

When clients blame themselves for something bad that happens, it's important for them to look for the proof that it's really their fault. Cognitive counselors like Dr. Aaron T. Beck often have clients draw a "responsibility pie" in which they draw a circle and divide it according to how much responsibility they have for the problem versus other people in their life. This concretely gets at the issue of guilt and responsibility that plagues so many people who are prone to depression. One of my clients who took 100 percent or full responsibility for a failed marriage made a list of evidence for and against this belief. While she often was difficult and argumentative, she also recognized that she begged her spouse to get counseling, which he adamantly refused. When she first drew a "responsibility pie," there was only one name in the circle and that was hers. The second time she did it, after making her list of pros and cons for and against the belief that she was 100 percent to blame, she marked off a quarter of the circle for her responsibility, leaving the other three-quarters for her husband. This new attitude dramatically lifted her mood by reducing her guilt feelings.

Second Opinion Technique

Sometimes clients can't gain perspective on a problem or know the right thing to do without talking to another person outside of the situation. This person can help them identify options they never knew existed. This second opinion may be a therapist or a trusted friend or colleague who has good judgment and the client's best interests at heart. Just as clients can use the Second Opinion technique in solving problems, they can also use it in wrestling with upsetting thoughts to get a new perspective on the situation. As George Herbert wrote, "The best mirror is an old friend." A good friend can reflect the client's needs and feelings in a way that gives the client a perspective on a problem he or she didn't have before. So, for example, tell clients when they have trouble doing a Stress Diary, get stuck on coming up with positive answers, or can't identify their upsetting thoughts, to talk it over with a trusted friend, confidante, or therapist.

Be sure that the confidante has the client's best interests at heart, has good judgment and expertise, and is good at handling his or her own personal problems. Encourage clients to make any final decisions about what to do themselves. After all, they have to live with any decision.

Feeling Dictionary

The Toolbox's Feeling Dictionary defines feelings or emotions in terms of the thoughts that usually accompany them. It is based on the work of Dr. Albert Ellis and other cognitive therapists. Therapists may introduce clients to the technique with the following script:

> A Feeling Dictionary is invaluable for identifying upsetting thoughts, when you feel upset but don't know exactly why. So, when you feel bad, but don't know what is causing you to feel bad, use the Feeling Dictionary. *Feelings are often the "royal road" to thinking or cognition.* If you can identify your feelings when you're upset, you can also identify your thoughts, because certain upsetting thoughts usually correspond to particular feelings. Once you look up the thoughts that go with the feelings, you can then answer these thoughts in a positive way using techniques like the Stress Diary and Questions in Court to come up with a positive answer.
>
> Review the Feeling Dictionary whenever you feel upset. After you have found the feelings listed in your Stress Diary, look them up in the Feeling Dictionary to see if you are having any of the upsetting thoughts associated with that feeling. If you discover an upsetting thought that you're having from the Feeling Dictionary, write it down in a Stress Diary under "Upsetting Thoughts." Next, try to combat or "tame" the thought by developing a positive answer.

TOOLS FOR INTERPERSONAL COGNITIVE RESTRUCTURING

From an evolutionary perspective, it may be more natural for humans to talk and interact nonverbally with others than to write things down for personal contemplation. Additionally, many clients lack the literacy, psychological mindedness, and ability to gain perspective amid the fog of negative affectivity-related modes to successfully use structured activities like thought records or pro versus con lists in schema work and the like. For this reason, whenever possible QOLT brings significant others into the therapy to help clients challenge and dispute maladaptive or unhealthy beliefs and to reinforce positive schemas and rational responses offered in session. The latter is accomplished by encouraging clients to discuss their therapy insights and homework with significant others. Thus, clients may record their upsetting thoughts in a stream of consciousness manner, jot them down on a piece of paper, or simply recite them to the significant other in order to explore healthy alternatives. This is often not difficult, since schema work usually involves the same issues coming up over and over again before difficult schemas are managed or changed.

The Second Opinion Technique

The Second Opinion technique can be used along with thought records. In this respect it becomes a mainstay in cognitive restructuring and schema work even when formal thought records are not employed. The form of thought record in QOLT is called the Lie Detector and Stress Diary (discussed previously).

Picture Gallery of Supporters and Inspirers or Cheerleaders Technique

Another favorite cognitive restructuring tool is the Picture Gallery of Supporters and Inspirers technique in which clients assemble pictures of their friends and supporters—alive and deceased—along with inspiring ethical or religious figures and then post these on their computer or wall to gain inspiration and ideas for positive answers when struggling with difficult thought records, decisions, or negative feelings. Clients like to address pictures and ask things like, "Mom, what would you do or advise in this situation?" even when their "personal cheerleader" is deceased. Therapists can ask clients if their beliefs include a belief that deceased loved ones can be prayed or talked to. If so, this exercise can be done in that way. Alternatively, it can be done in a purely secular way as the client asks, "What would my loved one do or suggest I do or think in this situation?"

The Cognitive Error or Distortions/Biases Technique

The Cognitive Error or Distortions/Biases handout (J. S. Beck, 1995) can also be used by therapists to help create positive reframes or adaptive alternative thoughts and schemas in the context of a thought record and is available on the Toolbox CD. With the aid of the therapist, clients first identify distortions or errors associated with a specific negative thought/belief or schema in the thought record—called the Upsetting Thoughts column in the present Lie Detector thought record. Next, with the initial aid of therapists, clients develop a positive answer to the negative thought based on the distortion as when clients assume they will fail in boosting happiness in a valued area of life, invoke the Fortune Teller Error, and reframe their pessimism by asserting, "I am not a fortune teller. This effort may work out. I have never tried this way and I am older and wiser than I was in the past when everything I did seemed to fail."

Mindful Breathing: A Type of Mindfulness Training and Cognitive *Process* Intervention

The QOLT approach to Mindfulness Training is called *Mindful Breathing* (see client handout in the Toolbox CD). Mindful Breathing is useful in managing negative affects as clients strive to achieve their lifetime goals. It can also aid in relapse prevention in cognitive therapy (Segal, Williams, & Teasdale, 2002). Mindfulness Training, Mindful Breathing and meditation in QOLT are all viewed in part as training in learning to tolerate negative affects and as training in solitude; learning to be happy by oneself is a difficult but necessary skill for consistent and lasting happiness according to Csikszentmihalyi (1997).

Rationale for Mindful Breathing: The Mind as a River of Consciousness

People who worry too much, ruminate about problems *ad nauseum,* and are prone to the Big Three negative feelings of anger, anxiety, and depression need to control the *process* of anxious worry and depressive or angry rumination and not just try to challenge the *content* of every upsetting thought or worry that they experience. QOLT offers two such process interventions: Guide for Worry Warts and Mindful Breathing.

As mentioned earlier, in QOLT, the mind or consciousness is likened to a river. This raging or flowing river is full of flotsam, jetsam, jewels, and trash. Some of our thoughts and beliefs are positive jewels, full of truth and wisdom that help us move toward a more contented life. Other thoughts and beliefs are negative: trash or debris, that defeat us, plague us, and distract us from enjoying and partaking in the banquet of life. If consciousness is a river of debris, jewels, and neutral items, and if one waits long enough, feelings and thoughts will recede to the "background" of consciousness and eventually pass by or simply go away. States of bliss or extreme happiness never last; fortunately, this is also true of negative feeling states as in the Big Three. In this vein, Mindful Breathing is a way to watch the river in a more detached way. We can use it to learn to tolerate the distress associated with upsetting thoughts, images, and feelings and to allow negative thoughts and beliefs to pass by.

I Am Not My Depressive Thought or Anxious Impulse to Run Away or Attack

Detachment can increase when clients are taught to not identify parts of the river of consciousness with their personhood or core identity. Therapists may say, for example, since the river of consciousness is constantly flowing, we need not identify with any one thing in the river. The passive, nonjudgmental, "Nothing Human Disgusts Me" attitude/Tenet taken toward consciousness in Mindful Breathing or Meditation fosters an acceptance and deeper awareness of upsetting thoughts and impulses, since they are not seen as identified with the self. Hence, as passing debris in the river, these items are no more the self or who I am than a passing fancy to buy a new house or car. Additionally, awareness of the thoughts and impulses make them available for critical examination with Lie Detectors and thus, make them, if anything, less dangerous than if clients try to ignore or suppress them (see Thou Shalt Be Aware Tenet).

Occasional Meditation

Mindful Breathing is a technique for controlling negative affect and ruminations as clients go about their everyday activities. Occasional "Meditation" requires clients' full attention and is recommended as a way for clients to become aware of negative feelings and thoughts at those occasional times when they are too upset or confused or alexithymic to name exactly what it is that is disturbing them. As clients become aware of unpleasant thoughts and feelings during meditation, these thoughts can be challenged with the Lie Detector and controlled with Mindful Breathing. The QOLT approach to Meditation whether occasional or regular is detailed in the Toolbox CD handout, Mindful Breathing and Meditation.

Regular Meditation and Relaxation Rituals for Chronic Worry/Negative Affectivity

A regular or daily Relaxation Ritual (see the Toolbox CD entry) or Meditation Practice—even for only 10 minutes per day—is recommended as a system of emotional control for clients with high or chronic negative affectivity even though it requires a daily commitment of time and energy. Without a group as when done through a clinic, fitness club, YWCA/YMCA, church, temple, mosque, zendo, or Buddhist organization, daily meditation practice tends to fall by the wayside. Additionally, it is important to have friends and teachers to help when clients get discouraged with meditation practice or simply have questions. Many American Buddhist groups whether Insight-, Zen-, or Dzogchen-oriented make meditation "teachers" available to students for one-on-one instruction at no cost; the instruction can be wide ranging enough to include the discussion of mindfulness during the day, personal problems, and other practical aspects of the spiritual approach. Periodic retreats and "one-day sittings" are highly recommended and even necessary for some clients to really learn the skill of meditation. In contrast, Relaxation Rituals can be of immediate benefit to clients with much less practice.

Mindful Breathing Instructions to Convey to Clients

The goal of Mindful Breathing is to calm clients down a little, make them aware of intrusive thoughts that are unpleasant or self-defeating that they can explore and cognitively restructure later, take some of their attention away from these intrusive thoughts that are unpleasant or self-defeating, and thereby allow clients to focus all or most of their attention on the here and now or the present moment. With practice, clients attend more to what they have to do in the moment. They are more acutely aware of what is happening right now in their breathing, their body, and in the place where they are. It is a myth to say that mindfulness and meditation should always result in greater calm; the goal is greater awareness, not relaxation, although relaxation typically follows after clients have become aware of and have cognitively restructured their concerns, worries, and negative thoughts. For many, it is merely the recognition of certain ruts or negative cognitive patterns that clients become aware of, get tired of, and eventually learn to live with as "background noise" in their consciousness as in Shirley's frequent ruminations about the morality of her divorce given her marital vows made in her Presbyterian church to never leave the marriage. (Her schizotypal husband, a software engineer from Austin, was emotionally abusive, controlling, moved the family 20 times, and recently attempted to kidnap the children.)

The process of Mindful Breathing involves:

- Doing whatever needs to be done as in washing the dishes or straightening up your office. Everyday tasks can be completed while doing Mindful Breathing.
- Keeping one's posture as erect and still as possible when standing, walking, or sitting. Be sure to sit, stand, or walk as tall and erect as you can with your shoulders back and your back as straight as medically possible.[1]
- Concentrating on the:
  —Breath as it goes in and out of the nostrils—try to not breathe through the mouth.
  —Belly as it expands and contracts with the breath—clients can put a hand on their belly to make this more real.
  —Other parts of the body. This is an "in the body" rather than "out of body" experience. It is designed to make clients aware of all bodily sensations.
  —Sounds in the room.
  —Sights in the room.
  —*Favorite mantra:* Clients should repeat this mantra to themselves silently as they inhale and exhale: One word on the inhale and one word to yourself slowly as you exhale.

Some favorite mantras that I and my clients have found useful are included in Table 10.1.

The "No . . . Thought" word pair has helped worriers and ruminators in my practice as has "Here. . . . Now," which gently reminds clients to pay attention to the sights and sounds of the moment. Encourage clients to experiment with these mantras and to make up others on their own.

Table 10.1 Suggested Mantras for Mindful Breathing

Utter to yourself upon your . . . In-breath or inhalation	Utter to yourself upon your . . . Out-breath or each time you exhale
In	Out
Here	Now
(Say nothing)	Ah
Deep	Slow
1	2 . . . to 10
No	Thought
(Say nothing)	1 . . . to 10
(Say nothing)	One
Deep	Still
In-2-3	Out-2-3 (prevents hyperventilation)
(Say nothing and just breathe)	(Say nothing and just breathe)
Mer-	-cy
Let	Go (of judgments, worries, etc.)
Judge	Not
My	Movie

Dealing with Distractions

When practicing Mindful Breathing or Meditation, clients should gently and "endlessly" acknowledge intrusive thoughts and ruminations. Tell clients to greet them as they might an old friend who is not a favorite but whom they know nonetheless, and then gently refocus their attention to their breath, body, sound, or mantra. It is fine to spend the whole time in Mindful Breathing just redirecting attention from thoughts about the past or future to the present moment. Thoughts can range from "I'm a bad person" to "This is a waste" to "What shall I eat for lunch?"

Like grasshoppers in a Texas field, interfering thoughts will continually pop up or fly up in any mindfulness exercise or practice. This is just part of Mindful Breathing. Clients should be encouraged not to try to banish or suppress these interfering worries when they come. Instead, they should welcome them as they might an annoying relative who has come to visit. Teach clients to cope with ruminations by acknowledging them in the back of their mind as they then gently try to refocus their attention on the task at hand. Instruct clients to let the annoying worry or rumination stay in the back of their mind as they proceed with an activity. To gently refocus attention, clients may ask themselves:

- What am I doing?
- What are my goals for this situation?

By asking these questions, the abyss of ruminating about a troublesome issue is replaced by mindful concentration on the task at hand. It becomes, "I am cleaning the toilet and want to stay in this moment, and really make the bathroom nice." So if your clients ruminate too much or have a problem with negative feelings intruding on their activities, instruct them to ask themselves these questions over and over, whenever they get distracted from the task at hand.

By asking yourself, What am I doing? you can refocus your attention on the task at hand and try to do the best that you can at that task since, in mindfulness terms, the present moment is all that you have. It is the most important time in your life because it is all you have, the past being a memory and the future, a fantasy or expectation. By asking yourself, "What are my goals for this situation?"—the essence of QOLT is tapped since we are invited to consider an activity in terms of our personal goals. For example, a badgering father who loved to tell his teenage daughter how to raise her child, changed his behavior after realizing that his main goal was to provide his daughter with a safe and comfortable haven from an abusive boyfriend and not to teach her child-rearing skills. This change of heart saved a relationship that had turned sour.

A preoccupied businessman bathed his children at night in a mindful way, thereby managing his rampant worry and generalized anxiety disorder.

Remember, the goal of mindfulness is single-pointed concentration on whatever it is we are doing in *this* moment.

From Mindful Breathing to QOLT Meditation

Mindful Breathing can be expanded to a more intense Meditation session by instructing clients to:

- Sit erect in a chair and looking down at the floor with eyes open or closed—whatever is comfortable—using a timer while completing the other steps in Mindful Breathing. Lying on the floor with a pillow is okay to try if you do not find yourself falling asleep. Always tell clients to see a physician about how erect a posture to assume if they feel any pain or have had any back or other pain problems in the past.
- Be sure to sit as tall and erect as you can with your shoulders back and your back straight. Clients usually will not touch the back of the chair.
- Sit as still as possible, allowing short breaks to shift position or scratch an itch.
- Gently place the hands on the thighs.

The general effect should be sitting up expectantly, as if the client were an eager student about to raise his or her hand to answer a question in class.

The idea of Meditation is for clients to energetically meet and accept whatever comes to their mind or their life situation, trying their best to learn what they can and to make the best of the situation, and help others in their sphere as much as possible. Meditation posture also can be viewed like a lion poised to strike or pounce. It is athletic and demanding, building patience and tolerance and strength as we stay perfectly still, poised, tall, and ready for anything. In this sense, it is a metaphor for life, as clients await and welcome each moment. Indeed, experienced practitioners speak of meditating or doing zazen (Zen's term for meditation) 24/7, that is, very aware and alert to each unfolding moment of the day without judging things or trying to change them. The attitude taken toward the self is one of *loving-kindness*. *Loving-kindness* is taught first to your imperfect self and then to other people and the rest of the world.

Ideally, clients learn to accept any painful truth that greets them in meditation or elsewhere in their lives but yet remain ultimately optimistic that they will *survive and thrive* eventually, in whatever circumstances unfold (Blind Dumb Optimism and Meanings as Buses Tenets). They learn to accept that old worries, personal "demons"/frailties/pecadillos, unhealthy urges, and neuroses will revisit them for as long as they live. They learn to greet these unwelcome "guests" with calm and equanimity. They learn to rechannel the energy of strong emotions into their most cherished parts of life and constructive personal projects. They stop demanding perfection in anyone or in any situation and they stop trying to hold, possess, or control life, loved ones, or friends. Therapy is a must, a necessary adjunct to meditation for those of us with psychological disorders, unhappy temperaments or deep pain, hurts or wounds from childhood.

Meditation need not be an indoor exercise. Encourage clients to try going outside to walk leisurely, counting their steps to themselves, as they focus on walking and the surrounding sights and sounds. They may also use a mantra as they walk such as "Here. . . . Now."

Meditation can be done in a seated, walking, or recumbent/lying down position. When particularly distracted or upset, CDs or MP3 files geared toward assisting Meditation may be played such as those developed by the pioneering teacher, Jon Kabat-Zinn, at http://www.mindfulnesstapes.com. CDs by Jack Kornfield published by Soundstrue.com are highly recommended adjuncts that can be played in the car while driving, allowing for frequent review of mindfulness training. The client guide to Mindful Breathing and Meditation in the Toolbox CD contains further instructions for clients in expanding Mindful Breathing to full-blown QOLT Meditation.

QOLT Meditation as a Prelude to Prayer or Other Spiritual Practices

Mindful breathing or Meditation is an excellent prelude to prayer or some other type of contemplative spiritual practice as we first settle down, become aware of our issues and concerns that interfere with a focus on the moment and on The Divine, God, Ultimate Reality, Higher Power, the Tao, or Ground-of-Being. All major wisdom traditions or religions have contemplative or meditative prayer branches that clients may explore should Spiritual Life be an area of life that is important to them (see Feed the Soul Tenet). All major faith traditions have a type of silent prayer in which we simply sit still and listen for the Divine; indeed, this was a favorite prayer technique of Mother Teresa of Calcutta (1983).

The Guide for Worry Warts and the Over-Emotional: A Second Cognitive *Process* Intervention in QOLT

Over-emotionality is another QOLT term for neuroticism, emotional reactivity, emotionality, negative affectivity, and Negative Affect or Sensitivity Syndrome. People who worry too much, ruminate about problems *ad nauseum,* and are prone to the Big Three negative feelings of anger, anxiety, and depression need to control the *process* of anxious worry and depressive or angry rumination and not just try to fight or dispute or challenge with every upsetting thought or worry that they experience. Many researchers now see *anxious worry* as synonymous with *depressive* or *angry rumination;* in each case, clients obsess about their negative feelings whenever they experience them (McMillan & Fisher, 2004). Clients are urged to carry around the Guide for Worry Warts from the Toolbox CD to see if it can reduce the time they spend spinning their wheels with worry and rumination. Using the guiding rubric of "collaborative empiricism" (A. T. Beck et al., 1979), clients are encouraged to prove or to demonstrate to themselves that worry is unhelpful. For example, clients can be told to first alternate use of the Guide with their old habit of worrying in a constant or uncontrolled fashion, employing one approach or the other on alternate days of the week.

Based on the work of Adrian Wells and others (Wells & Papageorgiou, 2004), The Guide for Worry Warts involves a habitual routine for clients to follow when as they notice undue worry, anxiety (or other Big Three emotion), or rumination about a problem:

- As soon as you notice worrying about something, postpone the worrying by promising yourself that you will think about the problem later in the day during a set Worry Time.

- Plan a time during the day for 15 to 30 minutes of worrying. Try to do this Worry Time during the day when you are most relaxed and centered—for example, *after* exercising, relaxing, or at a time of day when you are at your best with high Inner Abundance.
- Outside of Worry Time, gently try to distract yourself from worries with:
  —Mindful Breathing or Meditation (see the Toolbox CD).
  —A service activity that benefits someone else such as calling a friend in need or helping out someone at the office.
  —Some activity that needs to be done.
  —Aerobic physical activity of any kind such as walking. Exercising for 30 minutes is especially helpful.

  Do not try to banish or suppress worries when they come. Welcome them as you might an annoying relative whom you have to see by acknowledging them in the back of your mind and then gently trying to refocus your attention on the task at hand. Let the annoying worry or rumination stay in the back of your mind as you proceed with an activity. To gently refocus attention, ask yourself, "What am I doing now? What is my goal?" thus, the abyss of ruminating about the perfect mate you let get away, becomes, "I am cleaning the toilet and want to stay in this moment, and really make the bathroom nice." The goal of mindfulness is single-point concentration on whatever it is you are doing in this moment.
- When the time for Worry Time arrives:
  —Try to avoid processing the worry with Worry Time. That is, decide if you really need to worry about anything. If you decide that you do not need to worry or process the worry, go on to your next activity for the day.
  —If you decide that you need to process the worry via Worry Time, set a time limit for your worrying. Eventually, try to allow yourself no more than 15 minutes to worry about your problem(s).
  —Be compassionate with yourself and very caring as you acknowledge each painful worry as you might a cut or bruise. That is, gently care for yourself and care for each worry by gently exploring the problem and how it might be managed or solved.
  —It can help to write each problem down, to brainstorm solutions via Five Paths or Lie Detector in the Toolbox CD, and then to pick a solution or so-

lutions to try that have the greatest chance for *long-term* success at a reasonable cost. It can help to ask a trusted friend about which solution or solutions seems to be the best to try out first. This is called the Second Opinion or Expert Friend Tenet/technique.
- Try to do some aerobic physical activity every day for 20 to 30 minutes. Do this at a comfortable pace—it is not necessary to set a speed record for yourself or to do this fast to get a mood calming effect and a reduction in worry. Start small as with a 5-minute walk and try to get a buddy to do the activity with regularly. The socializing aspect can help your faithfulness in doing the activity and the conversation does wonders for worry by itself.
- Try to develop other Relaxation Rituals—see the Toolbox CD for two possible Rituals—that you can count on to calm you down such as prayer, meditation, listening to music, pleasure reading, visiting with a close friend, or taking a bath. These too can have a great mood calming effect that reduces worry.
- Find your own way to Be the Peace and Calm You Seek. As hard as it is to believe, we all have a Calming Response within us just as we have the capacity for the Fight or Flight (Freeze, Faint, Tend, and Befriend) Stress Response.

TECHNIQUES FOR MANAGING ANGER

Besides the Anger Is the Enemy Tenet, QOLT approaches anger management with a full panoply of cognitive therapy techniques such as the thought record and schema work described here and in other cognitive therapy texts, especially Burns (1999) and Hightower (2002). Additionally, QOLT espouses the following general approach to anger management that was developed independent of Hightower's (2002) approach:

- Treat anger like an addiction or compulsive behavior, that is, a behavior that feels good but that is, ultimately, self-defeating in the long term. Anger robs clients of joy or satisfaction in the moment as they brood. It can also cause immunosuppression, tissue damage, heart disease, and other physical sequelae of chronic negative affect. A good assignment for this is the Pro versus Con technique.
- Always start with an overall case conceptualization. Clark and Beck's (1999) theory explicitly applies to

anger. What is the stressor, schemata leading to anger and other problems?

- Try to involve loved ones and significant others such as partners, family, and even coworkers and bosses in assessment and treatment when it is in the best interests of the client.
- Look out for underlying fragile self-esteem or defective person schemas. Underlying fragile self-esteem supported by Defective Person Schemas—see Schemas That Drive Us Crazy in the Toolbox CD— are often involved with chronic anger. Some clients cannot accept criticism in an area that threatens their concept of themselves. More secure clients can deal with criticism without self-defeating anger as they:
  —Correct an error without ever questioning their general worth as a person, or
  —Blow off a criticism that is clearly inaccurate and unjust.

In cases where self-esteem problems and negative self-schemas relate to anger problems, QOLT invokes Schema-Change Emotional Control techniques along with self-esteem treatments—see Chapter 12—when treating anger management problems whether or not angry feelings are expressed inappropriately though aggression.

Setting the Session Agenda with Pressing Problems in Anger Management

The following guidelines are suggested for in-session therapist demeanor in anger management cases:

- Limit sessions to a context of immediate and lifetime goals.
- Frame discussions of problem situations in terms of coping and prevention for the next time the client becomes angry.
- Empathize with client's feelings without endorsing how feelings were expressed.
- Discuss coping with an anger spiral.
- Discuss prevention of trigger situations.
- Discuss relapse prevention for the upcoming week.

Specific Anger Management Techniques

Specific anger management techniques are based on compulsive behavior/addiction treatments detailed in Chapter 13 under the Habit Control Program. All of

the following QOLT procedures have been useful in anger management:

- Self-Monitoring of Anger defined as behavior based on angry feelings, viewing each as a habit or addiction.
  —Habit Diary—Clients record urges, fantasies, and incidents of anger and aggression. Ask them about these at the start of each session to make sure they are keeping themselves safe.
  —Thought Records or Lie Detector forms and other cognitive therapy techniques.
- Arousal Reduction.
  —Relaxation Ritual.
  —Mindful Breathing.
  —Recreation Routine.
  —Regular Aerobic Exercise.
- Cognitive Restructuring and Philosophy of Life.
  —Cultivate Good-Natured Humor.
  —Empathy Training.
  —Vision Quest technique.
  —Tenets of Contentment and New Life Script.
  —Spiritual Life and Helping Interventions.
- Social Skills and Assertion Training.
  —QOLT Relationship Enhancement.
  —Awareness Building with Take-a-Letter.
  —Role-Play Problem Situations.
- Problem Solving.
  —Five Paths.
  —Second Opinion and Business Partner Metaphor for couples.
- Distraction using the Play List and other Play techniques.
- Relapse Prevention.
  —Role-Play Trigger Situations found in Habit Diary.
  —Develop a Relapse Emergency Checklist—see the Toolbox CD.

SCHEMA WORK IN QOLT: PROS VERSUS CONS, TENETS OF CONTENTMENT, AND LIFE SCRIPT TECHNIQUE

QOLT schema work incorporates the cognitive restructuring techniques reviewed previously as well as time-honored techniques of looking at the advantages (pros) versus disadvantages (cons) of a schema along the lines of Motivational Interviewing Therapy to build motivation for altering or abandoning a negative schema altogether. In disputing core negative schemas, QOLT suggests that clients complete the exercise, Schemas to Drive You Crazy, and review the diagram of Beck's theory to see the process an individual goes through in becoming clinically anxious, angry, or upset. After clients identify schemas and look at their Pros versus Cons, QOLT will have them explore positive alternatives by having them piece together an alternative from the Tenets of Contentment. The Tenets can be viewed as positive schemas that enhance well-being and activate the constructive mode in Beck's theory of psychopathology or "negative psychology." Although positive schemas must be found to dispute and replace negative schemas leading to psychopathology, therapists should encourage QOLT clients to embrace any and all Tenets or positive schemas that they can in the service of enhancing well-being and in the service of building a resilient philosophy of life. This approach to building a resilient philosophy of life is elaborated in greater detail in the Life Script technique, presented in Chapter 11.

CLINICAL ILLUSTRATION OF SCHEMA WORK: THE CASE OF TOM

The case of Tom was first introduced and illustrated in Chapters 3 and 6. Here we examine Tom's schema work. Although Tom overemphasizes the importance of work in his life, which is characteristic of perfectionistic clients who may also have a history of abuse or neglect, Tom aspires to a more balanced and fulfilling lifestyle of flow and meaning to include the recreation and friendships he has neglected, along with his love life, spiritual life, and health (lack of exercise, smoking, overeating, and problem drinking). He has bought into the positive psychology and nonpathology view of QOL theory that all valued areas of life contribute to the overall life satisfaction equation and that all must be honored or recognized by being included in his life priorities and daily schedule if he wishes to feel happier and less frenzied. Finally, Tom understood Beck's theory and how it applied to his case conceptualization shared in Chapter 6. He understood how stressors and schemas interact to create a witches brew of depression and other Big Three emotions along with genetic and other risk factors. He also understood that schema work was the key to successful cognitive therapy and that his *self* schemas were

abysmal (see Chapter 12 for Tom's schema work related to the self). Many of the positive schemas that Tom adopted came from the Tenets of Contentment (see Table 10.2) along with especially insightful thought records or Lie Detectors that he had completed on a daily basis while in therapy.

LIFE MANAGEMENT SKILLS NEEDED FOR SUCCESSFUL GOAL STRIVING IN QOLT

Clients can gain control of their lives and make steady progress in solving problems and in achieving life goals and subgoals, including happiness, if they are reasonably organized in how they manage their day-to-day affairs and especially their time. If their time is planned and managed so that small steps of progress toward goals are made every day (called Zen Steps to Success here)—or subgoals in the service of larger, long-term goals are achieved (e.g., Graded Task Assignment; A. T. Beck et al., 1979), then they will feel happier and more content instead of dysphoric and frustrated—feelings associated with unsuccessful goal-striving and coping. Indeed, successful goal striving is negatively reinforced to the extent that dysphoria and frustration are reduced with goal attainment. In QOLT, skills in managing day-to-day affairs and time in the service of goal striving define Life Management Skills, along with basic relationship skills or social skills required for any level of goal attainment. A modicum of ability in these skills is essential to happiness according to QOL theory, since happiness goal strivings will lead to naught without them. This is the rationale behind time management procedures in QOLT that are taught to both clinical and nonclinical populations.

Time Management

To change the circumstances in any valued area of life, clients have to carefully manage their time so that these priorities are addressed and not just forgotten. For example, when one client was trying to find time alone with her husband, it was essential for her and her husband to carefully plan how they managed their time in advance. This allowed them to regain the sense of intimacy that was lost once their schedules became completely consumed by their work and child-care responsibilities.

Table 10.2 Controlling Negative Emotions: Tenets Conducive to Emotional Control

Accept What You Cannot Change Principle

ACOAN Principle or Abuse or Neglect Principle

Anger Is the Enemy or Shift of Hate Principle

Avoid Stress Carriers or I Never Bother with People I Hate Rule

Balanced Lifestyle Principle

Be the Peace You Seek or Worry Warts Principle

Be Your Own Guru or Personal Wisdom Principle

Calculated Risk Principle

Can't Buy Me Love or Forget Fame and Fortune Rule

Care for My One Body Principle

Daily Vacation Principle

Depression Is Not Normal Principle

Don't Bring it Home or Work Spillover Principle

Don't Forgive Principle or Set Aside, Shelve, Accept or Forget Principle

Do the Right Thing or Clear Conscience Rule or When in Doubt, Don't Rule

Emotional Control or The Big Three Make Us Dumb Principle

Emotional Honesty Principle

Exercise or Take Their Medication Principle

Expect the Unexpected Principle

Face the Music Principle

Failure Quota Principle

Feed the Soul Principle

Fight for Much, Reap Frustration Principle

Fight the Power Principle

Find an Area or Go to Your Room Principle

Flow It Principle

The FOOBS Principle or Switch Out of FOOBS Principle

Get a Therapist Rule

Giving Tree or Self-Other Principle

The Grass Isn't Greener, It's Weeds Principle

The Great Compromise Principle

Habits Rule or Routines Rule

Happiness Diet Principle

Happiness Is a Choice Principle

How Kind Principle or Tender Hearted Rule

Humor Principle

I Can Do It Principle

I'll Think about That Tomorrow Principle

Inner Abundance Principle

Intellectual Masturbation Principle

Judge Not, You Don't Know Principle

Keep Busy with Flows or Happiness Takes Effort Principle

Keeping Up with the Jones Principle

Kiss the Past Goodbye Principle

Leisurely Pace and Lifestyle Principle

Li Po or Commune with Nature Rule

Love and Work Principle

"Mad Col." Disease Rule

Make Friends at Work Principle

Manage Your Time and Your Life Rule

Marching Orders Principle

Mental Health Day Technique

Mine the Moment or Attack the Moment Principle

Modest Goal or Flow Principle

Mutual Aid Society Principle

Never Good Enough or Lower Expectations Principle

No Conditions of Worth Rule

No Gossip/Criticism/Suggestions or Words as Daggers Rule

One-Thing-at-a-Time Principle (OTAAT)

Overthinking Principle

Personality Stays the Same or Happiness Set Point Principle

Pick Your Battles/Pick No Battles Principle or Yes, Boss/Yes, Dear Rule

Play It Safe Principle

Positive Addictions Principle

Process Goal Principle

(continued)

Table 10.2 *Continued*

Quality Time Principle	String of Pearls Practice and Principle
The Question Rule	Surrogate Family Principle
Relationship with Self or Self-Compassion Principle	Sweet Revenge Principle
Ride It Out, Read It Out Principle	Taoist Dodge Ball Rule
Routine Is Everything or Make It a Routine Principle	The Three Rs of Stress Management Principle
Second Opinion Principle or Technique	Thou Shalt Be Aware or Psychephobia Principle
See a Psychiatrist Principle	To Understand All Is to Forgive All or Empathy Principle
Selective Hedonism or Reasoned Passion Principle	Trust Principle
Self-Acceptance Principle	Under the Influence or Yes, Dear Rule
Serve Others Principle	We Are Family Principle
Share the Hurt behind the Anger Tenet	We're Not Okay and That's Okay Rule
Should-Want Principle	What Would My Role Model Do or Role Model Principle
Silence Is Golden or Organ Recital Rule	You Can't Have It All Principle or Curb or Ignore Desires Principle
Street Signs to Success Principle	
Stress Carriers or I Never Bother with People I Hate Rule	You Do It to Yourself or Terrorist Principle

Balanced Lifestyle Principle or Tenet

The positive psychology and nonpathology-oriented view of CASIO theory explains unhappiness from the assumption that all valued areas of life contribute to the overall life satisfaction equation and that they must be honored or recognized by being included in one's life priorities and daily schedule if a person wishes to feel happier. This can often mean painful choices as clients parcel their limited time toward their most important priorities, shelving many things or areas they might like to pursue if the days were longer. The process of balancing can take time in situations in which major life changes are in order as in changing jobs. In these cases, clients must stay optimistic that things will change with time and practice Emergency Inner Abundance while they are waiting. Supportive friends, coworkers, or spiritual communities can help in these difficult transitions from an unbalanced to a more balanced lifestyle. Lifestyle imbalance is a recurring theme in the professional self-care literature suggesting it is important to consider and address if people wish to boost their happiness or satisfaction. The Happiness Pie exercise expresses this principle in a powerful and pictorial way.

What may be unique to the QOLT approach to time management is that QOLT tries to make a connection in how people order their daily routines and their overarching life goals. Quality of life therapists should encourage clients to prioritize every day the things that they do so that they only spend time on those things that are of the greatest long-term importance to their quality of life. To paraphrase the saying "Put your money where your mouth is," clients are told, "Put your time and effort where your values are." In general, clients are encouraged to take an existential view in which each day is viewed as one of the last days of their lives and should be used to the utmost to further their goals and to provide some reasonable pleasure and satisfaction. They are also urged to think about their own death, clarifying what is important to them. Personal goals and related activities are enshrined in clients' schedules for each day.

The two basic QOLT tools for managing life and time are Quality Time, during which goals are recalled and the next day's activities are considered, and the more structured Daily Activity Plan (DAP) that, after some practice, is replaced by the Short-Form Activity Schedule or Daily Activity Plan (DAP-brief version). Both instruments are available in the Toolbox CD under "Daily Activity Plan."

Box 10.2 presents the DAP of LaKeithia, a 68-year-old disabled widow with a pronounced limp who cares

BOX 10.2
Daily Activity Plan (DAP): Clinical Example

Name: _____   Day of Week: _____   Date: _____

Instructions: Plan each day in the morning or the night before. Rate your satisfaction as soon as you can after an activity is done.

To Do List	Plan of Action	Actual Activities	
Rate each item 1 = Essential, must do today 2 = Important 3 = Can wait	Make a tentative schedule for the day.	Write down what you did and how satisfying it felt on a 0 to 10 scale with 10 being the highest satisfaction possible.	
1 Dress and eat	6:00 A.M.	6:00 A.M.	
1 Make hair appt.	6:30 *Get up and shower*	6:30	
1 Help son with hygiene problem	7:00 *Breakfast*	7:00 *Shower and dress*	*3*
1 Quality time	7:30 *Call hairdresser*	7:30	
3 Grocery shop	8:00 *Call Mae*	8:00	
1 Clean kitchen	8:30 *Help son*	8:30 *Coffee/breakfast*	*8*
2 Pick up house	9:00	9:00 *Help son with problem*	*2*
3 Laundry	9:30	9:30	
3 Watch TV sitcoms	10:00	10:00	
3 Ask Mae to lunch.	10:30 *Do laundry*	10:30 *Clean kitchen*	*7*
2 Make dinner	11:00	11:00	
2 Run new computer program	11:30 *Make lunch*	11:30 *Make hair appt.*	*8*
3 Pleasure read	12 noon	12 noon *Lunch alone*	*2*
3 Plan party	12:30 P.M. *Lunch with Mae*	12:30 P.M. *Call friend/plan party*	*9*
3 Call about computer class	1:00	1:00 *Watch TV and do laundry*	*0*
	1:30 *Shopping*	1:30	
	2:00	2:00 *Work on computer*	*7*
	2:30	2:30	
	3:00	3:00 *Pick up house*	*3*
	3:30 *Pick up house*	3:30 *Quality time/relax*	*8*

for her mentally retarded son. After considerable resistance, LaKeithia agreed to complete a Daily Activity Plan after two sessions of QOLT. As part of her Quality Time in the evening, LaKeithia planned what she wanted to do the next day by completing the first two columns of the DAP. In completing her to-do list, she wrote down everything that came to her mind that she wanted to accomplish during the next day. Then she went back over her list and rated each item 1, 2, or 3, depending on how important it was to get done the next day. Next, she made a tentative Plan of Action. This helps to mobilize clients and make sure that important things get done by giving them a concrete, though flexible, guide as to what they should do at what time during the next day. LaKeithia kept her DAP either in her purse or on her kitchen table so that after every activity or frequently during the day she could complete the third column of the DAP and write down the actual activity she engaged in as well as her satisfaction in doing that activity.

As can be seen from Box 10.2, LaKeithia seemed to gain a sense of pleasure and satisfaction from having her morning coffee, calling a friend in order to plan a party, and relaxing and collecting her thoughts during her regularly scheduled Quality Time. She also experienced satisfaction based on a feeling of accomplishment when she did some things that were, perhaps difficult, but necessary in her mind to maintain her home and appearance, such as cleaning the kitchen, and making an appointment to have her hair done. It appears she may have suffered by not following through on her plan to call her friend Mae to join her for lunch. She also had difficulty in communicating with her son as reflected in her low rating for "Help son with problem"; this rating alerted the health care professional to discuss this issue in more detail, and, in fact, teach LaKeithia more effective child management techniques for dealing with her profoundly retarded son. While watching TV appeared to do nothing for her mood, her newfound hobby of using the computer gave her some satisfaction even though she was afraid at first to try this recreational activity that seemed to be ideally suited to her disability.

One unique feature of the DAP is the "To-Do List" in the first column. Every day clients list the things they would like to accomplish for that day in this column. After a To-Do List is generated, the next column is filled out in preparation for the day. This is a tentative Plan of Action. It is best for clients to do both the

To-Do List and the Plan of Action either in the evening or first thing in the morning as part of their daily Quality Time. The final part of the Daily Activity Plan, the "Actual Activities" column, is something that should be filled out on an hour-by-hour basis. Just as with the Plan of Action or To-Do List, clients may express themselves in only a few words. Clients also rate the satisfaction they feel from doing different activities during the day. This is extremely important in alleviating depression and unhappiness. Satisfaction is defined in two different ways. It reflects pleasure as when a client visits a friend or eats an ice cream cone, or a feeling of accomplishment as when clients do something they've been putting off, as in cleaning the bathroom.

Just as LaKeithia did, at the end of each day (preferably during Quality Time) and during QOLT sessions each week, it helps for clients to review their Daily Activity Plans to look for patterns. Are there certain activities that give clients more satisfaction, pleasure, or feelings of accomplishments than others? Clients may want to increase the frequency of high-satisfaction activities. It is good for clients to have some "down time" for pure pleasure or a fun activity each day; one client did this by planning lunch with a friend each day. It's also important to determine the extent to which clients are getting things done that are related to overall goals. These "big goals" should be broken down into specific activities that will help clients to gradually move toward their goals (see Zen Steps to Success technique). Some of these "baby-step" activities should be in a client's schedule or DAP each day.

Clients should also take note of planned activities that are actually carried out in a day. If they have too many "1" rated activities that are not getting done each day, it may be that they are overcommitted and not prioritizing their day sufficiently to build a reasonable and workable schedule routine.

Many clients resist the structure of the DAP since they think that they can do what they want whenever they want. In fact, this unstructured approach usually makes depressed clients more depressed since they are notoriously poor at pacing themselves, that is, they always try to do too much in too little time. In addition to teaching clients how to pace themselves, the DAP provides a structure for clients to act on their insight once they have solved a problem or chosen a path to increase their quality of life in some area. Specifically, any problem solution or approach to increasing the quality of life should be reflected in a client's daily schedule to ensure that they really implement their insights, solutions, and strategies. Without making concrete changes in their everyday life, including taking risks and trying new ways of coping, clients will continue to feel dissatisfied and frustrated.

Another invaluable lesson learned from the DAP is that even the most unhappy and depressed clients will have moments of satisfaction, pleasure, and even joy during particular parts of certain days. Clients can accept this fact better when they show it to themselves than when a therapist might suggest it. It is important for clients to note times of pleasure or satisfaction on the DAP so that they can schedule more of these activities in the future in order to improve their mood or quality of life. This usually involves a more balanced approach to living in which clients regularly schedule some time for recreation and relaxation throughout their day. The DAP may also reveal simple problems in living that can be easily solved as in the case of the "night owl" client who realized that she could no longer stay up so late and still feel refreshed and alert in the morning. DAP records also typically reveal that clients are happier when they are busy than when they sit around or pursue passive recreation, such as watching TV.

Short Form Activity Schedule or Brief Daily Activity Plan (BDAP)

Once clients have completed Daily Activity Plans for 1 or 2 weeks, they can be switched to one of two more efficient plans for planning their daily activities. The BDAP drastically reduces the time blocks and complexity of the DAP giving clients major blocks of time during which tasks like going for a job interview or studying for classes must get done. The Short Form Activity Schedule is a simple option that involves Clients purchasing a 5 × 7 tablet of paper and each day listing the activities that they hope to accomplish that day on a sheet of paper. Clients start by listing necessary appointments that have already been scheduled and then add other routine tasks that must be done that day. Next, they may add other activities that relate to long-term goals. Once this list is complete, clients simply go down the list and rate only the top priority or "1" activities or the things that must be done that day and that can be reasonably accomplished. Clients may carry this list with them, adding to it during the day. They may also note any concerns or problems that

come up, which they can then forget about until their Quality Time at the end of the day. In addition to keeping some kind of activity schedule, clients should also purchase a date book that they can check every day for necessary and required appointments. Rather than over regimenting clients' lives, these basic time management procedures have a freeing effect as clients' sense that they are getting things done and still have time to play and relax.

TIME MANAGEMENT PRINCIPLES

The following Time Management Principles can be shared with clients whether an activity schedule is used or not:

- *Double time:* To reduce the stress in clients' lives it can be helpful, when possible, to estimate the time needed for doing a task and then double that time. This can give clients sufficient latitude to get things done in a relaxed way and to handle the inevitable obstacles or hassles that are likely to come up.
- *Delegate responsibility:* If there's anything that clients can delegate to others, other family members, children, coworkers, or administrative staff, it is often a good idea for them to do so in order to lighten their burden.
- *Say "no" to unreasonable requests:* Some clients become unhappy and depressed because their life is dominated by requests to do things for others, which leaves them with no time to address their own priorities. See Chapter 14 on Relationships for more techniques that can enable clients to set reasonable limits with others.
- *Prioritize and stick to a schedule:* It is often too easy for clients to get sidetracked in carrying out a schedule or Daily Activity Plan.
- *Build a modest schedule with time for both pleasure and accomplishment:* One key to happiness may be setting modest goals each day and attaining those goals. Challenge clients to sculpt a modest, but fulfilling, schedule of activities for each day that enables them to gain satisfaction in valued parts of life but does not overtax them to the point that their moment-to-moment quality of life is sacrificed.
- *FAT time:* For clients with families it is important for them to schedule time each week for: (1) **Family**

time when they can visit and recreate as a family; (2) **A**lone time when they can relax and "recharge their batteries" by themselves as with Quality Time; and (3) **T**ogether time when they spend time away from the kids with their partner. This "together time" should be like a date. The idea is to relax and talk as a couple in order to keep feelings of romance and closeness alive.

Zen Steps or Stepping Stones to Success Technique

The term *Zen Steps* refers to the walking meditation called *kinchin*—pronounced kin hin in which very small and slow steps are taken on the path to enlightenment, or specifically, in walking meditation. Additionally, Zen students carry out all activities slowly, carefully, and mindfully—that is, with the fullest attention possible (see Mindful Breathing) and for doing only one activity at a time. The concept of engineering or planning small success experiences to build clients' confidence in key areas of life as they progress toward personal goals provides rationale for Zen Steps or Stepping Stones or Baby Steps to Success technique—this is similar to the Graded Task Assignment (Beck, 1995; Beck et al., 1979).

To implement the Zen Steps technique, therapists and clients work together to break down clients major life goals into tiny, manageable Zen Steps or activities (or Baby Steps or Stepping Stones if clients prefer these metaphors). For example, a shy male client was asked by his psychologist to talk briefly to a grocery store checker in preparation for asking a woman out for coffee and, later, dinner. This example involved "shaping" as well as "Zen Steps to Success" since the client learned and practiced new Relationship Skills from the Toolbox CD in session before each homework assignment and since each assignment was a successive approximation to dating skills designed to provide natural reinforcement or a success experience. Therapists can often assess clients' skills through role-playing and behavioral rehearsal of assignments before such assignments are given to see what clients' capabilities really are (Frisch et al., 1982; Frisch & Froberg, 1987; Frisch & Higgins, 1986).

Another client, Jude, put great effort in studying a menu as preparation for a test that was part of getting a job as a waiter at a local restaurant. This involved a

Stepping Stone toward his career goal of becoming an engineer since it enabled him to begin saving money for college.

The essence of Zen Steps involves reducing the large steps needed to attain overall life goals like finding a satisfactory mate into "tiny," "little," short-term steps, subgoals and activities of a few years, months, weeks, and even minutes. This is vital for sustained motivation. It is only when clients and therapists break overwhelmingly large goals into tiny pieces or steps that clients can truly feel a regular sense of accomplishment that will keep them on their way toward a long-term goal.

Zen Steps is closely related to other QOLT techniques; for example, it is a useful addition to Five Paths, Lie Detector exercises (as Action Plans are broken down into small steps or "stepping stones"), and the Daily Activity Plan, in which lifetime goals and subgoals are represented in very specific daily activities and moves clients closer to long-term goals.

Basic Relationship and Social Skills

In QOLT, skills in managing day-to-day affairs and time in the service of goal striving define Life Management Skills, along with basic Relationship Skills or social skills required for any level of goal attainment. Relationship Skills are delineated and applied in Chapter 14. Additionally, specific Relationship Skills can be found on the Toolbox CD and important relationship attitudes and schemas like Emotional Honesty and the Favor Bank can be found in the Tenets of Contentment.

A PRIMER IN COGNITIVE THERAPY

The QOLT approach to life management and emotional skills training contains variations on venerable cognitive therapy approaches to managing negative affect such as the Lie Detector and the Daily Activity Plan. In many ways, the chapter thus far is a review of cognitive therapy for negative affects. What follows in this last section of the chapter is a review of the basics of cognitive therapy as presented by Aaron T. Beck and his colleagues as a quick review or reference for readers who wish to seamlessly combine cognitive therapy with positive psychology interventions such as those in QOLT. The basic techniques in Beck's cognitive therapy of psychopathology—they are no longer applicable only to depression (see Clark & Beck, 1999)—are presented here in the order of presentation to clients. Readers are also encouraged to consult J. S. Beck (1995), and available cognitive therapy books/treatment manuals for specific *DSM* disorders, treatments that have been empirically supported in clinical trials—for example, see http://www .apa.org/divisions/div12/rev_est/index.html as well as the web site and listserv associated with the Academy of Cognitive Therapy with Aaron T. Beck as honorary president, http://www.academyofct.org/Info /Zoom.asp?InfoID=187&szparent=154&szPath=Add1.

Cognitive Therapy: An Outline Showing the Necessary Steps in Chronological Order

- Assessment and case conceptualization—this is always the first step in cognitive therapy. Find stressors and possible schema a la Beck's theory that is summarized in Chapter 3 on QOL theory and is illustrated in the Toolbox CD as Beck Theory Diagram. This diagram should be shared with clients during the next step on cognitive therapy.
- Share case conceptualization with client.
- Activity scheduling.
- Thought record.
- Problem solving of external problems contributing to psychopathology—Five Paths worksheet, Couples/Family Therapy, explore practical solutions and do cognitive restructuring via logical analysis or hypothesis testing via collaborative empiricism. You are an investigative team.
- Dealing with vexing symptoms via problem solving and treatment manuals (A. T. Beck et al., 1979).
- Schema change later in therapy.
- Relapse prevention via Mindfulness Training and/or QOLT, which has a mindfulness training component along with other positive psychology techniques for finding fulfillment in 16 areas of life.
- Setting the agenda in cognitive therapy.
- Jointly determine overall and session by session goals for client based on answers to the following:
  —What issues does the client bring to the session including urgent concerns or emergencies? (Be ready to scrap your agenda for that of the client in emergencies.)

- For each session, help to set the agenda at the beginning by asking these key, pertinent questions:
  —How are you feeling this week? Your BDI score is . . .
  —What do you want to work on today?
  —Here is my tentative agenda. These are some things I'd like us to discuss. These skills should make you feel better by (give reasonable date). These skills should help you begin to reach your goals by (give reasonable date).
- In session, unstructured or structured cognitive restructuring.
- Homework Review.
- Assign homework for next week with the rationale that completing homework gives clients "more bang for their buck" or faster results:
  —Hypothesis testing of automatic thoughts, schemas.
  —Implementing solutions from problem solving.
  —Bibliotherapy.
  —CBT technique practice.

THE MAJOR COMPONENTS OF COGNITIVE THERAPY

Activity Scheduling

Activity Scheduling consists of hourly rating and recording of activities. Activities are rated in terms of satisfaction, mastery, or pleasure on a form such as Frisch's Daily Activity Plan that includes an additional feature of a prioritized to-do list. This is done at the start of therapy for a week or more especially when clients are severely depressed. Activities can be recorded without ratings for the first week of this cognitive therapy homework assignment.

Goals for activity scheduling include:

- *Assess clients' daily routines* to look for problems such as impoverishment that may contribute to anxiety, depression, substance abuse, and so on.
- *Hypothesis testing* of beliefs that underlie symptoms of passivity and hopelessness such as "Nothing is satisfying or enjoyable anymore" or "Nothing I can do can help me feel better."
- *Planning activities* each day with an eye toward a balance of should versus want activities and a higher

should/want ratio as recommended in Marlatt's Relapse Prevention Treatment. Increasing the number and duration of pleasurable activities is a treatment in and of itself for behaviorists and others—see Peter Lewinsohn and so on.
- Often a reinforcement survey schedule such as the Play List (see Toolbox and Box 16.1) is used to suggest pleasurable activities to schedule (Playing tennis in the mountains case).
- Schedule time to carry out problem-solving solutions as part of therapy or coaching homework.
- *Graded task assignments* may also be embedded in activity schedules as when the activity of job hunting is broken down into 10 segments such as buying a newspaper for its want ads in order to make some tasks less overwhelming.
- *Provide a structured and routine ritual for staying active,* accomplishing goals, socializing, and pursuing pleasurable acts each day.

Use of Thought Record in Sessions and in Homework: A Primary Avenue for Cognitive Restructuring

A Thought Record such as Lie Detector and Stress Diary in the Toolbox CD is a structured way of journaling that allows clients to be their own therapist by being aware of, evaluating, and, when appropriate, changing their own automatic thoughts and even schemas. Ancillary materials such as a list of key questions or cognitive errors—see Beck's Three Questions or list of Cognitive Errors or Frisch's Lie Detection Questions in the Toolbox CD can help clients come up with cognitively restructured healthy, realistic, and positive answers to immobilizing automatic thoughts associated with the Big Three of negative affect—anxiety, depression, and anger. For alexithymic clients and others who have trouble *identifying* their specific thoughts associated with the Big Three and other emotions, materials like the Feeling Dictionary in the Toolbox can be useful. The Thought Record is the most common tool for cognitive restructuring in Beck's cognitive therapy. The Lie Detector has an Action Plan/Hypothesis testing homework component not typically found in other thought records.

Goals in Using Thought Record
- Assess clients' online automatic thoughts in and of themselves and as clues to underlying schemas.

- Logical analysis and effective disputation of dysfunctional beliefs that underlie symptoms of anxiety, depression, substance abuse, and other psychopathology.
- In some cases, hypothesis testing of dysfunctional beliefs that underlie symptoms of anxiety, depression, substance abuse, and other psychopathology.
- Provide a structured and routine coping ritual for dealing with Big Three emotions.

Instructions for Using the Thought Record

Only after successfully completing a thought record during a session, may Thought Records (or most any other exercise in QOLT or cognitive therapy) be assigned as homework. When ready, clients may be instructed to complete a thought record whenever they feel upset, preferably at the time that they are upset even if this means excusing themselves briefly from other activities.

Downward Arrow Technique. To get at schemas and other key "underlying" negative thoughts related to a thought record, try the Downward Arrow technique. My version is to simply repeatedly ask "And what does that mean or say about your self-esteem and future?" in response to every negative thought a client presents until you feel that you have gotten to the key issue, core schema or mode, or at least something that can be worked on in the session.

Use of the Cognitive Error or Distortions/Biases Handout to Facilitate Cognitive Restructuring

The Cognitive Error or Distortions/Biases Handout can also be used by therapists to help the process of coming up with positive reframes or adaptive alternative thoughts and schemas in the context of a thought record. The list of errors used here is reprinted in the Toolbox CD with permission from Dr. Judith Beck from her book (Beck, 1995).

With the aid of the therapist, clients first identify distortions or errors associated with a specific negative thought/belief or schema in the Thought Record—called "Upsetting Thoughts" column in the present Lie Detector thought record. Next, with the initial aid of therapists, clients challenge the thought by relating it to particular Cognitive errors or biases. Clients are taught to develop a "positive answer" or reframe to the negative thought based on the related cognitive distortion or error. For example, when clients assume or predict that they will fail in boosting happiness in a valued area of life, they may identify this reasoning as the "Fortune Teller Error," and reframe their pessimism by asserting, "I am not a fortune teller. I cannot predict the future. This effort may work out. I have never tried this approach and I am older and wiser than I was in the past when everything I did seemed to fail."

Problem Solving and Assessment in Cognitive Therapy

Cognitive therapy procedures involve the self-monitoring of thoughts and assumptions, logical analysis in which dysfunctional thoughts are disputed through logical argument, and hypothesis testing in which negative assumptions are challenged through "real-world" experiments aimed at testing their veracity (Hayes, Nelson, & Jarrett, 1987). According to both Persons and Bertagnolli (1999) and Frisch (1992), problem solving may constitute a little-recognized fourth component of cognitive therapy that is repeatedly mentioned in the "treatment manual" (Beck et al., 1979). According to A. T. Beck, "external," "situational," or "practical" problems or "precipitants" related to depression usually involve perceived losses at home, work, or school such as divorce or a business failure. The resolution of even simple and circumscribed problems either through consultation with the therapist or an appropriate "medical, legal, financial, or vocational" expert can in itself alleviate depressive symptoms. For example, the manual describes the case of a beleaguered homemaker whose "symptoms quickly disappeared" (p. 204) once she secured help with household chores. According to the manual, the focus of cognitive therapy at any given time is either a "target symptom" of depression such as passivity, sadness, or negative thoughts or an external problem situation, which seems to cause, maintain, or intensify depressive symptoms. Initially, the focus is on specific depressive symptoms targeted for treatment. With less severe depressions, or once acute symptoms have been relieved, the focus is on external problems related to the depression. In more recent works (e.g., DeRubeis & Beck, 2001) and videotapes of Dr. Beck, problem solving around external problems seems characteristic of cognitive therapy throughout the course of treatment even

when clients are suicidal. Empirical studies have also pointed to the need for comprehensive problem assessment and treatment in dealing with depressed patients, suggesting that different problems and skill deficits can cause depression and that treatment should be aimed at the particular problems of a particular client in order to be effective (McKnight, Nelson, & Hayes, 1984; Persons & Bertagnolli, 1999).

Cognitive therapists at time have observed a "snowball effect" in which improvement of one problem or symptom will somehow lead to changes in other areas (A. T. Beck et al., 1979; J. S. Beck, 1995). The Five Paths handout and exercise in the Toolbox CD involves one approach to problem solving that can be used in cognitive therapy. Whatever scheme of problem solving—for example, see pioneer, Thomas D'Zurilla, Marvin Goldfried, or Arthur Nezu's work—that is used should be applied in two ways over the course of cognitive therapy:

- Problem Solving of External Problems contributing to psychopathology—explore practical solutions and do cognitive restructuring via logical analysis or hypothesis testing via collaborative empiricism in which you, the therapist, are part of an investigative team with the client.
- Problem Solving with vexing Symptoms—Treatment Manuals such as J. S. Beck (1995) and A. T. Beck et al. (1979). For example, clients may decide to walk their dogs just before bedtime because this works effectively for them even though it is not a standard initial insomnia technique.

Schema Change Methods in Cognitive Therapy

The goal of schema change methods is to assess, evaluate, and modify clients' underlying negative schemas or core beliefs that feed the current episode of psychopathology and put them at risk—a negative schema is a diathesis in diathesis-stress theory terms—for future episodes. In other words, Negative Schemas are risk factors or cognitive vulnerabilities for future depression. Slight modifications rather than wholesale change are often sufficient and a more realistic therapy goal. Such minor modification can still have a prophylactic effect as when a perfectionist tries or dares to do a *very good* job in all he does rather than a *perfect* job in his pursuits.

Schema assessment can be accomplished in the following ways that are listed here and discussed in the context of the FOOBS Tenet of Contentment in the Toolbox CD:

- Underlying core beliefs can be abstracted by repeated themes/situations in Thought Records and issues raised in session.
- Instruments like the DAS and Young Schema Questionnaire, may have "treatment planning utility" even with poor psychometrics (Hayes, Nelson, & Jarrett, 1987). That is, they may help clients become aware of core schema or schema clusters/modes even when they are unscored and just examined item by item for patterns or possible schemas or modes.
- Going over the Schemas That Drive Us Crazy handout in the Toolbox CD with clients, especially after Thought Records have been kept for a while.

Here are some ways to dispute and challenge, and change negative schemas:

- Effective evaluation of negative thoughts and schemas via Hypothesis Testing and Logical Analysis of schemas that underlie symptoms of anxiety, depression, substance abuse, and other psychopathology. Foremost among these is what Frisch calls the Pro versus Con technique of simply listing the pros and cons of living in accord with a schema, highlighting the self-defeating aspects of negative schemas.
- Schemas can also be changed as one might change automatic thoughts via use of Thought Records at times such as QOLT's Lie Detector, a structured way of journaling that allows clients to be their own therapist by being aware of and changing their own automatic thoughts and even schemas. Ancillary materials such as a list of key questions—see Lie Detector Questions—and typical cognitive errors/biases—see Cognitive Errors—can help clients come up with cognitively restructured healthy and positive answers to immobilizing schemas associated with the Big Three of negative affect—anxiety, depression, and anger. The Lie Detector Questions go beyond the venerable "Three Questions" handout used by therapists in numerous cognitive therapy trials to include questions related to anxiety disorders (Barlow 2002), and questions that can speed the process of coming up with positive reframes for nega-

tive thoughts in a thought record or journal. For alexithymic clients and others who have trouble identifying their specific thoughts and schemas associated with the Big Three and other emotions, materials like the Feeling Dictionary can be useful.

- Schemas can be evaluated and changed by acting against them a la Ellis's Shame-Attacking exercises, Kelly's Fixed Role Therapy, or more recent Exposure Treatments such as Foa's Prolonged or Imaginal Exposure. This acting against schemas to show that they are not necessary to success is essentially hypothesis testing in the cognitive therapy sense.
- "Historical Review" (DeRubeis & Beck, 2001): Examine family of origin or F-O-O sources of schemas and how they are no longer adaptive, that is they have become FOOBS—see FOOBS Tenet in the Toolbox CD. For example, "Six Shotgun Junction" was essentially rejected by her mother for no rational reason, leading her to self-hate and a negative self-evaluation. Her defective self schema was activated by her husband's extramarital affair, leading to a suicidal crisis in which she drove to the small town of Buffalo, Texas, checking into a hotel with an assumed name and carrying in her husband's six shotguns. The origins of her depression included many incidents over the years in which she was slighted by her mother and in which her sister and her family were not. A discussion of these incidents showed "Six" that her schema was based on a fallacy since as a mother she knew that there was no rational reason to reject a child from birth.

Other useful resources for learning how to do schema work include Chapter 12 of "the Manual" of Beck et al. (1979), Chapter 6 of Barlow (2002), Chapter 6 of Persons et al. (2001), and Chapters 10 through 14 in Burns (1999) for a veritable transcript of how to dispute some of the most common negative schemas faced by clinicians. Most importantly, as discussed in Chapter 3 here, Clark and Beck (1999) discuss an elaboration of earlier theories in terms of schemas and schema clusters called *modes*.

Part Three
AREA-SPECIFIC INTERVENTIONS

CHAPTER 11

Goals-and-Values and Spiritual Life

WHEN TO APPLY AREA-SPECIFIC INTERVENTIONS LIKE GOALS-AND-VALUES IN QOLT

Area-specific interventions, such as those for the area of Goals-and-Values discussed in this chapter, are applied in QOLT whenever clients express dissatisfaction with the area and when it is clear that the area is important to a client. Even if clients have not expressed a particular area as being important, the therapist may suggest to clients that they target the area for intervention if it seems important in the overall context of the client's therapy. Graciella, for example, appreciated being exposed to Goals-and-Values interventions when the therapist suggested it. Her therapist had noted that Graciella's initial Vision Quest exercise lacked goals for her marriage even though she felt stranded at home alone while her husband put in long hours at the office. Furthermore, the therapist noted that Graciella had only listed two vague life goals in her initial assessment. The therapist suggested to Graciella that she could achieve a greater overall sense of life satisfaction if she targeted Goals-and-Values as an area of life to work on in QOLT.

DEFINITIONS

In QOLT, Goals-and-Values, also referred to as "Philosophy of Life," are defined as your beliefs about what matters most in life and how you should live, both now and in the future. This includes your goals in life, what you think is right or wrong, and the purpose or meaning of life as you see it (Frisch, 1994). Spiritual Life may or may not be an important part of a person's Goals-and-Values. In QOLT, Spiritual Life is defined as spiritual or religious beliefs or practices that you pursue on your own or as part of a like-minded spiritual community.

Having clear-cut Goals-and-Values and a sense of purpose seem essential both to happiness in general and a daily sense of satisfaction and contentment (Ed Diener, personal communication, July 25, 2005). The Find a Meaning Tenet is always shared with clients whether in written form or orally via the therapist since it is central to understanding why Goals-and-Values matter to happiness. This Tenet also includes some options and examples of Goals-and-Values that clients may wish to consider in identifying their own personal Goals-and-Values.

Find a Meaning/Goal Principle: A Core Tenet of Contentment Related to Goals-and-Values

This Tenet is one of the "three pillars" of QOLT and was first introduced in Chapter 7. We all need a guiding vision of what matters most in life and how we should live, both now and in the future. Whether secular, spiritual, or both, this guiding vision answers the question, "What is the meaning or purpose of life?" These Goals-and-Values are basic and essential to a sense of security and happiness.

Goals-and-Values include your personal and career goals for the future. Identifying some lifetime goals for yourself is an essential part of QOLT. The QOLI and Vision Quest exercise are designed to help you identify life goals. Once identified, the idea is to think about and recall your lifetime goals daily as you plan your days and your life. Also try to embrace beliefs, habits, and routines that help you in this endeavor and shun those influences, habits, beliefs, and routines that block your progress. Even the media, books, and TV that you watch or consume may help you or hinder you in your "diet" of influences needed for change and reaching personal goals.

More Secular Purposes.   Secular purposes in life beyond the self are often seen as sacred or spiritual callings by believers in these paths to fulfillment. Secular purposes can include raising a family, pursuing excellence in our work or hobbies, fighting for a cause we believe in, and even avidly following a nontheistic faith or philosophy as in being a fervent Bright, Humanist, Buddhist, Universist, or Unitarian. For some, the idea of fulfilling their own potential—self-actualization—is a useful goal along with just enjoying life to the fullest. Still and all, some meanings beyond the self seem necessary to happiness even if there is a selfish component as in raising children, a wonderful type of life work. Of course, multiple meanings and goals are typical, leaving room for both altruistic and more selfish pursuits.

Purely secular meanings can be reflected in QOLT areas of life such as love, children, creativity—defined broadly as originality in any area of human endeavor and service to others. The need for secular meaning can spring from the existentialist assumption that since life has no inherent or absolute meaning, we must, therefore, invent one and dedicate ourselves to a meaning in order for our lives to cohere, make sense, or be coherent. Psychologist Alfred Adler held this position as did the existential philosophers, Jean Paul Sartre and Albert Camus (Yalom, 1980).

More Spiritual and Religious Meanings and Goals.
While not important to everyone, religious and spiritual activities can greatly enhance a person's satisfaction with life and deserve consideration by all of us interested in boosting our happiness or contentment. In the most un-evangelical way imaginable, the Dalai Lama, spiritual leader of the Dzogchen lineage of Buddhism, an exile from his home country of Tibet by Communist China, speculates in the *Art of Happiness* that we should have as many religions as people in the world because all of us have different personalities and spiritual needs! He goes on to say that Buddhism is not for everyone and that we can be quite principled and moral without any religion at all as

long as we adhere to general ethical principles. QOLT defines spiritual life *broadly* as spiritual or religious beliefs or practices, that you pursue on your own or as part of a like-minded community. For those who value and want a spiritual life, QOLT proselytizes for a spiritual life or journey in which those interested freely explore spiritual meaning systems, practices, and communities until one finds one—or more—that is truly inspiring, uplifting, and personally meaningful. A religion or spiritual life should provide some useful personal answers for those of us spiritual pilgrims looking for causes and meanings beyond our own selfish desires as well as selfish tips on how to understand, live, and cope with an often insane world of conflicting beliefs, tremendous beauty, and horrific hatred and violence.

For those interested, QOLT advocates a search for a Spiritual Life that is renewing, invigorating, and inspiring. It should function in the same way that a love relationship should, as a shelter or safe haven in the storm of life. It should also function as a refueling station, inspiring us, making us feel good about ourselves and girding our loins, that is, giving us confidence and optimism to cope with the challenges of our life. Speaking of optimism, the quintessential positive psychology trait, what forum could be better suited for its cultivation than a spiritual community, practice, and belief system? Whatever spiritual approach or approaches are embraced, they should be followed and practiced on a daily basis for 5 to 20 minutes in order to get its maximum happiness-producing effect. Spiritual beliefs can be reviewed and need to be followed, rituals and practices can and need to be practiced, and spiritual guidance needs to be put into action for Spiritual Life to have a real benefit in terms of increased happiness or contentment. Being part of a like-minded spiritual community can also be extremely important, even essential.

Our Spiritual Life may be most powerful and fulfilling if it includes a community of spiritual friends and teachers who can support us and whom we can support—helper therapy principle—as we try to walk the walk of a spiritual approach 24/7, even with our most difficult family members and work colleagues. This more complete spiritual approach, including a community of like-minded people whom we socialize with on a regular basis, a particular teacher/leader or spiritual friend who sees the goodness and potential in you, and the belief system of the approach can completely change our lives, making us much more happy and fulfilled. Consider the success of Alcoholics Anonymous (AA) as well as the myriad communities and approaches from Judaism to Christianity to Islam, Hinduism, and Buddhism—American or Eastern. A spiritual life and discipline with regular, preferably daily practice for even 5 to 10 minutes, can make you more patient and kind, but likely will not change your basic temperament, personality, and potential happiness range or set point.

Happiness-Enhancing Goals-and-Values. You may wish to consider adopting some of the Tenets of Contentment themselves as part of your Goals-and-Values. All of the Tenets are meant to foster a life of greater happiness and contentment. The Tenets, *Happiness Matters* and *Happiness Is a Choice,* may be especially important for you to adopt if being happy is important to you.

Put Your Time Where Your Values Are. What may be unique to the QOLT approach is that QOLT tries to make a connection in how clients order their daily routines and their overarching life goals. To paraphrase the saying "Put your money where your mouth is," clients are told, "Put your time and effort where your values are." This sub-tenet or corollary of *Find a Meaning* suggests that we as therapists try telling clients to "Enshrine your personal goals with related activities in your schedule for each day *so that your acts follow your Goals-and-Values.*" Such a schedule constitutes your "Marching Orders" for the day and can really help in the process of "sculpting" days that fit your innermost values and personal goals (see Meanings Are Like Buses; Marching Orders Principle and Feed the Soul Principle).

CONSONANCE AND CONSISTENCY AMONG THERAPY AND LIFETIME GOALS IN QOLT

QOLT attempts to be more holistic and comprehensive than other cognitive-behavioral approaches in its insistence that therapy goals be considered in the context of clients' personal lifetime goals and in its attempt to explicitly connect therapy to lifetime goals whenever possible. In fact, in a variation on the Motivational Interviewing technique of William Miller and his colleagues (Miller & Rollnick, 2002), whenever possible, the therapist should build clients' motivation for therapy by showing how the activities of therapy will help clients achieve lifetime goals. Clients are much more likely to cooperate with treatment if they see therapy as a way to further their own ends. In many ways, this is the essence of a strong therapeutic or working alliance.

Conflicting Goals

Whenever conflicts are found among these goals, the therapist should attempt to resolve the conflicts with the client. In general, there should be consistency and a clear connection among all of a client's goals so that any current goals (and activities) of the client are consistent with the client's lifetime goals. For example, Peter decided to delay goals for his home building business after seeing that his all-consuming job and preoccupation at work made him so distracted at home that he was unable to enjoy time with his new infant daughter or his wife—his incipient alcohol problems and Generalized Anxiety Disorder were treated with empirically supported techniques at the same time as this positive psychology examination of life goals and priorities.

How to Generate Goals-and-Values: Vision Quest and the QOLI

Positive goals for life and for therapy in QOLT are generated primarily through the use of the Vision Quest technique and the QOLI in the beginning assessment phase. In using QOLI results, QOLT therapy goals are easily generated by asking clients about areas of dissatisfaction on their computer-generated Weighted Satisfaction Profiles (see Chapters 3 and 5). Therapy and lifetime goals can also be generated with the Vision Quest technique. Detailed instructions and illustrations on how to use the Vision Quest technique with clients are described in Chapter 5. The Vision Quest exercise is also available on the Toolbox CD.

Checking Outcomes with Vision Quest

After undertaking Goals-and-Values interventions with clients, the Vision Quest exercise can be completed again to assess changes and improvements in goals that guide QOLT. For example, many clients put the pursuit of happiness as a life goal priority only after being exposed to the Tenet, Happiness Matters.

TWEAKING AND EXPANDING CLIENT'S GOALS-AND-VALUES WITH THE TENETS OF CONTENTMENT EXERCISE

QOLT offers both general and specific guidance to clients choosing life Goals-and-Values. The Vision Quest technique and the QOLI are rather open ended exercises designed for clients to generate their own Goals-and-Values for areas of life that they value or cherish since goal attainment or satisfaction in valued areas of life will indeed lead to greater overall happiness and satisfaction with life—see Chapter 3 for theory and supportive studies. Additionally, QOLT puts forth the Tenets of Contentment and the Tenets of Contentment exercise as specific happiness- or contentment-fostering Goals-and-Values based on the literature and the authors' clinical and positive psychology practice. Most clients are unaware of some key Tenets precisely because they are not familiar with the happiness literature and because they are unused to the mind-set that cultivating and guarding our basic happiness and contentment are worthy life goals in and of themselves, even when we are pursuing altruistic goals aimed at serving and helping others; this mind-set is reflected in the Happiness Matters Tenet. Clients can easily modify existing goals and add new Goals-and-Values by merely following the instructions in the client version of the Tenets located in the Toolbox CD and in the client companion book to this one, *Finding Happiness*. Both sources recommend that clients peruse the Tenets in a leisurely way to find ones that may be useful to their unique life situation. These Tenets can be added to clients Goals-and-Values generated from Vision Quest or the QOLI, a process that enriches clients goals in depth and breadth.

In QOLT, area-specific Tenets may be presented to clients orally, especially for clients with reading difficulties, in the form of reading homework assignments, or both. The following is an example of how to present Tenets to clients:

> The Tenets of Contentment are attitudes or proverbs that, if followed closely, may dramatically increase your happiness and satisfaction in an area of life that you care about. Tenets can be viewed as positive schemas or core beliefs that can enhance our happiness according to the ASIO portions of the CASIO model of life satisfaction. I am going to ask you to decide on some Tenets or attitudes that you would like to try out and follow for a few days or a week to see if they really fit your value system and boost your sense of happiness, calm, or contentment.

After considering and trying some of these Tenets on for size, I will ask you to choose which ones to add to your overall value system, Vision Quest life goals, or New Life Script. Once you adopt a Tenet, it may be something you review regularly during Quality Time, or something that you pull out of your pocket or purse or e-mail when you are feeling upset during the day. These Tenets are new ways to look at problems or areas of your life that really boost your happiness.

Finally, I will challenge you to think of ways to put your personal list of Tenets into action in specific ways as part of your every day routine. The happiness effect of a Tenet can be boosted if you not only read over, think about, or believe in your Tenets, but also if you put them into practice by a specific action or behavior in which you do or say something specific related to the Tenet. For example, some people may choose to adopt a Tenet that considers happiness, good relationships with others, and service to others or to humankind as important qualities. These folks may put these concepts into practice by deciding to say hello with eye contact and a smile to everyone they encounter each day.

To remind yourself of the Tenets you have chosen to add to your routine, you may wish to put these on your computer desktop so it pops up each time you restart your computer. You may also post your favorite Tenets onto your refrigerator or dresser as a daily reminder. Simply reviewing these Tenets in a comfortable chair can constitute a Relaxation Ritual to use as you puzzle through a difficult feeling or time of day.

SPECIFIC TENETS USEFUL FOR DEVELOPING SPECIFIC, CHALLENGING, AND DOABLE GOALS FOR CLIENTS

A list of Tenets related especially to the development of satisfying Goals-and-Values can be found in Table 11.1. Therapists may share some or all of the Table 11.1 Tenets with clients either orally or in writing. The list is helpful for clients who may have glossed over a useful Tenet in their own perusal of the Tenets.

HAPPINESS TENETS: SPECIFIC TENETS ADDRESSING HAPPINESS PER SE AND ITS CULTIVATION OR ENHANCEMENT

QOLT recommends that clients consider making happiness a life goal or priority. This can be accom-

Table 11.1 Tenets Conducive to Identifying Specific, Challenging, and Doable Goals-and-Values (in Alphabetical Order)

Ask Your Death Tenet	Happiness Matters Principle
Balanced Lifestyle Principle	I Can Do It Principle
Be True to Your School Principle: BETTY'S Way	Kiss the Past Goodbye Principle
Be Your Own Guru or Personal Wisdom Principle	Live Your Dream or 24/7 Principle
Calculated Risk or Reasoned Passion Principle	Love Many Things Principle
Do the Right Thing or Clear Conscience Rule or When in Doubt, Don't Rule	Marching Orders Principle
	Modest Goal or Flow Principle
Feed the Soul Principle	Never Good Enough or Lower Expectations Principle
Fight for Much or Reap Frustration Principle	One-Thing-at-a-Time Principle
Find a Cause Principle	PRF Principle
Find a Meaning/Find a Goal Principle	Process Goal Principle
Forget Fame and Fortune Rule	Quality Time Principle
Get Organized Principle	You Can't Have It All Principle
Happiness from Achievement Principle	

plished most simply by asking clients to consider adopting the Happiness Matters Tenet as a personal goal or value. While all of the Tenets are aimed ultimately at enhancing clients' happiness and life satisfaction, some Tenets directly address the topic of happiness per se. A list of these so-called Happiness Tenets can be found in Table 11.2 (for a shorter, alternate list see the top 30 Tenets of Contentment in Chapter 9). Therapists may share some or all of these Tenets with clients either orally or in writing. Clients may wish to make their own "top 10" list of happiness boosting Tenets as part of the Tenet of Contentment exercise in the Toolbox CD.

INTERVENTIONS FOR INCREASING HAPPINESS AND SATISFACTION WITH GOALS-AND-VALUES

A client's lifetime goals and strategies should be reflected in his or her daily routine in order to insure that concrete progress toward goals is achieved. It is very helpful, for example, for clients to schedule homework assignments given by their therapist for a specific day and time as when a client schedules a specific time each day to chat with an attractive person as a way of building up dating skills. The Daily Activity Plan (DAP) discussed in Chapter 10 provides an excellent format for clients to manage their time in a way that furthers their goals each and every day.

Patterns of Concern in Specific Areas of Life for Pure Positive Psychology and Clinical Samples

Written comments in the narrative portion of the QOLI allow respondents to identify specific barriers to happiness and concerns with respect to specific areas of life. The authors' published research involving over 4,000 clients and participants (Frisch, 1992, 1994; Frisch et al., 2005) and his continuing informal content analysis of the QOLI with over 500 clinical and positive psychology clients, including lawyers, physicians, police personnel, and university student life professionals, form the basis for statements of patterns found in client explanations for unhappiness in each area of life assessed by the QOLI (and included in QOL theory). Thus far, patterns of concern with respect to particular areas of life seem similar for pure positive psychology and clinical samples, although this hypothesis needs more formal empirical

Table 11.2 Happiness Tenets: Tenets Most Conducive to Happiness (in Alphabetical Order)

Affirm the Spark (in Others) Principle

Assume the Best in Others Principle

Balanced Lifestyle Principle

Be with People or Relationship Immersion Principle

Blind Dumb Optimism Principle

Bosom Friends Principle

Cocoon It Rule

Color Purple Principle

Daily Vacation Principle

Depression Is Not Normal Principle

Don't Bring It Home or Work Spillover Principle

Don't Forgive Principle or Set Aside, Shelve, Accept, or Forget Principle

Do What You Love or Tune in to What Turns You on Principle

Exercise or Take your Medication Principle

Fight for Much, Reap Frustration Principle

Fight the Power Principle

Find a Friend, Find a Mate Principle

Find an Area or Go to Your Room Principle

Flow It Principle

Get Organized Principle

Giving Tree or Self-Other Principle

Glow of Peace Tenet

The Grass Isn't Greener, It's Weeds Principle

The Great Compromise Principle

Habits Rule or Routines Rule

Happiness Diet Principle

Happiness Equation Tenet

Happiness from Achievement Principle

Happiness Habits Principle

Happiness Is a Choice Principle

Happiness Matters Principle

Happiness Spillover Principle

How Kind Principle or Tender Hearted Rule

Humor Principle

I Can Do It Principle

I'll Think about That Tomorrow Principle

I'm Going to See My Friends at Work Principle

Inner Abundance Principle

Judge Not, You Don't Know Principle

Keep Busy with Flows or Happiness Takes Effort Principle

Keeping Up with the Jones Principle

Kill Them with Kindness or Love Bomb Principle

Kiss the Past Goodbye Principle

Leisurely Pace and Lifestyle Principle

Life Satisfaction Breeds Job/Work Satisfaction Principle

Li Po or Commune with Nature Rule

Live Your Dream or 24\7 Principle

Love Many Things Principle

Love What You Do Principle

Love and Work Principle

Manage Your Time and Your Life Rule

Mental Health Day Technique

Mine the Moment or Attack the Moment Principle

No Mayo, Pickles, or Mustard Rule

Nothing Human Disgusts Me or Acceptance Principle

One-Thing-at-a-Time Principle (OTAAT)

Overthinking Principle

Personality Stays the Same or Happiness Set Point Principle

Pick Your Battles/Pick No Battles Principle or Yes, Boss/Yes, Dear Rule

Pick Your Friends Principle

Pocket of Time to Relax Principle

Positive Addictions Principle

Process Goal Principle

Quality Time Principle

The Question Rule

Relationship with Self or Self-Compassion Principle

Routine Is Everything or Make It a Routine Principle

Selective Hedonism or Reasoned Passion Principle

Table 11.2 *Continuued*

Self-Acceptance Principle	Tangled Web or Web of Support or Love Where You Are Principle
Sensate Focus/Savor or Vary Your Pleasures to Avoid Adaptation Tenet	Taoist Dodge Ball Rule
Serve Others Principle	Thank Everyone for Everything Principle
Share the Hurt behind the Anger Tenet	The Three Rs of Stress Management Principle
Socializing Doubles Your Pleasure	Thou Shalt Be Aware or Psychephobia Principle
Stop Second Guessing Principle	To Understand All Is to Forgive All or Empathy Principle
Street Signs to Success Principle	Trust Principle
Strength It Principle	Under the Influence or Yes, Dear Rule
Stress Carriers or I Never Bother with People I Hate Rule	We Are Family Principle
String of Pearls Practice and Principle	We're Not Okay and That's Okay Rule
Success Principle	What Would My Role Model Do or Role Model Principles
Surrogate Family Principle	You Can't Have It All Principle or Curb or Ignore Desires Principles
Taking Your Emotional Temperature or Assessing Progress and Prospects Principle	You Do It to Yourself or Terrorist Principle

validation. This and all subsequent area-specific chapters describe the patterns found for each particular area.

Goals-and-Values Concerns and Treatments

With respect to Goals-and-Values, both clinical and positive psychology or nonclinical clients report difficulties in formulating, following, and achieving key personal goals and ethical standards. Depressive symptoms of excessive guilt over transgressions and suicidal thoughts may also be expressed. Interventions useful in this area include developing short- and long-term career goals, conducting a cognitive rehearsal of tasks needed to achieve long- and short-term goals; completing the Zen Steps to Success exercise (see discussion that follows); implementing strategies for achieving goals; cognitive restructuring immediate fears of failure; and referring clients to ministers, priests, and rabbis known to be tolerant in order to clarify religious questions (e.g., "Can I ever be forgiven for divorcing my abusive alcoholic hus-

band?") and alleviate guilt. Evaluating depressogenic philosophical assumptions and values or schemas by weighing their advantages and disadvantages (Pro versus Con technique—illustrated at the end of this chapter) has also been helpful as in the case of a client who decided it was not wrong to leave an unhappy marriage of 20 years given his wife's adamant refusal to discuss problems, make changes, or pursue marital therapy.

Cognitive techniques must usually be supplemented with behavioral techniques to effectively challenge self-defeating or maladaptive philosophies of life. Perfectionistic clients benefit from experimenting with less ambitious short-term and intermediate goals. Religious clients often benefit from church involvement in two ways: (1) church can provide a major recreational and social outlet, buffering the client from the major life stresses usually associated with depression (Abramson et al., 1989); and (2) religious beliefs are often extremely adaptive, comforting, and helpful in encouraging clients to either make change efforts or accept intractable problems such as physical disabilities or relationship problems that have proved impervious to change.

SPECIFIC TECHNIQUES FOR GOAL SETTING AND VALUES CLARIFICATION

Ask Your Death Tenet and My Most Feared Obituary Technique

In much the same way, the Ask Your Death Tenet and My Most Feared Obituary technique can help clients develop meaningful standards (the **S** in CASIO), priorities (the **I** in CASIO) and goals (the Goals-and-Values part of life). Ask Your Death Tenet can be found in the Toolbox CD along with the other Tenets. In My Most Feared Obituary clients write an obituary for themselves based on living a long life without positive changes in their current standards, priorities, goals, and lifestyle. They are urged to map a life trajectory based on a complete lack of effort to better themselves and a life based on current or increasing levels of day-to-day stress. They are asked to record or write a life of hitting bottom or deterioration in line with their worst habits and inclinations. The effects of negative habits of thought and behavior are projected far into the future as clients picture the worst possible scenario much as the specter of the future haunts Ebenezer Scrooge in Dickens' *A Christmas Carol.* Such "time projection" as Arnold Lazarus called it, is highly motivating to clients who have been resistant to change. An optional second obituary exercise consists of an Obituary of Aspiration, reflecting how clients would most like to be remembered after their passing. The two obits may be compared for the different standards, priorities, and goals implied by each. Prominent display of the My Most Feared Obituary where clients can see it, perhaps during Quality Time, or on the start-up menu of their computers, seems to motivate those clients who seem to be floundering without real direction in life or in QOLT.

Sand Timer Technique.   Some clients have responded well to a small sand timer on their desk or kitchen table as a reminder of their limited time on earth and the need to pursue goals today in the present moment; clients will turn over the timer whenever they think of it, as a compelling reminder in the same way that meditators use bells and gongs to remind them of the need to maintain a mindful state of mind.

Zen Steps Technique

Once generated, a clients' lifetime goals should be further broken down into very small steps and subgoals for the next year, month, week, and day. A. T. Beck et al. (1979) call this a Graded Task Assignment. In QOLT, this concept is presented as Zen Steps to Success. Essentially, Zen Steps refer to very small and deliberate steps taken in the service of a goal, that is, Zen walking or *kinhin* meditations. Some clients prefer to think of this as Stepping Stones or Baby Steps to Success in which deliberate small steps are taken toward a goal, one at a time, without worry or regard for the myriad steps to follow. Zen Steps is in keeping with the proverb, "a journey of a thousand miles, begins with one small step" (see Chapter 10 for further discussion of Zen Steps).

Life goals can be further whittled down into manageable pieces with Five Paths. The Five Paths (to Happiness) exercise can be used by therapists and clients to develop specific activities that can be completed in as little as 15 to 30 minutes aimed at moving clients closer to their goals. For example, the goal of pursuing a career in mental health may begin with a 5-minute phone call to a family friend who is a psychologist or social worker to get a feel for the work and to ask about typical salaries and job opportunities. The goal of finding a romantic partner in life can begin with the baby or Zen step of a homework assignment in which the therapist instructs the client to begin greeting and speaking with grocery clerks in order to build social skills and confidence. Each baby step a client is asked to take toward a goal (e.g., find a life partner) or subgoal (e.g., begin dating) should be planned and "programmed" by the therapist to be simple, doable, and highly likely to succeed. When unsuccessful, the therapist and client should analyze the activity for any possible mistakes by the client and then rehearse the assignment before it is done again. The operant technique of shaping is involved here in so far as clients competencies are *gradually* built-up and rewarded over time; each assignment is geared to the client's current level of competency in order to minimize the risk of failure. This technique gives clients the "taste" of success in small doses thereby building their confidence as they gradually move toward major life goals such as finding a love relationship or a meaningful career. By shaping responses and gradually achieving small subgoals, the therapist arranges for a series of life tests without big failures, an ideal way to learn and progress in any life endeavor.

Schema Work and the New Life Script Technique

According to Dr. Denise Davis, a schema is a "deeply held (often unconscious) belief that exerts a strong influence on behavior." Schemas include our basic, fundamental rules for living. They are our most deeply held beliefs about ourselves, others, and the world. They are core beliefs about what matters most and how the world operates. Taken together, all of our core beliefs or schemas make up our "Life Script" or what Alfred Adler called our "life plan." Our Life Script, like a script given to an actor, tells us how we should live in our own personal drama of life. This script has both positive and negative beliefs. The Life Script technique teaches clients how to identify negative schemas in their Life Script and how to write a New Life Script of healthy, happiness-enhancing beliefs. In addition to positive beliefs from clients, various Tenets of Contentment can make up the New Life Script of positive schema.

The New Life Script technique involves the following steps:

1. Clients write an *Old* (current) Life Script or a list of the self-defeating and upsetting beliefs that block their happiness and fulfillment in parts of life they care about. Give clients copies of the Schemas to Drive You Crazy handout in the Toolbox CD to further identify some of their self-defeating beliefs. Repeated themes in therapy sessions and the Lie Detector exercises can also suggest pervasive negative schemas that need modification.
2. Clients write a *New* Life Script of contentment that directly challenges and replaces all unhealthy core beliefs; therapists can use the Primer in Cognitive Therapy in Chapter 10 to review ways to effectively challenge negative schemas.
3. Positive schemas from the Tenets of Contentment are added to clients' New Life Scripts.
4. Clients test out or act on their New Life Script and notice any changes in their level of happiness and success in life.
5. Evaluation of scripts. The New Life Script is revised until clients are satisfied with the scripts' happiness-producing properties or effects.

Step 4 in which clients test out or act on their New Life Script in their everyday life is a difficult key step in the Life Script exercise and in any cognitive therapy schema work. Clients are told to enact the New Life Script they have developed by reading and reviewing the script on a daily basis and by being mindful of the script as they go about their daily routine. Specifically, the therapist should ask the clients to act "as if" the script were "true" and to consciously apply these new healthy beliefs to everyday life situations. This often involves clients "play acting" as they assume a new "identity" similar to George Kelly's Fixed Role Therapy. For example, one client taught herself to confine her worrying to her daily Quality Time and acted "as if" she were a relatively calm person instead of the fretful "worry wart" she previously thought herself to be. Throughout her day, whenever she became aware of a worry, she would make a mental note to think about the worry during her Quality Time and then try to distract herself by getting fully involved with the task at hand and by doing Mindful Breathing. While this new script and identity felt awkward at first, with practice, the client felt comfortable with the role as though it expressed her true self.

It is important for the therapist to constantly remind clients of positive changes brought about from acting out their New Life Script. In addition, clients must be encouraged to recall these successes for themselves in order for the difficult process of schema change to be effective. Clients should also be told to accept the fact that relapses into the Old Life Script are to be expected. These lapses should be interpreted to clients as a natural part of the change process.

In cases with limited time for therapy, clients can use the Tenets of Contentment by themselves to build a happiness-fostering New Life Script without ever writing an Old Life Script or rewriting unhealthy core beliefs into healthy core beliefs. While it is best for clients to know their Old Life Script *before* constructing a new one, some clients lack the patience or ability to do this even with the assistance of a therapist. In these cases, the therapist can simply ask clients to circle or list Tenets that clients agree may be helpful for them in becoming happier and more successful in their daily life. This list essentially becomes a client's New Life Script, which he or she can test out and revise periodically. Of course, clients must agree with and really believe in any healthy belief or Tenet for it to be effective in enhancing their quality of life. Chapter

10's discussion of schema work offers additional suggestions applicable to guiding clients as they build new and more positive life scripts.

New Life Script Technique: A Clinical and Positive Psychology Example

Tom's New Life Script centered on self-related schema and is excerpted in Chapter 12 on Self-Esteem. Pam was a decorated and highly respected math/science teacher as well as a perfectionist with subclinical depression that never met the *DSM* criteria. Box 11.1 illustrates the results of her effort to rewrite unhealthy core beliefs or schemas into a healthy New Life Script using the familiar two-column approach of many Thought Records such as QOLT's Lie Detector in which Upsetting Thoughts/ Unhealthy Core Beliefs are *reframed* into Positive Answers/New Healthy Core Beliefs.

New Life Script and Summary of QOLT: The Pure Positive Psychology Case of Jesse

Jesse, an Austin physician, had an interest in personal growth and positive psychology. Along with a few signs of subclinical depression she grappled with some personal problems or quality of life issues that she felt threatened her competence as a dermatologist and threatened her relationships with her boyfriend and "gal pals." After reading *Finding Happiness*, the client-version of this book, she wrote the following New Life Script that summarizes much of QOLT:

> I value contentment, learning, and caring toward others above everything else. I live a balanced lifestyle including daily or weekly Quality Time, relaxation, and reflection as well as time for recreation, friends, hobbies, and times to just "do nothing." When upset or lapsing into depression and worry, I do 30 minutes a day of Quality Time. I see Quality Time as a comfort, time to relax and take care of me so I can get centered and be there for others. I have decided to mend my "fretful, joyless ways." I've also decided to ignore all global self-evaluations of myself or others and to stick to Quality of Life Therapy and its principles in my day-to-day life. This includes the belief that one can change long-standing, destructive, emotional, behavioral, and thinking habits. This includes the belief that happiness is a strength that can be bolstered when I apply my strengths and skills to parts of life I care about. It also includes the belief that worry is never fruitful; that I am equal to others and worthwhile no matter what I achieve in life, that I don't have to de-

> pend on a few others for support; that life is a suspense drama or adventure to be lived out in an unself-conscious, non-evaluative way; that I can cope with anything that happens and that I need not fret all the time about potential problems until they actually happen; that life should be lived in the present fully and that the simple pleasures in life are most important, including spending time with loved ones. I do not identify my personhood or basic self-worth with my career, my lover, my patients, my coworkers, or the Temple I belong to and I don't worry about what other people think about me. I keep my own counsel about what truly matters in life and try to be spontaneous, loving, and curious in my day-to-day activities. I appreciate all I have in the present without lusting after greater wealth, prestige, or love. I see myself as a competent professional, regardless of what others say, and can see myself growing in happiness and having fun for the rest of my life. I count my blessings daily and take risks all the time to open myself to others and to learn. I challenge or ignore negative thoughts of worrying, putting myself down, comparing myself with others, perfectionism, and workaholism. When working I become thoroughly task- and process-oriented, losing self-awareness and fretting as I get into the "flow" of whatever I am doing in the moment. I look with compassion on my weaknesses and failings and those of others as I try to "forgive and forget." I save worries and concerns for time-limited periods of Quality Time. The rest of the time I am living my life, rather than worrying about it or planning for the future! I want to serve others and enjoy life instead of trying to control and fix everything. I am goal-striving and forward-looking, recalling each day's success experiences. I look for commonalties, not differences, between myself and others and use this "common ground" as a basis for developing trust, mutual interests, and for reducing suspicion of others.

> I commit myself to a life dedicated to self-discovery, self-caring, self-honesty, joy, pleasure, accomplishment, personal contentment, and reasonable service to others. I affirm my commitment to stop evaluating myself and other people as a whole—evaluating only behaviors in the spirit of forgiveness, compassion, and love. I eschew all fretting and worrying, and distract myself from problems that I cannot change or have made a plan to deal with. I strive to be a balanced, professional role model to medical students and other docs—one who does a little, consistent studying of current trends but who also provides a lot of caring, clinical wisdom, compassion, and humor to my patients.

> I assert my right to exist and to feel worthwhile and deserving of happiness, irrespective of my errors, failings, ignorance, or achievements. I accept responsibility for my mistakes, take corrective action, and then forget

BOX 11.1
Pam's New Life Script Worksheet

Unhealthy Core Beliefs from Old Life Script

1. I'm a lousy teacher and not doing my job unless there are no problems and all students and colleagues agree with me.

2. Those who criticize me do not like or respect me.

3. I'm not a good enough teacher, Jew, friend, or wife.

4. I'm a "shit" and a bad person for ever getting upset and depressed.

5. I'd be much happier in new circumstances. I need a new husband, a new job, and a nicer place to live. I can't be happy here. My circumstances make me depressed.

6. Without my job, achievement, and the respect of other people, I am nothing.

7. I must be extremely active in extracurricular activities and continue to win awards for my teaching. I also need to do my share of administrative work and always be courteous in how I relate to students, colleagues, administrators, friends, and family. I must be nice all the time and feel relaxed, content, and happy!

New Healthy Core Beliefs to Include in New Life Script

1. I am a good teacher by both my school's standards and my own. I choose not to let work worries dominate my life. Problems and interpersonal conflicts are to be expected and don't mean that I'm no good. "Failures" don't get good teaching evaluations at the end of the year!

2. I really do not know. This may be true . . . It is natural and a part of life to conflict with other people with different backgrounds, values, or needs. Maturity is determined by how we handle conflict, not by its absence.

3. I choose to accept me as I am without any further changes or alterations. I'm no better or worse than anybody else and deserve the same respect and understanding that others do.

4. Everyone gets upset. Depression is the "common cold" of psychological problems. I'm only making things worse by insisting that things be different than they are. Accept that you're depressed and move on!

5. Don't blame others or circumstances for your mood. Blame your thoughts and behaviors that you can control. I've been at peace and happy in these circumstances before. What can I do to make things better?

6. Self-respect is all I need to survive and thrive. Achievement alone won't do it for me.

7. As a fallible, person I'll make mistakes, and have setbacks in reaching personal goals and in gaining self-control. These lapses only prove I'm human. I can always "get back on the horse" and do better next time when I feel bad again or start to do something wrong.

(Continued)

8. I must earn the right to a happy, contented existence by always being productive and nice to other people.

8. Being happy is based on an assertion of self-acceptance, self-respect, and hope. It is not something to be "earned" through achievement or perfection. I deserve to be happy just because I'm alive along with every other living thing in the world.

9. I can't do what it takes to make my life more enjoyable and happy.

9. I <u>can</u> control my thoughts, feelings, and actions (not the rest of the world), no matter how often I claim or feel I cannot.

10. I must be special, unique, better than everyone else, the common "slobs" who aren't well-known, wealthy, and always right.

10. It is an unnecessary burden to feel that I must be better than others. Being *Good Not Great* is freeing. Get into the flow of life and pursue what you enjoy. If fame or fortune follow, great. If not, that's okay too. I'm no better or worse than anyone else. I'm a mix of good, bad, and neutral. I choose to accept myself as I am without any further changes or alterations even though I may try to better myself.

11. I can never find a consistent interest outside of work. I should bring my work home with me to do a good job.

11. My leisure time is important and my own to do with as I please. If I don't develop a more balanced lifestyle, I'll be depressed and ineffective both at home and at work! I am someone who values both work and play and who has a balanced life incorporating both of these elements. If I try to recreate as hard as I try to work, I'll find some hobbies I can stick with.

12. Pam added the following Tenets of Contentment to her *New Life Script* as beliefs and practices—she reviewed them daily—that kept her from becoming clinically depressed and made her a happier person:

- Ask Your Death Tenet
- Be the Peace You Seek or Worry Warts Principle
- Be with People or Relationship Immersion Principle
- Bosom Friends Principle
- Can't Buy Me Love or Forget Fame and Fortune Rule
- Cocoon It Rule
- Color Purple Principle
- Depression Is Not Normal Principle
- Don't Bring It Home or Work Spillover Principle
- Emotional Honesty Principle

- Exercise or "Take Your Medication" Principle
- Expert Friend
- Face the Music Principle
- Favor Bank
- Feed the Soul Principle
- Flow It Principle.
- Giving Tree or Self-Other Principle
- Happiness Is a Choice Principle
- Happiness Habits Principle
- Happiness Matters Principle
- Lower Expectations Principle—see Never Good Enough Principle
- "Mad Col." Disease Rule
- Make Friends at Work Principle
- Mental Health Day Technique
- Modest Goal or Flow Principle
- No Gossip/Criticism/Suggestions or Words as Daggers Rule
- OTAAT or One-Thing-at-a-Time Principle
- Overthinking Principle
- Self-Acceptance Principle
- You Do It to Yourself or Terrorist Principle

it. I assert my right to pursue what is best for me, rejecting societal values that I feel are destructive and dehumanizing like competition over cooperation and measuring worth by external standards like wealth and productivity. I realize that only I can make me happy and that I can always find new and rewarding relationships, even if I lose some current relationships.

I assert my faith in my own ability to change long-term cognitive, thinking, emotional, and behavioral habits. I accept the Happiness Is a Choice Tenet of Contentment as I accept the responsibility for creating and changing intense negative feelings by changing my distorted perceptions and attitudes (as well as my behavior and situations or circumstances). I look at my feelings and thoughts as "hypotheses" or theories about the world to be explored, rather than "facts" that I must accept. I accept that life is an adventure that necessarily will include frustrations, occasional boredom, and moments of real joy. I assert the right to be human and make mistakes, do hurtful things, and to not always be correct in this uncertain world. I accept the fact that I can't control other people and the future and that all I can do is control my own thoughts and actions as I pursue a "process" rather than "outcome" orientation to

life. I accept the challenge to be genuine, open, and risk-taking. I accept the complexity of juggling and serving different and sometimes competing demands, goals, and values at the same time. I refuse to hate myself when I neglect one area for another, as when I put more effort into work than my personal life and vice versa. I make modest goals each day that are easily attainable and yet challenging. My first Goal-and-Value is self-caring, inner abundance, and self-respect, which allows me to serve others better and to do everything else I want to do in my life with greater joy and skill.

I take responsibility for my thoughts, feelings, and behavior. If they are hurtful to me or others, I strive to accept them, change them, and minimize the hurt. I have a vision of who I want to be and what goals I want to accomplish in this one life I have to live. Until I alter these goals, I honor my commitments and visions of who I want to be today, tomorrow, 10 years from now, and when I die. This includes a monogamous commitment to Jim (boyfriend), to a healthy body, to a clear, contented mind, to the role of physician, to the role of "part-time social crusader" and witness of personal values who gives time to social causes and tries to make society better but never lets these efforts interfere with some time for basic self-reflection and time for Play. I am also committed to being a loyal friend and relative, and a respecter of each person's human dignity and worth.

I strive to keep demands on myself to a minimum and try to live a life of joy and wonder, like a suspense drama in which I determine my character. When confronted with problems, I strive to accept reality, choose a course of action that is in my best long- and short-term interest and act to make it happen as I implement my choice. I accept my situation and feelings no matter how scary, confused, or bad they may seem—Thou Shalt Be Aware Tenet. I also choose to act in accordance with my Goals-and-Values and philosophy-of-life. I take pride in my independence and my ability to care for myself, manage my affairs, and carry out the responsibilities I have chosen in one life on earth. I make the most of each day and moment as I realize that someday I will be dead and that I will be dead a very long time!

Jesse recorded this script and played it on her Ipod while driving to work each morning and, at times, as part of her Quality Time. These constant reminders and reviews of her new happiness-producing or, as she called it, "inner peace" Goals-and-Values helped her to "stay on the path" of QOLT.

Pros-versus-Con Technique

Before clients can challenge and revise an unhealthy core belief or schema, they must be convinced that the belief hurts or threatens their well-being (J. S. Beck, 1995; see Primer in Cognitive Therapy in Chapter 10). The therapist and client should discuss the advantages and disadvantages of any self-defeating belief, especially when clients seem ambivalent about giving up a particular belief. It helps for clients to list advantages and disadvantages as part of homework assignments (Pro-versus-Con Technique in the Toolbox). For example, a very successful, but driven, workaholic client examined his belief that, "Work is the most important thing in my life. It's okay and helpful to bring my work home with me and think about it all the time." On the positive side, he was very successful in his work. The disadvantage of this belief, however, was that he often came home tired, spent, and preoccupied with his work to the point that his family perceived him as if he were a "ghost." His wife was extremely angry with his lack of emotional availability and threatened divorce. An examination of these pros and cons led the client to give up his belief, putting family before work since his family was ultimately his main source of fulfillment. As is usually the case with perfectionists, he performed as well or better at work once he stopped bringing it home with him.

CHAPTER 12

Self-Esteem

"Total self-love and acceptance is the only foundation for happiness" according to the self-help writer, John Bradshaw. While overstating the case, basic self-acceptance and satisfaction with the self are closely related to satisfaction and happiness with life in general (see, for example, Alex Michalos, 1991, pioneering studies of students in 39 countries). Recalling from Chapter 3 that happiness wells forth when positive affects/satisfactions outweigh negative feeling experiences, it may be that self-esteem impacts happiness as much through negative as positive affect. Self-*dis*like or "negative self-evaluation" (Frisch, 1998a) is a modern scourge that is integral to the experience of negative affect, especially depression (Clark & Beck, 1999; Frisch, 1998a). The curse of self-hate or low self-esteem is all too common in both clinical and pure positive psychology clients. In CASIO terms, many do not measure up to their own standards of performance and achievement (Frisch, 1992). At times, it seems clearly rooted in parental rejection, maltreatment, or neglect as in the case of humorist, Jonathan Winters, whose drunken father berated him mercilessly. For others, it may amount to self-blame for a miserable temperament of negative affectivity, neuroticism, over-emotionality, or chronic bad moods (Clark, Vittengl, Kraft, & Jarrett, 2003). Whatever the roots, our clients need to see themselves as, in the words of family therapy pioneer, Virginia Satir, "basic miracles worthy of love." QOLT offers several paths to increasing self-esteem.

THE SUCCESS PATH TO SELF-ESTEEM

In QOLT, Self-Esteem is defined as liking and respecting yourself in light of your strengths and weaknesses, successes and failures, and ability to handle problems (Frisch, 1994). It may be impossible to separate one's sense of self-worth from one's actions (Bandura, 1986). This means that we may improve clients' self-esteem by helping them to act in accord with the standards of behavior that they have set for themselves in valued areas of life. Clinical and positive psychology experience and research suggest that the Success Path may be the most effective in building self-esteem, self-efficacy, and self-confidence. Specifically, research with the QOLI suggests that clients experience low self-esteem due to their perceived failure to meet their own standards of performance and success in valued areas of life such as work, school, love relationships, parenthood, weight control and physical appearance, friendships, ethical conduct, coping with life problems, and *psychological self-control* or the ability to manage and control symptoms of psychological disturbance such as depression, anxiety, and substance abuse (Frisch, 1992). The Success Path to greater self-esteem overcomes this sense of failure and demoralization (Frank & Frank, 1993) by building clients' competencies in valued areas of life and programming success experiences in these areas through real-life homework assignments.

The primary way to implement this treatment strategy using QOLT is to select the interventions appropriate to each area of life that is highly valued by each individual client. Therefore, a quality of life therapist can expect a dramatic increase in client self-esteem as a by-product of teaching clients how to gain satisfaction in the parts of life they deem most important. Clients will feel better about themselves when they are succeeding in the parts of life they care about. As the adage proclaims, "nothing succeeds like success" (in building self-esteem). For example, if a client's perceived "failure" in a marriage is eating away at the client's self-esteem, a successful course of QOLT couples therapy can both heal the client's marriage and the client's fragile sense of self-worth.

If success experiences in valued areas of life can increase self-esteem, "failure" experiences in the same areas can be expected to deflate a person's sense of self-worth. For this reason it is important that the therapist engineer or plan small, almost foolproof success experiences and homework using the Zen Steps to Success technique described in Chapter 10. It can help for the therapist to set process rather than outcome goals for the client; for example, a client can be congratulated for treating a business customer with courtesy and respect even though the customer may refuse to make a deal or acts rudely to the client in return (see Process Goal Tenet).

Recalling Successes on the Success Path

Often clients, especially those who are discouraged or depressed, will feel down on themselves or unhappy not because they have failed in important areas of life, but because they have lost touch with their successes. Whether due to mood-dependent memory, in which clients only seem able to retrieve unhappy memories, or other factors, unhappy and depressed clients tend to focus all their awareness on their shortcomings, failures, and worries. One important way to counteract this tendency and to thereby improve self-esteem is by using cognitive restructuring techniques such as the Lie Detector and Stress Diary described in Chapter 10. The BAT exercise and the Success Log are two additional tools designed to increase clients' self-esteem by making them more aware of the positive factors about themselves and their life, such as their strengths, successes, good fortune, and simple pleasures that they may be taking for granted.

In presenting these techniques to clients, it is important for the therapist to emphasize that these techniques are aimed at fostering a "normal," healthy, and modest level of self-respect, which is absent in people with low self-esteem. The exercises are not designed to make clients conceited or arrogant. As Erich Fromm observed in *The Art of Loving,* truly selfish and conceited people are as incapable of loving themselves as they are other people. In fact, a sense of self-respect and positive self-esteem are prerequisites for loving other people. Clients should be told that people with

positive self-esteem are the most generous toward others because they have nothing to prove and feel secure in themselves as persons.

Success Log

A specific technique for pursuing the Success Path to Self-Esteem by increasing clients' *awareness* and *recall* of accomplishments in life is to keep a daily record of success experiences. This technique is based on the pioneering work of Lynn Rehm of the University of Houston who has found that simply recording one's success experiences can be a powerful antidote to clinical depression; Rehm's related self-control therapy is an empirically based treatment for clinical depression.

The essence of the Success Log technique is to make self-recognition for accomplishment and self-praise a habit. Clients give themselves credit for the little things they do each day. They "pat themselves on the back" as soon as they do something right, think a pleasant thought, or have a pleasant experience. These moment-to-moment self-affirmations can help them tip the balance of positive and negative thoughts favorably so that their consciousness is less dominated by the self-downing ruminations that feed and foster pessimism, low self-esteem, and depression. Perhaps a 2 to 1 ratio of positive to negative thoughts is needed to promote basic contentment and emotional health.

To keep a Success Log, clients simply list any personal accomplishment, any experience of joy or pleasure, or any positive thought about themselves or their circumstances that they experience during the day. Instruct clients to write down these "success experiences" as soon as they happen or shortly thereafter to obtain the maximum effect of positive mood and self-esteem. This technique is especially helpful when clients are feeling discouraged or demoralized. For example, one computer operator for a large bank was able to move her Quality of Life Inventory score from "Very Low" to "Average" as a result of keeping a Success Log on a daily basis for 2 weeks. This is significant progress for measure of positive psychology or "positive mental health" that means more then merely the absence of depressive or "negative" indicators (see Chapter 5). Writing down her small and large successes, accomplishments, and positive experiences each day challenged her core belief that she was somewhat inadequate and unable to function. (While at risk for clinical depression, this was a pure positive psychology case in terms of a complete absence of DSM

BOX 12.1

Success Log: Positive Psychology Example

Name: _Janine McGillicuddy_   Date: _Friday, December 13, 2024_

Instructions: Pay attention to any big or small successes or accomplishments you have throughout the day. Also note any positive or pleasant experiences you have which can also be seen as a kind of accomplishment in terms of happiness. Also jot down any positive thoughts you have about yourself and your circumstances. As soon as you can, jot down these successes, pleasant experiences, and positive thoughts. You may stop to recall 3 successes in your day, whenever your mood starts to drop whether you have this form handy or not.

1. _Packed a lunch for the first time in three weeks._

2. _Sketched a brief outline for the Credit Card Program. A big first step!_

3. _A nice talk with parking lot attendant. I'm silent today. Felt good to connect._

4. _Thought to myself, "You have a great stamina and persistence to get things done."_

5. _What a beautiful sunset—all pink and orange._

6. _Made coffee for Jeff (husband) instead of letting him do it._

7. _Thought to myself, "I'm an intelligent, caring woman."_

8. _Got our mortgage refinanced at just the right time to save a bundle._

9. _Erin and Andrew, we have great kids._

10. _I'm going to enjoy dinner out with the girls tonight. I got great pals . . ._

11. _I did it! Hurray! Finished debugging Latice Program._

---

disorders both at the time of treatment and in her past.) Her completed Success Log from 1 day is illustrated in Box 12.1. (A blank form can be found in the Toolbox CD that accompanies this book.)

IMPORTANCE OF WRITTEN HOMEWORK AND THE DAILY ACTIVITY PLAN

Completing a Daily Activity Plan (DAP) can have the same effect as the Success Log in building self-esteem in that it shows clients concrete evidence of their accomplishments during the day as well as any experiences of pleasure, achievement, or satisfaction. In general, written homework assignments serve an invaluable function as indisputable evidence, which is often more convincing to clients than any verbal arguments of persuasion offered by their therapists.

STRENGTHS AND GRATITUDE IN QOLT: ILLUSTRATION WITH THE BAT TECHNIQUE

The BAT technique is another Success Path intervention aimed at improving clients' happiness and satisfaction with the self or Self-Esteem by improving recall of positive personal characteristics, strengths, accomplishments, and life circumstances. The BAT exercise represents a specific way clients can increase their Self-Esteem and positive affect by fostering an awareness of their talents, strengths, accomplishments, and blessings with the latter amounting to a Gratitude exercise in positive psychology parlance (Seligman, 2002; see the Thank Everyone for Everything and String of Pearls Tenets in the Toolbox CD for two additional gratitude exercises in QOLT).

BAT is also a strengths exercise in the classic positive psychology sense, in that, clients are asked to identify positive traits, strengths, and, in contrast to Seligman (2002), personal skills or accomplishments. Any of the Tenets of Contentment that clients consistently follow are considered positive psychology strengths in QOLT. Additionally, QOLT offers its own list of strengths based on the pioneering work of Peterson and Seligman (2004) along with some key Tenets of Contentment. The list of strengths in QOLT can be found in Table 12.1. Clients are taught to regard any word or phrase from the list that applies to them as a personal strength.

Because of the phenomenon of mood-congruent memory, clients often "forget" or lose awareness about positive things when upset, because their memories and thoughts match their bad mood. For example, a friend may look like a devil or angel depending on one's mood when thinking about him or her (Myers, 2000). The BAT technique or exercise helps clients to remember good things about themselves and their accomplishments in both the recent (today) and distant past so that they do not get too hopeless or down on themselves. The BAT exercise is more complex than the Success Log and seems to have greater happiness boosting properties. It is ideal for clients who seem to need more than the Success Log to improve their happiness and satisfaction with the self. Theoretically, it may boost overall life satisfaction as clients use the first two columns to recall success experiences in valued areas of life. BAT may also alter clients' stories and memories of the past in a positive way for we know that any remembering or recall can alter memories. To use the BAT technique, provide clients with the following instructions, which explain its purpose and mechanics:

> When upset, we often forget about important things as our memories and thoughts fit the bad mood we are in. BAT helps you to remember some good things about

yourself and your life so that you do not get too hopeless or down on yourself. To build a Happiness Habit of self-esteem, gratitude, and self-confidence, write down as many things as you can in each column. Carry your BAT list with you or post it somewhere prominently so you can see it several times a day. Whenever possible, add to your BAT list and edit it each day: The more you think about this, the better you will remember these positive parts of your life and yourself. Such "cognitive work" can help to boost your self-image or satisfaction with yourself. Recalling your strengths, accomplishments, and blessings from the past may even alter or soften some of your unpleasant memories as you start to think of your past in new ways.

Quick BAT Happiness Booster. After having some success with BAT, busy clients can often boost their happiness during the day by doing a truncated BAT exercise that dispenses with the BAT form completely. When feeling frustrated or unhappy, instruct clients to simply stop and recall 3 BAT items from the three categories of blessings, accomplishments, and traits. My clients often use their fingers to count off 3 Blessings, Accomplishments, and Traits. It helps for them to cite any accomplishments from their day whether small or large.

Case Example Using the BAT Technique

Mary, a clinically depressed and suicidal teacher of Mexican-American descent, used the BAT technique to great effect. A statewide award for excellent teaching exacerbated Mary's perfectionism and exorbitant work demands, leading to a crisis when her husband found her on their couch with a loaded .357 magnum revolver held to her head. QOLT, including a course of cognitive therapy for her depression, led to a remission of Mary's depressive episode with no reoccurrence reported for over 1 year. Mary completed the BAT exercise as part of her treatment. She carried around her completed BAT in her purse, pulling it out to review and to add to each column whenever she began to "feel like a hopeless loser." When especially down, Mary started from scratch, checking her ability to recall blessings, accomplishments, and positive traits and talents by comparing her latest BAT with those completed earlier in her treatment. Box 12.2 on page 192 presents one of Mary's many BAT exercises.

The BAT exercise may boost happiness on many levels. First, the technique forces clients to attend to the successes they have in life and to their positive personal

Table 12.1   Strength List in QOLT

Friendly and Affirming of Other People	Good Problem Solver
Kind, Loving, Loyal, Generous, or Sympathetic to Others	Good Common Sense, Good Judgment, Problem Solving and Decision Making in Practical Everyday Matters
Very Generous and Giving Toward Others	Cautious and Careful
Accepting and Nonjudgmental of Others	Creative or Original
Self-Disciplined and Cautious about What I Say to Avoid Hurting People	Artistic
Thoughtful toward Others	Can Make and Keep Close Friends
Thoughtful toward the Group or Society (Good Team Player)	Spiritually Gifted; Spiritually at Peace, Kind, or Forgiving
Gentle, Quiet, and Respectful of Others	Spiritually Gifted and In-Tune with What Really Matters in Life; Spiritually-Based Kindness, Patience, Optimism
Ethical, Honest, Fair, Straightforward	Good at Enjoying Life
Funny, Humorous, Playful, Fun to Be With	"Mindful" or Able to Focus All of My Attention on the Present Moment Rather Than Worry about the Past or Future
In Love with Learning New Things	
Modest, Humble, Forgiving	Not Obsessed with Fame or Fortune, Not Overly Concerned about Making Money or Achieving Fame
Able to Fix Things, Mechanically Gifted	
Self-Calming and Emotionally Intelligent in Controlling Feelings of Depression, Anxiety, or Anger (Good Emotional Control)	Lover of Animals
	Lover of Nature
Optimistic about Life and the Future	Lover of Children
Full of Energy and Enthusiasm	Nurturing of Others, Loves to Teach and Help Others Grow in Skill
A "Person on a Mission" in Life, That Is, a Person with Clear-Cut Life Goals-and-Values	
Self-Disciplined in Moving toward Long-Term Goals (Farsighted), Able to Control Self, Make Good Choices, and Steadily Move Toward Long-Term Goals	Lover of Social Justice, Good Fighter for Justice, Crusader for Social Justice or the Environment, Dedicated Citizen of the Community and the World
	Courageous or Brave
Self-Disciplined in Work Habits	A Person with Many Outside Interests
Self-Disciplined in Personal Habits Like Weight Control	Very Knowledgeable; Wise
Self-Disciplined and Cautious About What I Say to Avoid Hurting People	Loyal, Caring, Fair
	Consistently Happy or Content
Good Self-Control *in General*	Consistently Kind, Grateful, or Forgiving
Good Organizer, Well-Organized; Very Organized; Conscientious about Getting Things Done	Humble or Modest
Hard Working and Reliable; Persistent in Getting Things Done	Good Self-Esteem
Neat and Clean	
Able to Take Good Care of Myself and Keep Myself Healthy— Good Fitness Habits or Inner Abundance	

Note: Clients are asked to regard *any word* or *phrase* from the list that applies to them as a personal strength. Clients are also asked to regard the *Tenets of Contentment* as an additional list of strengths; thus, any Tenet that clients regularly practice is seen as a personal strength.

BOX 12.2

Clinical Example of Mary's Completed BAT Exercise

Instructions: When upset or unhappy, we often forget about important positive things in our life. Our memories and thoughts tend to fit the bad mood we are in. To build a Happiness Habit of self-esteem, gratitude, and self-confidence, write down as many things as you can in each BAT column. Keep your list handy or posted where you can see it often. Whenever you think of it, add to the list. The more you remember and dwell on these things, the more positive you will feel about your life and yourself. Happiness booster exercise: Even without this form, try to stop and recall 3 BAT items whenever you can throughout your day; use your fingers to count off 3 Blessings, Accomplishments, and Traits. Remember also that your *Talents and Traits* can be applied to any area of life you care about to boost happiness in that area (Strength It Tenet and Strength Exercise).

Blessings Count your blessings—the big and little things I'm grateful for.	Accomplishments Big and little things I got done *today* and accomplished in the past.	Talents, Traits, and Tenets Big and little things that I am good at and that people like about me.
Friends	High School diploma	Excellent teacher
Family	College degree	Great sense of humor
A good home	8 years married	Loving wife, mother, and person to all I meet
A good job	Landed a good job	Good listener who does String of Pearls Tenet
My face	Bought a house	Good cross-stitcher
Enough money to live on	Made good friends	Good with computers
A job I believe in	Well-liked by colleagues	Can make curtains
Flexible work schedule	Money saved for retirement	Animal lover
Nice church	Won Best Teacher award	Very organized at work and home
Chance to travel	Taught math and science to hundreds of students	Artistic
Darkroom to pursue my photography		Assertive with great social skills. I practice the How Kind Tenet: kind , loving, loyal, generous, fair, and sympathetic to others
		Witty and fun to be around
		Smart, ethical, and honest
		Persistent in getting things done; not obsessed with fame or fortune

---

characteristics or strengths and virtues to use positive psychology terminology. If done on a daily or routine basis, satisfaction with one's self and regard for oneself should improve in keeping with the rationale for the Success Path to Self-Esteem. Additionally, the blessings or gratitude component of BAT can make clients feel better by taking their attention off of themselves, thereby reducing the self-focused attention associated with painful rumination, negative affectivity, and depression (Frisch, 1998b). Emmons and McCullough (2003) found that practicing grateful thinking on a regular basis can enhance concurrent well-being. In their seminal paper on happiness, Lyubomirsky, Sheldon, et al. (in press) speculate on how gratitude may increase happiness and contentment. According to them, gratitude promotes the savoring of positive life experiences and situations, so that the maximum satisfaction and enjoyment is distilled from one's circumstances. This practice may directly counteract the effects of "hedonic adaptation" (see Sensate Focus/Savor Tenet), by helping people extract as much appreciation from the good things in their lives as possible. In addition, the ability to appreciate the positive aspects of their life circumstances may also be an adaptive coping strategy by which people distract themselves from tragedies. The practice of gratitude may also be incompatible with the experience of negative emotions, and thus may reduce experience of the Big Three emotions (anger, depression, anxiety).

DON'T ASK PATH TO SELF-ESTEEM

The second path to Self-Esteem, called the "Don't Ask Path," suggests that clients stop asking themselves whether they are worthwhile or measure up as whole persons because, as numerous leaders in the field such as Albert Ellis and Aaron T. Beck have pointed out, this is a meaningless question that takes on the impossible task of boiling down the thousands of good, bad, and neutral actions people make into some global or overall evaluation of their worth as a person (A. T. Beck et al., 1979). The Don't Ask Path can be presented to clients in the following way:

> Quality of Life Therapy assumes that we generally do our best in life situations given our limited skills and awareness at the time. Since people do many good, bad, and neutral things, they should never and cannot meaningfully rate themselves as a whole based on any of these particular acts. As Dr. Aaron T. Beck says, the self is made of many "little I's," including hundreds of traits, actions, and experiences. There is not one global "I" that can be rated meaningfully even though in our simplified minds it feels like there is. We are just too complicated as people to be given an overall rating of good or bad. Bad or imperfect acts don't make you a bad or inadequate person anymore than the thousands of good or neutral things you do make you a good or neutral person. People who rate their overall goodness based on a few behaviors are guilty of the cognitive mistake called "overgeneralization." So while you may criticize yourself for a particular act or something you did, the Don't Ask Path suggests that you never confuse yourself with the act. Thus, you can hate the act without hating yourself. You can evaluate particular performances or things you do but never rate yourself as a whole.

To sum up, this path to Self-Esteem discourages clients from asking "Do I have positive self-esteem?" or "Am I a worthwhile person?" Instead, this path focuses on an evaluation of specific performances in particular areas at particular times, such as when clients ask themselves, "Did I handle that interaction well with my child?" or "Did I do a good job on this particular work project?" This approach frees clients to get on with the central questions of, "What do I want in life?" and "How can I get it?" instead of being stuck trying to answer the complicated question of, "Am I worthwhile?"

When worries about self-worth intrude into one's consciousness, QOLT prescribes Mindful Breathing, from the Toolbox CD and Chapter 7, to aid clients in getting on with everyday activities.

SELF-ACCEPTANCE PATH

The third path to greater self-esteem and satisfaction is called the Self-Acceptance Path—summarized here and in the Self-Acceptance Tenet of Contentment—and is based on arguments made by Albert Ellis and Beck's group (A. T. Beck et al., 1979). Both the Don't Ask and Self-Acceptance Paths may require cognitive therapy schema work as discussed in Chapter 10 on emotional control skills in order to take or be effective. Consultation with clergy can also reinforce this approach.

In the case of the Self-Acceptance Path or strategy, clients decide that they have worth or value independent of what they may do in life and are reminded to include this in any thought records or New Life Scripts that they may write. This assertion of, "I accept myself and assert that I am worthwhile," can be based on rational or theological grounds. For example, clients may decide that all creatures of the earth are entitled to feel basically good about themselves and have the right to feel happy. Thus, they may assert that just by virtue of the fact that they are alive, they are entitled to feel good about themselves, worthwhile, and deserving of happiness and self-respect. In this case, the therapist can suggest to clients that they have the right to exist and be happy just as any other living creature does. It is not something that they have to earn through any achievements. As with all the paths of self-esteem and other cognitive arguments in QOLT, the therapist should merely offer these different viewpoints to clients to see which ones the client may agree with and may be willing to "test out" by acting "as if" the belief were accurate for a week or two. It is important that clients believe or "buy into" a particular argument or path to self-esteem for it to be effective in the same way that it is essential that they believe a positive answer written in a stress diary for it to prove effective.

In teaching clients this path to positive self-esteem it is helpful to reframe the problem as a problem in clients' relationships with themselves. Clients don't often think in these terms but how they relate to themselves is just as important as how they relate to other people. Too often clients with low self-esteem treat themselves worse than they treat strangers or loved ones. In this sense they need to learn to practice the *Reverse Golden Rule* that says, "Do unto you what you do unto others (when you treat them with basic decency and respect)." As Theodore Rubin has said, we must be in a "state of grace" with ourselves in order to be content and able to love and serve others. Thus, therapists should emphasize to clients that the principle of self-acceptance requires that clients start to treat themselves as they would a valued friend. This means never giving up on themselves and a commitment to Inner Abundance, that is, always taking care of themselves to meet their basic needs for rest, good nutrition, fulfilling work, or some "calling" to help others and the world, rewarding relationships, and recreational outlets.

Clients may also be helped to reason that since they always do their best, given their limited understanding, awareness, and skills—see QOLT theory of change presented in Chapter 4—they can never be judged as generally bad people for simply making mistakes. You may recall that the rationale for QOLT or its theory of change suggests that clients always do their best given their limited awareness, understanding, and skills. Thus, if clients always do their best, given their limited awareness and skills at the time, it is unfair and irrational for them to blame and hate themselves for mistakes that they make. The therapist can tell clients "you wouldn't have made these mistakes if you were really aware of how destructive they were and if you knew better ways of coping. I want you to adopt the philosophy of the author Will Campbell and say to yourself, 'I reserve the right to be wrong.' "

Another rational or "logical persuasion" justification for clients to like and accept themselves is based on the assumption that people are not equal to their acts or behaviors. Thus clients' actions are just what they do or what their "self" does to meet its goals given its limited abilities and awareness. In this sense, clients can be urged to separate the concepts of the inner or core self versus behaviors or strategies the self uses to try to meet its goals and get its needs met in valued areas of life. By making and believing in this distinction, clients' self-worth is never "on the line" when they make mistakes since "the self" is a separate entity from behaviors, which are but the means that the self uses to accomplish its ends given the self's limited awareness and understanding as a fallible, imperfect human being.

It is important for therapists to emphasize to clients that self-acceptance does not mean self-complacency. Just because clients don't condemn themselves for making wrong, bad, or hurtful acts, they can still admit these to themselves and try to change their behavior. In fact self-acceptance makes it easier for clients to admit their mistakes since their overall self-worth is never on the line. Too often when clients equate their self-worth with never making a mistake, they never admit the mistake, which leads them to continue hurtful or self-destructive behaviors over and over again. In other cases, when they do finally admit to a mistake they can be overwhelmed with guilt and self-hate to the point that they never really fix the problem and get on with their lives. In a sense, this is one of the biggest advantages of the self-acceptance path: It helps clients to get on with their life. In fact, numerous authors define happiness or the meaning of life as finding things that one cares about, forgetting oneself, and enjoying oneself while pursuing these interests or commitments to the hilt. It is necessary for clients and others to forget about themselves or "lose themselves" in order to feel centered, content, and "in flow" for the tasks that they care about in life. When clients learn to accept themselves, they can quickly learn from their mistakes and get back into the flow of life as they become task-oriented rather than self-oriented or unduly "self-focused" (see QOL theory of depression in Chapter 2). Patients may also use a theological justification to pursue this path when they decide that, "God loves me no matter what I do; therefore, I have basic self-worth."

To summarize, the Self-Acceptance Path gives clients rational or logical arguments for accepting, liking, and esteeming themselves independent of anything they do. The rational arguments, based on QOLT and Ellis include: (1) You are entitled to feel good about yourself because you are alive and have the same rights to happiness and self-esteem as any living creature; (2) you can never think less of yourself for your actions since you always do the best you can in a situation given your limited skills and awareness. Since you can't do better than your best and since you always try to do your best, putting yourself down as a person for some action is irrational and unfair; and (3) my actions are independent of my self; actions are the means by which the self tries to accomplish goals. Since my actions are independent of my self, it is unfair and irrational to put my self down when my actions are incorrect, mistaken, or hurtful.

Cooperation with Clergy and Spiritual or Religious-Based Arguments for Self-Acceptance

Numerous religious traditions provide a theological justification for positive self-esteem by asserting that a personal God loves and accepts each person independent of his or her actions, suggesting that people must be inherently good and worthwhile. This sentiment has been presented crudely on placards declaring, "God made me and God don't make no junk." Clients who spontaneously think of this justification are encouraged to evaluate its effectiveness in boosting self-esteem if recalled routinely. When clients have spiritual concerns related to guilty or self-hating thoughts, QOLT will refer them to clergy from their tradition when they know that the clergy member will present this message in a loving and accepting way.

Revising Childhood Recordings Technique

A specific technique for pursuing the Self-Acceptance Path involves the Revising Childhood Recordings technique—also see related FOOBS Tenet and Life Script technique from Chapters 9 and 11. This technique is in many ways built upon the cognitive therapy technique of historical review (see Chapter 10) in the service of self-referential schema change. For many clients, low self-esteem stems from adverse childhood experiences. Many children see their parents as gods. They took everything their parents said ("You're no good.") and did (abuse and neglect) as the "gospel truth" about themselves. For many clients, low self-esteem is a result of replaying these childhood "recordings" that their parents and significant others, including siblings and peers, impressed upon their psyches at an early age.

The Revising Childhood Recordings technique challenges clients to trace the source of their low self-esteem to childhood experiences, to take responsibility for persecuting themselves with the same old saw in the present, and then to challenge and revise these recordings or schema that make them feel that they are no good or a bad person today. To do this technique, ask clients to think about their childhood experiences. In session, ask them to state ways they put themselves down or engage in negative self-talk. See if they associate the voice and language that they use in their self-talk with a particular person or persons in their past. Discuss the origins of the negative self-talk and have them then write down these messages and challenge them through the Lie Detector, Stress Diary, or New Life Script exercises or by; reviewing the Tenets of Contentment.

Don't Blame the Victim: A Clinical Example

Bianca always blamed herself for her parents' bad marriage, believing that she was a "difficult child" who pushed them apart. She replayed this childhood recording on repeat mode throughout her life. Whenever a relationship problem developed in her life, this negative schema/mode was reactivated and she blamed herself entirely for the problem. After thinking about the source of her childhood recordings, Bianca realized that her irritable, alcoholic mother had abused her and called her "no good," when in fact she was a very obedient, "good," and joyful child. She also realized that she wasn't to blame for her parents' marital woes. In essence, Bianca took the advice of the English cognitive therapist, Dorothy Rowe, who says that for many, the key to overcoming depression is to "call a spade a spade" by blaming their parents instead of themselves for the problems they experienced in their families while growing up. Too often people blame themselves for problems in their families in order to protect the image they have of their parents as loving caretakers who knew what they were doing as they raised us. Unfortunately, the price of this inappropriate or excessive self-blame is often low self-esteem and unhappiness.

SUMMARY FOR CLIENTS OF SELF-ACCEPTANCE PATH FOR MANAGING CLIENT CONCERNS ABOUT SELF-ESTEEM

The Self-Acceptance Path can be summarized in the following script, which can be shared with clients for inclusion in their Goals-and-Values or New Life Scripts described in Chapter 11:

> I accept me with all my faults, uncertainties, and mistakes. I believe in me as a doctrine or assertion of faith. Who is more important in life that I am? I deserve to be treated with self-respect. I've done much good already in my life. Bad or imperfect acts don't make me a bad person. I am no better or worse than anyone else since I always do my best, given my limited skills and understanding. I have worth independent of my performance and, by definition, my performance and everyone else's will be less than average half the time. I see mistakes as a chance for me to learn and grow rather than as an indictment of my worth as a person. All humans make mistakes. It's only a disgrace if I define it as a "disgrace" and insist that I be perfect all the time.

SELF-SYMPATHY AND LOVING-KINDNESS MEDITATION FOR EMERGENCY BOUTS OF SELF-HATE OR LOW SELF-ESTEEM

The Self-Sympathy reading and exercise is popular with clients with low self-esteem who value quiet reflection time to renew and review progress in QOLT. It is a wonderful daily "practice" or exercise that may continue for a week or more when clients seem particularly plagued with thoughts of self-hate and disparagement. Therapists may share the Toolbox CD copy of the exercise with clients:

> To carry out this exercise, simply read this to yourself or play a recording of it in a quiet place that is free from distractions. Allow yourself time to think about and repeat each group of statements as they slowly "sink in":
>
> 1. You must care for and treasure yourself in order to extend that caring to others. Find a comfortable place to sit or lie down and begin by focusing on your breathing without trying to control it in any way. Just feel the breath as it enters and leaves your body. As you lie down to relax and meditate for the next 10 to 30 minutes—you may set a kitchen timer if it helps—focus deeply on accepting and loving yourself "warts and all."

> 2. *Read the following out loud to yourself:* I accept me with all my faults, uncertainties, and mistakes. I believe in me as a doctrine or assertion of faith. Who is more important in life that I am? I deserve to be treated with self-respect. I've done much good already in my life. Bad or imperfect acts don't make me a bad person. I am no better or worse than anyone else since I always do my best, given my limited skills and understanding. I have worth independent of my performance and, by definition, my performance and everyone else's will be less than average half the time. I see mistakes as a chance for me to learn and grow rather than as an indictment of my worth as a person. All humans make mistakes. It's only a disgrace if I define it as a "disgrace" and insist that I be perfect all the time.
>
> 3. Make peace with your body as a vehicle for pleasure, movement, and activity. Reject "lookism" as you refuse to judge your outer shell, your body, and see it and your inner character and feelings as evolving processes and not static "things" to be judged by a culture that wants to profit from your insecurity.
>
> 4. No one is more worthy of inner peace, caring, and compassion than you are.
>
> 5. Recall with great sympathy for yourself, the hurts and pain that you have worked through to get this far in life.
>
> 6. Laugh to yourself as you recall mistakes you made—how human and typical! *No big deal.* No, there are no "takeovers" in life. But you can live with that. We've all blundered at times.
>
> 7. Put aside thoughts of your enemies for a time and their actions toward you. Forgive, forget, or just ignore them during this exercise. Come back to you and your need for loving-kindness and understanding after all you have been through. Let go of hurts, fears, and concerns with imperfection in yourself, others, or your world for a time.
>
> 8. Think of things you are grateful for, the blessings in your life as well as your positive talents and traits.
>
> 9. Bask in your accomplishments for a moment; really *luxuriate* and *feel* the things you have achieved large and small. Take pride in your victories against the odds.
>
> 10. Focus on your breathing without trying to control it in any way. Just feel the breath as it enters and leaves your body for a few minutes, keeping a calm steady attitude of loving-kindness toward yourself.
>
> 11. Read this secular *Prayer for Loving-Kindness* to yourself or out loud: May I spend this day in sympathy and kindness toward myself, the self that has

done so much against the odds. . . . May I accept and try to love what is offered to me every moment of this day, including imperfect people and circumstances, content to live simply without trying to change or judge myself or others. May I gently refuse to indulge self-downing thoughts and attacks. May I renounce those influences from others or the media that breed unnecessary worry and pain for me. May I give up and let go of those worries and behavior patterns in myself that just make me miserable in the long run. May I constantly recall each of my "little" accomplishments today, including this exercise. May I carry this attitude of loving-kindness toward myself and others with me throughout the rest of the day.

RELATIONSHIP PATH TO SELF-ESTEEM

As we will see in Chapter 14, supportive social relationships may be the closest thing to the "holy grail" or a "sure thing" that positive psychology can offer as a universal vehicle to happiness. In keeping with this finding, the Relationship Path is a fourth path to self-esteem or greater satisfaction with ourselves, which consists of encouraging clients to cultivate close supportive and loving relationships in which they can be open, honest, and "real," and still be accepted, respected, and loved.

Loving friends, family, fellow hobbyists or spiritual seekers, and coworkers who know clients well and love and accept them, despite their frailties, weaknesses, or peccadilloes, can sometimes do more than years of psychotherapy to counter feelings of "badness," inferiority, and low self-esteem. As evolutionary psychologists have told us, we are social animals who are exquisitely sensitive to the group or those around us. Social or group pressure has an enormous impact on how good we feel about ourselves (Diener & Seligman, 2002). For this reason, we can maximize our happiness and satisfaction with ourselves by cultivating supportive relationships in all areas of life we care about, actively avoiding those who unfairly criticize, judge, or berate us since their influence is corrosive to our self-esteem (see I Never Bother with People I Hate Tenet). While certainly useful, cognitive techniques are no substitute for being with people who care for and love us *as much as possible every day* or for avoiding the "psychonoxious," or people who will always put us down or judge us negatively.

QOLT techniques for developing and maintaining relationships (see Chapter 14) are essential to this path to Self-Esteem and its maintenance. To pursue this path, therapists help clients build up the kind of close, affirming relationships that provide incontrovertible evidence and reassurance that one is valued and respected and so cannot be worthless. Service groups, self-help groups, spiritual groups, and therapy groups can be invaluable in helping clients to build these positive relationships, support groups, or Surrogate Families (see Tenets). Encourage clients to experiment by attending these groups to see if they can find supportive friends. In particular, spiritual groups are designed to lovingly accept visitors and so can be ideal for clients seeking affirmation and pastimes (see Feed the Soul Principle).

Two important techniques useful in pursuing the Relationship Path to Self-Esteem are the Set Up a Test and Second Opinion techniques discussed in Chapter 10. Clients who hate or dislike themselves seek a second opinion from other respected friends, family, or colleagues about their worth or value as a person. By finding others to "positively mirror" and affirm them, clients gain powerful evidence *against* the belief that they are somehow unworthy and "no good." They have essentially Set Up a Test of their Defective Person Schema and found evidence for the schema to be lacking—this and other schemas can be found in the Toolbox CD as Schemas That Drive You Crazy. Close relationships are particularly powerful for this purpose since in these cases clients reveal much about themselves and yet are still liked and cared for by the other person. In essence, a positive relationship with a respected other suggests to clients that they can't be so bad if a good and decent person likes and accepts them even when he or she knows them well, "warts and all."

A major criticism of this approach to self-esteem or to enhancement of satisfaction with the self, is that it is not as "elegant" (to use Albert Ellis' term) or foolproof as say, the Don't Ask Path in which one need not depend on others' reactions to define or support his or her worth in any way. While this may be true, the Relationship Path works for people who do not respond to other paths. Our biological heritage may make it impossible for many of us to withstand severe social disapproval; Diener and Seligman (2004) review evidence to this effect in work contexts.

The Relationship Path may be a powerful happiness and self-esteem booster for other reasons. Following the Relationship Path, for example, requires other happiness-boosting activities such as being with other people and serving or Helping others in some way. This may make its mechanism of effectiveness more comprehensive and complex than it appears at first blush. If pragmatism is used as the criterion for "truth," as it is by so many therapists and by the cognitive-behavioral paradigm per se, the Relationship Path deserves attention as a potential vehicle to greater self-acceptance and satisfaction. And, after all, some clients simply do not or cannot understand logical persuasion approaches to self-esteem.

THE FIFTH OR HELPING PATH TO SELF-ESTEEM

Happiness researcher, Sonja Lyubomirsky, and her colleagues (2004) have speculated on the many benefits of helping to the helper, sometimes called the helper-therapy principle, suggesting that acts of helping and service to others may foster a positive perception of others and one's community, an increased sense of cooperation and interdependence with other people, and an awareness of one's good fortune, presumably as one makes downward social comparisons, as in recognizing that the plight of a homeless person is much worse than one's own situation. Helping often involves socializing, thereby satisfying a basic human need that, by itself, may boost one's sense of satisfaction, contentment, and happiness. People who help, often by being kind to others (see String of Pearls Tenet) may even change their self-perception in positive ways, thereby boosting Self-Esteem. Perhaps helpers feel more satisfied with themselves and even like themselves more as they begin to view themselves as dispositional helpers, that is, as caring and good people, in general, and not merely an opportunistic client trying a homework assignment. For this mechanism of action, helpers presumably must eventually find an avenue of helping and service to call their own—see Chapter 17 for suggestions.

Shocked by the boredom and loneliness of his retirement, Raymond, turned a homework assignment to try volunteering as a disaster caseworker with the local Red Cross into a burning passion that outlasted his therapy by several years. He really was able to Find a Meaning (see Tenets of Contentment) in his Helping routine or habit that made him feel better about himself along with the other benefits just discussed. Helpers may also come to feel more confident, efficacious, in control, and optimistic as they see their helping efforts bear fruit. Helpers may get another self-esteem boost by the reaction that they get from others while helping. When people being helped express liking, gratitude, and appreciation for helpers' acts of generosity, helpers cannot help but feel good and worthwhile as individuals, perhaps debunking well-entrenched family-of-origin schema—called FOOBS in the Tenets—that they are no good and incompetent. This interaction pattern of helping followed by appreciation from the person being helped may begin a self-perpetuating and self-sustaining cycle of prosocial reciprocity, leading to lasting improvements in self-esteem and happiness, all of which are valuable in times of stress and need for helpers, according to Lyubomirsky, Sheldon, et al. (in press).

Similar to the Relationship Path, the major criticism of this fifth approach to self-esteem is that it is not as elegant or foolproof as, for example, the Don't Ask Path in which one need not depend on others or on other roles or activities to define or support his or her worth in any way. Invoking the rubric of pragmatism, this largely unexplored path deserves attention and study since it seems to affect the self-esteem and regard of clients who have been impervious to other means. Additionally, many of us define ourselves and our worth by what we do or how we behave (Bandura, 1986; Kornfield, 2001). There are always opportunities for service or Helping for those clients who define themselves in these terms.

WALKING THE PATHS WITH THE TENETS OF CONTENTMENT

The Tenets of Contentment are invaluable in reinforcing the Self-Acceptance and other paths to self-esteem presented here. Table 12.2 presents a summary of those Tenets most related to building self-esteem.

CASE EXAMPLE OF SELF-ESTEEM INTERVENTIONS AND SCHEMA WORK BY TOM

Tom understood Beck's theory and how it applied to the case conceptualization of his low self-esteem. He

Table 12.2 Tenets Useful in Promoting Self-Esteem

Accept and Enjoy Your Body	Keep Busy with Flows or Happiness Takes Effort Principle
Accept What You Cannot Change Principle	Kiss the Past Goodbye Principle
ACOAN Principle or Abuse or Neglect Principle	Leisurely Pace and Lifestyle Principle
Blind Dumb Optimism Principle	Live Your Dream or 24/7 Principle
Bosom Friends Principle	Men Are Just Desserts (and Women Are Just Desserts) Principle
Care for My One Body Principle	Mental Health Day Technique
Cocoon It Rule	Mine the Moment or Attack the Moment Principle
Do the Right Thing or Clear Conscience Rule or When in Doubt, Don't Rule	Modest Goal or Flow Principle
Expert Friends Principle	Mutual Aid Society Principle (see also Role Model Friends Principle)
Feed the Soul Principle	Never Good Enough or Lower Expectations Principle
Fight for Much, Reap Frustration Principle	No Conditions of Worth Rule
Find a Friend, Find a Mate Principle	Nothing Human Disgusts Me or Acceptance Principle
Find a Meaning Principle	One-Thing-at-a-Time Principle (OTAAT)
Flow It Principle (see also Modest Goal Principle)	Overthinking Principle
The FOOBS Principle or Switch Out of FOOBS Principle	Pick Your Friends Principle
Get a Therapist Rule	Relationship with Self or Self-Compassion Principle
Giving Tree or Self-Other Principle	Ride It Out, Read It Out Principle
Habits Rule Rule or Routines Rule Rule	Self-Acceptance Principle
Happiness Diet Principle	Stop Second Guessing Principle
Happiness from Achievement Principle	Street Signs to Success Principle
Happiness Is a Choice Principle	Strength It Principle
Happiness Matters Principle	Stress Carriers or I Never Bother with People I Hate Rule (see also "Mad Col." Disease Rule)
Humor Principle	Surrogate Family Principle
I Can Do It Principle	We're Not Okay and That's Okay Rule
Inner Abundance Principle	You Do It to Yourself or Terrorist Principle
Intellectual Masturbation Principle	

understood how stressors and schemas *interact* to create the Witches Brew of Depression and other Big Three emotions. He learned that schema work was the key to successful cognitive therapy and that his self-schemas were abysmal—the childhood roots of Tom's low self-esteem and horrendous self-schemata are detailed at the end of Chapter 3. Accordingly, Tom experimented with the techniques described in this chapter and waded through countless thought records, that is, Lie Detector and Stress Diaries (Chapter 10), that he did related to self-esteem to come up with the following New Life Script or schema for self-esteem:

No kid is good or bad. Only dumb parents with a kid they didn't want or plan for and with zero skills would say something like that to a beautiful two-year-old like me or any other kid. Thanks, Dad, for telling me that you guys wanted me aborted! But I *was* a beautiful child, full of energy and a zest for life, like any kid. . . . There was and is nothing wrong with me except that I was born in the wrong place at the wrong time. No one is perfect all the time and even if I were, it wouldn't make a difference to Dad who doesn't give a shit about me. I see the love showered on my Expert Friends (from Tenets) who fuck up and still are adored and loved by their cheerleader parents. You were different, Dad. You had no business having kids. As you said, I was an accident, an inconvenience to you and Mom. Anyway, decent parents love their kids despite their screw ups. We learn from mistakes and I am learning from mine.

I hereby accept and adopt the Self-Acceptance, Serve Others, Love Many Things, and the Process Goals Tenets as part of my New Life Script or philosophy of life. This means that I will never again give up on me or be so damn judgmental toward myself. I can be a good guy and a good teacher who nurtures kids in a po-dunk town instead of being a workaholic maniac at some Ivy League university like you want me to Dad, except that is bullshit, too, cause I wouldn't be making enough money as you have in your infinite wisdom, misery, and suicidality recommend. Jesus, give me a break and don't tell me about your shit anymore. I'm the kid, remember? You might give me a break. I'm not your therapist and I have my own Surrogate Family (in Tenets) including a new improved Mom to watch over and support me as I watch out for them.

I'm an alright guy. As I heard in Sunday school but never believed till now, "God made me and God doesn't make junk." It is sick and warped to try to sum up a person as good or bad anyway. I finally accept that I perpetuate the bullshit in my head that came from you and god knows where else. It is my bullshit now and I choose to repudiate it whenever it comes into my head. I will do Mindful Breathing to cope with those times of misery until I get a chance for some Quality Time, exercise, and prayer or meditation to zap it completely.

Overemphasizing work is characteristic of clients like Tom with perfectionism, obsessive compulsive personality traits, and a history of abuse or neglect (see ACOAN Tenet).

As a result, of his QOLT, Tom changed his basic Goals-and-Values, aspiring to a more balanced and fulfilling lifestyle of flows and meanings—see Balanced Lifestyle Tenet—to include the spirituality, recreation, friendships, and love life that he had sorely neglected along with basic health and self-care—in the form of exercising more while smoking and overeating less. With the help of QOLT, Tom bought into the positive psychology view of QOL theory, which says that *all* valued areas of life contribute to our life satisfaction equation and so therefore must be "honored" or paid attention to if we wish to be reasonably not rapturously happy. In this vein, Tom gained much from finding an affirming but non-fundamentalist church that provided avenues for service and Helping by teaching and tutoring immigrant children from Mexico as well as a "conflict-free" avenue for Spiritual Life development.

CHAPTER 13

Health

The World Health Organization defines health as "a state of complete physical, mental, and social well-being and not merely the absence of disease or infirmity" (World Health Organization, 1948). In keeping with this definition, the goal of health care today is to improve clients' QOL in addition to affecting a biological cure for physical illness or disability (Frisch, 1998a; Hyland, 1992; Muller, Montaya, Schandry, & Hartl, 1994). QOL is increasingly viewed as an essential health care outcome or "medical endpoint," which is at least as important as symptomatic status and survival in evaluating the effectiveness of any health care intervention. For this reason, general medicine and health psychology researchers are saying that biological measures of health should be supplemented with QOL and happiness measures to adequately represent the health of an individual or a group (American College of Physicians, 1988; Berzon, 1998; Diener & Seligman, 2004; Faden & Leplege, 1992; Fallowfield, 1990; Frisch et al., 1992; Ogles et al., 1996).

QOLT defines *positive mental health* as happiness with its core constituents of life satisfaction and preponderance in the frequency of positive affect experiences over negative affect. Either happiness overall or one of its core constituents qualify as an indicator of positive mental health in QOL theory (see Chapter 3).

FURTHERING POSITIVE MENTAL HEALTH AND HAPPINESS HYGIENE THROUGH QOLT

Therapists can boost clients' positive mental health in two ways:

1. Expose clients to the entire QOLT program or at least those procedures presented in Part II of this book, since QOLT in general is designed to increase human happiness in a lasting way.
2. Expose clients to the Tenets of Contentment pertaining to happiness.

Specifically, therapists can boost clients' positive mental health by having clients:

- Review the Tenets of Contentment pertaining to happiness,
- Choose Tenets that they would like to incorporate into their personal philosophy of life (or New Life Script as described in Chapter 11), and
- Evaluate whether acting on these Tenets in specific ways on a day-to-day basis actually leads to greater well-being on tests like the QOLI.

Happiness Fosters Better Physical Health and Adjustment to Chronic Conditions

In QOLT, health is defined "as being physically fit, not sick, and without pain or disability" (Frisch, 1994). The aphorism, "you don't know what you've got until its gone" clearly applies to Health, something most people take for granted until a problem develops. Still, many people in poor health with chronic diseases and disabilities are able to cope and to adapt to their conditions and find other avenues to happiness and satisfaction with life in spite of their infirmities. Only those with very severe and multiple disabilities that hamper the simplest activities of daily living seem to suffer significant losses of happiness that are never regained. Even this group, however, has some resilient souls who practice Happiness Habits to the point that they experience their life as meaningful and fulfilling. For example, many veterans I have counseled have built meaningful lives of joy and contentment despite horrific injuries. Diener and Seligman (2004) review a host of studies confirming the view that happiness may help people adjust to chronic health problems like chronic pain and COPD, taking away some of the sting or negative impact that these conditions can have.

In a similar vein, Diener and Seligman (2004) have built a convincing case for the notion that happiness can do more than lessen the pain of chronic physical diseases and disabilities. That is, the findings from numerous studies support the view that happiness contributes directly to everyday physical health. For example, greater happiness seems to bestow a greater immunity to colds and flu viruses. Greater happiness also seems to contribute to longevity; that is, the happier we are, the longer we live. Perhaps happiness as much as exercise or physical activity is a bona fide "fountain of youth." Boosting our happiness may also improve our physical health and longevity. Rather than relaxation and biofeedback, perhaps happiness or well-being interventions should be the "aspirins" that behavior medicine specialists routinely dispense to those who are sick or disabled by either an acute or chronic condition.

In light of the foregoing health and happiness connection and in light of a new emphasis or concern on positive mental health, QOLT considers the area of health to be a crucial component to improving QOL or subjective well-being. Additionally, since Emotional Control skills amount to a regimen of "negative mental health hygiene," this concept, too, is considered under the general rubric of health.

FREQUENT HEALTH CONCERNS EXPRESSED BY CLIENTS

The problems expressed by clients with respect to health on measures like the QOLI generally fall within three categories: (1) Poor fitness and health habits or "addictions." QOLT adopts the cognitive-behavior nomenclature in viewing addictive behaviors as compulsive behaviors that often respond to operant and cognitive interventions such as those laid out in Cognitive Therapy for Substance Abuse (A. T. Beck, Wright, Newman, & Liese, 1993). Typically, the problems of being overweight and "out of shape," that is, in need of exercise, are seen as impediments to satisfaction in the area of Health. Some clients also cited problems with addictions to alcohol, drugs, and so on; (2) Chronic illness or disability such as back prob-

lems, impaired hearing and eyesight in older persons, coronary heart disease, and allergies; and (3) recent acute health problems, including recent illness, injury, and surgery such as ulcers, kidney stones, or pain from an automobile accident.

HABIT CONTROL PROGRAM FOR POSITIVE AND NEGATIVE ADDICTIONS

The QOLT Habit Control Program can be used to increase almost any positive health habit like exercise—dubbed the fountain of youth by Myers (2004) and others for its aging delay properties—or decrease any negative Health habit like overeating or drinking too much alcohol after work, thereby increasing one's satisfaction with Health. In addition, the program can be used to control or eliminate other problem behaviors such as poor study habits in school or procrastination at work that are not directly related to health. As is true of QOLT in general and habit control interventions in particular, QOLT should not commence until clients have been medically examined and cleared by their physician for QOLT. Additionally, unhealthy habits or "negative addictions" that meet the criteria for a DSM disorder such as alcohol dependence or cocaine abuse, are always treated with cognitive therapy for the DSM disorder in addition to QOLT. Finally, the Basket-of-Eggs exercise from QOLT, is used in the Habit Control Program as it is in all area-specific intervention programs in light of the O factor in the CASIO model of life satisfaction, which predicts a general increase in life satisfaction when satisfaction is boosted in areas not of immediate concern.

The Habit Control Program of QOLT involves six steps that can easily be adapted and followed for any particular healthy or unhealthy behavior that a client wants to either increase or decrease. The six steps are:

1. *Build commitment,* motivation, and Inner Abundance to change the habit a client wants to change.
2. *Record "TAC"* or the Triggers, Actions, and Consequences related to the habit.
3. *"Take a new TAC"* or plan and implement new ways to handle the Triggers, Actions, and Consequences of the habit, using the latest principles of behavior modification.
4. *Stress Management and Problem Solving* for difficulties that discourage healthy habits or help to feed or maintain unhealthy habits.

5. Develop and implement a *plan to prevent relapses* and to maintain a client's gains once the habit is under control.
6. Develop a *plan for coping with a relapse* should it occur.

Step One: Building Commitment, Motivation, and Inner Abundance

The biggest mistake a *therapist* can make in trying to change a client's habit is to try to change the behavior too soon. Unhealthy habits may reflect other difficulties such as a lack of time for socializing, recreation, or play. Unhealthy habits may also reflect a stressful lifestyle, depression, marital unhappiness, or frustration at work. Never begin the Habit Change Program before functionally assessing and conceptualizing a case (see ACT model, for example) to see all of the factors maintaining the habit, including negative reinforcement as in stress-related dysphoria subsiding whenever the unhealthy habit is indulged.

Likewise, the biggest mistake a *client* can make in trying to change a habit is to try to change the behavior too soon. Clients should wait until they are absolutely sure that they are willing to spend the time and effort to really change this habit. The therapist should ask the client, "Are other areas of your life under sufficient control and stable enough that you have the time and energy to devote to changing this habit or behavior?" If the answer to this is, "No," it may be best to wait until the rest of the client's life is more stable.

Inner Abundance and Problem Solving

Before the rigors of habit change are undertaken, clients need a foundation of Inner Abundance—share and discuss this Tenet. Inner Abundance can be usefully augmented here by implementing QOLT for other—non-Health—valued areas of life in keeping with **O** in the CASIO strategy and the Basket-of-Eggs exercise, both from Chapter 8. Essentially, clients need to look to other areas of life for greater satisfaction as they undergo the often slow and difficult process of habit change.

Before any habit change, clients must be taking excellent care of themselves a la Inner Abundance with outside major stressors under some modicum of control and stability. In this vein, therapists' functional assessment may allow them to "jump the gun," doing some Stage 4 work to prevent the sabotage of change

efforts by clients and their environment. Problem solving for difficulties that help to "feed," maintain, or reinforce unhealthy habits or that discourage healthy habits can do much to forestall a disastrous failure, recalling Mark Twain's quote, "Quitting smoking is easy. I've done it a hundred times." The last thing clients need is another failure. Marjorie, a software designer from Austin, pursued couples therapy for a volatile marriage. Only when this source of stress and trigger for emotional eating was stabilized did she pursue the Habit Change Program for weight management.

In addition to answering the question, "Are you ready?" the building commitment and motivation phase involves making a detailed list of the pros and cons for changing the habit and not changing the habit (Pro versus Con technique). Consider both the long- and short-term consequences of either changing the habit or not changing the habit. For the sake of motivation, it's important for clients to make a long list of advantages for changing the behavior. It is also important for them to develop counterarguments to each of the disadvantages they can come up with for changing the behavior.

Step Two: Record TAC

To gain control over their habit, clients must learn to keep precise records of when and where the habit occurs. The motto here is that *clients have to count it to control it.* QOLT and cognitive-behavior therapists feel that habits are controlled by three factors, that is, the T, A, C of TAC. The first factor, T, stands for *Triggers* or antecedent situations or feelings or events (also called "discriminative stimuli") that encourage a behavior or habit to occur by "setting the occasion for reinforcement"; that is, triggers signal clients (often unconsciously) that it is likely to feel good and to be rewarding for them to engage in a habit in a particular situation or condition. Consider the example of overeating (a bad habit or unwanted behavior). The TAC model suggests that a client keep track of situations that trigger, encourage, or elicit overeating behavior. Very often this involves things like feeling bad, being alone, or going out to eat. Whatever the habit they're trying to change, clients must learn to keep some form of diary to record the triggers for that behavior so that these triggers or their reaction to these triggers can be changed. For example, overeaters may keep a food diary of when and where they eat as well as the type and amount of food along with its caloric content, fat content, or both. If clients learn from their diary-keeping or self-monitoring that they eat any high-fat food in sight, they may hide these triggers by putting the food away and not leaving it out on the counter as a temptation.

The A part of the TAC model refers to *Action* or the specific behavior or habit that clients want to change. This too must be recorded and thus made conscious for habits to be changed. For example, if clients are trying to lose weight, this would include keeping track of their eating behavior by counting the number of calories and kinds of food that they eat.

The C refers to the *Consequences* for the action, behavior, or habit in which clients engaged. For unwanted behaviors there is very often an immediate positive payoff for the behavior, as in the case of the binge eater who feels emotionally soothed and relaxed immediately after a binge, only to feel guilty and disgusted with him- or herself later on! Clients must clearly understand the positive and negative consequences of their habit in order to learn how to manipulate it and thereby control or eliminate unwanted habits.

During this self-monitoring period, clients record, for at least one to two weeks, the habit that they wish to learn how to control. Whatever record keeping method used, it must include all three of the TAC factors and it is best to arrange to record these aspects of the habit as close to the time the habit occurred as is possible. The Habit Diary (see Figure 13.1) may be used to record the TAC factors associated with any positive or negative "addiction" in either clinical or pure positive psychology clients.

Step Three: Take a New TAC: Planning and Implementing the Habit Change Program

The third step in the Quality of Life Habit Control Program involves using the information clients have gathered in the record keeping stage (Step 2) to design and carry out a behavior modification program to change the habit. The goal is to come up with strategies that will: (1) change the Triggers for or responses to the habit clients want to control in a way that encourages healthy habits and discourages unhealthy habits; (2) change the Actions, behaviors, or habit itself in the way that clients desire; and (3) change the Consequences for doing the habit or behavior in such a way as to encourage healthy actions and discourage unhealthy actions.

One strategy for modifying triggers is to avoid trigger situations. For example, a client who likes to "pig out" when eating out should not go out to eat until the eating behavior is under better control. The client may also narrow triggers by limiting the trigger situations in which the undesired habit is engaged. For example, if the client likes to overeat in front of the TV or in other rooms of the house, the client may make a rule such that he only eats (or overeats!) in the kitchen or dining room without distractions so that he will be more aware of how many calories he is consuming at a sitting.

Actions or bad habits also can be changed by developing incompatible behaviors. An incompatible behavior is an action that prevents the occurrence of some other, unwanted behavior. For example, a client took up horseback riding on Saturday afternoons, a behavior incompatible with her usual routine of watching movies and overeating!

Name: *Jane Doe*   Date: *02/08/08*

Triggers	Actions	Consequences
9/5/25 1:30 P.M. Sitting with Ginny in the smoking section of the bar after lunch. Feeling nervous and thinking "I really need a cigarette. One won' hurt."	Smoked 5 cigarettes	Feel relieved, relaxed, and a little "high" from the beer and cigarettes. Feel good and think "It's great to have a heart-to-heart talk with Ginny about our work problems."

Figure 13.1 Habit Control Diary example.

It is extremely important that clients develop positive rewards or reinforcement for any successes they achieve in the Habit Control Program. This is the C or Consequences part of the TAC model. Encourage clients to be creative in coming up with ways to lavish themselves with praise and rewards for any successful change efforts they make. One client, for example, rewarded herself for her success in exercising and adhering to her diet by giving herself 20 minutes a day to read a "trashy" Nora Roberts novel.

Clients may also "self-reward" or reinforce as they fill out their Habit Diaries and take note of occasions where a healthy behavior occurred and an unhealthy habit or behavior was resisted and did not occur. This self-reward often consists of positive thoughts (like "I didn't! I'm succeeding. I *can* control this. Good job") and the positive feelings associated with these thoughts.

In general, a positive reinforcement or reward refers to any event or consequence that follows a behavior and that maintains or strengthens the behavior. Strengthening the behavior means that the likelihood or probability of the behavior occurring in the future is increased. It helps to brainstorm with clients and make a list of positive rewards they can use to reinforce healthy habits or to reinforce behaviors that are incompatible with unhealthy behaviors. The Play List available on the Toolbox CD can be used in this regard. In addition, an action or behavior that the client does frequently, can be used to reinforce a new action or habit (Premack It Principle). For example, a client who has been addicted to methamphetamine and who is trying to foster the positive addictions of jogging and socializing, may reward herself with a half-hour of TV watching (something she frequently does) after she runs or visits a friend each day. Whenever a client cannot think of a positive reward for a behavior, suggest he or she simply "Premack it" by following the new, low-frequency behavior with a high-frequency behavior the client already engages in often (Premack It Principle, named after the operant psychologist David Premack who first wrote of this law of reinforcement). Social support and praise is often a powerful reinforcer for clients that can be tapped by including significant others or people trying to overcome a similar addiction in a client's Habit Control Program or both. The therapist may counsel these others in ways to support, encourage, and frequently praise the client for his or her efforts at habit control. In general, the removal of positive reinforcers or re-

wards (a type of punishment), the removal of aversive or unpleasant stimuli (negative reinforcement), or the presentation of an aversive or unpleasant stimulus (a second type of punishment) contingent upon or following a response is ineffective or impractical in self-directed, outpatient Habit Control Programs.

Step Four: Stress Management and Problem Solving for Related Problems

The first step in changing any unhealthy habit or addiction is to gain control of the problem behavior by using behavior modification strategies to attack and change trigger situations, unhealthy actions, and consequences that foster the addiction. Once this is done, it is also important to analyze and identify any underlying or related life problems or stresses that help to maintain the addiction or bad health habit by generating negative feelings that the addictive behavior will temporarily reduce or eliminate—an ACT model case formulation as described in Chapter 5 can help in this process. Lie Detector and Stress Diaries, discussions of the whys and wherefores of addictions, along with the results of functional analyses through use of the Habit Diary, will often point to personal failure, low self-esteem, perfectionism, or a failure to live up to impossible standards of performance—(the $\underline{S}$ in CASIO)—in valued areas of life that clients care about such as work, school, relationships, and physical appearance, and associated extremes in the Big Three negative emotions or the so-called "Negative Affect Syndrome" hypothesized by Barlow (2002) and discussed in Chapter 10. In complex cases like these, self-esteem interventions from Chapter 12, anti-perfectionism interventions like the Good-Not-Great technique from Chapter 8, and the Lifestyle and Emotional Skill training from Chapter 10 actually become part of the habit control treatment.

In terms of perfectionism, no one has done a better job of showing the connection between the failure to meet the exorbitant expectations of affluent Western societies for appearance and success and addictions or compulsive behaviors than Roy Baumeister (1991). In his book, *Escaping the Self*, Baumeister shows how public one's failures are, as if people are doing a career/school/appearance "strip tease" to the world in which everyone can easily see everyone else's mistakes and shortcomings, as though they were broadcast on the evening news. At the same time, nothing succeeds like compulsive behaviors such as problem drinking, overeating, and bulimia to give people a vacation from themselves and their failure ruminations. Combined with some distracting activity like watching television or surfing the net, "addictions" or compulsive behaviors relieve individuals of painful self-awareness such as the self-focused attention of the mildly and clinically anxious and depressed after a disappointment or failure experience (Barlow, 2002; Clark & Beck 1999; Frisch, 1998b). In these cases, cognitive therapy and QOLT interventions aimed at disputing negative self-schema and gaining distraction from self-defeating depressive and anxious rumination via positive addictions like Mindful Breathing and Meditation or almost any engaging alternative activity can be helpful (Lyubomirsky & Tkach, 2004; McMillan & Fisher, 2004).

Stress Management in QOLT consists of problem solving with the Five Paths exercise, regular Quality Time to relax and recreate, regular (and preferably daily) aerobic physical exercise, good nutrition (which builds up the body's capacity to handle stress), and building social support systems, including good friends, family, coworkers, and people clients may know through social clubs, churches, temples, synagogues, or other social groups (see Chapter 14 on Relationships). Lifestyle changes, including time management is also involved, such as the use of a daily schedule to make sure that clients' time is used wisely (see Chapter 10). For example, an accountant used the Five Paths strategy to successfully deal with her prescription drug addiction. Specifically, after completing the exercise, she decided to reduce her daily work schedule from 12 to 14 to 8 to 10 hours, which made her less tired, irritable, and prone to using drugs.

In cases where clients' addictions are caused or maintained by other psychological symptoms or problems (i.e., dual diagnosis) and by quality of life problems (also known as problems in living), the Habit Control Program should be supplemented with empirically validated, disorder-specific treatments.

Step Five: Relapse Prevention or Maintenance and the Personal Stress Profile

The fifth step in the QOLT Habit Control Program is to develop strategies designed to maintain the gains clients have made after eliminating unhealthy behaviors or starting positive behaviors. A good mainte-

nance program recognizes the high likelihood of a relapse and tries to set up a plan to prevent them.

One key maintenance or relapse prevention strategy is to write down any high-risk situations or triggers for repeating an unwanted behavior once it has been controlled and eliminated and then to problem solve around specific ways to either avoid those situations or to prevent the problem behavior from recurring in these situations. For example, one high-risk situation for a bulimic client was to wake up at three o'clock in the morning when anxious about something, go downstairs, and engage in some kind of a sedating binge of overeating. After recognizing this high-risk relapse situation, the client was able to develop a detailed plan for handling this occasional insomnia. The client decided not to go downstairs when unable to sleep and to instead read and relax in the study without the temptation of food around. The client also developed a quick and reliable Relaxation Ritual in the form of a tape that when played quickly took the "edge" off the anxiety and made the client less desperate to raid the refrigerator. This example illustrates the essence of good relapse prevention: One identifies high-risk situations and then develops the skills and confidence needed to handle the situations in such a way as to avoid relapsing into unhealthy habits. Any situation that may prompt clients to fall back into old, unwanted behavior patterns constitutes a high relapse situation; they should make a plan for each of these situations that come to mind and practice the plan until they have it down cold. Such plans can be developed using the strategies and techniques of Chapter 22 on Maintenance and Relapse Prevention, as well as by completing the Relapse Prevention worksheet included on the Toolbox CD. The Personal Stress Profile (also available on the Toolbox CD) helps clients to identify internal signs of stress that may trigger a relapse. Clients are then taught how to identify these signs as an *Early Warning Signal* or a cue to do something positive to reduce the stress, thereby reducing the likelihood of a lapse or relapse. The Relapse Prevention worksheet helps clients to formulate ongoing and trigger-specific coping plans in order to further reduce the likelihood of relapse. Since the likelihood of relapse can never be completely eliminated, and since it remains high months after conquering many addictions, clients must be prepared for dealing with the possibility of lapses or relapse.

Step Six: Coping with Relapse

Relapse is the rule rather than the exception in habit change and control. Expect clients to relapse and to even recycle through the six stages of the Habit Control Program when they are trying to change particularly difficult habits. It is good to help clients plan for and accept lapses and relapses and not to be unduly alarmed when they occur. It is important that they accept a momentary lapse and maintain an attitude of compassion, forgiveness, and practical problem solving, rather than getting down on themselves for a lapse. Encourage clients in the midst of a lapse to try to relax and reconsider some of the strategies they utilized earlier in their efforts to control or eliminate the habit. The Relapse Emergency Checklist, available on the Toolbox CD, can be completed by the client and therapist in concert in order to establish a concrete, overlearned routine for dealing with the emergency of a lapse or relapse into a destructive habit or addiction. By carrying this with them, clients are always armed and ready for a situation in which they find themselves resuming a habit that they had worked so hard to eliminate. If followed, the Relapse Emergency Checklist will literally "wear out" a client and will outlast any urge to relapse since it presents such a lengthy array of activities for positive coping in relapse situations. Lie Detector and Stress Diaries are also invaluable in helping clients cope with momentary lapses and in preventing lapses from turning into "collapses" or a return to destructive addictions. Above all, encourage clients not to give up hope but get back on the wagon of personal growth and change after a lapse into a bad habit. Some researchers have suggested that often a few relapses are almost necessary for clients to learn and hone the skills needed to eliminate or control a habit for good (Witkiewitz & Marlatt, 2004).

PAIN AND CHRONIC HEALTH PROBLEMS

Research shows a reciprocal or two-way relationship between health and quality of life (see Diener & Seligman, 2004, for review). Thus, better health can improve clients' quality of life. In addition, as clients' quality of life improves, their perception of health will often improve. Perhaps clients with chronic health and pain think and talk about health problems less, that is, give fewer "organ recitals" when they are satisfied and occupied with other areas of life. The $\underline{O}$ in the CASIO strategy for dealing with health dissatisfaction has been very effective. That is, clients have increased their overall quality and even their health satisfaction by trying to improve their happiness in areas of life besides health. For example, one client improved her Play satisfaction by taking up bicycling after she permanently injured her knees while running. After 6 months, her Health satisfaction increased (along with her overall happiness), even though the condition of her knees did not improve one bit! Evidently, she accepted her knee problem and became less concerned about it after finding a new hobby to replace her running. Another client, crippled by arthritis, had a similar experience after she started taking classes in creative writing at a local community college; her increased Learning satisfaction made her less aware of and worried about her arthritis even though her physical condition remained unchanged. Each of these clients came to their "solutions" using the Basket-of-Eggs worksheet, which can be routinely administered to clients with chronic health problems.

Helping Routine for Chronic Health Problems

Helping Routines (see Chapter 17) and activities can give a focus and a purpose as well as a huge happiness boost to clients who are coping with the onset of a chronic physical disability or chronic illness; such activities give a sense of satisfaction, and a chance to socialize that distracts clients from their obsessive focus on their own pain and suffering.

Of course, these and any other suggested QOLT interventions should be *in addition to* an evidence-based cognitive therapy approach for chronic pain.

Management of Stress, Emotions, and Lifestyle

The stress management procedures included in the Habit Control Program discussed in this chapter as well as the skills in Chapter 10 have been invaluable to clients with either chronic or transient pain, illness, disabilities, or injuries experienced by people with low Health satisfaction. Relaxation Rituals and the Five Paths exercise have been especially well-received by chronic pain patients. It also is helpful for pain patients to apply the Habit Control Program to increase positive health habits, such as walking or sitting up. Relaxation Rituals can attack general physical tension patients with chronic pain experience, which exacerbates their physical pain. This coupled with Habit Control Programs and therapy aimed at increasing physical activity have been useful.

Clients in pain must also force themselves to be more active; sitting around doing nothing gives them time to think about and focus on their pain. If they are able to get mobilized a little bit so that they can get involved in active recreational or work activities, the pain will often recede from the forefront of their consciousness. Here the Baby Steps to Success technique described in Chapter 4 is helpful. After a severe illness, injury, disability, or surgery, it can be good for clients to very gradually increase the amount of walking or sitting up they do each day, lavishly rewarding themselves for every increment of progress (such interventions should be approved by clients' physicians in advance).

The Habit Control Program also can be used to reduce unwanted pain behaviors such as the overuse of narcotic medicine for pain control. Here, a "Pain Cocktail" strategy of taking pain medication at a regular time during the day rather then whenever one feels pain can be extremely effective. It is also helpful to use a Relaxation Ritual or to do a Stress Diary and the Problem-Solving worksheet techniques to reduce the psychological worries and anxiety that often increase pain.

Often clients have to start over and rebuild their lives after some major health problem limits their ability to function in key areas of life such as Work, Relationships, and Recreation. In starting over, they may need to reevaluate their overall Goals-and-Values and proceed step-by-step through all the 16 areas of life in QOLT in order to gradually rebuild their lives into something fulfilling. For example, Martin, who was confined to a wheelchair after a serious car accident, experienced this as he changed careers from construction work to teaching. He could teach in a wheelchair (something he had always wanted to do but was afraid he was unable to do), but he could no longer do construction work after his car accident.

Clients must develop more realistic expectations (**S** strategy of the CASIO model) as they pursue interests they used to have before a chronic and serious illness or disability set in or occurred. This reordering of their lives can be referred to as *Lifestyle Modification*. Clients must modify their lifestyle and daily routine to accommodate major physical and health limitations. Although this can be frightening, the research suggests that people with serious injuries and chronic illnesses can usually restore themselves to the level of happiness or quality of life they enjoyed before their illness or injury in as little as a year's time.

Problem Solving as a Health Intervention

Problem solving through completion of the Five Paths exercise (from Chapter 8) can be effective in ameliorating health concerns in concert with clients' physicians. One client felt significantly less depressed after changing her shift work schedule, which cured her insomnia, and being referred to an allergist for the treatment of debilitating allergies. This case illustrates what Beck (1979) calls the "speck in the eye syndrome" (p. 227) in which an unresolved practical problem contributes significantly to psychological distress and depression. Table 13.1 lists the Tenets of Contentment that are particularly useful in addressing Health concerns.

Table 13.1 Tenets with Attitudes, Schemas, and Practices Conducive to Greater Satisfaction with Health

Accept What You Cannot Change Principle

ACOAN Principle or Abuse or Neglect Principle

Anger Is the Enemy or Shift of Hate Principle (see also Don't Forgive Principle)

Ask Your Death Tenet

Assessing Progress and Prospects Principle (see also Taking Your Emotional Temperature Principle)

Assume the Best in Others Principle

Avoid Stress Carriers or I Never Bother with People I Hate Rule

Balanced Lifestyle Principle

Be the Peace You Seek or Worry Warts Principle

Be True to Your School Principle: BETTY'S Way

Be with People or Relationship Immersion Principle

Bosom Friends Principle

Care for My One Body Principle

Cocoon It Rule

Color Purple Principle

Daily Vacation Principle

Depression Is Not Normal Principle

Don't Bring It Home or Work Spillover Principle

Don't Forgive Principle or Set Aside, Shelve, Accept or Forget Principle Do What You Love or Tune in to What Turns You on Principle

Do the Right Thing or Clear Conscience Rule or When in Doubt, Don't Rule

Emotional Control or the Big Three Make Us Dumb Principle

Emotional Honesty Principle Exercise or Take your Medication Principle

Expect the Unexpected Principle

Face the Music Principle

Failure Quota Principle

FAT Time Principle

Fight for Much, Reap Frustration Principle

Fight the Power Principle

Find an Area or Go to Your Room Principle

Find a Friend, Find a Mate Principle

Find a Meaning/Find a Goal Principle

Flow It Principle

The FOOBS Principle or Switch Out of FOOBS Principle

Get a Therapist Rule

Get Organized Principle

Giving Tree or Self-Other Principle

Habits Rule Rule or Routines Rule Rule

Happiness Diet Principle

Happiness Equation Tenet

Happiness from Achievement Principle

Happiness Habits Principle

Happiness Is a Choice Principle

Happiness Matters Principle

How Kind Principle or Tender Hearted Rule

Humble Servant or Servant Leader Principle

Humor Principle

I Can Do It Principle

I'll Think about That Tomorrow Principle

I'm Going to See My Friends at Work Principle

Inner Abundance Principle

Intellectual Masturbation Principle

Judge Not, You Don't Know Principle

Keep Busy with Flows or Happiness Takes Effort Principle

Kiss the Past Goodbye Principle

Leisurely Pace and Lifestyle Principle

Life Satisfaction Breeds Job/Work Satisfaction

Li Po or Commune with Nature Rule

Live Your Dream or 24/7 Principle

Love and Work Principle

Love Many Things Principle

Love What You Do Principle

"Mad Col." Disease Rule Make Friends at Work Principle

(continued)

Table 13.1   *Continued*

Men Are Just Desserts (and Women Are Just Desserts) Principle	Should-Want Principle
Mine the Moment or Attack the Moment Principle	Silence Is Golden or Organ Recital Rule
Modest Goal or Flow Principle	Socializing Doubles Your Pleasure
Never Good Enough or Lower Expectations Principle	Stop Second Guessing Principle (see also Cocoon It Principle)
One-Thing-at-a-Time Principle (OTAAT)	Street Signs to Success Principle
Overthinking Principle	Strength It Principle
Personality Stays the Same or Happiness Set Point Principle	Stress Carriers or I Never Bother with People I Hate Rule (see also "Mad Col." Disease Rule)
Pick a Role Model for a Friend Principle	
Pick Your Battles/Pick No Battles Principle or Yes, Boss/Yes, Dear Rule	String of Pearls Practice and Principle
	Surrogate Family Principle
Pick Your Friends Principle	Sweet Revenge Principle (see also Don't Forgive Principle)
Play It Safe Principle (see also Pick Your Battles)	Taoist Dodge Ball Rule
Pocket of Time to Relax Principle	The Three Rs of Stress Management Principle
Positive Addictions Principle	Thou Shalt Be Aware or Psychephobia Principle
Process Goal Principle	To Understand All Is to Forgive All or Empathy Principle
Quality Time Principle	Trust Principle
The Question Rule	We're Not Okay and That's Okay Rule (see also Personality Stays the Same Principle)
Relationship with Self or Self-Compassion Principle	
Ride It Out, Read It Out Principle	What Would My Role Model Do? or Role Model Principle
Second Opinion Principle or Technique	You Can't Have It All Principle or Curb or Ignore Desires Principles
Serve Others Principle	
Share the Hurt behind the Anger Tenet	

CHAPTER 14

Relationships

IT IS THE RELATIONSHIP THAT HEALS

Over the years, therapists from Carl Rogers to Irving Yalom have maintained that the active ingredient of effective psychotherapy is the relationship. A positive therapist-client relationship is central to cognitive therapy, especially in treating clients with personality disorders (A. T. Beck, Freeman, Davis, & Associates, 2004; Beck, 1995). In terms of clinical and positive psychology clients, positive social relationships may be the most powerful ingredient of the "happiness stew" or "salad" (my favorite metaphors for happiness and happiness interventions); in any case, it seems a necessary ingredient or part of human happiness, although it may be insufficient by itself to ensure deep and lasting happiness or contentment (Diener & Seligman, 2002, 2004).

DEFINING RELATIONSHIPS IN QOLT

As seen in the characters of Huck Finn and Jim in *The Adventures of Huckelberry Finn,* we can endure almost anything with friendships to keep us going; for Luo and his friend, it enabled them to endure their "reeducation" in a Chinese peasant village from which they schlepped dripping backpacks of feces up a mountainside to fertilize a field at a higher elevation only to be drenched in feces by journey's end. According to the novel, *Balzac and the Little Chinese Seamstress,* these high school graduates were considered intellectuals deserving of punishment in the eyes of Chairman Mao (Sijie, 2001). In QOLT, Friends (or Friendships) are defined as the people (not relatives) you know well and care about who have interests and opinions similar to yours. Friends have fun together, talk about personal problems, and help each other out (Frisch, 1994). In QOLT, friendship is the model for *all* fulfilling relationships, even committed love relationships and marriage. Indeed QOLT hopes that a client's lover is indeed his or her best friend since the relationship will be deeper, more fulfilling, and long lasting, if it is (Gottman & Silver, 1999). In QOLT, Love (or Love Relationship) is defined as a very close romantic relationship with another person. Love usually includes sexual feelings and feeling loved, cared for, and understood (Frisch, 1994).

QOLT also considers relationships with clients' children, relatives, coworkers, deceased or unavailable loved ones, and the self. Some of the same general Relationship Skills and Tenets (both available for clients in the Toolbox CD) apply to these and other relationships that people value, although specific skills and Tenets may also be called for if these relationships are to flourish. For example, while the mutual respect and closeness of friendship ideally characterize relationships with children, these relationships also include the exercise of parental authority and limit setting and in no way is a "friendship between equals."

CORE TENETS AND RELATIONSHIP SKILLS: THE BUILDING BLOCKS OF RELATIONSHIP ENHANCEMENT IN QOLT

The Four-Step process of Relationship Enhancement in QOLT is built and predicated on a thorough reading and understanding of the Core Tenets of Contentment for Relationships and the largely behavioral, Relationship Skills in QOLT.

A listing of these Tenets and instructions for their use can be found in Table 14.1: Core Relationship Tenets and Tenets for Finding Love and Making New Friends.

The definition and details of the core Tenets must be mastered by therapists and shared with clients before efforts at boosting satisfaction in relationships can commence. Emotional Honesty and Favor Bank involve a set of values, a philosophy of relationships, that is central to all relationship enhancement in QOLT. Expert Friend delineates a central tool for finding and improving relationships that rests on a bedrock finding of positive psychology. String of Pearls gives clients a way to approach daily interactions that serves two functions: (1) maintains and enriches clients' face-to-face interactions each day and (2) constitutes a *Helping Routine* for QOL enhancement that is elaborated in Chapter 17.

Table 14.1 Core Relationship Tenets and Tenets for Finding Love and Making New Friends

The definition and details of these Tenets can be found in Chapter 9 and in the Toolbox CD. Copies for clients can be found in the companion volume for clients, *Finding Happiness* (Frisch, 2006) and/or made from the Toolbox CD. Therapists are encouraged to read over the Tenets to identify and prescribe *additional* Tenets to those presented here in order to suit the needs of particular clients and their particular relationship problems with Romantic Partners, Spouses, Children, Friends, Relatives, Coworkers, the Self, and Deceased or Unavailable Loved ones. The same may also be done with respect to the specific *Relationship Skills* of QOLT that may also be found in the Toolbox CD.

Core Relationship Tenets for Use in All Relationships:
- Emotional Honesty
- Favor Bank
- Expert Friend
- String of Pearls

Additional Useful Tenets for Finding Love and Making New Friends:
- Find a Friend, Find a Mate Principle
- Men Are Just Desserts (and Women Are Just Desserts) Principle
- Relationship with Self or Self-Compassion Principle
- Pick Your Friends Principle
- Failure Quota Principle

Emotional Honesty Principle

The Emotional Honesty Principle is defined as a deep awareness of and honesty with oneself about what is wrong in a relationship, careful decision making about whether to share concerns or not, and, when deciding to share concerns, using QOLT skills and Tenets to express concerns in an honest, but considerate, compassionate, and respectful way that preserves the relationship as much as possible. These components constitute a three-step process:

1. Developing a deep emotional awareness and understanding of one's hurts, feelings, and wants in a troubled relationship. This is the goal of the core technique of Take-a-Letter 1 (explained later in this chapter) and is also reflected in the QOLT Tenet of Thou Shalt Be Aware, that is, individuals must face relationship problems head on and in an unflinching manner whether they decide to change them or not. This awareness process itself can be very helpful and healing, hence the usefulness of Take-a-Letter 1 even with those who are deceased or unavailable.

Emotional honesty also includes an individual's role and responsibility in creating relationship problems and not just that person's innermost feelings about the relationship.

Building a deep awareness of our feelings and our role in a relationship dispute requires some Quality Time away from the situation. Expressing anger in the moment when a person is very upset and lacks perspective, is not recommended in QOLT, although it is recognized that this often happens. Individuals can be honest about problems in ongoing relationships and still be optimistic about their capacity for happiness in general; as this book demonstrates there are myriad paths to contentment and happiness.

2. Deciding what to do if anything based on a deep awareness of the relationship. Because no one is graced with "immaculate perception" and because people can be clueless about their role in creating relationship problems, the Second Opinion technique in which individuals seek counsel about what happened and how to deal with it is highly recommended in QOLT. Whenever possible, it is best to consult a relationship expert, someone adroit at handling these situations who also has your best interests at heart and can keep a secret. Friends, loved ones, and therapists can often serve in this role. No matter how much advice is

given, however, QOLT says the buck stops with you, since the individual must live with the consequences of his or her actions. For example, although often helpful, Second Opinions can be ineffective or even harmful, in that they may irritate the antagonist and make matters much worse. Thus, when deciding what actions, if any, to take when confronting a relationship difficulty, individuals must consider their rights in a situation and others' capacity to change. Often saying and doing nothing may be the best option, such as in work relationships in which the antagonist has no willingness or motivation to change.

John Gottman, marriage researcher, estimates that about two-thirds of problems between couples are "perpetual" or unsolvable (Gottman & Silver, 1999). Still individuals may feel it is worth the try to share their hurts, feelings, and wants with the person causing them distress. This is fine as long as they carefully consider the possible negative as well as positive consequences.

Emotional honesty depends on believing in some basic human rights in communication and in how individuals should live their lives. It is helpful to see if personal rights have been violated in a situation as a first step in giving a person the confidence and assurance that he or she is justified to raise an issue. Nevertheless, QOLT and its relationship approach of Emotional Honesty, recommend Compassionate and Considerate Speech when sharing hurts, feelings, and wants with another person. Individuals have the human and relationship right: (1) to act in ways that promote dignity and self-respect as long as others' rights are not violated in the process; (2) to be treated with respect; (3) to say no and to not feel guilty; (4) to experience and express feelings; (5) to take time to slow down and think; (6) to change their minds; (7) to ask for what they want; (8) to do less than they are humanly capable of doing; (9) to ask for information; (10) to make mistakes; and (11) to feel good about themselves.

3. Sharing hurts/feelings/wants: Applying relationship skills to problem situations or relationships. If an individual decides to share his or her concerns about a relationship problem with the antagonist, QOLT and emotional honesty recommend that that individual practices and implements QOLT Relationship Tenets (see Tenets of Contentment and Relationship Skills found in the Toolbox CD). QOLT recommends retreating from angry situations when possible to avoid "poisoning" the relationship with insults that can never be taken back and to think about what brought about the problem. Using state of the art communication skills may not guarantee success, but it will increase the odds of success; Interestingly, Gottman and Silver (1999) contradict themselves on the importance of communication skills, saying that they are irrelevant early in their book and then resurrecting them later as they give advice on how to deal with relationship problems. Take-a-Letter 2 is the core technique in QOLT for preparing to confront the antagonist in a dispute by marshalling the Tenets and Relationship Skills of QOLT, many of which have been empirically supported in research (e.g., see Frisch & Froberg, 1987).

Favor Bank or Favor Bank of Good Will from Good Deeds Principle

This is a foundational relationship mind-set and skill in QOLT. Tom Wolfe, in his novel, *Bonfire of the Vanities,* talks about the "favor bank" system, in which Irish cops, judges, and lawyers do favors for each other with the understanding that when they need a favor their "friends" will come through for them because everyone has a full bank account of favors from each other. A full bank account of favors means that others have done so many helpful and kind things for us, that we are more than willing to return the favor.

It is helpful to think of relationships in terms of the Favor Bank metaphor. Indeed, QOLT assumes that the Favor Bank system is really the way of the world in relationships. QOLT views all relationships through this Favor Bank lens of mutuality and reciprocity. That is, QOLT assumes that every relationship has a "bank account" of good feelings that builds up as individuals do favors for their friends, loved ones, and coworkers. Usually, when people are in conflict, this bank account of good feelings is depleted or empty. To resolve disputes, it helps to build the bank account back up by doing genuine favors and little things to please or help the people they care about or work with in their lives. Even when there is no conflict, it's good to regularly, even daily, make efforts to please and help others to keep the Favor Bank full. This helps ensure that people will be treated fairly, considerately, and generously when problems or disagreements inevitably come up and they need a favor in return or a spirit of compromise and fairness and kindness as they negotiate a dispute.

The Favor Bank in many respects boils down to the concept of "What have you done for me lately?" which can be distasteful to some positive psychologists and other idealists who conceive of at least some relationships of unconditional positive regard. Except in cases of disability, such as in Alzheimer's disease, people expect relationships of reciprocity in which individuals take turns doing favors for each other, meeting each other's needs, and responding to others' requests for help (see Mutual Aid Society Tenet). Once Favor Banks are full on both sides of a relationship, it is pleasurable to do things for each other so the question of what have you done for me lately never comes up. Helping is not a burden hanging over someone's head. However, if people stop giving basic satisfactions to others that they know they are fully capable of giving, the relationship atrophies.

Even if they do not need a favor, building up a Favor Bank account with others is a social lubricant that makes daily interactions pleasant and rewarding. Just saying hello to someone for whom an individual has done a favor in the past brightens the interaction. One way to do a favor is to always, Thank Everyone for Everything (see Tenet). That is, anytime anyone does something special or helpful, the recipient should say thanks in a sincere and kind way. This can include doing something for that person, even if the person was just doing his or her job.

Starting with the groundbreaking work of social worker Richard Stuart in *Helping Couples Change* and his Love Days intervention, this general concept has been applied to couples in a rather contrived way. Modifying this intervention, you might give an assignment to a client saying:

> This homework involves doing at least one small thing a day that we know will please, affirm, or ease the burden of our lover/partner. Commit yourself to doing a favor or "act of love" whenever you think of it or have a break in your schedule (a quick e-mail or phone call could qualify). It's important to be sincere in doing favors; if you do them grudgingly, it will ruin their positive effects. It's best for partners in a love relationship to do the Favor Bank technique at the same time.

Clients should never feel compelled to do a favor they are uncomfortable with.

In QOLT, the Favor Bank goes way beyond structured assignments. The Favor Bank is a philosophy of relationships that clients are taught to always keep in mind and to act on in a routine and habitual way.

QOLT therapists ask clients to always have the Favor Bank of Good Will concept in their mind as they constantly remind themselves to thank and to do thoughtful/kind things for the people in their life that they interact with day after day. It is too easy and terribly mistaken to take these everyday people, including lovers and partners, for granted and to live without this Mind-Set of Constant Gratitude and Kindness Doing. As they do favors, they should not selfishly look for a payoff now or necessarily even in the future. We dispense kindness and happiness because it is fun and makes us feel good. We certainly notice, however, how smoothly things go when we do need to ask for something. We appreciate it when others seem to do kindnesses in return for us. However, when people do something kind for others, it is more likely that others will do kind things for them. The String of Pearls Principle and Practice (see Tenets and Helping) is a similar concept that is less selfish than the Favor Bank approach.

Expert Friend Principle

Always, choose one or more friends who are in your same life situation and who are doing really well at handling the challenges and minefields associated with your situation and time of life. This may be the most important key to "Aging Well," according to Harvard psychiatrist George Vaillant (2002). It can also be crucial to young stay-at-home moms or career women lawyers as well as mid-career male accountants with young children at home. Whatever your situation, do not take the easy route of befriending folks who simply like you or are easy friends to make. Indeed, the most accepting groups can be those who have failed to find happiness such as those people in school and university settings who drown their sorrows with alcohol and drugs. Instead, pick friends you look up to, who are role models of who you want to be, and who cope well with the stresses and strains of their and your stage of human development. You may need to woo these friends as you would a spouse, but you only need one or two of them and the payoff is enormous. Expert Friends who are role models are fonts of wisdom on how to cope with the tragedies of life like sickness and death as well as the mundane details of finding a good pediatrician if you have children or climbing the corporate ladder. As the Bible proverb says, "Walk with the wise and you will become wise." QOLT also says, "You are who you hang out with." Our friends say a lot about who we are and who we will become.

THE BUILDING BLOCKS OF RELATIONSHIP ENHANCEMENT: QOLT RELATIONSHIP SKILLS

The Relationship Skills outlined and used in QOLT represent an attempt to capture the best from social skills training clinical trials, including some early work by Frisch and his colleagues (Frisch & Froberg, 1987; Frisch & Higgins, 1986; Frisch & McCord, 1987; Frisch et al., 1982). The work of Jacobson and Christensen (1996) and Gottman and his colleagues (Gottman, 1994; Gottman & Silver, 1999) also inform and inspire this compilation, although it should be noted that Gottman contradicts himself by repeatedly recommending the use of communication skills for both solvable and perpetual problems after first claiming that they are useless based on studies of etiology and not treatment outcome (e.g., see pp. 149–155, 158, 201 in Gottman & Silver, 1999). Finally, these skills have been honed through feedback both from my clinical and positive psychology practice. Therapists need to be thoroughly familiar with these skills in order to be ready to suggest particular skills to particular clients and to rehearse the same in session. What follows is a discussion of the Relationship Skills to be used with clients—a list for client use can be found in the self-help version of this book, *Finding Happiness*, and in the Toolbox CD. The skills here are listed and discussed in alphabetical order.

Behavior Change Request

When asking for changes in a relationship, ask a person to change specific behaviors, instead of making vague and general requests. For example, you may say to your partner, "I'd like you to wash the dishes on the weekends when I'm working," instead of, "I'd like you to be more helpful around the house." Tell the person exactly what you would like him to DO or SAY differently. In coming up with a specific behavior change request, it can help to picture what the new behavior would look like to an outsider or on a videotape. Be prepared to make a Mutual Compromise and

to not get everything you want; this is the price you pay for an equal, noncoercive relationship with another person who will often have different needs and wants than you.

Compliment

Compliment means saying something nice about another person, especially after they do something that pleases you. It is an essential way to encourage someone to keep doing or to repeat doing what pleases you. To compliment or praise effectively: (1) Be specific about what it was you like about the person's behavior; (2) do it as soon as you can after someone behaves the way you like; (3) do it *often*. Go out of your way to praise or compliment someone you care about; and (4) be *sincere*. Don't say it unless you mean it, or else your praise will soon mean nothing. When you deliver praise, *look directly* at the other person so he knows you really mean it.

Constructive Criticism

This skill reduces the chance that someone will get angry and defensive in response to your criticism. It involves 2 steps:

1. *Compliment the person.* Find something you *really* like or appreciate about the person.
2. *Give specific criticism.* State the specific behaviors of the other person that bother you. Say exactly what the person will do or say that bothers you. Do not attack the person in a general way as when you use trait labels like "lazy," or "inconsiderate." For example, you may say to a friend, "I really like it when we get together and talk (compliment), but you never call me to get together (specific criticism). Next time, I'd like it if you called me to set up a time to get together (Behavior Change Request)."

Dress Rehearsal

Practice or repeatedly role-play a difficult social situation before it happens. You may write out a script of what might be said or make a list of communication skills you want to use. Once this is done, practice the skills in your imagination, in front of a mirror, on an audiotape, or with a friend. This technique is very effective for giving speeches, asking someone out on a date, preparing to discuss a problem with a boss or coworker, or any other stressful social situation. Roleplaying reduces anxiety and increases social poise in real-life situations.

Favor Bank

It is helpful to think of relationships in terms of the favor bank metaphor. Every relationship has a "bank account" of good feelings that builds up as we do favors for our friends, loved ones, and coworkers. Usually, when we are in conflict, this bank account of good feelings is depleted or empty. In order to resolve disputes, it helps to build the bank account back up by doing genuine favors and little things to please or help the people we care about or work with in our lives. Even when there is no conflict, it's good to regularly, even daily, make efforts to please and help those we care about and work with to keep the Favor Bank (see Tenets) "full." This helps to ensure that we'll be treated fairly, considerately, and generously when problems inevitably do come up.

The Favor Bank technique skill involves doing at least one small thing a day that we know will please, affirm, or ease the burden of a loved one, friend, or coworker. To implement the technique, make a list of 10 small things you could do for the person you wish to favor. One list of favors to please a partner includes "do the dishes, call partner at work to say I love you, bring food home for dinner, initiate making love, leave a love note in the partner's car, snuggle while watching TV, and bring partner a cup of coffee in the morning." After making a Favor List, play "detective" by doing the favors and seeing if they really are pleasing to the other person. You may even let the other person see your list and give you ideas as to what favors please the most. Commit yourself to doing a favor or "act of love" at least once a day either indefinitely or during a period of time that you're trying to work out problems in a relationship. It's important to be sincere in doing favors; if you do them grudgingly, it will ruin their positive effects. It's best for both partners in a love relationship to do the Favor Bank technique at the same time. Also, never feel compelled to do a favor you are uncomfortable with.

Feeling Statements

Feeling statements are I-statements that involve sharing feelings. We can really get people's attention and increase their willingness to change their behavior when we can tell them how their behavior makes us feel. Feeling statements typically begin with the words, "I feel . . ." For example, you may say, "I feel hurt, angry, and unappreciated when you refuse to make time for us to go out together alone without the kids." The Feeling Dictionary discussed in the context of controlling negative emotions in Chapter 10 and available in the Toolbox CD can help you to figure out exactly how you are feeling so you can tell others. Regularly sharing feelings and personal concerns is an essential part of Emotional Honesty and close, personal relationships. When you are angry, it is important to share the feelings behind (or in addition to) the anger that you feel.

Fess Up

This technique is a powerful tool for defusing anger and hostile criticism from others. Fess Up involves admitting to any part of another's criticism that we can and stifling our urge to counteract when criticized. For example, if your partner calls you a "slob," you may resist the temptation to counterattack and admit a mistake by saying, "I haven't picked up my dirty clothes this week. I'm sorry." A counteract only escalates the anger on both sides of an argument.

I-Statements

Part of being Emotionally Honest means owning up to your feelings and opinions. To do this, it is helpful to start the sentences with the word "I." I-statements make others less defensive. They open the door to compromise and problem solving by suggesting that your statements are opinions, not proven facts and could be wrong or mistaken. I-statements are definitely more effective than You-statements that attack the other person and make them defensive and angry. For example, it's better to say, "I feel frustrated, like you just don't care when I give you work to do and you don't finish it," than to say, "You never see any projects through."

Lie Detector and Stress Diary

Relationship problems almost always include errors in our perceptions and misunderstandings. For example, we often attempt to "mind-read" our partners and jump to false conclusions about their intentions and feelings for us. Do a Stress Diary whenever you feel upset about a relationship. This will help you to see the patterns of thoughts and behavior that get you into trouble with the other person. You can use this information to plan some constructive problem solving with the other person. One client saw a pattern when she would demand more time and intimacy from her husband; he would withdraw. After identifying this pattern and problem solving with her husband, they developed a regular routine that would allow for them to both have time together and time alone.

Making Conversation

Being able to make "small talk" or conversation is an essential social skill. It helps in getting to know strangers and in maintaining existing relationships. This skill is really made of many specific subskills, including Pay Attention! Wake up! and Respond! (my updated version of "active listening"). Other important conversation skills include the following:

- *Greeting:* Always say "hello" to people you see. Make eye contact, smile, and even shake hands if it's appropriate. Make it a habit to give a friendly greeting to anyone you run into during the day. People will appreciate the thoughtfulness and you will become less shy and self-conscious around others.
- *What turns you on?* One of the best ways to overcome shyness and to make others like you is to tune into what "turns" the other person "on." It also broadens your horizons as you learn what "makes other people tick." The key to good conversation is asking people about the things that are important to them. You know you're on a "hot" or important topic when the person gets enthusiastic or talkative. Ask about the other person's interests, family, work, and hobbies. Find out what he or she is excited about and "zero in" on these topics in conversation. This shows consideration for others, which

they will appreciate. It also helps you forget yourself and your nervousness about making conversation.

- *Open-ended questions:* To keep a conversation going, ask questions that start with words like "what, when, where, how, and why." Memorize these words. They are the key to open-ended questions, or questions that can't be answered with a simple "yes" or "no." For example, you may ask, "How do you think the president (or your favorite sports team) is doing?" "What made you pick business for a career?" "Where are you from?" "What do you like to do for fun?" or "How do you like this weather?" It helps to ask questions relevant and appropriate to the setting you're in. For example, in a restaurant you may ask someone, "What's good on the menu here?" or "What kind of food do you like?" Keep it light, even superficial, as you make conversation with someone you don't know very well. The goal is to be pleasant and show an interest in the other person. The goal is not to "bare your soul" or give someone the "third degree" with embarrassing, personal questions. Take a moment to plan, even practice, what you might say before you get together with a person.
- *Follow-up questions:* To keep a conversation going, ask further questions about what has already been said in the conversation. For example, after finding out why a person moved into the area, you could ask "How do you like it here?"
- *Changing the topic:* It's important to change topics for conversations to continue to flow smoothly. Once a subject has been exhausted, ask an opened-ended question about something else relevant or appropriate to the situation.
- *Sounds of silence:* It's easy to get "spooked" by long, "pregnant" pauses in conversations. Above all, try to relax, take some deep breaths, and realize that pauses are normal and won't ruin the conversation. Use the time to think of new or related topics to talk about. For example, ask yourself, "What else is this person interested in that I could ask about?"
- *Good goodbyes:* Try to end conversations on a positive note by saying something like, "It's been nice visiting," or "Let's get together soon." A farewell handshake and smile with direct eye contact also helps to end a conversation on a positive note. Remember, if you really want to get together again, this is the time to either get a phone number or make

a date to get together again at a specific date, place, and time. In early dating relationships, it often helps to plan "low stress" and "low cost" meetings like a "date" to have coffee or lunch together. This allows both parties to "check each other out" without investing an entire evening.

Night on the Town

While this skill is particularly suited to those in a love relationship, it can also be relevant to other relationships such as close friends or children. Night on the Town refers to a commitment you make to spend some time each week or month alone with a loved one with whom you want to build a more positive relationship. In the context of a love relationship this involves a couple going out as if on a "date" during a courtship period. The idea is that you never stop "courting" each other. By going out on some kind of a date, you reaffirm and rekindle loving, romantic feelings toward each other. These "dates" do not have to be expensive; a walk in a park or dinner at McDonald's can serve the purpose.

Pay Attention! Wake Up! and Respond!

Wake up and pay attention. Listening in an active rather than a passive way means paying close attention to what another person says and making sure that the other person knows that you are listening and understanding his or her point of view. *This skill should be used in combination with all of the skills discussed in this list.* Show you are really listening by looking directly at the person speaking (Look into My Eyes), sitting quietly in your chair, facing the other person with your body, and leaning forward rather than sitting back. Try sitting knee to knee and almost "eyeball to eyeball" with a partner and spouse when either of you have trouble paying attention during problem-solving discussions (Nonverbal Attention Signals). Try to really understand what the other person is thinking and feeling (Empathy). Make sure you understand the person by repeating his or her message in your own words. Paraphrase what the other person says to his or her satisfaction, before you state your opinion about a problem. For example, you may paraphrase your boss by saying, "Tell me if I'm wrong, but I hear you saying that when I'm late, you feel like I don't take our work

seriously. Do I have that right? (Boss agrees.) Okay, now I'd like to give you my view of the problem. . . . (Paraphrasing)." You can show the other person that you are really listening by asking thoughtful questions. A good question tells the other person you are listening, and not just thinking of what you are going to say next (Questioning). *Whatever else, drop what you are doing and respond to someone as if you really care about him or her and his or her viewpoint.* Blowing off or dismissing another is the way to poison a relationship for life. If your goal is to work together, make an effort to really connect, and converse and visit on a daily basis.

Persistence

Use this skill in situations where you feel that there is no room for compromise and where others are pressuring you to change your mind. Persistence means calmly repeating your position on an issue over and over again. You may sound like a broken record or a broken ipod that plays the same selection over and over. This will prevent you from being manipulated unfairly by others. To show that you have some appreciation for the other person's viewpoint, combine Pay Attention! Wake up! and Respond! (an updated version of active listening) with Persistence. For example, "I hear that it's your car and that you want to drive us home, but I'm not willing to drive with someone who's had as much to drink as you have."

Positive Attitude/Mind-Set

The following Principles of Emotional Honesty will help you prepare mentally for difficult social situations. Having a positive attitude will help you display positive behaviors and communication skills to the fullest. Go over these principles before you face a difficult social situation.

- You have the right to be Emotionally Honest, which means you have the right to express your feelings, opinions, and wishes to the people in your life as long as you do so in a considerate and respectful way that does not violate the rights of others. It is usually better to express your feelings in a considerate way than to keep them to yourself.

- Relationships matter. It is worth the effort to make things better in our relationships with other people.
- Be optimistic about change. No matter how hopeless things have been in the past, the relationship may change using a new approach. Using the skills of Emotional Honesty will increase your chances of being heard and getting what you want from other people. Engage yourself in a "Willing Suspension of Disbelief" as you entertain the possibility that there is hope for your relationship and that your partner is not hopelessly flawed or defective in his or her character; most couples in distress feel negative about their partners and hopeless about the future, even those couples who achieve healthy, long-lasting, and satisfying relationships. Expect and plan for your partner to resist change efforts at first. This is normal and not a sign of "failure."
- Different people with different needs, values, and backgrounds will always disagree. Expect conflict and don't blame people with whom you disagree for being obstinate or "impossible." Try to be a patient problem solver. You cannot have a relationship without having problems. It is not the differences or problems that we have that make or break a relationship; it is how we handle these differences, or how we problem solve that make or break a relationship. Successful couples learn to accept each other's differences and to negotiate a lifestyle where each partner gets some of his or her needs met, that is, mutual compromise.
- The other person is not all bad or all to blame. Try and act *as if* this is true even if you don't believe it entirely; this attitude can open up the lines of communication.
- Both parties in a relationship conflict are responsible for both the problem and the solution.
- Think of what you can do for your partner in addition to what you want him or her to do for you. It is especially helpful for you to do positive things for your partner before asking him or her for any changes. Follow the *Golden Rule of Relationship Change* that says, "I'll consider your requests for behavior change, if you'll consider mine." Create a *Mutual Admiration Society* among loved ones, especially partners (and in other relationships) in which you regularly and sincerely tell them what you like, admire, and appreciate about them. Maintain a rate of five positive interactions for every single negative interaction to maintain satisfaction and commitment (Gottman, 1994).
- Avoid fighting or talking when you or your partner or antagonist are extremely angry. Angry words and hurtful actions damage the relationship and can never be taken back completely. You will eventually destroy a relationship if you try to get what you want by "bullying" the other person with anger, threats, put downs, guilt, or physical aggression. In intensely angry situations with your partner it is best to leave for at least 30 minutes in order to calm down and collect your thoughts. Agree to resume your discussion at a specific time within 24 hours. Try to stop fighting and to start calm, rational problem solving in your relationships.
- Focus on the present and future and not the past. Instead of seeking revenge over past wrongs, focus specifically on what each of you can do or say differently to make things better now and in the future.
- Make sure your nonverbal communication matches what you say. For example, asking to help someone in a sarcastic, angry way nullifies the request to help.
- Love relationships work best if each partner has an equal say in deciding important issues like how to raise the children, how to spend money, and so on.
- *Emotional honesty:* The core relationship skill and principle in QOLT is Emotional Honesty defined as deep awareness and honesty with oneself about what is wrong in a relationship, a careful decision about whether to share concerns or not, and, when it is decided to share concerns, the use of Relationship Skills and Tenets (from the Toolbox CD) to express concerns in an honest, but considerate, compassionate, and respectful way that preserves the relationship as much as possible (see Emotional Honesty in the Toolbox CD Tenets for details).
- You have the right to choose *not* to be Emotionally Honest when the effort isn't worth it, you are sure the person will not respond positively, or you are certain that the other person will be terribly hurt, and so on.
- To develop counterarguments (e.g., do a Stress Diary) to dispute irrational thoughts like: "The honeymoon should last forever," "The situation is hopeless," "Lovers shouldn't disagree," "My lover should fulfill all my needs for companionship and intimacy," "If my partner loved me, he would figure out what I need without asking me."
- "Having affairs," "cheating," or "infidelity" seriously threaten any committed love relationship. Affairs destroy trust and distract couples from dealing with relationship problems.

- Learn to accept and live with relationship problems that do not respond to repeated, serious efforts at change.
- Limit discussions of problems to 30 minutes and try to have five positive interactions for every negative interaction in order to preserve a love relationship (Gottman, 1994).

Problem Solving

The Five Paths to Happiness worksheet in the Toolbox CD includes instructions for its use in problem solving with couples and with others—coworkers, relatives, family members—trying to solve or manage a relationship conflict. Try to use Five Paths or keep its guidelines in mind whenever you discuss a relationship problem. Regular problem solving to maintain the health of a relationship is comparable to regular visits to a dentist to maintain your teeth: The problem solving is difficult and unpleasant, but essential to keeping the relationship alive.

To begin problem solving, make a "problem-solving appointment" of 15 to 30 minutes and plan to discuss only one problem at a time (you can make another appointment to discuss additional problems). Approach the person you are having a conflict with, whether it be your partner, a coworker, or a friend. Tell him that something is bothering you and that you would like to discuss it at his convenience. Before you bring up what is bothering you, try to genuinely compliment the person about something he has said or done that you have appreciated in the past. This softens the blow of criticism. Next, be brief and specific as you tell the person what exactly he does or says that bothers you; using I-statements and Feeling Statements as you describe the problem. For example, you may say, "I feel angry and hurt when you leave me alone at parties and go and talk to people on your own." Use the 'Fess-Up technique to say how you contribute to the problem. For example, you may say, "I know I am shy and have a hard time talking at parties, but it hurts my feelings when you leave me alone and go talk to other people."

Suggest that you use the steps in the Problem-Solving worksheet to work on the problem since it outlines an approach that research has shown to be helpful. Share a copy of the worksheet with all of those involved in the conflict. Go through each step together. It can help for everyone to sign or initial the worksheet when you are done and a solution or "change agreement" has been made. The best solutions are specific, stating what each person will do and say differently as well as when and how often these changes will occur. Decide when you want to discuss how the change agreement/solution is working and whether it needs to be negotiated. Of course, you may experiment with this procedure, adding or subtracting steps depending on what works best for you. Encapsulate or draw a circle around conflicts by limiting problem-solving discussions to 30 minutes and by keeping interactions positive once they are over.

Second Opinion

This technique involves asking a trusted friend with great social skills the best way to act in a tough social situation. You then can weigh the consequences of his actions and decide for yourself how you wish to handle the situation. Because none of us is graced with what Nietzsche called "immaculate perception" and because we can be quite clueless about our role in creating relationship problems, the Second Opinion technique in which we get counsel about what is happening in a relationship dispute and how to deal with it is highly recommended in QOLT. Where possible, it is best to consult a relationship expert (see Expert Friend Tenet), someone adroit at handling these situations who also has your interests at heart and can keep a secret; researchers have used this approach for a long time with success (Frisch & Froberg, 1987). Friends, loved ones, and therapists can often serve this role. Friends and loved ones who really know you and perhaps the history of the conflict are especially useful. Additionally, Second Opinions are often helpful in choosing specific CASIO changes in areas of life that we care about. Second Opinions are often essential in doing any cognitive work, that is, in changing attitudes, beliefs, schemas, or upsetting thoughts.

Take-a-Letter

Along with Problem Solving, this is the most important relationship change technique in Quality of Life Therapy. Take-a-Letter 1 involves writing an uncensored letter in which you share your innermost thoughts, feelings, hurts, and wants with the person you are in conflict with. You may be completely open and honest in writing Take-a-Letter 1 since it is kept confidential and *never* shared with the addressee!

In addition to your uncensored feelings, tell the person exactly what she or he has done to hurt you and how you would like him or her to change. If you have difficulty writing, you can do the Take-a-Letter 1 exercise by speaking into a tape recorder, talking to a mirror, or talking to an empty chair and pretending the other person is there. The goal of this exercise is to make you fully aware of the hurts, feelings, and wants you have about your "antagonist." It is only when we are fully aware of our hurts and feelings that we can begin to understand, accept, feel better about, and possibly solve a relationship.

The Take-a-Letter 1 exercise can improve a relationship by itself without any direct communication between the parties involved. For example, some people feel less angry, more understanding, and accepting or forgiving of parents who have fallen short after writing a Take-a-Letter 1. In these cases, the person often improves her relationship with her parents by changing her attitude and behavior without asking for any corresponding change in her parents' behavior. By itself, Take-a-Letter 1 can also be a useful component in Grief Resolution Therapy. Whether a loved one or "antagonist" has died or left the area, you can process your feelings toward this person with a Take-a-Letter 1. In cases of the death of a loved one, add a section to your letter saying how you feel the deceased would want you to live your life now that they are gone. At the end of "grief letters," be sure to say goodbye to the deceased with the understanding that you will stay loyal to him or her by recalling and gaining inspiration from your memories of him or her. Unhealthy grief can further be reduced by reading the Take-a-Letter 1 at the deceased person's gravesite on a weekly basis, forcing yourself to visit any persons or places that remind you of the deceased, talking at length about the deceased and your feelings to those who will listen, and allowing yourself 30 minutes or so a day to immerse yourself in your grief as you go through memorabilia, such as pictures and letters, in a private place. Once the specified period of mourning is completed each day, try to get involved in other activities as you get on with your life.

More typically, the Take-a-Letter 1 exercise is conducted as a preparation for Take-a-Letter 2, which involves direct, emotionally honest communication with the person you are having a conflict with. Take-a-Letter 1 prepares you for direct confrontation by making you fully aware of the hurts, feelings, and wants you have with respect to your "antagonist." It can also, at times, reveal distorted or unrealistic thinking and expectations that can be dealt with by means of a structured journal like a Lie Detector and Stress Diary (Toolbox CD). You and no one else must make the final decision as to whether you wish to share your hurts, feelings, and wants directly with your "antagonist." Consider both the short- and long-term consequences—both positive and negative—in making your decision. While the communication skills of Emotional Honesty greatly increase your chances of being heard and responded to by others, they cannot guarantee this. In fact, the relationship may stay the same or even get worse once sensitive issues are raised. Take-a-Letter 2 can be delivered either as a letter in writing or in the form of a face-to-face talk with your "antagonist." In either case, you should anticipate the different ways in which the letter may be received and practice either in your mind or through role-playing how you may respond to the person you're in conflict with in an emotionally honest way. Realize that in some cases delivery of the Take-a-Letter 2 is only the beginning of a campaign to improve a relationship. Thus, it is important that you anticipate some resistance to your change efforts and plan to gently but persistently share your concerns until they have been fully heard and discussed. It can be helpful to get a Second Opinion on the tactfulness, effectiveness, and emotional honesty of your Take-a-Letter 2 by allowing a trusted friend or therapist to see it before it is delivered.

Take-a-Letter 2 involves writing an emotionally honest letter in which you openly acknowledge your feelings and make a request for behavior change, but do so in a considerate and courteous manner. The goal here is to help the relationship grow rather than to punish or hurt the other person. Keeping that in mind, Take-a-Letter 2 should be composed using the other skills in this dictionary that are designed to promote emotionally honest communication. As much as possible, it is important to refrain from using labels, put downs, threats, and demands in composing Take-a-Letter 2. It's also best not to dwell on the past and instead to focus on making specific Behavior Change Requests of the other person. It's also important to include some compliments and positive feelings in this second letter so that the other person isn't overwhelmed by criticism.

Time Out

Whenever you are too angry or upset to think clearly and whenever you feel more like hurting your partner than rationally solving a problem together, call a Time Out. Time Out means leaving a tense social situation for at least 30 minutes in order to avoid saying or doing something that may hurt the relationship. Before you leave the situation, tell you partner why you need a time out and agree on a time to finish discussing the problem within the next 24 hours. For example, you may say, "I'm too angry and upset to talk right now. Instead of saying something ugly I'll regret later, I'd like to cool off for a while and get back to you when I'm feeling better. Let's get back together in an hour to discuss it again."

After calling a time out it is your responsibility to do things that you know will help you to calm down and to view your partner more as an equal partner than the "enemy" who deserves to be "punished." This may be accomplished by doing a Stress Diary, a Relaxation Ritual, a pleasant and distracting recreational activity (see Play List), or aerobic exercise. Keep a list or essay handy (and share it with your partner) that details all of the positive qualities of your partner so you can refer to it when discouraged about the relationship (Love Letter technique). Since things said in anger can never be totally forgotten and can *permanently* poison a relationship, it is useful to call a Time Out whenever you feel "out of control" in your anger toward someone.

Tit for Tat

To increase the chance of getting what you want, give the other person what he wants—at least as much as you can. We all expect different things from relationships so do not assume that what you like is what your friend, coworker, or lover likes, wants, or needs from you.

Vision Quest Exchange

In a Love Relationship or close friendship, it is important that we are aware of our partners' or friends' innermost hopes, dreams, and fears. This exercise simply involves completing, exchanging, and discussing Vision Quest exercises with your close friend or partner. It is a beginning exercise in QOLT for couples and other loved ones.

Workable Compromise or Win-Win

Being Emotionally Honest does *not* mean always refusing to give in. Whenever you feel your self-respect is not threatened, offer a workable or mutual compro-

mise to the other person; that is, offer a compromise that meets both of your needs to some extent. Too often we see situations as "either you lose or I lose." The fact is that both parties can often "win" or satisfy some (but not all) of their needs at the same time. Be creative in designing compromises that result in "you win, I win" situations. This skill is essential in love relationships. Compromise is the price we pay to be close to others whose needs and wants will always differ from ours to some extent. Truth to tell, a compromise can be completely one-sided and still be highly adaptive as in cases where one partner is simply unable to compromise in return or give in at all. For example, clients with severe social anxiety disorder are often too impaired to socialize to any extent with their partners. Perhaps more important than love, is Tolerance and acceptance of differences in our loved ones. Tolerance is a central sub-skill to Workable Compromise.

FOUR STEPS OF RELATIONSHIP ENHANCEMENT[1] IN QOLT

QOLT includes a host of positive schema, emotional control techniques, and communication skills aimed at establishing or improving relationships with romantic partners, friends, children, relatives, and coworkers. A basic four-step approach is presented first, followed by specific modifications for a variety of subgroups. The four steps are:

1. Awareness building, cognitive restructuring, and goal setting
2. Skill building and the practice of communication skills and relationship-oriented Tenets
3. *Get Happy Strategy* or QOLT for other valued areas of life in keeping with <u>O</u> in CASIO strategy and the Basket-of-Eggs technique
4. Application of Skills and Tenets to relationships in everyday life and Evaluation of Change Efforts

Step 1: Awareness Building, Cognitive Restructuring, and Goal Setting

Before clients can tackle a relationship problem, they have to become fully aware of their thoughts and feel-

---

[1] The relationship enhancement part of the term QOLT Relationship Enhancement is used as a descriptive label for the treatment goal of the procedures and is unrelated to other approaches similarly named such as that of Guerney or Markman. No disrespect is intended toward the many authors who have used this label in the past.

ings and decide exactly how they want the relationship to be different. As part of this process encourage clients to develop goals for how they want the relationship to be different, laying out *specifically* what they or the other party may *do or say* differently to make the relationship better. In order to set goals for the relationship, clients have to decide on what their rights are in this situation, what's fair to expect from the other person, and what they can reasonably expect to change in the relationship. But setting goals should really come after getting in touch with their deepest feelings, hurts, and desires for the relationship. One of the best ways to accomplish this is through the Take-a-Letter technique.

The Take-a-Letter technique is one of the most powerful interventions in QOLT. It involves writing two letters to someone with whom a client is having a conflict. The first letter is never sent to the person. The second letter is used only if clients decide to talk to their "adversaries" in a relationship problem and is designed to be shared with a client's "antagonist" either in person or through the mail. Since Take-a-Letter 2 is part of the skill building part of relationship enhancement it will be discussed as part of skill building in Step 2 of Relationship Enhancement.

Take-a-Letter 1 involves writing an uncensored letter in which clients bare their soul to the addressee. They need to realize that this letter will not be sent and write their innermost thoughts, feelings, hurts, and wants about the other person. In addition to their uncensored feelings, clients tell the person exactly what he or she did to hurt them and how they would like him or her to change. Clients with difficulty in writing, can speak into a tape recorder or talk to an empty chair, pretending the other person is seated there. In therapy, this "Empty Chair Approach" is most effective in eliciting core feelings and *emotions,* including thoughts and schemas. This *Royal Road to Meaning Principle* of QOLT suggests that strong emotion is a sign that core schemas and negative thoughts are engaged as part of this emotional constellation or mode (D. A. Clark & Beck, 1999). For this reason, QOLT never shies away from strong emotion. Its expression is encouraged as a first step to understanding core schema that may or may not need alteration. An example of Take-a-Letter 1 is shown in Box 14.1.

Step 2: Skill Building and the Practice of Communication Skills

Once clients' feelings and beliefs about a relationship of concern are on the table or fully understood, QOLT proceeds to Step 2. In this phase, clients must first decide for themselves what, if anything, to further do about the relationship of concern. This presupposes that they have done something already by becoming more aware of their hurts, feelings, and wants from completing Take-a-Letter 1. At this stage, therapists may guide or assign clients a Five Paths worksheet to help them decide for themselves, how, if at all, to act to change or improve a relationship of concern. As late, great couples researcher Neil Jacobson used to say, the choices a partner has in responding to a problem or difference in the relationship often boil down to four options: "Dig it, Change it, Suck it up, or Split!"

QOLT therapists would never presume to recommend a course of action since it is the clients who must live with the consequences of their decisions. When clients decide to confront someone about a relationship problem and are willing to assume the risk of negative consequences should their attempts at emotional honesty fail, the skill building and the practice of communication skills associated with this phase of intervention commences. This is begun with the understanding that although QOLT skills and Tenets can dramatically increase the odds of success in being heard in a relationship dispute, they do not guarantee that the other person will decide to change his or her behavior.

Clients who decide not to confront "antagonists" often feel more at peace about the relationship for having gone through the process of Take-a-Letter 1. As in the case of a son and his parents who chose not to confront a family member who had severed all contact with the family after a bitter family argument and after displaying narcissistic and borderline personality traits within the family for years. Similarly, clients whose "antagonists" are unavailable or deceased also feel more at peace about the relationship for having gone through the process of Take-a-Letter 1.

Wendy's Decision. After writing Take-a-Letter 1 Wendy completed a Five Paths worksheet focused on the problem of how to proceed in her relationship with her father. After discussing her results and the pros and cons of further action with her therapist, she decided to proceed with Take-a-Letter 2 and to confront her father with her concerns. Part of Wendy's decision to confront her father involved thinking about what was the fair and reasonable thing to do in this situation or relationship. After considering her

BOX 14.1

Case Illustration of Take-a-Letter 1

Wendy had been bullied, criticized, and berated by her father throughout the 35 years of her life. It all came to a head with the birth of her third child who suffered from spina bifida, a serious physical disability that resulted in almost constant illnesses and medical problems in her daughter. Wendy was clinically depressed and enraged at her father who continued to make unreasonable demands on her time and who criticized her parenting and her weight during one of the most difficult times in her life. Here is the letter Wendy wrote (but did not send) to her father:

Dear Dad,

You have made my life miserable for as long as I can remember. The unhappy memories of you overshadow any good times we had. Most of the time when you speak to me or even look at me all I see is your disappointment and disapproval in me. The message I have received over and over is that I don't measure up and that I never will. Well screw you!

As a child you very seldom allowed me to voice my opinion, and when I did, I was put down even more or laughed at. You were always too busy to attend my school programs, my piano recitals, but you always had time to play golf or go fishing on your own. Granddad took me fishing, told me stories, took me to the store, let me mow the grass, and talked to me when I was down. He hugged me when I needed it. All these things I wished you could do for me, but you never did. You were a failure as a father.

When I became a teenager, you and I began having worse problems. My friends were never able to meet your approval. You never trusted me or believed what I had to say. I wasn't allowed to date or go out much with my friends. I felt like I was living in a cage. I tried to move out for a while and then came back home. Instead of being sympathetic, you kicked me out. Finally, I left for good. Thanks for your "support"! With friends like you, who needs enemies?

To this day you don't seem to think I make good decisions and are very quick to let me know this. Why are you so bitter and ugly to me and the rest of the family all the time?

When I finally moved to Austin to try to be my own person, you punished me by not calling me or contacting me for four months. When I became pregnant, you refused to believe my explanation and decided to take over my life once again. You and Mom decided you would raise my baby since I could never be a "good Christian wife or mom." After a lot of struggle, I did take charge of my life again with my new daughter, but you were not impressed. You kept telling me how you knew I would fail again! You bastard!

When I remarried you told my husband that he was getting the "short end of the stick." Thanks a lot!

Now when I visit you, you get up and go to your shop to be alone. When you do play with my kids, you quickly get angry with them and put them down just like you did me when I was growing up. Don't pull that crap on them!

I want to hear some encouragement, approval, and acceptance from you. I want to see you happy instead of depressed and bitter all the time. You should spend more time with my kids and enjoy being around them more. I am confused, hurt, and angry with you. I just don't know how to handle the situation anymore.

With love and hate,

Wendy

rights and responsibilities, as well as those of her father, she decided that it was fair and just for her to ask for her father to engage in some behavior change. She also decided she would share her feelings with her father even though she risked alienating him forever. Things had become so bad she decided that it would be better to risk severing all ties than to let the situation continue as it was. By staying neutral concerning her decision, the therapist avoided being attacked should her efforts at rapprochement fail.

Relationship History. An invaluable tool in relationship work is the Relationship History technique in which clients list their history of relationships peculiar to a particular type of relationship, such as friends or love relationships, by jotting down the names of persons, dates of relationships, and relationship details, patterns, and lessons for the future. One client, Debbie, did this with respect to Love only to find a pattern of attaching herself to "loser men," including drug users and dealers, who would negotiate reality for her as she faced a particular developmental challenge or task such as making friends in high school or college. In the end, Debbie felt emotionally retarded for the lack of skill development in these areas as she hid behind her socially forceful men, often in an alcoholic haze. More subtle relationship patterns can jump out at clients if they record or write down their relationship histories. When Wendy did this, she discovered a pattern of being a doormat to men in authority, a template she created based on her relationship with her father. In therapy, Wendy decided that fixing the relationship with her dad was a golden opportunity to break the mold for similar relationships. A change in such a pattern can be schema changing and transforming.

Take-a-Letter 2. After completing a relationship history, clients complete Take-a-Letter 2 as part of Step 2. Recall that, unlike Take-a-Letter 1, clients will share this letter with the person with whom they are in conflict. Therapists should discuss, practice, and role-play with clients how clients will deliver Take-a-Letter 2, selecting as many relevant and useful Relationship Skills from the Toolbox CD as they can. An example of Take-a-Letter 2 in action is illustrated in Box 14.2, drawing on the case of Wendy discussed earlier.

Performer Metaphor. The operative metaphor for this part of Step 2 is that of a performer, as in a fighter, gymnast, pianist, or dancer who must learn and practice his or her skills before getting in the ring/gym/auditorium to display their wares.

Choosing Skills and Tenets. When Wendy decided to share her concerns with her father in order to bring about constructive change in the relationship, her therapist asked her to read about the QOLT philosophy of relationships as expressed in Emotional Honesty, String of Pearls, and Expert Friend in the Core Rela-

tionship Tenets listed in Table 14.1. Besides the Core Tenets presented in Table 14.1, she and her therapist used homework and in session time to review all of the Tenets for ones applicable to her situation with her father. For example, she chose the FOOBS Principle as useful for dealing with relatives in general and her father in particular. Points of confusion and disagreement were discussed in session as a master list of useful Tenets was then constructed in therapy along with a list of key Relationship Skills.

Drawing heavily on Relationship Skills in QOLT and Tenets in the Toolbox CD, Wendy and her therapist next composed an Emotionally Honest Take-a-Letter 2 that would actually be shared with her father. In this letter Wendy, translated the vague yearning for love and encouragement she expressed in Take-a-Letter 1 into very specific Behavior Change Requests (from Relationship Skills). She also decided to focus more on the present and future rather than all the wrongs her father had committed in the past. Because she wanted to preserve the relationship with her father, she also decided to cut out the insults and tone down some of her anger. Wendy consciously incorporated many of the communication skills that she thought would increase the chance of her father really hearing her concerns and responding in a positive way.

Wendy and her therapist devoted time to discuss, practice, and role-play how she would deliver her Take-a-Letter 2 to her dad, selecting as many relevant and useful Relationship Skills from the Toolbox CD as they could. She warmed to the idea that she was like a fighter getting ready for a "bout" with her dad. Therapists using this metaphor also make it clear that the object of an emotionally honest confrontation is to repair a relationship and not to hurt the "antagonist" by inflicting either figural or literal blows. In keeping with the metaphor, Wendy accepted that she needed to learn and practice cognitive and behavioral skills before getting in the ring with her dad.

Specifically, as the therapist and Wendy prepared, they utilized the Dress Rehearsal technique from Relationship Skills in the Toolbox CD by role-playing and practicing emotionally honest ways to deal with her father after he received the letter. After this practice, Wendy felt that she could deal with any reaction her father might have in a fairly calm direct way without losing her temper and attacking, thereby further damaging the relationship. She was impressed enough with what she was learning, that she

BOX 14.2

Wendy's Take-a-Letter 2

Dear Dad,

I've been wanting to talk to you for some time but find it hard to put the words in the right order. This letter will hopefully open a door of communication between us.

Life has changed very dramatically for me since Lindsey's birth, as you well know. In seeing my psychologist, things are getting easier to cope with. I have been taking a good look at myself, and some areas clearly need work.

Dad, I love you dearly and discovered that I have put you very high on a pedestal. Somehow, I always expected you to be perfect and to fit <u>my mold</u> of what <u>I</u> wanted for a dad. I have come to realize that this was unfair to you, selfish, unrealistic; and a sure-fire way to be disappointed.

I also feel that you have done the same thing to me in that I have always felt that I could never measure up to your expectations of a daughter. I don't know how you feel, but I cannot continue this way anymore. Our relationship has me feeling hurt, angry, depressed, resentful, disappointed, and uncomfortable. My impression of you is that you are bitter, angry, resentful, ready to die, hopeless, bored, and depressed. You seem to have a lot of problems of your own and I'm very sympathetic to that. I can't, however, change them for you.

We cannot change the past but we can deal with the present and the future. I love you and would like to see us work out a better and happier relationship. I would like to feel more comfortable around you. The way things are now is too uncomfortable and stressful for me.

I have come to realize as a parent that it is not easy bringing up kids. This gives me sympathy for what you had to put up with as a parent. My dream of how I would be the "perfect parent" has been shattered by reality. I have and will make mistakes too! Mistakes are easy to make; however, admitting to them and correcting them can be very hard.

Listed below are some changes I would like to see in your behavior: As you read these, please keep in mind that I am just asking for the kind of courteous behavior anyone would expect from another person:

1. When we are visiting and the baby has a behavior problem, please come to me about it instead of disciplining her yourself.
2. Please do not tell me how to care for my girls, or put me down when you disagree with my methods.
3. Allow me the benefit of the doubt to succeed instead of seeing me as sure to fail. Specifically, if you think I will fail at something I try, please keep these doubts to yourself.
4. Do not make any more jokes about my weight or figure.

I need your support and encouragement now more than ever. Just as I have made a list of Behavior Change Requests, I would also like for you to let me know what I could do to make our relationship better from your perspective. I really liked our last visit. You were smiling, holding, and playing with my girls, and willing to have a nice conversation with me. It felt great not to be teased about my weight. Please let me know what <u>I</u> can do to help us stay close.

It is not my intention with this letter to hurt you, put you down, or be disrespectful. I just want to share my feelings and wants with you in private. I love you dearly and hope you will respond to me in the way that you feel most comfortable with. Let's talk about this letter together when you get a chance.

Love,

Wendy

even planned to share a copy of the Relationship Skills in QOLT from the Toolbox CD with her father if he responded positively to her efforts to communicate.

Step 3: Get Happy Strategy or QOLT for Other, Nonrelationship, Valued Areas of Life in Keeping with O in CASIO and the Basket-of-Eggs Technique

Relationship Enhancement usually includes QOLT for other, nonrelationship, valued areas of life in keeping with O in CASIO and the Basket-of-Eggs technique because relationship change is a difficult process and because satisfaction in other areas of life and the inner abundance that goes with this oftentimes takes the pressure off of the relationship of concern to meet all of the needs ascribed to it by partners. Emily for example, was like a bird locked in a gilded cage in so far as her rich husband kept her in the country away from people, loaded her up with chores, and rarely visited home because of his software business. After doing the Basket-of-Eggs exercise in the Toolbox CD, her slow going therapy went smoother as she pursued other friendships, hobbies, and a fitness program to meet some of her needs. By inviting her husband to share in her dove hunting hobby, she also extended an olive branch of peace to a war torn partner. When time is limited, this step may amount to simply assigning the Basket-of-Eggs exercise from the Toolbox CD as homework along with the Five Paths Summary Cheat Sheet.

This *Get Happy* yourself or *Get Happy In General Strategy* is also part of Work, Money, and Relapse Prevention interventions in QOLT. It is based on the empirically supported assumption that happier people are more successful in relationships, their work, and even in making money (see the beginning of this chapter along with Chapters 1, 15, and 20 for citations of supportive research). Become a happier person by attending to all the areas of life you care about. Become a happier person by practicing Inner Abundance and Quality Time on a regular basis. Become a happier person by becoming more self-sufficient outside of the relationship of concern and you'll be more skillful and effective in the relationship of concern. For example, you'll be less desperate and more centered and calm in the relationship of concern if you are getting important needs met elsewhere in your life and are high in Inner Abundance. However, even the most skillful, centered, and attractive person can be rejected by another.

QOLT skills increase the chances of success without any guarantees. Ultimately, you can influence but cannot control another person.

Step 4: Applying Communication Skills and Tenets in Everyday Life and Evaluating Change Efforts

Once clients have practiced what they want to say in a difficult situation to the point where they feel ready for anything, it is time for them to bite the bullet and talk to the person directly about their feelings and concerns. Sharon, for example, worked mightily at being emotionally honest in every situation in which she felt uncomfortable with excellent results. In a situation in which her sister yelled at her to help her with her homework, Sharon held her ground by saying, "I'll help you with your homework if you stop yelling at me and treating me like a doormat." After this, her sister gained a new respect for her that continues to this day. She gently got rid of a boy badgering her for a date by saying, "I'm really flattered by your interest, but I'm really not interested in dating right now." By using the Making Conversation skill (see Relationship Skills in the Toolbox CD), she learned the art of small talk and gradually overcame her social phobia of talking to people in social situations; an overture she made in a European History class led to a relationship with a nonabusive man who would become her husband. Sharon was also successful in employing emotional honesty to set limits with her domineering (though loving) parents; for example, she rejected their efforts to choose her college and future career for her. In the case, of Wendy, Box 14.3 illustrates what happened after she delivered her Take-a-Letter 2 to her father.

Evaluation of Change Efforts. Once clients have practiced Emotional Honesty with a coworker, friend, or loved one, they should take stock and evaluate how successful their efforts have been. This is the second part of Step 3. If clients still have problems in a relationship after trying to be Emotionally Honest, they may repeat the four steps in Relationship Enhancement until they experience the changes that they desire. Whatever happens, clients should not be led to expect big changes right away. Relationship change is a gradual process of mutual accommodation that takes time, often weeks or months; this is the rationale for Step 3 along with Inner Abundance. Interestingly, it jibes with the

---

BOX 14.3

Wendy Enters the Ring

Wendy and her therapist implemented Step 3 of QOLT Relationship Enhancement by having Wendy mail the Take-a-Letter 2 she had written to her father. She also sent a copy to her mother so that she could help facilitate change and know what was going on. Wendy was afraid that her father would tear the letter up and never talk to her again. Rather than getting angry, however, Wendy heard from her mother that her father cried when he received and read the letter.

A few days later, her father called her to get together to discuss the letter. During this conversation, Wendy used a form of *extremely* active listening called *Pay Attention! Wake Up!* and *Respond!* along with Persistence from *QOLT Relationship Skills* to empathize with her father at the same time that she gently repeated her requests for behavior change. From that day forward, her father treated both her and her children with great respect and consideration. Although her father was still depressed and irritable at times, he was careful not to express his irritation at Wendy or her family.

When heated disagreements arose, Wendy simply retreated, reviewed the tenet of Emotional Honesty and QOLT *Relationship Skills* to formulate a response to her dad. She then practiced or role-played the response with her husband or in front of a mirror before confronting her father in an Emotionally Honest way. These disagreements were rare and invariably Wendy and her dad would reach a Workable Compromise (from *Relationship Skills*) that would resolve the problem between them. Once when particularly upset, Wendy actually wrote a script of what she wanted to say to her father, referring to her notes as she discussed the problem in-person.

---

technique of self-care and getting needs met outside the relationship that cannot be met in the relationship in Jacobson and Christensen's (1996) approach.

Dealing with Failure. Finally, clients should be prepared for the possibility that their relationships of concern may *not* be amenable to change. No matter how considerate, skillful, and persistent they are about improving a relationship, they can't be successful if those involved will not cooperate. Once they've realized that a relationship cannot be changed, it may be best to reevaluate all of their relationships and life-goals in order to answer the question, "Where do I go from here?" This process can be called getting on with your life. One way to take stock in this way is through readministration of the Vision Quest technique as well as the Basket-of-Eggs exercise.

SPECIAL APPLICATIONS OF RELATIONSHIP ENHANCEMENT

The QOLT's four-step procedure for Relationship Enhancement is basically the same for relationship problems with couples/romantic partners in love, friends, children, relatives, and coworkers:

- Awareness-building, cognitive restructuring, and goal setting.
- Skill-building and the practice of communication skills and relationship-oriented Tenets.
- Get Happy In General Strategy or QOLT for other valued areas of life in keeping with **Q** in CASIO strategy and the Basket-of-Eggs technique.
- Application of skills and Tenets to relationships in everyday life.

A few modifications and additions can be suggested for each of these groups. As a general rule, for example, whenever possible, all parties in a relationship conflict should be included in the assessment and intervention/ treatment of relationship problems. In terms of Step 3, the therapist shows a keen interest in the personal development and quality of life of each member of the system, including spouses and children, for example.

When it is not possible to include significant others in treatment, the procedures described in the case of Wendy may be applied without modification. For example, a client in a distressed marriage whose partner refuses to come for therapy may attempt to improve the relationship in the same way that Wendy worked with her therapist to improve the relationship with her father who was unavailable to join in the therapy process himself.

MODIFICATIONS FOR COUPLES THERAPY

In *The Personal History of David Copperfield* (Dickens, 1991), once David's pretty but vacuous child bride, Dora, dies, his confidant, teacher, and dearest friend, Agnes Wickfield, takes Dora's place. Agnes has studied homework and read books for pleasure with David from the moment he comes to Canterbury to live with her and her father. He has come in order to attend school and to become an educated man after a frightening underclass existence at a funeral parlor and factory utilizing child labor. Agnes' tutoring and example moves David from the bottom to the top of his class. She imbues her environs with an atmosphere of goodness, peace, and truth, according to David. It seems natural, from a twenty-first century perspective that David and Agnes' almost brother-and-sister relationship and deep regard for each other evolves into love. A persuasive case can be made that Charles Dickens uses the pseudo-sibling romance in David Copperfield, serialized in 1848 and 1849, and other works as a means of promoting a model of marriage as a relationship between equals based on deep friendship (A. A. Ford, 2004), presaging the work of psychologists like Neil Jacobson, John Gottman, and Gayla Margolin by about 150 years.

Dickens' model notwithstanding, as the old blues song says, "I've *never* heard of lovers that could be best friends." And yet this is precisely the model for successful long-term marriages and committed relationships in QOLT. That is, couples need first and foremost to be very close friends, preferably best friends. This model is based on the pioneering research of John Gottman who observes that happy marriages are based on deep friendship, mutual respect, equality in decision making, as well as deep fondness and admiration (Gottman, 1994; Gottman & Silver, 1999; also see and Jacobson & Christensen, 1996; Jacobson & Margolin, 1979). This sentiment or value system underlying QOLT for couples is spelled out in a key Tenet:

Romantic Friendship or Take the Sex Out of Marriage Rule: QOLT assumes that long-term committed love relationships depend first and foremost on a deep friendship in which partners are essentially best friends who

work hard at the relationship as if it were paid employment, and who compromise and forgive endlessly to borrow a phrase from Mother Teresa. Try to be the exception to the old lament, "I've Never Heard of Lovers Who Could Be Best Friends." QOLT maintains that sex in successful committed relationships is a symptom or expression of what the relationship is like outside of the bedroom, hence, couples therapists' interest in the last time a couple has made love. If it has been 6 to 12 months the couple may already be psychologically divorced.

Although the basic steps for Relationship Enhancement is the same for couples as it is for individuals, therapists may need to make some modifications as outlined here. Adaptations and modifications are outlined next under each step of Relationship Enhancement:

Step 1: Awarenss-Building Modifications

An Initial Assessment of each partner's and the couple's awareness of problems and strengths in the relationship is made in two, 1.5-hour sessions. The first conjoint session is followed with individual sessions for each partner, using the following procedures for Relationship Enhancement:

- *Conjoint session outline and procedure:* The QOLT therapist assesses the couple's awareness of the problems and strengths in their relationship by asking the following questions at the start of the conjoint session:
  —What brought you here today for relationship enhancement counseling?
  —What problems do you see in the relationship?
  —What are your goals for therapy? Be specific—how would positive changes look on TV? What would each of you *do or say* different?
  —What individual goals for growth does each of you have outside of the relationship?
  —What are things that your partner has done or still does that you really appreciate and that make you want to do things for him or her in return?
  —What strengths do you admire now in your partner?
- Homework Assignment given to each partner:
  —Make an appointment for an individual session with the therapist to discuss personal growth issues.
  —Take-a-Letter 1 and 2.
  —Vision Quest exercise with the understanding that it will be shared with partner.

—Vision Quest Exchange in which each partner allows the other partner to read and discuss his or her Vision Quest exercise.

—QOLI for QOL assessment and FESS to screen for possible *DSM* disorders.

—Read Emotional Honesty and Favor Bank Tenets of Contentment.

- *Individual session outline and procedure:* The QOLT therapist assesses each partner's awareness of the problems and strengths in the Love relationship and in their own individual life by following these steps in the individual session with the understanding that there will be no secrets kept from the partner not present:

—Therapist asks, "What problems do you see in the relationship? What are your goals for therapy?"

—Review Take-a-Letter 1 and 2 homework from couples session.

—Review Vision Quest exercise, QOLI and FESS homework from couples session as a way to discuss possible individual goals for growth outside of the relationship, beyond what was mentioned in the initial conjoint session.

- Homework Assignment given to each partner:

—Make an appointment for a second conjoint session with the therapist to discuss assessment results and to decide whether to proceed with QOLT for couples.

—Revise Take-a-Letter 2 for sharing at next couple's session.

Step 2: Skill Building Modifications

Step 2 involves a 1.5-hour conjoint session aimed at sharing assessment results and deciding on whether to proceed with QOLT for couples. Instructions for conducting this session follow:

- The QOLT therapist asks each partner to report on his or her solo sessions with the therapist and homework from the same session—QOLI, FESS, Take-a-Letter 2 (but not 1, which the therapist does not allude to)—with the partner.
- The therapist summarizes his or her view and list of problems and strengths in the couple and in each partner, including any *DSM* diagnoses that are applicable.
- The therapist describes an intervention plan of Relationship Enhancement if it seems clear that this couple could benefit; the intervention plan should also include concurrent treatment of any comorbid *DSM*

disorders with an empirically supported cognitive therapy approach. A Family Practice or Primary Care Model of Treatment is presented in which the therapist treats the entire family, including each partner separately for any *DSM* disorder, with the understanding that there will be no secrets kept from the partner not present and no secrets kept from parents in the family. Clients are told to expect relapses under stress after treatment is completed. These relapses will be treated with Booster Sessions as needed.

After couples have decided to proceed with QOLT for Couples, Step 2 involves ongoing conjoint sessions aimed at teaching Five Path problem solving using Relationship Skills and Tenets in session for eventual application at home (all three tools are available in the Toolbox CD). The goal here is to teach new routines and rituals for problem solving, communication, and for pure fun times devoid of problem discussion, criticism, or complaint—the **T** in FAT Time Tenet. When successful, a Five Path Routine or Ritual is established for solving or managing problems. It is expected that this effort will work for couples willing to take some responsibility for problems and to compromise on relationship disputes, but won't cure irresolvable or perpetual problems as identified by Gottman (1994). For these perpetual problems, some acceptance measures are instituted by the therapist, including a gratitude and count your blessings attitude in which the therapist regularly asks couples to reflect on what is right and good in the relationship as in Georgia's grudging appreciation for her "deadbeat" husband's efforts to be a super house-husband, getting the kids to the doctor and practices and to school each day.

At the start of each session on problem solving, couples are first asked about their shared efforts to boost satisfaction in other areas of life. By inviting each other to share in an upbeat effort at QOLT in non-relationship areas, partners create a conflict-free space to enjoy each other. All that is required is that partners share their efforts at greater happiness.

Although QOLT therapists teach Five Paths problem solving to bring about changes in relationships, they also model acceptance and routinely enact acceptance interventions (Jacobson & Christensen, 1996), realizing that many problems will never be completely managed or solved. Such interventions include:

Acceptance Interventions

- *Basic strategy:* Therapist models empathy and understanding and acceptance by being Rogerian or accepting of each partner's perspective regardless of issue.

—The Serenity Prayer Assignment for QOLT with Couples is often assigned as homework and discussed at the subsequent session. It plants the seeds for the understanding that many problems and habits are impervious to change. A blank copy with a clinical example can be found on the Toolbox CD.

—Therapist repeatedly asks for Soft Disclosures (see Relationship Skills) or feelings behind a partner's anger such as feeling lonely, hurt, unappreciated.

—Therapist may use Feeling Dictionary to teach couple how to identify and label their feelings.

—Positive reframe of inevitable differences between partners by therapist.

—Therapist urges self-care or Inner Abundance in which partners get appropriate needs met elsewhere, that is outside of the relationship (as when a husband finds a friend to share his opera interest with) and protect themselves during a fight as with a limited time out of 30 minutes to 24 hours.

—The QOLT therapist teaches Five Paths problem solving using the specific instructions for couples in Five Paths. Relationship Skills and Tenets are also explored in order for couples to identify which ones may be particularly applicable to a particular problem in problem solving. Beginning with noncontroversial or easy problems, the couple progresses to solving or managing more difficult problems with Five Paths until they reach criterion, that is, until they are consistently successful in solving problems with minimal therapist involvement.

Step 3: Modifications to *Get Happy Strategy*

Beginning with Step 1 and continuing throughout therapy, individual partners are assessed and queried as to their own personal goals and quality of life. The therapist will "check in" with individual partners to evaluate their efforts at pursuing personal goals outside of the relationship and their efforts at improving their happiness in general and through specific exercises such as Basket-of-Eggs in the Toolbox CD.

Step 4: Application to Everyday Life and Modifications

After couples are consistently successful in solving problems with minimal therapist involvement, the therapist begins to assign them homework to try at home on an ongoing basis with the understanding that the therapist will review their efforts for a few weeks and that booster sessions will be needed in times of stress in the future.

Homework in this step for each partner usually consists of:

- Bibliotherapy with Relationship Skills, all relevant Relationship Tenets.
- Basket-of-Eggs exercise. These efforts are to be shared in a light hearted way during the T of FAT time each week.
- Conduct Five Paths problem-solving sessions at home for real problems both as they arise and as part of a weekly problem-solving session as part of the FAT Time Tenet of Contentment.
- Write and sign a contract of behaviors if a partner is having trouble following through with solutions from Five Paths. Box 14.4 presents a sample contract to share with couples as an example.

QOLT RELATIONSHIP ENHANCEMENT FOR BUILDING NEW FRIENDSHIPS AND LOVE RELATIONSHIPS

I once had a client, Cliff Dancing, who was a timid 36-year-old woman who, like Bill Clinton, watched her father abuse her mother. She loved Rick Heimberg's protocol for social phobia and after many weeks took her role-played and rehearsed skills from Relationship Skills "on the road" or in vivo as we psychologists like to put it. All she had to do was to arrive at a dance to get asked to dance. In an ironic twist of fate that made me feel terribly guilty, she fell off the raised dance floor and broke her leg. Using Marsha Linehan's admonishment to make lemonade of lemons or negative outcomes, she took up the guitar while bedridden and really zeroed in on her schema work to good effect. After boldly whispering hi to a man she was interested in at a community college class, Cliff Dancing was married.

Damien or Third Pew on the Left attended an Episcopal church. After weeks of rehearsing basic social skills in approaching women, he mustered the gumption to sit next to a parishioner in the fourth seat of the third pew on the left. This candidate for dating had been screened by "Third Pew's" pastor who in concert with me encouraged this 42-year-old man to act against his social phobia.

BOX 14.4

Couples Contract Example from QOLT Relationship Enhancement

CONFIDENTIAL
Couples Contract
July 20, 2024

Darrell and Chelsea do hereby agree to this following contract on the 20th day of July 20, 2024:

- Chelsea and Darrell will go over their schedules daily being as respectful as they would be to a business partner.
- Darrell will hug and kiss Chelsea hello and goodbye.
- FAT Time, T Time, or Weekly Fun/Romantic date. Chelsea and Darrell will spend at least two hours a week together doing something mutually enjoyable like walking in the park or eating at an inexpensive restaurant.
- FAT Time, T Time for Weekly Problem-Solving Date. Chelsea and Darrell will spend quality time once a week discussing problems and schedules. Darrell and Chelsea will problem solve and brainstorm solutions for disagreements and not assume that the other doesn't care.
- Empathize don't problem solve for the other person: When Chelsea is upset, do not second guess her or give her advice. Just be supportive and say, "I'm sorry, how can I help?"
- Angry situations. Chelsea and Darrell will respond to one another with respect when they feel they are being yelled at, threatened, or criticized. The advisable response in a calm tone of voice should be: "I'm sorry, I love you. How can we get close again?"
- We will take a 2-hour time out if we are having a bad fight to be followed by sleeping in separate rooms or in a hotel.
- When all else fails, call our therapist for a booster session appointment—avoid threats or talking when angry.
- Chelsea will continue to work out in an effort to lose weight.
- Darrell will show Chelsea affection outside the bedroom.
- Assume nothing and tell the other exactly how you feel and what you feel.
- Beware of the cognitive distortion of Jumping to Conclusions . . .
- Darrell will increase his "hang time" with Chelsea and reassure her often that he loves her and cares for her.
- To prevent emotional leakage, Darrell, when angry or frustrated, thinking of ending the marriage, will go work out and do a 24-hour time out.
- Chelsea and Darrell will enjoy intimate moments initiated by Chelsea at least once a week if the above items are respected.

We agree to follow this contract daily.

_____

Darrell

_____

Chelsea

_____

Witness/Therapist

As evidenced by these case examples, the four-step Relationship Enhancement Procedures can be used to make new friends or establish a new relationship as well as improve existing relationships. At the same time, clients make efforts in therapy to establish new relationships, the therapist should encourage them to improve their satisfaction in non-relationship parts of life that they care about, especially self-esteem. This amounts to the Get Happy Strategy for relationship enhancement. In taking this two-pronged approach, the therapist can reduce clients' urgency for developing a love relationship or close friendship immediately and can also make clients more secure and attractive to the opposite sex as they cultivate varied interests and maintain positive self-esteem even when they are "alone." The therapist must sell clients on the idea that they must first work on their relationship with themselves in order to be emotionally secure even when they are alone and in order to attract high-quality friends and lovers who are "turned off" by desperate, unhappy, and disorganized people in search of a friend or mate to make them happy. In addition to the self-esteem strategies outlined in Chapter 12, the therapist may wish to introduce clients to the Lie Detector/Stress Diary, Problem-Solving worksheet, and Daily Activity Plan as tools for organizing their life and controlling negative emotions. Clients should also be encouraged to cater to themselves by keeping their apartment clean, preparing good meals or going out to a restaurant alone, and pursuing the same recreational activities they might engage in if they had a friend or lover to accompany them.

Therapists can role-play homework assignments in advance by teaching clients how to apply Relationship Skills from the Toolbox CD to every social situation in their life, which gives them an opportunity to practice and apply vital skills such as Making Conversation. At the same time clients develop a daily routine and attitude, which helps them feel good about themselves, the therapist can urge them to take up hobbies or join special interest groups. The idea is for clients to meet people while doing things that they enjoy or feel is important. This makes it more likely that they will find like-minded friends or partners, that is, people who share their particular interests and values. It also relieves some of the pressure to start a friendship or love relationship right away. Doing things in a group gives clients a chance to check people out before they pursue closer relationships. Also encourage clients to experiment with new groups or activities in order to find new friends. Urge them to adopt an attitude of "I'll try anything once" toward activities that may bring them closer to potential friends or partners.

The Internet can also be an excellent way for people to find new friends and potential love interests. There is no substitute for a reputable Internet dating service to find available folks in your geographical area. This does not mean that more traditional avenues of asking friends and loved ones to keep an eye out for potential dates is no longer useful. It does mean that technology is changing the way we meet and find people, adding to our arsenal of ways to find good friends and mates. Finally, encourage clients to consider the Tenets of Contentment listed in Table 14.1 as they begin to gain confidence in navigating the social scene, often for the first time.

RELATIONSHIP ENHANCEMENT WITH CHILDREN

In QOLT, relationships with children is defined as how you get along with your child (or children). Think of how you get along as you care for, visit, or play with your child (Frisch, 1994). Children involved in relationship conflicts should be assessed both individually and in the context of their family in order to identify any psychological disturbance, intellectual and developmental level, and ways of relating to parents and siblings. The three-step Relationship Enhancement Procedure is modified for children and adolescents in that after the "problem child" is assessed, the therapist goes through the three-step procedure with the *parent,* in the case of a single-parent household, or parents without the child or adolescent being present.

Parents are treated alone during the awareness building and skill-building phases so that they can freely explore their feelings about the child and so the therapist can teach basic parent training skills that are relevant and need to be applied to the family situation. The child or adolescent is invited to attend therapy sessions at the start of step three or the skill-application phase of Relationship Enhancement. At this point, cognitive-behavioral family therapy commences as the therapist monitors and coaches the parents in new, more effective ways of dealing with their child or adolescent. The therapist makes a special effort at this phase to inquire about and pursue reasonable goals that the child or adolescent has for the relationship with his or her parents. This in-session family therapy is conducted in a similar way to QOLT for couples described previously, using a Family Practice model.

QOLT Family Therapy is supplemented with regular homework assignments including a modification of the Favor Bank technique in which parents and, to the extent possible, the child or adolescent performs daily favors for each other. In addition, the family is coached on how to conduct Family Problem-Solving Sessions following the instructions in the Five Paths worksheet. The family is encouraged to hold these sessions whenever significant problems arise. Family Problem-Solving sessions can be used to discuss issues like family vacations, the assignment of household chores, allowances, and the use of the telephone or family car. In addition, the Night Out technique (from Relationship Skills in the Toolbox CD) is assigned such that the family as a whole spends regular, conflict-free recreational time together in order to deepen relationships and build-up the Favor Bank of positive feelings toward one another. In cases of severe psychopathology, individual therapy, medication, or both for the child or adolescent occurs concurrently with the Relationship Enhancement procedures described here. The therapist should advise parents to problem solve about ways to discipline their children or adolescents privately and then to apply their disciplinary measures as a united front or team. Parents are taught to avoid disagreeing about discipline in front of their children. They are also encouraged to emphasize rewards to encourage positive behavior and de-emphasize punishment for misbehavior, although this is often necessary.

In keeping with the Behavior Change Request instructions in QOLT Relationship Skills, parents are encouraged to be very clear about what specific behaviors they expect from their children and what consequences the children may expect if they do not comply. It is vital that parents *consistently* apply rewards or punishments to encourage or discourage specific behaviors and to do so consistently. By modeling the skills of Emotional Honesty in the context of family problem-solving sessions and at other times, parents may impart basic social skills to their children that they may apply effectively in other contexts for the rest of their life.

RELATIONSHIP ENHANCEMENT WITH RELATIVES

In QOLT, relationships with relatives is defined as how you get along with your parents, grandparents, brothers, sisters, aunts, uncles, and in-laws. Think about how you get along when you are doing things together like visiting, talking on the telephone, or helping each other out (Frisch, 1994). The three-step Relationship Enhancement procedures illustrated by the clinical case of Wendy at the start of this chapter can be implemented in the same way to enhance relationships with relatives. The reader will recall that Wendy, with the aid of her therapist, drastically improved her relationship with her father. As this case suggests, Relationship Enhancement techniques can be used to deal with relationship problems involving different relatives whether it be grandparents, parents, brothers or sisters, in-laws, and even aunts and uncles. Therapists should emphasize that clients can dramatically alter their relationship with relatives when clients change their attitudes and behaviors toward these relatives. This is true even when relatives are unaware of the change efforts being made by clients. Of course, when possible, it is best to involve all parties of the conflict, including any relatives, to be part of the assessment and intervention process. Finally, clients interested in improving relations with their relatives should be encouraged to review and internalize the Tenets of Contentment listed in Table 14.1.

RELATIONSHIP ENHANCEMENT WITH COWORKERS

We spend so much time at work that relationships there take on an added importance. The three-step Relationship Enhancement procedures illustrated by the clinical case of Wendy at the start of this chapter can be implemented in the same way to enhance relationships with coworkers or bosses. In some cases, coworkers or employers can be brought into sessions to good effect in the same way that both partners in a marriage are brought in for couples therapy.

Relationship Enhancement has been used in building positive relations among coworkers and between workers and their managers, as well as in managing specific conflicts at work. Administrative staff have used Relationship Skills from the Toolbox CD to give performance feedback in a straightforward but compassionate way. Individual professionals have been counseled in a positive psychology context to deal with interpersonal conflicts using the general and work-specific Tenets and Relationship Skills as in the case of a nephrologist who negotiated turf wars between his fellow nephrologists and the anesthesiologists and cardiac surgeons in his hospital. Likewise, a civil litigation attorney used the skills in harmonizing his work group as they moved to a new building in downtown Austin. Earlier, he negotiated reduced hours, leave time, and a continuation of salary to care for a parent with Alzheimer's disease.

Relationship Skills and Tenets (from the Toolbox CD) can be modified or expanded for work settings. For example, the Take-a-Letter 2 intervention can be much less personal in the work setting and still be effective. Using the Take-a-Letter 2 technique at work is useful when stressing the basic wants and needs of one professional to another with less disclosure of personal background, feelings, or hurts, which are more appropriate in being emotionally honest with intimates. When using relationship enhancement techniques at work, encourage clients to review and practice all of the Tenets of Contentment and Relationship Skills, in general since so many are applicable to work settings.

RELATIONSHIP ENHANCEMENT WITH SELF: EXERCISES IN SELF-SYMPATHY AND SELF-COMPASSION

As odd as it may sound, everyone has a relationship with themselves that is very important to overall happiness. Therapists should always be on the lookout for nonobvious signs of self-contempt or the lack of self-compassion and self-respect in clients. Techniques from this chapter can be usefully applied to exploring and improving this relationship. For example, as a self-sympathy and self-compassion exercise, clients can write a Take-a-Letter 1 to themselves, provided that they do this in a loving, compassionate way; this powerful exercise can become a stress-reduction ritual for those who tend to overwork or berate themselves chronically. Material from Chapter 12 on self-esteem should also be used in pursuing this important relationship that can, at times, be missed by relationship therapists and coaches. In addition, encourage clients to review and practice the Tenets of Contentment related to building a better relationship with oneself, especially Inner Abundance (see Table 14.1).

RELATIONSHIPS WITH DECEASED OR UNAVAILABLE LOVED ONES

As an exercise in grief resolution and as part of a treatment for Complicated Mourning or Bereavement, clients can write a Take-a-Letter 1 and Take-a-Letter 2 to deceased and unavailable loved ones. This unfinished business can also be addressed via Gestalt-like Empty Chair techniques or via imagery with one's eyes closed, imagining a conversation with the deceased or otherwise unavailable individual. The Association for Death Education and Counseling is an excellent resource for clients and therapists who are grieving. Interestingly, from a spiritual life perspective, many bereaved clients are now interested in making some type of spiritual contact with the deceased, a trend explored in this association along with many other resources and listservs and so forth (see the ADEC web site at www.adec.org). The Vision Quest exercise is also an invaluable tool for the bereaved who lack direction. In these cases it helps if the passively bereaved are challenged to carry on and reinvest in life in ways that the deceased would want them to. When working with clients to resolve relationships with deceased or unavailable individuals, encourage them to review and try out the Tenets of Contentment listed in Table 14.1.

CHAPTER 15

Work and Retirement

In QOLT, Work is defined as your career or how you spend most of your time. Clients may work at a job, at home taking care of their family, or at school as a student. Work includes duties on the job, the money earned (if any), and the people with whom clients work (Frisch, 1994). Therapists should emphasize to clients how some form of meaningful Work adds greatly to the quality of life of most people. One only has to review the hundreds of research studies showing the devastating impact of unemployment on happiness, satisfaction, and basic mental and physical health in order to appreciate the enormous impact of Work on our physical health, emotional health, and quality of life (see exhaustive review in Diener & Seligman, 2004). As George Vaillant found in his research, a stable work adjustment may be more important to clients' overall mental health and happiness than just about anything else, including problems in childhood, which mental health professionals like to emphasize so much (Vaillant, 2002).

Work seems to get a bad rap in Western cultures where Work is something to be minimized and avoided and where happiness is usually defined in terms of nonwork recreational activities; in contrast, Work in non-Western cultures is often seen as a source of fun and happiness (Diener & Suh, 2000). Clients and therapists may be missing out on understanding a tremendous source of potential happiness and satisfaction. What does Work do for us? If we are lucky and choose wisely, our Work can provide very enjoyable activities and a great amount of flow time, in keeping with David Myers's point that happiness is loving what you do. Therapists and clients must really understand the Flow It Tenet or Principle from the Toolbox CD in order to benefit from QOLT.

FLOW IT PRINCIPLE OR TENET

Along with the importance of close relationships with others, flow activities in which people actively do something challenging that fits their level of skill may be as close to the Holy Grail or the Key to happiness that science can offer right now (Csikszentmihalyi, 1997; Csikszentmihalyi & Hunter, 2003). As much as possible, we want to Flow It, that is, find and carry out flow activities or *flows* in all spheres of life and at all possible times—at home, with family and friends, in hobbies, at work and in retirement—in order to maximize our happiness and life satisfaction. Ask yourself this common survey question to find out if an activity is a flow for you—if it is, try to do it more often and try to do nonflows less often: Do you ever get involved in something so deeply that nothing else seems to matter, and you lose track of time? Many of our favorite activities are flows like making conversation with people, playing sports, or exercising—athletes refer to flow as in the zone, gardening, decorating, gaming, scrap booking, shopping, home improvement, surfing the net to answer a question, playing with children, arts and crafts, playing or listening to music; there is also a treasure trove of flows that each of us has never tried but need to in order to maximize our happiness like Helping, creative problem solving at Work, and trying out entirely new and active hobbies—see Play List in the Toolbox CD. Since we are all different, we must try out various activities several times to see if they are potential flows for us.

A flow is an activity that requires our total attention, we are not distracted with other worries or concerns. A flow is an activity with a definite challenge that requires us to use our maximum skill as in reading a book written at just our reading level or slightly above. In computer gaming, flow is playing a game you enjoy at a difficulty level that matches your skill level or exceeds it slightly. It cannot be too hard/challenging or too easy to be a flow; the activity must require all of your skills and attention to overcome an obstacle or challenge that is just slightly out of reach. Flow It may be the Holy Grail of happiness because you can use it even if you have a grumpy temperament/personality and, as long as you keep raising the challenges to fit your skill level, it *never* stops working. Too much chocolate or sex is cloying; flow is the gift that keeps on giving. You need only make the initial effort to start the activity and pick a goal or challenge that takes all of your skill and attention. This requires bigger challenges as your skill increases as when a gardener making solid color roses branches out to make a rainbow colored rose of three different colors. If you get too good, you may need to switch hobbies or flows entirely, but there is always one out there for each of us, a major source of joy or fulfillment if we just make the effort and say no to the easy but cloying pleasures of passive activities like TV.

Flows are activities that we do for their own sake, that are intrinsically rewarding. The state of consciousness that results while we do flows is the sense of total engagement, loss of time, and loss of self-consciousness or worry. The state of consciousness that results when the activity is over and we reflect back on it is a deep sense of satisfaction and happiness. "Flow-ers," folks engaged in flow activities, are, in a sense, too busy or immersed to feel happiness at the time; that comes later.

When feeling bored, unhappy, or discontented, we should be aware of the feeling and accept it fully but then make ourselves do something that has been challenging and engaging in the past. If not a past flow, we can try a potential new flow, practicing Mindful Breathing as we carry out the activity. Insert as many flows as you can into your Work and Play time every hour of every day.

OTHER BENEFITS OF WORK

Paid and, perhaps, volunteer Work may be essential to happiness precisely because it structures our day, leading or pulling us toward flows (Csikszentmihalyi, 1997; Frisch & Gerrard, 1981). Getting started in

flows may be our greatest challenge to experiencing more flows as we choose, say, between watching TV and writing a letter or e-mail. Work removes the element of choice, making us attend to our job duties many of which are "flow-ful" if we have chosen the job wisely—see Work That Satisfies in the Toolbox CD. The tragedy of happiness and flow is that we end up wasting many hours in nonflow, rather unsatisfying and unenjoyable activities like watching TV because they take so little effort to begin. Work gets us off our duffs, a requirement for engaging the world and finding flow. Besides giving needed structure to our days, Work gives us social contact with others, a proven happiness producer and even an antidote to depression (McLean & Hakstian, 1979). Work can also give us a means of achieving respect, and a source of engagement, challenge, and meaning (Diener & Seligman, 2004); in the words of Studs Terkel, "work is a search for daily meaning as well as daily bread, for recognition as well as cash, for astonishment rather than torpor; in short, for a sort of life rather than a Monday through Friday sort of dying." Even so called crummy or mundane jobs such as flipping burgers, cleaning houses, and clerking at a convenience store can be very satisfying and meaningful, providing great amounts of flow time for those whose skills and interests match the job (Csikszentmihalyi, 1997).

Besides being important to clients' happiness during working hours, satisfaction in their occupation "spills over" into their personal and home lives (Kahneman et al., 1999). So, if clients hate their work, they are often preoccupied and irritable at home as they "take their work home with them." On the other hand, satisfying work can make clients pleasant, content, and enthusiastic when at home or while recreating. A spillover effect can also be seen in so far as overall life satisfaction predicts future work performance and productivity up to 5 years in advance (Judge & Hulin, 1993; Judge & Watanabe, 1993).

For this reason, QOLT suggests that it may be useful for clients to embark on a happiness program like QOLT just as they might pursue a fitness program or further study in their field, since greater happiness and fulfillment can also lead to greater job productivity and even wealth (see Chapter 20).

Finally, a happiness spillover takes place at Work itself in so far as satisfaction with one's job seems to lead to greater productivity and even customer satisfaction (Diener & Seligman, 2004). For this reason, clients can increase their productivity if they can find ways to enjoy their work more, make it more interesting and challenging, and just appreciate it more moment to moment. For example, the Happiness Habit Tenet may keep clients balanced and sane when work problems arise and allow them to Mine the Moment (Tenet) at Work by finding joy and satisfaction in their jobs, whereas others cannot effectively plug in to the pockets of enjoyment at Work such as relationships, flow aspects of the work itself, and so forth. Of course, the happiness-worker productivity/customer satisfaction connection should be the clarion call for employers to find ways to foster happiness on the job and in the homes of their workers; a real concern and caring for workers' general happiness and well-being may also confer a competitive advantage in the increasingly competitive labor market of Western societies (Diener & Seligman, 2004).

WORK CONCERNS AND TREATMENTS

The New Global Economy

According to QOLT, a big part of Work involves pay and fringe benefits, that is, Money. As we will see in Chapter 20, QOLT says people need enough Money and material possessions to be sure that they can take care of their basic needs—like food, shelter, a safe neighborhood, medical care, a good education for their children—both now and in the future. Unfortunately, it is frequently the case that more and more money is needed to cover the basics of living, especially in urban areas, which leads to jobs with long hours and little security that sap clients' energy for other pursuits like family and friends and hobbies, leading to a decidedly less balanced lifestyle and a poor overall quality of life. Many of the pressures for overwork and the insecurity of jobs are caused by factors beyond clients' control.

Specifically, the new economy, although providing great deals for consumers at the click of a mouse button, has made everyone's job and income less secure as consumers and employers try to find the best deal in a global economy (Reich, 2000). Rank and seniority mean less today. The global high tech economy has also made people work much harder with longer hours at a frenzied pace as they try to make all the money while they can since they could be in a company that suddenly loses its place in the market due to the cut-

throat competition that is part of the global economy today. Especially workers in lower-tier jobs and workers who are not as talented, face greater uncertainty and hardship. For these reasons, therapists should be mindful that clients likely will have to change jobs during the course of their working years and will need career, professional, and personal—Reich emphasizes salesmanship and creative thinking on the job—skills that give them some modicum of stability and mobility in an intensely competitive global economy. Therapists should also confront clients both with the market forces pushing for overwork and highly stressful employment and with the consequences of their choices within the global marketplace. Reich offers some political solutions that go beyond the immediate needs of the moment, that is, to get the skills needed to get a good job. Nevertheless, as clients wait for and even work for market change to rein in some negative aspects of the global economy just as we dealt with the excesses of the Industrial Revolution, they must assess their Goals-and-Values, preferred lifestyle, and desire for balance among the sixteen areas of life as they consider their careers. Clearly, hard choices often have to be made in all valued areas of life, such as the number of children couples have and the quality of neighborhood, medical care, and education they wish to have on one hand, versus the income, necessities, and amenities they crave.

Clients typically cite one of five problems that interfere with their Work satisfaction:

1. Interpersonal conflicts with coworkers, the boss, or upper-level management;
2. The nature of the work itself that is unfulfilling;
3. Excessive work demands or "pressure"/stress;
4. Feeling inadequate in either finding a job or in doing the work; and
5. Job insecurity.

Less frequently, unemployment, a lack of necessary skills and education, low salary, and competition from a spouse's career are cited as problems. Clients in school typically complain of poor school performance either in terms of grades or the ability to learn, retain material, and show their knowledge on tests. Most often students attribute their subpar performance to distracting emotional problems, an internal and stable character flaw that makes learning difficult, a lack of motivation, a lack of career goals and direction, an overload of courses, "procrastination," or poor study habits.

QOLT offers specific interventions for addressing work concerns (in addition to the general CASIO strategies presented in this chapter). Specific strategies for increasing work satisfaction are divided into the following four areas (or steps): (1) choosing a career; (2) finding a job; (3) making the most of the job you have; and (4) planning for retirement.

Although therapists should help clients explore the advantages and disadvantages of major life decisions relating to Work (e.g., staying in their current job, retiring, or finding a new job) and other areas of life addressed in QOLT, this and all other major life decisions should be made by the client without any explicit recommendations by the therapist. As clients must face the consequences and live with the aftermath of any major life decisions, QOLT therapists should avoid dispensing specific advice on major life decisions.

CHOOSING A CAREER OR *PASSIONATE CALLING*

According to QOLT, clients' goal in choosing a career should be to find Work that, as much as possible, feels like play, seems to be a *Passionate Calling* in the sense that it feels like something perfectly suited to them, makes them feel passionate about work and eager to go to work each day, and fits with their overarching Goals-and-Values and purpose in life, whether this be spiritual or secular (see Find a Meaning Tenet). This values and calling approach is akin to Colozzi and Colozzi's (2000) approach, which fits well with positive psychology views of work (Seligman, 2002). QOLT is also inspired, in part, by Brown's (1995) values-based holistic model of life role choices and satisfaction.

Thus, clients should seek out Work that is challenging (but within their capabilities), enjoyable, meaningful, and absorbing; unfortunately, there is a dearth of data on the well-being impact of various occupations, perhaps reflecting a tunnel vision focus on income and required education (Diener & Seligman, 2004). For this reason, QOLT challenges clients to collect their own data on the intrinsic properties of various jobs and careers. The process of choosing a career becomes a serious and all-consuming project that also has a fun, kid in a candy store attitude in so far as therapists can help clients remain optimistic about finding an array

of choices from the panoply of potential occupations (e.g., see Herr & Cramer, 1992). Therapists may also present the exploration of career alternatives for their intrinsic properties and satisfaction, as clients shadow or observe professionals go about their work and interview them about the quality of life aspects and impacts of various jobs. For example, Carmen, an African American premed student found that specialties in dermatology and family practice medicine were the most family friendly and intrinsically satisfying to her after researching the alternatives and speaking with and observing doctors in various specialties. Although ER medicine was also very family friendly, it failed on the intrinsic satisfaction of the work front for Carmen who insisted on a less hectic and more predictable kind of medicine that allowed her to carefully consider treatment options in advance. Clients may also use the Work That Satisfies handout from the Toolbox CD to check out the extent to which jobs in general within a particular career path being considered have these satisfaction or happiness-producing qualities.

Secondarily, it is important for clients to find Work that will give them a decent and reasonable standard of living. Research shows a lavish standard of living usually adds little or nothing to feelings of contentment, so warn clients of the trap of getting into Work that is unpleasant in order to make more money than they need (Diener & Seligman, 2004). Finally, QOLT career counseling is culturally and diversity sensitive (see Luzzo, 2000; and Luzzo & McWhirter, 2001; for specific guidance on these issues) and is also developmentally sensitive and comprehensive as seen in the work of Herr and Cramer (1992). QOLT considers developmental factors and constraints in assessing and presenting career options to clients. As so much of life is spent pursuing Work, therapists should urge clients to make the process of choosing a career a serious and all-consuming project or adventure, realizing that unsuitable career paths can always be changed.

Identifying Potential Careers

QOLT moves from eliciting clients' general interest, goals, and values to a list of specific occupations to consider and explore. First, clients' Goals-and-Values should be clarified through the Vision Quest technique since this will often reveal clients' general life interests and career interests and since clients' Goals-and-Values will often limit which careers or jobs a client will consider. QOLT assumes that Work will be satisfying, in part, to the extent to which it is consistent with clients' overall Goals-and-Values. Secondly, the Career Clarification Questionnaire can be administered either by interview during the session or as a homework assignment. This questionnaire helps clients to identify their abilities, interests, and personality traits related to Work. These factors along with the client's Goals-and-Values help to determine the type of Work that is satisfying. The questionnaire also asks clients to reflect on the standard of living to which they aspire, other aspects of work, and a general question about Goals-and-Values that can substitute for the Vision Quest exercise when time is at a premium. Finally, the questionnaire asks clients to begin to consider specific jobs or occupations that might fit their interests that they would like to explore further. The third step in helping clients explore careers is to administer the Occupational Survey, which asks clients to evaluate specific jobs and careers based on their interests, skills/experience, and the extent to which a particular job or career would fit their particular personality and preferred lifestyle. In going over the results of the Occupational Survey it helps for therapists to emphasize to clients that they must further investigate any occupation of interest. All of these handouts are available on the Toolbox CD that accompanies this book. The following internet resources have also been invaluable to my clients:

Occupational Outlook Handbook—http://www.bls
.gov/oco
Occupational Information Network (O*Net)—http://
www.onetcenter.org
America's Career InfoNet—http://www.acinet.org
Career Resource Center—http://www.careers.org

Step four in helping clients to choose a career involves encouraging clients to get enough specific, accurate, and current information about each occupation they wish to explore so that they can make a final decision about which particular option to pursue. Therapists can assign homework to clients involving interviews with people in the job or careers that interest them and the teachers or professors responsible for training people in the occupations that interest the clients. These teachers and job holders should be asked about specific job duties, the typical 9-to-5 routine they experience, the strengths and weaknesses of the job or career, the current job market for particular positions, salaries, and prior experience, education, or training required to pur-

sue particular fields of interest. With respect to education and training, clients need to know how difficult it is to secure needed education and training as well as what this may cost in terms of time, money, and effort. Libraries and career counseling centers at local colleges or universities may also be consulted to answer these important questions.

An additional, even more direct, way for clients to check out the suitability of a particular job or career is to get work-related experience—whether paid or volunteer—or by taking classes in subjects related to the career. At times, the therapist or client must arrange for formal assessments to determine a client's suitability for particular jobs. For example, intelligence tests and achievement tests such as the Scholastic Aptitude Test for undergraduate college work, Graduate Record Examination for graduate-level study, or the LSAT for law school may be appropriate for evaluating clients' suitability to particular jobs or careers.

For example, one client "checked out" a career in mental health by interviewing psychologists and psychiatrists he knew, by volunteering at a local psychiatric hospital, and by taking an undergraduate course in abnormal psychology. After this "checking out" he decided that a career in clinical social work would best fit his interests, skills, personality, and preferred lifestyle. He is now a respected social worker in his community (despite several "false starts" in business and public relations work). Even when they have found areas in which they have skills and experience, clients should also determine whether their personality is a good fit for a particular job. In addition, tell clients to not be discouraged if they don't have skill or experience in a particular area of interest; given sufficient motivation they can often gain the experience and skill that they need for a particular occupation.

What follows is one approach to discuss career exploration with clients:

Before you settle on a particular job or career option I want us to explore it in detail so that you don't waste a lot of time preparing yourself for something that doesn't work out or that doesn't really suit you. Let's put our two heads together and see how we can find out what the current job prospects, salaries, and education or training requirements are for each job or career you're interested in. For example, if you're interested in being a computer operator, it would help if you could find friends or acquaintances in this career that you could take to lunch or interview to see what the job prospects in the field are like. In addition you want to ask people what the 9-to-5 routine is like on the job. It also helps to talk to teachers or professors in the field. For example, you may go to the local community college and talk to the instructors in the computing program to find out about available jobs and needed training. To get even closer to what the career or job would be like I'll ask you to consider doing some volunteer work or even getting a paid job related to the career you're interested in. It is especially good if this work-related experience allows you to "rub shoulders" with people in the field. It can also help for you to take a class in something like computers so that you can tell firsthand whether you have the interest or skills to really pursue this field. Too often people waste time in pursuing fields that just don't work out for them. You may find, for example, that you're great with computers and can get As in computer classes, but really hate working with them on a 9-to-5 basis. You can also find out that the salaries don't meet your standards. This information by itself can help you to drop this as an option, saving you all the effort, time, and money of getting trained as a computer operator and only then finding out what salaries are when you take your first job. Let's make finding a career or job that fits you a major hobby, job, or project for you right now. It could be like taking a class; every day you do a little reading or exploration to check out all of the jobs or career possibilities that you are interested in.

As therapists we can admonish clients about putting too much of an emphasis on pursuing money for its own sake (see Chapter 20) and on matching their temperament to the type of work. Unfortunately, even the most thrill-seeking and entrepreneurial clients may become miserable when self-employed or otherwise paid by commission or piecework. Even the most materialistic individuals may need to reconsider their dedication to work if other Areas of their life suffer as a result.

Finally, therapists should be careful not to oversell clients' ability to rise above the structure of many jobs and the particular psychonoxious organizational climate of many companies. Often clients need to decide for themselves, therapists should never try to make such decisions and only show potential consequences of actions. Clients must decide for themselves to exercise the <u>C</u> option in the CASIO model and change their circumstances by leaving their current job for a different type of work altogether or for a less psychonoxious work environment.

Step six in helping clients to choose a career or type of job to pursue involves helping clients to decide on one particular job or career path and then helping them make the necessary steps to get a job in their chosen field. It is important that clients realize that they can always change their mind about a particular career or job path. On the other hand, by "sitting on the fence" and not committing to a particular career path, they are dooming themselves to stagnation and frustration. Completing a Problem-Solving worksheet, either with a client in the session or as part of a client's homework assignment, can greatly aid the decision process. It is especially important for clients to weigh the short-term and long-term costs and benefits of particular career options. Once a career path has been chosen, clients can draw on the information they've already gained about particular jobs and careers to begin to make their career goals a reality (see Baby Steps to Success technique in Chapter 4).

Finding a Job

Once clients decide on a career path, they need to make decisions about the suitability of particular jobs. This is also an issue when clients have not yet settled on a career path, but need a job immediately to "pay the bills." Whereas financial necessity can require clients to quickly take a job, it can often take a year for clients to find a job that truly fits their personality, interests, and abilities; and that furthers them on the career path they have chosen. For this reason, therapists should urge clients to be patient. Have them do Stress Diaries when they are feeling upset and hopeless, and encourage them to keep outside interests and relationships going so that all of their "emotional eggs" are not in the one basket of Work (see Chapter 4, Basket-of-Eggs exercise).

In deciding which particular job to accept, help clients identify the features of the job that matter most. For example, it helps if the job relates to clients' overall career path whenever possible. Beyond this, research shows that overall job satisfaction is made up of specific "pieces" or characteristics such as the work itself (Is the work intrinsically satisfying to the client?), the pay, the prospects for promotion, the quality and availability of supervision, the workplace itself, job security, as well as relationships with coworkers. A major strategy of QOLT is to help clients find jobs that will allow them to enjoy a high quality of life, which is different for every client. These characteristics are based on findings in the literature (Argyle, 2001; Diener & Seligman, 2004;

Table 15.1   Work That Satisfies: Characteristics of Work That Satisfies

1. *Money.* Good pay and fringe benefits.
2. *Safety.* Physical security and safety.
3. *Good boss and "higher-ups."* Supportive supervisor or boss and "organizational climate." *Good supervisors* care about workers being happy in general. In fact, companies in the know realize that this increases productivity, morale, and even customer satisfaction. *Good supervisors* also carefully match duties to our positive strengths and abilities, encourage friendships on the job, and give workers the resources they need to get the job done. They lavish workers with praise and criticize carefully and constructively. They try to make the work as interesting and satisfying as possible while serving the needs of the organization. A *good climate* or atmosphere suggests a general concern for workers' general welfare and happiness that can be seen in specifics like flextime, the possibility of doing some work at home, employee stock options, on-site day-care, and good family leave policies.
4. *Knowing What to Do or Task Identity.* This means that the job has clear requirements for what needs to be done and clear information on how to do the work. We feel best having a job in which we can complete a clear and identifiable piece of work.
5. *Using Your Skills in a Variety of Tasks.* We flourish with a chance for *using our skills* in a *variety* of tasks or duties. This is the extent to which you can use the different skills and talents you have in executing your job, which both challenges you and prevents the job from becoming boring.
6. *Personal Control.* Opportunity for personal control in which you have some autonomy over doing your tasks without someone looking over your shoulder and "micro-managing" what you do.
7. *Social Relationships.* This involves the chance for regular interpersonal contact with others on the job as well as Supportive Relationships with Coworkers or the extent to which the people you work with get along together and help each other out. Supportive work environments in which folks trust and help each other are the most satisfying.
8. *Respect and High Status.* Having a job that is respected within the organization and outside of the organization is very satisfying. Having a job that is *highly* regarded, that has high status also contributes to satisfaction with the Work.
9. *Flow Potential or Intrinsic Satisfaction.* This is the extent to which the particular duties and tasks of a job are interesting, enjoyable, engage your full attention, and give a feeling of accomplishment once the duties or tasks are completed. The tasks should be challenging but not "over your head" in terms of skill. Additionally, you should not be asked to the impossible in terms of workload. A humane workload with reasonable time constraints will add to Intrinsic Satisfaction by giving you the chance to savor each step of satisfying work.
10. *Soulwork.* Sometimes called "task significance," this refers to the degree to which your job helps other people or has a positive impact on the lives of others. The term soulwork was coined by Sam Keen (1994); unfortunately, there is often an inverse relationship between this and the amount of pay.
11. *Fit with Overall Goals-and-Values.* Work that satisfies will fit well with QOLT's *Whole Life Perspective.* That is, the work will allow for some balance with other valued areas of life such as recreation, marriage, raising children, and friends. For example, for many, marriage and family life begins to suffer as we work more than 45 hours per week. Good work will also not ask us to violate our core values and ethical principles.

Note: Clients looking for a new job are encouraged to find jobs with as many of these characteristics as possible. They are also encouraged to negotiate for items that are not yet part of the prospective job. Clients can "enrich" their current job by problem solving around ways to introduce or maximize these characteristics into their present employment. Volunteer jobs or Helping activities (Chapter 17) may be chosen and enhanced using the same characteristics, except for Money.

Warr, 1999) and are summarized in Table 15.1 along with instructions for clients on how to use them either in finding a new job or in improving their satisfaction with existing jobs. A client-oriented version of Work That Satisfies is also available in the Toolbox CD.

The Job Search

After clients have decided on the kind of job that would best suit them, it is time to begin the job search. Therapists should encourage clients to look for jobs with other people so that they can encourage each other and "compare notes." Urge clients to treat the process of finding a job like an 8-hour-a-day job in and of itself. Encourage them to set "process" rather than "outcome" goals. For example, they may feel good about doing two job interviews a day, whether or not they receive offers from either of these potential employers. Using a Daily Activity Plan from the Toolbox CD and Chapter 10, clients can schedule job-finding activities throughout their day and still include some time for relaxation or recreation.

Encourage clients to ask family and friends for support and encouragement. Besides asking for emotional support, clients can ask their families to keep the telephone free and to help with transportation. Families and friends can also give job leads based on their job contacts and knowledge of the community.

It often helps for therapists to role-play job interviews with clients to reduce their anxiety and improve their skill. In addition to the communication skills listed elsewhere in this book, therapists should encourage the clients to be properly dressed and well-groomed for any job interviews.

Therapists should encourage clients to always try to arrange a face-to-face interview with a prospective employer. Even when told there are no openings, clients should ask to meet with someone in person such as a personnel manager, saying that they would still like to learn about the company and would like to meet face-to-face in case a future opening should occur. Clients may also use these meetings as opportunities to ask about other potential employers in the area who may have job openings. As many jobs are not advertised, therapists should encourage clients to visit any company in which they are interested in addition to those companies who have advertised positions in the newspaper or elsewhere. Clients should never rely solely on mailing resumes or telephone contacts in pursuing job leads. Clients should also be encouraged to regularly call back any employer they have visited or contacted to see if any new positions have opened.

Therapists can effectively use the analogy of dating to prepare clients to accept a certain "quota" or number of rejections before they find the job that is right for them. Job seekers like those in the "dating scene" also need to be persistent and thick-skinned in order to be most successful and to persevere in the process to the point necessary for success. Finally, it can help clients to have open letters of recommendation that they can present at the time of an initial application. These letters of reference from previous employers can be addressed simply to "To whom it may concern."

MAKING THE MOST OF THE JOB YOU HAVE

The CASIO Approach to Job Enrichment

By using the Five Paths technique, clients can often increase their work satisfaction by changing their thoughts, feelings, behaviors, relationships, and circumstances associated with their current job instead of trying to find a new job or career. As with all areas of life the Five Paths exercise can be used in two ways to boost satisfaction with Work:

1. To begin with, clients can complete Five Paths for the area of Work. This entails brainstorming ways to make the job more satisfying without specifying any Work problems or concerns. The Work That Satisfies handout is a useful aid in this context as clients can reflect on the extent to which their present job has some or all of the key characteristics of a satisfying job.
2. Additionally, clients can complete Five Paths for specific problems or concerns in the area of Work. If time permits, the therapist can assess the job for problems or areas that could be improved by interviewing clients about the nature of their work.

When time is available for a thorough assessment, therapists may ask clients about any difficulties on the job. The key job characteristics listed in the Work That Satisfies (Toolbox handout) may be reviewed with clients to see if their existing job has these key features. Problems raised by clients can be framed in terms of these characteristics. The Five Paths worksheet may be used in tandem with Work That Satisfies to problem solve about ways to enhance clients' current job in line with these characteristics, such as Sid, a thoracic surgeon, did in getting a local hospital to increase the autonomy of surgeons using the hospital.

Obvious solutions identified from Five Paths exercises have made huge differences in clients' Work satisfaction. Clients' work performance or satisfaction has been drastically improved with additional job training and education. For example, a beleaguered nurse felt like she died and went to heaven after insisting on specialized training for an ICU unit that she was assigned to against her wishes for months; she realized afterward that she simply lacked the necessary training to be an effective ICU nurse prior to receiving the training.

The Use of Five Paths to Change Work Circumstances

Using Five Paths as a guide, the actual circumstances of clients' work can be changed in an effort to increase their satisfaction with work. For example, job duties can be renegotiated, clients can move to a different section of a company, and new equipment or supplies may be obtained. Each of these strategies have been successfully used with police personnel, business marketing departments, and university student life professionals and staff.

Use of Nonpathological and Nonpejorative Labels to "Diagnose" Work Concerns

The second aspect of QOLT Work assessment involves additional assessment as to the nature of Work concerns beyond the characteristics of the Work as compared with the ideal characteristics identified in the Work That Satisfies handout. Nonpathology-oriented descriptions of Work problems based on a cognitive therapy functional analysis may be developed in concert with clients. Lowman's (1993) taxonomy, categories and descriptions are useful in this regard to share with clients in order to come to a common understanding of problems and strengths in the area of Work:

1. *Patterns of undercommitment to work:* Here clients are not reaching their potential on the job or are not performing their duties up to the standard of the organization. This category includes Underachievement in Work, which can be due to a poor fit between clients' skills or values and the job as presently conceived—poor person-environment fit with present job. Underachievement can also reflect problems with procrastination, fear of failure that is often related to self-esteem problems in general, antipathy toward the organization or particular administrators expressed in passive-aggressive behavior, that is foot-dragging in completing job duties up to standard.
2. *Patterns of overcommitment to work:* This problem consists of overinvolvement with work to the point that productivity, health—physical or mental—or both, is compromised. Slavish devotion to Work is so normative for our culture and is so often necessary for advancement and promotion (Lowman, 1993; Reich, 2000), that this diagnosis is only made if it is really affecting clients' work or health and is causing significant distress in clients, their superiors, or clients' families and loved ones. Difficulties with overcommitment often consist of job burnout, which so often is a euphemism for clinical depression. Here it is important to recall the admonition in QOLT to have clients assessed by their physicians and when possible, by a mental health professional prior to

conducting QOLT in a positive psychology or nonclinical context. The line between symptoms of clinical depression and meeting the full criterion set for Major Depressive Disorder is a thin one. For this reason, therapists need to be on the lookout for nonclinical difficulties becoming clinical problems in short order. Difficulties with perfectionism and obsessive-compulsive personality traits often contribute to patterns of overcommitment to Work.

Other problems of overcommitment can include workaholism defined here as a slavish devotion to work that is counterproductive in terms of job performance and that takes away from other important areas of life and relationships to the point of negative Work spillover to clients' home and family life. Problems with hostility and cynicism, perhaps the core dysfunctions in Type A personality, are often seen in cases of overcommitment. Here QOLT can be very useful in teaching optimism, emotional control, and balance in clients' lifestyle such that all cherished areas of life are honored with time and attention. Of course, particular work projects—like writing a book like this!—can be necessarily all consuming for limited time periods. In this case, Emergency Abundance is the prescription.

3. *Negative spillover from home to work:* Another pattern of concern or area for growth and improvement at Work can involve negative spillover from clients' homelife as in cases where marital or family distress affects clients' work performance. In these cases, family or couples therapy following the steps to Relationship Enhancement enumerated in Chapter 14 should be followed. Temporary situational stressors at Work include getting used to a new boss or reassignment of job duties, "crazy" bosses who are bona fide Stress Carriers (see Avoid Stress Carriers Tenet), and dysfunctional organizational climates.
4. *Dysfunctional organizations:* Too often in my positive psychology practice I have been asked to do training for workers that does not include upper management when upper management is part of the problem. When the structure and philosophy of the organization as expressed by superiors is antithetical to the characteristics of Work That Satisfies, the day-to-day effect on subordinates can be psychonoxious, making them miserable, fearful, hopeless, paranoid, or a combination of these. For example, Jason, a successful civil litigant in a large law firm got fed up with the firm's lack of concern for junior partners and the double standard in assigning impossibly high

caseloads on "underlings" while some partners did next to nothing. The only solution for Jason was a "jobendectomy" in which he was removed from his job, only to find a much more caring, equitable, and democratic firm in a city close to Austin. Michelline used the **C** CASIO strategy or what she called the "50 Ways to Leave Your Lover" strategy to leave a nursing job in which she was constantly asked to work in areas beyond her competencies. Too often clients waste years trying to influence organizational climates that are impervious to change. Individuals often simply are not powerful enough to change the climate of an organization determined by well-entrenched administrative professionals.

CREATIVITY APPROACH TO GREATER SUCCESS AND JOB ENRICHMENT

As viewed by Sternberg (2003) and others (Csikszenthimahalyi, 1997), creativity is a broad approach to problem solving that, when applied to work, can:

1. Solve important and vexing problems
2. Lead to deeper intrinsic satisfaction or greater flow at Work
3. Increase income, awards, and promotions at Work (Sternberg, 2003).

For this reason, QOLT recommends the application of Creativity Skills from the Toolbox CD and Box 19.1 from Chapter 19 to clients' work environment. The application may be to problems at Work or, in a pure positive psychology sense, to a Work situation that while not problematic, could be improved in terms of satisfaction, productivity, or both. To implement this strategy, simply discuss ways in which Creativity Skills may be applied to the client's work situation or problems.

Managing Relationship Difficulties with Coworkers and Supervisors: The Relationship History Technique

Work relationship difficulties are the culprit in firings and serious Work dysfunctions more than technical skill in the job itself (Reich, 2000). For this reason, therapists should ask about and assess closely, through role-playing (Frisch & Higgins, 1986), any and all relationship problems that clients report with coworkers and superiors. The Relationship History technique may also be used to assess such problems.

It is useful to take a relationship history from clients starting with their current job and moving back in time chronologically. Rebel with a Cause, a positive psychology client, was a highly successful plaintiff attorney who was plagued with angry conflicts at each of his past three jobs and in law school. Rebel's relationship history revealed a pattern of "in your face" confrontation and arrogance with colleagues, bosses, office staff, and even paralegals, in which he crassly told people of their shortcomings and the shortcomings of their professions. He was also hugely successful in products liability civil litigation earning millions of dollars in judgments for himself and the firms for which he worked. A historical review of the background of his negative schemas of perfectionism, entitlement, and hypercriticalness stemmed from a childhood in which he faced discrimination as a Jew in San Francisco—his basketball teammates refused to speak to him when they discovered his religious preference—and a mother who taught him to stand up for himself by loudly complaining whenever he felt mistreated or shortchanged in any way.

Using the Lie Detector from Chapter 10 as a journaling technique along with Relationship Enhancement from Chapter 14 that involved some trusted work friends and his spouse. Rebel's work problems were completely cured, allowing him time to advocate for the rights of Jews in appropriate forums. Rebel's rabbi was an invaluable resource, adjunct, or "tag-team therapist" in this regard. With Rebel's permission, his rabbi was used as a resource for making the QOLT interventions culturally sensitive, identifying effective versus ineffective approaches to verbal expression and activism along with challenging what the rabbi called Rebel's "victim mentality" or negative schemas.

Chapter 14 must be closely read and followed to help with interpersonal problems at Work. Particular Tenets of Contentment are also applicable to Work Relationship Problems and should be assigned as homework and discussed with clients. The Tenets related to Work are listed in Table 15.2.

PLANNING FOR RETIREMENT

Since Work is defined in terms of how you spend your time, it encompasses retirement, a crucial stage of life for more and more of the aging Baby Boom generation. Clients can be prepared for retirement or may deal with existing retirement problems by using

Table 15.2 Tenets with Attitudes, Schemas, and Practices Conducive to Greater Satisfaction with Work and Relationships with Coworkers and Superiors

Accept What You Cannot Change Principle

ACOAN Principle or Abuse or Neglect Principle

Affirm the Spark (in Others) Principle

Anger Is the Enemy or Shift of Hate Principle (see also Don't Forgive Principle)

Ask Your Death Tenet

Assume the Best in Others Principle

Avoid Stress Carriers or I Never Bother with People I Hate Rule

Balanced Lifestyle Principle

Be the Peace You Seek or Worry Warts Principle

Be True to Your School Principle: BETTY'S Way

Be with People or Relationship Immersion Principle

Be Your Own Guru Principle

Blind Dumb Optimism Principle

Calculated Risk Principle

Can't Buy Me Love or Forget Fame and Fortune Rule

Care for My One Body Principle

Cocoon It Rule

Color Purple Principle

Daily Vacation Principle

Depression Is Not Normal Principle

Don't Bring It Home or Work Spillover Principle

Do the Right Thing or Clear Conscience Rule or When in Doubt, Don't Rule

Don't Forgive Principle or Set Aside, Shelve, Accept, or Forget Principle

Do What You Love or Tune In to What Turns You On Principle

Emotional Control or the Big Three Make Us Dumb Principle

Emotional Honesty Principle

Exercise or Take your Medication Principle

Expect the Unexpected Principle

Face the Music Principle

Failure Quota Principle

FAT Time Principle

Favor Bank or Favor Bank of Good Will from Good Deeds Principle

Feed the Soul Principle

Fight for Much, Reap Frustration Principle

Find an Area or Go to Your Room or Principle

Find a Friend, Find a Mate Principle

Find a Meaning/Find a Goal Principle

Flow It Principle (see also Modest Goal Principle)

The FOOBS Principle or Switch Out of FOOBS Principle

Get a Therapist Rule

Get Organized Principle

Giving Tree or Self-Other Principle

Glow of Peace Tenet

The Grass Isn't Greener, It's Weeds Principle

Habits Rule Rule or Routines Rule Rule

Happiness Diet Principle

Happiness Equation Tenet

Happiness from Achievement Principle

Happiness Is a Choice Principle

Happiness Habits Principle

Happiness Matters Principle

Happiness Spillover Principle

How Kind Principle or Tender Hearted Rule

Humble Servant or Servant Leader Principle

Humor Principle

I Can Do It Principle

I'll Think about That Tomorrow Principle

I'm Going to See My Friends at Work Principle

Inner Abundance Principle

Intellectual Masturbation Principle

Judge Not, You Don't Know Principle

Keep Busy with Flows or Happiness Takes Effort Principle

Keeping Up with the Jones Principle (see also Cocoon It Rule)

Kill Them with Kindness or Love Bomb Principle

Kiss the Past Goodbye Principle

Leisurely Pace and Lifestyle Principle

Table 15.2 *Continued*

Life Satisfaction Breeds Job/Work Satisfaction

Live Your Dream or 24/7 Principle

Love What You Do Principle

Love and Work Principle

Love Many Things Principle

"Mad Col." Disease Rule

Make Friends at Work Principle

Manage Your Time and Your Life Rule

Marching Orders Principle (see also Find a Meaning/Find a Goal Principle)

Mental Health Day Technique

Mine the Moment or Attack the Moment Principle

Modest Goal or Flow Principle

Multiple Personality or Multiple Personality of Everyday Life Principle (see also FOOBS Principle)

Mutual Aid Society Principle

Never Good Enough or Lower Expectations Principle

No Conditions of Worth Rule

No Gossip/Criticism/Suggestions or Words as Daggers Rule

No Mayo, Pickles, or Mustard Rule

Nothing Human Disgusts Me or Acceptance Priniciple

One-Thing-at-a-Time Principle (OTAAT)

Overthinking Principle

The PCD Time for Couples Rule

Personality Stays the Same or Happiness Set Point Principle

Pick a Role Model for a Friend Principle

Pick Your Battles/Pick No Battles Principle or Yes, Boss/Yes, Dear Rule

Pick Your Friends Principle

Pocket of Time to Relax Principle

Positive Addictions Principle

PRF Principle

Process Goal Principle

Quality Time Principle

The Question Rule

Relationship with Self or Self-Compassion Principle

Ride It Out, Read It Out Principle

Role Model Friends Principle

Routine Is Everything or Make It a Routine Principle

Second Opinion Principle or Technique (see also Psychiatrist Principle)

Selective Hedonism or Reasoned Passion Principle

Self-Acceptance Principle

Serve Others Principle

Share the Hurt behind the Anger Tenet

Should-Want Principle

Silence Is Golden or Organ Recital rule

Socializing Doubles Your Pleasure

Stop Second Guessing Principle

Street Signs to Success Principle

Strength It Principle

Stress Carriers or I Never Bother with People I Hate Rule

String of Pearls Practice and Principle

Surrogate Family Principle

Success Principle

Sweet Revenge Principle

Take a Stand Principle

Tangled Web or Web of Support or Love Where You Are Principle

Taoist Dodge Ball Rule

Thank Everyone For Everything Principle

Thou Shalt Be Aware or Psychephobia Principle

The Three Rs of Stress Management Principl

To Understand All Is to Forgive All or Empathy Principle

Trust Principle

Under the Influence or Yes, Dear Rule

We Are Family Principle

We're Not Okay and That's Okay Rule

What Would My Role Model Do or Role Model Principle

You Can't Have It All Principle or Curb or Ignore Desires Principles

You Do It to Yourself or Terrorist Principle

QOLT intervention strategies associated with non-work areas of life that they value. In essence, therapists can enroll clients in QOLT starting from the very beginning with an assessment of life goals for their retirement as described in Chapter 5. All areas of life should be considered by using the Basket-of-Eggs technique as clients experiment with sculpting a fulfilling way of life in retirement. Helping interventions from Chapter 17 are particularly potent in maintaining fulfillment for those who miss their paid employment, although a return to gainful employment even on a limited part-time basis should always be considered in cases of extreme unhappiness in retirement. Work That Satisfies in the Toolbox CD and earlier in this chapter is invaluable in helping clients evaluate volunteer and Helping jobs or positions in addition to paid employment. Ideally, preretirement counseling is recommended to prevent retirement dissatisfaction from developing in the first place; unfortunately, clients often fail to plan for their most basic retirement needs, including financial needs, which can be addressed with Money interventions (see Chapter 20). Table 15.3 consists of a listing of Tenets with attitudes, schemas, and practices conducive to greater satisfaction with retirement. Like all area-specific listings of Tenets, these are shared with clients in an ongoing and collaborative process of identifying which Tenets "get them where they live," that is, really seem to be written just for them and their unique situation. In this vein, many clients end up writing their own Tenets or Tenet names, ones that seem to "fit them to a T" or exactly in terms of their psychology and life circumstances.

Table 15.3   Tenets with Attitudes, Schemas, and Practices Conducive to Greater Satisfaction with Retirement

Accept What You Cannot Change Principle	Kiss the Past Goodbye Principle
Ask Your Death Tenet	Love Many Things Principle
Be True to Your School Principle: BETTY'S Way	Mine the Moment or Attack the Moment Principle
Be with People or Relationship Immersion Principle	Pick Your Battles/Pick No Battles Principle or Yes, Boss/Yes, Dear Rule
Exercise or Take your Medication Principle	Positive Addictions Principle
Feed the Soul Principle	Self-Acceptance Principle
Find a Friend, Find a Mate Principle	Sensate Focus/Savor or Vary Your Pleasures to Avoid Adaptation Tenet
Find a Meaning or Find a Goal Principle	
Get a Therapist Rule	Serve Others Principle
Habits Rule Rule or Routines Rule Rule	Surrogate Family Principle
Keep Busy with Flows or Happiness Takes Effort Principle	The Question Rule

CHAPTER 16

Play

In the words of Henry David Thoreau, Evelyn lived a life of "quiet desperation." Her daily schedule consisted of unremitting drudgery. When not caring for a colicky baby, she pushed herself to do all the household chores, including all the washing for her family; scrubbing the floors; dusting, cooking, and performing countless favors for family members and friends. She cried quietly in my office when I first saw her, telling me how overwhelmed she felt and how guilty she felt for letting her friends down by not completing three dresses for an Easter pageant, two of which would be used by the children of her friends and one of which would be used by her oldest daughter.

Michelle, a prominent physician, had the same problem. She worked 70-hour weeks and refused to share her evening on-call hours with other physicians so that she could provide a "personal touch" to all of her patients. Like a predecessor, Sigmund Freud, she took it as a personal failure and attack whenever a patient would complain about her service and switch to another physician. To keep all of her patients happy, she would often spend a half-hour to an hour with a patient who was upset about something. This meant her office was always overflowing. Then there were the phone calls. She would return calls day or night and would talk at length to patients about their medical (and personal) problems, rather than offering a brief word of reassurance and instructing them to see her during regular office hours. Using the scheme developed by Alan Marlatt of the University of Washington, the ratio of Michelle's "should activities" to "want activities" seemed to be about 100 to 1 (see Should/Want Tenet in the Toolbox CD). Michelle had little or no time to spend alone with her husband or with her child, much less time to relax and to recreate on her own (she

was an avid reader and gardener). Lately, Michelle had been relying on "chemical vacations" to keep her going; that is, she would occasionally take controlled substances that she could easily obtain to help her function or go to sleep.

Both Evelyn and Michelle suffered from what I call "recreation deficits." If you examine the word recreation, it refers to "re-creating" ourselves. Indeed the *Oxford English Dictionary* (Simpson & Weiner, 1989) defines recreation as the action of re-creating oneself by some pleasant pastime or amusement.

To me it involves both "recharging our batteries" or renewing our enthusiasm for life and "making ourselves over," that is re-creating or improving ourselves so that we are more of the person we want to be. Michelle and Evelyn both saw that they were very far from being the kind of person they wanted to be. More pressingly, they had gradually eliminated all recreational activities in order to fulfill assumed obligations. No wonder they had trouble getting up in the morning! All they had to look forward to was unremitting and overwhelming work and obligations. They had not learned an important piece of human wisdom: *Just as people need food to eat and air to breathe in order to survive and be happy, they also need to recreate or Play.* This is not an optional activity. Rather it is something we need to sustain and refresh ourselves. We need rituals and routines for recreation just as we have routines for eating, bathing, brushing our teeth, sleeping, and working. These routines should be automatic so that we don't neglect our recreational needs. When such automatic rituals or Happiness Habits (see Tenets in the Toolbox CD) are established, the question each day becomes, "How and when shall I relax and recreate?" rather than, "I wonder if I'll have time today to kick back and relax?" The question becomes one of not *if* or whether I will recreate, but *when* will I Play or recreate.

Choosing not to recreate risks destroying your quality of life; something to which both Evelyn and Michelle can attest. Their depressions became so severe that they could not perform even their obligations without tremendous effort. They couldn't sleep, their appetite was gone, they had no interest in sex, and they were emotionally unavailable to the people who needed them, including their families and patients. The words of Bob Dylan's song, *Desolation Row,* apply to both Michelle and Evelyn; "Her profession was her religion, her sin was her lifelessness."

Too many clients—in both clinical and positive psychology—have become so consumed with their work, household chores, and personal care activities that they have eliminated time for recreational pursuits. Even restorative sleep gets slighted; clients often deprive themselves of a good night's sleep, only to be irritable, "walking zombies" the next day! No wonder they feel unhappy. In addition to quality of life research on the importance of recreation (e.g., see George Vaillant's and John Flanagan's research), the emerging field of leisure therapy, or leisure counseling, attests to the growing recognition that play and recreational pursuits are crucial to happiness.

Whereas the presence of recreation is clearly related to happiness, its absence is related to a host of medical and psychological *dis*orders. The kind of lifestyle imbalance experienced by Evelyn and Michelle, for example, creates tremendous stress and strain, which, in turn, contribute to a host of physical problems including heart disease, cancer, and strokes (Taylor, 2002). Mental health problems also abound—in addition to connections with anxiety, depression, and sexual difficulties, a lack of recreation has repeatedly been linked to problems of addiction, especially the abuse of drugs and alcohol (Taylor, 2002). As was the case with Michelle, many people turn to chemical substances for solace, comfort, and a quick fix when overwhelmed with obligations in a life devoid of recreation. Many other people with addiction problems have too much time on their hands, such that they turn to their addiction to fill up their time and to overcome feelings of boredom and restlessness. The ability to relax, have fun, and play is really an important life skill (Vaillant, 2002).

Recreational activities involving partners in a love relationship are related to higher *marital* satisfaction,

a key ingredient to the recipe of happiness for many people. Unfortunately, many mental health professionals and the medical establishment have too often neglected the area of recreational counseling, instead focusing on what's wrong in people's psyche and body rather than focusing on what is right and wrong about their day-to-day lifestyle and activities. In contrast, QOLT tries to focus some attention on the connection between everyday blessings, assets and strengths, everyday practical problems, like a lack of recreation or Play, unhappiness and serious physical and psychological problems such as depression, substance abuse, and cardiac disease (Csikszentmihalyi, 1997; Taylor, 2002; Vaillant, 2002).

How does recreation restore, renew, and re-create a person? For one thing, it gives the person a mini-vacation or holiday from the worries in his or her life. By getting totally lost, absorbed, and in "flow" while recreating, people can forget about their problems and build up their psychological reserves so that they can later face their problems with alacrity, enthusiasm, and new ideas for solving them. Another way in which recreation is renewing and invigorating is that it often gives people a sense of identity, pride, and status, as Michael Argyle of Oxford University has observed (Argyle, 2001).

We see this in adults and children who show skill in sports or who play musical instruments at recitals and concerts.

Another way in which recreational pursuits can add to happiness is through the socializing that often accompanies recreation. Socializing is a major antidote to depression. People tend to forget about their problems when socializing and often feel excited and affirmed by others. Because many recreational pursuits are done with other people, this relationship component adds to overall happiness and satisfaction. Involvement in recreational pursuits can alleviate negative affects and increase happiness by building self-confidence. As experiences of success accumulate over time, as in the case of clients who feel "too stupid" to read but then find that they can truly enjoy a certain genre of writing such as mystery novels, their confidence increases as they become more knowledgeable about their avocations; recreational activities can also reduce the self-preoccupation and self-hating putdowns that are so characteristic of unhappy, depressed people by shifting their focus from themselves to some intrinsically "fun" or flow activity. Much of the power of Play and recreation to build happiness comes from those moments of magic when we are, in the words of Marty Seligman, "one with the music," having found a *flow* or flow activity as defined in the Flow It Tenet and discussed in Chapter 15. Both clients and therapists need to be thoroughly acquainted with the concept of flow as expressed in both the Flow It and Frivolous Flow Tenets in the Toolbox CD. The former was discussed in depth in Chapter 15; the latter is presented here.

PLAY LIKE A KID OR FRIVOLOUS FLOW PRINCIPLE

A 5-year-old plays for hours in an empty cardboard box that is now a spaceship to the alien planet of Mordor. The poet Wordsworth said "the child is father to the man" in *Intimations on Immortality*. Jesus bade the little children to come forward. What can young children teach us? They can teach us to have a blast as we play unself-consciously at frivolous, fun games and flows—see Flow It—that are not productive work and that in no way add to our wealth or prestige. To paraphrase the Bible, unless you can play like a little child who is full of the joy and wonder of the world, who has a blast at pure fun activities with no merit, and who is blissfully unaware of how they are being judged, you will not enter the kingdom of happiness here on earth. A key to "aging well," is to pursue "fun and games" with gusto even as society sneers at us for being "over the hill" (Vaillant, 2002). QOLT holds that this is important our whole lives as we search for and find recreation, play, and flow activities that give us joy by engaging us totally and using all of our skills even when it does nothing for our reputation or our pocketbooks. Can you talk baby talk to your dog or cat as you play with them or train them for agility competitions? Can you color or paint shamelessly like you did as a child or sing at the top of your lungs or dance without lessons or putter around in your garden or read a trashy novel or play computer games just because they are fun, engaging flows that are intrinsically satisfying? Explore frivolous fun activities and flows throughout your life as you allow some time for yourself to simply play; limiting ourselves to "productive" hobbies or work, cuts us off from myriad sources of joy that this life offers—see Chapters 10 and 12 for ways to cope with naysaying or killjoy thoughts about pure play.

Pocket of Time to Relax Principle

People shouldn't wait for vacations. Rather, they should grab, steal, and enjoy brief pockets of time whether it be 5 to 30 minutes to take a walk, read a book, or call their partner to say hi. Intervals of pure play and relaxation are essential to happiness and contentment. No one can keep up a nonstop frenzied pace day in and day out.

DEFINITIONS

QOLT defines Play or recreation broadly as any nonwork, and usually nonpaid, activity that gives people relaxation, refreshment, fun, distraction, meaning, or ways to improve themselves, others, or their community. Specifically, Play is defined as what you do in your free time to relax, have fun, or improve yourself. This could include watching movies, visiting friends, or pursuing a hobby like sports or gardening (Frisch, 1994). Given the huge role of social relationships in happiness and given the huge antidepressant, anxiolytic, and anti-anger effects of socializing, Play that involves flows and/or social contact is particularly encouraged (Barlow, 2002; Diener & Seligman, 2004). Interventions aimed at the area of recreation are usually an essential part of treatment plans for clients with no time to relax; an inability to relax often related to worry and perfectionism; depression, anxiety, or anger problems; any addiction, workaholism, or Type A personality/hostility and cyncism; obsessive-compulsive personality disorder or traits; and psychophysiological disorders.

In addition to the Flow It Tenet and general CASIO strategies for improving life satisfaction with Play, QOLT offers a specific step-by-step approach to improving satisfaction with Play by creating a certain habit or routine for recreation.

ESTABLISHING A PLAY HABIT OR ROUTINE

Step 1: Build Motivation

As the start of this chapter suggests, recreation is a requirement for a contented human being and not an unnecessary frill. Unless clients agree with this,

Table 16.1   Tenets with Attitudes, Schemas, and Practices Conducive to Greater Play Satisfaction

Balanced Lifestyle Principle	Never Good Enough or Lower Expectations Principle
Be with People or Relationship Immersion	Overthinking Principle
Care for My One Body Principle	Play It Safe Principle
Color Purple Principle	Pocket of Time to Relax Principle
Creativity Routine Principle	Positive Addictions Principle
Daily Vacation Principle	Process Goal Principle
Do What You Love or Tune In to What Turns You On Principle	Quality Time Principle
Exercise or Take your Medication Principle	Relationship with Self or Self-Compassion Principle
FAT Time Principle	Ride It Out, Read It Out Principle
Feed the Soul Principle	Routine Is Everything or Make It a Routine Principle
Flow It Principle	Sensate Focus/Savor or Vary Your Pleasures to Avoid Adaptation Tenet
Habits Rule rule or Routines Rule Rule	
Happiness Habits Principle	Serve Others Principle
Humor Principle	Should-Want Principle
I Can Do It Principle	Socializing Doubles Your Pleasure
Inner Abundance Principle	Strength It Principle
Keep Busy with Flows or Happiness Takes Effort Principle	String of Pearls Practice and Principle
Leisurely Pace and Lifestyle Principle	Surrogate Family Principle
Li Po or Commune with Nature Rule	Tangled Web or Web of Support or Love Where You Are Principle
Love Many Things Principle	
Manage Your Time and Your Life Rule	The Three Rs of Stress Management Principle
Mental Health Day Technique	Thou Shalt Be Aware or Psychephobia Principle
Mine the Moment or Attack the Moment Principle	We're Not Okay and That's Okay Rule
Modest Goal or Flow Principle	You Can't Have It All Principle or Curb or Ignore Desires Principles

intervention in this area is destined to fail. Step 1 is aimed at cultivating "positive addictions" or Play Routines. Therapists would do well to consider this step as one in Motivational Interviewing as developed by Bill Miller and his colleagues at the University of New Mexico (Miller & Rollnick, 2002). To build motivation, start with a reading or discussion with clients of the Tenets related to Play in Table 16.1. In particular, discuss the Tenets as part of a therapy process of listing advantages and disadvantages to a commitment to Play activities in general and a specific daily and weekly Play Routine. The Pro versus Con Technique in the Toolbox CD and illustrated in Box 18.1 (on page 276) from Chapter 18 is ideal for this purpose, forcing clients to recall positive reasons for change and to list and dispute reasons to maintain the status quo.

Step 2: Identifying Play Interests and Possibilities That Fit with Personal Goals-and-Values

The second step is for clients to explore and identify all of their Play interests and flows. As is usually the case in QOLT, start with clients' overall Goals-and-Values from the Vision Quest exercise in the Toolbox CD and Chapter 5. As Freud said, "freedom is a terrible burden"; this is especially true in modern society with the overabundance of recreational options. One way to lessen the burden is to consider *plays*, QOLT's term for leisure activities, that are related to valued areas of life and even the goals associated with those areas.

After reviewing life Goals-and-Values, therapists challenge clients to choose some specific Play goals and activities that reflect their most cherished Goals-and-Values, their recreational interests, the time they have available—as determined by a look at their schedules or completed Daily Activity Plans. Michelle decided to spend at least 20 minutes a day in "free play" with her son. In this way she honored a major interest in her life, did it within the time that was available, and pursued something that reflected her most important Goals-and-Values, the goal of having a family and raising a son and being a good parent. Clients involved in a love relationship or who live with other family members and want to think of things to do with them should consider adapting their favorite activities to include those people. In keeping the FAT Time Tenet of Contentment, it is important for those with families to have recreational time Alone, Together with one's lover or partner, and with one's Family as a whole in order to have some fun and maintain these relationships, including the relationship clients have with themselves. As the Socializing Doubles Your Pleasure Tenet says, family members and friends can be brought along to enhance the pleasure of clients' play, as when the whole family goes for a walk or to a zoo. Of course, some clients want time alone or with friends *away* from their partners and/or kids for their Play time—see FAT Time Tenet. As therapists and clients generate lists of fun activities, it is vital that clients not be pushed into socially desirable activities or activities that most people find enjoyable but that many of your clients do not enjoy or even hate. It's vital for clients not to choose activities based on what others say or based on what clients think they *should* do; as is the case with reinforcers in general, what is fun for one person can be tedious or boring for another. If clients don't pursue hobbies that fit their unique interests and that result in deep flow or fun at the time, they run the risk of turning their Play time into drudgery as they pursue what Alan Marlatt of the University of Washington calls "should" instead of "want" activities.

Identifying plays. There are several ways that QOLT elicits potential plays in clients who may be at a loss to think of ways to recreate. For example, this is done informally by having clients think about leisure pursuits they have enjoyed in the past, or ones they have thought about pursuing and that still interest them. It may be more satisfying to pursue several play interests instead of just one—Love Many Things Tenet—as the philosopher, Bertrand Russell (1958) pointed out in *The Conquest of Happiness.* Second, the QOLT Play List in Box 16.1 and the Toolbox CD represents a more formal way to identify potential plays; a copy of the Play List for client use can be found in the Toolbox CD. The Play List is based on clinical experience and pleasant events lists developed in the past by Peter Lewinsohn and his colleagues at the University of Oregon.

Step 3: Problem-Solving Obstacles to Play

Step 3 involves problem solving around barriers or obstacles to Play satisfaction in the client's life. In my own informal research with several hundred clinical and positive psychology clients who are unhappy with the area of Play, I've found that most of them see a lack of time or simply failure to do the things they know they like to do even when they have the time, as the major obstacles to their satisfaction. Thus, clients felt they didn't have the time for things like golf, reading, or socializing, and even if they had the time, they just didn't do these activities. Clients who thought they didn't have enough time seemed to let other activities take priority, often leading to an impoverished, dull, and routine lifestyle dominated by work, as was the case of Evelyn and Michelle, presented at the start of this chapter.

Less often, depressed clients unhappy with Play said they couldn't enjoy the Play time they had because they didn't really know how to relax or what to do to enjoy themselves. Obviously, these people can overcome this obstacle simply by doing the earlier steps in this process. They especially need to generate a list of plays that are consistent with their Goals-and-Values. In some cases, like playing a musical instrument, a person may need some instruction and equipment (such as a guitar) before being able to test out whether a particular play is satisfying to them.

Other clients have problems with worry or guilt about taking time away from work, family, or household duties in order to relax and Play. These people often benefit from doing Lie Detectors—Chapter 10 and the Toolbox CD—to process their worries and negative thoughts and by doing Daily Activity Plans—Chapter 10 and the

BOX 16.1
Play List

Name: _____   Date: _____

Instructions: For most people, play or recreational activities are essential ways to relax, have fun, forget worries, be creative, learn something new, or improve themselves, others, or their community. These activities can renew and refresh us so that we perform better in our work and relationships. Circle the number next to every activity that you think you might enjoy as a recreational outlet. Do not think about what is best, most practical, or easy to do. Just circle any item that interests you or that you've enjoyed in the past. Circle activities in which you get so involved that you lose track of time—these are called flows in QOLT. While harder to get started, *active* recreational activities such as gardening are usually more satisfying and beneficial than *passive* activities such as watching television. When you are finished, choose some activities to try and see whether they are satisfying, fun, or pleasurable. Try to follow a Play or *Recreation Routine* or *Leisure Plan* in which you *regularly*—preferably daily even for just 5 minutes—engage in some of these activities in order to improve your overall quality of life. (*Note:* Many activities not directly associated with couples, families, or friends may be adapted and done with a partner, a family, or a friend(s). Some items are repeated on purpose.)

A. *Personal Pleasure and Renewal*

1. Blogging, Instant Messaging, or Text Messaging

2. Watching something special on TV or DVD

3. Computer Gaming

4. Watching a sports game or event

5. Shopping

6. Reading or watching something funny or interesting

7. Listening to music

8. Listening to the radio

9. Eating a nice meal, dessert, or snack

10. Having a drink, soda, or coffee

11. Viewing or reading something sexy (Erotica)

12. Visiting your favorite (or new) sections of a book, video, or music store

13. Playing cards or board games

14. Planning a day trip or vacation

15. Taking a day trip or vacation

16. Dressing up

17. Putting on comfortable clothes

18. Getting a massage

19. Going to a hair stylist

20. Getting a manicure

21. Having some time alone

22. Making up a pleasant daydream or fantasy

23. Looking at home videos or picture albums

24. Just sitting and relaxing

25. Taking a leisurely bath or shower

26. Sleeping in

27. Taking the day off

28. Staying up late, taking a nap, getting up early

29. Making a fire in the fireplace

30. Doing some pleasure reading

31. Playing bingo or gambling

32. Singing or dancing by yourself

Additional activities you enjoy: _____

_____

B. *Community Activities*

33. Going to a movie

34. Going to a play, show, or lecture

35. Going to a concert

36. Going to a bookstore

37. Visiting a park

38. Visiting neighbors

39. Going to a sporting event or game like football, basketball, baseball, or soccer

40. Going to a museum

41. Going to a botanical garden or aquarium

42. Going out to eat at a favorite restaurant

43. Going out to eat at a new restaurant

44. Going out for a drink, coffee, snack, or dessert

45. Doing something outside

46. Going shopping

47. Buying yourself something special

48. Buying someone else something special

49. Going to a garage, auction, or antique sale

(Continued)

50.   Shopping out of town

51.   Going window shopping for things you can't buy

52.   Taking a walk somewhere pretty or interesting

53.   Going sightseeing in the country

54.   Going sightseeing in the city

55.   Going to a coffee shop

Additional activities you enjoy: _____

_____

C. *Hobbies/Creative Outlets*

56.   Gardening

57.   Dancing

58.   Playing cards

59.   Drawing or painting

60.   Playing with, caring for, or watching pet(s)

61.   Taking music, painting, singing, dancing, acting lessons

62.   Playing a musical instrument

63.   Joining a singing or acting group

64.   Using the computer: including games, programs, Internet

65.   Doing needlework like sewing and knitting

66.   Doing woodworking

67.   Keeping a journal

68.   Writing a poem or story

69.   Going skating or rollerblading

70.   Doing arts and crafts

71.   Doing a crossword or jigsaw puzzle

72.   Hiking

73.   Birdwatching

74.   Doing photography

75.   Visiting or joining a hobby group

76.   Playing pool or ping pong

77.   Watching sports on TV

78.   Going to a sporting event or game

79.   Collecting stamps, coins, cards, etc.

80. Stargazing/astronomy

81. Boating or canoeing

Additional activities you enjoy: _____

_____

D. *Sports*

82. Golfing

83. Fishing or hunting

84. Joining a sports team like softball, volleyball, basketball, etc.

85. Playing soccer

86. Water skiing

87. Snow skiing

88. Playing racquetball or tennis

89. Bowling

90. Cycling

91. Hiking

92. Playing baseball, basketball, or football

93. Playing shuffleboard, badminton, croquet, or horseshoes

Additional sports you enjoy: _____

_____

E. *Learning/Reading*

94. Surfing the Web

95. Visiting a library

96. Visiting a bookstore

97. Going to professional or business meeting or conference

98. Reading work-related material

99. Taking a class

100. Running computer programs

101. Going to a lecture

102. Going to a museum

103. Reading the newspaper

104. Reading a favorite magazine

105. Reading a novel or mystery

(Continued)

106.   Reading interesting nonfiction books or magazines

107.   Reading about your hobbies and interests

108.   Looking at picture books

109.   Learning a new language

110.   Learning about computers

111.   Reading do-it-yourself books or magazines

Additional activities you enjoy: _____

_____

F.   *Socializing, Family Activities, and Helping Others*

Note: Write an F or C beside activities listed here and elsewhere that you think you might enjoy as a family or couple.

112.   Visiting/phoning a friend

113.   Visiting/phoning a date

114.   Visiting/phoning relatives

115.   Visiting/phoning partner

116.   Visiting/phoning children or grandchildren

117.   Visiting/phoning acquaintance

118.   Inviting over a friend, acquaintance, date, relatives, partner, children, or grandchildren

119.   Planning an outing with a friend, acquaintance, date, relatives, partner, children, or grandchildren

120.   Writing a letter or e-mail to a friend, acquaintance, date, relatives, partner, children, or grandchildren

121.   Going to a party

122.   Planning a party or get-together

123.   Playing with kids

124.   Reading to the kids

125.   Teaching/helping kids

126.   Taking family pictures and videos

127.   Flying a kite with the kids

128.   Wrestling, tickling, joking with kids

129.   Take kids somewhere they enjoy (e.g., amusement park)

130.   Going dancing

131.   Flirting

132.   People watching

133.   Taking a walk with someone else

134. Going to a professional business meeting or conference

135. Doing a favor for someone

136. Playing cards with someone or a group

137. Playing a game with someone

138. Planning a vacation with others

139. Taking a vacation with others

140. Visiting or joining a hobby group

141. Visiting or joining a social club

142. Visiting or joining church/temple/synagogue/mosque, etc.

143. Visiting or joining a community, political, or school group working on causes you believe in

144. Joining your neighborhood association

145. Helping to solve a local, state, national, or international problem

146. Doing something nice for someone

147. Buying someone a present

148. Giving money or things to a group or cause you believe in

149. Complimenting or thanking people in your life

150. Volunteering to help people you enjoy like children, old people, etc.

151. Joining a self-help group

152. Having a good conversation with someone

153. Talking to someone about your interests or things on your mind

154. Asking someone for help, advice, or support

155. Dressing up and going out on the town

156. Going on a picnic

157. Camping

158. Playing sports with others

159. Singing or dancing with someone

160. Asking someone you like to get together so they will ask you to go out later

Additional activities that would make you feel good or satisfied: _____

_____

G. *Health and Fitness*

161. Exercising

162. Working out at a health club

163. Going to an aerobic class

(Continued)

164.   Walking

165.   Jogging

166.   Swimming

167.   Lifting weights

168.   Trying to control or eliminate a bad habit

169.   Going to counseling

170.   Reading a self-help book

171.   Joining a self-help group

172.   Doing self-help exercises

173.   Doing Quality Time

174.   Doing a Relaxation Ritual

175.   Having a good cry

176.   Meditating/praying

177.   Sitting quietly for 30 minutes

178.   Getting 7 to 8 hours of sleep

179.   Eating three meals a day, including breakfast

180.   Getting a physical exam

Additional activities that would make you feel good or satisfied: _____

_____

H. *Spiritual and Religious Activities*

181.   Visiting or joining a church, temple, zendo, synagogue, mosque, etc.

182.   Praying or meditating

183.   Reading religious, spiritual, or inspirational literature

184.   Asking someone to pray for you

Additional activities that would make you feel good or satisfied: _____

_____

I. *Satisfying or Enjoyable Chores*

185.   Cook or bake something

186.   Fixing something

187.   Cleaning something up

188.   Doing a home improvement project

189.   Doing something you've put off but will feel great when it's over

190.   Dealing with a problem or challenge that has been bothering you

191. Completing do-it-yourself repairs or home improvement

192. Rearranging or decorating the house/apartment

193. Planning the day, including something that is fun or gives you a feeling of accomplishment

194. Planning a personal project

195. Planning a self-improvement project

Additional activities that would make you feel good or satisfied: _____

_____

J. *Couples Activities (for Romantic Partners)*

Note: For additional ideas, write a C next to activities listed at the beginning of this Play List—Sections A through I—that you think you might enjoy as a *couple.*

196. Going out on a "date" (without children)

197. Giving a massage or backrub

198. Taking the kids to a sitter and returning home for time together as a couple

199. Sharing a romantic dinner at home

200. Making time to visit

201. Taking a shower or bath together

202. Making love

203. Cuddling, kissing, or necking

204. Trying new approaches to lovemaking

205. Spending an evening at a hotel or motel—in or out of town (without children)

206. Sharing personal feelings and opinions

207. Reading together and discussing ideas

208. Reading out loud to each other

209. Wrestling, rough housing, or tickling each other

210. Flirting with each other

211. Complimenting each other

212. Planning something to do together

213. Visiting, calling, or messaging partner at work

214. Having lunch together

215. Making love during lunchtime

216. Taking a walk during lunchtime

217. Showing public displays of affection

218. Singing or play music together

(Continued)

219. Relaxing (for example, have breakfast and read the newspaper together on Sunday)

220. Watching the sun rise or set together

221. Going on a picnic together

Additional activities that would make you feel good or satisfied: _____

_____

Toolbox CD—that allowed them to schedule time for work and recreation so that they don't neglect their work too much when pursuing recreational activities.

Some clients seem unhappy with Play because they over-rely on television for entertainment. Television, in my experience, feeds the passivity and inertia of depression, making things much worse rather than better. The one exception is when people "titrate" or limit their television viewing and only watch a few select shows that are highly enjoyable. Generally, more active pursuits are better at boosting one's mood and happiness than sitting passively in front of the "boob tube."

Still other people had problems with an unwilling partner in pursuing activities. One of my patients with this problem used Five Paths from the Toolbox CD and finally came up with the solution to pursue some recreational activities on his own and not to let his spouse limit his highly enjoyable activities just because she didn't want to go along. Others effectively problem solve with their partner to find fun things to do that they *both* enjoy (see Relationship Skills like Workable Compromise from the Toolbox CD and Chapter 14). Many of my clients cite loneliness or a lack of love interest, friends, or a social group as a major obstacle to Play satisfaction; they have benefited most from the relationship-building strategies in Chapter 14 to build a social support network.

People with a lack of time often benefit from using the time management principles and Daily Activity Plan described in Chapter 10 and the Toolbox CD. These skills have taught many of my patients to assertively carve out time for recreation and Play activities that they felt didn't exist before. The best or "prime times" to recreate when no time seems available is in the early morning, lunchtime, and after work and before dinner for those working outside of the home.

Play or Die. Often negative core beliefs are an obstacle to Play satisfaction, as in the case of people who define their self-worth strictly in terms of how well they perform in their work. In these cases, major changes in their Life Script, Goals-and-Values, and attitudes are needed. For example, one of my workaholic clients, Raymond, would only recreate if he could prove to himself, through the use of the Daily Activity Plan and discussion with me and his wife, that such Play was essential to his mood control and marital satisfaction. It was only when he realized that his marriage would die and that he would be chronically depressed and plagued with ulcerative colitis if he did not start to recreate both by himself and with his family, that Raymond was able to follow a daily Play Routine.

Another obstacle to Play satisfaction is the core belief that clients can "have their cake and eat it too" by overworking ourselves in order to make money, have a high standard of living, and have "oodles" of time to relax, recreate, and renew themselves. Recent studies have found that the 40-hour work week is losing ground in the United States as people increasingly overload themselves with work. In many cases this cannot be helped; it is a matter of financial survival for many to work one, two, or even three jobs in order to make ends meet. In other cases, however, people are sacrificing quality of life for more Money and possessions even though once the basics are covered these factors have basically no impact on happiness or successful aging whatsoever (see Chapter 20). As a people, Western societies seem to grossly overestimate the standard of living and the amount of material possessions that they need to be happy. Additionally, many of us wish to have our cake and eat it too in terms of being slaves to work and wanting to feel deeply content and reasonably happy—the goal of QOLT. The truth is that for the most part, we *cannot* have our cake and eat it too. That is, if we consistently overwork ourselves and live a life of imbalance that ignores many valued areas of life, we will not be happy (I have seen some clients whose work is fun and flow to them who are content with work and a few friends or family as their hobby or Play Routine). Truly discontent workaholic clients are loathe to say no to Work projects and responsibilities even though this more than anything can make them happier. One is reminded of Fritz Perls' old saw that some "clients don't want to change; they come to therapy to learn how to live with their neurosis." Therapists must be careful since it is easy to be "fired" over this issue.

Other obstacles can get in the way of Play satisfaction such as a decided *lack* of money, unemployment, a demanding job that really demands all of clients free time in order for them to stay employed, a lack of ability, a physical disability, or even the weather. Creatively problem solving around each of these issues using Five Paths can overcome obstacles to Play satisfaction. For example, Money problems can often be overcome by finding inexpensive ways to recreate, as in the case of one of my clients who, though unemployed, was still able to go out on a "McDate" with his wife each week to McDonald's and for a walk in the park. A lack of ability or poor leisure skills can often be solved through taking classes in things like needlework, martial arts, digital photography, or painting.

At times, significant others object to leisure activities, a barrier that must be faced in order for Play to be fruitfully pursued. One couple I worked with negotiated with each other such that they would take turns exercising at a local health club while the other spouse watched their children. Such compromises and negotiations are crucial to both meet Play needs and keep relationships alive and positive.

Clients with a history of drug or alcohol abuse have learned to curtail Play activities that may trigger a relapse. For example, John, a recovering crank or methamphetamine user, avoided parties in which alcohol or drugs were available and even moved to a new part of town in order to make friends and pursue activities that did not involve drugs or alcohol. Generally, it is best for people who are recovering from addictions to wait at least a year or two before exposing themselves to any high-risk situation, if then.

Preventing Noncompliance or Relapse. As is done with any outside activity or homework that is a part of QOLT, always ask clients before they leave the office, "Tell me all the reasons you might give me next week for not doing your QOLT exercise?" Having this discussion in a way that shows clients how QOLT "homework" or more preferably "growth exercises" for the week are *intimately* related to reaching clients' goals in life for greater happiness and so on, does much to reduce homework noncompliance or "resistance." I always tell

clients that they will get more for their money, "more bang for their buck," if they experiment with growth exercises and activities *outside* of therapy or coaching sessions. This is how resistance or noncompliance is dealt with in QOLT and other cognitive therapy approaches.

Buddy System, Play Flows, and Premack It. A second way to dramatically improve compliance with play and other QOLT assignments and to, very importantly, routinize the activity, is for clients to find a friend, acquaintance, or buddy with whom to do the activity. Clients who exercise together are much more likely to continue on a routine basis. It also helps greatly if the play involves a flow for clients—see Flow It in the Toolbox CD and in Chapter 15—that is rewarded after completion with another high-frequency or highly rewarding activity such as having a meal—Premack It Principle. For example, many clients will not eat lunch or breakfast or get online until after they have exercised.

Step 4: Implement a Leisure Plan or Recreation Routine

Step 4 charges clients to develop and implement a specific Leisure Plan. This Plan should consider ways to overcome the barriers or obstacles to Play that clients identified in Step 3. The plan should also include some of the specific plays from Step 2 that best fit clients interests, the time available for recreation, and clients Goals-and-Values. Leisure Plans can benefit from the inclusion of the Play-related Tenets with attitudes, schemas, and practices conducive to greater Play satisfaction discussed in Step 1 and listed in Table 16.1. The Routine often involves the principles and exercises—Habit Diary—of the Habit Control Program delineated in Chapter 13 on Health. Recall that positive behaviors and positive addictions can be monitored, reinforced, and routinized as much as self-defeating behaviors can be eliminated using the Habit Control Program.

Step 5: Evaluate Efficacy or Whether Play Routine Was Carried Out and Increased Satisfaction

In Step 5, therapists and clients evaluate together whether a Play Routine was carried out completely and whether it increased client satisfaction with the area of Play. As problems are revealed in the implementation of plans in the real world, problems that were not anticipated in Step 3 or not dealt with successfully, Step 5 involves a simple repeat of Step 3.

CHAPTER 17

Helping

In QOLT, Helping (or *helping*) refers to helping others in need or helping to make your community a better place to live. Helping can be done on your own or in a group like a church, a neighborhood association, or a political party. Helping can include doing volunteer work at a school or giving money to a good cause. Helping means helping people who are not your friends or relatives (Frisch, 1994). As this definition implies, Helping can involve *service* to those in need or *civic action* to make the community or world a better place to live. Interestingly, in most world religions and wisdom traditions, nonrelatives and strangers are defined as one's sisters and brothers with service to these seen as a path to spiritual enlightenment. People flourish and prosper in communities where they act as if those strangers and neighbors are their brothers and sisters, that is, in communities where people help and trust each other, an increasingly rare thing in today's society (Diener & Seligman, 2004). Organized helping through high rates of volunteer activity, club memberships outside of work, and church membership, are also characteristic of happy communities, that is, communities with the happiest and most satisfied inhabitants (Helliwell, 2003; Putnam, 2001). One of the great services of positive psychology, may be to alert the general public as well as the physicians, counselors, and mental health professionals of the world that Helping and service to others is a *major* untapped source of joy, inner peace, and contentment.

HELPING HELPS THE HELPER PRINCIPLE

In QOLT, the myriad ways in which Helping activities benefit the helper (and not merely the "helpee" or re-cipient of help) is called the Helping Helps the Helper Principle. The idea of nourishing the self by helping others seems radical. Self-caring, self-nourishing, or achieving Inner Abundance through helping *others* seems foreign to traditional caregiving models in Western society of letting others serve and nourish those who need to be rejuvenated. Nevertheless, many wisdom traditions prescribe selfless service to others as a path to enlightenment, knowing God, or spiritual nirvana as effective and legitimate as contemplative prayer or arduous meditation practice (Kornfield, 2000; Merton, 1996b). This sentiment is expressed in diverse contemplative spiritual traditions, including Islamic Sufis, Jewish Kaballah practitioners, Buddhists, and Christian monastics. No less a venerated monk than Thomas Merton says that kindly and patient service to others, putting into practice the Christian commandment to love one's neighbor—a commandment of all great wisdom traditions—is "the only ascetic method given in the Gospels" (Merton, 1996b).

How Does Helping Lead to Greater Happiness?

Helping is associated with higher levels of well-being and life satisfaction. For example, those with memberships in voluntary organizations outside of work are happier than those who do not volunteer outside of work (Diener & Seligman, 2004; Myers, 1993). But how does helping lead to greater happiness?

Helping may help clients achieve greater happiness by allowing helpers to express their Goals-and-Values in concrete ways (as when an environmentalist gets involved in preserving green spaces in his community), by allowing for social contact, which in itself is a powerful happiness-booster and antidepressant (McLean & Hakstian, 1979), and by allowing helpers to feel efficacious as they see concrete progress among those whom they are helping as in literacy programs where immigrants who cannot speak English, gradually gain fluency in the language of their adoptive homeland. Helping can also allow for career exploration, which may ultimately increase satisfaction with Work, as when clients volunteer in areas related to their career interests to see if, in fact, a particular career would suit them. Helping activities can give clients an opportunity to practice and refine their social skills.

Helping activities can also give a focus and a purpose to clients who are going through major life crises and transitions, such as retirement, unemployment, widowhood, and the onset of a physical disability or chronic illness. For example, Maynard, a man who defined himself by his work lost his moorings in a retirement community far from home; only when he found a way to use his skills for others as a legal aid society volunteer and to be with "his people" at a Reformed Jewish Temple, did he find happiness and contentment.

Jazmin found joy in volunteering with children at a nearby private school, something that had nothing to do with her career as a lawyer; law was something she wanted to say goodbye to after retirement.

Sandy was a mess. She was a 30-year-old white, divorced probationer diagnosed with alcoholism and borderline personality disorder who accessed help through Baylor's psychology practicum in the rural Texas town of Paris. Sandy had lost everything important to her, including her husband, her job, and her relationship with her parents who were sick of her irresponsible and outrageous behavior. After her fifth time in an alcohol rehabilitation program, she finally decided that it was time to turn her life around. As part of her responsibilities in Alcoholics Anonymous (AA), she became a sponsor of a 19-year-old alcoholic who reminded her of herself at that age. For the first time in her life, she was given the responsibility for caring for and helping someone else overcome *her* addiction. This responsibility was to change her life. By "re-parenting" this teen, she bolstered her own sobriety skills, learned how to control her anger, and learned how to be socially appropriate with others. After all, she had to be a role model for this oppositional young woman whom she grew to love and care for as much as if she were her own child. She also found a home and identity in AA that she hadn't had either as a child in a chaotic home or as part of the drug culture. She became ambitious and interested in moving up within the organization of AA. She wanted to become

a drug and alcohol counselor herself. This was a far cry from her previous ambition of simply satisfying all of her appetites and telling the world to "go to Hell!" In the words of Marty Seligman, Sandra's Helping experience was "life changing." For her, volunteer work was not some "Yuppie frill" activity. It was a crucial part of her survival and recovery from alcoholism as well as a *passionate calling* or vocation—see Chapter 15—that gave her life meaning, purpose, and great satisfaction.

Happiness researchers, Sonja Lyubomirsky, and her colleagues (Lyubomirsky, Sheldon, et al., in press) have suggested that acts of helping and service to others may foster a positive perception of others and one's community, an increased sense of cooperation and interdependence with other people, and an awareness of one's good fortune, presumably as clients make "downward social comparisons," as in seeing the lot of a homeless person as much worse than their own. Helping often involves socializing, thereby satisfying a basic human need of us "social animals," which, by itself, may boost one's sense of satisfaction, contentment, and happiness; according to Diener and Seligman (2004) even introverts prefer to have other people around them even if they would rather not have to interact with those people in any great depth.

ESTABLISHING A HELPING ROUTINE

Step 1: Build Motivation

As the start of this chapter suggests, *helping* is a major, largely untapped, resource of contentment that costs little or nothing to begin. Unless clients agree with this, intervention in this area is destined to fail. Step 1 is aimed at cultivating a regular Helping Routine, which is more likely to be followed than occasional, irregular helping activities. Therapists would do well to consider this step as one in Motivational Interviewing as developed by Bill Miller and his colleagues (Miller, Rollnick, & Conforti, 2002) of the University of New Mexico. To build motivation, start with a reading or discussion with clients of the Tenets related to Helping in Table 17.1.

The most important Tenets to share with respect to Helping are:

- Serve Others Principle
- Giving Tree or Self-Other Principle
- String of Pearls Practice and Principle

Table 17.1   Tenets with Attitudes, Schemas, and Practices Conducive to Greater Helping Satisfaction

Balanced Lifestyle Principle	Inner Abundance Principle
Be True to Your School Principle: BETTY'S Way	Judge Not, You Don't Know Principle
Be with People or Relationship Immersion Principle	Kill Them with Kindness or Love Bomb Principle
Blind Dumb Optimism Principle	Leisurely Pace and Lifestyle Principle
Calculated Risk Principle	Love Where You Are Principle (see also Tangled Web Principle or Web of Support)
Color Purple Principle	
Empathy Principle (see also To Understand All Is to Forgive All Principle)	Make Friends at Work Principle
	Make It Routine Principle (see also Routine Is Everything Principle)
Expect the Unexpected Principle	
Expert Friend Principle	Meanings Like Buses Rule
Favor Bank or Favor Bank of Good Will from Good Deeds or Mindset of Constant Gratitude and Acts of Kindness Principle	Modest Goal
	No Gossip/Criticism/Suggestions or Words as Daggers Rule
Feed the Soul Principle	Play Like a Kid/Frivolous Flows Principle
Find a Goal Principle (see also Find a Meaning Principle)	Positive Addictions Principle
Flow It Principle	Role Model Principle (see also What Would My Role Model Do Principle)
Giving Tree or Self-Other Principle	
Glow of Peace Tenet	Serve Others Principle
Happiness Is a Choice Principle or Responsibility Principle	Socializing Doubles Your Pleasure
Happiness Takes Effort Principle (see also Keep Busy with Flows Principle)	Stop Second Guessing Principle
	Strengthen It Principle
How Kind Principle or Tender Hearted Rule	String of Pearls Practice and Principle
Humble Servant or Servant Leader Principle	Surrogate Family Principle
Humor Principle	Thank Everyone for Everything Principle
I Can Do It Principle	Trust Principle
I'm Going to See My Friends at Work Principle	You Are What You Do

Notice that the Serve Others Principle speaks of helping as an avenue to *meaning in life* from both secular and spiritual perspectives. Anecdotal evidence supports the view that what helps most is when the helper is doing the helping because it is a core value (see Goals-and-Values) that the person holds and not merely a way to selfishly boost his or her happiness. To rekindle such a value for helping, therapists can inquire about whether helping is or ever was an important personal value. When it has been, the philosophical or spiritual basis for this can also be explored and reinforced through "homework" as when a Catholic client read a biography of Dorothy Day as a way of getting in touch with her "catholic worker" roots that extolled the values of helping the poor in ways similar to that of Mother Teresa of Calcutta who also inspired this client's helping efforts. Indeed, from experience in teaching social service and helping classes at Baylor, the author shared some pertinent readings of Mother Teresa's with this client (Mother Teresa, 1985). QOLT therapists will often hook clients up with supportive clergy or readings from the clients' tradition that extol the value of helping without in any way "prescribing" a particular spiritual tradition or approach that would be insensitive, potentially very harmful to clients, and unethical according to ethical standards of various mental health disciplines. (See the American Psychological Association, 2002, for clear guidelines on cultural competence and respect for clients' religious and cultural identity.)

Serve Others Principle (or Tenet of Contentment).

Helping others day to day and making the world a better place to live can be a satisfying answer to the question of the meaning of life. According to several spiritual traditions, service *by itself* can lead to wisdom, and even enlightenment or nirvana. Serving Others or Helping in QOLT parlance can also be a major key to happiness for the giver. Service is a greater happiness booster than great food according to positive psychology researchers (Seligman, 2002). Service has also been found to prolong life. According to University of Michigan researchers, older adults who help or emotionally support friends, neighbors, or relatives reduce their risk of dying by nearly 60 percent even when the researchers controlled for the health, age, and gender of the helpers. Paid staff versus volunteer distinctions are likely meaningless so long as we see the work as really helping others. It may truly be better to give than to receive.

Most spiritual traditions stress service to others, giving those who serve both a life meaning to pursue and an avenue to reduce painful self-consciousness and self-focused attention, which is endemic to a materialist culture in which few of us measure up to the ideal. Self-consciousness and self-focused attention are also endemic to depression and anxiety problems, making it a relief to focus on helping others, on one's spiritual community, and on one's religious practices instead of the self. The emphasis on service is illustrated in the best-seller, *The Purpose Driven Life* (Warren, 2002) in which the author boldly proclaims that meaning in life from a Christian perspective goes way beyond any selfish concerns for self-actualization and the like. Similarly, the Zen master, Joko Beck says that spiritual maturity in Zen is characterized by an increasing focus on the welfare of others (and all sentient beings), and a decreasing concern for self.

The Giving Tree or Self-Other Principle has wisdom and relevance for pursuing fulfillment in all areas of life and is closely related to the Tenet of Inner Abundance. It is especially relevant, however, for those engaged in Helping Routines on a regular basis:

Giving Tree or Self-Other Principle.

Many people suffer from the *Giving Tree Syndrome;* they become depressed when overwhelmed by outside responsibilities. The Self-Other Principle suggests that we balance the time we devote to helping other people with time for ourselves or self-caring. Self-caring is not selfishness. It is a realistic understanding that we have some basic physical and psychological needs that have to be met before we can be there for anyone else or do anything else. Self-caring can be thought of as self-maintenance. We need to find a balance between extremes of total self-sacrifice and extreme narcissism or selfishness.

As Giving Tree suggests, clients need to approach their service commitments and appointments from a position of Inner Abundance lest they get easily irritated or burned out, thereby missing the happiness-boosting effects of helping and often leaving helpees in the lurch. As Frisch and Gerrard (1981) discuss, helpers must never promise things that they cannot deliver; they also found a relationship between helping as youth and helping and giving as adults, suggesting that Helping Routines started in children and youth may become lifelong habits.

String of Pearls as a Helping Routine or Practice.

All four foundational Tenets for *relationship satisfaction* in QOLT (see Chapter 14) are highly applicable to gaining helping satisfaction and success:

Emotional Honesty
Favor Bank
Expert Friend
String of Pearls

Of all of these, perhaps the most altruistic in tone and practice is String of Pearls. The String of Pearls practice is often cited by clients as a "majorly" helpful part of QOLT. It is an excellent beginning for those skeptical of the happiness-producing properties of Helping; for some, it makes up their entire Helping Routine in QOLT. The String of Pearls Practice and Principle or Tenet follows:

Fast as the rolling seasons bring
The hour of fate to those we love,
Each pearl that leaves the broken string
Is set in Friendship's crown above.

As narrower grows the earthly chain,
The circle widens in the sky;
These are our treasures that remain,
But those are stars that beam on high.
                                   —*Songs of Many Seasons,*
                                      Our Classmate, F.W.C.

In "Our Classmate," Oliver Wendell Holmes Sr. talks about the death of a loved one as the removal of a pearl from a pearl necklace with each pearl denoting a treasured relationship. QOLT speaks of metaphorically building a pearl necklace each day from the positive, kind, and loving interactions that we have with others. Think of every day as a series of interactions with others from loved ones to strangers on the street. Measure your day by these interactions. It can be fun to write them down to see all of the lives you touch or cross paths with each day. The String of Pearls Principle says that the goal each day is to be mindful of every social interaction; paying attention as one interaction starts, unfolds, stops, and another begins. *With each interaction, try to do no harm in terms of being surly or rude or ignoring others; besides doing no harm, try to be kind and responsive in each of your daily interactions. If you are kind, you can judge that interaction as a positive pearl for your necklace for the day.* It doesn't matter if others respond to these pearls of kindness; the pearls are counted even if the other person is too grumpy to accept them.

String of Pearls is meant to become a habit of kindness toward others in every interaction. This principle will become a habit or "no brainer," something we do without thinking that will build deep bonds with those we see on a regular basis (see Favor Bank) and will make us feel good about how we treat strangers. String of Pearls will also eliminate guilt from being rude or dismissive to others. As the How Kind and Serve Others Tenets say, being kind and decent is the essential fruit of most spiritual practices and is something that will brighten our day, increase our enjoyment and satisfaction with life and ourselves, and make the world a better place for others whose paths we cross. Try to be aware and to stop time while we are in these interactions so we can fully attend to the other person (see Mine the Moment Principle).

Using Tenets with Cognitive Therapy to Build Motivation for Routines. In particular, discuss the Tenets with clients as part of a therapy process of listing advantages and disadvantages to a commitment to Helping

activities in general and a specific daily and weekly *Helping Routine.* The Pro versus Con Technique in the Toolbox CD and illustrated in Table 18.1 from Chapter 18 is ideal for this purpose, forcing clients to recall positive reasons for change and to list and dispute reasons to maintain the status quo. Therapists may use clients' own past experiences in Helping and the points at the start of this chapter to build a case for the benefits of Helping.

Marty Seligman, the father of positive psychology, has students and clients compare the happiness-boosting properties of a pure pleasure activity like buying ice cream to a Helping or service activity. Invariably, the results of this Set Up a Test, a cognitive therapy exercise outlined in Chapter 10, is that clients are pleasantly surprised to experience greater satisfaction from Helping than from the selfish pleasure activity. QOLT uses the same or similar exercises to build motivation and to convince clients that Helping is a potentially inexhaustible source of lasting contentment, in contrast to ephemeral physical pleasures that are not lasting (see discussion in Seligman, 2002). To implement Set Up a Test, therapists help clients to plan and pursue some daily or weekly Helping activity over a short period of time (as in volunteering three or four times), observing, evaluating, and reporting back to therapists whether their mood, overall happiness, or other difficulties have improved.

Thought records like the Lie Detector from Chapter 10 can help to dispute killjoy thoughts that keep clients from Helping. Five Paths can help to develop practical rejoinders to starting Helping experiments such as lack of time, too much other work to do, or not knowing what to do for Helping.

Step 2: Identifying Helping Interests and Possibilities That Fit with Personal Goals-and-Values

The next step in building a Helping Routine is for clients to explore and identify all of their Helping interests and flows. As is usually the case in QOLT, start with clients' overall Goals-and-Values from the Vision Quest exercise in the Toolbox CD and Chapter 5. As Freud said, "freedom is a terrible burden"; this is true when selecting among the myriad options for Helping or service. One way to lessen the burden is to consider Helping activities that are directly related to clients Goals-and-Values—valued areas of life and even the *goals* associated with those areas. For example, Betsy who had spiritual reasons for respecting and caring for living nature, including animals, and was a pre-veterinarian student at Baylor volunteered at Fuzzy Friends, the only animal shelter within 100 miles that does not practice euthanasia. This boosted her Helping and, thereby, her overall life satisfaction considerably (see Chapter 3 for the theory for how satisfaction in each particular area contributes to the whole).

As the great psychologist George Kelly suggested with respect to psychological assessment, if you would like to know something about a client, you can simply ask. In this context, "simply ask" clients to recall social service, civic action, and other Helping pursuits they have enjoyed in the past, or ones they have thought about pursuing and that still interest them. After reviewing life Goals-and-Values, therapists may then proceed by challenging clients to choose some specific Helping activities that reflect their most cherished Goals-and-Values, their Helping or service interests, and the time they have available—as determined by a look at their schedules or completed Daily Activity Plans from Chapter 10. Julio decided to spend at least 20 minutes a day in "free play" with his son, allowing him to dictate exactly how they would play for those 20 minutes. In this way, he honored a major interest in his life, did it within the time that was available, and pursued something that reflected his most important Goals-and-Values, the goal of having a family, raising a son, and being a good parent.

Tiffany, a self-described agnostic humanitarian with a passion for the arts, volunteered for the local symphony and children's theatre that brought programs and training to schools whose budgets had squeezed out arts education.

Kristen, an evangelical Christian, increased her involvement in her church by teaching Sunday school to children whom she cared about deeply; as it turned out, she had been horribly neglected herself as a child.

Scott, an observant orthodox Jew, helped to raise money for the local Jewish community center; the associated socializing and "hobnobbing" with like-minded people both raised his happiness and lowered his depression in a way that other psychotherapies had failed to do.

The Helping activity for the latter three of these clients evolved into a new calling or passionate vocation for each person, a common occurrence in Helping interventions in which a type of volunteer work becomes a second career or hobby, giving clients a new focus during their off hours and flow-like distraction

from Big Three worries and emotions (also see Chapter 15 on finding a Calling in Work). Such volunteer positions can turn into paid employment for those who wish to pursue that option as well.

Because many clients and therapists are unaware of the strong happiness-boosting properties of Helping, therapists may ask some direct questions about Helping even when self-report measures indicate no problem. In fact, Helping Routines can be a useful all-purpose intervention or assignment in QOLT, regardless of particular clients' strengths or problems; it is also an effective cure-all for many clients who wish to meet people. This is particularly true of clients with subclinical habit problems—see Chapter 13—or Big Three emotional control problems, as well as clinical levels of depression, anxiety, social phobia, anger, and addiction (as in the case of drug or alcohol abuse). Clients with intractable work or relationship difficulties also benefit from Helping interventions that give a much needed respite from their problems at home or in the office.

QOLT therapists take the stance that the client must usually try a particular activity at least once in order to know for sure whether it is potentially pleasurable or satisfying. In this vein, therapists should encourage clients to adopt the attitude of "I'll try anything once" as long as they have some interest in the activity, as long as the activity is safe and fits with their overall life Goals-and-Values, and as long as the activity does not sabotage their progress in another area of QOLT. For example, it would be foolhardy for a recently abstinent client with alcohol problems to raise money for a favorite charity at a bar where they know that their former drinking buddies will pressure them to drink. At times, going over the Play List of possible recreational activities (in Chapter 16 and the Toolbox CD) will suggest Helping activities as in the case of a jogger who decided to volunteer at the races sponsored by a local running club.

Volunteer Job Enrichment and Finding the Best Helping Positions Available. Table 15.1 details job characteristics that, if maximized, can boost satisfaction and happiness in paid employment (a client version of "Work That Satisfies" is also available in the Toolbox CD). With the exception of Money, all of the characteristics of Work That Satisfies listed and discussed in Table 15.1 can be used to find and choose volunteer or Helping positions. In addition, clients' satisfaction with *existing* volunteer positions can be enhanced with

Work That Satisfies to the extent that current volunteer positions are "enriched" by adding characteristics from Table 15.1 to the current position. For example, Abby, a docent at an art museum and an usher at the local repertory company, chose her volunteer positions based on their fit with her Goals-and-Values and the positive organizational climate at both locations. She enriched the docent job further by arranging for several close friends with whom she could visit to work as well and share the experience (see Table 15.1 and the Socializing Doubles Your Pleasure Tenet).

Step 3: Problem-Solving Obstacles to Helping

Step 3 involves using Five Paths to problem solving around barriers or obstacles to Helping satisfaction. For example, in those instances where there truly is no time for Helping, Five Paths can be utilized to suggest alternatives, as in the case of a homemaker who arranged for time to be a teacher's aide at her childrens' school by joining a babysitting co-op and by asking her husband to watch their preschooler a few extra hours a week.

In my own informal research with several hundred clinical and positive psychology clients who are unhappy with the area of Helping, I've found that most of them feel stymied by under-involvement due to a lack of time, interest, or a compelling cause or issue. Some also did not know how to get involved, had become cynical about the value of service or political action, or lacked logistical support such as transportation. A few clients felt dissatisfied due to over-involvement in this area such that other priorities in life were beginning to suffer—see Balanced Lifestyle Tenet.

Pessimistic clients with a lack of time benefit from doing Lie Detectors to process their worries and negative thoughts and by doing Daily Activity Plans that allowed them to carefully schedule time in order to honor all of their commitments that reflected *all* of their valued areas of life. (Chapter 3 explains the roles of particular areas of life in clients' overall happiness or life satisfaction.) The time management principles described in Chapter 10 have enabled many of my clients to assertively carve out time for Helping activities that they felt didn't exist before.

Busy couples in need of more time together and couples with other relationship problems can effectively problem solve with their partner to find service activities that fit *both* of their Goals-and-Values that they can do *together* (see the Relationship Skills like Workable Compromise in the Toolbox CD and Chapter 14). For example, Martin and Annabel decided to volunteer at a local soup kitchen on holidays and at a food bank at other times. Harry and Janet got involved with precinct politics. Judith and Rodney started a local chapter of the Nature Conservancy along with a support group for parents of children with spina bifida, which their daughter suffered from. Frisch (1992) details a cognitive therapy case in which a shy client began a support group for parents of children with heart disabilities serious enough to make a common cold life threatening. Finally, overly dependent clients often benefit from pursuing Helping activities without their partners when those partners simply refuse to take part.

Social anxiety, poor social skills, or both are often an obstacle to Helping satisfaction when socializing is part of the service activity. In these cases, Relationship Skills from Chapter 14 and the Toolbox CD have to be combined with Helping interventions in order to establish a reliable and satisfying Helping Routine. Indeed, Helping activities are wonderful laboratories for clients with social anxiety to test out new skills and develop greater confidence.

***Resistance and Noncompliance:* If You Always Do What You've Always Done, You'll Always Get What You Always Got.** Anxious and depressed workaholics who claim to have "no time" for Helping can be told that the very fact that they believe they have no time is an indication that they may need to make time to try something new in order to reduce their symptoms, feel better, and maintain sources of satisfaction outside of work—see Balanced Life Tenet; QOLT suggests that if you always do what you've always done, you'll always get what you always got in terms of problems and unhappiness. The *Set Up a Test* approach discussed earlier can also help in combating therapeutic resistance or noncompliance. For example, a harried news reporter was shocked to discover that she was more focused and productive at Work when she "forced" herself to volunteer and help at a shelter for battered women.

As is done with any outside activity or homework that is a part of QOLT, always ask clients before they leave the office to, "Tell me all the reasons you might give me next week for not doing your QOLT exercise?" Having this discussion in a way that shows clients how QOLT "homework" or, preferably "growth exercise or activity" for the week is intimately related to getting their goals in life met for greater happiness, and so on, does much to reduce homework noncompliance with Helping assignments.

Buddy System, Helping Flows, and Premack It. A second way to dramatically improve compliance with Helping and other QOLT assignments and to, very importantly, routinize the activity, is for clients to find a friend, acquaintance, or buddy with whom to do the activity. Clients who volunteer at a hospice or mental hospital together are much more likely to continue on a routine basis. It also helps greatly if the Helping involves a flow activity for clients—see Flow It in the Toolbox CD and Chapter 15—that is rewarded after completion with another high frequency or highly rewarding activity such as having a meal—Premack It Principle. For example, Gail postponed breakfast every Friday until after she had delivered day-old bread to the local food bank. Driving served as a flow activity for her as she explored new routes around the city to complete her rounds.

Step 4: Implement a Helping Routine

Step 4 charges clients to develop and implement a specific Helping Routine. This plan should consider ways to overcome the barriers or obstacles to Helping that clients identified in Step 3. The plan should also include some of the specific Helping activities from Step 2 that best fit clients' interests, the time available for recreation, and clients Goals-and-Values. Helping Routines benefit from the inclusion of the Helping-related Tenets with attitudes, schemas, and practices conducive to greater Helping satisfaction discussed in Step 1 and listed in Table 17.1.

As mentioned earlier, the String of Pearls Practice or Tenet can be an excellent Helping activity to begin with for almost any client. For example, Paloma simply practiced String of Pearls from the Tenets for her Helping Routine; String of Pearls seemed perfect for her because it reflected her love and value of people and relationships and was highly efficient, that is, not time consuming in that it involved the normal interactions of her everyday routine. Furthermore, it touched on relationship goals and needs that she had for herself, thereby accomplishing several ends with one activity.

Step 5: Evaluate Whether Helping Routine Was Carried Out and Increased Satisfaction

In Step 5, therapists and clients evaluate together whether a Helping Routine was carried out completely and whether or not it increased client satisfaction with the area of Helping. In cases where problems are revealed in the implementation of plans in the real world that were not anticipated in Step 3, Step 5 involves a simple repeat of Step 3. In the positive psychology case of Paloma just discussed her routine was too successful. That is, her visiting with everyone she saw throughout the day became excessive, leading her to neglect some of her duties as an electrical engineer testing TV plasma screens. Using a tip from the Habit Control Program from Chapter 13, Paloma corrected her problem by "premacking" her work tasks for the day with String of Pearls visiting such that she would go no further than a kind greeting for those she encountered until after a major job task for the day was completed, after which she rewarded herself with a few minutes of conversation with a colleague or a server at the in-house coffee shop and so on. This modification led to a real enrichment of her job and Work life, according to Paloma and her boss who noticed an improved attitude of kindness and even greater productivity in Paloma.

CHAPTER 18

Learning

HOW CAN LEARNING MAKE US HAPPIER?

In the thirteenth century, searching for a way to overcome the loss of the love of his life Beatrice, Dante Alighieri found just one path that healed: the path of learning in general and the study of philosophy in particular. After a lifetime of pursuing this path, he decided that human beings could only be satisfied and happy if their intellectual and Learning needs were met (Lewis, 2001). In QOLT, Learning is defined as gaining new skills or information about things that interest you. Learning can come from a variety of activities, from reading books to taking classes on subjects such as history, car repair, or computers (Frisch, 1994). Love of learning for its own sake or as a means to an end as in professional training seems to be a universal human strength or motivation no doubt related to our desire for mastery (Peterson & Seligman, 2004). The democratization of learning through the Internet makes it a potential avenue for growth and happiness around the globe. Increasingly advanced Learning and education are requirements for careers involving high flow and intrinsic satisfaction as well as a good standard of living—see Chapters 15 and 20 on Work and Money, respectively. Some level of Learning and education are requirements of many satisfying jobs that compensate those in the field with a salary that provides an adequate standard of living. Likewise, Learning may be an avenue of deep satisfaction related to a fervent avocation such as bridge or golf.

LEARNING PROBLEMS OR DISSATISFACTIONS

Clinical and positive psychology clients often see a need for further education and training, but feel unable to pursue this because of financial constraints, a lack of time, more important priorities such as educating their children, or because they feel they lack the intelligence or ability in an area of interest. Some clients see their poor school performance as the main obstacle to their satisfaction with Learning. They may attribute their poor performance to a variety of factors, ranging from a lack of intelligence or ability, to distracting emotional problems, lack of motivation, or poor study habits. Occasionally, clients may express a desire to take nonacademic courses for recreational purposes, such as classes in ceramics or cooking.

ASSESSMENT RELATED TO LEARNING: THE QOLT WHOLE LIFE PERSPECTIVE ON LEARNING AND CAREER

When a client's Learning is career related and tied to long-term goals like gaining entry to a profession, it helps to have a specific career goal in mind at the start. Thus, the QOLT Work strategies for choosing a career (see Chapter 15 and the Occupational Survey) and Goals-and-Values (e.g., Vision Quest technique) can be very helpful as initial Learning interventions. A career focus can make even the most boring and difficult course tolerable because individuals can see a direct connection between their performance in that course and their future career. For example, many psychology majors have difficulty completing the required statistics course, or even understanding why it is a required part of the curriculum. But when students realize that to get into graduate school and ultimately realize their dream of becoming a psychologist, they must take this course, it motivates them to hunker down, focus their attention, and do what it takes to pass the class. Even a vocational career or long-term goals can guide clients through a maze of learning hoops that they must figuratively jump through to gain the level of proficiency that they desire. For example, the hobby of dog agility training specifies numerous complex levels of proficiencies that partners—that is handlers or humans and their canine agility partners—must meet in order to progress to the next level. Devotees must plan out a detailed curriculum of skill training for themselves and their dogs in order to succeed in this hobby. Those who plan and train poorly with little consultation from Expert Friends—from the Tenets—in the sport can spend months in frustration as they fail to successfully navigate the required courses at agility meets in their area.

Other Learning Strategies

The general strategy or intervention to enhancing Learning satisfaction in QOLT is to establish a Learning Routine or regimen that moves clients toward their long-term Learning goals in a gradual way that minimizes stressors and failures by carefully planning small, incremental experiences of success. Therapists initially ask clients to identify the kinds of learning experiences they want for themselves and then collaboratively brainstorm with clients using Five Paths (see Toolbox) around ways to achieve goals and to handle potential obstacles along the way. Behavioral and cognitive skill training are usually both required. For example, very often obstacles consist of negative thoughts and self-schemas of incompetence or stupidity. Judith was anxious about studying computer science at the university even though she knew that taking advanced classes would greatly enhance her technical abilities. Her pay would also increase as business manager for a thriving group practice of thoracic surgeons. In addition, she felt she also lacked the time and money to take the classes she needed. After completing several Lie Detector and Five Path worksheets from the Toolbox CD to combat her defeatist attitude that she could never learn advanced computing and programming skills, Judith and her therapist set up some experiments to challenge her beliefs—see Set Up a Test from Chapter 10. Specifically, she talked to several friends and colleagues in computing and asked them to show her some of the ropes of advanced computer operation that she needed to get ahead at her office—see Second Opinion and Expert Friend Tenets in

the Toolbox CD. As a result of these cognitive interventions and perfunctory computer skills training, Judith realized that her feelings of incompetence were unfounded and proceeded to master the skills she needed; she found the time and money to pursue her studies in computing using the financial and temporal budgeting techniques offered in Chapters 20 and 10, respectively.

Many QOLT techniques, such as Five Paths, Zen Steps to Success, Relationship Skills, Vision Quest, Occupational Survey, and Set Up a Test, are useful in addressing client's Learning concerns. Therapists use these techniques cognitively to challenge clients' feelings of inadequacy with respect to their ability to learn, intelligence, and ability to effectively study. For example, a math phobic nurse successfully completed a newly required math course for continuing education in a university after debunking her assumptions that she was too "dumb" and more intimidated by the subject than her classmates. Specifically, these assumptions were rejected once she successfully completed a timed arithmetic subtest of an intelligence test administered by her therapist and discovered that her classmates were equally concerned about their performance in the class. Furthermore, her core belief in her math stupidity was traced and challenged via historical review to her abusive father who had attacked her mercilessly whenever she asked for help with homework as a child.

CREATIVITY APPROACH TO GREATER SUCCESS AND SATISFACTION IN LEARNING

According to Sternberg (2003) and others (Csikszenthimahalyi, 1997), creativity is a broad approach to problem solving that, when applied to learning and school difficulities, can:

1. Solve important and difficult problems
2. Lead to deeper intrinsic satisfaction or greater flow in school and other learning situations
3. Increase academic success as well as success in other Learning pursuits (Sternberg, 2003).

For this reason, QOLT recommends the application of Creativity Skills from the Toolbox CD and Box 19.1 from Chapter 19 to clients' learning pursuits. The application may be to problems at school or other learning situations or, in a pure positive psychology sense, to a Learning situation that, while not problematic, could be improved in terms of performance, satisfaction, or both. To implement this strategy, simply discuss ways in which Creativity Skills may be applied to the client's Learning situation or problems.

School Failure Problems

Many clients are disappointed because of their poor school performance. It can be helpful for these clients to get independent assessments of their abilities by a mental health professional who knows how to administer intelligence and achievement tests. Remedial education and paid tutors may be required for some students with learning problems to succeed in traditional academic programs. Parents usually find this well worth the price. For a more specific ability, such as music, parents and clients try finding respected teachers in the field through word-of-mouth referrals in their community or beyond. These expert teachers are then asked to be evaluators of the student's abilities in the field.

Too often, full-time college students don't look at school as a job, which it should be for those who fail by not putting in the hours that they need to succeed. Those who look at school as a job in which they put in at least 8 to 12 hours a day, whether they're in class or not, are much more likely to succeed. Even if they are taking only one class, it can help to define their school job requirements specifically, such as "I will study 3 hours outside of class for every hour I'm in class." Since tests usually cover material not discussed in class, this studying outside of class is a *must* for success in demanding high schools and universities.

ESTABLISHING A LEARNING ROUTINE

Step 1: Build Motivation

As the start of this chapter suggests, some level of Learning and education is a requirement for many satisfying jobs with a good standard of living. Learning may also be valued as an end in and of itself or as an avenue of joy related to a fervent avocation such as bridge. Unless clients see a direct connection between Learning skills and satisfaction and their overall life goals and happiness, intervention in this area is destined to fail. For this reason, once it has been established that learning dissatisfaction exists, therapists at the outset try to help clients view their Learning dissatisfaction as an important contributor to their overall unhappiness and poor or low quality of life.

Step 1 is aimed at building motivation for developing and carrying out Learning Routines. Therapists would do well to consider this step as one in Motivational Interviewing as developed by Bill Miller of the University of New Mexico. To build motivation, start with a reading or discussion with clients of the following Core Tenets related to Learning:

• Find a Meaning/ Find a Goal Principle
• Love What You Do Principle
• Expert Friend Principle
• Play Like a Kid/Frivolous Flows Principle

Next, proceed to a discussion of all of the Tenets related to Learning in Table 18.1. In particular, discuss the Tenets as part of a therapy process of listing advantages and disadvantages to a commitment to Learning activities in general and a specific daily and weekly Learning Routine (Pro versus Con technique). It is also helpful for the therapist to ask clients about their current learning activities and their history in school. A client copy of the Pro versus Con exercise is available in the Toolbox CD; a clinical example of a completed Pro versus Con exercise appears in Box 18.1 on page 276.

Step 2: Identifying Learning Interests and Possibilities That Fit with Personal Goals-and-Values

This step is for clients to explore and identify all of their Learning interests and flows. As is usually the case in QOLT, start with clients' overall Goals-and-Values from the Vision Quest exercise in the Toolbox CD and Chapter 5. The procedures for identifying a career or Calling from Chapter 15 must be applied to all clients with job and career advancement concerns. As Freud said, freedom is a terrible burden; this is especially true in modern education with the overabundance of occupational, disciplinary/major, and even interdisciplinary options in fields like quality of life research. One way to lessen the burden is to consider only Learning activities or educational options that

Table 18.1   Tenets with Attitudes, Schemas, and Practices Conducive to Greater Satisfaction with *Learning*

Ask Your Death Tenet

Attack the Moment or Mine the Moment Principle

Balanced Lifestyle Principle

Be the Peace You Seek or Worry Warts Principle

The Big Three Makes Us Dumb Principle—Emotional Control Principle

Blind Dumb Optimism Principle

Calculated Risk Principle

Care for My One Body Principle

Cocoon It Rule

Creativity Routine Principle

Curb or Ignore Desires Principles (see also You Can't Have It All Principle)

Daily Vacation Principle

Don't Bring It Home or Work Spillover Principle

Do What You Love or Tune in to What Turns You on Principle

Exercise or Take your Medication Principle

Expect the Unexpected Principle

Expert Friend Principle

Face the Music Principle

Failure Quota Principle

Find a Meaning/ Find a Goal Principle

Flow It Principle

The FOOBS Principle or Switch Out of FOOBS Principle or the Multiple Personality or Multiple Personality of Everyday Life

Get Organized Principle

Habits Rule Rule or Routines Rule Rule

Happiness from Achievement Principle

Happiness Is a Choice Principle or Responsibility Principle

Happiness Matters Principle

Happiness Set Point Principle (see also Personality Stays the Same Principle)

Humor Principle

I Can Do It Principle

Inner Abundance Principle

Intellectual Masturbation Principle

Kiss the Past Goodbye Principle

Leisurely Pace and Lifestyle Principle

Live Your Dream or 24/7 Principle

Love What You Do Principle

Love Where You Are Principle (see also Tangled Web Principle or Web of Support)

Lower Expectations Principle (see also Never Good Enough Principle)

Manage Your Time and Your Life Rule

Meanings Like Buses Rule

Mental Health Day Technique

Modest Goal Principle

No Conditions of Worth Rule

One-Thing-at-a-Time Principle (OTAAT)

Overthinking Principle

Play Like a Kid/Frivolous Flows Principle

Pocket of Time to Relax Principle

Process Goal Principle

Quality Time Principle

The Question Rule

Role Model Principle (see also What Would My Role Model Do Principle)

Second Opinion Principle or Technique

Self-Acceptance Principle

Stop Second Guessing Principle

Strength It Principle

Success Principle

Thou Shalt Be Aware or Psychephobia Principle

The Three Rs of Stress Management Principle

You Are What You Do

Note: In cases of Tenets with two names, they are listed by the first name (with the second name following).

BOX 18.1

Pro versus Con Technique: Clinical Example

Name: _____   Date: _____

Part I Instructions: This exercise builds motivation for managing negative habits, "addictions" or what psychologists call "compulsive behaviors" like smoking or overeating. Another Health concern is to build "positive addictions" like daily physical activity such as walking. This exercise can build motivation for positive addictions as well. Finally, this exercise can help build motivation for positive habits or *routines* you are trying to start in areas like Helping, Learning, Creativity, Play or recreation. The *Pro versus Con Technique* can help build the motivation you need to stay on track and accomplish your life goals and objectives. To do this technique, first write out an Objective or Goal at the top of a piece of paper having to do with a *habit* or *routine* that you would like to stop, manage better, or increase. Next, divide the sheet of paper into two columns, writing "Pro" over the left column and "Con" over the right column. Under the "Pro" column, write all the reasons you can think of (at <u>least</u> five) why achieving this goal or establishing this habit would be good for you. Under the "Con" column, be honest about listing all the reasons why you don't want to pursue this goal or cultivate this habit. Steve's Pro vs. Con exercise is written below:

Pros or Advantages of Reaching My Goal	Cons or Disadvantages of Reaching My Goal
I'll be a better teacher.	*I don't have to do this to keep my job.*
I'll get a pay raise.	*I don't have the time.*
I'll feel less burned out by learning new ideas.	*I'm too lazy.*
I'll meet some new fellow-teachers and may meet a potential friend or girlfriend.	*I may fail.*
I'll move a one small "Zen step" closer to getting my Master's degree.	
I'll be less bored at night with a class to study for.	

Case Note: By keeping a list of these advantages and disadvantages taped to his refrigerator, Steve stopped "raiding" the refrigerator and studied more in the evenings. After thinking about the "cons" of taking the class, Steve also had well rehearsed counterarguments on the "tip of his tongue" so that he could not use a "Con" reason as an excuse not to study. For example:

Part II Instructions: Build motivation further by challenging your Cons from Part I. For each Con, write why is wrong for you or a bad idea.

Cons or Disadvantages to Positive Change	Counterargument to Con or Why Con Is a Bad Idea
I don't have to take this class to keep my job.	*No, but I* do *have to do it to advance or get a raise! Anyway, I'm not happy to just "get by" at work. I need a challenge to stay "fresh" and sharp as a teacher. If I "Flow It" (see Tenet) and make my all day job a "flow," I'll be happy all day, every day! You lose flow without increasing the complexity of something so I need this class to keep teaching interesting and rewarding.*

are related to valued areas of life and even the goals associated with those areas. For example, some clients from working class families, refuse to leave the immediate geographical area for further education because it means too great a separation from their families and extended families. Learning for its own sake along with Learning related to avocations or hobbies, that is, Frivolous Flows, is also tied to specific interests or areas of study that must be identified in order to proceed to the next step of developing a *Learning Routine.*

After reviewing clients' life Goals-and-Values, therapists proceed by challenging them to choose some specific Learning goals and activities that reflect their most cherished Goals-and-Values, their interests, and the time they have available—as determined by a look at their schedules or completed Daily Activity Plans. Most often these relate to the following options of:

- Formal education related to clients' Work or career from a regionally accredited college or community college.
- Formal or informal continuing education related specifically to one's Work or career as in nurses, social worker, surgeons, and insurance salespeople taking seminars to keep up with their respective professions.
- Formal education related to clients' Play, pastimes, or hobbies apart from any Work responsibilities that they might have.
- Informal education related to clients' Play, pastimes, or hobbies apart from of any Work responsibilities that they might have.

For example, Marvin went to community and technical college to gain draftsman and mechanic skills since he could not afford or qualify for sufficient financial aid to area colleges. With much guidance and support, Melissa was accepted with a full scholarship to Princeton, after being discouraged from going away to school by her "blue and pink collar" parents who secretly wanted her around for friendship in the absence of a loving marriage. Julian took classes in animation at a technical school as a form of Play or fun and as a break from a difficult job as an insurance adjuster.

Identifying Learning Goals and Activities. There are several ways that QOLT therapists can elicit potential Learning activities from clients who may be at a loss to think of ways to find outlets for Learning. For example, this may be done informally by having clients think about avenues of Learning that they have enjoyed in the past, or ones they have only thought about pursuing and that still interest them.

For Mark, a depressed client who had been working as a hair stylist, Learning meant going to a local community college to study nursing in order to increase the prestige and pay of his Work. For George, an insurance adjuster, Learning meant taking classes and workshops in order to keep up with the new developments in the insurance field. For Angie, taking classes in piano and studying needlework on her own was an important expression of Learning, self-care, and Inner Abundance in her otherwise harried life, making her a more loving mother and wife in the process.

In contrast, Mike had to find his Learning opportunities outside of the usual places like local universities, community colleges, or technical schools. He was interested in learning more about his hobbies of running and martial arts. By asking people at work and friends at his Temple, he was able to find an expert in Aikado karate who was willing to take him on as a student in return for Mike's help in teaching some of his karate classes for young people. After attending a few local running races, Mike joined a runners' club and learned how to prepare for his first marathon. Pursuing Learning opportunities takes good problem-solving skills and often, good relationship skills as well. The "detective" work of exploring local resources can be enjoyable and exciting for clients, while getting them used to taking risks in order to improve their happiness, an essential skill in Quality of Life Therapy.

Step 3: Problem-Solving Obstacles to Learning

Step 3 involves problem solving with the aid of Five Paths around barriers or obstacles to Learning satisfaction in the client's life.

Poor Study Skills and Classroom Performance. Many clients effectively use the Expert Friend or the Second Opinion Tenet from the Toolbox CD to learn more about good study habits. In the former instance, clients talk to friends who do well in school and ask them for tips on study routines, taking notes, and taking tests. An often neglected source of information is the course instructor. Student clients are taught to think of their instructors as their employee since their tuition dollars are paying teacher salaries. This encourages some unassertive clients to visit instructors during office hours to make specific appointments for the same purpose. Use the Relationship Skills of Emotional Honesty (Chapter 14) to teach clients to ask their instructor specific questions such as:

- How can I best study for your tests?
- What material do you emphasize on tests? Are Powerpoint lectures more important than information from the text?
- Would you look at my notes to see if they are adequate?
- What *kind* of questions will be on your tests—multiple choice, short-answer, essay, or a combination of these?
- Would you please explain these points from your lecture and the text that I am unsure of?
- Do you know of a good tutor I could hire to help me in this class?
- Given my current grades, do I have a chance at the grade I want or would I be better off to drop the class and start over?
- What kind of career options exist for this area of study? Is the job market good?
- May I assist you in your research in order to learn more about this area and in order to get a letter or recommendation for graduate school?
- Would you go over my test with me to help me see what I did wrong?
- Can you recommend a good graduate or professional school in this area? Do I have the qualifications to get in?

A lack of ability or skill in Learning or school can also be solved through classroom instruction or bibliotherapy on study skills or reading comprehension—two essential skills for success in traditional learning environments. In keeping with the rationale for two-track QOLT layed out in Chapter 1, evidence-based treatment for adult or child ADHD and other learning disabilities and problems is often necessary for educational success for clients with these disabilities.

Some clients have problems with worry or guilt about taking time away from work, family, or household duties in order to pursue Learning. These clients often benefit from doing Lie Detectors—Chapter 10

and the Toolbox CD—to process their worries and negative thoughts and by doing Daily Activity Plans—Chapter 10 and the Toolbox CD—that allow them to schedule time for Work, family responsibilities, and Learning so that they don't neglect their work or family too much when furthering their education or knowledge base. Family or couples therapy can work wonders in clarifying expectations among family members vis à vis the Learner in the family. For example, Millicent had problems with an unwilling partner in pursing further education and Learning. Using Five Paths and single sessions with QOLT therapists, the partners agreed to "take turns" pursuing courses and degrees with Millicent going first.

Clients with a lack of time for either vocational or avocational Learning often benefit from using the time management principles and Daily Activity Plan described in Chapter 10 and the Toolbox CD. These skills have taught many clients to assertively carve out time for Learning activities that they felt didn't exist before.

Take a B or Divorce.   Often negative core beliefs are an obstacle to Learning satisfaction, as in the case of people who define their self-worth strictly in terms of how well they perform in their educational classes. In these cases, major changes in their Life Script, Goals-and-Values, and attitudes are needed. For example, one of my perfectionist clients, Jamie, who insisted on all A's in her coursework, through the use of a Good-Not-Great worksheet in the Toolbox CD and in Chapter 8 and through a session with her and her husband, decided that accepting a B in her coursework would not impact her professional placement in occupational health medicine and was essential to her mood control and marital satisfaction. It was only when she accepted that her husband would end their marriage if she did not devote less time to her studies, that she decided to "live with" lower grades to gain credentials in her new medical subspecialty and sustain her marriage.

Other obstacles can get in the way of Learning satisfaction such as a lack of money to pay for classes, a job that demands all of clients' free time in order for them to stay employed—making further education impossible—a lack of academic ability or motivation sufficient to pass required classes, and the presence of a physical disability like MS that requires greater accessibility to classrooms. Creatively problem solving around each of these issues using Five Paths can overcome obstacles to Learning satisfaction. For example, Randy, an Iraq War vet with two amputated legs successfully lobbied a college president to make a Sciences building more accessible or risk adverse publicity and even a lawsuit.

Preventing Noncompliance in Learning Assignments. As is done with any outside activity or homework that is a part of QOLT, always ask clients before they leave the office: "What are all the reasons you might give me next week for not doing your Learning exercise?" Having this discussion in a way that shows clients how QOLT homework for the week is intimately related to getting their goals in life met for greater happiness, and so on, does much to reduce homework noncompliance. This is how resistance or noncompliance is dealt with in QOLT and other cognitive therapy approaches.

Buddy System, Learning Flows, and Premack It. A second way to dramatically improve compliance with Learning and other QOLT assignments and to, very importantly, routinize the activity, is for clients to find a friend, acquaintance, or buddy with whom to do the activity. Clients who go to school and study together are much more likely to continue successfully. It also helps greatly if the Learning involves a flow for clients—see Flow It in the Toolbox CD and in Chapter 15—that is rewarded after completion with another high frequency or highly rewarding activity such as having a meal—Premack It Principle. For example, many clients will not eat lunch or breakfast or get online until after they have studied their favorite flow subjects of English literature and history.

Step 4: Implement a Learning Plan or Routine

Step 4 charges clients to develop and implement a specific Learning Plan or Routine. This Plan should consider ways to overcome the barriers or obstacles to Learning that clients identified in Step 3. The plan should also include some of the specific Learning goals and activities from Step 2 that best fit clients interests, the time available for further education, and clients' Goals-and-Values. A Learning Plan can benefit from the inclusion of the Learning-related Tenets with attitudes, schemas, and practices conducive to greater Learning satisfaction discussed in Step 1 and listed in Table 18.1. The therapist should encourage the client to actually engage in a particular Learning activity at least once in order to know for sure whether he or she finds it pleasurable or satisfying. Ask the client to adopt the attitude of "I'll try anything once" when it comes to Learning opportunities that fit their Goals-and-Values.

Step 5: Evaluate Whether Learning Routine Was Carried Out and Increased Satisfaction

In Step 5, therapists and clients evaluate together whether a Learning Routine was carried out completely and successfully—Did clients pass a GED exam, a required course, or continuing education class?—and whether or not it increased clients satisfaction with the area of Learning. In cases where problems are revealed in the implementation of plans in the real world that were not anticipated in Step 3, Step 5 involves a simple repeat of Step 3.

CHAPTER 19

Creativity

REDEFINING CREATIVITY TO CLIENTS

In his biography of Walt Whitman, David Reynolds (1996) writes that Whitman was "tarred, feathered, and ridden out of town by angry Long Islanders after he was accused of sodomy." Out of the torpor that ensued, emerged poems of ecstasy as Whitman, the "poet of America" began to establish himself. Perhaps we create to master our fate, overcome disappointments, and conquer personal demons. This model has been applied to other creative minds such as Van Gogh and John Lennon (Coleman, 1992). In Lennon's case, his album with the Plastic Ono Band was released on December 11, 1970, after therapy with Arthur Janov. The album speaks of an art born out of pain and in keeping with the Thou Shalt Be Aware Tenet. Speaking of his parents, Lennon says, "They didn't want me, so they made me a star." Lennon's father, a merchant shipman, abandoned his mother. His mother subsequently abandoned him to her sister, Aunt Mimi, after a stepfather refused to have him living in the same house (Coleman, 1992). Unfortunately, many clients never consider Creativity as an avenue of self-expression, self-healing, self-realization, and satisfaction. Why?

Narrow definitions of Creativity focus on a magical and inherent virtuoso skill in the arts, such as, painting or playing a musical instrument. This narrow definition can be a major obstacle to creative expression and satisfaction in clients. If clients assume that they can only be creative in these few particular areas after years of instruction aimed at a ridiculously high level of perfection, they may never pick up a paintbrush or even sing in the shower. QOLT therapists present a broader and less perfectionistic view of creativity to clients, brainstorming with them on ways to be creative in all areas

of life, including their recreation/Play, relationships, job, community, caring for children and frail elders, cooking, decorating, or even planning dinner parties and other gatherings.

A BROADER, LESS PERFECTIONISTIC DEFINITION

In QOLT, Creativity is defined as using your imagination to come up with new and clever ways to solve everyday problems or to pursue a hobby like painting, photography, or needlework. This can include decorating your home, playing the guitar, or finding a new way to solve a problem at work (Frisch, 1994). This definition is purposefully broad, allowing for creativity in many different types of activities. The QOLT definition, like that of Sternberg (2003), emphasizes ability to assertively go beyond given information and imagine new and exciting ways of reformulating old problems. Creativity is most simply creative or original problem solving in any or all spheres of life. It often involves self-expression or the expression of clients' unique and original ideas. Similarly, Irving Yalom (1980) in *Existential Psychotherapy* sees broadly defined creativity as a major avenue of life meaning and purpose:

> The creative path to meaning is by no means limited to the creative artist. The act of scientific discovery is a creative act of the highest order. Even bureaucracy may be approached creatively. . . . A creative approach to teaching, to cooking, to play, to study, to bookkeeping, to gardening adds something valuable to life. (p. 436)

Just as we may be creative or artistic in painting a painting, writing a poem, or doing needlework or photography, we may be equally creative in solving everyday problems at work or home. We can creatively stretch a paltry budget to plan a nice meal or a party. The writer Ann Cushman (1992) also defines creativity broadly; "most of us . . . assume that creativity means taking up pen or paintbrush, when in truth creativity can mean anything from innovation on the assembly line to an afternoon stroll that turns into an improvisation for an audience of one." The artist Suzy Gablik (1991) suggests in her book, *The Reenchantment of Art,* that we broaden our definition of artistic expression. She believes that we can develop and apply our creative potential in order to foster healthy relationships and even address pressing social problems such as environmental destruction, poverty, and homelessness.

BENEFITS OR WHY CREATIVITY MATTERS

These broad definitions of Creativity as a means of self-expression and problem solving are visible in everyday acts in all parts of life and the fact that Creativity is important to the happiness of many as revealed in psychological tests like the QOLI, flies in the face of the conventional wisdom that creative self-expression may not be particularly important to the average person or even to our society. First of all, more clients identify creativity as important to their happiness when presented with the broader definition of Creativity used here. They crave a way to express their uniqueness, originality, viewpoints, and feelings as they deal with pressures of conformity in their Work and social roles. They search for creative solutions to problems at work and at home. Additionally, in my work, with both poor and affluent clients, I see many cases in which creative problem solving or a creative outlet has had a snowball effect, leading to a new passion or pastime and greater self-understanding, energizing clients in all of their pursuits, and conferring a general self-confidence.

As a potential hobby, Frivolous Flow (see Tenet), or pastime, creative self-expression can be a major ingredient of a client's *happiness stew* whether the client is retired, in school, or in a demanding profession (Csikszentmihalyi & Hunter, 2003; Vaillant, 2002). For example, visual arts projects like painting and drawing are an oasis of calm, flow, and satisfac-

tion in the competitive, hurly burly world of adolescence (Csikszentmihalyi & Hunter, 2003). As viewed by Sternberg (2003) and others, creativity is a broad approach to problem solving that when applied to work, learning, and school difficulties, can solve important and vexing problems, leading to deep intrinsic satisfaction, external accolades and promotions, and increased income (Csikszentmihalyi, 1997; Sternberg, 2003). Finally, as an approach to its traditional domain of artistic self-expression in the arts, creativity is essential (Sarason, 1990).

COGNITIVE INTERVENTIONS TO ENCOURAGE CREATIVE SELF-EXPRESSION AND PROBLEM SOLVING IN ALL AREAS OF LIFE

Not a Magical Inborn Talent

Even if we believe that creativity is a crucial part of happiness for many, to the extent we need pastimes and flows as well as new solutions to problems at home and work, we must overcome the idea that the capacity for creative expression is possessed only by a talented few, damning the rest of us to be spectators or *consumers* rather than *creators* of art. (The same may be said of sports.) Like social and positive psychologist, Mike Csikszentmihalyi (1997), psychologist Seymour Sarason (1990) directly challenges this belief in his book, *The Challenge of Art to Psychology.* He states that "artistic activity is a unique, universal potential of *all* humans. . . . All people have the capacity to derive satisfaction from artistic activity in some way at some level" (p. 1). Sarason goes on to point out how our society has mistakenly de-emphasized the importance of creativity in our educational system and how we are sometimes told that we lack talent merely because we cannot create "carbon copy" representations of the world through art. Thus, if we can't draw an exact likeness of our parents or a scene in nature, we are taught to believe, erroneously, that we have no creative or artistic ability.

Too often the "extravagant creativity of childhood" is crushed by the demands of realism and practicality are imposed by parents, schools, and society. In contrast, art saturates daily living in many non-Western cultures. As the Balinese put it, "We have no art, everything we do is art." QOLT maintains that creativity is an important part of being human, a vital force for many without which we can exist but not truly live. While many of us have become alienated from it, the damage is not irreversible. We may tap and develop our creative skills and potential if we first accept the view of leading scholars that Creativity is a skill that can be developed. We may then tap and develop our creative potential if we are willing to simply let our guard down. This may involve "shame attacking" exercises in the Albert Ellis sense, as we experiment with creative self-expression despite harsh criticism regarding the quality of our work from ourselves and others.

Creativity Routine Rationale

The following is one way to present the QOLT view of creativity and art to clients:

> Many of us have been told we are dumb, stupid, or inadequate when it comes to being an artist or doing something creative. Art used to be something that *everyone* did as a way of saying who they are and creating something unique and different from other people. The art world is full of examples of acclaimed works by so-called "primitive artists" like Grandma Moses who had little or no training for what has traditionally been defined as "art." Anyone who has personal and unique thoughts and feelings can express them creatively in traditional or nontraditional ways. Additionally, creativity is increasingly seen by psychologists as a way to solve problems in life and not just an avenue of self-expression or telling the world how you see things. *Can you think of ways that you have been or could be creative? Could any of this make you a happier person? I guess we won't know for sure unless we test it out . . .*

A structured thought record like the Lie Detector in the Toolbox CD is sometimes necessary to combat clients' killjoy thoughts about Creativity. For example, many clients successfully combat negative automatic thoughts with challenges like "the goal of recreational art or creativity is to simply relax and forget yourself and your troubles by immersing yourself into some flow or activity that you find compelling." According to this view of the arts, it doesn't matter what other people think of clients' art if *they* find it to be a satisfying release from the tensions of the day. Of course, the only way clients will really know if creative art-

work can help them to be happier or more satisfied is if they try it.

Collaborative Empiricism in Testing Negative Schemas about Your Creative Potential

The therapist can overcome obstacles to creative pursuits by presenting QOLT's *alternative view* of creativity and art and then by encouraging clients to Set Up a Test (see Emotional Control techniques in Chapter 10) to see if a creative activity might give them a feeling of accomplishment or pleasure. In keeping with Zen Steps to Success discussed in Chapter 10, therapists should start small, with "sure fire" activities that take little time.

In-Session Creativity Homework

Rather than getting bogged down with clients in arguing whether creativity could be fulfilling, the therapist would do well to pull out some drawing pencils, clay, finger paints, or a karaoke machine to *test* the client's assumption in the real world. Allowing clients to dance or play air guitar to a favorite song of theirs is also a possibility—either in session or as homework. Participant modeling by the therapist can also reduce the risk of the client's perception of failure. If comfortable enough to do so, the therapist can do an activity with the client thereby modeling the type of creativity aimed at *losing the self* in a flow experience aimed at having fun, instead of an exercise in perfectionism, ruminative self-criticism, and "torture." To be consistent and honest, any homework or personal growth exercises or assignments should be started with clients in session to increase the odds that they are understood and will be completed outside of the session.

Sharing Research Findings to Challenge Assumptions

Clients may also feel encouraged that there is research to suggest that creative activities can be flows (see Flow It Tenet), activities that give deep satisfaction and that result in a loss of self-consciousness, worry, and time whenever we do them. Creative acts of self-expression and problem solving can also raise self-esteem, self-confidence, and enthusiasm for life in anyone including teenagers, older persons, persons of color, uptight

White people such as the author, positive psychology clients, and those with psychological disturbances, below-average intelligence, or disadvantaged status (Flanagan, 1978; Sarason, 1990; Vaillant, 2002). These same authors and others present evidence that *anyone's* creativity can be discovered, enhanced, and developed through some initial instruction and encouragement. Clients may test out this assumption themselves by taking a low-cost creative arts class at a community college or getting instruction from a friend.

Creative Homework

Therapists can help clients explore their creativity with simple assignments like "Make a drawing with crayons or markers," or "Write a poem, story, or journal entry and bring it to the next session." "Write a poem about your work problem or existential angst." In giving these assignments, the therapist should emphasize that art is meant to be playful, energizing, or relaxing and that perfectionism and criticism destroy the potential fun.

QOLT therapists may, at times, give homework assignments in creativity that have nothing to do with the traditional arts. For example, a depressed client felt a deep sense of satisfaction and accomplishment after she cleaned and decorated her house in, what was for her, a new and creative way. Another client congratulated herself on her creativity in using the Five Paths to fashion a new work schedule for her nursing colleagues that would honor most of their needs and priorities.

Creating a Nonperfectionist Space

Quality of Life Therapy asks that clients not be perfectionists in their creative pursuits. Clients should be told to trust their intuition and to paint, write, or dance whatever they are feeling in the moment. Clients should also be urged to "create boldly" in so far as they don't cross things out and focus on the *process* rather than the final product and its quality or perfection—see Process Goal Tenet.

Try asking clients to create a thematic scrap book page, poem, painting, dance, story, or song for the pure pleasure of doing it instead of trying to impress someone with the quality of the work. If the work of art engages us fully, is relaxing or energizing, and allows us to express something unique and important about our-

selves, then it is successful, according to the definitions used in QOLT. That is, the process is more important than the product, although *primitive art* products are noteworthy and valuable, too. Again, recall the work of Grandma Moses.

Encourage clients not to "psycho- or over-analyze" their creative products but simply to enjoy them (Overthinking Principle). Clients should also be reminded that special talent and training is not necessary and that they can develop their own unique approach to artistic creation. Finally, clients should be encouraged to establish a regular Creative Routine or ritual for their creative pursuits or art, so that they may gain the relaxation and flow benefits on a regular basis—see Frivolous Flow Tenet.

CREATIVITY SKILL TRAINING AND PRACTICE

The cognitive interventions just discussed are combined with 16 specific skills culled from the author's theory and practice and from the literature that may reliably enhance clients' Creativity, creative problem solving, or creative self-expression across all domains of human endeavor from art to science to business (Csikszentmihalyi, 1997; Sarason, 1990; Sternberg, 2003). Although more research is needed, QOLT assumes that these same skills can enhance creative problem solving in everyday matters at home and work and even in relationships. Box 19.1 lists *Creativity Skills* to encourage self-expression and problem solving. Also see Relationship Skills in the Toolbox CD and in Chapter 14 for cultivating Creativity in the sphere of *relationships*.

CREATIVITY ROUTINE

Step 1: Build Motivation

As the start of this chapter suggests, for those who value it, Creativity is a vital part of overall happiness and contentment. Since many clients are not aware of the relationship between creative satisfaction and their overall quality of life, therapists should remind clients of this when possible, using for example, Weighted

BOX 19.1

Creativity Skills to Encourage Creative Self-Expression and Problem Solving in all Areas of Life

Instructions: Creativity refers to using your imagination to come up with new and clever ways to solve everyday problems or to pursue a hobby like painting, photography, or needlework. This can include decorating your home, playing the guitar, or finding a new way to solve a problem at work (Frisch 1994). *Creativity is most simply creative or original problem solving in all or any sphere of life.* Creativity is viewed by leading psychologists as something that can be learned, cultivated, and even *chosen*. As a potential hobby or *Frivolous Flow*—see Tenet, creative self-expression can be a hugely important ingredient of our overall happiness. As an approach to work, learning, and school, *creativity* can solve vexing problems, leading to accolades, promotions, and increased income. As an approach to its traditional domain of artistic expression, creativity is essential. Adopt the attitude of "I'll try anything once" and search for a Creativity Routine, habitual activity, or positive addiction that gives you a chance to express yourself in a creative way on a daily basis. Include as many of the following skills for developing and maintaining creativity that you can use:

1. Stay optimistic about your ability to become more creative. Remember that creativity can be learned, cultivated, and even chosen.
2. Try to think of new and clever ways to solve everyday problems or to pursue a hobby—this is all that creativity amounts to.
3. Be willing to take risks and to go against the traditional ways of seeing and doing things. Appeals to do things as we have always done them fall on deaf ears for creative problem solvers.
4. Carve out a lot of uninterrupted time when you are at your best for creative pursuits.
5. Have the courage to disagree with others and even your own old ways of thinking as you come up with new ways to define and solve problems.
6. Fall in love with problems, allowing yourself the time and patience to mull them over in a relaxed but persistent way.
7. Use the Five Paths exercise to analyze, mull over, and generate solutions to problems in a relaxed but persistent way.
8. Be assertive about getting the time, resources, training, and help that you need to pursue your creative pursuits.
9. Design work spaces and other parts of your environment so that they are inviting and encourage your creative pursuits.
10. Find creative flows or activities that have clear-cut goals and that take all of your attention so that time passes quickly and you stop thinking about yourself—see *Flow It Tenet*. In other words, find ways to be creative that totally mesmerize or engross you.
11. Cultivate creativity by pursuing one or more *Frivolous Flows* or hobbies—see Tenets.
12. Harness or preserve some of your highest energy and enthusiasm each day for creative pursuits.
13. Bring an open, playful, curious, but highly focused mind to problem solving to creatively solve problems from a digital art project to discussing a serious conflict with your teenager. Focus requires long stretches of time to look at the problem in different ways with complete concentration and without hurrying.
14. Put your ego on the shelf as you grapple with problems; the truly creative people are humble problem solvers fascinated by the problems they encounter—see *Humble Servant Tenet*.
15. Stay open and sensitive to new possibilities of viewing and doing things.
16. Persevere through trials and tribulations. Do not give up easily when problems arise that seem to defy any type of creative solution. Learn to live with difficulties as you attempt to solve them by taking breaks and by spending time on problem solving—Expert Friends can be invaluable here as can simple time for reflection. Make time to sit and mull over difficult problems. Brainstorm (see Five Paths) creative solutions to problems in all spheres of life whether in a ceramics studio or the lunchroom at work.

Satisfaction Profiles and ratings from the QOLI introduced in Chapter 5. For many, creativity is also an untapped source of happiness that can be learned and developed to an extent in everyone. Unless clients agree with this, intervention in this area is destined to fail. Step 1 is aimed at cultivating *positive addictions* or Creativity Routines. Therapists would do well to consider this step as one in Motivational Interviewing as developed by Bill Miller and his colleagues at the University of New Mexico (Miller & Rollnick, 2002). To build motivation, start with a reading or discussion with clients of the Skills and Tenets related to Creativity in Box 19.1 and Table 19.1, respectively. In particular, discuss the *Creativity Skills* and Tenets as part of a therapy process of listing advantages and disadvantages to a commitment to Creativity, in general, and to a specific daily or weekly *Creativity Routine*. The Pro versus Con technique in the Toolbox CD and illustrated in Box 18.1 from Chapter 18 is ideal for this purpose, forcing clients to recall positive reasons for change and to list and dispute negative reasons for the status quo.

Step 2: Identifying Creativity Interests and Possibilities That Fit with Personal Goals-and-Values

The second step in developing a *Creative Routine* is for clients to explore and identify all of their Creativity interests and flows. As is usually the case in QOLT, start with clients' overall Goals-and-Values from the Vision Quest exercise in the Toolbox CD and Chapter 5. Consider ways to pursue satisfaction in each valued area of life with the skills of Creativity or creative problem solving—see Creativity Skills in Box 19.1.

After reviewing life Goals-and-Values, therapists proceed by challenging clients to choose some specific Creativity goals and activities that reflect their most cherished Goals-and-Values, their creative interests, and the time they have available—as determined by a look at their schedules or completed Daily Activity Plans. Aaron wrote poems about his problems at Work as a way to gain perspective and new ideas about solutions—as he had not discussed these problems with anyone before he found the exercise very useful and fulfilling in keeping with the work of Pennebacker and his colleagues (Pennebacker & Stone, 2004). As the Socializing Doubles Your Pleasure Tenet says, family members and friends can be included in creative pur-

suits as Helen and Don, two design engineers for Hewlett-Packard did in forming a family "oldies" "garage band" with their older children. Paraphrasing the popular spiritual adage, Helen and Don, assert that "the family that plays together, stays together."

Identifying Creative Activities or Flows in Home, Work, and Leisure/Play. There are several ways that QOLT therapists may elicit potential *Creative Activities or Flows*. For example, this is done informally by having clients think about creative pursuits they have enjoyed in the past, or ones they have thought about pursuing and that still interest them. Clients are also challenged about ways to be creative problem solvers on the job, at work, and in relationships. Finally, the Play List in Chapter 16 and the Toolbox CD has been invaluable in suggesting creative *flows* to clients.

Step 3: Problem-Solving Obstacles to Creativity

Step 3 involves problem solving with *Five Paths* around barriers or obstacles to satisfaction with Creativity. In my own informal research with clinical and positive psychology clients who are unhappy with the area of Creativity, I've found that most of them see a lack of time or talent as the major obstacles to their satisfaction. Thus, clients felt they didn't have the time for things like painting, home redecoration, or playing a musical instrument. Others felt artistically "stupid" or "retarded"; for these an education about the definition of creativity used in this chapter was necessary to get the therapy back on track.

Some clients have had problems with worry or guilt about taking time away from work, family, or household duties in order to pursue Creativity flows or activities. These clients often benefit from doing Lie Detectors to process their worries and negative thoughts and by doing Daily Activity Plans that allow them to schedule time for Work and Creativity so that they don't neglect their Work and so on as a result of increased Creative activities. Those who found ways to be Creative *in their jobs* felt wonderful about "killing two birds with one stone" as they boosted their happiness in several areas at once.

The time management principles and Daily Activity Plan described in Chapter 10 have helped many clients to assertively carve out time for Creativity that they felt didn't exist before. Additionally, clients who haven't

Table 19.1   Tenets of Contentment with Attitudes, Schemas, and Practices Conducive to Greater Satisfaction with Creativity

Attack the Moment or Mine the Moment Principle

Balanced Lifestyle Principle

Be the Peace You Seek or Worry Warts Principle

Be Your Own Guru or Personal Wisdom Principle

The Big Three Makes Us Dumb Principle—Emotional Control Principle

Blind Dumb Optimism Principle

Calculated Risk Principle

Cocoon It Rule

Color Purple Principle

Commune with Nature Rule (see also Li Po Rule)

Creativity Routine Principle

Curb or Ignore Desires Principles (see also You Can't Have It All Principle)

Daily Vacation Principle

Don't Bring It Home or Work Spillover Principle

Do What You Love or Tune in to What Turns You on Principle

Exercise or Take your Medication Principle

Expect the Unexpected Principle

Expert Friend Principle

Face the Music Principle

Failure Quota Principle

Find a Goal Principle (see also Find a Meaning Principle)

Flow It Principle

The FOOBS Principle or Switch Out of FOOBS Principle or the Multiple Personality or Multiple Personality of Everyday Life

Get Organized Principle

Habits Rule Rule or Routines Rule Rule

Happiness from Achievement Principle

Happiness Is a Choice Principle or Responsibility Principle

Happiness Matters Principle

Happiness Set Point Principle (see also Personality Stays the Same Principle)

Humor Principle

I Can Do It Principle

I'll Think about That Tomorrow Principle

Inner Abundance Principle

Intellectual Masturbation Principle

Kiss the Past Goodbye Principle

Leisurely Pace and Lifestyle Principle

Life Satisfaction Breeds Job/Work Satisfaction

Live Your Dream or 24/7 Principle

Love What You Do Principle

Love Many Things Principle

Lower Expectations Principle (see also Never Good Enough Principle)

Make It Routine Principle (see also Routine is Everything Principle)

Manage Your Time and Your Life Rule

Mental Health Day Technique

Modest Goal

No Conditions of Worth Rule

One-Thing-at-a-Time Principle (OTAAT)

Overthinking Principle

The PCD Time for Couples Rule

Pick a Role Model for a Friend Principle

Play Like a Kid/Frivolous Flows Principle

Pocket of Time to Relax Principle

Positive Addictions Principle

Process Goal Principle

Quality Time Principle

The Question Rule

Relationship with Self or Self-Compassion Principle

Role Model Principle (see also What Would My Role Model Do Principle)

Second Opinion Principle or Technique

Self-Acceptance Principle

Sensate Focus/Savor or Vary Your Pleasures to Avoid Adaptation Tenet

Stop Second Guessing Principle

Strength It Principle

Success Principle

Thou Shalt be Aware or Psychephobia Principle

The Three Rs of Stress Management Principle

Note: In cases of Tenets with two names, they are listed by the first name (with the second name following).

known *how* to be Creative in a particular area of interest have benefited from taking classes in hobbies like arts and crafts, ceramics, scrap booking, painting, photography, or needlework.

Another obstacle to Creativity satisfaction is the desire for an immediate boost or "high" from a new creative outlet when, in fact, it may take time to feel most of the benefits of creative pursuits as was true for Ron, a business executive who took 2 months to be satisfied in his progress in acrylic and oil painting. Clients often need the therapist's encouragement to persevere through the early skill building phases of traditional artistic creative outlets.

Preventing Noncompliance or Relapse.

As is done with any outside activity or homework that is a part of QOLT, always ask clients before they leave the office: "Tell me all the reasons you might give me next week for not doing your QOLT exercise." Having this discussion in a way that shows clients how QOLT homework is intimately related to getting their goals in life met for greater happiness and so on does much to reduce homework noncompliance. If possible, begin exercises in session to elicit problems or negative, killjoy thoughts associated with the exercise.

Socializing Doubles Your Pleasure, Creativity Flows, and Premack It.

A second way to dramatically improve compliance with Creativity and other QOLT assignments and to, very importantly, routinize the activity, is for clients to find a friend, acquaintance, or buddy with whom to do the Socializing Doubles Your Pleasure Principle. This Tenet can be shared with clients after finding its separate listing in the Toolbox CD folder labeled Tenets in Separate Documents that displays Tenets in alphabetically arranged Word documents so that individual Tenets may be easily viewed and assigned. Clients who participate in a cross stitch class, a photography course, community theatre, or karaoke group *together* are much more likely to continue on a routine basis. It also helps greatly if the Creativity involves a flow for clients—see Flow It in the Toolbox CD Tenets and in Chapter 15—that is additionally rewarded after completion with another, higher frequency or highly rewarding activity such as having a meal—Premack It Principle. For example, many clients will not eat lunch or breakfast or get online until after they have written poetry or done some arts and crafts project.

Obstacles to Traditional Artistic Creative Pursuits.

Clients must be reminded over and over that creativity is a teachable skill and that the flow *process* is more important than the artistic *outcome* or product. The artist Ann Cushman (1992) has valuable advice for clients struggling to pursue traditional creative outlets:

- *Trust your intuition.* Whether you're writing, painting, or singing, dancing, daydreaming, or just talking to a friend, it is crucial to honor your initial impulses—the raw, uncensored vitality of your first thoughts—which your internal critic will usually try to censor.
- *Stay in the present.* Forget about painting what you planned to paint. . . . The wellspring of creativity is accessible only if you stay attuned to the here and now. If you're terrified, express terror. If you're angry, let your anger form your creation. Boredom is a sure sign you're not staying in the moment (see the Mine the Moment Tenet of Contentment in Chapter 7).
- *Do not cross out.* Don't erase what you've written, even if you've changed your mind. Don't paint over something you've done. If you're improvising with a partner, don't negate your partner's contributions, but build on them even if you don't like them. Create boldly, without afterthoughts or regrets.
- *The process is what matters, not the product.* Feeling empty inside, we often want to reassure ourselves by creating something other people can admire. But what we're really hungering for, whether we know it or not, is a sense of aliveness, of deep contact with the sacred mystery of our lives. The goal is not to produce a masterful painting, story, poem, or song. The reason to create is the sheer pleasure and power of doing it, the vibrant aliveness that comes when we're contacting and expressing our true self. In this view, the product is simply a by-product, a relatively harmless side effect of the creative process.
- *Don't analyze what you've done.* People paint an image and they want to know where it came from and what it means about them. They want to show it to people and ask them what they think about it. They make it so important, while really the whole process is about not making important what comes out of you.
- *Realize that special talent is not necessary.* It is not necessary to spend years acquiring technical skills before launching your creation. In fact, an arsenal

of painstakingly accumulated techniques can be a hindrance because you'll be tempted to rely on what you've learned rather than reinventing your approach spontaneously, moment by moment.

- *Practice, practice, practice, practice.* Although you don't need talent, you do need perseverance—the courage to confront again and again the blank notebook, the empty canvas, the expectant eyes of the audience. The freedom with which you play must be balanced by the discipline that you return to day after day. The term "practice" can be misleading. Practice must be approached diligently, but not as a means to an end, rather as an end in itself.

Step 4: Implement a Creativity Plan or Routine

Step 4 charges clients to develop and implement a specific *Creativity Routine.* This plan should consider ways to overcome the barriers or obstacles to Creativity that clients identified in Step 3. The plan should also include some of the specific ways to be creative developed as part of Step 2; that is, outlets that best fit clients' interests, the time available for Creativity, and clients' Goals-and-Values. Creativity Routines benefit from the inclusion of Creativity-related Tenets of Contentment discussed in Step 1 and listed in Table 19.1.

Step 5: Evaluate Whether the Creativity Routine Was Carried Out and Increased Satisfaction

In Step 5, therapists and clients evaluate together whether a *Creativity Routine* was carried out completely and whether or not it increased client satisfaction with the area of Creativity. As problems are revealed in the implementation of plans in the real world, Step 3 for dealing with obstacles to satisfaction is simply repeated here as part of Step 5 until such obstacles are managed or removed entirely.

To many clients, satisfaction with Creativity or any other area of life hinges on Money and what it can bring them in the way of needed skills, equipment, and security. Fortunately, as we shall see in the next chapter, clients and the general public over-estimate the influence of money and our standard of living on personal happiness.

CHAPTER 20

Money and Standard of Living

> Annual income of twenty pounds with an annual expenditure of nineteen and six results [in] . . . happiness; an annual income of twenty pounds with an annual expenditure of twenty pounds and six results [in] . . . misery.
>
> —From Charles Dickens' *David Copperfield*

MONEY ISN'T WHAT IT'S CRACKED UP TO BE

In QOLT, Money or standard of living has three components: (1) It is the money you earn; (2) the things you own (like a car or furniture); and (3) the belief that you will have the money and things that you need in the future (Frisch, 1994). Findings from research show that you can't "buy" happiness after a certain modest amount (Diener & Seligman, 2004). For example, while respondents from the *Forbes* list of the 400 richest Americans score high on well-being surveys (Diener, Horwitz, & Emmons, 1985), research shows that they are no happier than the Maasai, a traditional East African herding people who live in huts made from cow dung (Biswas-Diener, Vitterso, & Diener, 2003). Furthermore, the wealth of affluent Western nations has grown exponentially for over 40 years, while overall happiness and satisfaction with life have stayed the same; and Western countries have experienced a tenfold increase in clinical depression (Diener & Seligman, 2004; Easterbrook, 2004; Myers, 2000).

While the research supports the view that being rich adds little to our happiness, it also supports Aristotle's idea that some limited moderate wealth *is* important to happiness. In QOLT terms, we need enough money and material possessions to be sure that we can take care of our basic needs—such as food, shelter, a safe neighborhood, health care, and a good education for our children if we have them. Gaining wealth beyond this

level seems to have little, if any, impact on our happiness or quality of life. Furthermore, if we look at Money as only one ingredient in our entire "happiness stew," the impact of Money on our overall happiness is dwarfed by *other* ingredients or areas of life like relationships that contribute much more to our overall happiness and life satisfaction than material wealth (Diener & Seligman, 2004).

Money for a Rainy Day or How Money Soothes

Richard Lazarus of the University of California, Berkeley, has suggested a reason why a basic standard of living is important: Moderate wealth may be a necessary buffer against stress or stressors in our life. It may be that having a decent standard of living helps us to manage stress and increase our happiness by increasing the options we have for coping with problems, including the option of seeking professional assistance and services when they are required, such as those times when we need a good lawyer, doctor, or a better school for our children (Lazarus, 1991).

Money Can't Buy Me Love

Research shows that those who's Goals-and-Values emphasize money and possessions aren't as happy as those who do not (Diener & Seligman, 2004). While money can be seen as a means to support a family or a charity, a focus on gaining wealth for its own sake may be self-defeating in terms of our own happiness and quality of life. Perhaps the most materialistic among us neglect other ingredients of the happiness stew, becoming a slave to work, for example, to the neglect of some of the other areas of potential happiness. Additionally, what it takes to make a lot of money can be a very unpleasant and aversive use of our time. The pursuit of wealth often involves unpleasant tasks performed in an isolated, highly competitive, and aversive environment.

For example, in the cutthroat business of selling real estate, coworkers may steal clients and long hours of showing prospective buyers homes are often fruitless. My client, Jeremy, for example, spent a year showing homes to a wealthy buyer who could never be satisfied enough to actually buy a house, settling instead for an apartment, something he said he would never do! The pressure of commission-based income leads many of us to focus on the unpleasantries of work more and more, with little or no time for friends, family, or pastimes. The self-employed can become very much like the rats we observed in undergraduate psychology experiments who worked to exhaustion pressing a lever on fixed ratio or variable ratio schedule of reinforcement for essentially miniscule rewards in the form of tiny food pellets that delivered only occasionally after huge amounts of work.

Money Problems

In analyzing clients' concerns about their standard of living expressed on the QOLI, clients typically report problems in budgeting and the need for greater income to pay for basic necessities. In the case of young adults, financial independence from their parents is often a major goal.

Interventions

In advising clients, Quality of Life Therapy therapists should suggest that first and foremost, we try to be happier and more content with life, in general, so that we can think more clearly about financial plans and problems and so that we can be more productive at work—see Happiness Can Buy Money Strategy that follows. Next, we find out what basic financial resources we need to be happy and then use all the tools at our disposal, in order to be sure that those needs are met, both now and in the future. More specifically,

QOLT prescribes five strategies for maintaining or increasing clients' standard of living and thereby becoming more satisfied with the area of Money. Therapists are urged to share the following strategic possibilities with clients as part of negotiating a mutually agreed upon intervention plan for Money.

1. *Get Happy or Happiness Can Buy Money Strategy.* While it seems true that money can't buy you happiness, it seems like greater happiness can buy you money! Happier people seem to have more initiative and productivity at work and their customers are more satisfied as well (Diener & Seligman, 2004). For this reason, one strategy for boosting clients' happiness with Money and for increasing their income is to advise them to follow QOLT in all areas of life so that they become happier people in general. Additionally, greater happiness and Inner Abundance will lead to a clearer awareness of what is important in life and better decision making with respect to money—see Tenets. This *Get Happy in General* strategy is also used to boost satisfaction in Relationships and Work; indeed, it may be useful in all areas of life.

2. *Choose a CASIO Strategy and Key Tenets.* Choose among the five CASIO strategies in Five Paths and the myriad Tenets associated with Money in order to boost satisfaction with Money.

3. *Learn and Practice Basic Money Management Skills.* This includes the ability to balance a credit card account and a checkbook, make a budget, and plan for the future financially, including retirement and other long-term goals such as buying a house or car. QOLT offers some tools in this regard as do the computer software programs of *Microsoft Money Deluxe 2005* and *Quicken 2005 Premier.*

4. *Ask for Money or Financial Advice.* Using Emotional Honesty (see Tenets), assertively seek out any financial assistance or "in-kind" services to which we are entitled. For example, ask for charitable or government assistance for which we may qualify. This may also include asking for reasonable assistance and loans from family and friends or, at times may involve asking for reasonable assistance, loans, and raises from employers. The Relationship Skills in the Toolbox CD and Chapter 14 can be invaluable in this regard. Assertively seek out and ask for *advice* about

Money matters from making a budget to applying for a loan, to retirement planning.

5. ***Choose the Right Career or* Passionate Calling.** According to QOLT, clients' goal in choosing a career should be to find Work that, as much as possible, feels like play, seems to be a Passionate Calling in the sense that it feels like something perfectly suited to them, makes them feel passionate about work and eager to go to work each day, and fits with their overarching Goals-and-Values and purpose in life, whether this be spiritual or secular or both. To this definition of an optimal career from Chapter 15 we now add a criterion for fulfilling work; Urge clients to choose a career that is both intrinsically satisfying *and* profitable enough to provide for the income and benefits necessary for basic financial satisfaction and security. QOLT career counseling (see Chapter 15) can help in this regard.

Money in Context or Whole Life Assessment

Whole Life Assessment is a hallmark of QOLT that prescribes looking at problems or growth goals for one area of life in the context of all life goals and areas of life. Before choosing any Money interventions, therapists must do an assessment of the situation to discover the exact nature of money problems as in CASIO terms for example and, most importantly, to see the role of Money in the context of clients' *other* life goals and valued areas of life (see Areas of Life in the Toolbox CD). Specifically, the therapist and client should together examine the client's overall Goals-and-Values for the present and long-term with the Quality of Life Inventory or QOLI and Vision Quest techniques. Other problems in living such as an impending divorce or a *DSM* disorder should be considered in formulating an overall conceptualization a la the ACT model in Figure 6.1 of Chapter 6. Money problems can be usefully recast or understood in terms of the 5 elements of the CASIO model. In particular, CASIO related problems with Money may be examined with the What's Wrong? assessment in the Toolbox CD. In sum, gain an understanding of clients' overall life goals and quality of life and how these may relate to Money. Next, consider *all* of the possible sources or causes of clients' dissatisfaction with standard of living and *only then* choose among the five intervention strategies.

Based on your assessment findings and conceptualization as to what is causing the clients' unhappiness with Money, diverse treatments may be employed. At times, all five Money intervention strategies may be called for when, at other times, a single cognitive intervention will suffice, such as when clients' standards are unrealistically high (a useful intervention for this problem is the Good-Not-Great exercise in the Toolbox CD). In another straightforward intervention example, some clients who rob themselves of FAT Time (see Tenets) for relaxation with **F**amily, **A**lone time for golfing or reading a book, and **T**ogether time to keep courting and dating their partners, have drastically improved their overall quality of life by simply working less and slightly lowering, rather than raising, their productivity and standard of living. This option was revealed through Five Paths and the Good-Not-Great exercises from Chapter 8 aimed at the area of Money.

INCREASING GENERAL HAPPINESS OR LIFE SATISFACTION

Get Happy or Happiness Can Buy Money Strategy

While Money may not buy happiness, happiness can buy money. If we can make ourselves happier overall by following QOLT, we may become more financially successful (Diener & Seligman, 2004). Part of the money-happiness connection that we see in research findings, reflects the fact that happier people seem to go out and make more money than unhappy people; general contentment seems to give us more initiative and productivity at work. For example, Diener and Seligman (2002) report that higher cheerfulness in college freshmen related to higher incomes earned by these same freshman 19 years later when they were in their late 30s. While we cannot ignore the effect of personality attributes like extraversion in studies like this, it is also true that some extraversion or at least Happiness Habits can be *taught* as through the approach outlined in this book. For this reason, one strategy for boosting clients' happiness with Money and for increasing their income, is to enjoin them to follow the entire QOLT in order to be happier people in general. This is such a fun and easy path, that clients asked to do it never seem to object. It seems that there may be financial rewards for being a well-rounded person (Diener & Seligman, 2004).

APPLYING TENETS AND CASIO STRATEGIES TO MONEY

Choose a Five Path or CASIO Strategy

Choose among the five CASIO strategies in order to boost satisfaction with Money. It can be especially fruitful to emphasize the four strategies, that is, the ASIO in CASIO that do not involve making or even saving more money. For example, the Lie Detector and Stress Diary that relate to the Changing Attitudes strategy have been very helpful in enabling clients to solve financial problems via Action Plans and to manage their worry and depressive ruminations about finances (see also Worry Warts Tenet and Mindful Breathing skill in the Toolbox CD).

How Much Is Enough? Intervention

This is a standard setting intervention (the **S** in CASIO) that can have a snowball effect on many areas of life (also called Beware of What You Wish For exercise). Clients should be reminded that being very wealthy seems to have no appreciable effect on quality of life or happiness. It is likely that we adapt to greater income quickly in so far as yesterday's luxuries become today's necessities. After the basics are covered, rising wealth just leads to rising standards, aspirations, and expectations; even our definition of "the basics" will change once we get used to an income level far above what we need for comfortable living and financial security.

When overall happiness is the goal as in the Happiness Matters Tenet, then it is best if our income and aspirations can be frozen at current levels if this is adequate for our needs—both now and during retirement—with the goal of cost-of-living adjustments up until retirement only. Put another way, *if clients can target an income that takes care of their basic needs as their standard for happiness with Money, wish for no more, and consciously devalue Money in importance— the **I** in CASIO—with respect to other areas of life* like relationships that have a much greater impact on overall happiness anyway, their overall happiness may be greater along with greater satisfaction with Money per se. This intervention can also free up time and energy

spent chasing the "almighty dollar" for other valued areas of life leading to a more Balanced Lifestyle—see Tenet. Recall that the CASIO model assumes that it's best to attend to *all* areas of life we care about rather than to slavishly honor or involve ourselves with only one, the common scenario of unhappy workaholics; even those lucky enough to have work that is loved and that feels like play need other areas of fulfillment such as relationships to be fully satisfied and content.

Further CASIO Interventions

To proceed with other CASIO interventions, first ask clients to carefully assess their budgetary needs both now and in the future so that Five Paths can then be applied to the problems and shortfalls that are revealed. Visits to financial planners with impeccable long-term reputations in the community can be part of the homework connected with this intervention, invoking the Second Opinion technique.

Choose a CASIO Strategy and Key Tenets

Clients need additional motivation and guidance to carry out CASIO strategies aimed at boosting satisfaction with Money. Reading over relevant Tenets can help in this regard. Table 20.1 lists some important Tenets for them to consider when setting lifetime and immediate goals for Money and when handling money.

LEARN AND PRACTICE BASIC MONEY MANAGEMENT SKILLS

As the quote from the start of this chapter suggests, clients must learn to live within their financial means to be satisfied with their standard of living. To live within their means, clients must know how much money they have and be able to spend it, or budget it, in a way that does not overextend them financially. Clients must be able to save money for important purposes. Clients must know how to balance a credit card or debit card account and a checkbook or operate a money management computer program to see exactly where they stand financially at any given time.

Money management skills include the ability to balance a charge card statement or a checkbook, make a budget, and plan for the future financially, including retirement and other long-term goals such as buying a

Table 20.1 Tenets with Attitudes, Schemas, and Practices Conducive to Greater Satisfaction with Money

Accept What You Cannot Change Principle	I Can Do It Principle
Ask Your Death Tenet	I'll Think about That Tomorrow Principle
Attack the Moment or Mine the Moment Principle	Inner Abundance Principle
Balanced Lifestyle Principle	Keeping Up with the Jones Principle
Be the Peace You Seek or Worry Warts Principle	Kiss the Past Goodbye Principle
Be True to Your School Principle: BETTY'S Way	Leisurely Pace and Lifestyle Principle
Be Your Own Guru or Personal Wisdom Principle	Life Satisfaction Breeds Job/Work Satisfaction
The Big Three Makes Us Dumb Principle-Emotional Control Principle	Live Your Dream or 24/7 Principle
Calculated Risk Principle	Lower Expectations Principle (see also Never Good Enough Principle)
Clear Conscience Rule (see also Do the Right Thing Rule or When in Doubt, Don't Rule)	Manage Your Time and Your Life Rule
Cocoon It Rule	Marching Orders Principle
Creativity Routine Principle	Meanings Like Buses Rule
Curb or Ignore Desires Principles (see also You Can't Have It All Principle)	Mental Health Day Technique
Do What You Love or Tune in to What Turns You on Principle	Modest Goal
Exercise or Take your Medication Principle	One-Thing-at-a-Time Principle (OTAAT)
Expect the Unexpected Principle	Pick a Role Model for a Friend Principle
Expert Friend Principle	The Question Rule
Face the Music Principle	Second Opinion Principle or Technique
Find a Goal Principle (see also Find a Meaning Principle)	Stop Second Guessing Principle
Habits Rule Rule or Routines Rule Rule	Strength It Principle
Happiness from Achievement Principle	Thou Shalt Be Aware or Psychephobia Principle
Happiness Is a Choice Principle or Responsibility Principle	The Three Rs of Stress Management Principle
Happiness Spillover Principle	You Are What You Do

house or car. Quality of Life Therapy therapists should be willing and able to teach clients and to check clients' work when it comes to these basic money management skills. Besides the material here on budgeting, computer software programs such as *Microsoft Money Deluxe 2005* or *Quicken 2005 Premier* can help clients with budgeting and other money management skills.

Expert Friends and Diagnosing Dementia from a Checkbook Register. Norma Jean's positive psychology counseling turned clinical in nature when it was found that she was unable to balance her checkbook after doing it successfully for 50 years. After conducting a dementia screening assessment that turned out positive, I arranged for Second Opinion dementia evaluation performed by a specialist that revealed that Norma Jean was in the early stages of Dementia of the Alzheimer Type. This development meant that an Expert Friend (see Tenet) was needed to manage Jean's financial affairs. In Norma Jean's case, it was her son who stepped up to help out. In less dramatic circumstances, couples often designate one partner who is more adept or skillful in Money matters to manage their financial affairs. While often unavoidable, therapists should encourage such couples to still discuss Money goals, the current financial picture, and how both partners can get full access to all financial documents and records as a couple. Too much financial power in the hands of one partner can jeopardize the equality in decision making that is so vital to the health of love relationships in QOLT.

Making a Budget with Your Client

When assessment of Money dissatisfaction in clients reveals inadequate budget skills, QOLT advocates teaching your clients to make a budget. For example, QOLT has helped clients who chronically overspend to learn how to make and stick to a budget, one that takes care of their immediate day-to-day expenses and also includes arrangements and savings for any long-range financial goals. The Toolbox CD handout, Budget Skills, is displayed in part in Box 20.1. It teaches some rudimentary budgeting skills. It can be assigned to clients as part of their regular homework. Note the QOLT Money Management Plan for Couples in the box. This is an important aspect of budgeting in QOLT.

Adherence to the Budget

Therapists themselves can evaluate clients' adherence to proposed budgets if a financial planner has not been hired. This need not be complicated or intimidating to math phobic therapists because the proof is in the pudding or the outcome of the budgeting. In essence, therapists need only ask clients a few questions in the weeks after a budget has been implemented:

- Are you paying all of your bills on time?
- Are you overspending or going over your budget at all?
- Do you wait to pay *variable* budget items only after your *fixed* expenses are paid? The therapist may ask chronic overspenders, "Are you willing to cut up your credit card and experiment with a debit card or cash only system?"

Applying Habit Control and Activity Schedule Interventions to Money and Budget Problems

Adhering to a budget and paying bills promptly can be facilitated with activity scheduling (see Daily Activity Plan in the Toolbox CD and Chapter 10) and with the Habit Control Program (see Habit Diary in the Toolbox CD and Chapter 13). With respect to latter, the habit to be controlled may be overspending or lack of adherence to the budget rules each month, that is, after fixed expenses are paid, only the remaining salary is used for variable expenses. Clients with severe budgeting problems would do best to cancel and destroy all of their credit cards.

ASK FOR MONEY OR FINANCIAL ADVICE

Using the Relationship Skills in the Toolbox CD and in Chapter 14, therapists can teach clients to assertively seek out and ask for any financial advice, financial assistance, or "in-kind" services to which they are entitled, such as asking for charitable or government assistance for which they may qualify. This may also include asking for reasonable assistance and loans from family and friends at times or loans, and/or raises from employers so that clients are paid a fair wage. Government and charitable programs are equipped to provide cash or "in-kind" services that can significantly boost clients' standard of living. "In-kind" services include items or services that are provided directly to a person instead of giving someone the money to buy these things themselves such as food, clothing, shelter, day care, or home care services for children and adults with and without disabilities, and medical equipment.

The Relationship Skills in Chapter 14 along with the core Tenets of Emotional Honesty and Favor Bank can be invaluable in this regard. For example, Ellen, kept records of her part-time hours, case outcomes, and fees paid as part of her work for a prestigious law firm. After making herself indispensable to the firm and following the Favor Bank dictum of returning favors from colleagues whenever she could, Ellen was able to parlay her contribution into a huge raise based on a study she did of competitive salaries in the area. By using the Relationship Skills, especially Emotional Honesty, she never came across as shrill or unreasonable in her requests, making it hard for the partners not to acquiesce to her proposal for a raise.

One unemployed client, Steve, decided that he was not a "worthless freeloader" for thinking about getting assistance for his family, including his wheelchair-bound son. After learning and practicing the relationship en-

BOX 20.1
Budget Skills

Name: _____   Date: _____

Instructions: This handout teaches you how to make and stick to a budget. Specific advice for couples and others who share a household is offered at the end of this handout. A good budget takes care of your immediate day-to-day expenses and also includes saving for future goals, such as your retirement, buying a house, or buying a car. When possible, it is also important to maintain an emergency or reserve savings account for unexpected bills like car repairs and for bills that are paid on a quarterly or biannual basis like car insurance. Ideally, people should save enough money to cover all of their expenses for 3 to 6 months in case of an emergency such as becoming seriously injured or sick. (Disability insurance is also available to deal with this particular emergency.)

INCOME ASSESSMENT

The first step in budgeting is to determine the yearly income of your household. Add up the salaries of everyone living in your house and also consider other sources of income such as investment income. Next, make a list of your expenses, separating variable from fixed expenses. Fixed expenses are things that you have to pay in order to live and that cost the same amount each month. This would include things such as your rent or house payment, insurance premiums, and installments on loans that you are paying off. Put all of your expenses in monthly terms. For example, if you pay $800 in car insurance every year, you would compute this fixed expense as $800/12 or $66.67 each month. Be sure to consider all of the following items when computing your fixed expenses:

Fixed Expenses	Annual Amount	Amount per Month
Rent or House Payment	_____	_____
Property Taxes	_____	_____
Internet Service Provider	_____	_____
Federal, State, Social Security Taxes	_____	_____
Life Insurance	_____	_____
Health and Accident Insurance	_____	_____
House and Contents Insurance	_____	_____
Auto Insurance	_____	_____
Loan Payments (Debt Service)	_____	_____
Car Payment(s)	_____	_____
Child Support	_____	_____
Hobby Club Dues	_____	_____
Charitable and Religious Contributions	_____	_____
Other_____	_____	_____

(Continued)

DETERMINING VARIABLE EXPENSES

Next, compute your variable expenses. These are flexible expenses in which the amount that you spend is not fixed every month and includes things like your utilities (remember that you do have control over how hot or how cold you keep the house), entertainment expenses, the amount of money you give to charities, the amount of money you spend for travel or vacations, food, clothing, phone calls, savings, personal allowances, car expenses, household expenses (furniture, appliances, repairs), investments, and schooling.

Money Diary Technique

A great way to get a realistic, comprehensive, and accurate picture of your flexible expenses is to keep a *Money Diary* for one month in which you record every dime you spend and note what you spent it on. One way to facilitate this is to save every receipt you get during this period and try to pay for items with cash, check, or a debit card only. The *Money Diary* is very effective in revealing hidden expenses like the money spent at the candy machine, coffee shop, convenience store, local bar and grill, or making online purchases.

Sometimes these variable expenses can come as quite a shock and can "break the bank" as when you get a huge heating bill in the winter. To reduce the shock and devastation of these large bills, utility companies will often average your bill based on the previous year, making payments much more even from month to month. Be sure to consider all of the following potential expenses when figuring your variable expenses:

Variable Expenses	Annual Amount	Amount per Month
Savings (pay yourself first)	_____	_____
Food at Home	_____	_____
Meals on the Job	_____	_____
Coffee, Candy, and Snacks at Work	_____	_____
School Lunches	_____	_____
Meals Out	_____	_____
Electricity	_____	_____
Gas/Heating	_____	_____
Water/Sewage/Garbage	_____	_____
Cell Phone	_____	_____
Internet Service	_____	_____
Family Clothing	_____	_____
Uniforms	_____	_____
Dry Cleaning/Laundry	_____	_____
Home Cleaning Supplies	_____	_____
Auto Repairs/Tags/Inspections	_____	_____
Gasoline	_____	_____
Car Maintenance/Oil/Lube	_____	_____
Bus Fares/Ride Share/Parking	_____	_____

Child Care	_____	_____
School (Tuition/Supplies)	_____	_____
Allowances	_____	_____
Household Expenses	_____	_____
Barber/Beauty Shop	_____	_____
Books/Newspapers/Magazines	_____	_____
Movies/Sporting Events/Cable TV	_____	_____
Gifts/Parties/Holidays	_____	_____
Cigarettes/Tobacco/Alcohol	_____	_____
Babysitter	_____	_____
Hobbies/Club Dues	_____	_____
Record/Book Clubs	_____	_____
Doctor/Hospital	_____	_____
Dentist	_____	_____
Drugs/Medicine	_____	_____
Bank Charges	_____	_____
Postage	_____	_____
Personal Care	_____	_____
Taxes	_____	_____
Pet Care	_____	_____
Other _____	_____	_____

hancement steps in Chapter 14, Steve found a charitable agency that provided his son with an expensive wheelchair (which his health insurance would not cover). After repeated efforts, he also secured social security disability payments for his son. A local church made it possible for his son to go to a day camp in the summer, giving the client needed time to study and work a part-time job. Steve cut back to part-time work after he applied for and won a scholarship to study auto mechanics from a local technical college. In looking at his long-term Goals-and-Values it was clear that he loved the idea of being a mechanic and needed the extra money it would give his family.

A Million Ain't Enough: Seeking Money Advice from Outside Consultants

Seeking and finding financial advice can be as daunting as asking for Money per se for clients. As a therapist you can encourage clients to find consultants with im-peccable reputations of effectiveness and ethical behavior. Clients may then use Relationship Skills to hire a consultant. This amounts to clients' using the Second Opinion technique and Tenet to get expert aid on handling their money and possessions. Certified financial planners, accountants, and budget, credit, and debt counselors can give clients useful advice for managing their money. For example, Jeremy was told by a financial planner that being a millionaire was no longer enough to ensure his super-wealthy lifestyle and retirement plans. Fifty million would be required! On a more realistic note, the Consumer Credit Counseling Service (CCCS) offers free or low-cost financial services that are especially helpful for clients who have lost control of their finances and are seriously in debt. CCCS will also help anyone develop a budget and financial plan; it is the only nationwide nonprofit credit and financial counseling service with 850 offices across the United States. (In order to find the closest office call 800-388-CCCS.) Clients can also call their local Better

Business Bureau for the names of other nonprofit financial counseling services in the area. Nonprofit agencies are often preferable to profit-making credit-counseling agencies since the "nonprofits" have low or nonexistent fees and since many creditors refuse to negotiate with profit-making credit counseling agencies.

For clients who have trouble balancing a checkbook, it is important that they assertively ask their banker for help and advice whenever their account is overdrawn. Many banks have "800" phone numbers that clients can call 24 hours a day to quickly find out the current balance of their account, the last five checks received by the bank, and the last three deposits received by the bank. A counselor from the Consumer Credit Counseling Service (CCCS) will also help with this problem at little or no cost—clients in the United States may reach them by calling (800) 388-2227.

Finding reputable computer software programs such as *Microsoft Money Deluxe 2005* or *Quicken 2005 Premier* for help with budgeting and other Money Management Skills also fits the rubric here of using outside consultants to get needed financial skills and advice.

CHOOSE THE RIGHT CAREER

Helping clients find a career, *PASSIONATE CALLING,* or vocation that is both intrinsically satisfying and profitable enough to provide for the income and benefits that they need for basic financial satisfaction and security is a daunting task. QOLT career counseling discussed in Chapter 15 on work can help therapists implement this suggestion with clients.

STORM CLOUDS ON THE HORIZON: THE FUTURE OF MONEY

One of my great concerns is that future research will confirm what I have begun to see in my practice: clients reporting that more and more money is needed to cover the basics of living, especially in urban areas (some of my clients travel from Dallas, Austin, and Houston). Increasingly, moderate wealth may not be enough to cover the American so-called middle-class lifestyle. Additionally, as we discussed in Chapter 15

on Work, the new global economy, while providing great bargains for consumers at the click of a mouse button, has made many of our jobs and income less secure as consumers and employers try to find the best deal in a global economy (Reich, 2000). In CASIO terms, our **S**tandards of fulfillment for money may rise as it costs more and more to secure the American dream. One way to control these costs is to live in a less expensive community; however, we must factor in the loss of close friends and relatives when deciding where to settle, especially as having supportive relationships is one of the most important ingredients of happiness (Diener & Seligman, 2004). Additionally, smaller communities do not have the job options that big cities afford when we need to find new employment.

What Have You Done For Me Lately

Rank and seniority mean much less today than in the past. That is, for employers and consumers of our skills, it is much more about what have you done for me lately in terms of your ability to sell yourself, your skills and services, and your innovative new ideas that will get the consumer to switch to *your* company or professional group, devastating competitors and all of *their* professional and nonprofessional staff who thought *they* had some job security (Reich, 2000). In turn, this volatile market pushes us to overwork because many of us want to make and save as much money as we can *now* in case we lose our job.

Therefore, feelings of job insecurity and the rising costs of basics could make moderate wealth insufficient for our satisfaction with Money. If we then have to devote even more time to work, we will have even less time for the *balanced* lifestyle. In this "rob Peter, to pay Paul" scenario, we will have less time for relationships, spiritual life, and pastimes—any of the nonfinancial endeavors we value, thereby driving down our overall happiness, especially since Money cannot fully compensate for a lack of fulfillment in other areas like relationships. If this scenario comes to pass, clients will need to be much more strategic about choosing careers, eliminating luxuries from their budgets, and finding bargains in necessities like health care and education. Ultimately, political action may be the only way to improve the situation—see Fight the Power Tenet.

CHAPTER 21

Surroundings: Home, Neighborhood, and Community

> You ask me why
> I live on Green Mountain.
> I smile
> and make no reply
> for my heart is free of care.
>
> Peach-blossom petals
> flow down mountain streams
> To earths and skies beyond Humankind.
> —LI PO (A.D. 699–762)

THE QUALITY OF LIFE WHERE YOU LIVE

Our physical and interpersonal surroundings are too often ignored by therapists preoccupied with clients' inner experience even though research has demonstrated that surroundings directly impact life satisfaction and mood. Both therapists and clients need to be aware that surroundings, defined in QOLT as our homes, neighborhoods, and communities, can have a profound impact on our mental and physical well-being. For example, researchers have found that overcrowding in such diverse places as dormitories, prisons, high-rise apartment buildings, submarines, and aircraft carriers can lead not only to dissatisfaction but also to behavioral and health problems, including higher mortality rates. Other research has shown that families living in high-rise apartments feel less safe, less satisfied, more socially isolated, and less empowered to change building policies. Those living in high-rise apartments also have less privacy and aren't as inclined to let their children go outside to play as those in low-rise apartment buildings. We flourish and prosper in communities where we help and trust each other, which is increasingly rare in the United States. Communities with the best

quality of life and the happiest and most satisfied members, are those who have high rates of volunteer or Helping activities, club memberships outside of work, and religious activities (Diener & Seligman, 2004; Helliwell, 2003; Putnam, 2001). Knowing and trusting your neighbors is becoming a quality-of-life indicator by itself, a vanishing sign of greater contentment and well-being in the United States (Diener & Seligman, 2004). Increasing unhappiness in the United States seems to be due in part to the breakdown in social relationships such as in knowing and feeling connected with our neighbors (Twenge, 2002). Ironically, this decline in social well-being is happening at the same time that wealth or objective material well-being is increasing (Myers, 2000).

LOVE IT, LEAVE IT, OR FIX IT STRATEGIES

In addition to the general CASIO strategies such as Five Paths, QOLT offers three area-specific strategies for helping patients to improve their satisfaction with their surroundings. In QOLT parlance, these three strategies are summarized as the Love It, Leave

It, or Fix It strategies. (The strategies for surroundings are reminiscent of those independently coined by the late Neil Jacobson with respect to couples in turmoil, that is, "Dig it, Change it, Suck it up, or Split.") The Love It strategy entails appreciating and accepting our surroundings. Sometimes clients can boost their satisfaction by learning to accept, appreciate, and enjoy what they have without pining for something different or better—see Curb Desire Tenet. Their satisfaction can grow as they explore and become more aware of positive aspects of their surroundings, as in the case of many clients who become more aware of recreational, educational, child development, or singles' outlets in their community, which they never knew existed.

The Leave It strategy involves leaving our surroundings if necessary, such as when a family moves to a safer neighborhood after finding it impossible to reduce or control the amount of crime in their old neighborhood.

The Fix It strategy involves improving one's surroundings, as when clients clean up and redecorate their home, join neighborhood associations aimed at reducing the amount of crime, or organize a block party in order to get to know neighbors. More specifically, Marlon organized his neighbors to form a Neighborhood Watch Program. Judy, a depressed widow, who lived alone, alleviated her anxiety and insomnia caused by a recent burglary by installing a home security system. Another client, Jennifer, used the Relationship Skills from the Toolbox CD and Chapter 14 to mobilize neighbors to lobby local government officials to increase the police protection and garbage collection in her neighborhood.

HOME

Quality of Life Therapy defines home as your house or apartment and the yard around it. Our homes are the most important places in our lives. We look to our home as a place for refuge, recreation, and rejuvenation. Like a good relationship, our home is our refuge, against the stressors of the outside world, including the dangers of the street and the stresses of our work life. The importance of home may be increasing; social scientists and market researchers have found that people are spending more time "nesting" in their homes

and less time venturing outside for recreation. With the advent of the Internet, we have the world, or at least a virtual world, at our fingertips without having to leave the comforts of our home.

The physical setting of our home can also influence our life satisfaction in other areas of life such as recreation, play, and interaction with others. Research has found, for example, that over half of our recreational time is spent *inside* the home. If there are not specific places in the home set aside for recreation, such as a den or family room, the opportunity for and satisfaction with play and social contact with children, friends, and our partner can be greatly diminished.

In keeping with our definition of satisfaction judgments from Chapter 3, home satisfaction is often a function of the discrepancy perceived between the physical qualities of home and the *ideal* of what we would like these qualities to be. These qualities can include things like the number of rooms, the home's layout, décor, general condition, age and location, architectural style, and the size of the home's lot.

Physical characteristics interact with clients' personality traits to determine home satisfaction. For example, perfectionist clients are often unhappy with homes that others would find adequate. Demographic factors also play a part in determining which physical characteristics clients find satisfying. For example, single and older individuals tend to prefer apartment living, while most others prefer a single-family home.

Time and Space Territory Techniques for Overcrowding

A large number of people per square foot defines overcrowding that impacts our satisfaction with our homes. Research has demonstrated that the more people are crowded into the same space—higher "household population densities," the more stress, unhappiness, and even serious social problems such as delinquency may manifest. Privacy is important in a home and can be secured by rotating a particular space among family members as when computer access is limited to certain times of day for each family member (Time Territory technique) or by limiting particular activities to particular places, such as when an adolescent is admonished to play her music in her bedroom with the door closed (Space Territory technique).

Overlap among Home, Money, and Work Concerns

On the Quality of Life Inventory, clients who feel dissatisfied with their homes usually can trace their unhappiness to the physical layout of the house, their desire for a new home or residence, or their conflicts with others in the home. Some clients also see their homes as unattractive, in need of remodeling or repair, or too small; unfortunately, at the same time, they also often feel unable to afford to redecorate or move, pointing out the common overlap among Home, Money, and Work concerns. Clients living with (unrelated) roommates often dislike the lack of space, privacy, and quiet relative to those who live alone. In addition, roommates blame Home dissatisfaction on conflicts over issues like mess, noise, lack of privacy, or the intrusion of boyfriends or girlfriends into the home's limited space.

Applications of the Love It, Leave It, or Fix It Strategies to the Home

A depressed client, Steeler, used the Fix It, or Improving Surroundings strategy, to boost his home satisfaction by carrying out a plan to clean and redecorate his house. Using the Zen Steps to Success technique from Chapter 10, he worked as little as 20 minutes a day on improving his house. Each small success experience, as when he bought a painting for an empty living room wall and threw out two boxes of broken knickknacks and unnecessary papers, tested Steeler's negative assumption that he was a "slob who could never change"; Steeler's satisfaction with and pride in his home increased along with his self-esteem and confidence that he really could improve things by himself.

Another client, Mac, improved his home's atmosphere by resolving some relationship problems with his roommates, drawing upon the techniques for relationship enhancement in Chapter 14. Melody used the *Home Improvement Plan*, to change sleeping arrangements so that her toddler no longer slept with her and her husband. She also used the Space Territory technique to establish a designated play area in the den where the family could interact socially. Another positive outcome of this intervention, which came about in the course of a Five Path positive psychology counseling session, was that the designated play area also limited the children's clutter and noise to one room of the house.

As is the case with most home changes, Melody consulted and compromised with her housemates before implementing any solutions or interventions. She relied on the Skills and Tenets in the Toolbox CD (especially, Mindful Breathing, Silence Is Golden Tenet, and Emotional Control Tenet to carry out her negotiations because her drug withdrawal, history of emotional abuse, and chronic negative affect made it easy for her to anger and alienate others).

Campion's home needed repairs and decorating but she could not afford it. Using Zen Steps, she focused her attention on work and money strategies of finding a job and then budgeting her earnings. Finally, she asked for help by securing a home improvement loan to get the money she needed to make the necessary improvements.

Marjorie, a single mother and a television reporter scored in only the 15th percentile on the Quality of Life Inventory. Marjorie used the Leave It or Leaving Surroundings strategy to deal with her Home problem. After failing with Time Territory and Space Territory techniques for overcrowding, she and her children moved to a bigger house so that she was no longer "overrun" by her kids and unable to find any private space for herself.

Champagne Tastes with a Beer Pocketbook

Terry, a depressed accountant, used the Love It or Accepting Surroundings strategy to increase her home satisfaction. After much soul-searching and an updated Vision Quest and Tenets of Contentment exercise, she lowered her **S**tandards (the **S** in CASIO) and the **I**mportance that she assigned to her Home surroundings in determining her happiness (the **I** in CASIO) in a way that made her family relationships more important than a rich standard of living and a palatial house. Before her reevaluation of the problem, Terry had felt embarrassed by her modest home because it did not measure up to the house her brother had built. By adjusting her priorities and lowering her standards for a satisfactory home, Terry was able to feel more satisfied without moving or spending any money. In addition, she began spending more time at home with her family. It seems that Terry simply had not been home enough before to appreciate its positive features, including its antique furniture, spacious yard, and large picture windows.

NEIGHBORHOOD

QOLT defines Neighborhood as the area around your home, how nice it looks, the amount of crime in the area, and how well you like the people in evaluating your neighborhood (Frisch, 1994). Research has found that the characteristics of noise, the attractiveness of buildings, the upkeep of the yards, the mixture of homes and businesses, and the amount of green space all affect our neighborhood satisfaction. A major obstacle to neighborhood satisfaction is not feeling safe. This is especially true of clients living in high-crime urban areas or in isolated rural communities. The more rundown areas of town, besides being unsafe, are also seen as being unattractive with a lack of natural beauty. Also, in "bad neighborhoods," neighbors are often seen as loud, rude, and noisy.

We Are Family

Relationship Skills from the Toolbox CD have been essential for some clients to learn how to get along with their neighbors whom we do not choose anymore than we choose our families of origin (see We Are Family and Surrogate Family Tenets). In a positive psychology workshop, Tabitha decided to use her new-found skills in Emotional Honesty along with a sneaky **C** strategy from CASIO and Five Paths to "mend the fence" and rebuild her relationship with her neighbor, Jane, whose dog barked at and accosted Tabitha and her family on a daily basis. It seems that one day, Tabitha lost her temper with the dog and yelled at Jane. With Quality Time reflection using Five Paths, Tabitha realized that she could get reacquainted with Jane by letting her son cross the street to play with Jane's two boys. With time, Jane accepted Tabitha's apology for losing her temper about the dog. It seemed that she simply had to be civil and nice to Tabitha now that their kids were regular playmates, a common pattern among neighboring families who overcome prejudices and petty grudges when their children intermingle and play together.

Building Neighborhood and Community Relationships: A Fertile Strategy for Greater Happiness

Trying to invest more time in neighborhood relationships may be an effective "secret weapon" (an **O** strategy in CASIO terms), because the payoff in terms of greater happiness in several areas can be great (Diener & Seligman, 2004). For example, Jody, an anesthesiologist with odd hours of work decided to socialize more with her neighbors whom she had ignored and taken for granted because they "weren't important enough." After spending more time with her neighbors, she felt a belongingness to and an appreciation for her Neighborhood, which included the neighbors who shared her German ethnic heritage. While the research shows that, in general, people no longer rely on their Neighborhood as their main source for making friends and socializing, it is still an important part of Neighborhood satisfaction for many clients, particularly those who live in neighborhoods with people of similar cultural backgrounds. Additionally, clients may build up their reserves by reversing this trend since neighbors like coworkers are a wonderfully proximate and available resource for socializing and close friendships.

Helping and Serving the Neighborhood and Community: A New Innovative Strategy for Greater Neighborhood and Community Satisfaction

Investing time in Neighborhood and/or Community service or Helping activities often as part of a larger *Helping Routine*—see Chapter 17—is an innovative, perhaps even counterintuitive strategy for improving our surroundings that can boost satisfaction in myriad ways in myriad areas of life. Happiness researchers, Sonja Lyubomirsky and her colleagues (Lyubomirsky, Sheldon, et al., in press) have suggested that acts of Helping and service to others may constitute an attitude change strategy—**A** in CASIO terms—by creating a positive perception of the people in one's neighborhood and community. This should increase satisfaction with these areas because the tenor of relationships is a key characteristic in judging our neighborhoods and communities. This local community service can also be expected to lead to an increased sense of cooperation and interdependence with other people, and an awareness of one's good fortune, presumably as clients make downward social comparisons, for instance, in seeing the lot of say a homeless person's situation as much worse than their own (Frisch, 1998b; Lyubomirsky, Sheldon, et al., in press). Helping often involves socializing, a key ingredient in most clients' *happiness stew*—see Relationship Chapter 14.

QOLT assumes that both service and relationship enhancement strategies for boosting satisfaction with our surroundings are Fix It strategies since the social characteristics of clients' neighborhoods change and are altered or fixed as a result of the interventions; of course, a case can be made for viewing these as Love It or accepting, appreciating strategies since the denizens of clients' neighborhoods and communities remain the same.

Love It Case Examples for Greater Neighborhood Satisfaction

Many clients boost their neighborhood satisfaction by learning to accept, appreciate, and enjoy their neighborhood as it is, without pining for something different or better. Howard's satisfaction grew as he explored the parks, ball fields, restaurants, and bars in his neighborhood instead of merely "crashing" after work in his Atlanta suburb with his wife and dogs in their four-poster bed at home. Merriam become more aware and appreciative of her neighborhood, as she researched the courses of study offered to working people at the prestigious Rhode Island School of Design near her home in Providence.

Leave It Case Examples for Greater Neighborhood Satisfaction

A single father of three, Donny, used the Leave It or Leaving Surroundings strategy to move his family away from a Neighborhood in which "alcoholics take over the playground from the kids and where it wasn't safe for his kids to play outside." He also bemoaned the presence of "druggies, thieves, and prostitutes" in the Community and their negative impact on his children. On the other end of the spectrum, an insurance magnate was counseled to consider research supporting the idea that living in a wealthy gated community or neighborhood was actually counterproductive. Interestingly enough, those who are wealthy are much happier on average living in a middle class neighborhood (Hagerty, 2000).

COMMUNITY

QOLT defines community as the whole city, town, or rural area where you live, including how nice the area looks, the amount of crime in the area, and how well you like the people. It also includes places to go for fun like parks, concerts, sporting events, and restaurants. You may also consider the cost of things you need to buy, the availability of jobs, the government, schools, taxes, and pollution (Frisch, 1994). Likewise, community services like fire and police protection, garbage collection, and sewage treatment must be effective and responsive to feedback and suggestions from citizens. Finally, the most satisfying and effective communities are embedded in a nation-state or government that is stable, democratic, responsive to citizens, subject to the rule of law with little if any corruption, respectful of human rights, and characterized by national institutions that really work as in transportation departments that maintain and expand needed highways and defense departments that can really defend the country and its citizens from terrorist threats and so on (Diener & Seligman, 2004). Organized helping through high rates of volunteer activity, club memberships outside of work, and church membership are also characteristic of happy communities, that is communities with the happiest and most satisfied inhabitants (Helliwell, 2003; Putnam, 2001). Clients who take the Quality of Life Inventory can often trace their community dissatisfaction to a perceived lack of available job opportunities, safety from crime, like-minded people, cultural amenities, good restaurants, and singles and recreational outlets.

COMMUNITY APPLICATIONS OF THE LOVE IT, LEAVE IT, OR FIX IT STRATEGIES

Assessment Using the Neighborhood/ Community Checklist

Therapists can ascertain which aspects of clients' communities are positive or negative and thereby which intervention strategy to use by having their clients complete the Neighborhood/Community Checklist in the Toolbox CD and Box 21.1. Because it is so brief, the Checklist can be quickly administered as part of a homework assignment or in session.

BOX 21.1

Neighborhood/Community Checklist

Name _____   Date _____

Instructions: To understand and reduce your unhappiness with your neighborhood or community, read the following list of community characteristics; complete the checklist separately for your community or neighborhood. This checklist is completed for (circle one): Neighborhood/Community.

   If a characteristic is true of your current community or neighborhood, check the Current column to the left of the item. If a characteristic is very important to your Ideal of a good neighborhood or community, check the Ideal column to the left of the item. Next, go over your responses and choose either the "Love It," "Fix It," or "Leave It" strategies for improving your satisfaction with your neighborhood or community. To practice the "Love It" strategy, go over the features checked in the Current column; you can learn to appreciate your community more by reminding yourself of its positive features, accepting its negative characteristics, and comparing it to communities that are clearly worse. To practice the "Fix It" strategy, read over the items checked in the Ideal column and circle those characteristics you would like to help fix, improve, or foster in your present community. For example, you may start a Neighborhood Watch Program to lower the crime rate or campaign against higher taxes. To do the Leave It strategy, make a list of communities or neighborhoods that have many of the characteristics that you checked in the Ideal column. Next, problem solve with *Five Paths* to choose a particular community or neighborhood to move to.

	Current	**Ideal**	**Community/Neighborhood Characteristic**
1.	_____	_____	Suburban
2.	_____	_____	Urban
3.	_____	_____	Rural
4.	_____	_____	"Edge city" or town outside of big city
5.	_____	_____	Low cost of living
6.	_____	_____	Friendly people with similar values
7.	_____	_____	People involved in community services and politics
8.	_____	_____	Safety from crime
9.	_____	_____	Not very crowded
10.	_____	_____	Good privacy
11.	_____	_____	Low noise
12.	_____	_____	Little or no pollution
13.	_____	_____	Good weather
14.	_____	_____	Good schools
15.	_____	_____	Close, affordable medical care and hospitals
16.	_____	_____	Attractive
17.	_____	_____	Close to nature
18.	_____	_____	Close to mountains

19.	_____	_____	Close to water
20.	_____	_____	Close to a big city
21.	_____	_____	Good shopping centers nearby
22.	_____	_____	Good transportation systems
23.	_____	_____	Few traffic jams
24.	_____	_____	Low local taxes
25.	_____	_____	Good local government
26.	_____	_____	Good state government
27.	_____	_____	Good services like street maintenance and fire protection
28.	_____	_____	Good recreational facilities like parks and playing fields
29.	_____	_____	Good restaurants
30.	_____	_____	Good entertainment like sports teams, concerts, plays, and museums
31.	_____	_____	Good opportunities to meet single people
32.	_____	_____	Good health clubs nearby
33.	_____	_____	Chance to pursue favorite hobbies such as birdwatching, fishing, singing groups, skiing, etc.
34.	_____	_____	Plenty of things to do for fun
35.	_____	_____	Close to children
36.	_____	_____	Close to parents
37.	_____	_____	Close to other relatives
38.	_____	_____	Close to work
39.	_____	_____	Good church, temple, synagogue, mosque nearby
40.	_____	_____	Nice, affordable housing
41.	_____	_____	Good appreciation on houses, neighborhood
42.	_____	_____	Good economic climate with job growth, etc.
43.	_____	_____	Other _____

Community Interventions: Fix It
Case Examples

The Fix It or Improving Your Surroundings strategy often involves social and political action as clients lobby the "powers that be" to improve community services and recreational opportunities, reduce tax burdens, and improve fire and police protection, garbage collection, street maintenance, and schools—see Fight the Power Tenet. Katie created her own cultural and social outlet by convincing a local night club and coffee house and bookstore to allow local musicians, such as herself, to play folk music one night each week. Another client, Laura, improved her Community satisfaction by forming a support group for parents of children with serious heart disease (Frisch, 1992). In the act of doing this, she also met her Helping needs because she created an important community resource. In addition, she also increased her confidence in relationships by exercising the leadership and the social skills necessary to recruit families for the group and to enlist the support of area physicians. Another client, Jim, a stock broker, reduced his dissatisfaction and anxiety by successfully blocking a major development project that would have dramatically reduced the "green space" around his

Community, obstructing the view of and access to a park from his own backyard.

Love It Community Examples

The Love It or Appreciating/Accepting Surroundings strategy can also be used to help clients reduce Community-related unhappiness. Therapists should challenge clients to aggressively test their hypothesis or belief that "there is nothing to do" in the Community. This belief often functions as an untested excuse for not taking interpersonal risks. It can help for therapists to challenge clients to become immersed in their Community in order to ferret out any potential sources of satisfaction. Specifically, clients can "immerse" themselves by assiduously reading local newspapers, watching local news broadcasts every night, and attending local community events in order to find recreational and social outlets that will meet their needs. Many clients fail to use important social outlets such as area health clubs, singles clubs, churches, and hobby groups because of social anxiety and social skill deficits. Cognitive restructuring through tools like the Stress Diary and social skills training through tools like Relationship Skills can increase their participation in Community activities. For example, one client was pleasantly surprised when she read about a production of a Eugene O'Neill play at a local community college that proved to be part of a small, but vibrant, theatre community in her town. Another client gave up her belief that her Community could not meet her needs when she found a professional feminist women's organization after feeling "desolate and alone" for over a year.

Leave It Community Examples

The Leave It or Leaving Your Surroundings strategy for communities is typified by clients moving to the city or to suburbs, depending on their preferences. Perhaps too often therapists fixate on trying to change clients rather than their environment in order to effect positive change when the latter alternative is much more doable and efficient—see Personality Stays the Same Tenet. In this vein, a gay client, Jeremy, decided to sell his business in a conservative small town and move to Dallas in order to pursue a romance, a vi-brant night life, and a more active and supportive gay community.

Assessing and Intervening in the Larger "Communities" of County, State, Nation, and the World

It is possible to extend community interventions to areas beyond our immediate community of say ten to fifty miles. This is important when clients are disaffected with their entire county, state, or country. It is also an issue for clients with dual citizenship or the means and desire to move to another country. Therapists must be alert to these larger possibilities by asking whether clients wish to extend their change efforts to these larger Communities. Meredith successfully blocked the development of a coal-burning power plant and drag boat racing riverfront development leading to greater satisfaction with her county as well as a new social outlet as a result of her civic action efforts. Indeed, she formed a countywide environmental watchdog group in Austin that continues to this day, 5 years after its formation.

Complex Relationships: The Intersection of Neighborhood, Community, Work, and Money

Preserving or boosting clients' happiness requires complex choices as important areas of life often overlap and interact with each other in complex and interdependent ways. For example, while the research shows that being rich is not important for happiness, it also supports the idea that we need enough money and material possessions to be sure that we can take care of our basic needs—like food, shelter, a safe neighborhood, good medical care, and a good education for our children—both now and in the future.

Furthermore, money allows for more options in coping with unexpected problems or tragedies, including the option of seeking professional assistance and services when they are required, such as those times when we need a good lawyer, a good doctor, or a better school for children who are struggling academically or in need of a safer and saner school environment. As more and more wealth seems to be needed to secure financial peace of mind especially in urban areas some clients in consultation with their therapists choose a less expensive Community or Neighborhood to live in as a way to control or reduce costs while keeping the possibility of a satisfying job or career with many flows—see Flow It Tenet. In contrast, other clients flee to the city to find high-flow Work opportunities that simply don't exist elsewhere, while other clients work as nomads in jobs untethered to a particular location as they follow their partner or family so that loved ones may find fulfilling work in safe communities.

OTHER INTERVENTIONS: APPLYING SKILLS, TENETS, AND FIVE PATH STRATEGIES TO SURROUNDINGS

A Trial and Error Approach

In order to gain a fresh perspective on their home, neighborhood, or community, encourage clients to consider and to apply all possible and relevant Skills (from the Toolbox CD), Tenets, and CASIO Strategies. When clients are stymied by a problem or obstacle to surroundings satisfaction, this usually takes the form of a trial and error hunt for "the" skill, Tenet, or exercise from the Toolbox CD that seems to hold a useful "answer" for either solving or managing a problem. For example, when finances are limited, it can be especially fruitful to emphasize the **ASIO** strategies in CASIO from Chapter 8 that do *not* involve spending large sums of money for redecorating or moving. In this vein, the *Lie Detector and Stress Diary* have been very helpful in improving clients' satisfaction with their surroundings. For example, Sam and Shirley reframed their "luxury house lust" with a *Lie Detector and Stress Diary* and realized that Shirley's desire for a more expensive home reflected her anxiety about finances and the need to have their assets handy in the form of a tangible asset like an expensive home. Shirley grew up in a "hand to mouth" existence and never lived in a house that her family owned. She had the mistaken notion that a house gives the best investment return for either long- (retirement) or short-term (saving for a car) goals. After completing *Five Paths* and pursuing the *Second Opinion Tenet* with a financial planner, Shirley and Sam realized that they would be lucky to break even on a long-term investment in a "fancy" house and could make much more money in a reputable mutual fund or even certificate of deposit or T (treasury) bill.

Jeremy and Laetitia worked on solving the many problems of listing their condo with a realtor and of finding a better apartment to suit the Goals-and-Values of their lifestyle with *Five Paths*. They further managed their worry and depressive ruminations about finding something in Manhattan on their limited budget using the *Lie Detector* and associated *Lie Detector Questions* in the Toolbox CD to generate a *Positive Answer* or reframe that they could really believe. In the process of looking, they used the *Guide for Worry Warts* and *Mindful Breathing* from Chapter 10 and the Toolbox CD to ward off feelings of gloom and doom. In the end, they settled for a smaller apartment in Brooklyn, which they reframed as a stepping stone a la *Zen Steps* to an eventual Manhattan address, a doable and likely move in 5 years after each of them had received anticipated promotions.

Tenets Conducive to Greater Satisfaction with Home, Neighborhood, and Community

Clients often need additional motivation and guidance to carry out CASIO and other strategies aimed at boosting satisfaction with their surroundings. What follows in Table 21.1 are some important Tenets for them to consider when setting and pursuing goals for greater happiness with their surroundings. These Tenets include attitudes, schemas, and practices particularly conducive to greater satisfaction with home, neighborhood, or community.

Table 21.1 Tenets with Attitudes, Schemas, and Practices Conducive to Greater Satisfaction with Home, Neighborhood, or Community

Accept What You Cannot Change Principle

Ask Your Death Tenet

Balanced Lifestyle Principle

Be True to Your School Principle: BETTY'S Way

Be with People or Relationship Immersion Principle

Be Your Own Guru or Personal Wisdom Principle

The Big Three Makes Us Dumb Principle—Emotional Control Principle

Blind Dumb Optimism Principle

Calculated Risk Principle

Clear Conscience Rule (see also Do the Right Thing Rule or When in Doubt, Don't Rule)

Cocoon It Rule

Color Purple Principle

Commune with Nature Rule (see also Lin Pao Rule)

Creativity Routine Principle

Curb or Ignore Desires Principles (see also You Can't Have It All Principle)

Don't Bring It Home or Work Spillover Principle

Do What You Love or Tune in to What Turns You on Principle

Equality Principle

Expect the Unexpected Principle

Expert Friend Principle

Face the Music Principle

FAT Time Principle

Fight for Much, Reap Frustration Principle

Fight the Power Principle

Find a Goal Principle (see also Find a Meaning Principle)

Flow It Principle

Get Organized Principle

Giving Tree or Self-Other Principle

The Grass Isn't Greener, It's Weeds Principle

Habits Rule Rule or Routines Rule Rule

Happiness from Achievement Principle

Happiness Is a Choice Principle or Responsibility Principle

Happiness Matters Principle

Happiness Spillover Principle

Happiness Takes Effort Principle (see also Keep Busy with Flows Principle)

Humor Principle

I Can Do It Principle

Inner Abundance Principle

Intellectual Masturbation Principle

Judge Not, You Don't Know Principle

Keeping Up with the Jones Principle

Kill Them with Kindness or Love Bomb Principle

Kiss the Past Goodbye Principle

Leisurely Pace and Lifestyle Principle

Live Your Dream or 24/7 Principle

Love Many Things Principle

Lower Expectations Principle (see also Never Good Enough Principle)

Manage Your Time and Your Life Rule

Modest Goal

One-Thing-at-a-Time Principle (OTAAT)

Overthinking Principle

Pick Your Battles/Pick No Battles Principle or Yes, Boss/Yes, Dear Rule or Under the Influence Principle

Positive Addictions Principle

Process Goal Principle

Quality Time Principle

The Question Rule

Reasoned Passion Principle (see also Selective Hedonism Principle)

Relationship with Self or Self-Compassion Principle

Role Model Principle (see also What Would My Role Model Do Principle)

Second Opinion Principle or Technique

Self-Acceptance Principle

Table 21.1 *Continued*

Serve Others Principle	Success Principle
Socializing Doubles Your Pleasure	Take a Stand Principle
Stop Second Guessing Principle	Thank Everyone for Everything Principle
Street Signs to Success Principle	Thou Shalt Be Aware or Psychephobia Principle
Strength It Principle	The Three Rs of Stress Management Principle
String of Pearls Practice and Principle	We Are Family Principle
Surrogate Family Principle	

CHAPTER 22

Relapse Prevention and Maintenance

QOLT invokes the same model of relapse prevention (Witkiewitz & Marlatt, 2004) that is used in addiction treatment and research. Clients in QOLT can falter, lapse, relapse, or collapse into myriad *DSM* symptoms and disorders. The scope of the problem of clinical relapse is large even for disorders that do not involve substance dependency or abuse; for example, even after full recovery from a depressive episode, 80 percent of clients with a recurrent depressive history will relapse again (Jarrett et al., 2001). Of course, pure positive psychology clients may lapse after QOLT into happiness-depleting, dysfunctional, self-defeating, and so-called "unhealthy" or negative personal habits of choosing overly challenging or unrewarding circumstances, thinking, feeling, and behaving that had been remediated earlier with QOLT. In this vein, QOLT is concerned with two types of relapse: (1) unhappiness relapses and; (2) *DSM* disorder relapses. Just as we watch for and assess relapse urges in clinical clients with *DSM* disorders, QOLT advocates a watchful eye for relapse urges in positive psychology clients who seem to be losing gains in life satisfaction or seem to be relapsing into old habits that are ultimately *happiness-depleters*. To anticipate and minimize the lasting effects of these lapses and relapses, QOLT prescribes the building of life skills such as goal striving in valued areas of life throughout treatment as well as detailed skill training at the end of treatment aimed at preventing and coping with relapses that bring clients back to the lower levels of functioning, happiness, and quality of life seen at the start of QOLT.

Four QOLT Strategies

1. *Get Happy* in General Strategy. The initial strategy for relapse coping and prevention in QOLT is for clients, first with and then without therapist assis-

tance to apply QOLT to all valued areas of life to build a *Happiness Reserve,* a bulwark against future stresses and triggers for relapse with significant dissatisfactions or unhappiness. Valued areas of unhappiness or dissatisfaction take priority because they may constitute triggers for relapse. It is very helpful for clients to have a copy of the companion book, *Finding Happiness* (Frisch, 2006), to refer to when doing this in preparation for the time when their therapist or coach is no longer administering acute or initial treatment/intervention. Essentially, this strategy for boosting clients' success in preventing and coping with relapse is for therapists to advise them to follow QOLT in all areas of life after formal treatment/intervention is completed so that they may become happier people *in general.*

By simply continuing QOLT for valued areas of life, clients maintain critical skills and foster daily Inner Abundance, an essential bulwark against (Hamlet's) "slings and arrows of outrageous fortune," that is, outside stressors that are so notorious for triggering relapses across various *DSM* disorders and within positive psychology and organizational situations.

Certain elements of QOLT are especially useful in battling or preventing relapse. Applying the Basket-of-Eggs and related O strategies of CASIO of Chapter 8, will maximize the happiness and life satisfaction reserves that clients may draw on when stressors rear their ugly heads or arise. This *Happiness or Satisfaction Reserve* or *Bank* is akin to the Favor Bank described in Chapter 14 except in this case the reserve helps the *Inner Happiness Economy* of the person instead of furthering interpersonal harmony. The Emotional Control skills and Tenets detailed in Chapter 10 are especially important as clients continue to hone or at least maintain their skills in dealing with negative affect, often the biological harbinger or concomitant of external stressors that is equally notorious for fomenting relapse.

The Relationship Skills and Tenets of Chapter 14 are invaluable to teaching ways to handle another cause of relapse, interpersonal problems. Clients must be armed with Emotionally Honest and effective social skills for resisting peer pressure to resume happiness depleting habits. Misery loves company in the form of miserable and unhappy friends and acquaintances who threaten the gains of both high-functioning positive psychology clients and more functionally impaired clients with *DSM* disorders. This is one among many instances where the application of the chemical dependency based model of Witkiewitz and Marlatt (2004) demonstrates its wide applicability to other *DSM* and pure positive psychology challenges to relapse. Since any client in QOLT can be persuaded by friends to relapse into happiness-depleting patterns in the absence of any "addictive," compulsive behavior, or other *DSM* disorder. For example, Anthony, a skilled surgeon, relapsed into temper outbursts due to overwork. He took on more than his share of surgeries and office visits, working much more than either of his partners. He couldn't say no to these two arrogant partners with "God-complexes," necessitating booster sessions in QOLT in order to control the temper outbursts and regain the happiness and composure he had won earlier.

2. Happiness Habits or Positive Addictions Strategy. The second QOLT strategy teaches clients to apply the Habit Control Program of Chapter 13 (Health) to their most useful and powerful—in terms of happiness-boosting properties—Happiness Habits of QOLT that are thereby recast as positive habits or "addictions" in need of care and nurturance throughout their lives.

3. Lifelong Therapy or Booster Sessions. The third QOLT strategy enjoins therapists to apply QOLT continuation phase and QOLT maintenance phase treatment as long as necessary for cases with chronic or reoccurring *Happiness-Depleting Habits* or psychological disturbance as in *DSM* disorders. The third QOLT strategy for relapse coping and prevention in QOLT is for therapists to apply QOLT continuation phase and QOLT maintenance phase

treatment for those clinical cases with chronic or reoccurring *DSM* symptoms and disorders.

4. Relapse-Specific Skills Training Strategy. The fourth QOLT strategy for relapse coping and prevention in QOLT is for clients, first with and then without therapist assistance, to apply the *QOLT Relapse-Specific Skills* and *Tenets* of this chapter pertinent to coping with relapse and relapse prevention.

RATIONALE AND PROPOSED MECHANISM OF ACTION

The rationale for and proposed mechanism of action for relapse prevention in QOLT is that QOLT gives clients a positive focus and framework for pursuing life goals in all areas of life that they care about. It is expected that this *Goal Striving* (see Chapters 3 and 10) toward life goals will continue well after therapy has ceased. Since most QOLT interventions and skills are routinized into habits to be practiced and reinforced on a daily basis, it is expected that some of these Happiness Habits (see Tenets) will continue long after treatment is over. This should maintain activation of the constructive mode even during times of stress, thereby staving off relapse as defined above for both clinical and pure positive psychology clients. For those times when stressors are sufficient to disrupt key Happiness Habits learned during the course of QOLT, clients will have been taught two specific sets of skills or routines to follow and exercises to complete contained in this chapter—one routine is aimed at coping with a relapse that "breaks through" and a second routine is for preventing relapses before they occur. Finally, one of the options presented to clients, especially to those with indicators of chronicity to their *DSM* disorders is therapist-assisted continuation or maintenance treatment.

QOLT FOR RELAPSE PREVENTION IN COGNITIVE THERAPY

QOLT is seen as a way to boost the acute treatment response of clients undergoing evidence-based cognitive therapies for *DSM* disorders, in part, because of QOLT's hypothesized activation of the constructive mode, a necessary part of successful cognitive therapy according to the latest formulation of cognitive theory expanded now to include most psychopathology and not just clinical depression (D. A. Clark & Beck, 1999; also see details in Chapter 3). As discussed earlier and in Chapter 1, QOLT also has a role to play in relapse prevention.

Specifically, when treating clients with *DSM* disorders, QOLT assessments are readministered—aimed at fine-tuning interventions and charting progress as discussed in Chapter 5. They have showed progress indicative of treatment success and therefore the approaching end of acute phase treatment. These final or near final assessments of the acute treatment phase, document change in a psychometrically sound way and provide data useful for implementing the four relapse coping and prevention strategies presented at the beginning of this chapter. With respect to the latter, the assessments are used to make a new conceptualization following the procedures of Chapters 5 and 6 that detail progress to date as well as areas to consider for further growth—potential pockets of fulfillment and residual *DSM* symptoms—and relapse prevention planning. The four relapse prevention strategies are then implemented. Special consideration and procedures are implemented for clients with recurrent *DSM* disorders as in a history of three or four episodes of the disorder including the latest episode for which clients sought QOLT.

LIFELONG THERAPY OR BOOSTER SESSIONS: CONTINUATION, MAINTENANCE, AND RELAPSE PREVENTION IN CLINICAL CLIENTS WITH CHRONIC DISORDERS

Continuation phase psychotherapy (especially cognitive therapy) and maintenance phase psychotherapy in the service of relapse prevention are being explored as psychologists observe the efficacy of similar phased treatments in pharmacotherapy trials and as psychologists face the problems of: (1) relapse prevention and the need for maintenance phase treatment; that is, the problems of frequent relapse, chronicity, or high reoccurrence of many disorders like depression and; (2) the need for continuation phase treatment; that is, how to treat residual symptoms at the end of acute phase treatment in order to prevent a likely relapse based on these symptoms

(Jarrett et al., 2001; Rush & Kupfer, 2001). Evidence exists supporting the efficacy of intervention in the continuation and maintenance phases of treatment for depression and, to a lesser extent, anxiety and body image disorders; specifically, fewer relapses and reoccurrences are characteristic of clients given continuation- or maintenance-phase treatment (Fava & Ruini, 2003; Jarrett et al., 2001; Rush & Kupfer, 2001). In some cases, a positive psychology intervention has been combined with cognitive therapy in the service of relapse prevention (Fava & Ruini, 2003). For this reason and in light of the constructive mode postulated in Clark and Beck's current theory, QOLT is recommended as a comprehensive positive psychology intervention alternative for say monthly continuation and maintenance phase treatment sessions when such monthly *follow up* sessions are feasible. Box 22.1 presents the specific definitions and QOLT procedures associated with each phase of treatment based on the description offered by Rush and Kupfer (2001). The procedures of Box 22.1 constitute expression of the third QOLT strategy for relapse coping and prevention in QOLT presented at the start of this chapter. Some pure positive psychology clients will need lifelong QOLT or periodic booster sessions in QOLT. These clients are the chronically unhappy or those who, after finding happiness, tend to repeatedly relapse into subclinical depression or unhappiness and Happiness-Depleting Habits or behavior patterns such as pessimism or compulsive workaholism.

RELAPSE-SPECIFIC SKILLS FOR BOTH CLINICAL AND POSITIVE PSYCHOLOGY CLIENTS

Maintaining Gains: Pretermination Counseling

To anticipate and minimize the lasting effects of these lapses or relapses, QOLT prescribes detailed discussions at the end of treatment aimed at identifying useful interventions along with specific interventions for preventing and coping with relapses.

Before termination, the therapist should ask the client to reflect on what specifically has helped in treatment both during sessions and outside of therapy. This can be followed with a discussion of ways in which the client can maintain or even further the gains they have made. Clients should be encouraged to *Act as*

BOX 22.1

Description of Acute Phase, Continuation Phase, and Maintenance Phase
QOLT Treatment with Clinical Populations with Recurrent *DSM* Disorders

ACUTE PHASE TREATMENT WITH EMBEDDED RELAPSE PREVENTION TRAINING

- *Acute Phase* refers to the initial treatment of any psychological disturbance or DSM disorder. Most treatment ends here due to cost and time constraints.

- Goal is symptom remission and restoration of quality of life and psychosocial functioning to previous levels or higher along with skills in *Being One's Own Therapist* so that QOLT clients can establish life skill routines or *Happiness Habits* that will prevent relapse as long as they are enacted. Additionally, clients will learn skills applicable to preventing and coping with lapses and relapses per se—see Chapter 22.

- Evidence-Based Treatment such as cognitive therapy and/or medication treatment response is boosted or augmented with QOLT positive psychology interventions aimed at activating the construction mode (Clark & Beck, 1999) just as lithium or thyroid hormone is used at times to augment the impact of SSRIs in pharmacotherapy (Rush & Kupfer, 2001).

CONTINUATION PHASE TREATMENT

- *Continuation Phase* refers to clinicians' estimate of the natural, untreated course or typical duration of a disorder's episode after which it would remit spontaneously, that is, without formal treatment. This estimate usually lasts 4 to 9 months in cases of depression (Rush & Kupfer, 2001) and is often based on clients' reports of the typical duration of previous untreated episodes of disturbance (Rush & Kupfer, 2001).

- Refers to some modicum of treatment such as monthly sessions offered after acute treatment and during clients' continuation phase.

- Goal: Treatment of *residual* symptoms of disorder left over from the acute phase of treatment and especially, relapse prevention; more specifically, prevent the return of the most recent full blown episode of psychological disturbance that was successfully treated to a large extent in the acute phase of treatment.

- In QOLT, monthly treatment sessions involve either QOLT positive psychology interventions aimed at activating the construction mode (Clark & Beck, 1999) *or* the *combination* of positive psychology interventions with evidence-based cognitive therapy and/or medication treatment.

MAINTENANCE PHASE TREATMENT

- *Maintenance Phase* refers to the period of time after the acute and continuation phases of treatment when clients with a recurrent disorder, such as three or more episodes of depression, are at high risk for relapse. This phase and the treatment associated with it can last from 1 or 2 years to a lifetime for clients with a highly recurrent or chronic disorder.

- Goal: Relapse prevention; more specifically, prevent the return of *new episodes* of psychological disturbance in clients with recurrent or chronic DSM disorders.

- In QOLT, monthly treatment sessions involve QOLT positive psychology interventions aimed at activating the construction mode (Clark & Beck, 1999) *or* the combination of positive psychology interventions with evidence-based cognitive therapy and/or medication treatment.

Their Own Therapist or Coach as they continue applying the attitudes and coping skills that have been helpful in therapy to their everyday life. The client should be reminded that the goal of therapy is to make the therapist obsolete in so far as the therapist is trying to teach the client ways that he or she can help themselves. Of course, the therapist should emphasize to the client that she or he is available as a resource for "booster sessions," occasional consultations, continuation treatment, or full-blown relapses.

Clients may be encouraged to know that coping skills treatment such as QOLT and other cognitive-behavioral approaches have been found to be effective in preventing relapses because these models teach clients practical self-help skills that they can use to maintain their gains and either cope with or prevent relapse (Witkiewitz & Marlatt, 2004). Learning and practicing coping skills can, in a metaphorical sense, "inoculate" or "immunize" clients from breaking down or relapsing in future stressful situations. Therapists should, however, prepare clients for the possibility of relapses. In general, the therapeutic strategy is to "normalize" the relapse as something to be expected so that clients do not get discouraged or give up.

Coping with Relapse: Rationale

Before termination, the therapist should work with the client to plan for relapse prevention as well as to develop a plan for coping with a relapse should it occur. The following therapy transcript demonstrates one approach to introducing the topic:

> While you've done a great job in dealing with your growth plans, problems, and symptoms in therapy, I'd like for us to develop a plan for coping with relapses. In many ways, the skills and attitudes that you've learned in therapy have made you your own therapist or coach. Still, especially during periods of severe stress, you may revert to your old way of thinking, feeling, and behaving. You've built a style of coping over the years. You're forging a new path to personal growth now, but it will take time and practice for this new style to be comfortable enough for you to stay with during times of stress. For example, even those who have successfully quit lifetime habits of smoking or alcoholism typically have numerous lapses or relapses before they develop their skills sufficiently to maintain abstinence. The same goes for Happiness Habits and the symptoms of various clinical disorders in the *DSM*. In addition, research indicates that most people

aren't really stable in their abstinence until they have been abstinent for a year and a half or more. Any mental health disorder or quality of life problem can reemerge if we're stressed enough.

> It's important to have the right attitude and a plan for dealing with a lapse or relapse. A relapse is just a sign that your skills and awareness have not developed enough yet to give you a consistent quality of life. So, should you have a relapse, say to yourself, "I'm going to get back on the horse of Quality of Life Therapy, redo the exercises that helped in the past, try to figure out why I lapsed, and expand my understanding and skills so that I will have fewer or no lapses in the future." Use a lapse as a signal or wake up call to take some Quality Time, perhaps a Mental Health Day—from the Tenets—and do some major Inner Abundance work; pull out your copy of Finding Happiness to recall these ideas. Experiencing a lapse or relapse is just a sign that you are human. It is not a sign that you are a complete failure or a hopeless case. A lapse need not turn into a relapse or total collapse. Recall during these "down" times of a lapse or relapse, the days and weeks of success achieved in therapy. Perhaps do the BAT exercise in Chapter 12 to remind yourself of your successes, strengths, and value as a person. Recall your past treatment successes—Nothing can take that away from you. You did it once; you can do it again. This is the attitude you need to deal effectively with a relapse. This attitude and other tips for limiting and overcoming relapses are in the Relapse Emergency Checklist (in the Toolbox CD), which I'd like you to complete as part of a personal growth exercise for our next session. The Checklist has room for any suggestions that you or your Expert Friends—from Tenets—have for coping effectively with a relapse along with other ideas that have helped previous clients in your situation. Once you complete the Checklist, you will have a plan that you can immediately implement should you find yourself backsliding into your old negative habits, thoughts, and feelings. I can go over your Checklist with you to be sure that we leave nothing out that could be of benefit.

Use of Metaphor

The metaphor of horseback riding can help to communicate the attitude clients need to deal effectively with relapses. Clients can be told that self-improvement or efforts at personal growth is like learning to ride a horse. Clients may get "knocked off the horse" by stresses or temptations in their life. They may revert to their old ways for a time. This is to be expected and is a normal part of the process. It's okay to "fall off the horse," so to speak, and have a relapse. No one learns to ride perfectly right away. It takes persistence and practice. Tell clients that if stress knocks them off the "horse" of positive change, they should get up, dust themselves off, and get back on using the positive coping skills they have already learned and, if necessary, developing new ones in order to further their quest.

Relapse Emergency Checklist

The Relapse Emergency Checklist is an essential tool for coping with relapses that can be found in the Toolbox CD. If possible, therapists may begin completing the checklist with clients in session. It is also helpful to go over the Relapse Emergency Checklist *after* clients have first completed it in order to help clients brain storm with Five Paths on new steps that can help them to cope effectively with a relapse situation, to check for errors or omissions, too add useful strategies that clients might not have considered, and, finally, to clearly verify to themselves and to clients that this is a realistic plan of action should clients find themselves in a relapse situation. It can also help for clients to *practice* their plan for dealing with a relapse in their imagination, in real life, or in a therapy session. For example, the therapist can role-play challenging situations with others using the ideas from Chapter 14 on Relationships. Box 22.2 contains the *Relapse Emergency Checklist.*

Relapse Prevention

While clients need skills for coping with relapses, it is infinitely preferable to prevent relapses from occurring in the first place. As part of termination, therapists and clients should invoke the Habit Control Program of Chapter 13, viewing Happiness Habits as "positive addictions" and discuss the triggers for relapse and develop a coping plan (which could consist of skill training, practice, and/or role-playing) for dealing with them. Triggers consist of a variety of situations, thoughts, feelings, or behaviors that may increase the likelihood of the client backsliding into old, self-defeating problems and symptoms.

Kelly Brownell of Yale uses the metaphor of a forest ranger to communicate to clients the task of relapse prevention (Brownell, 2004). The goal of forest rangers is to prevent forest fires and to put fires out before they spread and do major damage (think of the old "Smokey the Bear" TV commercials). The fires are like relapses. Just as forest rangers try to take control of the forest to prevent or put out fires, clients need to take control of their lives and of high-risk trigger situations in particular in order to prevent lapses and to minimize or "stomp out" fires or relapses that do occur. Like the forest ranger, clients must be "eternally vigilant" for situations, thoughts, feelings, or behaviors that may lead them to lapse or relapse. Clients must be prepared for high-risk trigger situations and have a plan to deal with these situations should they occur. Part of this "forest ranger" job is to stay calm in a crisis and maintain a positive, optimistic attitude. As previously discussed, lapses must be viewed as an inevitable part of the human change process and not a sign of failure. Techniques for "stomping out" fires or relapses as soon as they occur are discussed in the context of the Relapse Emergency Checklist.

Early Warning Signs and the PSP—Personal Stress Profile—Instrument

As described in the Habit Control Program in Chapter 13, triggers may consist of situations, thoughts, feelings, or behaviors. One of the best ways for clients to prevent relapses is to become more sensitive to the way in which they experience stress. In a sense, any stressor may function as a trigger for relapse in so far as it creates distress in a client and puts demands on her coping resources. If clients can learn to identify the unique ways in which they experience stress in the early stages, they can use this awareness to short-circuit their stress response, thereby preventing a lapse or relapse. This approach to relapse prevention encourages clients to react to their early signs of stress as a signal to exercise positive coping strategies instead of "sitting back" and watching their stress escalate to the point of a relapse into old, destructive ways of coping. Clients can also use their awareness of early signs of stress to identify trigger situations in their life that make them uncomfortable and that may, therefore, precipitate a lapse or relapse. Therapists may facilitate clients' awareness of their internal signs of stress by asking them to complete the Personal Stress Profile (PSP) from the Toolbox CD (see also Box 22.3 on p. 320).

BOX 22.2
Relapse Emergency Checklist

Name: _____   Date: _____

Instructions: Circle the *thoughts* and *activities* that you believe will best help you to positively cope with a lapse into old patterns and problems so that the lapse does not turn into a complete relapse or collapse. Add your own thoughts and activities and carry this checklist with you at all times. At the first sign of a lapse, find a quiet place to review this checklist. Repeat each thought and carry out each activity until the lapse has stopped and until the urges to lapse gradually subside—as they always do. When feeling out of control, go over your list with a trusted friend or professional who can help you to implement the activities on the checklist.

1. Get out of the situation. If necessary, make an excuse, leave and go somewhere else, even outside or to a bathroom, to calm down and collect your thoughts.

2. Call or visit a friend, family member, or counselor who will support you in your efforts to maintain the gains you've made and who cares about you, "warts and all." Consult your list of who to call and keep calling until you reach someone.

Name	Contact Info
1. _____	_____
2. _____	_____
3. _____	_____
4. _____	_____
5. _____	_____

3. Recall the reasons why you've tried to change destructive thoughts, feelings, or behaviors. Consult the list below:

Advantages of Staying with My Quality of Life Therapy Program

1. _____   6. _____
2. _____   7. _____
3. _____   8. _____
4. _____   9. _____
5. _____   10. _____

4. Distract yourself and wait out urges by doing something fun or engaging somewhere else.

5. Exercise.

6. Take a walk.

7. Go to bed, lie down, and relax.

8. Forgive yourself and get back "on the wagon" of Quality of Life Therapy.

9. Remember that staying happy takes practice. What can you learn from the mistake?

10. Imagine yourself as you were before the lapse.

11. Write in your journal.

12. Do a *Lie Detector and Stress Diary*.

13. Ask yourself, "What's bugging me?" and tackle the problem. A lapse is just a distraction from a problem or bad feeling. What problem am I not facing right now?

14. Do a *Five Paths* problem-solving exercise.

15. Listen to music.

16. Make tea or coffee.

17. Have a healthy snack.

18. Identify the trigger, make a plan for the future, and forget it.

19. Never give up on your ability to regain control. You did it before.

20. Stand up for yourself and say "No!" to the urges to lapse.

21. Think "How will I feel in the morning? Is a relapse worth the cost of lower self-respect and confidence?"

22. STOP! You worked too hard to "chuck" it all now.

23. Take responsibility for your thoughts and behavior, which you *do* have control of.

24. Stop denying that this hurts you in the end.

25. Remember that this is a lifelong project. One lapse won't kill you.

26. Surf the net or look at a newspaper, picture book, or magazine.

27. Urges and temptations are like a wave. They build up and then subside. Wait it out.

28. For just 10 minutes, agree that you'll do something else and not indulge the urge.

29. Do a Relaxation Ritual or *Play/Creativity/Learning/Helping Routine*.

30. Think positive. You can get through this and eventually Survive and Thrive.

31. Think of how you'll pay for this later.

32. Just do one thing at a time . . . and forget the rest.

(Continued)

33. Ask yourself "What's bugging me . . . really?"

34. Take the time to calm down and get back on the wagon. What is more important than your health?

35. Do a chore. Get back to your routine.

36. Find friends or hobbies as a way to cope with stress.

37. You can be happy without relapsing.

38. Make this a challenge for greater self-esteem, self-caring, forgiveness, and creativity in finding new ways to cope and solve problems.

39. Remember that no one is perfect. It's human and natural to make mistakes.

40. Use the lapse as a signal to leave and do something else.

41. Take a shower or a bath.

42. Recall the benefits of staying with the program.

43. Take 30 minutes of quality time alone.

44. Take a bike ride.

45. Go for a drive.

46. Look at family picture files or albums.

47. Stop making excuses.

48. Go to a meeting of a self-help group.

49. Go to a religious service.

50. Do something nice for someone.

51. Buy a gift for yourself or someone else.

52. Do something nice and healthy for yourself.

53. Daydream about something you like.

54. Do QOLT exercises and readings.

55. Read through *Finding Happiness.*

56. Read over old notes from counseling sessions.

57. Ask a friend to come over and just be with you.

58. Play with your children.

59. Play with your partner or a friend.

60. Play with your pet.

61. Do volunteer work.

62.. Go to the office and catch up.

63. Take deep breaths for 5 minutes.

64. Remember it's never easy, but you can get back to where you were.

65. Take pride in your relationships. Do something to keep these alive.

66. Stop stuffing the anger, fear, hurt, sadness, or grief away.

67. Rent a video or watch a movie.

68. Ask what would my role model do and then do it!

69. Do something with your hands—knit, draw, do the dishes, lift weights—anything.

70. Read the Tenets of Contentment.

71. Do a *Daily Activity Plan* for the time between now and the time when you go to bed.

72. Stand up to others pressuring you to lapse.

73. Use the *Habit Control Program* to get back to where you were.

74. Make time to figure out what went wrong and to fix it. This is important.

75. _____

76. _____

Post-PSP Procedures

Therapists should go over the clients' completed Personal Stress Profiles or PSPs in order to add their own ideas and to identify the clients' signs and "symptoms" (whether physical, feelings, thoughts, images, or behaviors) of stress. It is especially important for therapists to try to identify the very first signs of stress, since the earlier they are identified, the greater the likelihood for minimizing the temptation to lapse. Kristie, for example, learned that she began to clench her teeth in the early stages of an anger outburst. This awareness was pivotal in her efforts at change since she learned to identify this *Early Warning Signal* and act immediately to diffuse the situation with a positive coping response.

Once clients have learned to identify which PSPs can be viewed as internal or inner personal triggers for relapse, therapists should encourage them to begin identifying external or "situational" triggers. This can be accomplished in many ways. For example, during a session, the therapist can ask clients to identify challenging trigger situations that they will face once therapy has been terminated. In addition, therapists should lend their expertise and give their opinions as to the likely trigger situations and challenges that the client may face once therapy is terminated. Previously completed Lie Detectors may also be reviewed

BOX 22.3
Personal Stress Profile (PSP)

Name: _____   Date: _____

Instructions: Each of us responds to stress in unique ways. If you can learn to pay attention and to notice the signs of stress early, before you get too upset, you can "nip" stress "in the bud." You can use your early signs of stress as an early warning signal, to stop, figure out what's going on, and apply new positive coping techniques. The more you practice applying new coping skills, the more automatic and comfortable they will become. The first step is to identify your unique signs of stress, your Personal Stress Profile or PSP. Think about the times that you have gotten upset lately. Picture the incident in your imagination as if you were watching it on a video. "Rewind" the image to just before you started to get upset and notice your early signs of stress. Identify your Personal Stress Profile by circling the items below that apply to you when you feel stressed. With practice, you will use these signs as cues to cope in positive ways.

Physical Sensations

1. Muscle tension
2. Headache
3. Back pain
4. Sweaty or clammy hands
5. Sweating
6. Heart pounding
7. Tightness across chest
8. Chest pains
9. Teeth clenching
10. Cold or numb feet or hands
11. Hard to breathe
12. Dizzy
13. Nausea
14. Vomiting
15. Diarrhea or constipation
16. Dry mouth
17. Feeling tired
18. Trembling or shaking
19. Muscle spasms
20. Feeling hot

21. Blushing

22. Feel numb or dead all over

23. Skin irritation

24. High blood pressure

25. Not hungry

Other _____

Feelings

26. Uptight

27. Scared

28. Worried

29. Anxious

30. Restless

31. Overwhelmed

32. Confused

33. Annoyed

34. Irritated

35. Frustrated

36. Angry or mad

37. Disappointed

38. Hurt

39. Tired

40. Sad

41. Depressed

42. Lonely

43. Hopeless

44. Jealous/envious

45. Guilty

46. Ashamed

47. Bored

48. Lazy

49. Disgusted with Self

50. Overexcited

51. Miserable

Other _____

(Continued)

Thoughts/Images

52. Frequent worrying about problem(s)

53. Thinking "Something bad is going to happen"

54. "I'm doomed"

55. "I'm out of control"

56. "The worst is going to happen"

57. "I couldn't survive if the worst happened"

58. "I can't stand this"

59. "I can't cope with this"

60. "It's hopeless"

61. "There is nothing I can do to make things better"

62. "I'm bad, no good"

63. "I give up. To hell with it. I don't care anymore"

64. Visualizing a car or plane crashing

65. Visualizing worst fears coming true. Specify _____

_____

66. Having suicidal thoughts

67. "This is unfair and I shouldn't have to take it"

Other _____

Actions or Behaviors

68. Hand wringing

69. Pacing

70. Biting nails, tapping feet, playing with your hair, or other nervous habit

71. Problems concentrating or staying on task

72. Losing temper easily

73. Acting aggressively

74. Hurrying or rushing

75. Putting things off

76. Frequent checking that everything is all right or going well

77. Problems sleeping

78. Feeling lazy

79. Passivity

80. Procrastination

81. Crying spells

82. Abusing illegal or prescription drugs

83. Overeating

84. Over-drinking

85. Engaging in addictive or compulsive Behavior (specify) _____

_____

86. Acting impulsively

87. Losing control

88. Doing something foolish or self-defeating

Other _____

to identify potential trigger situations. Finally, clients can be asked to simply keep a diary of situations during the week in which they feel tempted to give up their efforts at change and to revert to old self-destructive patterns of thinking, feeling, and behaving. It is also useful to go over any lapses that have occurred over the course of therapy. It is especially important for the therapist and client to identify the *behavior chain* or sequence of behaviors that eventually led up to the relapse. For example, Greg identified a trigger situation as "staying up too late" even though it occurred a full 24 hours before a relapse into problem drinking. Greg identified a pattern in which he woke up tired and irritable due to a lack of sleep, went to work, got into a fight with a coworker due to his increased irritability, began to feel hopeless and angry, and was afraid about what would happen as a result of his disagreement. Feeling stressed, he accepted an invitation from a friend to go out for pizza. Out of his frustration over what had happened at work, he concluded that his change efforts were hopeless, and wound up sharing five pitchers of beer with his friend.

Once personal and situational triggers have been identified, clients must develop a coping plan for them. It is important for the therapist to assess whether clients have the necessary skills and confidence to exercise their plans. In some cases, clients may need to learn and practice new skills, as in the case of clients who lack social skills and who are socially pressured to resume their addictions.

Relapse Prevention Worksheet

The Relapse Prevention worksheet from the Toolbox CD provides a structure for clients to list relapse triggers as well as corresponding trigger-specific coping plans. These coping plans can include any techniques used during the course of QOLT in addition to new ideas designed to avoid, eliminate, or diffuse internal or situational triggers. The second part of this worksheet allows clients to list ongoing or day-to-day activities that they believe will help them to maintain their gains. The therapist should help and encourage clients to include techniques used during the course of QOLT in both Parts One and Two of the Relapse Prevention worksheet. The following QOLT techniques have been particularly helpful to clients in relapse prevention: Habit Diaries from Chapter 13 and the Toolbox CD, Quality Time, Five Paths to Happiness problem-solving worksheet, Lie Detector and Stress Diary, Daily Activity Plan, Relaxation Rituals, Crying Time, Good-Not-Great technique, Basket-of-Eggs technique, Success Log, Relationship Skills, Recreation Routine, Habit Control Program, and New Life Script. Box 22.4 illustrates a clinical example of a completed *Relapse Prevention* worksheet.

New Life Script Rewritten and Focused on Relapse Prevention

The New Life Script summary of positive goals, values, and schemas from Chapter 11 can be rewritten

---

BOX 22.4
Clinical Example of Relapse Prevention Exercise

Name: *Morgan*   Date: *February 13, 2010*

Part I: Encouraging Happiness Habits and Positive Addictions with Encouragers or Positive Triggers

Instructions: List any people, situations, QOLT exercises, or internal thoughts, feelings, or behaviors that may *trigger* or encourage you to engage in *Happiness Habits* and other positive addictions like greater physical activity from QOLT. Use this list to design your environment and circumstances to expose yourself to these positive influences as much as possible. Make these encouragers or *positive triggers* a part of your immediate environment on an ongoing basis in order to maintain your progress in QOLT and your current level of quality of life, satisfaction, and happiness.

1. *Daily* Quality Time *and* Inner Abundance *alone to go over my life goals, personal values, and reasons for personal growth and self-improvement. Apologize and take a hot bubble bath with a* Lie Detector *after I've gotten upset, mad, and slipped (lapsed) by being too harsh with Austin (son).*

2. *Do* Take-a-Letter *and* Five Paths *to resolve disagreements with Jerry (husband). Also, do monthly* Night Out, Favor Bank *(daily),* Compliment, *and* Making Conversation—*from Relationship Skills—to keep up five positive interactions for every negative one in my marriage.*

3. *Start taking classes at the community college to serve my goal for a career with flow working as a "vet tech" with the animals I love.*

4. *Paste my New Life Script and Street Signs to Success on my mirror or listen to a DVD of it in the car once a week.*

5. *Stay in touch with friends and plan some fun with one of them monthly.*

6. *Write a Take-a-Letter #1 to Mom and Dad to get my hurt feelings out and better understand my problems (even though they are deceased).*

7. *In keeping with the Basket-of-Eggs (Chapter 8), do some volunteer work and go back to needlework as my "therapy" and flow hobby.*

8. *Never give up on me. I've done it before. Lapses are just part of the journey (of life and growth). I hereby forgive me and vow to get back on the horse of QOLT any time I falter. No big deal. We all make mistakes and this'll work out damn it. Rome wasn't built in a day!*

9. *Keep Dr. Frisch's picture in my wallet as I do the* What Would My Role Model Do *thing (tenet) by asking myself "WWDFD" or "What Would Dr. Frisch Do?" If this doesn't work, I've got Dr. Frisch's phone number on speed dial in my cell phone.*

Part II: Discouraging or Negative Triggers for Happiness—Depleters and Negative Addictions—Clinical Example

Instructions: List any situations or internal signs of stress (as from your Personal Stress Profile), thoughts, feelings, or behaviors that may encourage you to lapse or relapse into negative thoughts, feelings, behaviors, or habits For each *trigger*, write down a plan of things you can do to manage with, cope, or eliminate the trigger so as to avoid a lapse or relapse. If necessary, practice your coping plan until you are sure that you can apply it in real life.

Trigger for Relapse (Including Negative Circumstances, Situations, Thoughts, Feelings, Behaviors)	Trigger-Specific Coping Plan (Including QOLT Techniques)
Situations Involving Austin, My Toddler	
1. (from PSP *in Toolbox*) *Teeth clenched, "I want to slap you, you little monster." Anger*	*Say "I'm too upset to talk about this now. Go to your room and I'll come talk to you in a little while." Take a bath and Quality Time break. Call a friend over to "keep me safe from hitting Austin."*
2. *I remind Austin (son) that he may not drink his drink in the car and must wait until we get home to eat. He opens the lid on his Coke anyway and spills it on his sister who is crying.*	*Keep your eyes on the road. Take some* Mindful Breaths. *Say, "Jerry (husband), I need you to handle this one as we talked about." Problem solve with Jerry about this problem away from the kids when we get home.*

---

and focused on relapse prevention. A subclinically depressed physician interested in positive psychology, Jesse did precisely this. She reviewed her New Life Script each week as part of her relapse prevention plan. The script amounted to an excellent summary of QOLT and can be found at the end of Chapter 11.

RELAPSE PREVENTION AND COPING WITH RELAPSES: FURTHER RESOURCES

Clients typically choose chapters from *Finding Happiness* along with Toolbox CD Skills, and related Tenets for additional skills and guidance for success in relapse prevention and coping with relapses. Table 22.1 lists Tenets with attitudes, schemas, and practices most conducive to greater success in maintaining gains in QOLT, relapse prevention, and coping with break-through relapses. Clients may read these along with ones chosen and even written by themselves as part of an individually tailored plan most likely to succeed in preventing or coping with relapse to old happiness-depleting behaviors, thinking patterns, and psychonoxious environments such as those characterized by social isolation, disparagement, or cynicism/pessimism.

Table 22.1 Tenets with Attitudes, Schemas, and Practices Conducive to Greater Success in Maintaining Gains in QOLT, Relapse Prevention, and Coping with Break-Through Relapses

Abuse or Neglect Principle or ACOAN Principle	Equality Principle
Accept What You Cannot Change Principle	Exercise or Take your Medication Principle
Acceptance Principle or Nothing Human Disgusts Me Principle	Expect the Unexpected Principle
Anger Is the Enemy or Shift of Hate Principle	Expert Friend Principle
Ask Your Death Tenet	Face the Music Principle
Assessing Progress and Prospects Principle or Taking Your Emotional Temperature	Failure Quota Principle
	FAT Time Principle
Attack the Moment or Mine the Moment Principle	Favor Bank or Favor Bank of Good Will from Good Deeds or Mindset of Constant Gratitude and Acts of Kindness Principle
Avoid Stress Carriers or I Never Bother with People I Hate Rule	
	Feed the Soul Principle
Balanced Lifestyle Principle	Fight for Much, Reap Frustration Principle
Be the Peace You Seek or Worry Warts Principle	Find an Area or Go to Your Room or Principle
Be with People or Relationship Immersion Principle	Find a Friend, Find a Mate Principle
Be Your Own Guru or Personal Wisdom Principle	Find a Goal Principle (see also Find a Meaning Principle)
The Big 3 Makes Us Dumb Principle—Emotional Control Principle	Flow It Principle
	The FOOBS Principle or Switch Out of FOOBS Principle or The Multiple Personality or Multiple Personality of Everyday Life
Blind Dumb Optimism Principle	
Bosom Friends Principle	Get a Therapist Rule
Calculated Risk Principle	Get Organized Principle
Can't Buy Me Love or Forget Fame and Fortune Rule	Giving Tree or Self-Other Principle
Care for My One Body Principle	Habits Rule Rule or Routines Rule Rule
Check-In with Friends Principle	Happiness Diet Principle
Clear Conscience Rule (see also Do the Right Thing Rule or When in Doubt, Don't Rule)	Happiness Equation Tenet
	Happiness Is a Choice Principle or Responsibility Principle
Cocoon It Rule	Happiness Matters Principle
Color Purple Principle	Happiness Set Point Principle (see also Personality Stays the Same Principle)
Commune with Nature Rule (see also Li Po Rule)	
Daily Vacation Principle	Happiness Spillover Principle
Depression Is Not Normal Principle	Happiness Takes Effort Principle (see also Keep Busy with Flows Principle)
Don't Bring It Home or Work Spillover Principle	
Don't Forgive Principle or Set Aside, Shelve, Accept or Forget Principle	How Kind Principle or Tender Hearted Rule
	Humble Servant or Servant Leader Principle
Do What You Love or Tune in to What Turns You on Principle	Humor Principle
Emotional Honesty Principle	I Can Do It Principle
Empathy Principle (see also To Understand All Is To Forgive All Principle)	I'll Think about That Tomorrow Principle

Table 22.1 *Continued*

Inner Abundance Principle

Intellectual Masturbation Principle

Judge Not, You Don't Know Principle

Kiss the Past Goodbye Principle

Leisurely Pace and Lifestyle Principle

Live Your Dream or 24/7 Principle

Love Many Things Principle

Love Where You Are Principle (see also Tangled Web Principle or Web of Support)

Lower Expectations Principle (see also Never Good Enough Principle)

Make Friends at Work Principle

Make It Routine Principle (see also Routine Is Everything Principle)

Manage Your Time and Your Life Rule

Meanings Like Buses Rule

Mental Health Day Technique

Modest Goal

Mutual Aid Society Principle

No Conditions of Worth Rule

No Gossip/Criticism/Suggestions or Words as Daggers Rule

No Mayo, Pickles, or Mustard Rule

Organ Recital Rule (see also Silence is Golden Rule)

One-Thing-at-a-Time Principle (OTAAT)

Overthinking Principle

The PCD Time for Couples Rule

Parent-Teacher Support Principle

Pick a Role Model for a Friend Principle

Pick Your Battles/Pick No Battles Principle or Yes, Boss/Yes, Dear Rule or Under the Influence Principle

Pick Your Friends Principle

Play It Safe Principle

Play Like a Kid/Frivolous Flows Principle

Pocket of Time to Relax Principle

Positive Addictions Principle

Process Goal Principle

Quality Time Principle

The Question Rule

Reasoned Passion Principle (see also Selective Hedonism Principle)

Relationship with Self or Self-Compassion Principle

Ride It Out, Read It Out Principle

Role Model Principle (see also What Would My Role Model Do Principle)

Romantic Friendship or Take the Sex Out of Marriage Rule

Second Opinion Principle or Technique

See a Psychiatrist Principle

Self-Acceptance Principle

Serve Others Principle

Share the Hurt Behind the Anger Tenet

Should-Want Principle

Socializing Doubles Your Pleasure

Stop Second Guessing Principle

Street Signs to Success Principle

Strength It Principle

String of Pearls Practice and Principle

Surrogate Family Principle

Sweet Revenge Principle

Take a Stand Principle

Taoist Dodge Ball Rule

Terrorist Principle (see also You Do It to Yourself Principle)

Thank Everyone for Everything Principle

Thou Shalt Be Aware or Psychephobia Principle

The Three Rs of Stress Management Principle

Trust Principle

We Are Family Principle

We're Not Okay and That's Okay Rule

You Are What You Do

References

Abbe, A., Tkach, C., & Lyubomirsky, S. (2003). The art of living by dispositionally happy people. *Journal of Happiness Studies: An Interdisciplinary Forum on Subjective Well-Being, 4,* 385–404.

Abeles, R. P., Gift, H. C., & Ory, M. G. (Eds.). (1994). *Aging and quality of life.* New York: Springer.

Abramson, L. Y., Metalsky, G. I., & Alloy, L. B. (1989). Hopelessness depression: A theory-based subtype of depression. *Psychological Review, 98,* 358–372.

Abramson, L. Y., Seligman, M. E. P., & Teasdale, J. D. (1978). Learned helplessness in humans: A critique and reformulation. *Journal of Abnormal Psychology, 87,* 49–74.

Ahrens, A. H. (1987). Theories of depression: The role of goals and the self-evaluation process. *Cognitive Therapy and Research, 11,* 665–680.

American College of Physicians. (1988). Comprehensive functional assessment for elderly patients. *Annals of Internal Medicine, 109,* 70–72.

American Psychiatric Association. (2000a). *Diagnostic and statistical manual of mental disorders* (4th ed. TR). Washington, DC: Author.

American Psychiatric Association. (2000b). *Handbook of psychiatric measures.* Washington, DC: Author.

American Psychological Association. (2002). Ethical principles of psychologists and code of conduct. *American Psychologist, 57*(12), 1060–1073.

Anderson, B. L., Kiecolt-Glaser, J. K., & Glaser, R. (1994). A biobehavioral model of cancer stress and disease course. *American Psychologist, 49,* 389–404.

Andrews, F. M. (1974). Social indicators of perceived quality of life. *Social Indicators Research, 1,* 279–299.

Andrews, F. M., & Inglehart, R. F. (1979). The structure of well-being in nine western societies. *Social Indicators Research, 6,* 73–90.

Andrews, F. M., & Robinson, J. P. (1991). Measures of subjective well-being. In J. P. Robinson, P. R. Shaver, & L. S. Wrights-man (Eds.), *Measures of personality and social psychological attitudes* (pp. 61–114). San Diego, CA: Academic Press.

Andrews, F. M., & Withey, S. B. (1976). *Social indicators of well being: American's perceptions of life quality.* New York: Plenum Press.

Argyle, M. (1999). Causes and correlates of happiness. In D. Kahneman, E. Diener, & N. Schwarz (Eds.), *Well-being: The foundations of hedonic psychology* (pp. 61–84). New York: Russell Sage.

Argyle, M. (2001). *The psychology of happiness* (2nd ed.). London: Routledge.

Aristotle. (2000). *Nicomachean ethics* (R. Crisp, Ed. & Trans.). New York: Cambridge University Press.

Arns, P. G., & Linney, J. A. (1995). Relating functional skills of severely mentally ill patients to subjective and societal benefits. *Psychiatric Services, 46,* 260–265.

Awad, A. G. (1992). Quality of life of schizophrenic patients on medications and implications for new drug trials. *Hospital and Community Psychiatry, 43,* 262–265.

Babigian, H. M., Cole, R. E., Reed, S. K., Brown, S. W., & Lehman, A. F. (1991). Methodology for evaluating the Monroe-Livingston capitation system. *Hospital and Community Psychiatry, 42,* 913–919.

Baltes, P. B., & Baltes, M. M. (Eds.). (1990). *Successful aging: Perspectives from the behavioral sciences.* New York: Cambridge University Press.

Bandura, A. (1986). *Social foundations of thought and action: A social-cognitive theory.* Englewood Cliffs, NJ: Prentice-Hall.

Barlow, D. H. (2002). *Anxiety and its disorders: The nature and treatment of anxiety and panic* (2nd ed.). New York: Guilford Press.

Barlow, D. H., Allen, L. B., & Choate, M. L. (2004). Toward a unified treatment for emotional disorders. *Behavior Therapy, 35,* 205–230.

Baruffol, E., Gisle, L., & Corten, P. (1995). Life satisfaction as a mediator between distressing events and neurotic impairment in a general population. *Acta Psychiatrica Scandinavica, 92,* 56–62.

Baumeister, R. F. (1991). *Escaping the self: Alcoholism, spirituality, masochism, and other flights from the burden of selfhood.* New York: Basic Books.

Beck, A. T. (1979). *Cognitive therapy and the emotional disorders.* New York: Plume.

Beck, A. T. (1996). Beyond belief: A theory of modes, personality, and psychopathology. In P. M. Salkovskis (Ed.), *Frontiers of cognitive therapy* (pp. 1–25). New York: Guilford Press.

Beck, A. T. (1999). *Prisoners of hate: The cognitive basis of anger, hostility, and violence.* New York: HarperCollins.

Beck, A. T., Freeman, A. A., Davis, D. D., & Associates. (2004). *Cognitive therapy of personality disorders* (2nd ed.). New York: Guilford Press.

Beck, A. T., Rush, A. J., Shaw, B. F., & Emery, G. (1979). *Cognitive therapy of depression.* New York: Guilford Press.

Beck, A. T., Wright, F. D., Newman, C. F., & Liese, B. S. (1993). *Cognitive therapy for substance abuse.* New York: Guilford Press.

Beck, J. S. (1995). *Cognitive therapy: Basics and beyond.* New York: Guilford Press.

Ben-Porath, Y. S. (1997). Use of personality assessment instruments in empirically guided treatment planning. *Psychological Assessment, 9,* 361–367.

Berzon, R. A. (1998). Understanding and using health-related quality of life instruments within clinical research studies. In M. J. Staquet, R. D. Hays, & P. M. Fayers (Eds.), *Quality of life assessment in clinical trials* (pp. 3–15). Oxford, England: Oxford University Press.

Bigelow, D. A., Brodsky, G., Stewart, L., & Olson, M. (1982). The concept and measurement of quality of life as a dependent variable in evaluation of mental health services. In G. J. Stahler & W. R. Tash (Eds.), *Innovative approaches to mental health evaluation* (pp. 345–366). New York: Academic Press.

Biswas-Diener, R., Vitterso, J., & Diener, E. (2003). *Most people are pretty happy, but there is cultural variation: The Inughwit, the Amish, and the Maasai.* Manuscript submitted for publication.

Bowlby, J. (1985). The role of childhood experience in cognitive disturbance. In M. J. Mahoney & A. Freeman (Eds.), *Cognition and psychotherapy* (pp. 181–200). New York: Plenum Press.

Bowling, A. (1991). *Measuring health: A review of quality of life measurement scales.* Philadelphia: Open University Press.

Bradburn, N. M. (1969). *The structure of psychological well-being.* Chicago: Aldine.

Brickman, P., & Campbell, D. T. (1971). Hedonic relativism and planning the good society. In M. H. Appley (Ed.), *Adaptation-level theory* (pp. 287–305). New York: Academic Press.

Brickman, P., Coates, D., & Janoff-Bulman, R. (1978). Lottery winners and accident victims: Is happiness relative? *Journal of Personality and Social Psychology, 36,* 917–927.

Brief, A. P., & Nord, W. R. (1990). Work and nonwork connections. In A. P. Brief & W. R. Nord (Eds.), *Meanings of occupational work* (pp. 171–199). Lexington, MA: Lexington Books.

Brown, D. (1995). A values-based model of facilitating career transitions. *Career Development Quarterly, 44,* 4–11.

Brownell, K. D. (2004). *The LEARN® Program for Weight Management* (10th ed.). Dallas, Texas: American Health Publishing Company.

Burns, D. (1999). *Feeling good* (Rev. Ed.). New York: HarperCollins.

Campbell, A. (1981). *The sense of well-being in America.* New York: McGraw-Hill.

Campbell, A., Converse, P. E., & Rogers, W. L. (1976). *The quality of American life.* New York: Russell Sage.

Cantril, H. (1965). *The pattern of human concerns.* New Brunswick, NJ: Rutgers University.

Carlbring, P., Setling, B. E., Ljungstrand, P., Ekselius, L., & Andersson, G. (2001). Treatment of panic disorder via the internet: A randomized trial of a self-help program. *Behavior Therapy, 32,* 751–764.

Carver, C. S., & Scheier, M. F. (1990). Origins and functions of positive and negative affect: A control-process view. *Psychological Review, 97,* 19–35.

Chambliss, C. H. (2000). *Psychotherapy in managed care: Reconciling research and reality.* Boston: Allyn & Bacon.

Cheavens, J. S., Feldman, D. B., Gum, A., Michael, S. T., & Snyder, C. R. (in press). Hope therapy in a community sample: A pilot investigation. *Social Indicators Research.*

Clark, D. A., & Beck, A. T. (1999). *Scientific foundations of cognitive theory and therapy of depression.* New York: Wiley.

Clark, M. P., & Mason, T. W. (2001). Implementation of a comprehensive system of program evaluation: The Iowa State University experience. *Journal of College Student Development, 42,* 28–35.

Clark, L. A., Vittengl, J., Kraft, D., & Jarrett, R. B. (2003). Separate personality traits from states to predict depression. *Journal of Personality Disorders, 17,* 152–172.

Cleary, P. (1996). Future directions in quality of life research. In B. Spilker (Ed.), *Quality of life and pharmacoecomonics in clinical trials* (2nd ed., pp. 73–78). New York: Lippincott-Raven Press.

Coan, R. W. (1977). *Hero, artist, sage, or saint? A survey of views on what is variously called mental health, normality, maturity, self-actualization, and human fulfillment.* New York: Columbia University Press.

Coleman, R. (1992). *Lennon: The definitive biography.* New York: Perennial Currents.

Colozzi, E. A., & Colozzi, L. C. (2000). College students' callings and careers: An integrated values-oriented perspective.

In D. A. Luzzo (Ed.), *Career counseling of college students: An empirical guide to strategies that work* (pp. 63–91). Washington, DC: American Psychological Association.

Cornell, J. E., Saunders, M. J., Paunovich, E. D., & Frisch, M. B. (1997). Oral health quality of life inventory (OH-QoL). In G. Slade (Ed.), *Assessing oral health outcomes: Measuring health status and quality of life* (pp. 135–149). Chapel Hill: University of North Carolina Press.

Cottraux, J. (1993). Behavioral psychotherapy applications in the medically ill. *Psychotherapy and Psychosomatics, 60,* 116–128.

Cowen, E. (1991). In pursuit of wellness. *American Psychologist, 46,* 404–408.

Crits-Christoph, P., & Connolly, M. B. (1997). Measuring change in patients following psychological and pharmacological interventions: Anxiety disorders. In H. H. Strupp, L. M. Horowitz, & M. J. Lambert (Eds.), *Measuring patient changes in mood, anxiety, and personality disorders: Toward a core battery* (pp. 155–190). Washington, DC: American Psychological Association.

Crowley, M. J., & Kazdin, A. E. (1998). Evaluation in clinical practice: Clinically sensitive and systematic methods of treatment delivery. *Journal of Child and Family Studies, 7,* 233–251.

Crowne, D. D., & Marlowe, D. (1960). A new scale of social desirability independent of psychopathology. *Journal of Counseling Psychology, 24,* 349–354.

Csikszentmihalyi, M. (1990). *Flow: The psychology of optimal experience.* New York: Harper & Row.

Csikszentmihalyi, M. (1997). *Finding flow: The psychology of engagement with everyday life.* New York: Basic Books.

Csikszentmihalyi, M., & Hunter, J. (2003). Happiness in everyday life: The uses of experience sampling. *Journal of Happiness Studies, 4,* 185–199.

Cummins, R. A. (2003). Normative life satisfaction: Measurement issues and homeostatic model. *Social Indicators Research, 64,* 225–256.

Cushman, A. (1992). Are You Creative? *Utne Reader, 50,* 52–60.

Davis, E. E., & Fine-Davis, M. (1991). Social indicators of living conditions in Ireland with European comparisons. *Social Indicators Research, 25,* 103–365.

Davison, G. C., Neale, J. M., & Kring, A. M. (2004). *Abnormal psychology* (9th ed.). Hoboken, NJ: Wiley.

DeNeve, K. M., & Cooper, H. (1998). The happy personality: A meta-analysis of 137 personality traits and subjective well-being. *Psychological Bulletin, 124,* 197–229.

Denney, D. R., & Frisch, M. B. (1981). The role of neuroticism in relation to life stress and illness. *Journal of Psychosomatic Research, 25,* 303–307.

Derogatis, L. R., & Lynn, L. L. (1999). Psychological tests in screening for psychiatric disorder. In M. E. Maruish (Ed.), *The use of psychological testing for treatment planning and outcome assessment* (2nd ed., pp. 41–80). Mahwah, NJ: Erlbaum.

DeRubeis, R. J., Tang, T. Z., & Beck, A. T. (2001). Cognitive therapy. In K. S. Dobson. *Handbook of cognitive-behavioral therapies* (2nd ed., pp. 349–392). New York: Guilford Press.

Diamond, R., & Becker, M. (1999). The Wisconsin quality of life index: A multidimensional model for measuring quality of life. *Journal of Clinical Psychiatry, 60,* 29–31.

Dickens, C. (1947). *The personal history of David Copperfield.* Oxford: Oxford University Press.

Diener, E. (1984). Subjective well-being. *Psychological Bulletin, 95,* 542–575.

Diener, E. (2000). Subjective well-being: The science of happiness and a proposal for a national index. *American Psychologist, 55,* 34–43.

Diener, E. (2003). What is positive about positive psychology: The curmudgeon and Pollyanna. *Psychological Inquiry, 14,* 115–120.

Diener, E., & Diener, M. (1995). Cross-cultural correlates of life satisfaction and self-esteem. *Journal of Personality and Social Psychology, 68,* 653–663.

Diener, E., Diener, M., Tamir, M., Kim-Prieto, C., & Scollon, C. (2003). *A time-sequential model of subjective well-being.* Unpublished paper. Champaign, IL.

Diener, E., Emmons, R. A., Larsen, R., & Griffen, S. (1985). The satisfaction with life scale. *Journal of Personality Assessment, 49,* 71–75.

Diener, E., Horwitz, J., & Emmons, R. A. (1985). Happiness of the very wealthy. *Social Indicators Research, 16,* 263–274.

Diener, E., & Larsen, R. J. (1984). Temporal stability and cross-situational consistency of affective, behavioral, and cognitive responses. *Journal of Personality and Social Psychology, 47,* 580–592.

Diener, E., & Larsen, R. J. (1993). The experience of emotional well-being. In M. Lewis & J. M. Haviland (Eds.), *Handbook of emotions* (pp. 405–415). New York: Guilford Press.

Diener, E., & Oishi, S. (2003). Are Scandinavians happier than Asians? Issues in comparing nations on subjective well-being. In E. Columbus (Ed.), *Politics and economics of Asia.* Hauppauge, NY: Nova Science.

Diener, E., Scollon, C., & Lucas, R. E. (2004). The evolving concept of subjective well-being: The multifaceted nature of happiness. In P. T. Costa & I. C. Siegler (Eds.), *The psychology of aging.* New York: Elsevier Publishing.

Diener, E., & Seligman, M. E. P. (2002). Very happy people. *Psychological Science, 13,* 81–84.

Diener, E., & Seligman, M. E. P. (2004). Beyond money: Toward an economy of well-being. *Psychological Science in the Public Interest, 5*(1), 1–31.

Diener, E., & Suh, E. M. (Eds.). (2000). *Culture and subjective well-being.* Cambridge, MA: MIT Press.

Diener, E., Suh, E. M., Lucas, R. E., & Smith, H. L. (1999). Subjective well-being: Three decades of progress. *Psychological Bulletin, 125,* 276–302.

Dimsdale, J. E., & Baum, A. (Eds.). (1995). *Quality of life in behavioral medicine research*. Hillsdale, NJ: Erlbaum.

Donahue, E. M., Robins, R. W., Roberts, B. W., & John, O. P. (1993). The divided self: Concurrent and longitudinal effects of psychological adjustment and social roles on self-concept differentiation. *Journal of Personality and Social Psychology, 64*, 834–846.

Dworkin, R. H., Hartstein, G., Rosner, H. L., Walther, R. R., Sweeney, E. W., & Brand, L. (1992). A high-risk method for studying psychosocial antecedents of chronic pain: The prospective investigation of herpes zoster. *Journal of Abnormal Psychology, 101*, 200–205.

Easterbrook, G. (2004). *The progress paradox: How life gets better while people feel worse*. New York: Random House Trade Paperbacks.

Eickman, L. S. (2004). *Eating disorders, cognitive behavior therapy, and beyond: Innovation and critical analysis of cognitive behavioral therapy for treating eating disorders in a college counseling center*. Unpublished Manuscript. Baylor University at Waco, TX.

Eidelson, R. J., & Eidelson, J. I. (2003). Dangerous ideas: Five beliefs that propel groups toward conflict. *American Psychologist, 58*, 182–192.

Ellwood, P. M. (1988). Shattuck lecture—Outcomes management: A technology of patient experience. *New England Journal of Medicine, 23*, 1549–1556.

Emmelkamp, P. M. (1982). *Phobic and obsessive-compulsive disorders: Theory, research, and practice*. New York: Plenum Press.

Emmons, R. A. (1986). Personal strivings: An approach to personality and subjective well-being. *Journal of Personality and Social Psychology, 47*, 1105–1117.

Emmons, R. A., & McCullough, M. E. (2003). Counting blessings versus burdens: An experimental investigation of gratitude and subjective well-being in daily life. *Journal of Personality and Social Psychology, 84*(2), 377–389.

Endicott, J., Nee, J., Harrison, W., & Blumenthal, R. (1993). Quality of life enjoyment and satisfaction questionnire: A new measure. *Psychopharmacology Bulletin, 29*, 321–326.

Eng, W., Coles, M. C., Heimberg, R. G., & Safren, S. A. (2001a). Quality of life following cognitive behavioral treatment for social anxiety disorder. *Depression and Anxiety, 13*, 192–193.

Eng, W., Heimberg, R. G., Hart, T. A., Schneider, F. R., & Liebowitz, M. R. (2001b). Attachment in individuals with social anxiety disorder: The relationship among adult attachment styles, social anxiety, and depression. *Emotion, 1*,365–380.

Etcoff, N. (1999). *Survival of the prettiest*. New York: Doubleday.

Evans, D. R. (1994). Enhancing the quality of life in the population at large. *Social Indicators Research, 33*, 47–88.

Faden, R., & Leplege, A. (1992). Assessing quality of life: Moral implications for clinical practice. *Medical Care, 30*, 166–175.

Fallon, P., Katzman, M. A., & Wooley, S. C. (1994). *Feminist perspectives on eating disorders*. New York: Guilford Press.

Fallowfield, L. (1990). *The quality of life: The missing measurement in health care*. London: Souvenir Press.

Fava, G. A., & Mangelli, L. (2001). Assessment of subclinical symptoms and psychological well-being in depression. *European Archives of Psychiatry and Clinical Neuroscience, 251*(8), 1147–1152.

Fava, G. A., & Ruini, C. (2003). Development and characteristics of a well-being enhancing psychotherapeutic strategy: Well-being therapy. *Journal of Behavior Therapy and Experimental Psychiatry, 34*, 45–63.

Feinberg, J. (1992). *Freedom and fulfillment*. Princeton, NJ: Princeton University Press.

Ferrans, C. E. (2000). Quality of life as an outcome of cancer care. In C. Yarbro, M. Frogge, & M. Goodman (Eds.), *Cancer nursing: Principles and practice* (5th ed., pp. 243–258). Boston: Jones and Bartlett.

Ferrans, C. E., & Powers, M. J. (1985). Quality of life index: Development and psychometric properties. *Advances in Nursing Science, 8*, 15–24.

Ferrans, C. E., & Powers, M. J. (1992). Psychometric assessment of the Quality of Life Index. *Research in Nursing and Health, 15*, 29–38.

Fibel, B., & Hale, W. D. (1978). The generalized expectancy for success scale: A new measure. *Journal of Consulting and Clinical Psychology, 46*, 924–931.

Finley, J. (Producer). (2003). *Christian meditation: Entering the mind of Christ* (CD Recording No. AF00679D). Boulder, CO: Sounds True.

Flanagan, J. C. (1978). A research approach to improving our quality of life. *American Psychologist, 33*, 138–147.

Flanagan, J. C. (1982). Measurement of quality of life: Current state of the art. *Archives of Physical Medicine and Rehabilitation, 63*, 56–59.

Folkman, S., & Moskowitz, J. T. (2000). Positive affect and the other side of coping. *American Psychologist, 55*, 647–654.

Ford, A. A. (2004). *The quest for egalitarian relationship: Charles Dickens and the pseudo-sibling romance*. Unpublished dissertation. Baylor University, Waco, TX.

Ford, J. D., Fisher, P., & Larson, L. (1997). Object relations as a predictor of treatment outcome with chronic posttraumatic stress disorder. *Journal of Consulting and Clinical Psychology, 65*, 547–559.

Ford, J. D., & Kidd, P. (1998). Early childhood trauma and disorders of extreme stress as predictors of treatment outcome with chronic posttraumatic stress disorder. *Journal of Traumatic Stress, 11*, 743–761.

Foster, R. J. (1988). *A celebration of discipline*. San Francisco: Harper San Francisco.

Frank, J. D., & Frank, J. B. (1993). *Persuasion and healing: A comparative study of psychotherapy* (3rd ed.). Baltimore, MD: The Johns Hopkins University Press.

Freud, S. (1989). Civilization and its discontents. In P. Gay (Ed. & Trans.), *The Freud reader* (pp. 722–772). New York: Norton. (Original work published 1929)

Frey, B. S., & Stutzer, A. (2001). *Happiness and economics: How the economy and institutions affect human well-being.* Princeton, NJ: Princeton University Press.

Frisch, M. B. (1992). Use of the Quality of Life Inventory in problem assessment and treatment planning for cognitive therapy of depression. In A. Freeman & F. Dattilio (Eds.), *Comprehensive casebook of cognitive therapy* (pp. 27–52). New York: Plenum Press.

Frisch, M. B. (1993). The Quality of Life Inventory: A cognitive-behavioral tool for complete problem assessment, treatment planning, and outcome evaluation. *Behavior Therapist, 16,* 42–44.

Frisch, M. B. (1994). *Manual and treatment guide for the Quality of Life Inventory or QOLI®.* Minneapolis, MN: Pearson Assessments (formerly, National Computer Systems).

Frisch, M. B. (1998a). Quality of life therapy and assessment in health care. *Clinical Psychology: Science and Practice, 5,* 19–40.

Frisch, M. B. (1998b). Documenting the effectiveness of employee assistance programs. *Employee Assistance Research, 2,* 2–5.

Frisch, M. B. (2000). Improving mental and physical health care through quality of life therapy and assessment. In E. Diener & D. R. Rahtz (Eds.), *Advances in Quality of Life Theory and Research* (pp. 207–241). New York: Kluwer Academic.

Frisch, M. B. (2002). A quick screen for DSM-IV disorders: The essential symptom approach. In L. VandeCreek & T. Jackson (Eds.), *Innovations in clinical practice: A source book* (pp. 375–384). Sarasota, FL: Professional Resources Press.

Frisch, M. B. (2004a). Use of the QOLI or Quality of Life Inventory in quality of life therapy and assessment. In M. R. Maruish (Ed.), *The use of psychological testing for treatment planning and outcome assessment: Vol. 3. Instruments for adults* (3rd ed., pp. 749–798). Mahwah, NJ: Erlbaum.

Frisch, M. B. (2004b). *Teaching positive psychology.* Paper presented to the Third Annual International Positive Psychology Summit, Washington, DC.

Frisch, M. B. (2006). *Finding happiness with Quality of Life Therapy: A positive psychology approach.* Woodway, TX: Quality of Life Press. E-mail contact: michael_frisch@baylor.edu.

Frisch, M. B., Clark, M. P., Rouse, S. V., Rudd, M. D., Paweleck, J., & Greenstone, A. (2005). Predictive and treatment validity of life satisfaction and the Quality of Life Inventory. *Assessment, 12*(1), 66–78.

Frisch, M. B., Cornell, J., Villanueva, M., & Retzlaff, P. J. (1992). Clinical validation of the Quality of Life Inventory: A measure of life satisfaction for use in treatment planning and outcome assessment. *Psychological Assessment: A Journal of Consulting and Clinical Psychology, 4,* 92–101.

Frisch, M. B., Elliot, C. H., Atsaides, J. P., Salva, D. M., & Denney, D. R. (1982). Social skills and stress management training to enhance patients' interpersonal competencies. *Psychotherapy: Theory, Research, and Practice, 19,* 349–358.

Frisch, M. B., & Froberg, W. (1987). Social validation of assertion strategies for handling aggressive criticism: Evidence for consistency across situations. *Behavior Therapy, 2,* 181–191.

Frisch, M. B., & Gerrard, M. (1981). Natural helping systems: A national survey of Red Cross volunteers. *American Journal of Community Psychology, 9,* 567–579.

Frisch, M. B., & Higgins, R. L. (1986). Instructional demand effects and the correspondence among self-report, naturalistic, and role-play measures of social skill as influenced by instructional demand. *Behavioral Assessment, 8,* 221–236.

Frisch, M. B., & MacKenzie, C. J. (1991). A comparison of formerly and chronically battered women on cognitive and situational dimensions. *Psychotherapy, 28,* 339–344.

Frisch, M. B., & McCord, M. (1987). Sex role orientation and social skill: A naturalistic assessment of assertion and conversational skill. *Sex Roles, 17,* 437–448.

Frisch, M. B., & Sanford, K. P. (2005). *Construct validity and the search for a unidimensional factor solution: Factor analysis of the Quality of Life Inventory in a large clinical sample.* Unpublished paper. Baylor University, Waco, TX.

Fromm, E. (1956). *The art of loving.* New York: Harper & Row.

Fuhrer, M. J. (2000). Subjectifying quality of life as a medical rehabilitation outcome. *Disability and Rehabilitation, 22,* 481–489.

Gablik, S. (1991). *The reenchantment of art.* New York, NY: Thames and Hudson.

Gatchel, R. J. (2002). Psychophysiological disorders: Past and present perspectives. In R. J. Gatchel & E. B. Blanchard (Eds.), *Psychophysiological disorders* (2nd ed.). Washington, DC: American Psychological Association.

Geigle, R., & Jones, S. B. (1990). Outcomes measurement: A report from the front. *Inquiry, 27,* 7–23.

George, L., & Bearon, L. (1980). *Quality of life in older persons.* New York: Human Sciences Press.

George, M. S., Ketter, T. A., Parekh, P. I., Horowitz, B., Herscovitch, P., & Post, R. M. (1995). Brain activity during transient sadness and happiness in healthy women. *American Journal of Psychiatry, 152,* 341–351.

Gilman, R., & Huebner, E. S. (2000). Review of life satisfaction measures for adolescents. *Behavior Change, 3,* 178–183.

Gladis, M. M., Gosch, E. A., Dishuk, N. M., & Crits-Christoph, P. (1999). Quality of life: Expanding the scope of clinical significance. *Journal of Consulting and Clinical Psychology, 67,* 320–331.

Goleman, D. (1995). *Emotional intelligence: Why it can matter more than IQ.* New York: Bantam Books.

Gonzales, L. R., Lewinsohn, P. M., & Clarke, G. N. (1985). Longitudinal follow-up of unipolar depressives: An investigation of predictors of relapse. *Journal of Consulting and Clinical Psychology, 53,* 461–469.

Gottman, J. M. (1994). *What predicts divorce*. Hillsdale, NJ: Erlbaum.

Gottman, J. M., & Silver, N. (1999). *The seven principles for making marriage work*. New York: Crown.

Grady, K. L., Jalowiec, A., White-Williams, C., Pifarre, R., Kirklin, J. K., Bourge, R. C., et al. (1995). Predictors of quality of life in patients with advanced heart failure awaiting transplantation. *Journal of Heart and Lung Transplantation, 14*, 2–10.

Grant, G., Salcedo, V., Hynan, L. S., & Frisch, M. B. (1995). Effectiveness of quality of life therapy. *Psychological Reports, 76*, 1203–1208.

Grebner, S., Semmer, N. K., & Elfering, A. (2003). *Working conditions and three types of well-being. A longitudinal study with self-report and rating data*. Manuscript submitted for publication.

Groenland, E. (1990). Structural elements of material well-being: An empirical test among people on social security. *Social Indicators Research, 22*, 367–384.

Gurin, G., Veroff, J., & Feld, S. C. (1960). *Americans view their mental health*. New York: Basic Books.

Guyatt, G. H., & Jaeschke, R. (1990). Measurements in clinical trials. In B. Spilker (Ed.), *Quality of life assessment in clinical trials*. New York: Raven Press.

Guyatt, G. H., Walter, S., & Norman, G. (1987). Measuring change over time: Assessing the usefulness of evaluative instruments. *Journal of Chronic Disease, 40*, 171–178.

Hadas, M. (Ed.). (1958). *The stoic philosophy of Seneca: Essays and letters of Seneca*. New York: Doubleday.

Hagerty, M. R. (2000). Social comparisons of income in one's community: Evidence from national surveys of income and happiness. *Journal of Personality and Social Psychology, 78*, 746–771.

Harter, J. K., Schmidt, F. L., & Hayes, T. L. (2002). Business-unit-level relationship between employee satisfaction, employee engagement, and business outcomes: A meta-analysis. *Journal of Applied Psychology, 87*, 268–279.

Hayes, S. C., Nelson, R. O., & Jarrett, R. B. (1987). The treatment utility of assessment: A functional approach to evaluating assessment quality. *American Psychologist, 42*, 963–974.

Headey, B. W., Holmstrom, E. L., & Wearing, A. J. (1985). Models of well-being and ill-being. *Social Indicators Research, 17*, 211–234.

Headey, B., Kelley, J., & Wearing, A. (1993). Dimensions of mental health: Life satisfaction, positive affect, anxiety, and depression. *Social Indicators Research, 19*, 63–82.

Headey, B., & Wearing A. (1992). *Understanding happiness: A theory of subjective well-being*. Melbourne, Australia: Longman Cheshire.

Heimberg, R. G. (2002). Cognitive-behavioral therapy for social anxiety disorder: Current status and future directions. *Biological Psychiatry, 51*, 1101–1108.

Helliwell, J. E. (2003). How's life? Combining individual and national variables to explain subjective well-being. *Economic Modeling, 20*, 331–360.

Herr, E. L., & Cramer, S. H. (1992). *Career guidance and counseling through the life span* (4th ed.). New York: Harper-Collins.

Hibbard, M. R., Gordon, W. A., & Kotherap, L. M. (2000). Traumatic brain injury. In F. M. Dattilio & A. Freeman (Eds.), *Cognitive-behavioral strategies in crisis intervention* (2nd ed., pp. 219–242). New York: Guilford Press.

Hightower, N. (2002). *Anger busting 101: The new ABC's for angry men and the women who love them*. Houston, TX: Bayou Publishing.

Hohmann, A. A. (1996). Measurement sensitivity in clinical mental health services. In L. I. Sederer & B. Dickey (Eds.), *Outcome assessment in clinical practice* (pp. 161–168). Baltimore: Williams & Wilkins.

Hope, D. A., Heimberg, R. G., Juster, H. R., & Turk, C. L. (2000). *Managing social anxiety: Client workbook*. San Antonio, TX: Psychological Corporation.

Horowitz, L. M., Strupp, H. H., Lambert, M. J., & Elkin, I. (1997). Overview and summary of the Core Battery Conference. In H. H. Strupp, L. M. Horowitz, & M. J. Lambert (Eds.), *Measuring patient changes in mood, anxiety, and personality disorders: Toward a core battery* (pp. 11–56). Washington, DC: American Psychological Association.

Huebner, E. S. (1994). Preliminary development and validation of a multidimensional life satisfaction scale for children. *Psychological Assessment, 6*, 149–158.

Huebner, E. S., Drane, W., & Valois, R. F. (2000). Levels an demographic correlates of adolescent life satisfaction reports. *School Psychology International, 21*, 281–292.

Hughes, G. J. (2001). *Aristotle on ethics*. London: Routledge.

Hyland, M. E. (1992). A reformulation of quality of life for medical science. *Quality of Life Research, 1*, 267–272.

Inglehart, R. (1990). *Culture shift in advanced industrial society*. Princeton, NJ: Princeton University Press.

Jacobson, N. S., & Christensen, A. (1996). *Integrative couple therapy*. New York: Norton.

Jacobson, N. S., & Margolin, G. (1979). *Marital therapy*. New York: Brunner/Mazel.

Jacobson, N. S., & Truax, P. (1991). Clinical significance: A statistical approach to defining meaningful change in psychotherapy research. *Journal of Consulting and Clinical Psychology, 59*, 12–19.

Jahoda, M. (1958). *Current concepts of positive mental health*. New York: Basic Books.

Jakubowski, P., & Lange, A. J. (1978). *The assertive option*. Champaign, Illinois: Research Press.

Jarrett, R. B., Kraft, D., Doyle, J., Foster, B. M., Eaves, G., & Silver, P. C. (2001). Preventing recurrent depression using cognitive therapy with and without a continuation phase. *Archives of General Psychiatry, 58*, 381–387.

Jenkins, C. D. (1992). Assessment of outcomes of health intervention. *Social Science and Medicine, 35,* 367–375.

Johnson, J. R., & Temple, R. (1985). Food and Drug Administration requirements for approval of new anticancer drugs. *Cancer Treatment Report, 69,* 1155–1157.

Judge, T. A., & Hulin, C. L. (1993). Job satisfaction as a reflection of disposition: A multiple source causal analysis. *Organizational Behavior and Human Decision Processes, 56,* 388–421.

Judge, T. A., Thoreson, C. J., Bono, J. E., & Patton, G. K. (2001). The job satisfaction-job performance relationship: A qualitative and quantitative review. *Psychological Bulletin, 127,* 376–407.

Judge, T. A., & Watanabe, S. (1993). Another look at the job satisfaction-life satisfaction relationship. *Journal of Applied Psychology, 78,* 939–948.

Kahneman, D. (1999). Objective happiness. In D. Kahneman, E. Diener, & N. Schwarz (Eds.), *Well-being: The foundations of hedonic psychology* (pp. 3–25). New York: Russell Sage.

Kahneman, D., Diener, E., & Schwarz, N. (Eds.). (1999). *Well-being: The foundations of hedonic psychology.* New York: Russell Sage.

Kalichman, S. C., Kelly, J. A., Morgan, M., & Rompa, D. (1997). Fatalism, current life satisfaction, and risk for HIV infection among gay and bisexual men. *Journal of Consulting and Clinical Psychology, 65,* 542–546.

Kaplan, R. M. (1988). Health-related quality of life in cardiovascular disease. *Journal of Consulting and Clinical Psychology, 56,* 382–392.

Kassinove, H., & Sukhodolsky, D. G. (1995). Anger disorders: Basic science and practice issues. In H. Kassinove (Ed.), *Anger disorders: Definition, diagnosis, and treatment.* Washington, DC: Taylor & Francis.

Katschnig, H. (1997). How useful is the concept of quality of life in psychiatry. In H. Katschnig, H. Freeman, & N. Sartorius (Eds.), *Quality of life in mental disorders* (pp. 3–16). New York: Wiley.

Katschnig, H., & Angermeyer, M. C. (1997). Quality of life in depression. In H. Katschnig, H. Freeman, & N. Sartorius (Eds.), *Quality of life in mental disorders* (pp. 137–148). New York: Wiley.

Kazdin, A. E. (1992). *Research design in clinical psychology* (2nd ed.). New York: Macmillan.

Kazdin, A. E. (1993a). Evaluation in clinical practice: Clinically sensitive and systematic methods of treatment delivery. *Behavior Therapy, 24,* 11–45.

Kazdin, A. E. (1993b). Treatment of conduct disorder: Progress and directions in psychotherapy research. *Development and Psychopathology, 5,* 277–310.

Kazdin, A. E. (1994). Methodology, design, and evaluation in psychotherapy research. In A. E. Bergin & S. L. Garfield (Eds.), *Handbook of psychotherapy and behavior change* (4th ed., pp. 19–71). New York: Wiley.

Kazdin, A. E. (2003). *Research design in clinical psychology* (4th ed.). Boston: Allyn & Bacon.

Keen, S. (1994). *Hymns to an unknown God.* New York: Bantam.

Keane, T., & Solomon, S. (1996). *Assessment of PTSD: Report on the NIMH/National Center for PTSD Consensus Conference.* Washington, DC.

Keyes, C. L. M. (2005). Mental health and/or mental illness? Investigating axioms of the complete state model of health. *Journal of Consulting and Clinical Psychology, 73,* 539–548.

Kocsis, J. H., Zisook, S., Davidson, J., Shelton, R., Yonkers, K., Hellerstein, D. J., et al. (1997). Double-blind comparison of sertraline, imipramine, and placebo in the treatment of dysthymia: Psychosocial outcomes. *American Journal of Psychiatry, 154,* 390–395.

Koivumaa-Honkanen, H., Honkanen, R., Koskenvuo, M., Viinamaki, H., & Kaprio, J. (2002). Life dissatisfaction as a predictor of fatal injury in a 20-year follow-up. *Acta Psychiatrica Scandinavia, 105,* 444–450.

Koivumaa-Honkanen, H., Honkanen, R., Viinamaki, H., Heikkila, K., Kaprio, J., & Koskenvuo, M. (2001). Life satisfaction and suicide: A 20-year follow-up study. *American Journal of Psychiatry, 158,* 433–439.

Kolotkin, R. L., Head, S., Hamilton, M., & Chie-Kit, J. T. (1995). Assessing impact of weight on quality of life. *Obesity research, 3,* 49–56.

Koocher, G. P., & Keith-Spiegel, P. (1998). *Ethics in Psychology: Professional standards and cases* (2nd ed.). New York: Oxford University Press.

Kornfield, J. (2000). *After ecstasy, the laundry: How the heart grows wise on the spiritual path.* New York: Bantam Books.

Kozma, A., Stone, S., & Stones, M. J. (2000). Stability in components and predictors of subjective well-being. In E. Diener & D. R. Rahtz (Eds.), *Advances in Quality of Life Theory and research* (pp. 13–30). New York: Kluwer Academic.

Kozma, A., & Stones, M. J. (1978). Some research issues and findings in the study of psychological well-being in the aged. *Canadian Psychological Review, 19,* 241–249.

Lazarus, R. S. (1991). *Emotion and adaptation.* New York: Oxford University Press.

Lazarus, R. S., & Folkman, S. (1984). *Stress, appraisal, and coping.* New York: Springer.

Lehman, A. F., Ward, N. C., & Linn, L. S. (1982). Chronic mental patients: The quality of life issue. *American Journal of Psychiatry, 1271–1276.*

Lewis, R. W. B. (2001). *Dante.* New York: Viking.

Lewinsohn, P., Redner, J., & Seeley, J. (1991). The relationship between life satisfaction and psychosocial variables: New perspectives. In F. Strack, M. Argyle, & N. Schwartz (Eds.), *Subjective well-being* (pp. 141–169). New York: Plenum Press.

Linn, J. G., & McGranahan, D. A. (1980). Personal disruptions, social integration, subjective well-being, and predisposition toward the use of counseling services. *American Journal of Community Psychology, 8,* 87–100.

Loftus, E., & Ketcham, K. (1994). *The myth of repressed memory.* New York: St. Martin's Griffin.

Lowman, R. (1993). *Counseling and psychotherapy of work dysfunctions.* Washington, DC: American Psychological Association.

Lucas, R. E., Clark, A. E., & Georgellis, Y. (2003). Reexamining adaptation and the set point model of happiness: Reactions to changes in marital status. *Journal of Personality and Social Psychology, 84*(3), 527–539.

Lucas, R. E., Diener, E., & Suh, E. (1996). Discriminant validity of well-being measures. *Journal of Personality and Social Psychology, 71,* 616–628.

Ludden, J., & Mandell, L. (1993). Quality planning for mental health. *Journal of Mental Health Administration, 20,* 72–78.

Luminet, O. (2004). Measurement of depressive rumination and associated constructs. In C. Papageorgiou & A. Wells (Eds.), *Depressive rumination: Nature theory and treatment* (pp. 187–215). West Sussex, England: Wiley: Chichester.

Lundh, L., & Sinonsson-Sarnecki, M. (2001). Alexithymia, emotion, and somatic complaints. *Journal of Personality, 69,* 483–510.

Luzzo, D. A. (Ed.). (2000). *Career counseling of college students: An empirical guide to strategies that work.* Washington, DC: American Psychological Association.

Luzzo, D. A., & McWhirter, E. H. (1999). Sex and ethnic differences in the perception of educational and career-related barriers and levels of coping efficacy. *Journal of Counseling and Development, 79*(1), 61–67.

Lykken, D. (1999). *Happiness: The nature and nurture of joy and contentment.* New York: St. Martin's Griffin.

Lyubomirsky, S., King, L., & Diener, E. (in press). Happiness is a good thing: A model of the benefits of chronic positive affect. *Psychological Bulletin.*

Lyubomirsky, S., Sheldon, K. M., & Schkade, D. (in press). Pursuing happiness: The architecture of sustainable change. *Review of General Psychology.*

Lyubomirsky, S., & Tkach, C. (2004). The consequences of dysphoric rumination. In C. Papageorgiou & A. Wells (Eds.), *Depressive rumination: Nature theory and treatment* (pp. 21–42). Hoboken, NJ: Wiley.

Maslow, A. (1982). *Toward a Psychology of Being* (2nd ed.). New York: Van Nostrand Reinhold.

Matarazzo, J. D. (1992). Psychological testing and assessment in the 21st century. *American Psychologist, 47,* 1007–1018.

McCrae, R. R., & Costa, P. T., Jr. (1990). *Personality in adulthood.* New York: Guilford Press.

McCrae, R. R., Costa, P. T., Jr., Ostendorf, F., Angleitner, A., Hrebíčková, M., Avia, M. D., et al. (2000). Nature over nurture: Temperament, personality, and lifespan develop-

ment. *Journal of Personality and Social Psychology, 78,* 173–186.

McGee, H. M., O'Boyle, C. A., Hickey, A., O'Malley, K., & Joyce, C. R. B. (1990). Assessing the quality of life of the individual: The SEIQoL with a healthy gastroenterology unit population. *Psychological Medicine, 21,* 749–759.

McGregor, I., & Little, B. R. (1998). Personal projects, happiness, and meaning: On doing well and being yourself. *Journal of Personality and Social Psychology, 74,* 494–512.

McLean, P. D., Hakstian, A. R. (1979). Clinical depression: Comparative efficacy of outpatient treatments. *Journal of Consulting and Clinical Psychology, 47*(5), 818–836.

McMillan, D., & Fisher, P. (2004). Cognitive therapy for depressive thinking. In C. Papageorgiou & A. Wells (Eds.), *Depressive rumination: Nature theory and treatment* (pp. 241–258). Hoboken, NJ: Wiley.

McNamara, J. R., & Booker, D. J. (2000). The abuse disability questionnaire: A new scale of assessing the consequences of partner abuse. *Journal of Interpersonal Violence, 15,* 170–183.

McKnight, D. L., Nelson, R. O., & Hayes, S. C. (1984). Importance of treating individually assessed response classes in the amelioration of depression. *Behavior Therapy, 15*(4), 315–335.

Meehl, P. E. (1992). Factors and taxa, traits and types, differences of degree and differences in kind. *Journal of Personality, 60,* 117–174.

Mehnert, T., Krauss, H. H., Nadler, R., & Boyd, M. (1990). Correlates of life satisfaction in those with disabling conditions. *Rehabilitation Psychology, 35,* 3–17.

Meichenbaum, D. (1994). *Clinical handbook for assessing and treating PTSD.* Waterloo, Ontario, Canada: Institute Press.

Mendlowicz, M. V., & Stein, M. B. (2000). Quality of life in individuals with anxiety disorders. *American Journal of Psychiatry, 157,* 669–682.

Merton, T. (1996a). *Contemplative prayer.* New York: Doubleday.

Merton, T. (1996b). *Life and holiness.* New York: Doubleday.

Michalos, A. C. (1983). Satisfaction and happiness in a rural northern resource community. *Social Indicators Research, 13,* 225–252.

Michalos, A. C. (1991). *Global report on student well-being: Vol. I. Life satisfaction and happiness.* New York: Springer-Verlag.

Miller, I. W., Keitner, G. I., Schatzberg, A. F., Klein, D. N., Thase, M. E., Rush, A. J., et al. (1998). The treatment of chronic depression: Pt. 3. Psychosocial functioning before and after treatment with sertraline or imipramine. *Journal of Clinical Psychiatry, 59,* 608–619.

Miller, W. R., & Rollnick, S. (2002). *Motivational interviewing* (2nd ed.). New York: Guilford Press.

Miller, W. R., Rollnick S., & Conforti, K. (2000). *Motivational interviewing: Preparing people for change* (2nd ed.). New York: Guilford Press.

Millon, T. (1987). *Manual for the MCMI-II.* Minneapolis, MN: National Computer Systems.

Mirin, S. M., & Namerow, M. J. (1991). Why study treatment outcome? *Hospital and Community Psychiatry, 42,* 1007–1012.

Mother Teresa. (1985). *Words to love by.* Notre Dame, Indiana: Ave Maria Press.

Moras, K. (1997). Toward a core battery for treatment efficacy research on mood disorders. In H. H. Strupp, L. M. Horowitz, & M. J. Lambert (Eds.), *Measuring patient changes in mood, anxiety, and personality disorders: Toward a core battery* (pp. 301–338). Washington, DC: American Psychological Association.

Moreland, K. L., Fowler, R. D., & Honaker, L. M. (1994). Future directions in the use of psychological assessment for treatment planning and outcome evaluation: Recommendations and predictions. In M. E. Maruish (Ed.), *The use of psychological testing for treatment planning and outcome assessment* (pp. 581–602). Hillsdale, NJ: Erlbaum.

Morganstern, J., Labouvie, E., McCrady, B. S., Kahler, C. W., & Frey, R. M. (1997). Affiliation with Alcoholics Anonymous after treatment: A study of its therapeutic effects and mechanisms of action. *Journal of Consulting and Clinical Psychology, 65,* 768–777.

Muller, A., Montaya, P., Schandry, R., & Hartl, L. (1994). Changes in physical symptoms, blood pressure, and quality of life over 30 days. *Behavior Research and Therapy, 32,* 593–603.

Myers, D. G. (1993). *The pursuit of happiness.* New York: Avon.

Myers, D. G. (2000). *The American paradox.* New Haven, CT: Yale University Press.

Myers, D. G. (2004). *Psychology* (7th ed.). New York: Worth.

Myers, D. G., & Diener, E. (1995). Who is happy? *Psychological Science, 6,* 10–19.

Nelson-Gray, R. O. (1996). Treatment outcome measures: Nomothetic or idographic? *Clinical Psychology: Science and Practice, 3,* 164–167.

Newman, F. L., Ciarlo, J. A., & Carpenter, D. (1999). Guidelines for selecting psychological instruments for treatment planning and outcome assessment. In M. E. Maruish (Ed.), *The use of psychological testing for treatment planning and outcome assessment* (2nd ed., pp. 153–170). Mahwah, NJ: Erlbaum.

Nhat Hanh, T. (1999). *The heart of Buddah's teaching.* New York: Broadway Books.

Nozick, R. (1989). *The examined life.* New York: Simon & Schuster.

Ogihara, T., Ozawa, T., & Kuramoto, K. (1991). Usefulness of the beta-blocker carteolol and its effect on quality of life in elderly hypertensive patients. *Current Therapeutic Research, 49,* 38–46.

Ogles, B. M., Lambert, M., & Masters, K. (1996). *Assessing outcome in clinical practice.* Boston: Allyn & Bacon.

Ogles, B. M., Lunnen, K. M., & Bonesteel, K. (2001). Clinical significance: History, application, and current practice. *Clinical Psychology Review, 21,* 421–446.

Othmer E., & Othmer, S. C. (1994). *The clinical interview using DSM-IV* (Vol. 1). Washington, DC: American Psychiatric Press.

Oxford English Dictionary. (1989). Oxford, England: Oxford University Press.

Papageorgiou, C., & Wells, A. (2004). Nature, functions, and beliefs about depressive rumination. In C. Papageorgiou & A. Wells (Eds.), *Depressive rumination: Nature theory and treatment* (pp. 3–20). Hoboken, NJ: Wiley.

Patterson, J. T. (1996). *Grand expectations: The United States, 1945–1974.* New York: Oxford University.

Paunovic, N., & Ost, L. (2001). Cognitive-behavior therapy vs. exposure therapy in the treatment of PTSD in refugees. *Behaviour Research and Therapy, 39,* 1183–1197.

Pavot, W., & Diener, E. (1993). Review of the satisfaction with life scale. *Psychological Assesement, 5,* 164–172.

Pelham, B. W. (1995). Self-investment and self-esteem: Evidence for a Jamesian model of self-worth. *Journal of Personality and Social Psychology, 69,* 1141–1150.

Pennebacker, J. W., & Stone, L. D. (2004). Translating traumatic experiences into language: Implications for child abuse and long-term health. In L. J. Koenig, & L. S. Doll (Eds.), *From child sexual abuse to adult sexual risk: Trauma, revictimization, and intervention* (pp. 201–216). Washington, DC: American Psychological Association.

Perls, F. S. (1971). *Gestalt therapy verbatim.* New York: Bantam Books.

Persons, J. B. (1989). *Cognitive therapy in practice: A case formulation approach.* New York: W. W. Norton & Company.

Persons, J. B., & Bertagnolli, A. (1999). Inter-rater reliability of cognitive-behavioral case formulations of depression: A replication. *Cognitive Therapy and Research, 23,* 271–283.

Persons, J. B., Davidson, J., & Thompkins, M. A. (2001). *Essential components of cognitive-behavior therapy for depression.* Washington, DC: American Psychological Association.

Peterson, C., & Seligman, M. E. P. (Eds.). (2004). *Character strengths and virtues: A handbook and classification.* New York: Oxford University Press.

Petry, N. M., Petrakis, I., Trevisan, L., Wiredu, G., Boutros, N. N., Martin, B., et al. (2001). Contingency management interventions: From research to practice. *American Journal of Psychiatry, 158,* 694–702.

Plato. (2001). *Plato's Republic* (B. Jowett, Trans.). New York: Agora Publications.

Pohl, R. B., Wolkow, R. M., & Clary, C. M. (1998). Sertraline in the treatment of panic disorder: A double-blind multicenter trial. *American Journal of Psychiatry, 155,* 1189–1195.

Putnam, R. (2001). *Bowling alone: The collapse and revival of American community.* New York: Simon & Schuster.

Rabkin, J. G., Griffin, K. W., & Wagner, G. (2000). Quality of life measures. In A. J. Rush & H. A. Pincus (Eds.), *Handbook of psychiatric measures.* Washington, DC: American Psychiatric Association.

Rapaport, M. H., Endicott, J., & Clary, D. M. (2002). PTSD and quality of life: Results across 64 weeks of sertraline treatment. *Journal of Clinical Psychiatry, 63,* 59–65.

Rehm, L. P. (1988). Self-management and cognitive processes in depression. In L. B. Alloy (Ed.), *Cognitive processes in depression* (143–176). New York: Guilford Press.

Reich, R. B. (2000). *The future of success.* New York: Vintage Press.

Reisman, J. M. (1966). *A history of clinical psychology* (Enlarged ed.). New York: Irvington.

Reynolds, D. S. (1996). *Walt Whitman's America: A cultural biography.* New York: Vintage.

Rice, R. W., Frone, M. R., & McFarlin, D. B. (1992). Work-nonwork conflict and the perceived quality of life. *Journal of Organizational Behavior, 13,* 155–168.

Rouse, S. V., Butcher, J. N., & Miller, K. B. (1999). Assessment of substance abuse in psychotherapy clients: The effectiveness of the MMPI-2 substance abuse scales. *Psychological Assessment, 11,* 101–107.

Rush, A. J. (2000). *Sequenced treatment alternatives for resistant depression: STARD research protocol.* Unpublished manuscript.

Rush, A. J., & Kupfer, D. J. (2001). Strategies and tactics in the treatment of depression. In G. O. Gabbard (Ed.), *Treatments of psychiatric disorders* (3rd ed., Vol. 2, pp. 1417–1442). Washington, DC: American Psychiatric Association.

Russell, B. (1958). *The conquest of happiness.* New York: Liveright Publishing Corporation.

Safren, S. A., Heimberg, R. G., Brown, E. J., & Holle, C. (1997). Quality of life in social phobia. *Depression and Anxiety, 4,* 126–133.

Salek, S. (Ed.). (1998). *Compendium of quality of life instruments.* New York: Wiley.

Sarason, S. B. (1990). *Challenge of art to psychology.* New Haven, CT: Yale University Press.

Schimmack, U., Diener, E., & Oishi, S. (2002). Life-satisfaction is a momentary judgment and a stable personality characteristic: The use of chronically accessible and stable sources. *Journal of Personality, 70,* 345–385.

Schipper, H., Clinch, J., & Powell, V. (1990). Definitions and conceptual issues. In B. Spilker (Ed.), *Quality of life assessments in clinical trials.* New York: Raven Press.

Schnurr, P. P., Friedman, M. J., Lavori, P. W., & Hsieh, F. Y. (2001). Design of Department of Veterans Affairs Cooperative Study No. 4230: Group treatment of posttraumatic stress disorder. *Controlled Clinical Trials, 22,* 74–88.

Schwartz, R. C. (2001). *Introduction to the Internal Family Systems Model.* Oak Park, IL: Trailheads Publications.

Schwarz, N., & Strack, F. (1999). Reports of subjective well-being: Judgmental processes and their methodological implications. In D. Kahneman, E. Diener, & N. Schwarz (Eds.), *Well-being: The foundations of hedonic psychology* (pp. 61–84). New York: Russell Sage.

Seeman, J. (1989). Toward a model of positive health. *American Psychologist, 44,* 1099–1109.

Segal, Z. V., Williams, J. M. G., & Teasdale, J. F. (2002). *Mindfulness-based cognitive therapy for depression: A new approach to preventing relapse.* New York: Guilford Press.

Seligman, M. E. P. (2002). *Authentic happiness.* New York: Free Press.

Shafranske, E. P. (1996). Introduction: Foundation for the consideration of religion in the clinical practice of psychology. In E. P. Shafranske (Ed.), *Religion and the clinical practice of psychology* (pp. 1–20). Washington, DC: American Psychological Association.

Shehan, C. L. (1984). Wives' work and psychological well-being: An extension of Gove's social role theory of depression. *Sex Roles, 11,* 881–899.

Sheldon, K. M., & Elliot, A. J. (1999). Goal striving, need-satisfaction, and longitudinal well-being: The self-concordance model. *Journal of Personality and Social Psychology, 76,* 482–497.

Sheldon, K. M., Elliot, A. J., Kim, Y., & Kasser, T. (2001). What is satisfying about satisfying events? Testing 10 candidate psychological needs. *Journal of Personality and Social Psychology, 80,* 325–339.

Sheldon, K. M., & Houser-Marko, L. (2001). Self-concordance, goal-attainment, and the pursuit of happiness: Can there be an upward spiral? *Journal of Personality and Social Psychology, 80,* 152–165.

Shiner, R. L. (2003). *Development and happiness.* Paper presented at the second International Positive Psychology Summit, Washington, DC.

Sijie, D. (2001). *Balzac and the little Chinese seamstress* (I. Rilke, Trans.). New York: Anchor Books.

Simon, L. (1998). *Genuine reality: A life of William James.* New York: Harcourt Brace.

Simpson, J. A., & Weiner, E. S. (Eds.). (1989). *The Oxford English dictionary* (2nd ed.). Oxford: Oxford University Press.

Sirgy, M. J. (2002). *The psychology of quality of life.* Dordrecht, The Netherlands: Kluwer Academic.

Snyder, A. G., Stanley, M. A., Novey, D. M., Averill, P. M., & Beck, J. G. (2000). Measures of depression in older adults with generalized anxiety disorder: A psychometric evaluation. *Depression and Anxiety, 11,* 114–120.

Snyder, C. R., & Lopez, S. (Eds.). (2002). *Handbook of positive psychology.* New York: Oxford University Press.

Snyder, C. R., & Lopez, S. (Eds.) (in press). *Handbook of positive psychology* (2nd ed.). New York: Oxford University Press.

Spilker, B. (1996). *Quality of life and pharmacoecomonics in clinical trials* (2nd ed.). New York: Lippincott-Raven Press.

Stanard, R. P. (1999). The effect of training in a strengths model of case management on client outcomes in a community mental health center. *Community Mental Health Journal, 35,* 169–179.

Sternberg, R.-J. (2003). *TI: Wisdom, intelligence, and creativity synthesized.* New York: Cambridge University Press.

Stewart, A. L., & King, A. C. (1994). Conceptualizing and measuring quality of life in older populations. In R. P. Abeles, H. C. Gift, & M. G. Ory (Eds.), *Aging and quality of life* (pp. 27–54). New York: Springer.

Stewart, A. L., Ware, S. E., Sherbourne, C. D., & Wells, K. B. (1992). Psychological distress/well-being and cognitive functioning measures. In A. L. Stewart & J. E. Ware (Eds.), *Measuring functioning and well-being: The medical outcomes study approach* (pp. 102–142). Durham, NC: Duke University Press.

Strupp, H. H. (1996). The tripartite model and the Consumer Reports study. *American Psychologist, 51,* 1017–1024.

Strupp, H. H., & Binder, J. L. (1984). *Psychotherapy in a new key: A guide to time-limited dynamic psychotherapy.* New York: Basic Books.

Strupp, H. H., & Hadley, S. W. (1977). A tripartite model of mental health and therapeutic outcomes. *American Psychologist, 32,* 187–196.

Suldo, S., & Huebner, E. S. (2005). *Very satisfied youth: Advances in quality of life research.* New York: Springer.

Sullivan, M. (1992). Quality of life assessment in medicine: Concepts, definitions, purposes, and basic tools. *Nordic Journal of Psychiatry, 46,* 79–83.

Szalai, A., & Andrews, F. M. (Eds.). (1980). *The quality of life: Comparative studies.* Beverly Hills, CA: Sage.

Tatarkiewicz, W. (1976). *Analysis of happiness.* Hague, The Netherlands: Martinus Nijhoff.

Taylor, S. E. (2002). *Health psychology.* New York: McGraw-Hill.

Taylor, S. E., & Brown, J. D. (1988). Illusion and well-being: A social psychological perspective on mental health. *Psychological Bulletin, 103,* 193–210.

Telch, M. J., Schmidt, N. B., Jaimez, T. L., & Jacquin, K. M. (1995). Impact of cognitive-behavioral treatment on quality of life in panic disorder patients. *Journal of Consulting and Clinical Psychology, 63,* 823–830.

Terry, D. J., Mayocchi, L., & Hynes, G. J. (1996). Depressive symptomotology in new mothers: A stress and coping perspective. *Journal of Abnormal Psychology, 105,* 220–231.

Truong, M. (2003). *The book of salt.* Boston: Houghton Mifflin.

Turk, D. L., Mennin, D. S., Fresco, D. M., & Heimberg. (November, 2000). *Impairment and quality of life among individuals with Generalized Anxiety Disorder.* Paper presented at the annual meeting of the Association for Advancement of Behavior Therapy, New Orleans, LA.

Twenge, J. M. (2000). The age of anxiety? The birth cohort change in anxiety and neuroticism, 1952–1993. *Journal of Personality and Social Psychology, 79,* 1007–1021.

Vaillant, G. (2002). *Aging well.* New York: Basic Books.

Valois, R. F., Zullig, K. J., Huebner, E. S., & Drane, J. W. (2001). Relationship between life satisfaction and violent behaviors among adolescents. *American Journal of Health Behavior, 25,* 353–366.

Veenhoven, R. (1984). *Conditions of happiness.* Boston: Reidel.

Veenhoven, R. (1993). *Happiness in nations: Subjective appreciation of life in 55 nations 1986–1990.* Rotterdam, The Netherlands: RISBO—Erasmus University.

Veenhoven, R. (1996). Developments in satisfaction research. *Social Indicators Research, 37,* 1–46.

Veenhoven, R. (1999). Quality-of-life in individualistic society: A comparison of 43 nations in the early 1990s. *Social Indicators Research, 48,* 157–186.

Veenhoven, R. (2003a). Arts of living. *Journal of Happiness Studies, 4,* 373–384.

Veenhoven, R. (2003b). Hedonism and happiness. *Journal of Happiness Studies, 4,* 437–457.

Vitaliano, P. P., Dougherty, C. M., & Siegler, I. C. (1994). Biopsychosocial risks for cardiovascular disease in spouse caregivers of persons with Alzheimer's disease. In R. P. Abeles, H. C. Gift, & M. G. Ory (Eds.), *Aging and quality of life* (pp. 145–159). New York: Springer.

Wagner, E. H., Schoenbach, V. J., Orleans, C. T., Grothaus, L. C., Saunders, K. W., Curry, S., et al. (1990). Participation in a smoking cessation program: A population-based perspective. *American Journal of Preventive Medicine, 6,* 258–266.

Walker, A. (1982). *The color purple.* New York: Harcourt.

Walker, L. E. A. (1994). *Abused women and survivor therapy.* Washington, DC: American Psychological Association.

Ware, J. E. (1986). The assessment of health status. In C. H. Aiken & D. Mechanic (Eds.), *Applications of social science to clinical medicine and health policy* (9th ed.). New Brunswick, NJ: Rutgers University Press.

Ware, J. E. (2004). SF-36 health survey update. In M. R. Maruish (Ed.), *The use of psychological testing for treatment planning and outcome assessment: Vol. 3. Instruments for adults* (3rd ed., pp. 693–718). Mahwah, NJ: Erlbaum.

Warr, P. (1999). Well-being and the workplace. In D. Kahneman, E. Diener, & N. Schwarz (Eds.), *Well-being: The foundations of hedonic psychology* (pp. 392–412). New York: Russell Sage.

Warren, R. (2002). *The purpose-driven life.* Grand Rapids, MI: Zondervan.

Watson, G. (1930). Happiness among adult students of education. *Journal of Educational Psychology, 21,* 79–109.

Wells, A., & Papageorgiou, C. (2004). Metacognitive therapy for depressive rumination. In C. Papageorgiou & A. Wells (Eds.), *Depressive rumination: Nature theory and treatment* (pp. 259–273). Chichester, West Sussex, England: Wiley.

Wenger, N. K., & Furberg, C. D. (1990). Cardiovascular disorders. In B. Spilker (Ed.), *Quality of life assessments in clinical trials.* New York: Raven Press.

Wessman, A. E., & Ricks, D. F. (1966). *Mood and personality.* New York: Holt, Rienhart, & Winston.

Williams, R. (1998). *Anger kills: Seventeen strategies for controlling the hostility that can harm your health*. New York: HarperTorch.

Witkiewitz, K., & Marlatt, G. A. (2004). Relapse prevention for alcohol and drug problems. *American Psychologist, 59,* 224–235.

Wolfe, T. (1988). *The bonfire of the vanities*. New York: Bantam Books.

Woody, S. R., & Adessky, R. S. (2002). Therapeutic alliance, group cohesion, and homework compliance during cognitive-behavioral group treatment of social phobia. *Behavior Therapy, 33,* 5–27.

World Health Organization. (1948). World Health Organization constitution. In *Basic documents*. Geneva, Switzerland: World Health Organization.

Wortman, C. B., & Silver, R. C. (1987). Coping with irrevocable loss. In A. Baum, C. J. Frederick, I. H. Frieze, E. S. Shneidman, & C. B. Wortman (Eds.), *Cataclysms, crises, and catastrophes: Psychology in action* (pp. 185–235). Washington, DC: American Psychological Association.

Yalom, I. (1980). *Existential psychotherapy*. New York: Basic books.

Yardley, J. K., & Rice, R. W. (1991). The relationship between mood and subjective well-being. *Social Indicators Research, 24,* 101–111.

Zullig, K. J., Valois, R. F., Huebner, E. S., Oeltmann, J. E., & Drane, J. W. (2001). Relationship between perceived life satisfaction and adolescents' substance abuse. *Journal of Adolescent Health, 29,* 279–288.

Author Index

Subject Index

Lightning Source UK Ltd.
Milton Keynes UK
27 October 2010

161949UK00001B/2/P